CRIMINAL LAW
Principles and Cases

Fifth Edition

CRIMINAL LAW
Principles and Cases

Fifth Edition

Thomas J. Gardner
Attorney at Law

Terry M. Anderson
Professor of Law,
Creighton University School of Law

West Publishing Company
St. Paul   New York
Los Angeles   San Francisco

CREDITS

Copyediting: Julie Bach
Interior Design: Lois Stanfield
Artwork: Gloria Langer

Photo Credits:

7 AP/Wide World Photos; **29** AP/Wide World Photos; **33** AP/Wide World Photos; **46** AP/Wide World Photos; **71** Frost Publishing; **106** UPI/Bettmann Newsphotos; **133** UPI/Bettmann Newsphotos; **134** AP/Wide World Photos; **142** (left) UPI/Bettmann Newsphotos; **142** (right) AP/Wide World Photos; **152** AP/Wide World Photos; **182** AP/Wide World Photos; **203** American Correctional Association; **220** AP/Wide World Photos; **266** UPI/Bettmann Newsphotos; **288** AP/Wide World Photos; **300** AP/Wide World Photos; **318** AP/Wide World Photos; **342** AP/Wide World Photos; **349** James L. Shaffer; **369** UPI/Bettmann Newsphotos; **412** AP/Wide World Photos; **416** AP/Wide World Photos; **447** UPI/Bettmann Newsphotos; **451** AP/Wide World Photos; **453** (both) AP/Wide World Photos; **461** Eileen Gardner; **474** James L. Shaffer; **502** AP/Wide World Photos; **509** AP/Wide World Photos; **511** UPI/Bettmann Newsphotos; **529** AP/Wide World Photos; **555** AP/Wide World Photos; **568** UPI/Bettmann Newsphotos; **570** Eileen Gardner; **581** United Nations/Jane Schreibman/Frost Publishing; **593** AP/Wide World Photos; **599** UPI/Bettmann Newsphotos; **604** AP/Wide World Photos

EXPLANATORY NOTE

The author has attempted to present the general principles of criminal law in this textbook. However, because of the variance in state statutes and court decisions from state to state, it is recommended that students and officers consult with their legal advisers before assuming that principles of law applicable in other jurisdictions exist in their states.

COPYRIGHT © 1975,
1980, 1985, 1989   By WEST PUBLISHING COMPANY
COPYRIGHT © 1992   By WEST PUBLISHING COMPANY
                         610 Opperman Drive
                         P.O. Box 64526
                         St. Paul, MN 55164-0526

99 98 97 96 95 94   8 7 6 5 4 3

Library of Congress Cataloging-in-Publication Data

Gardner, Thomas J., 1921–
    Criminal law : principles and cases / Thomas J. Gardner, Terry M.
  Anderson.— 5th ed.
      p.   cm.
    Includes index.
    ISBN 0-314-92953-3 (hard)
    1. Criminal law—United States—Cases.   I. Anderson, Terry M.
  II. Title.
  KF9218.G36   1991
  345.73 —dc20   91-26344
  [347.305]   CIP

To three very fine young men:

Bill Thomas Feldman
Alexander Gardner Anderson
Brain Patrick Demet

Contents

| Preface

In this fifth edition of the text we have retained what we believe to be the best features of prior editions. We continue to mix textual exposition with case abstracts and quotations as the principle method of development. Where appropriate we have deleted or replaced questions and problems at chapter endings. Finally, we have added some of what we believe to be the most important developments in criminal law which have occurred since the fourth edition. We are certain each instructor will add other new and important developments.

A course in criminal law is more than the study of the elements of criminal offenses, however important knowledge of those elements may be for practical purposes. We think that students should recognize at the earliest opportunity the fundamental role the criminal law plays in our democratic process, and the limits that process places on government's power to use the criminal law. We have therefore continued to present the material with an early emphasis on these aspects of the traditional criminal law course.

We understand that some instructors may wish to cover the material in Part Two after coverage of specific crimes. Indeed, some might conclude that material may be eliminated completely in an introductory course. However, we think the tide of current events bears out our decision to include these materials where we do. We seem to be at a period in our history where there is occurring a general shift from an emphasis on individual rights to a more structured society. If that is so, it must surely surface in renewed tensions between the criminal law and individual liberty, as it has already done in privacy, religion, free speech, abortion, and other cases. We think it is vital our students understand these changes, and that we present them accurately.

Many students may wish to go beyond the case abstracts and statutory selections, and consult primary legal sources found in law libraries. We encourage that, but advise those students to first become familiar with the sources available. To do so we recommend Teply, *Legal Research and Citation,* third edition (West, 1989).

We hope teachers and students alike will find this new edition to be a constructive and interesting tool in their study of the criminal law.

Finally, the authors wish to acknowledge their debt to the following criminal law teachers, each of whom took valuable time to critique the fifth edition: Harry Balfe, Montclair State; George E. Green, Mankato State University; Patrick J. Hopkins, Harrisburg Area Community College; Albert D. Kirby, East Carolina University; Marc Neithercutt, California State University-Hayward; George P. Orvis, University of Alabama-Birmingham; Joseph M. Pelicciotti, Indiana

University-Northwest. Their comments and suggestions greatly assisted the authors in deciding what to change and what to keep in the text.

Terry Anderson wishes to thank Creighton Law School, Faculty Research Fund, for financial support given him in his work on this project. He also wishes to thank his colleagues on the Creighton law faculty for their advice and guidance.

Thomas J. Gardner
Terry M. Anderson

Introduction

Despotism has been defined as the anarchy of lawless rulers, and anarchy as the despotism of lawless crowds. The fifty-five men who met at the Philadelphia Convention in 1787 feared both extremes as they wrote a proposed new constitution for their society which was in crisis because of severe economic, political and foreign problems.

The Constitution that emerged from the Philadelphia Convention continues to be used today as the supreme law of the land. Its vitality is attributed to the fact that it permits a balance to be maintained between individual liberties and the collective needs of the society; between personal freedoms and the need for public order; and the between the right to different lifestyles and the need for some degree of uniformity.

This Constitution and the system of government established under it have served the American people well for more than two hundred years. It is not a perfect system of government because there never has been and never will be an absolutely perfect government in this world. Under this system Americans have emerged from the ten years of the severe depression of the 1930s and the four years of intense war in the early 1940s to become the most prosperous and affluent people in the world. Americans are also the freest people in the world as they enjoy more personal, economic , social and political freedom than any other people in the world.

Rational men since the early Greek philosophers have recognized that personal freedoms are never absolute. The personal freedoms of one person end when his or her activities come into conflict with the rights and freedoms of other persons or are contrary to the over-all needs and good of the society as expressed by the statutes and laws. The cliche that "your freedom extends as far as the end of my nose" is sometimes used to express the limited concept of freedom. Therefore, in a democratic society, government must regulate conduct to a limited extent, by use of criminal and civil laws, to ensure the rights and freedoms of the society as a whole.

Only a responsible society may be free. Persons in the society must generally respect the rights and dignities of their fellow men. They must also recognize their obligations and duties toward the society as a whole. In a democracy, this means bowing to the will of the majority upon occasion, because in a democracy as in a marriage, the individual does not always get his or her own way if the marriage or the democracy is to survive.

The 18th-century member of British Parliament, Edmund Burke, expressed this requirement of responsibility in a democracy in this way:

Men are qualified for civil liberty in exact proportion to their own disposition to put moral chains upon their own appetites. Society cannot exist unless a controlling power upon will and appetite be placed somewhere and the less of it there is within, the more there is without. It is ordained in the external constitution of things that men of intemperate minds cannot be free. Their passions forge their fetters.

Personal freedoms and rights may be infringed on in many ways. The elderly persons who do not venture out of their homes at night because of the fear of being criminally assaulted have had their personal freedoms infringed on. The victims of a crime have had their rights infringed on. There is always the possibility in a democracy that the government (or one of the agencies of government) will abuse the power and authority vested in it and will infringe upon the liberties and rights of the people. Overseas, totalitarianism in the form of Fascist, Nazi and Communist governments have presented severe threats to the free people of the world.

The struggle for freedom and liberty goes on constantly in all democracies. American history is a record of this struggle and of the efforts to define the rights of the individual. Criminal law is a study of the authority of government to regulate conduct within constitutional limitations so that maximum freedoms and liberties may be enjoyed by all.

Thomas J. Gardner
Terry M. Anderson

Part One

Basic Concepts of Criminal Law

Chapter One

CRIMINAL LAW GENERALLY

A. Introduction to Criminal Law

Does the United States Have a Serious Crime Problem?

For many years the United States has had a crime rate that exceeds any of the other industrial democracies. In many American cities, murder rates have soared, with experts blaming drugs and the use of deadlier weapons.[1] The United States leads all other industrial democracies in criminal homicides.[2]

While the use of cocaine and coke is down dramatically among recreational users and young Americans, the drug problem in the United States remains serious and is reflected in crime rates.[3] The rate of imprisonment in the United States is now reported to be the highest in the world, with more than one million Americans in jails or prisons, either awaiting trials or serving time.[4]

In the Spring 1991 issue of *The Prosecutor,* the president of the National District Attorneys Association pointed out that for the first time in American history the chance of being a victim of a violent crime for an American is now greater than the chance of being involved in an automobile accident.

Former Illinois Governor James R. Thompson stated while he was cochairman of the National Violent Crime Task Force that:

> The threat of violent crime has reached epidemic proportions. The statistics have gone off the charts; and it does not require a litany of shocking examples to recognize that each crime statistic represents a victimized human being, a shattered life, or a broken family. The time has come to take a unified approach to the problem of violent crime. The magnitude of the threat to our domestic tranquility requires a consensus reaction.

* * *

> Violent crime is exacting a fearful toll in the communities of our nation. Millions of our fellow citizens are being held hostage by their fear of crime and violence. Though violent crime can strike anyone, it most frequently affects the poor, the old, and the residents of the inner cities—precisely those persons who are least able to protect themselves. Even those who can afford a suburban residence or a privately guarded city apartment often find themselves defenseless on the streets.[5]

President George Bush pointed out in 1991 that more Americans are killed every year in some American cities than were killed on the entire Kuwaiti front during the Gulf War; in that sense, the war was safer than the streets of America.

Countries in the free world[6] have always sought to ensure freedom through a system of laws that would protect the basic rights of individuals within their societies. Although public order is primarily a function of state governments and municipalities, domestic tranquility cannot be achieved without the public's cooperation.

As a first step toward seeking public order, laws are enacted. Laws are rules created by government for the orderly functioning of an organized society. Criminal laws are rules of conduct that forbid specific acts or, in some instances, require certain acts. Criminal laws are distinguished from civil laws primarily

---

Government Regulation of Conduct

Government May Regulate Conduct by Means of:

1. Civil offenses created by statutes or ordinances that usually punish specifically forbidden conduct only by fines or forfeiture (for example, speeding is ordinarily a civil offense punishable by a fine and forfeiture of points)

2. Criminal offenses that may be punished by imprisonment

---

because violations of criminal laws can be punished by imprisonment or other severe penalties.

The Goals of a Democracy

Through a system of laws, a democracy seeks to translate its basic principles and ideals into achievable goals. One of these goals is that of achieving public order and domestic tranquility. To achieve these goals and remain a nation of laws requires a fine tuning in the balancing of the rights of individuals with the compelling needs of the society as a whole.

Criminal justice systems operate most successfully in democracies in which the majority of the people believe that the system and the laws are fair and that the system can operate efficiently and effectively.[7]

Laws Should Be the Will of the People

In a democracy, laws should be a product of the will of the people. Laws are enacted by the duly constituted representatives of the people. They are enforced, administered, and interpreted by civil servants and elected officials in other branches of government. In the United States, those branches are:

1. *The legislative branch.* Laws (including criminal laws) are enacted by the legislative branch. The chief executive officer participates in the legislative process by signing or vetoing proposed laws. State governors and the U.S. president provide leadership on many proposed laws by either supporting or opposing them and providing information about proposed laws.
2. *The executive branch.* Agencies within the executive branch of government administer and enforce laws. Law enforcement agencies are found within the executive branch of government and are charged with the enforcement of criminal laws, in addition to performing other duties.
3. *The judicial branch.* Persons who are charged with crimes have a right to be tried before a judge or a jury in a court in the judicial branch of government. Fact finders (jury or judge) determine the ultimate issues in cases presented to them. The issue of guilt or innocence is dealt with by

the jury (if the case is tried before a jury). Judges in the United States have the power of judicial review in determining the constitutionality of laws or ordinances.

Public policy and laws are determined through democratic political processes. Debates as to what the law should or should not be take place constantly in democracies. Law enforcement officers do not make laws. Their traditional tasks are to enforce laws and maintain public order. They are also called on to provide a wide range of other public services, such as dealing with family disputes, coping with community tensions, guiding community crime prevention efforts, and providing aid in time of emergencies or disasters.

Public and Private Law

Laws can be classified as either private or public laws. Private laws deal with relationships between individuals in which the government has only an indirect interest. Included in this group are such laws as the law of domestic relations (marriage, divorce, etc.), contract law, real estate law, and the law of private inheritance.

The government has a more direct interest in public laws and, in most instances, has specific responsibilities. Some examples of public law are public health laws (purity of foods and drugs, sanitation, etc.), vehicular and traffic laws, laws of criminal procedure, and criminal laws.

In early England, such offenses as robbery, theft, and murder were classified as private laws because it was believed that these offenses affected only the individual victims and did not directly affect the state. Victims or their families or clans would usually retaliate with violence if they knew who the offender was. They also had the alternative of bringing legal action against the offender. During the reign of Henry II (1154–89), English law first recognized that crime was more than a personal affair between the victim and the perpetrator, and that punishment should not be left largely to private enforcement. Today, criminal law is public law in both England and the United States, since it is recognized that crimes are offenses not only against the victim, but also against society. Criminal actions in the United States are brought only by the government, whereas the victim of the crime (or the heirs) may initiate a civil action against the offender. English law, however, has carried over some of the old concept; thus, if the government decides not to initiate a criminal action, the victim may retain a private attorney and initiate both a criminal and a civil action.

The Subfields of Criminal Law

Law is a means to an end. To have an orderly society, there must be rules (law) controlling and governing the limits of individual behavior. American criminal law is made up of a number of subfields. *Substantive criminal law,* with which this book concerns itself, is one of those subfields. It concerns the conduct, acts, and omissions that have been designated as crimes. The acts (or omissions) plus the mental state and other essential elements are the ingredients that constitute a crime.

Criminal procedure is another subfield of criminal law. It consists of the steps that governmental agencies follow from the criminal incident through pun-

To have an orderly society, there must be rules (law) controlling and governing the limits of individual behavior. Here police move in to arrest demonstrators outside the Minneapolis Federal Building. (See chapter 15 for material on the limits of lawful demonstrations.)

ishment of the offender. Other courses of study dealing with criminal procedure are criminal investigation, criminal evidence, and arrest, search, and seizure.

Criminology and criminalistics are fields that are separate from but related to substantive criminal law. *Criminology* is the sociological and psychological study of (a) the causes of crime, (b) the control of crime, and (c) the conditions under which criminal law developed. *Criminalistics* is the professional and scientific discipline directed to the recognition, identification, individualization, and evaluation of physical evidence by application of the natural sciences. Criminology is a branch of sociology; criminalistics is the application of science to criminal investigation and encompasses forensic science.

Substantive Criminal Law

Substantive criminal law is an important branch of public law. It defines the standards of conduct that the society and the community require for the protection of the community as a whole. It establishes the standards necessary to preserve public order and to protect property rights. It protects the right of individual privacy and the right to move about freely without fear of molestation. It does this primarily by defining conduct that is unacceptable and punishable.

In ancient times and on the frontiers in America, people had to protect themselves and thus moved about armed with weapons. If the law could not (or would not) punish an offender, the victim or family and friends would take on the punishment of the offender. Such retaliations could trigger blood feuds that went on for years between families and clans.

With the establishment of a system of laws and the growth of public confidence in the ability of the criminal justice system to preserve ordered liberty, people have generally ceased taking the law into their own hands. Public confidence that government, as an agent of the people, has the ability and the desire to maintain public order is an indispensable ingredient of a successful criminal justice system.[8]

Legal Wrongs

Legal wrongs are either civil or criminal. A *civil wrong* is a private wrong (such as a tort or a contract violation) done to a person or property; a *criminal wrong* is one in which the state and the public have declared an interest. Ordinarily, when a private wrong occurs, only the injured party or the party's representative may seek civil redress in a civil court of law. In almost every large American community there are three or four times as many civil courts, hearing civil cases in which private wrongs are alleged, as there are criminal courts, hearing cases involving public wrongs. In cases of public wrong, the state may either begin a criminal action in a criminal court or take the alleged public wrong into a civil court, as is done occasionally in obscenity, antitrust, or consumer fraud cases.

Distinction Between a Crime and a Tort

A *tort* is a civil wrong done to a person or to his or her property. The law of torts is the closest of the civil private laws to that of criminal law. Often the same wrong may constitute both a tort and a crime. For example, battery, rape, theft, criminal libel, and criminal damage to property are all torts and also crimes. Both civil actions by the injured parties and criminal actions by the state may be brought against the offenders. The offenders may be convicted of the crime in a criminal court and then in a civil court found to be civilly liable and ordered to pay compensatory and punitive damages to the victims for the torts that were committed.

Legislative Designations of Crime

Reasons a Legislative Body Might Designate Specific Conduct as Criminal

- To protect the public from violent or dangerous conduct
- To protect public health
- To maintain public order
- To protect the right of privacy of individuals
- To protect public morality
- Because there appears to be no other way in which to promote a desired public policy

Reasons a Legislative Body Might Not Designate Specific Conduct as Criminal

- It is not within the power of the government to prohibit such conduct
- The conduct in question is constitutionally protected
- There is no demand by influential public or private groups or individuals for the regulation of such conduct
- It would not be economically feasible to enforce a law criminalizing such conduct
- It would not be politically popular to pass a law criminalizing such conduct

A man who has thrown rocks at the windows of a private building, breaking ten windows and injuring one of the occupants before he is stopped, has committed both crimes and torts. Not only may a criminal action be brought against him for his conduct, but civil tort actions may also be brought against him by the person who was injured and by the person whose property was damaged. However, a man who has seriously injured another person in an automobile accident, in which the police and a prosecutor determine that there was neither a criminal violation nor criminal negligence, cannot properly be charged with a crime. In this case, only a civil action may be brought by the injured person or his or her representative. If the defendant were found to be civilly liable, this would then be an example of a tort that was not also a crime.

B. THE CRIMINAL LAW AND THE MORAL LAW

Criminal laws are strongest when they reflect the moral and ethical beliefs of the society. Murder, for example, is considered morally wrong, and most people would not murder another person even if it were not forbidden by all American jurisdictions. Murder, then, is forbidden not only by the criminal law, but also by the moral law. This moral or ethical commitment to the law is known as the "law behind the law." The importance of the "law behind the law" lies in the fact that it compels most people to conform to standards necessary for public order regardless of whether a police officer is watching them. Public order is not possible without the "law behind the law," as there are not enough police to enforce criminal law without this moral and ethical backing. Without moral or ethical commitments, who would watch the watchman or who would "police the police"?

The standards set by moral laws are generally higher than those set by criminal laws. Moral law attempts to perfect personal character, whereas criminal law, in general, is aimed at misbehavior that falls substantially below the norms of the community. Criminal conduct is ordinarily unjustifiable and inexcusable.

Criminal law alone cannot bring all conduct into conformity with the standards expected by the community. Society uses many sanctions besides criminal law to encourage and coerce people to behave properly. A person with a good job and savings knows that a substantial money judgment could be obtained against

---

Distinguishing Crime, Tort, and Moral Wrong

Type of Wrong	Court Determining Wrong
Crime A public wrong against society	Criminal court
Tort A private wrong against an individual or individuals	Civil court
Moral wrong Violation of a moral or religious code	No punishment unless the moral wrong is also a crime or tort

A crime may also be a tort and a moral wrong. For example, murder is a crime, a tort, and also a moral wrong.

him if he assaults, rapes, or libels other people. A spouse beater could end up in a divorce court instead of a criminal court. A person who is rude, abusive, and vulgar will lose friends and social standing. An employee who cannot get along with other people or who punches another employee in the face could be fired by the employer. Suspension of a driver's license and the revocation of a tavern license are other examples of sanctions used to regulate behavior.

Criminal codes do not include all the general moral concepts of society. The issue of which moral concepts should be embodied in a criminal code is primarily a political question, although courts may override lawmakers when constitutional issues are involved. For example, to many Americans, abortion is a moral wrong, but the U.S. Supreme Court has ruled on the constitutional limitations of the states' and the federal government's power to criminally forbid abortion in *Roe v. Wade*[9] (see chapter 12). This decision, like any other U.S. Supreme Court decision, could be set aside by an amendment to the U.S. Constitution that would give the federal and state governments full power to legislate in this area. Whether such an amendment would have sufficient support to be proposed and ratified is a political question for the Congress and the state legislative bodies.

The Eighteenth Amendment is an example of another dilemma that every democratic society faces. What social and governmental controls should be used to regulate the manufacture, sale, and consumption of alcohol? In 1918–19 a substantial number of Americans believed that consumption of intoxicating liquors was immoral and caused considerable social harm. They mustered sufficient political support to propose and ratify the Eighteenth Amendment forbidding the manufacture, sale, and consumption of intoxicating liquors except for

Why a Person Would or Would Not Commit a Crime

Why a Person Would Not Commit a Crime	*Why a Person Would Commit a Crime*
Moral or ethical commitment to obey the law ("law behind the law")	Neither moral nor ethical restraints are sufficient
Fear of arrest and punishment	Belief that he/she can get away without detection, arrest, and punishment
Social and peer pressures, of friends, associates, family, and community	Peer pressure
Fear of embarrassment to self, family, and friends	Belief that detection can be avoided, so there will be no embarrassment
Lack of motive or compelling drive to commit crime (no compelling desire to steal, murder, assault, rape, etc.)	Compelling desire or motive to achieve illegal objective (narcotic addiction, for example, provides motive for person who would probably not otherwise commit crime)
Lack of opportunity, or lack of capacity or skill to commit crime	Opportunity presents itself and person has capacity and skill
Fear of economic sanction: • loss of job, promotion • lawsuit and damages • loss of license, such as driver's license, tavern, lawyer, doctor, nurse, etc.	Crime can be a quick, easy way of obtaining money, drugs, power, or other objectives. Even if caught, the odds are good that the person will not go to prison. Very few persons convicted of nonviolent felonies go to prison.

limited uses. However, a significant number of Americans did not see anything morally wrong with having a glass of beer or a highball, thus creating a market for contraband, which the underworld readily supplied. The lesson learned from this situation was that if a significant number of people oppose and will not comply with a criminal law, enforcement of such law can run into serious difficulties.

Consider the following examples that further illustrate other moral dilemmas:

EXAMPLE 1: In 1983, a young woman entered a crowded New Bedford, Massachusetts, tavern to purchase cigarettes. Men in the bar grabbed her and commenced gang-raping her. Other tavern patrons watched and some cheered. No one came to her aid or called the police. If this incident occurred in your state, could any of the witnesses be charged with a criminal offense?

EXAMPLE 2: In 1964, Kitty Genovese was murdered in New York City in an attack that lasted some 35 minutes. More than 38 persons were in nearby apartments, with most witnessing the attack. Had the police been called immediately, or had someone come to her assistance, Kitty Genovese could have been saved. If this incident occurred in your state, could any of the witnesses be charged with a criminal offense?

The Principle That There Can Be "No Punishment Without a Law for It"

A basic principle of both English and American law is that no one can be lawfully punished for his or her conduct (or omission) unless that conduct has been clearly made a crime by statutory or common law of that jurisdiction. The Latin maxim *Nulla poena sine lege* ("no punishment without law") long ago established this principle.

Although it is impossible for the state to enumerate in detail each act (or omission) that the legislature seeks to forbid, the criminal statute may describe generally the act or acts forbidden (or required). However, the criminal statute must be directed at a defined evil (or wrong) and must be written clearly enough to provide notice as to what acts are forbidden (or required).

Therefore, in view of the principle that there can be "no punishment without a law for it," the following questions must be asked before any person is arrested, charged with a crime, or convicted: *What has the person done that violates the statutes of your state? Was the person legally (not just morally) obligated to act and did he fail to perform his legal (not moral) duty?*

In view of these principles, did the witnesses in Examples 1 and 2 commit acts in violation of criminal laws in your jurisdiction? The answer would depend upon the laws of your state and whether they imposed a duty upon the witnesses to act. Parents are legally obligated to help their children. The common law requires that husbands come to the assistance of their wives. Unless your state has a statute imposing an obligation on bystanders to come to the assistance of people in distress, there is no legal duty.

Civil Liability of Witnesses to Crimes

Witnesses to crimes are not criminally liable unless they perform acts that make them parties to the crime (see chapter 4, Criminal Liability).[10]

Are witnesses civilly liable for failure to act or to render aid in some form? The general rule of law is that there is no civil liability.[11] Public and private organizations, however, must exercise ordinary care in providing adequate security for customers, tenants, and others who are lawfully on their premises. This relationship creates a duty to aid and protect.

Because the tavern employees in Example 1 did not come to the aid of the woman being sexually assaulted, the tavern is civilly liable to the woman. A civil lawsuit was filed for this breach of duty to the woman, who was a customer and lawfully on the premises.[12]

C. CLASSIFICATION OF CRIMES

Many acts have been designated as criminal offenses in the United States. The President's Commission on Crime reported in 1966 in *The Challenge of Crime in a Free Society* (p. 18) that the federal government alone has designated more than 2,800 offenses as crimes and noted that "a much larger number of State and local" offenses exist.

The large number of crimes in the United States may be classified as follows:

1. According to their sources, as statutory, common law, administrative, or constitutional crimes (see chapter 2)
2. As felonies or misdemeanors, which determines the method in which they are tried and, in many states, affects the law of arrest for such offenses. Many states classify felonies and misdemeanors as Class A, Class B, etc. In this way, punishment standardized as a class B felony is generally a twenty-year felony, a class C felony is a ten-year felony, etc. (see material below on Felony and Misdemeanor.)
3. According to the harm or wrong that occurs (see your state criminal code for classifications of crime, such as "crimes against the person," "crimes against property," etc.)

Felony and Misdemeanor

The felony-misdemeanor classification is the most common classification used for crimes. In old English common law, crimes were classified as either treason, felony, or misdemeanor. Treason was the most serious of the three, with the lands of the traitor being forfeited to the king on conviction. The felon's land might also be forfeited, but usually he did not meet so horrible a death as the traitor. Ironically, under early English common law, those who were charged with a misdemeanor could call witnesses in their favor and have the assistance of counsel, whereas those who were charged with a felony did not have these rights.

As the years went by the classification of treason faded away because people were rarely charged with the crime. In 1967, the English Parliament decided that the distinction between felonies and misdemeanors had become so blurred that all distinctions between the two classes were abolished by the Criminal Law Act of 1967. The English now use the classification of arrestable and nonarrestable offenses. An English police officer has no power to arrest for the latter without a

"Good Samaritan" Laws

Broadly Defined, "Good Samaritan" Laws Include Statutes that Fall into the Following Categories:

1. Practically all states have enacted "Good Samaritan" laws that encourage doctors and other health practitioners to aid injured or ill strangers. Such statutes do not encourage acts of heroism or impose a duty to aid, but rather they eliminate fear of malpractice suits that had discouraged doctors and others from rendering assistance to those who had been injured or were ill.

2. The New Bedford (Mass.) bar room rape incident caused some American states to enact "Good Samaritan" statutes requiring persons to come to the aid of a victim if they can do so without endangering themselves. This could be simply calling the police. Violations of such American laws are generally punished by a small fine. Many European countries have similar statutes that include possible jail sentences. It is reported that violations of the French statute could result in up to five years in prison.

3. Another form of a "Good Samaritan" law is a statute passed by Maryland in 1982: "Any person witnessing a violent assault upon the person of another may lawfully aid the person being assaulted by assisting in that person's defense" (Art. 27, Sec. 12A). This statute and others authorizing force in self-defense or the defense of another *do not impose a duty* to come to the assistance of another. See the 1982 case of *Alexander v. State* in Chapter 6, in which a prisoner in a Maryland penitentiary saw two guards subduing another prisoner and was charged with assaulting the guards when he physically intervened. The prisoner used this Maryland statute in his defense arguing his conduct was lawful.

warrant, which limits the arrest authority of British police. But British officers have considerably more search authority than do American officers.

For procedural purposes, England now classifies crimes as summary and indictable offenses. *Summary offenses* are minor criminal charges tried before a magistrate having summary jurisdiction. A number of offenses that were previously felonies were made summary offenses. There is no right to a jury trial for a summary offense. Serious offenses, which are now referred to as *indictable offenses,* are all tried before a jury. This is possible because English jury procedures are much faster than those used in impaneling a jury in the United States. The distinction between serious and minor crimes is maintained in England, but the main distinction today lies in the right to have the offense tried with or without a jury.

The automatic forfeiture of the land of an offender was never used as a punishment for serious offenses in the United States, and treason was never used as a classification separate from felonies and misdemeanors. The classification of minor crimes as misdemeanors and serious crimes as felonies has always been used in the United States, and it has been the responsibility of legislatures to determine which crimes are misdemeanors and which are felonies. The legislatures have added many new felonies to the original list of common law felonies. Most of these new felonies are offenses not known at common law, but there are instances of common law misdemeanors becoming statutory felonies.

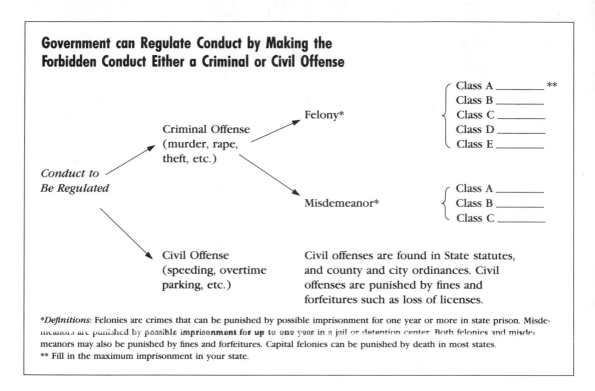

Government can Regulate Conduct by Making the Forbidden Conduct Either a Criminal or Civil Offense

Conduct to Be Regulated

Criminal Offense (murder, rape, theft, etc.)

Felony*

Class A _____ **
Class B _____
Class C _____
Class D _____
Class E _____

Misdemeanor*

Class A _____
Class B _____
Class C _____

Civil Offense (speeding, overtime parking, etc.)

Civil offenses are found in State statutes, and county and city ordinances. Civil offenses are punished by fines and forfeitures such as loss of licenses.

*Definitions: Felonies are crimes that can be punished by possible imprisonment for one year or more in state prison. Misdemeanors are punished by possible imprisonment for up to one year in a jail or detention center. Both felonies and misdemeanors may also be punished by fines and forfeitures. Capital felonies can be punished by death in most states.
** Fill in the maximum imprisonment in your state.

Effect of the Felony-Misdemeanor Classification Today

In the United States, whether a crime is a felony or a misdemeanor is important for the following reasons:

1. Public policy has made a felony a more serious offense than a misdemeanor. Imprisonment in a state prison and a longer term of imprisonment could be imposed for a felony. A felony conviction on a person's record could seriously affect his or her entering any of the professional fields. It would seriously stand in the way to obtaining employment in any law enforcement agency, or entering the armed forces of the United States. It would prevent employment with any law enforcement agency. It would prevent the obtaining of a commission with the U.S. armed forces. It might affect credit rating or ability to adopt a child. A misdemeanor conviction would not ordinarily have these effects.[13]

2. Law enforcement officers in states using the "in-presence" requirement for misdemeanor arrests may not make an arrest for a misdemeanor not committed in their presence. An arrest for a felony may be made if the officer has reasonable grounds to believe that the person has committed the felony, regardless of whether the offense was committed in the officer's presence.

EXAMPLE: An officer in a state using the "in presence" requirement is sent to a department store, where the store security man tells him that he saw X shoplift a $25 item. Because the offense is a misdemeanor and did not occur in the officer's presence, the officer ordinarily may not make an arrest.

In the example given the officer could obtain the identification of the person and then "order the person in," that is, instruct him to report to the office of a prosecuting attorney at a given time. If the officer has reasonable grounds to believe that the person (a) will not report in as required, or (b) will cause injury to himself or others unless immediately arrested, or (c) will cause damage to property, the officer may then make an immediate arrest if the officer's jurisdiction uses these circumstances as exceptions to the "in presence" requirement rule.

3. A person charged with a felony has a right to a preliminary hearing (or a "presentment or indictment of a grand jury").[14]

4. In most states, citizens would have no authority to make an arrest for a misdemeanor under their "citizen arrest" power unless the law of the state permitted an arrest for a breach of the peace committed in the citizen's presence.[15] However, a citizen may generally arrest for a felony committed in his or her presence unless the statutes or common law of the state (or jurisdiction) provide otherwise.

Crimes of Commission as Distinguished from Crimes of Omission

Most criminal laws are written like most of the Ten Commandments. They forbid specific conduct. Do not murder. Do not rob. Do not rape. Such offenses are called crimes of commission. All persons are told by the law that they should not commit (do) the specific conduct that is forbidden.

All states also have a few laws that impose upon persons an obligation and a duty to act under certain circumstances. A motorist who is involved in an accident is legally obligated to stop, render assistance, and identify himself or herself. Failure to comply with these demands of the law is a crime of omission (failure to do a required act).

Before an officer makes an arrest, or a prosecutor issues a criminal complaint, each must ask themselves: (a) what did the person do that violated a specific criminal statute? Or, (b) what duty did the person fail to perform that he or she was legally obligated to?

White-collar Crimes

Such crimes as murder, rape, robbery, auto theft, battery, and larceny are ordinarily classified as "street crimes." Crimes that do not involve direct physical violence but are crimes of personal or corporate gain may be classified as "economic crimes," "business crimes," or "commercial crimes" (or "crimes in the suites").

The term *white-collar crime* was originated in the 1930s by sociologist Edwin H. Sutherland to indicate the nonviolent crimes of personal enrichment committed by people in their work or occupation or, occasionally, in defrauding other people or governmental agencies. These crimes may be committed in offices, banks, financial institutions—anywhere money, securities, or anything of value is handled by white-collar employees. As this type of crime is sometimes committed by "yuppie-type" persons, such crimes are also occasionally called "yuppie" crimes. Cheating, dishonesty, and corruption can also be found among blue-collar workers, but generally blue collar workers do not have access to as much money as either white-collar or yuppie criminals. Professor Sutherland

When Failure to Act is a Crime: Crimes of Omission

Statute number
of the offense
in your state.
(If not a crime,
indicate status
of this conduct
in your state.)

1. Failure to remain at the scene of a vehicular accident in which a person
   was involved (Also list other responsibilities of the person required in
   your state)
2. Failure to aid an officer when requested to do so   _____
3. Failure to report the death of a child   _____
4. Failure to report the location of a human corpse   _____
5. Failure by parent, guardian, etc. to provide adequate food, clothing, shelter, medical care, supervision, etc. for a child in his/her care when harm
   results or might result   _____
6. Failure by parent, guardian, etc. to come to the aid of a child in his/her
   care when such aid would not place the adult in any serious danger   _____
7. Failure to aid, come to the assistance, or to summon police for crime victim by a person who knows that a crime of bodily harm has occurred
   when such aid would not place the person in any serious danger   _____
8. Failure to leave or withdraw when ordered by a public official who has
   declared that an unlawful assembly exists   _____
9. Failure to "move on" or to leave a place when properly and lawfully ordered to do so by a law enforcement officer   _____
10. Failure to properly identify oneself and explain one's conduct when prop-
    erly and lawfully ordered to do so by a law enforcement officer (see
    sec. 250.6 Loitering or Prowling of the Model Penal Code)   _____
11. Failure to submit to a breathalyzer test (or other similar test) when prop-
    erly and lawfully requested to do so by a law enforcement officer   _____
12. Failure to obey a proper and legal order of a court (see chapter 21, on
    contempt)   _____
13. Homicide by omission (see the Ford Pinto case in chapter 5)   _____

originally intended the term white-collar crime more as a classification of offenders than as a classification of offenses. However, the term seems to be used today
more as a classification of offenses.

Victimless Crimes

The term *victimless crimes* is used to designate crimes that do not have a victim
in the sense that murder, robbery, rape, battery, and theft do.

Most victims of reported crimes are cooperative with the police and anxious
that the offender be apprehended. The victimless crime is a crime committed by
two or more persons, both of whom readily participate in the crime. Such offenses include narcotics violations, gambling, prostitution, homosexual acts, and
liquor violations. For example, X sells heroin to Y (an addict) in X's apartment. No
one else is present. The transaction is a crime, but the offense is unlikely to come

---

Examples of Victimless Crimes used by Many or All States*

Drug violations

Public drunkenness (decriminalized by many states)

Prostitution

Gambling (many forms of gambling now legalized)

Obscenity offenses involving consenting adults

Fortune-telling

Dueling (both parties consent but can result in victim)

Loan-sharking (when both parties voluntarily enter agreement)

Examples of Victimless Crimes that Have Been Abolished by Many States

Fornication
Adultery
Homosexual relations
Cohabitation

Between consenting adults in a nonpublic place

Examples of Victimless Crimes that Have Been Declared Unconstitutional

Use of contraceptives (even by married couples)—*Griswold v. Connecticut,* 381 U.S. 479 (1965)

Possession of or reading obscene material in privacy of one's home—*Stanley v. Georgia,* 394 U.S. 557 (1969)

California made drug addiction a crime in and of itself—*Robinson v. California,* 370 U.S. 660 (1962)

*Some persons point out that society is the "victim" of many of these offenses.

---

to the attention of the police because there is no victim and neither X nor Y have any intention of disclosing their criminal act.

The Criminal Justice Standards and Goals Report states that the "nature of some victimless crimes makes them excellent targets for organized crime." The report advises that "[s]tates and localities should exercise caution in considering the legalization or decriminalization of so-called 'victimless crimes' . . . because there is insufficient evidence that legalization or decriminalization of such crimes will materially reduce the income of organized crime."[16]

D. GENERAL LIMITATIONS ON CRIMINAL LAWS

States Have Broad Power to Enact Criminal Laws

The U.S. Supreme Court stated that "[b]roadly speaking, crimes in the United States are what the law of the individual States make them, subject to (constitutional) limitations. . . ."[17]

States, therefore, have broad authority to create criminal laws. But criminal laws cannot violate rights of persons protected or granted by the U.S. Constitution (or the constitution of that state). States cannot criminalize conduct protected by the First Amendment freedoms of speech, religion, or the freedom to move about freely (see chapters 11, 12, and 13). Nor could a state impose a punishment that violates the Eighth Amendment prohibition against "cruel and unusual punishment" (see chapter 8). Chapters 6 and 7 on defenses also present other constitutional limitations. Other general limitations on criminal laws follow.

Ex Post Facto Laws

A state legislature could not create a new crime in November and make the law retroactive so as to punish conduct occurring in September or October of that year. Article 1, Sections 9 and 10 of the U.S. Constitution prohibit federal and state governments from enacting ex post facto laws. Most state constitutions also forbid such laws. Ex post facto (after the fact) restrictions apply only to criminal laws. Therefore, a state legislature may pass a new tax law and make it retroactive. Taxpayers would not like this and political reactions could result in the defeat of elected officials, but such a law would not involve constitutional violations (unless the tax law was enforced by criminal penalties).

The ex post facto clause forbids the following: (a) creating a criminal law and making it retroactive so as to make conduct before the enactment of the law a criminal violation; (b) laws that aggravate a crime retroactively (for example, making a misdemeanor a felony as of a date six months before the enactment of the legislation); (c) laws that increase the punishment for a crime retroactively; and (d) laws that alter the legal rules of evidence and permit conviction on less or different testimony than the law required at the time of the commission of the offense.

The ex post facto clause protects conduct that is innocent when performed and requires that "persons have a right to fair warning of conduct which will give rise to criminal penalties . . ." (U.S. Supreme Court in *Marks v. United States,* 430 U.S. 188, 97 S.Ct. 990, 992 (1977)).

An ex post facto law is, then, a retroactive criminal law that works to the detriment of the defendant charged with an offense. However, a retroactive law that benefits a defendant is not forbidden. For example, a state legislature may pass a retroactive law that reduces a felony to a misdemeanor. In such case, the defendant would not challenge the validity of the law.

In the 1977 case of *Dobbert v. Florida,*[18] the U.S. Supreme Court reviewed the ex post facto cases that had come before that Court over the years. In the *Dobbert* case the defendant was sentenced to death under a Florida statute that was revised after the defendant's crimes to afford more, not less, protection. The penalty of death was part of the statute before the crimes and was retained in the statute after the crimes were committed. The Supreme Court affirmed the defendant's conviction, as the new statute provided him with more, rather than less, judicial protection than did the old statute.

Bill of Attainder

Article 1, Sections 9 and 10, also forbid Congress and the states from enacting any bill of attainder. A *bill of attainder* is a legislative act that inflicts punishment without a judicial trial. In 1965, the U.S. Supreme Court stated the history of the bill of attainder in *United States v. Brown:*

> The bill of attainder, a parliamentary act sentencing to death one or more specific persons, was a device often resorted to in sixteenth, seventeenth and eighteenth

century England for dealing with persons who had attempted, or threatened to attempt, to overthrow the government. In addition to the death sentence, attainder generally carried with it a "corruption of blood" which meant that the attained party's heirs could not inherit his property. The "bill of pains and penalties" was identical to the bill of attainder, except that it prescribed a penalty short of death, e.g. banishment, deprivation of the right to vote, or exclusion of the designated party's sons from Parliament. Most bills of attainder and bills of pains and penalties named the parties to whom they were to apply; a few, however, simply described them. While some left the designated parties a way of escaping the penalty, others did not. The use of bills of attainder and bills of pains and penalties was not limited to England. During the American Revolution, the legislatures of all thirteen States passed statutes directed against the Tories; among these statutes were a large number of bills of attainder and bill of pains and penalties.[19]

By forbidding bills of attainder, the Constitution limits legislatures to the task of rule making and gives to the courts the function of determining whether rules have been violated. In the *Brown* case, the defendant was a San Francisco longshoreman and an officer of his union. He was an open and avowed Communist and was charged and convicted of violating the Labor-Management Reporting and Disclosure Act of 1959, which made it a crime for a member of the Communist party to serve as an officer or an employee of a labor union. In a 5-4 decision, the Supreme Court held that the Reporting and Disclosure Act of 1959 was a bill of attainder, and stated that "Congress must accomplish such results by rules of general applicability. It cannot specify the people upon whom the sanction it prescribes is to be levied. Under our Constitution, Congress possesses full legislative authority, but the task of adjudication must be left to other tribunals."

Legislative bodies, however, have the power to punish for contempt for such acts as disrupting or immobilizing their vital legislative functions (see chapter 22 and the 1972 U.S. Supreme Court case of *Groppi v. Leslie* in that chapter).

Void-for-Vagueness

In writing a criminal statute or ordinance, a legislative body must use clear and precise language that gives fair and adequate notice as to the conduct that is forbidden (or required). If the language of a statute or ordinance is vague, it may be held unconstitutional under the "void-for-vagueness" doctrine.

The void-for-vagueness test asks whether a statute or ordinance on its face "is so vague that men of common intelligence must guess at its meaning and differ as to its application."[20] A vague criminal statute or ordinance creates uncertainty as to what the law requires and may have some or all the following results:

1. It may trap those who desire to be law-abiding by not providing fair notice of what is prohibited.[21]

2. It may cause arbitrary and discriminatory enforcement, since those who enforce and apply the law have no clear and explicit standards to guide them.[22]

3. When a vague statute "abut(s) upon sensitive areas of First Amendment freedoms, it operates to inhibit the exercise of (those) freedoms. Uncertain meaning inevitably leads citizens to steer far wider of the unlawful zone ... than if the boundaries of the forbidden areas were clearly marked.[23]

Overbreadth

Criminal statutes and ordinances may also be held to be unconstitutional if the manner in which they are written violates the Overbreadth Doctrine. In 1967, the U.S. Supreme Court stated that overbreadth "offends the constitutional principle that a governmental purpose to control or prevent activities constitutionally subject to state regulation may not be achieved by means which sweep unnecessarily broadly and thereby invade the area of protected freedoms."[24] A vague statute or ordinance may be overbroad if its uncertain boundaries leave open the possibility of punishment for protected conduct and thus lead people to avoid such protected activity in order to steer clear of violating the uncertain law.[25] However, a clear and precise statute may also be overbroad if it prohibits constitutionally protected conduct.

The void-for-vagueness test and the overbreadth test are separate and distinct. However, when First Amendment rights are at issue, the U.S. Supreme Court uses the two tests in a manner that makes them virtually one doctrine. From the cases, it can be stated that statutes and ordinances that regulate conduct must comply with the following requirements:

1. Fair and adequate notice must be given as to the conduct that is forbidden (or required).
2. A precise standard of conduct must be specified in terms of results that can reasonably be expected.
3. The statute or ordinance cannot permit or encourage arbitrary and discriminatory law enforcement that may result in erratic and arbitrary arrests and convictions.
4. The statute or ordinance cannot violate or infringe on rights that are secured or granted by the U.S. Constitution.

The following are some of the cases in which the Supreme Court has applied these doctrines:

COATES v. CITY OF CINCINNATI
Supreme Court of the United States (1971) 402 U.S. 611, 91 S.Ct. 1686

In this case, the Court declared unconstitutional a Cincinnati ordinance that made it illegal for three or more persons assembled on a city sidewalk to "annoy" those passing by. The Court stated:

Conduct that annoys some people does not annoy others. Thus, the ordinance is vague, not in the sense that it requires a person to conform his conduct to an imprecise but comprehensible normative standard, but rather in the sense that no conduct is specified at all.

PAPACHRISTOU v. CITY OF JACKSONVILLE
Supreme Court of the United States (1972) 405 U.S. 156, 92 S.Ct. 839

The Supreme Court held the following Jacksonville ordinance unconstitutionally vague:

Rogues and vagabonds, or dissolute persons who go about begging, common gamblers ... common drunkards, common night walkers ... lewd, wanton and lascivious persons ... common railers and brawlers, persons wandering or strolling

*around from place to place without any lawful purpose or object, habitual loafers
... shall be deemed vagrants.*

BOARD OF AIRPORT COMMISSIONERS v. JEWS FOR JESUS, INC.
Supreme Court of the United States (1987) 482 U.S. 569, 107 S.Ct. 2568

The Court held that an airport regulation that forbade a minister of the "Jews for Jesus"
group from distributing free religious literature was so broad it "prohibits even talking and
reading, or the wearing of campaign buttons or symbolic clothing." The Court further held:

* * *

*A statute may be invalidated on its face, however, only if the overbreadth is "sub-
stantial."* Houston v Hill, *482 U.S. 451, 107 S.Ct. 2502, 96 L.Ed.2d 398 (1987).*

* * *

*The requirement that the overbreadth be substantial arose from our recognition
that application of the overbreadth doctrine is, "manifestly, strong medicine,"*
Broadrick v Oklahoma, *supra, at 613, 37 L.Ed.2d 830, 93 S.Ct. 2908, and that "there
must be a realistic danger that the statute itself will significantly compromise
recognized First Amendment protections of parties not before the Court for it to be
facially challenged on overbreadth grounds."* City Council v Taxpayers for Vincent,
466 U.S. 789, 801, 80 L.Ed.2d 772, 104 S.Ct. 2118 (1984).

* * *

CITY OF HOUSTON v. HILL
Supreme Court of the United States (1987) 482 U.S. 451, 107 S.Ct. 2502

A city ordinance that made it unlawful to "in any manner . . . interrupt any policeman in the
execution of his duty," was held to be so unusually broad that it authorized police officers
to arrest virtually anyone who might annoy them while they were on official business. The
Court held the ordinance "accords the police unconstitutional discretion in enforcement."
(One observer pointed out that under this ordinance, a citizen who interrupted a policeman to tell the officer of a bank robbery could lawfully be arrested.)

KOLENDER v. LAWSON
Supreme Court of the United States (1983) 461 U.S. 352, 103 S.Ct. 1855

The Supreme Court held that

> *"[A] penal statute [must] define the criminal offense with sufficient definiteness
> that ordinary people can understand what conduct is prohibited and in a manner
> that does not encourage arbitrary and discriminatory enforcement."*[26]

GRAYNED v. CITY OF ROCKFORD
Supreme Court of the United States (1972) 408 U.S. 104, 92 S.Ct. 2294

> *[L]aws [must] give the person of ordinary intelligence a reasonable opportunity to
> know what is prohibited, so that he may act accordingly.*

LANZETTA v. NEW JERSEY
Supreme Court of the United States (1939) 306 U.S. 451, 59 S.Ct. 618

> *No one may be required at peril of life, liberty or property to speculate as to the meaning of penal statutes.*

WARREN v. STATE
Supreme Court of Florida (1991) 572 So.2d 1376

Kathleen Warren was charged with keeping "a house of ill fame resorted to (for) the purpose of prostitution or lewdness" as forbidden by Florida statute 796.01. The Supreme Court of Florida found that the words "prostitution" and "lewdness" were words that could be understood by persons today but held that:

> *... the term "ill fame" might have been sufficiently understandable when the legislature first adopted this statute in 1868, it is now outdated. Section 796.01 does not provide an objective standard for differentiating between permitted and prohibited conduct and fails to provide fair notice in language relevant to today's society. Therefore, we hold that section 796.01 is unconstitutionally vague ...*

"Status" Crimes

A state may regulate and control the use of such drugs as heroin, cocaine, crack, etc. in a number of different ways. The government may (and does) forbid the importing or manufacturing of the drugs; the law forbids possession and transportation of the forbidden drugs; the sale, use, or possession of such drugs is also forbidden. All of these specific acts (conduct) have been determined to be harmful to others or to the society as a whole. But can a state make addiction to heroin, cocaine, or crack, by itself, a crime?

To do something about its increasing heroin problem in the late 1950s, California passed a law making heroin addiction, by itself, a crime. The issue before the U.S. Supreme Court in the 1962 case of *Robinson v. California*[27] was whether a person could be arrested and convicted for what he or she is (or was). The U.S. Supreme Court considered the question as to whether a state could make a "status" or a "chronic condition" a crime in itself.

In pointing out the many ways in which government may legitimately attack the evils of narcotics trafficking, the U.S. Supreme Court reversed the defendant's conviction. In holding that a state law that made "status" of narcotic addiction a criminal offense for which an offender might be prosecuted and imprisoned at any time, the Court held that such a criminal statute inflicted a "cruel and unusual punishment" in violation of the Eighth and Fourteenth Amendments of the U.S. Constitution. The Court stated that "even one day in prison would be a cruel and unusual punishment for the 'crime' of having a common cold."

In the 1968 case of *Powell v. Texas*,[28] the defendant was an alcoholic with approximately one hundred arrests for acts of public intoxication. In this case, the defendant argued that because he was compelled to drink and because he could not control his "status," the state did not have the power to punish him for his acts of public intoxication. The U.S. Supreme Court, however, affirmed Powell's conviction holding that he was arrested and convicted for what he did (being drunk in a public place) and that Powell was not convicted for what he was (status). In refusing to extend the rule of law that had been established in the case of *Robinson v. California,* the Supreme Court held:

> Traditional common-law concepts of personal accountability and essential considerations of federalism lead us to disagree with appellant. We are unable to conclude, on the state of this record or on the current state of medical knowledge, that chronic alcoholics in general, and Leroy Powell in particular, suffer from such an irresistible compulsion to drink and to get drunk in public that they are utterly unable to control their performance of either or both of these acts and thus cannot be deterred at all from public intoxication.

"Equal Protection of the Laws"

If a state made the crime of burglary in that state applicable only to males, the first man charged with burglary in that state would challenge the statute arguing that it violated the Fourteenth Amendment requirement of "equal protection of the laws." Women could commit burglary in that state, but for the same conduct a man could be convicted and sent to jail.

The "equal protection of the laws" clause of the Fourteenth Amendment requires that states must treat all persons alike, not only in enacting criminal and civil laws, but also in enforcing rules. For example, probably all states have consanguinity laws forbidding marriages between brothers and sisters (and other close relatives). Consanguinity laws apply to all persons, regardless of status, race, or religion.[29] They represent a valid exercise of the police power of a state because children born to closely related parents are more apt to be deformed.

But can a state make it a crime for black persons to marry white persons, or for persons of different races to live together? A few of the Southern states had such laws in the early 1960s, which applied only to white and black persons committing the specific acts that were forbidden. Can states forbid marriage between members of different races (miscegenation laws)? This issue was presented to the U.S. Supreme Court in the following case.

LOVING v. VIRGINIA
Supreme Court of the United States (1967) 388 U.S. 1, 87 S.Ct. 1817

Richard Loving, a white man, and Mildred Jeter, a black woman, were lawfully married in Washington, D.C. They then moved to the State of Virginia which forbade interracial marriages. The Lovings were criminally indicted and pleaded guilty to the charges. They were sentenced to one year in jail. However, the trial judge suspended the sentence on the condition that the Lovings leave Virginia and not return for twenty-five years. The convictions and sentences were appealed to the U.S. Supreme Court. The Court noted that "Virginia is now one of 16 States which prohibit and punish marriages on the basis of racial classifications." In declaring such laws unconstitutional, the U.S. Supreme Court held:

* * *

> *These statutes ... deprive the Lovings of liberty without due process of law in violation of the Due Process Clause of the Fourteenth Amendment. The freedom to marry has long been recognized as one of the vital personal rights essential to the orderly pursuit of happiness by free men.*

Marriage is one of the "basic civil rights of man," fundamental to our very existence and survival. . . . To deny this fundamental freedom on so unsupportable a basis as the racial classifications embodied in these statutes, classifications so directly subversive of the principle of equality at the heart of the Fourteenth Amendment, is surely to deprive all the State's citizens of liberty without due process of law. The Fourteenth Amendment requires that the freedom of choice to marry not be restricted by invidious racial discriminations. Under our Constitution, the freedom to marry or not marry, a person of another race resides with the individual and cannot be infringed by the State.

These convictions must be reversed. It is so ordered.

* * *

Questions and Problems for Chapter 1

1. X and his wife, Y, were involved in an automobile accident in which X was not at fault in any way. However, their ten-year-old child was seriously injured. A doctor at the scene of the accident told X and Y that the child could be saved with immediate medical attention. However, because of their religious beliefs, X and Y refused to allow their child to be treated. The child died the next day. Could X and Y be charged? What could the charge be?

2. M is hired by a family that is going on vacation to take care of their ninety-year-old grandmother. M is to feed and give daily medication to the elderly woman, who cannot get out of bed. After three days on the job, M quits without notifying anyone and takes another job. The elderly woman dies because she did not receive medication or food and water for two days. Should M be charged with a criminal offense? Specify. (For a discussion of criminal imputability for negative acts, see pp. 591–610 of *Perkins on Criminal Law,* 2d ed. [Mineola, N.Y.: Foundation Press, 1969].)

3. A five-year-old child is in sudden peril when a big wave hits him while in shallow water at the beach. Each of the following could have saved him with no risk to himself but all fail to come to the child's assistance. Indicate the legal liability of each and whether he can be charged in your state with the death of the child.
   a. the father of the child
   b. the lifeguard on duty
   c. a stranger sunning on the beach who took pictures of the child's death

4. In a bad storm over your state, a plane lost most of its power 50 miles from the closest landing field. To lighten the load, the crew threw out baggage and other items. When this was not enough, the crew, in desperation, began to throw passengers off the plane. Had not 20 of the 40 passengers been thrown off, the pilot would not have been able to land the plane safely. Should the crew be congratulated for saving the plane, or charged with the deaths of the passengers who were killed?

5. Ten-year-old Johnnie is punished by his mother for eating all the cookies in the cookie jar. Which of the following instructions by the mother, given just before she left the house for an hour, would not violate the void-for-vagueness principle?
   a. "Be a good boy, Johnnie."
   b. "Don't do anything naughty, Johnnie."
   c. "Don't go into the cookie jar, Johnnie."
   d. "Don't eat anything and spoil your appetite because we are going to have dinner in an hour."
   e. c. and d. are correct

Explain your answer.

6. Michael was almost 18 years old. Around midnight on a summer's night, he approached a 16½-year-old girl, Sharon, and her sister as they waited at a bus stop. The girls had been drinking. Michael and Sharon moved away from the others and began to kiss. When Sharon objected to Michael's sexual advances, Michael struck her in the face. Sharon then submitted to sexual intercourse. If the California prosecutor had charged Michael with rape, the State would have had a very difficult time obtaining a criminal conviction. Therefore, based on the statements of the parties and witnesses (and other evidence),

Michael was charged with violating California's "statutory rape" law. This law in California forbade sexual intercourse with a female under 18 (who is not a wife of the perpetrator). Another term for this offense is "SIWAC" (sexual intercourse with a child). As the statute makes men alone criminally liable, Michael attacked the statute as violating "equal protection of the laws." Does California have a valid state interest in enacting a "statutory rape" law and making it applicable to men only? Explain. *Michael M. v. Superior Court of Sonoma City,* 450 U.S. 464, 101 S.Ct. 1200 (1981).

Notes

1. See the article "Murder rate soars higher across US" in the 12/20/90 issue of the *Milwaukee Journal.*

2. See the *New York Times* articles "U.S. is by Far the Leader in Homicide" (6/27/90) and "More Americans Are Killing Each Other" (12/31/89).

3. See the 1/25/91 *New York Times* article "Cocaine Use Found on the Way Down Among U.S. Youths: Middle-Class Drug Crisis May Have Run its Course in the 80s, Experts Say."

The Chairman of the U.S. House Select Committee stated in December, 1987 that "We have more drugs on our streets than we have ever had before." Reports show that tens of thousands of tons of heroin, cocaine, and marijuana are smuggled into the United States every year. "Anytime you have 1 out of 10 Americans using or abusing drugs," the chairman of the Drug Law Enforcement Coordinating Group stated, "you have a problem that won't be solved overnight." It is estimated that 23 million Americans are thought to be routine drug users.

4. See the 1/7/91 *New York Times* article "Rate of Imprisonment in U.S. Is Cited as Highest in World."

5. Former Governor Thompson's remarks appear in the *Journal of Criminal Law and Criminology,* 73 (1982): 867.

6. Before the dramatic changes and new freedoms in the countries of Eastern Europe, only about one-third of the world's population enjoyed civil and political liberties. The other two-thirds did not have civil and political liberties classified as living in a free society.

7. See James Q. Wilson's book, *Thinking About Crime* (New York: Basic Books, 1983), in which he states that "the average citizen thinks it obvious that one major reason why crime has increased is that people have discovered they can get away with it." This reflects a belief that the criminal justice system is neither efficient nor effective.

8. Failure to protect citizens breeds crime. When the government fails to protect citizens, some persons are likely to take the law into their own hands. An example of private justice (vigilantism) may have occurred in a New York subway in December 1984. Bernhard Goetz told New York police that he believed that he was about to be robbed and that he produced a gun, shot his presumed assailants, and then left the scene. A New York grand jury would not indict Goetz for the shooting, but did indict him for the illegal possession of a hand gun. He was convicted and punished for that offense.

9. 410 U.S. 113, 93 S.Ct. 705 (1973).

10. Witnesses may not be arrested unless they are party to a crime. But witnesses may be detained to obtain their identities and the information that they have regarding the crime. However, if a witness to a crime encourages the perpetrator to commit the crime, the witness could be charged as an aider and abetter to the crime (see chapter 4 of this text).

11. See 65 C.J.S. Negligence, sec. 63 (106) (1966), and Restatement (2d) of Torts, sec. 314 (1965).

12. See Restatement (2d) of Torts, sec. 314A, "Special Relations Giving Rise to a Duty of Aid or Protect."

13. When good reasons are given, state governors are likely to grant a pardon for a felony or misdemeanor conviction. The pardon will wipe the slate clean for the person. Depending upon the law of the state, governors have the authority and power to grant clemency in different ways. They may grant a pardon, or commute, or modify a sentence. Such clemency could be conditional if authorized by the state law.

14. Fifth Amendment to the U.S. Constitution.

15. Some states authorize store employees to arrest persons for shoplifting, which in most cases is a misdemeanor or is charged as an ordinance violation. The shoplifting statutes of other states authorize the store employees to detain the suspect until the police (or sheriff) arrive.

16. National Advisory Committee on Criminal Justice Standards and Goals Report on Organized Crime, pp. 218–219.

17. *Rochin v. California,* 342 U.S. 165, 168, 72 S.Ct. 205, 207 (1952).

18. 432 U.S. 282, 97 S.Ct. 2290, 21 CrL 3159 (1977).

19. 381 U.S. 437, 85 S.Ct. 1707 (1965).

20. *Connally v. General Construction Co.,* 269 U.S. 385, 46 S.Ct. 126 (1926).

21. See *Papachristou v. City of Jacksonville,* 405 U.S. 156, 162, 92 S.Ct. 839, 843 (1972), and *United States v. Harriss,* 347 U.S. 612, 617, 74 S.Ct. 808, 811 (1954).

22. See *Coates v. City of Cincinnati,* 402 U.S. 611, 614, 91 S.Ct. 1686, 1688 (1971), and *Shuttlesworth v. Birmingham,* 382 U.S. 87, 90–91, 86 S.Ct. 211, 213–214 (1965).

23. *Grayned v. City of Rockford,* 408 U.S. 104, 109, 92 S.Ct. 2294, 2299 (1972).

24. *Zwickler v. Koota,* 389 U.S. 241, 250, 88 S.Ct. 391, 396 (1967).

25. See *Grayned v. City of Rockford,* 408 U.S. 104, 109, 92 S.Ct. 2294, 2299 (1972), and *Dombrowski v. Pfister,* 380 U.S. 479, 486, 85 S.Ct. 1116, 1120 (1965).

26. See also *Watts v. State,* 463 So.2d 205 (Fla. 1985) and *State v. Ecker,* 311 So.2d 104 (Sup.Ct.Fla. 1975). The New York loitering and prowling statute fell in the 1988 case of *People v. Bright,* 71 N.Y.2d 376, 520 N.E.2d 1355 (1988).

27. 370 U.S. 660, 82 S.Ct. 1417 (1962).

28. 392 U.S. 514, 88 S.Ct. 2145 (1968).

29. State statutes also often provide that marriage licenses may be issued to women beyond childbearing age who wish to marry a close relative. Under such statutes, two first cousins could marry if the woman meets the requirements of the state statute.

Chapter Two

PURPOSES, SCOPE, AND SOURCES OF CRIMINAL LAW

A. Purposes of Criminal Law

Background of the American Criminal Justice System

People in all societies have the inherent right to protect their society and those living in that society from vicious acts that threaten either the society or the people. All societies in the history of the world have exercised this inherent right and have had either written or unwritten laws forbidding and punishing acts (or omissions) considered detrimental to the group or the individual.

From colonial days up through World War I, the criminal codes of the various American states were generally small and usually embodied only those crimes that were considered serious wrongs against the society. Because these criminal laws were used to define and enforce public morality, the traditional attitude of lawyers and judges was that a crime was essentially a moral wrong.

The United States in those days was primarily an agricultural society with a much more simple style of life than that of today. Since most people lived in rural areas or small towns, the criminal codes could confine themselves primarily with conduct that was considered a serious threat to society. In those days, religious institutions, the family, and social pressure from the neighborhood and the town were generally capable of regulating behavior in other respects.

The 1920s saw the beginnings of the rapid change of the United States from an agricultural society to an industrial society. This transformation, plus the unbelievable array of economic, social, and political changes that accompanied it, hastened the arrival of today's mass industrial society. With these changes, there was a lessening of the influence of American religious institutions, the community, and the home in molding and shaping behavior (particularly of youth) to the standards expected by society. To compensate for this change, many new criminal laws were enacted. The burden of maintaining public order and safety gradually shifted.

Today, the American criminal justice system is very large and assumes a greater role than ever before. Fear and concern for crime has caused many changes. Everyone takes precautions today that were not taken thirty years ago. Doors are locked. Businesses and corporations take sophisticated measures to protect their employees, customers, and property. Private security personnel now outnumber law enforcement personnel. Alarm systems in businesses, homes, schools, and vehicles are common. Private attempts to deal with crime have become an important complement to the criminal justice system.

General Purposes

The general purposes and objectives of American criminal law can best be expressed by the U.S. Constitution, which is the supreme law of the land. The Preamble to the Constitution states that the purposes of the Constitution (and government) are to "establish Justice, insure domestic Tranquility, ... promote the general welfare and secure the Blessing of Liberty to ourselves and our Posterity." The U.S. Supreme Court has stated that the "most basic function of any government is to provide for the security of the individual and of his property."[1]

The U.S. District Court for the District of Columbia expressed the objective and purpose of criminal law in these terms in the first degree murder case of *United States v. Watson:*

Theodore Bundy, shown here in 1978, was executed for the murder of a twelve-year-old girl in Florida. He was also sentenced to death for the slayings of two sorority sisters at Florida State University in Tallahassee, and is believed to have murdered over thirty other young women in five Western states. He reportedly confessed to some of these murders in what some officials state was an attempt to obtain a stay of execution from the electric chair.

The object of the criminal law is to protect the public against depredations of a criminal. On the other hand, its purpose is also to prevent the conviction of the innocent, or the conviction of a person whose guilt is not established beyond a reasonable doubt. The Court must balance all these aims of the trial. This view was eloquently stated by Mr. Justice Cardozo in *Snyder v. Commonwealth of Massachusetts,* 291 U.S. 97, 122, 54 S.Ct. 330, 338, 78 L.Ed. 674: "... justice, though due to the accused, is due to the accuser also. The concept of fairness must not be strained till it is narrowed to a filament. We are to keep the balance true."[2]

Criminal Law and the Right of Privacy

The criminal justice system and criminal law are essential in protecting the right of privacy that we treasure for ourselves and for our families. In discussing the right and the expectation of privacy, the U.S. Supreme Court wrote the following in 1967:—"The protection of a person's general right of privacy—his right to be let alone by other people—is, like the protection of his property and his very life, left largely to the law of the individual States."[3]

B. The Permissible Scope of Criminal Laws in the United States

Although criminal law and the criminal justice system are essential parts of the rule of law in a democracy that provides for basic freedoms, they are often used

---

Goals and Purposes of Criminal Law and the Criminal Justice System

1. To discourage and deter people from committing crimes.
2. To protect society from dangerous and harmful people.
3. To punish people who have committed crimes.
4. To rehabilitate and reform people who have been convicted of crimes.

---

as instruments of suppression in a totalitarian state. Instead of ensuring freedom, criminal law in a dictatorship is often used to maintain the regime in power and to legalize a rule of terror and brute force. In a democracy, the criminal justice system and criminal law cannot master the people. They can be used only to serve the people. Therefore, there must be constitutional limits of the power of government to regulate the conduct of its citizens through the use of criminal law.

The Use of the Police Power to Maintain Public Order

Each state is responsible for the maintenance of public order and public safety within that state. To do this, the state must enact criminal laws and a criminal justice system under the "police power" of that state. The "police power" is an inherent power vested in each state. The Tenth Amendment of the U.S. Constitution provides that "the powers not delegated to the United States by the Constitution, nor prohibited by it to the States, are reserved to the States respectively or to the people."

The term "police power" refers to the broad legislative power of a state to pass laws that promote the public health, safety, and welfare. In the 1949 case of *Kovacs v. Cooper,* the U.S. Supreme Court stated:

> The police power of a state extends beyond health, morals and safety, and comprehends the duty, within constitutional limitations, to protect the well-being and tranquility of a community. A state or city may prohibit acts or things reasonably thought to bring evil or harm to its people.[4]

In the 1974 case of *Village of Belle Terre v. Boraas,* the Supreme Court sustained a zoning ordinance restricting land use to one-family dwellings, stating:

> The police power is not confined to elimination of filth, stench, and unhealthy places. It is ample to lay out zones where family values, youth values and the blessing of quiet seclusion, and clean air make the area a sanctuary for people.[5]

Limitations on the Use of the Police Power of the State to Regulate Conduct

In enacting criminal laws through the use of the police power, the state is regulating the conduct of citizens within the state by telling them what they may not do or what they must do. The state may not regulate conduct arbitrarily.

In enacting criminal law, the state must be able to show:

1. That there is a compelling public need to regulate the conduct the state seeks to regulate, and that the power to regulate is within the police power of the state. The U.S. Supreme Court held in *Lawton v. Steele* that

"it must appear, first, that the interests of the public generally . . . require such interference; and, that the means . . . are not unduly oppressive upon individuals."[6]

2. That the law does not contravene the U.S. Constitution or infringe on any of the rights granted or secured by the U.S. Constitution or the constitution of that state.

3. That the language of the statute (or ordinance) clearly tells people what they are not to do (or what they must do) and that the law prohibits only the conduct that may be forbidden.

The following examples are used to illustrate these limitations. Suppose the following states create the following offenses as misdemeanors:

- State A enacts a law requiring that all people in the state go to a church of a specific religion every Sunday.
- State B enacts a law forbidding skateboarding and breakdancing.
- State C enacts a law forbidding the sale, use, or possession of any tobacco product.
- State D enacts a law requiring operators and passengers of motorcycles to wear protective headgear.

Not only would State A violate First Amendment rights to the freedom of religion by passage of a law of this nature, but also this statute is not within the police power of a state, as it serves no valid function of government.

Regulation of skateboarding and breakdancing could be done by governmental units, such as cities and school districts, for public safety reasons and to minimize interference with pedestrian and motor vehicle traffic. As there is no compelling public need to completely forbid such conduct because of public health, safety, or morals, such regulations could hardly stand under attack. The right to be free of interference by government was stated as follows in 1975:

No right is more sacred, or is more carefully guarded, by the liberty assurance of the due process clause than the right of every citizen to the possession and control of his own person, free from restraint or interference by the state. The makers of our Constitution conferred, as against the government, the right to be let alone—the most comprehensive of rights and the right most valued by civilized man.

* * *

However, personal freedoms are not absolute, and the liberty guaranteed by the due process clause implies absence of arbitrary interferences but not immunity from reasonable regulations.[7]

* * *

State C could show that its regulation is within the police power of the state because medical studies show that the use of tobacco products does affect peoples' health. To date, states and cities have not outlawed smoking completely. Rather, they have prohibited smoking in parts (and some places all) of public buildings. Enforcement of a complete ban has not been advocated by any group, as it would be very difficult if not impossible to enforce. A total ban on smoking could lead to the kind of lawlessness associated with attempts to outlaw alcohol in the 1920s.

Many states have passed statutes requiring motorcyclists and their passengers to wear protective head and eye gear. The issue of the constitutionality of these statutes has come before many state courts. The majority rule is that such statutes are a valid exercise of the police power of the state. The Wisconsin Supreme Court followed the majority rule in *Bisenius v. Karns*[8] and the issue was appealed to the U.S. Supreme Court, where the appeal was dismissed for want of a federal question.

Not all courts, however, have gone along with the majority rule. The Supreme Court of Illinois held in *People v. Fries*[9] that requiring operators and passengers to wear protective gear is beyond the police power of the state because the protection is for the person wearing the gear rather than for the public generally. A municipal court in Ohio ruled that there was no substantial relation to public health, safety, morals, or the general welfare, and that the statute was a denial of motorcyclists' liberty under the Fourteenth Amendment. The court stated that "included in man's 'liberty' is the freedom to be as foolish, foolhardy or reckless as he may wish, so long as others are not endangered thereby."[10]

Actor Gary Busey and others helped defeat a proposed California law that would compel motorcycle riders to wear helmets. After Busey received a severe head injury in a motorcycle accident in 1988, Busey changed his mind and now advocates using helmets to prevent what he calls "slam-dancing" with a cement curb.

C. Sources of Criminal Law

Substantive criminal law can be found in the following sources, each of which will be discussed in the following pages:

1. Most criminal law is found in the statues of each state and in the statutes of the federal government.
2. Criminal law can also be found in commercial, sanitation, health, financial, and tax administrative regulations that have criminal sanctions. These regulations are enacted by state and federal administrative and regulatory agencies.
3. A few sections of state constitutions and one section of the U.S. Constitution contain criminal law.
4. Criminal law, on rare occasions, can be found today in the common law of some states.

1. Common Law Crimes

As the common law was the first and earliest source of criminal laws, it is presented first. And because the historic source of American criminal law lies in the common law of England, it is necessary to review the development of criminal law in England and in the American colonies.

When the English kings gained control of the whole of England in the Middle Ages, royal judges began deciding civil and criminal cases throughout all of

The principal source of state criminal law is the state legislature. Each state legislature considers additions and changes to its criminal code every year. Here, a chamber of the Connecticut legislature is considering a matter in session.

England, thus supporting the Crown by preserving the peace and dispensing justice. Few people in those days could read or write, and England was not yet a democracy. The king, the judges, and the ecclesiastical authorities played important roles not only in creating (sometimes inventing) criminal laws, but also in defining the elements and the scope of the criminal offenses. Judges became familiar with the general customs, usages, and moral concepts of the people and based judgments on them. In doing so, the judges determined which customs and moral concepts should prevail as law.

By the early 1600s, there were only a few criminal statutes, and the criminal law of England was made up primarily of the mandatory rules of conduct laid down by the English judges. In formulating the common law crimes of England, the royal judges believed that their decisions represented the best interests of the king and of the country as a whole. These decisions became the common law of England. As authoritative precedents, they were followed and applied in future cases wherever English common law was used and followed.

During this period of development of the criminal law in England, the English Parliament enacted a few criminal statutes, such as embezzlement, false pretense, and incest. The English ecclesiastical courts (religious courts) formulated and punished offenses that violated the moral code but that were not public offenses, such as private acts of fornication, adultery, and seduction.

The English settlers who began colonizing America in the early 1600s brought with them the English common law. This formed the basis of the law in each of the individual colonies. Modifications and adjustments were made to meet the needs of the frontier life of each of the colonies. A great deal of discretion was vested in colonial governors, councils, and judges with respect to the enforcement and scope of offenses and with respect to the creation of new laws. However, for the most part, English common law crimes continued as the common law crimes in each of the colonies.

During the American Revolution and for some time after, there was a great deal of hostility toward the English in America, and this hostility extended to the common law. Justice Hugo L. Black of the U.S. Supreme Court referred to this situation in his 1958 dissenting opinion in *Green v. United States,* in which he stated:

> Those who formed the Constitution struck out anew free of previous shackles in an effort to obtain a better order of government more congenial to human liberty and welfare. It cannot be seriously claimed that they intended to adopt the common law wholesale. They accepted those portions of it which were adapted to this country and conformed to the ideals of its citizens and rejected the remainder. In truth, there was widespread hostility to the common law in general and profound opposition to its adoption into our jurisdiction from the commencement of the Revolutionary War until long after the Constitution was ratified.[11]

Many American lawyers and judges knew the value of many of the English common law principles, which at that point had been developing for more than two hundred years. But the public wanted American law for Americans, and many changes were thus made by the new state legislative bodies, which transformed the English common law into statutory law.

Common Law Crimes in the United States

Most American states have used common law crimes (judge-made crimes) in their early histories. Some of these crimes were taken from English common law; others were modified versions of English common law crimes; and others were created by judges in those states.

In 1812, the case of *United States v. Hudson and Goodwin*[12] came before the U.S. Supreme Court. The defendants were charged with the common law crime of criminal libel because they wrote in a newspaper that the president of the United States and the Congress had secretly voted $2 million as a present to Napoleon Bonaparte. There was no federal statute making libel a crime, but criminal libel was a common law crime. The Supreme Court pointed out that state courts could punish a person for a violation of the common law crime of libel under their police power if they chose to adopt and incorporate the offense as part of the crimes of that state. But the Supreme Court held that federal courts had only that power and jurisdiction given to them by the U.S. Constitution and the Congress and had no power to adopt common law crimes. The rule that there are no federal common law crimes has been affirmed many times over the years. In 1949, Justice Robert H. Jackson wrote that "it is well and wisely settled that there can be no judge-made offenses against the United States and that every federal prosecution must be sustained by statutory authority."[13]

Today in the United States, more than half the states have abolished common law crime within their jurisdictions. In the states that have not abolished common law crimes, it is unusual for a person to be charged with a common law crime, because all state legislative bodies have enacted hundreds of statutory criminal offenses. A prosecutor who is charging a statutory offense is on much safer ground

Development of Criminal Law in the United States

English criminal law as developed in the common law of England
by English judges who adopted customs and usages

1st Stage in the American Colonies

Use of English common law as it came
across the Atlantic with the early settlers

⇩

2nd Stage in the Independent American States Under the Articles of Confederation

Enactment of common law crimes into statutes and ordinances by newly created American legislative bodies	Continued use of other common law crimes in either their original or modified forms

⇩

3rd Stage with the Establishment of a Federal Form of Government
Under the Present Constitution of the United States

Further definition of crimes by state legislatures with the creation of many new crimes in the past 50 years	Diminished use of common law crimes in all states with more than half the states abolishing common law crimes	In 1812, the U.S. Supreme Court held that federal courts had no authority to adopt common law crimes. Therefore, all federal criminal prosecutions "must be sustained by statutory authority."

than he or she would be in charging a common law crime, which immediately leaves the charge vulnerable to attack. The following 1972 case illustrates the type of attack that may be made on common law crimes.

STATE v. PALENDRANO
Superior Court of New Jersey (1972) 120 N.J. Super. 336, 293 A.2d 747

The defendant (a woman) was indicted and charged in New Jersey with violating two statutory offenses and the common law crime of being a common scold. The defendant was found innocent of the two statutory offenses and made the following arguments against the common law crime of being a common scold:

1. *That a common scold[14] is no longer a crime in New Jersey.* The court agreed, stating, "Most, if not all, of the elements of being a common scold are found in our present Disorderly Persons Act. To the extent that they are not found, such conduct is no longer an offense and is ignored by the law."
2. *That the charge is unconstitutionally vague and therefore unenforceable under the "due process" concepts of the Fourteenth Amendment of the U.S. Constitution.* The court agreed that the meaning of the term "common scold" has been all but lost over the years and thought that the average citizen should not be required to carry a pocket edition of Blackstone with him to ascertain what conduct was forbidden by law.

3. *That since only a woman can be a common scold the offense is a blatant violation of the equal protection requirement of the U.S. Constitution.* The Court agreed, stating that "the discrimination between the sexes is obvious. It is senseless. It is unconstitutional under the Equal Protection Clause."

Why Retain Common Law Crimes Today?

England retains and prosecutes a moderate number of common law crimes. However, it must be kept in mind that England, unlike the United States, has no written constitution, and that an act of Parliament is the supreme law of the land. English courts do not have the power to declare an act of Parliament unconstitutional. Nor does England use the federalist system of government under which a federal court system determines and imposes on state courts constitutional standards relating to criminal laws.

The English criminal justice system has operated remarkably well. This is probably one of the reasons Parliament has not incorporated the remaining common law crimes of England into statutory form. Parliament also has apparently been satisfied with the judicial definition of these common law crimes and the limited number of prosecutions that charge common law crimes. There is no question of the constitutionality of such common law crimes in England, and the reasoning seems to be, "Why change that which is working well?"

Relatively few common law crimes exist today in the twenty or so American states that have not abolished common law crimes. Some argue that these common law crimes should be retained to fill any possible loopholes and gaps that might exist in the statutory criminal codes of the states that have not abolished common law crimes. This argument, however, is weak in view of the results that occurred in the 1972 New Jersey "common scold" case.

Distinction Between Common Law Crimes and Common Law Rules of Criminal Procedure

Common law crimes are acts defined as crimes by judges; statutory crimes are crimes created and defined by a legislative body. Common law rules of criminal procedure are judge-made rules of criminal procedure having to do with such subjects as arrest, search, and seizure. In most states, the law having to do with entrapment is common law and is likely to remain so. There are also many statutory rules of criminal procedure that have been enacted by legislative bodies.

The abolition of common law crimes in more than half the states does not mean that common law has been abolished. Abolishing common law crimes does not affect in any way the common law rules of criminal procedure or the civil common law rules that are used in civil courts. These rules remain in effect in all states unless the state legislative bodies pass laws changing them.

2. Statutory Crimes

After the American Revolution, the new American state legislatures began converting common law crimes to statutory form. Through the police power of the state, they had the power to amend, affirm, change, extend, abolish, modify, or alter any common law crime or rule. In many instances, state legislatures kept the common law crime intact by merely restating the law in statutory form. In other

Important Documents of the English-Speaking World

Magna Carta: 1215

A civil war in England forced King John to sign the Magna Carta (great document), which provided:

- No criminal "trial upon ... simple accusation without producing credible witnesses to the truth therein."
- "No freeman shall be taken, imprisoned ... except by lawful judgment of his peers or the law of the land."

The Writ of Habeas Corpus developed as a result of Magna Carta. This greatest writ in the English-speaking world was first used in its common law form. Its present form probably came into existence through an act of the English Parliament in 1679.

Mayflower Compact: 1620

As the *Mayflower* rode at anchor off Cape Cod, some of the passengers threatened to go out on their own, without any framework of government. To avoid this threat of anarchy, the *Mayflower Compact* agreed that. "We ... doe ... solemnely and mutually ... covenant and combine our selves together into a civil body politike for our better ordering and preservation ... and by vertue hereof to enact ... such just and equall lawes ... unto which we promise all due submission and obedience."

English Bill of Rights: 1689

Because of the numerous attacks on personal liberty, the English Parliament forced King James II to abdicate, and Parliament produced a Bill of Rights. This document served as a guide for Americans, as it provided that:

- "Suspending laws ... without consent of Parliament is illegal."
- "Keeping a Standing Army within the Kingdom in Time of Peace unless it be with Consent of Parliament is against the law."
- "Election of Members of Parliament ought to be free."
- "Freedom of Speech ... ought not to be impeached or questioned."

Declaration of Independence: July 4, 1776

After King George declared the American colonies to be in a state of rebellion and the English Parliament forbade all trade with the colonies, an eloquent statement of the American democratic creed was made in the *Declaration of Independence:*

> We hold these Truths to be self-evident, that all Men are created equal, that they are endowed by their Creator with certain unalienable Rights, that among these are Life, Liberty, and the Pursuit of Happiness.—That to secure these Rights, Governments are instituted among Men, deriving their just powers from the Consent of the Governed, that whenever any Form of Government becomes destructive of these Ends, it is the Right of the People to alter or to abolish it, and to institute new Government, laying its Foundation on such Principles, and organizing its Powers in such Form, as to them shall seem most likely to effect their Safety and Happiness.

U.S. Constitution: ratified 1788

Because of the failure to achieve a workable government under the Articles of Confederation, delegates from the American States met in Philadelphia in 1787. George Washington presided for months over the debates and arguments that led to the adoption and ratification of the Constitution used by the United States since that time.

The Bill of Rights (first ten amendments) was made part of the U.S. Constitution in 1791. See Appendix A of this text for applicable sections of the U.S. Constitution.

All of the original thirteen States and the U.S. Constitution guarantee and protect the Writ of Habeas Corpus. (See Article I, Section 9, of the U.S. Constitution.)

instances, legislatures created new crimes by forbidding and punishing conduct that was not a crime at common law. In still other instances, they redefined the common law crime by changing elements of the crime or removing common law limitations and extending the crime to cover conduct not included in the common law crime. If the common law punishment was considered too severe, changes were made in the degree or form of punishment. Attempts were made to clarify areas of doubt or uncertainty in common law crimes.

Practically all criminal laws that are enforced today are statutory laws enacted by legislative bodies. Many of today's statutory crimes were unknown at common law. Most of these criminal laws have been enacted in the past thirty or forty years to meet the problems of our mass industrial society.

3. Administrative Crimes

In 1911, the case of *United States v. Grimaud*[15] came before the U.S. Supreme Court. Congress had passed a statute authorizing the Secretary of Agriculture to make regulations concerning the use of government forests in order to preserve and maintain these areas as forest reserves. Violation of regulations created by the Secretary of Agriculture was made a criminal offense by the Congress. The defendant grazed his sheep on U.S. forest lands without first obtaining a permit as required under a regulation issued by the Secretary of Agriculture. As the federal courts were divided on the question of whether a violation of such regulation constituted a crime, the government appealed the case to the U.S. Supreme Court.

The Supreme Court held that Congress may constitutionally delegate to an administrative agency the power to make regulations that are enforced by criminal penalties established by that legislative body. The Court stated that the Secretary did not exercise the legislative power of declaring the penalty or fixing the punishment for grazing sheep without a permit, but the punishment is imposed by the act itself. The offense is not against the Secretary, but as the indictment properly concludes, "contrary to the laws of the United States and the peace and dignity thereof."

Today, it is well established that the Congress and most state legislatures may delegate to an administrative agency the power to make rules, and the legislature may provide by statute that such rules may be enforced by criminal penalties. In a few states, this procedure has been held to be unconstitutional. But in the majority of states, criminal laws may be created by the legislature establishing the framework and the administrative agency providing the specific regulation or rule within that framework. The delegation of such authority is constitutional in the majority of the states if:

1. the legislative act sets forth sufficient standards to guide the administrative agency, and the act provides for criminal penalties for the violation of the administrative regulations created within the guidelines, and if

2. the administrative agency stays within the guidelines established by the legislative body in creating rules enforced by the criminal penalties; but

3. the rules of the administrative agency "must be explicit and unambiguous in order to sustain a criminal prosecution; they must adequately inform

those who are subject to their terms what conduct will be considered evasive so as to bring the criminal penalties of the Act into operation"[16] and

4. the determination (adjudication) of whether there has been a violation of the "administrative crime" is made by a court with proper jurisdiction and is not made by the administrative agency.

Publication of Administrative Rules Having Criminal Sanctions

People who are subject to the criminal law cannot be presumed to know the law if information as to the contents of the law is not available to them. This information is ordinarily available at public libraries or from governmental agencies on request. However, in 1933 and 1934, information as to the administrative rules having criminal sanctions was sometimes not readily available from any source. The National Recovery Agency (NRA) and other New Deal agencies of the federal government were issuing regulations having criminal sanctions at an unprecedented rate because of the economic emergency that existed at the time. A committee of the American Bar Association (ABA) estimated that the NRA alone issued 2,998 orders in a one-year period and that these regulations were made known to the public through 5,991 press releases. Lawyers had to inform themselves of the law by reading the newspapers and hoping that the reporters had accurately reflected the facts. The ABA committee reported as follows:

> The total legislative output by, or in connection with, this one administrative agency staggers the imagination. Any calculation involves guess-work but a safe guess would be that the total exceeds 10,000 pages of 'law' in the period of one year ... Under these circumstances not only citizens but even lawyers are helpless in any effort to ascertain the law applicable to a given state of facts. The presumption of knowledge of the law becomes, to term it mildly, more than violent. Is it too much to expect that before these legislative enactments be given force and effect, they be subjected to simple formalities such as those suggested in the committee's conclusion?[17]

In 1935, the Federal Register Act was passed, and in 1936 the Federal Register, designed for the publication of administrative orders and regulations, came into being.

Common Law, Statutory, and Administrative Crimes

Common law crimes	Are custom, usage or moral values, and concepts of a community built up over a period of many years	plus	Adoption by judges of these customs or concepts in court decisions as crimes.
Statutory crimes	Are enactment of bills by a legislative body	plus	Signing of the bills by the chief executive officer (governor or president).
Administrative crimes	Are enactment of sufficient guidelines by a legislative body that are signed into law by the governor or president	plus	Authorized regulatory agencies create rules within the guidelines established by law.

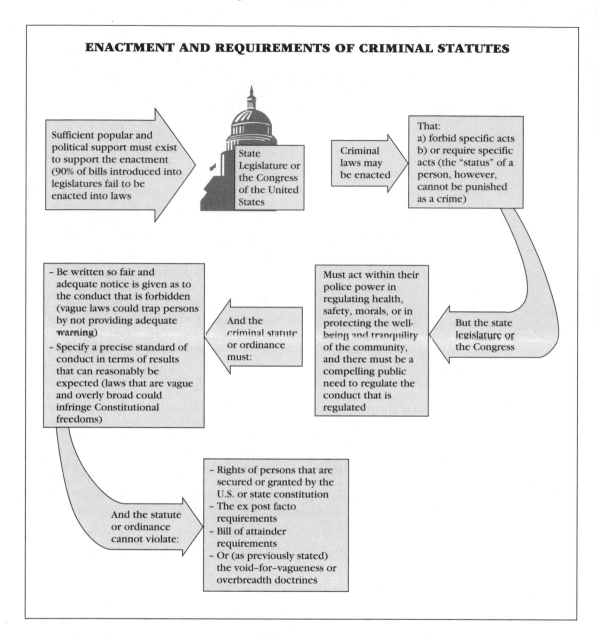

ENACTMENT AND REQUIREMENTS OF CRIMINAL STATUTES

Sufficient popular and political support must exist to support the enactment (90% of bills introduced into legislatures fail to be enacted into laws

State Legislature or the Congress of the United States

Criminal laws may be enacted

That:
a) forbid specific acts
b) or require specific acts (the "status" of a person, however, cannot be punished as a crime)

- Be written so fair and adequate notice is given as to the conduct that is forbidden (vague laws could trap persons by not providing adequate warning)
- Specify a precise standard of conduct in terms of results that can reasonably be expected (laws that are vague and overly broad could infringe Constitutional freedoms)

And the criminal statute or ordinance must:

Must act within their police power in regulating health, safety, morals, or in protecting the well-being and tranquility of the community, and there must be a compelling public need to regulate the conduct that is regulated

But the state legislature or the Congress

And the statute or ordinance cannot violate:

- Rights of persons that are secured or granted by the U.S. or state constitution
- The ex post facto requirements
- Bill of attainder requirements
- Or (as previously stated) the void-for-vagueness or overbreadth doctrines

4. Criminal Laws Created by Constitutions

The U.S. Constitution and state constitutions contain many provisions having to do with the rights of people within their jurisdictions, and they specify the criminal procedures that may or may not be used. They generally leave the definition of crimes to legislative bodies and the courts. The only sections of the U.S. Constitution that forbid or define conduct that is criminal are:

Article III, Section 3
(1) Treason against the United States, shall consist only in levying War against them, or in adhering to their Enemies, giving them Aid and Comfort. No Person shall be

convicted of Treason unless on the Testimony of two Witnesses to the same overt Act, or on Confession in open Court.

(2) The Congress shall have Power to declare the Punishment of Treason.

Thirteenth Amendment

Section 1. Neither slavery nor involuntary servitude, except as a punishment for crime whereof the party shall have been duly convicted, shall exist within the United States, or any place subject to their jurisdiction.

Section 2. Congress shall have power to enforce this article by appropriate legislation.

State constitutions are usually considerably longer than the U.S. Constitution and contain more details. In addition to provisions having to do with treason and forbidding the holding of people in involuntary servitude, state constitutions may also forbid such conduct as dueling, cockfighting, and other offenses that concerned legislative bodies years ago.

5. Interpretation of Criminal Statutes

Criminal penalties were severe in the early history of the United States and England. The death penalty and long mandatory prison terms were common punishments for felonies. Because of the severity of these penalties, a rule of strict construction or strict interpretation of criminal laws came into existence. Under this rule, the courts would take the narrowest possible view in interpreting the offense and in determining the scope of the crime charged. Under the circumstances, this had a great deal of merit.

However, when state legislatures began reducing the number of mandatory sentences and reducing the severity of the punishment, many courts continued to use the rule of strict construction. This resulted in the occasional acquittal of offenders who had clearly violated the spirit and letter of the statutory law, but who were not successfully prosecuted because of the strict construction (interpretation) of the statute. Legislative bodies then began to attempt to anticipate every possible narrow interpretation that the courts might place on new statutes. As a result, the statutes became wordy and cumbersome.

In order to write criminal laws in simpler and clearer language, some legislative bodies began abolishing the "strict construction" rule by statute, so that they could avoid artificial and cumbersome language in proposed new criminal codes. Following are two examples of such statutes:

Texas: The provisions of this Code shall be liberally construed, so as to attain the objects intended by the Legislature: The prevention, suppression and punishment of crime.[18]

New York: The general rule that a penal statute is to be strictly construed does not apply to this chapter, but the provisions herein must be construed according to the fair import of their terms to promote justice and effect the objects of the law.[19]

The Effect of Interpretation on Enforcement of Criminal Laws

A newly enacted criminal statute or ordinance must be read and interpreted by law enforcement officers having enforcement responsibility. Their interpretation of the statute or ordinance in most instances determines the initial scope of enforcement.

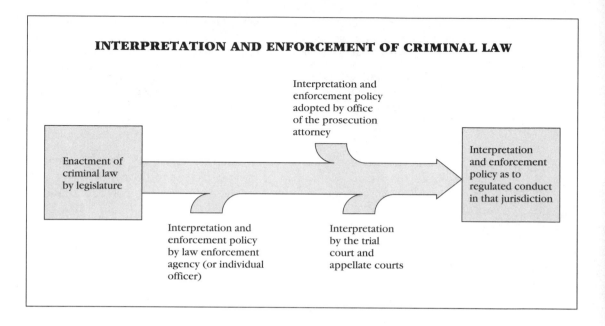

If, for example, a statute or ordinance applies only to conduct in a "public place," that phrase would need interpretation if it were not clearly defined in the legislation. After an individual officer or a law enforcement agency took some action based on the definition of a public place, a prosecutor might also have to interpret the phrase. The final definition of a public place would have to be made by the courts, unless the legislative body amended the statute or ordinance with a further clarification of the phrase.

Many criminal codes contain lists of definitions of words and phrases, in order to provide for uniform interpretations. In addition, many court decisions concern themselves with the interpretation of words and phrases. The task of interpreting words and phrases that have not been defined, however, remains for law enforcement officers and prosecutors. Their interpretation in many instances determines enforcement practices.

In determining what interpretations should be made of criminal statutes and ordinances, consideration should be given to the intent and expectation of the legislative body. For example, in many jurisdictions, most forms of gambling not authorized by state statutes are illegal. However, the President's Commission on Crime points out that it is apparent that state legislatures "neither intend nor expect that such statutes be fully enforced." As a result, gambling statutes in most states (if not all) are interpreted so as not to apply to friendly neighborhood poker games and other forms of social gambling.

Questions and Problems for Chapter 2

1. Indicate whether the following conduct constitutes a crime in your jurisdiction. If so, what would be the specific charge? Also, indicate how you, as a law enforcement officer, would handle each situation.

a. You are sent to a home in which a mother of two teenage daughters complains that the man who lives next door has set up a telescope on his second-floor rear porch and trains it on her daughters as they are sunbathing in their backyard.

b. You are sent to a street on which two men are standing on a public sidewalk late at night watching a woman undress who has forgotten to pull down her bedroom shades.

c. You are sent to an apartment in which male residents are questioning a man they found

standing in the backyard area of the apartment building. The man was not window peeping, but as it was midnight, the occupants of the apartment building are concerned. The man states that he was looking for a friend but can name no one who lives in the apartment building or in the neighborhood.

Notes

1. *Lanzetta v. New Jersey,* 306 U.S. 451, 455, 59 S.Ct. 618 (1939).

2. 146 F.Supp. 258, 262 (D.D.C. 1956).

3. *Katz v. United States,* 389 U.S. 347, 88 S.Ct. 507 (1967).

4. 336 U.S. 77, 69 S.Ct. 448 (1949).

5. 416 U.S. 1, 94 S.Ct. 1536 (1974).

6. 152 U.S. 133, 14 S.Ct. 499 (1894).

7. *Bykofsky et al. v. Borough of Middletown,* 401 F.Supp. 1242, Affr. Fed. Ct. of App., 535 F.2d 1245, Review denied U.S. Supreme Court, 89 S.Ct. 2033, 97 S.Ct. 394 (1976).

8. 42 Wis.2d 42, 165 N.W.2d 377 (1969), and appeal dismissed 395 U.S. 709 (1969). Other majority-rule decisions are *Commonwealth v. Coffman,* 453 S.W.2d 759 (Ky. 1970); *Penney v. City of North Little Rock,* 248 Ark. 1158, 455 S.W.2d 132 (1970); *State v. Albertson,* 93 Idaho 640, 470 P.2d 300 (1970); *Love v. Bell,* 171 Colo. 27, 465 P.2d 118 (1970); *State v. Lee,* 51 Hawaii 516, 465 P.2d 573 (1970); *State v. Cushman,* 451 S.W.2d 17 (Mo. 1970); *State v. Laitinen,* 77 Wash.2d 130, 459 P.2d 789 (1969); *State v. Eitel,* 227 So.2d 489 (Fla. 1969); *City of Albuquerque v. Jones,* 87 N.M. 486, 535 P.2d 1337 (1975). In 1977, the Wisconsin legislature repealed the law requiring that adult operators and passengers of motorcycles wear protective head gear. This was in response to political lobbying and large demonstrations against this requirement.

9. 42 Ill.2d 446, 250 N.E.2d 149 (1969).

10. *State v. Betts,* 21 Ohio Misc. 175, 252 N.E.2d 866 (Franklin Mun. Ct., Ohio, 1969).

11. 356 U.S. 165, 78 S.Ct. 632 (1958).

12. 11 U.S. (7 Cranch) 32, 3 L.Ed. 259 (1812).

13. *Krulewitch v. United States,* 336 U.S. 440, 69 S.Ct. 716 (1949).

14. Blackstone defines a common scold as a troublesome and angry woman who by her brawling and wrangling among her neighbors, breaks the peace, increases discord and becomes a nuisance to the neighborhood. Depending on the situation, such conduct might be a violation of a state disorderly conduct statute, but the statute cannot be addressed only to a woman.

15. 220 U.S. 506, 31 S.Ct. 480 (1911).

16. *M. Kraus & Bros., Inc. v. United States,* 327 U.S. 614, 66 S.Ct. 705 (1946).

17. American Bar Association's Special Committee on Administrative Law, 59 A.B.A.Rep., pp. 552–555 (1934).

18. Vernon's Penal Code of the State of Texas, Art. 1.26.

19. McKinney's Consolidated Laws of New York, Annotated, Sec. 5.00.

ESSENTIAL ELEMENTS OF A CRIME

Since the development of common law and up until modern times, all crimes consisted of two essential elements: (1) the physical act or omission, and (2) a mental requirement known as criminal intent or purpose. Some writers refer to such crimes as "true crimes." Today, true crimes continue to make up a considerable number of crimes in any criminal code.

With the industrialization of the United States, modern legislative bodies began creating criminal laws that did not require the mental element essential to "true crimes." This relatively new type of crime is called a "strict liability" crime, or regulatory offense. Strict liability crimes can be found in criminal laws pertaining to traffic violations, narcotics, liquor, sanitation, hunting, and pure food laws. In strict liability crimes, the government does not have to prove intent or purpose and must show only that the accused performed the act (or omission) charged or brought about the results that are alleged and shown.

A. Crimes Requiring Proof of Mental Fault

Before a person may be convicted of a crime that requires proof of mental fault, the government must prove beyond a reasonable doubt:

For many years, gambling was forbidden in all states except Nevada. This 1949 photo shows gamblers being arrested in New Jersey, and money being confiscated from them. Gambling offenses today are typically "strict liability" crimes.

1. *The external physical act.* That the conduct or act forbidden by the law of the jurisdiction was in fact committed by the defendant,
2. *The internal mental element.* That the act (or omission) was accompanied by a state of mind required by the criminal statute.

The Latin term *actus reus* (guilty act) is used by the courts and writers to describe the essential physical act, and the term *mens rea* (guilty mind) is used to describe the essential mental requirement. This mental requirement of criminal intent is embodied in criminal statutes in the following degrees:

- intentionally (the highest degree of mental fault)
- knowingly
- recklessly
- negligently

The U.S. Supreme Court has never created and announced a doctrine requiring proof of *mens rea* in all crimes and in all cases before an accused can be held accountable for his or her acts.[1] Therefore, the states are generally free to create criminal laws that do not require proof of *mens rea* or to create criminal laws requiring different degrees of mental fault or mental guilt. But if a degree of mental guilt is made an element of the crime by law, the prosecutor must then prove this essential element of the crime.

Necessity for the Concurrence of the Act and the Required Mental Element

Thinking of committing a crime without performing a criminal act is not a crime. If a person with criminal thoughts does nothing to carry out his or her thoughts, no crime has occurred. Government can not punish thoughts alone. To show that a "true crime" has occurred, the state must show that the external physical act and the internal mental state essential to that crime occurred at the same time. Even crimes like conspiracy where two or more persons share their thoughts about a crime require that the conspirators do at least one physical act in furtherance of the conspiracy. (See chapter 4, section A.)

In some instances, an act without the required mental state (guilty mind) is no crime. A person incapable of entertaining the required criminal mind because of legal insanity has not committed a crime. Or, a student who picks up someone else's book or briefcase by mistake has performed a physical act, but if there is no guilty or criminal state of mind necessary for the crime of theft, no crime has been committed. However, suppose that the student keeps the book or briefcase for two days and then, realizing the mistake, decides to keep the property. The taking and keeping of the property for two days has been a continuous act in the eyes of the law. The crime of theft occurred when the intent to deprive the true owner of permanent possession concurred with the act of taking and retaining possession.

Although the forbidden act and the guilty mind must concur, the results do not necessarily have to take place at the same time.

EXAMPLE: While A is on vacation, X rigs a spring gun to A's front door (forbidden act), setting it with the intention that A be killed when he opens the door (guilty mind). Two weeks after the spring gun is set in place, A returns from vacation and is shot and killed when he opens his door.

Elements of Crime

*Crimes May Consist of Combinations of the Three Human Activities
of Thought, Communication, and Actions (or Conduct)*

Thoughts alone cannot be punished as crimes However, thoughts could constitute the required mental element *(mens rea)* for verbal offenses or acts that have been designated as crimes.

Communications (words, etc.) may be offenses in themselves or may be combined with either thoughts or actions to constitute crimes. (See chapter 10, The Limits of Free Speech.)

Human acts alone may constitute "strict liability" crimes, in which all that is required is that the state show that the defendant committed a forbidden act (or omission). When it is required that the state prove a specific mental element *(mens rea),* the state must then prove the required intent, purpose, or knowledge that is an essential element of the crime.

In the example given, the *actus reus* and the *mens rea* concurred, but the results did not occur until A opened the door two weeks after the act with intent to kill was performed.

The Forbidden Act or Omission *(Actus Reus)*

Most criminal laws forbid specific acts, and a few punish the failure to carry out a legal duty. The act forbidden or commanded by the law is set out in the definition of each particular offense, usually in terms of the harm or the wrong that occurs. In the crime of murder, it is the death of the victim caused by the defendant's forbidden act (or omission) that is the harm and the wrong. In the crime of larceny, it is the loss of personal or movable property caused by the defendant's wrongful taking and carrying away that is the harm and the wrong.

The manner in which the harm or wrong can be caused varies considerably. A murder can be committed by use of a gun, a knife, a blow, or poison, or by any one of many different acts. The harm or the wrong done usually varies from crime to crime, but sometimes two crimes embody the same harm or wrong. All criminal homicides share the same harm or wrong, which is the death of a person. These crimes differ from one another primarily because of the differing states of mind of the offender at the time he or she causes the harm or wrong (the death of another person).

Actus Reus for Different Elements of "Parties to a Crime"

Chapter 4 explains the different categories of the criminal liability of "parties to a crime." These categories are (a) the person who actually commits the crime, (b) the person who aids and assists in the commission of the crime, and (c) the person who conspires in the planning of the crime.

Each of these categories have different *actus reus* elements.

EXAMPLE: A hires B and C to murder X. A tells B and C how and where he wants X to be murdered. B is the vehicle driver and look-out while C commits the murder.

C's act in killing X is the *actus reus* of the direct commission of the crime. B's acts as aider and abettor are the *actus reus* of assistance. A jury could easily find that all three men (particularly A) conspired and agreed in the planning of the murder, which is the *actus reus* of agreement.

The state has the burden of proving beyond a reasonable doubt the *actus reus* element of every offense, and the jury must unanimously agree that the state has proved the *actus reus* elements before they may find a defendant guilty.

Because the *actus reus* element for each category is different, the jury must agree unanimously on which *actus reus* or which category the state has proven.

The Guilty Mind (Mens Rea)

A cardinal principle of criminal law pertaining to "true crimes" was long ago expressed in Latin as *actus non facit reum nisi mens sit rea* (an act does not make a person guilty unless the mind is guilty).

The term *mens rea* also means evil intent, criminal purpose, and knowledge of the wrongfulness of conduct. It is also used to indicate the mental state required by the crime charged, whether that be specific intent to commit the crime, recklessness, guilty knowledge, malice, or criminal negligence.

Criminal liability usually requires "an evil-meaning mind (and) an evil-doing hand."[2] But the late Justice Robert H. Jackson complained of the "variety, disparity and confusion" of judicial definitions of the "requisite but elusive mental element" required in the proof of crimes. In 1970, the National Commission on Reform of Federal Criminal Laws complained of the "confused and inconsistent ad hoc approach" of federal courts to this problem and called for a new approach.

In the 1980 case of *United States v. Bailey,*[3] the U.S. Supreme Court pointed out that at "common law, crimes generally were classified as requiring either 'general intent' or 'specific intent.' This . . . distinction, however, has been the source of a good deal of confusion." Because of this problem, the Court pointed out that there has been a movement away from the common law classifications of *mens rea.* Citing Section 2.02 of the Model Penal Code and LaFave and Scott's book, *Criminal Law* (St. Paul: West Pub. Co., 1972), the Court suggested the following "in descending order of culpability: purpose, knowledge, recklessness, and negligence."

The following example illustrates situations in which the harm done is the same in all cases, but the mental element varies:

EXAMPLE: X, a construction worker, is working on the fourth floor of a building under construction in the downtown area of a city. His conduct caused the death of W, who was hit on the head by a crowbar as he was walking on the sidewalk past the building.

1. X deliberately dropped the heavy crowbar so as to hit W on the head.
2. X did not want to kill anybody but wanted to see the people scatter when he dropped the crowbar to the sidewalk.
3. X threw the crowbar at another worker in a fight, but missed. The crowbar fell, killing W on the sidewalk below.
4. X came to work drunk and accidentally pushed the crowbar off the edge of the building.
5. Another worker called for the crowbar and X threw it to him, but the throw was bad and the crowbar hit W on the sidewalk below.

Innocent Acts That, If Done With Forbidden Intent, Are Crimes

Innocent Acts	Forbidden Intent	Resulting Crimes
Possession of a tool or other instrumentality	To use such a device to break into a depository or building and steal therefrom	Possession of burglarious tools
Traveling in interstate or foreign commerce	To avoid prosecution for a state felony, or to avoid giving testimony in such a prosecution	Fugitive felon or witness violation; 18 U.S.C.A. sec. 1073 & 1074(a)
Use of U.S. mail, telephone, or interstate wire facilities	To participate through racketeering in an enterprise	RICO violation; 18 U.S.C.A. sec. 1961–68
Transporting a female "through or across" the state of New Jersey	With the intent to engage in prostitution	N.J.S.A. 2A:133–12
Use of the U.S. mails	To advance a fraudulent scheme	Mail fraud; 18 U.S.C.A. sec. 1341
Use of fictitious name or address	To further a fraudulent mail scheme	18 U.S.C.A. sec. 1342
Association with other people and even membership in an organization that advocates the overthrow of government by force or violence is not punishable	Unless there is knowledge of the aim to use force or violence in the overthrow of government and there is shown to be an intent to bring it about	18 U.S.C.A. sec. 2385
Entering a train	With intent "to commit any crime or offense against a person or property thereon"	18 U.S.C.A. sec. 1991
Going on "any military, naval, or Coast Guard reservation, post, fort, arsenal, yard, station, or installation	For any purpose prohibited by law or lawful regulation"	18 U.S.C.A. sec. 1382
Teaching or demonstrating the use, application, or making of a firearm, explosive, or incendiary device, or a technique capable of causing injury or death	"Intending that the same will be unlawfully employed for use in, or in furtherance of, a civil disorder which may in any way or degree obstruct, delay, or adversely affect commerce," or the performance of any federally protected function	18 U.S.C.A. sec. 231(a)(1)
Travel in interstate or foreign commerce	With intent to incite a riot (statute requires an overt act, but such act could be a lawful act)	18 U.S.C.A. sec. 2101(a)(1)

6. X was knocked unconscious when a crane collapsed, causing him to drop the crowbar, which hit and killed W.

In your jurisdiction, what degree of criminal liability should X be charged with in each example with respect to his conduct and mental state? As a jury could be the final judge in determining whether the "evil-meaning mind (and) evil-doing hand" existed, what arguments could a prosecutor and defense lawyer make to prove their cases?

See *United States v. Gypsum Co.*,[4] in which the U.S. Supreme Court stated that in the case of most crimes, "the limited distinction between knowledge and purpose has not been considered important."

In *United States v. Bailey*,[5] the Supreme Court stated that in a "general sense, 'purpose' corresponds loosely with the common-law concept of specific intent, while 'knowledge' corresponds loosely with the concept of 'general intent.' "

Proving the Criminal Intent or Criminal State of Mind

When criminal intent or another mental element is an essential element of a crime, the state has the burden of proving the required *mens rea*. Proof of the mental element may be made by:

1. Showing the acts of the defendant and the circumstances that existed at the time of the crime. As most people know what they are doing and also know the natural and probable consequences of their acts, a judge or jury may reasonably infer that the defendant intended the natural and probable consequences of his or her deliberate acts.[6] Thus, a person who pointed a loaded gun at another person and pulled the trigger knew what he or she was doing and desired the natural and probable consequences of the acts.

2. Producing evidence to show the statements of the defendant at the time of the crime as well as statements made after the crime. Statements of a defendant before or after a crime may be incriminating and may include admissions or a confession of guilt.

Only rarely is written evidence of intent or purpose of a defendant available to the state. The following jury instruction on intent was approved by the Fifth Circuit Court of Appeals in the 1975 case of *United States v. Durham*:

> It is reasonable to infer that a person ordinarily intends the natural and probable consequences of his knowing acts. The jury may draw the inference that the accused intended all of the consequences which one standing in like circumstances and possessing like knowledge should reasonably have expected to result from any intentional act or conscious omission. Any such inference drawn is entitled to be considered by the jury in determining whether or not the government has proved beyond a reasonable doubt that the defendant possessed the required criminal intent.[7]

Although it is reasonable to infer that a person ordinarily intends the natural and probable consequences of his or her knowing and deliberate acts, there is no inference that a person intends results that are not the natural, reasonable, or probable consequences of a voluntary act.

The Requirement of Scienter

"Scienter" is sometimes made an essential element of a crime that the state must prove beyond a reasonable doubt. *Scienter* is a legal term meaning a degree of knowledge that makes an individual legally responsible for the consequences of his or her acts. Scienter is alleged in a criminal complaint through charging that

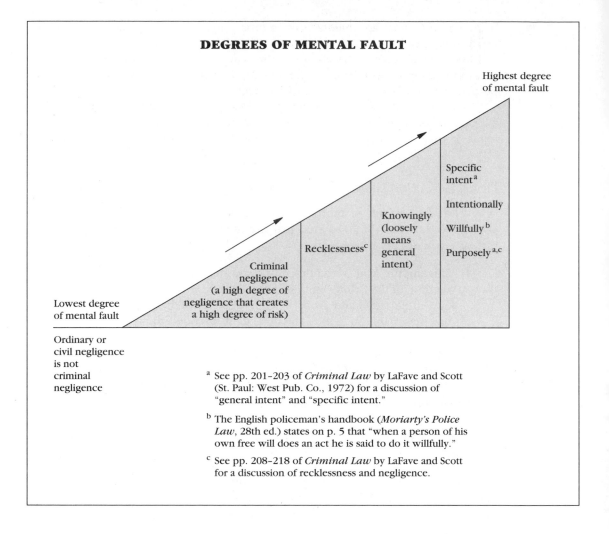

DEGREES OF MENTAL FAULT

Highest degree
of mental fault

Specific
intent[a]

Intentionally

Knowingly
(loosely
means
general
intent)

Willfully[b]

Purposely[a,c]

Recklessness[c]

Criminal
negligence
(a high degree of
negligence that creates
a high degree of risk)

Lowest degree
of mental fault

Ordinary or
civil negligence
is not
criminal
negligence

[a] See pp. 201–203 of *Criminal Law* by LaFave and Scott
(St. Paul: West Pub. Co., 1972) for a discussion of
"general intent" and "specific intent."

[b] The English policeman's handbook (*Moriarty's Police
Law*, 28th ed.) states on p. 5 that "when a person of his
own free will does an act he is said to do it willfully."

[c] See pp. 208–218 of *Criminal Law* by LaFave and Scott
for a discussion of recklessness and negligence.

the accused person had sufficient knowledge to know that his or her act was unlawful. Examples of crimes in which state statutes most often require scienter are:

- in battery or assault to a law enforcement officer, knowledge that the victim is a law enforcement officer
- in refusing to aid a law enforcement officer, knowledge that the person requesting assistance was a law enforcement officer
- in obstructing a law enforcement officer, knowledge that the person obstructed was a law enforcement officer
- in receiving stolen property, knowledge that the property received was stolen property
- in possession of obscene material, knowledge of the nature of the material
- in bribery of a public officer or a juror, knowledge that the person was a public official or juror
- in harboring or aiding a felon, knowledge that the person aided was a felon

EXAMPLE: As you are driving your car down a busy street, you see a hitchhiker. You pick up the hitchhiker and a mile down the road, you are stopped by police. The hitchhiker had committed an armed robbery of a store minutes before you picked him or her up in your car. What scienter element must be shown to justify your arrest and conviction for either the offense of party to the crime of armed robbery or harboring and aiding a felon?

The following cases have appeared before the U.S. Supreme Court in recent years.

UNITED STATES v. FEOLA
Supreme Court of the United States (1975) 420 U.S. 671, 95 S.Ct. 1255

Feola and others assaulted two men. Feola argued that he did not know the men he assaulted were undercover federal agents and, for that reason, his convictions of assaulting federal officers should be reversed.

In their "assault on law enforcement officer" statutes, most states require proof of scienter (knowledge that the victim was a law enforcement officer). But the U.S. Congress did not put this element into the federal crime of assaulting or battering a federal officer.

The U.S. Supreme Court refused to read the scienter element into the federal crime written by the U.S. Congress. The Court pointed out that the defendants may have been surprised when their victims turned out to be federal officers but that they knew from the beginning that the planned course of conduct was unlawful. The Court held:

> *A contrary conclusion would give insufficient protection to the agent enforcing an unpopular law, and none to the agent acting under cover.*

UNITED STATES v. FALU
Federal Court of Appeals, Second Circuit (1985) 776 F.2d 46, 38 CrL 2142

Strick Liability

The federal "schoolyard statute" 21 U.S.C.A. Sec. 845a (a) provides for doubling the sentence of a person convicted of selling drugs within 1,000 feet of an elementary or secondary school. The federal statute does not require the government to prove a defendant had knowledge of the school's proximity. Perez sold heroin to a federal undercover agent brought to him by his friend, Falu. The sale occurred within 1,000 feet of a public school that could not be seen from the location where the sale occurred. Perez and Falu were convicted of "knowingly or intentionally" selling the heroin. Perez directly committed the crime and Falu was an aider and abettor to the crime. Increased penalties were given to both defendants under the "schoolyard statute" as Congress' clear purpose was to deter drug distribution in and around schools. The Court of Appeals affirmed the convictions and increased penalties holding:

* * *

> *The defendant argues that without a requirement that a defendant be aware of the key element under the schoolyard statute, namely, proximity to a school, the statute fails to provide fair notice that the prohibited conduct is subject to enhanced penalties. Falu attempts to distinguish the schoolyard statute from a statute like 18 U.S.C.A. Sec. 111, which makes assaulting a federal officer a federal offense regardless of the defendant's knowledge of the victim's identity. See U.S. v. Feola, 420 U.S. 671, 684 (1975). Section 111, he argues, seeks to effectuate the legislative aim— protection of federal officers—directly, while the schoolyard statute operates only indirectly to benefit school children.*

* * *

> *The purpose of the statute is clear from a reading of the legislative history. Congress sought to create a drug-free zone around schools; whether it chose to do so directly or indirectly is not particularly relevant. According to its sponsor, the provision was designed to "deter drug distribution in and around schools," including transactions which "take place in remote outdoor areas, at local hangouts, or at nearby homes or apartments," thereby helping to "eliminate outside negative influences" around schools.*

* * *

The Motive for Committing a Crime

Motive and intent are sometimes thought of as being one and the same. However, in the law there is a clear distinction between the two. Intent is the mental purpose or design to commit a specific act (or omission), whereas motive is the cause, reason, inducement, or why an act is committed.

EXAMPLE: A man entered a crowded tavern, and when he saw the person he was looking for, he went up to the man and killed him by plunging a large knife into his body.

When this case was tried, the state easily proved intent to kill through the many eyewitnesses to the crime (that is, the jury easily inferred intent to kill from the action of the defendant). But the state had no admissible evidence as to motive (why the defendant sought out the victim and killed him). However, the state had inadmissible hearsay evidence that the victim had sold the defendant a bad batch of heroin. The heroin caused the defendant to become ill. As soon as the defendant could get on his feet, he went out and killed the supplier of the heroin.

Intent is an essential element of many crimes and must be proved beyond reasonable doubt when required. Motive is not an element of any crime and the state does not have to show why a person committed a crime. To place the burden of proving motive on the state would make it unreasonably difficult to obtain a conviction in some cases.

Motive, however, is always relevant evidence that, if available to the state, can be used to show why the person committed the crime. In this sense, motive can be used to help prove intent or another degree of *mens rea,* in that it provides the trier of fact with more information and may remove doubt, by answering the question "why." However, motive alone would not be sufficient to convict. But a person may be lawfully convicted even if there is no motive or if a motive cannot be shown.

Criminal homicides are committed for different motives, such as hatred, anger, greed, and revenge. However, homicide and other offenses may be committed for "good" motives. Robbing a bank to give the money to the poor and needy is still a crime, even if the stolen funds are used for a good purpose.

Newspapers give a great deal of publicity to mercy-killing cases (euthanasia). However, "(t)he mother who kills her imbecile and suffering child out of motives of compassion is just as guilty of murder as is the man who kills for gain, since each intentionally takes another human life."[8] Although motive is not relevant to the issue of guilt or innocence, it can be a factor in sentencing. The defendant who kills in a rape-murder case or in the course of a robbery could receive and serve a much longer sentence than a mercy-killing defendant, who killed because of love and compassion.

B. Strict Liability Crimes

In enacting statutes to enforce rules having to do with traffic, liquor, purity of food, hunting, and narcotics offenses, modern legislative bodies often choose not to create "true crimes," but rather strict liability (or liability without mental fault) statutes.

Except for narcotic offenses, the penalties for strict liability offenses are usually lighter. The offenders are often not generally considered criminals in the true sense of the word, and the state is not required to carry the burden of proving criminal intent or other mental fault. The defendant is liable regardless of his or her state of mind at the time of the act.

The motor vehicle codes, hunting regulations, and the food and liquor laws of all states probably contain strict liability statutes. A bartender cannot ordinarily use as a defense the fact that the person to whom he sold liquor looked twenty-two when in fact the person was only seventeen. The driver of an overweight truck cannot argue that the company scales were faulty; nor can an adult male, in most states, argue that he did not know the age of the fifteen-year-old girl with whom he had sexual intercourse.

In referring to strict liability crimes, the U.S. Supreme Court pointed out that "Congress has rendered criminal a type of conduct that a reasonable person should know is subject to stringent public regulation and may seriously threaten the community's health or safety."[9]

Other cases illustrating strict liability crimes are:

UNITED STATES v. FREED
Supreme Court of the United States (1971) 401 U.S. 601, 91 S.Ct. 1112

Congress has made it a criminal offense to receive or possess unregistered hand grenades. In affirming that the government does not have to prove that a defendant knew the hand grenades were unregistered, the court stated:

> *[O]ne would hardly be surprised to learn that possession of hand grenades is not an innocent act.*

UNITED STATES v. DOTTERWEICH
Supreme Court of the United States (1943) 320 U.S. 277, 64 S.Ct. 134

A corporate officer can violate the Food, Drug, and Cosmetic Act when his or her firm ships adulterated and misbranded drugs even "though consciousness of wrongdoing be totally wanting."

LIPAROTA v. UNITED STATES
Supreme Court of the United States (1985) 471 U.S. 419, 105 S.Ct. 2084

After finding that fraudulent trafficking in food stamps does not threaten public health or safety, the U.S. Supreme Court held that the government must prove that a defendant knew that his or her purchase or possession of food stamps was in a manner unauthorized by law.

The defendant in this case was a businessman who purchased food stamps for amounts less than the face value of the food stamps.

Strict Liability Laws that Seek to Protect Children

The age of a minor is an essential element of such crimes as SIWAC (sexual intercourse with a child), contributing to the delinquency of a child, liquor laws, child porn laws, or giving or selling a minor a pistol, drugs, alcohol, beer, cigarettes, etc.

Such laws seek to protect children. To provide further protection to children, many states take away the defense of mistake of age from some or all of the offenses that seek to protect children. When this defense is taken away, defendants can not argue that they made an honest mistake as to the age of a child. (See chapter 7 for a discussion of the defenses of honest mistake of law or fact.)

By taking away the defense of honest mistake as to the age of a child, the state then makes the offense a strict liability offense and defendants can be proven guilty by showing only that they committed the forbidden act.

EXAMPLE: An adult has sex with a minor. The state only has to show that the sex occurred and the age of the parties. Consent cannot be used as a defense by the adult, as the minor is incapable of giving consent. Mistake as to the age of the minor cannot be used if this defense is prohibited by state law.

In the following 1990 case, the defendant hired a minor to dance nude in her place of business:

STATE v. WHITE
Court of Appeals of Minnesota (1990) 464 N.W.2d 585

After checking the identification of a young woman, Eve White hired her to dance nude on her bookstore dance floor. White testified that she honestly believed that the dancer was twenty-six years old, but the prosecutor and the police showed she was seventeen years old. The court held that White could not use the defense of consent or an honest mistake of age of the minor, as these defenses are taken away in the Minnesota crime of "promoting, employing, using, or permitting a minor (to engage in) a sexual performance." (Minn. Stat. 617.246.). In affirming the conviction, the Court of Appeals stated:

> . . . *States may create strict liability by defining criminal offenses without an element of scienter. . . . This exclusion has also been upheld in forbidding interstate transportation of persons to engage in immoral practices. . . .*

> * * *

> *A well-established body of case law has upheld statutes that exclude mistake of age as a defense to sexual conduct between an adult and a child under the statutory age of consent. . . .*

> * * *

> *An additional body of case law has upheld strict liability offenses in the area of public welfare, including food and drug legislation. . . .*

> *The specific effect of removing the mistake of age defense is to put the promoter of a sexual performance at greater peril. Although the severity of the penalty factors into the overbreadth analysis, it does not compel a finding that the statute is overbroad. . . .*
>
> *Despite the severity of excluding a good faith defense of mistake of age, we conclude that the statute is not unconstitutionally overbroad. We reach this conclusion because the statute affects expressive conduct rather than speech, contains a scienter requirement for the content of the performance, and potentially deters only a limited amount of conduct.*

* * *

(In 1991, the U. S. Supreme Court agreed to hear the case of *White v. Minnesota*. See 49 CrL 3090.)

C. Proximate Cause or Causation

Crimes are defined in terms of conduct that is forbidden (or required) and the mental state existing at the time of the forbidden act (or omission). Crimes are also defined in terms of the harm done or the wrong that occurs. For example, without any reason X strikes W a hard blow on the face with intent to injure him. The following different results may occur:

1. For a week, W has a black eye that heals without any medical attention (misdemeanor, ordinance battery, or assault).
2. W loses his eye and has a scar on his face (felony aggravated battery or assault, or maybe mayhem if elements of state crime can be proven).
3. W is knocked unconscious and remains in a coma for days in a hospital. There is a great deal of bleeding but no disfiguration (aggravated battery or assault).
4. W is killed immediately when he falls backward and strikes his head against a hard object (wrongful act manslaughter).
5. W's face is cut and bruised. He does not take care of the wound and an infection develops that causes W's death two weeks after the blow.
6. W's face is cut and bruised, and an ambulance is called to take him to a hospital. On the way to the hospital, the ambulance is involved in a traffic accident and W is killed.

Proximate cause (or causation) must be shown beyond a reasonable doubt by the state. The state must show that the unlawful and wrongful act of the defendant was the ordinary and probable cause of the harm that resulted. The harm to the victim could occur immediately, such as in a situation where a defendant shot a victim at point-blank range causing immediate death. Or, the defendant's acts could set off a chain of events where the criminal acts contributed to the victim's death days or weeks after the crime.

However, where death is caused by an intervening cause completely unrelated to the acts of a defendant, there then is no criminal liability. In the first four examples, the causal relationship between X's wrongful act and the wrong and harm that occurred is apparent. However, in examples 5 and 6, there were intervening causes that brought about the death of W.[10] The following cases reflect state court rulings on causation:

PEOPLE v. BRACKETT
Supreme Court of Illinois (1987) 117 Ill.2d 170, 510 N.E.2d 877

The defendant (a twenty-one-year-old male, 6 feet 3 inches tall and 170 pounds) broke into the home of an eighty-five-year-old woman. He beat and raped the woman, remaining in her home for hours. At a hospital, she was treated for a broken arm, broken rib, bruises on face, neck, arms, trunk, and inner thighs. After the victim left the hospital, she was transferred to a nursing home where she refused to eat. The smallness of her nasal passages prevented the insertion of a nasal feeding tube. The victim became weaker and the family was called to the nursing home believing death was imminent. While an attempt was being made to feed her small amounts of pureed food on a spoon, she choked to death on the food. The victim died more than a month after the rape. A doctor testified that the amount of air in the victim's lungs was insufficient to expel the food from her trachea. In addition to rape, deviate sexual assault and aggravated battery, the defendant was convicted of felony murder. In affirming the murder conviction, the court held:

※ ※ ※

It is a matter of common knowledge that a person can accidentally choke to death while eating. Moreover, that type of accidental death could be the type of intervening cause which would relieve a defendant of criminal responsibility for death. . . . The courts in Illinois have repeatedly held that an intervening cause completely unrelated to the acts of the defendant does relieve a defendant of criminal liability. . . . The converse of this is also true: when criminal acts of the defendant have contributed to a person's death, the defendant may be found guilty of murder. . . . It is not the law in this State that the defendant's acts must be the sole and immediate cause of death. Causal relationship is a question of fact which should be left to the trier of fact . . . and we will not disturb this verdict unless this evidence is so unreasonable, improbable and unsatisfactory as to leave a reasonable doubt as to defendant's guilt. . . .

* * *

Contrary to the defendant's contentions, we believe this is precisely the kind of case where the defendant takes his victim as he finds him. There are many cases in this State where the victim's existing health condition contributed to the victim's death. However, [so long as the defendant's acts contribute to the death there is still sufficient proof of causation, despite the preexisting health condition.]. . . . It appears to this court that a person's advanced age is as significant a part of his existing health condition as diabetes or hardening of the arteries.

* * *

The trier of fact was entitled to find that the defendant, a 21-year-old male, 6 feet 3 inches tall and 170 pounds, who battered and raped an 85-year-old woman, set in motion a chain of events which contributed to her death.

* * *

We hold here that the defendant did not have to foresee that this victim would die from asphyxiation in order to be guilty of felony murder.

* * *

SEAGROVES v. STATE
Supreme Court of Tennessee (1955) 198 Tenn. 633, 281 S.W.2d 644

Where it appears that it is equally probable that death resulted from one cause as from another, and the defendant is not responsible for one of the causes, then any determination of the cause of death cannot be speculative and conjectural, and the evidence will be held insufficient to support a verdict of guilty.

DUNCAN v. STATE
Court of Appeals of Alabama (1942) 30 Ala. App. 356, 6 So.2d 450

If death was due solely and exclusively to natural cause, i.e., heart failure, with the blow in no way contributing to or accelerating it, then, under the indictment, there was no homicide, and at most (if the blow was wrongful) the defendant would only be guilty of some degree of assault.

STEVENS v. UNITED STATES
Court of Appeals of the District of Columbia (1969) 249 A.2d 514

(T)he causal connection must be proven beyond a reasonable doubt and not by mere conjecture and speculation.

STATE v. NOSIS
Court of Appeals of Ohio (1969) 22 Ohio App.2d 16, 257 N.E.2d 414

The victim was a sixty-five-year-old man who blew his horn several times when passing the defendant on a highway. This angered the defendant, who challenged the victim to a fight at the next stoplight. The victim's wife asked the defendant to leave her husband alone because he had a bad heart. However, the defendant followed the victim and his wife several miles to their suburban home, where he argued and made menacing gestures in the driveway, after being warned again of the victim's bad heart. When the wife went inside to call the sheriff, her husband collapsed and died less than an hour later of a heart attack. In charging the defendant with manslaughter, the prosecutor acknowledged that the defendant had not struck the deceased but argued that the defendant's threats and gestures amounted to an assault. Moreover, the defendant knew of the victim's heart condition. The prosecutor argued that the defendant could have reasonably anticipated that the threats were likely to result in death. In affirming the manslaughter conviction, the court stated:

> *Unlawful killing . . . may be established by proof of assault, or of menacing threats . . . which proximately caused death, when death could be reasonably anticipated by an ordinarily prudent person as likely to result from such conduct while possessed with knowledge of a heart ailment of the victim.*

STATE v. NESTER
Supreme Court of West Virginia (1985) 336 S.E.2d 187

Essential Elements of a "True Crime"

The Essential Elements that State Must Prove in Showing that a "True Crime" was Committed

- the **act** element—the forbidden act (or failure to act)

- the **harm** element—the wrong done (killing, physical injury, property damage, loss, etc.)

- the **mental** element—the state of mind required for the crime (the guilty mind)

- the **cause** element—that the harm done was the natural and probable result of the wrongful act

Some crimes require proof of additional essential elements, such as scienter, possession (actual or constructive), etc.

STATE v. TURK

Court of Appeals of Wisconsin (1990) 154 Wis.2d 294, 453 N.W.2d 163

Defendants in both cases drove vehicles while intoxicated. Collisions occurred. A passenger in the Wisconsin case was seriously injured and a passenger in the West Virginia case was killed. The drivers in both states were charged with these results while driving under the influence.

The Courts in both cases rejected arguments that the failure of the passengers to wear seat belts intervened between the intoxicated operation of the vehicles and their injuries. The Wisconsin Court adopted the reasoning of the Supreme Court of West Virginia, which held:

> *The appellant . . . contends that the victim's failure to wear his seatbelt was an independent, intervening cause of the victim's death. This contention seriously distorts the definition of an intervening cause. An intervening cause is a new and independent force which breaks the causal connection between the original act or omission and the injury, and itself becomes the direct and immediate cause of the injury . . . The fact that the victim did not take precautionary steps which may have prevented his eventual demise is not an intervening cause.[2]*

The Ancient "Year-and-a-Day" Murder Rule

The "year-and-a-day" rule goes back hundreds of years in the law to 1278 when medical science was primitive.[11] Sir William Blackstone described the rule before the American Revolutionary War as follows: "In order . . . to make the killing murder, it is requisite that the party die within a year and a day after the stroke (blow) received, or cause of death administered; in the computation of which the whole day upon which the hurt was done shall be reckoned the first."[12]

A defendant therefore could not be convicted of murder if his victim did not die within a year and a day. Because of modern medical science and the skills of doctors and nurses, victims are most often on their feet and home if they can

---

2. To say otherwise could absolve a murderer if it could be shown the victim was not wearing a bullet-proof vest.

survive the first few weeks after a criminal assault. However, victims sometimes do not die until a long time after a criminal assault, as illustrated in the following case:

STATE v. HEFLER
Supreme Court of North Carolina (1984) 310 N.C. 135, 310 S.E.2d 310

The defendant drove a car after he drank a lot of beer, swallowed Quaaludes, and smoked marijuana. While intoxicated in this way, the defendant hit a jogger with his car, seriously injuring the man. The man never regained consciousness and died more than fourteen months after being run down by the defendant. The defendant was not charged until after the victim's death. The North Carolina courts held that the "year-and-a-day" rule applied only to murder cases and would not extend the rule to the involuntary manslaughter charge of which the defendant was convicted.

The Supreme Court of North Carolina pointed out in the *Hefler* case that the "year-and-a-day" rule is a statute of limitations upon the commencement of murder actions. The *Hefler* case, however, is very unusual in that Hefler was not criminally charged until more than fourteen months after the criminal act. Most suspects who seriously injure other persons in criminal acts are immediately taken into custody. If a suspect is in custody, a prosecutor must issue a criminal charge or release the person. When a criminal charge (or charges) is issued, the "speedy trial" requirements commence running. In most states "speedy trial" means that a defendant must be tried within 90, 100, or 120 days. Failure to try a defendant within this time limit is a complete defense to the criminal charges (see chapter 7).

Therefore, in such cases, prosecutors charge attempted murder, aggravated assault (or battery), injury by intoxicated use of a motor vehicle, etc. and go to trial on lesser charges. Defense lawyers are not likely to waive "speedy trial" and wait until a victim dies.[13]

D. POSSESSION AS AN ESSENTIAL ELEMENT

All states make the possession of certain objects a criminal offense. Examples of such crimes are the carrying of concealed weapons (CCW), possession of illegal drugs, possession of burglary tools, etc. "Actual possession" means that the object is either on the defendant's person, or within reach and under his or her immediate control and domination.

Because of public safety, all states forbid carrying an unauthorized concealed weapon (see chapter 12). "Carrying" requires a showing of actual possession. If a pistol is in the trunk of the car and not within the immediate reach and control of a person, it is not within actual possession.

Illegal drugs could be in "actual possession" of a defendant, or a defendant could have "constructive possession" of the drugs. The term *constructive possession* is used to indicate control over property and objects that the defendant does not have in actual possession. The object may be in his or her car parked two blocks away, in a desk drawer in the home or office, or in a suitcase stored

---

Possession as an Essential Element

Possession May Be	*Possession May Be*	*Possession of a Controlled Substance May Be*
a. actual, or b. constructive (not in actual possession)	a. in one person (sole), or b. joint (in possession of more than one person)[14]	a. of a "usable amount," or b. of a "trace amount," or c. within the body of the suspect d. a combination of any of the above

Most states will not permit a criminal conviction for drug possession based only on a showing of illegal drugs within the body of a defendant. Some states will not sustain a conviction of drug possession on a showing of "trace amount" alone. Combinations of the above are stronger cases. (Also see chapter 20 on Drug Abuse.)

---

somewhere for which he or she has a baggage claim check or key. Constructive possession would not be sufficient to sustain a conviction for carrying a concealed weapon, as a showing of actual possession is necessary. However, constructive possession would sustain a conviction for the possession of contraband, such as narcotics. The rules for the search of objects in a suspect's actual possession differ somewhat from the rules pertaining to the search for objects constructively possessed by a suspect.[15]

The mental element that must be proved in possession offenses is generally that of "intentionally" or "knowingly." These mental elements are usually easy to prove because a person with a loaded revolver or two pounds of marijuana in his or her pocket cannot argue convincingly that he or she did not know that the contraband was in actual possession. The intent to possess, then, is a state of mind existing at the time the person commits the offense. In seeking to determine the state of mind of the alleged offender in order to decide whether an intent existed, the jury or the court may base its decision on the defendant's acts, conduct, and other inferences that can be reasonably deducted from all the circumstances.

Possession is one of the rights of ownership of property. Criminal statutes do not require that ownership be proved. A person who possesses heroin may or may not be the owner of the heroin. Possession of personal property is presumptive evidence of ownership, and if the possession is accompanied by the exercise of complete acts of ownership for a considerable time, it is strong evidence of ownership. When objects and articles are in a vehicle, dwelling, or a business place, in the absence of evidence showing otherwise, there is a strong inference they are in the constructive possession of the person controlling the vehicle, dwelling, or business place. Therefore, heroin found in an apartment that is searched under the authority of a search warrant is in the constructive possession of the person controlling and occupying the apartment, unless the person can show otherwise. (Also see chapter 20 on Drug Abuse.)

When Drug Testing Shows that a Person Has Illegal Drugs in His or Her Body

Persons on parole or probation, professional athletes, airline pilots, and persons in other occupations could be obligated to take drug tests. If reliable or confirmed tests show that a person has drugs in his or her body, this person could either be required to enter a drug treatment program, or could enter such a program voluntarily. This person could be suspended from or lose his or her job. As occurred in the 1988 summer Olympics in Korea, such a person could lose his or her gold medal. The results of such tests could be used as evidence to convict the person of driving a vehicle (motor vehicle, aircraft, watercraft, train, etc.) under the influence. If the person is on probation or parole, his or her probation or parole could be revoked and the person sent to jail or prison.

But when drug tests show the presence of heroin, cocaine, or crack in a person's body, would this evidence be sufficient in itself to obtain a conviction for possession of the illegal substance? This was the issue presented to the Minnesota Court of Appeals in the 1986 case of *State v. Lewis.*[16] Laboratory results from a urine sample showed that the defendant had morphine in his body. The only other evidence used in obtaining Lewis's conviction on illegal possession of morphine was the testimony of a police officer that he observed what he believed were "needle marks on the inside elbow of both of Mr. Lewis' arms." After reviewing other similar cases in the United States, the Court reversed, quoting other courts as follows:

* * *

Discovery of a drug in a person's blood is circumstantial evidence tending to prove prior possession of the drug, but it is not sufficient evidence to establish guilt beyond a reasonable doubt.

* * *

Once a controlled substance is in the human system it is beyond the control which the uniform act contemplated. The deleterious effects of the drug are already in progress. What the act seeks to prevent has occurred. The "controlled substance" is no longer susceptible to the control the act seeks to regulate.

* * *

E. The Use of Presumptions and Inferences in Criminal Law

Presumptions are used in criminal law. The first and earliest presumptions were common law presumptions created by courts. In modern times, most newly created presumptions are created by legislative bodies. The best-known presumption, and probably the oldest, is the presumption of innocence until proven guilty. The presumption of innocence until proven guilty is a rebuttable presumption (rebuttable presumptions may be overcome by evidence proving otherwise). The presumption of innocence may be overcome by evidence showing that a defendant is guilty beyond a reasonable doubt.

Some writers identify another form of presumption, called "conclusive presumption." A *conclusive presumption* is a statement of substantive law that cannot be overcome with evidence showing otherwise. There are few conclusive presumptions; probably the best known is the rule of law that a person under age

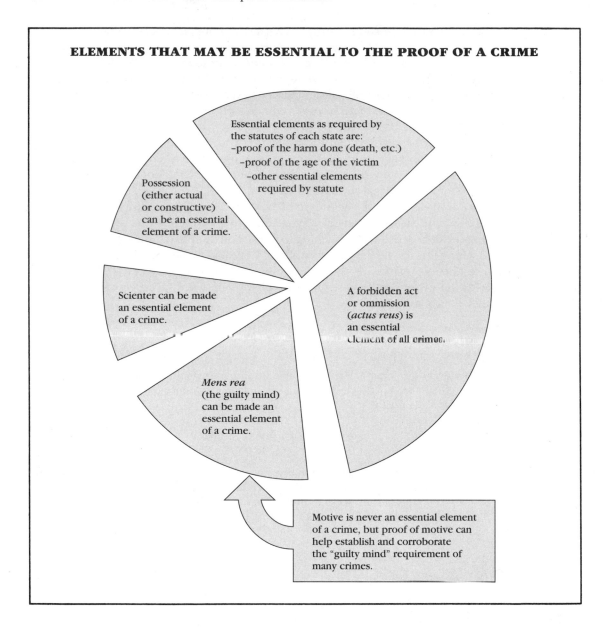

ELEMENTS THAT MAY BE ESSENTIAL TO THE PROOF OF A CRIME

Essential elements as required by the statutes of each state are:
-proof of the harm done (death, etc.)
-proof of the age of the victim
-other essential elements required by statute

Possession (either actual or constructive) can be an essential element of a crime.

Scienter can be made an essential element of a crime.

A forbidden act or ommission (*actus reus*) is an essential element of all crimes.

Mens rea (the guilty mind) can be made an essential element of a crime.

Motive is never an essential element of a crime, but proof of motive can help establish and corroborate the "guilty mind" requirement of many crimes.

seven has not reached the age of reason and therefore is not capable of committing a crime.

Functions of Presumptions

Presumptions are created to permit orderly civil and criminal trials. The Supreme Court of Pennsylvania[17] and the Supreme Court of Indiana[18] defined the function and legal significance of presumptions as follows:

A presumption of law is not evidence nor should it be weighed by the factfinder as though it had evidentiary value. Rather, a presumption is a rule of law enabling the party in whose favor it operates to take his case to the jury without presenting evidence of the fact presumed. It serves as a challenge for proof and indicates the party from whom such proof must be forthcoming. When the opponent of the presumption has met the burden of production thus imposed, however, the office of the presumption has been performed; the presumption is of no further effect and drops from the case.

Inferences Distinguished from Presumptions

A *presumption* is a deduction or conclusion that the law expressly directs that the trier of fact (jury or judge) *must* make. As most presumptions may be disputed, they may be outweighed or overcome with evidence showing otherwise. Unless presumptions are overcome with other evidence, judges and jurors *must* accept the presumption as true.

The purpose of civil and criminal trials is to determine the truth of the issues presented to the fact finder. Criminal trials commence with the presumption that the defendant is innocent. To overcome this presumption, the state must present evidence proving beyond a reasonable doubt in the minds of the jury the guilt of the defendant. Each essential element of the crime charged must be proved beyond a reasonable doubt.

Fact finders (juries and judges) must use good common sense and their knowledge of everyday life. In their reasoning process, juries and judges must use *inferences*. An inference is a conclusion or deduction that a jury or judge *may* draw from a fact or a group of facts presented to them. A common inference used in criminal trials is that persons intend (desire) the natural and probable consequences of their deliberate acts. The following example is used to illustrate:

EXAMPLE: X is charged with the attempted murder of Y. X is a 170-pound, thirty-year-old man who did the following:

Facts	Conclusions that logically may be inferred from facts
a) Reliable witnesses testify that X repeatedly attempted to hit Y on or about Y's head with a baseball bat. Bystanders stopped X.	X intended to kill Y and would have done so had not Y protected himself until X was restrained.
b) Same facts as stated in (a), except that X used a rolled-up newspaper to strike at Y.	An intent to kill cannot be inferred from the facts.

The Inference that All Persons Are Sane, Normal, and Competent

Another important inference concludes that all persons are sane, normal, and competent. Adult witnesses in civil and criminal cases are inferred to be sane, normal, and competent. However, an attorney could challenge this inference. (The exception to this inference is very young children who may not be able to remember and communicate about events that occurred weeks and months prior to the trial.)

Defendants in criminal cases are also inferred to be sane, normal, and competent. This inference can also be challenged. It is reported that all state and

Fact Patterns from which Permissible and Impermissible Inferences Can Be Drawn

Inferences must be used to prove intent in criminal cases because direct proof (statements, confessions, etc.) is seldom available. Juries must use their good common sense and draw inferences from the evidence presented. The following cases illustrate:

Conduct

Defendant forced a young girl into a secluded area and forced her to take off her clothes and lie on the ground. He threatened her with a gun as he loosened his pants. Nothing was said of his intent and he fled at this point.	Attempted sexual assault in the first degree?	Yes, see *Green v. Connecticut,* ___ A.2d ___ . Review denied U.S. Supreme Court, 36 CrL 4178 (1985)
In the middle of the day, defendant was seen walking out of an empty warehouse by police. Defendant was cooperative, did not run, and had nothing in his possession. He told police that he had to go to the toilet and entered the building looking for a lavatory.	Can an inference of intent to steal be drawn to justify a conviction of burglary (illegal entry with intent to steal)?	No, see *Commonwealth v. Muniem,* 225 Pa.Super. 311, 303 A.2d 528 (1973)
Police with a search warrant stop a United Parcel Service truck carrying more than two hundred parcels on city delivery. The warrant authorizes the opening of one of the parcels, which was found to contain two pounds of heroin.	Can an inference be drawn based on this information to conclude there is probable cause to justify an arrest of the UPS driver by the police?	No
X is present in a store while the store was robbed.	Would mere presence at the scene of a crime justify an arrest?	No, further information would be needed
A murder is committed and only two people were at the scene of the crime. They could have committed the crime together, or one could be guilty and the other innocent.	Would these facts justify a conclusion that probable cause exists to arrest either or both?	Yes, see Restatement of Torts (2d) Sec. 119 (1965)
Defendant was one of the crew aboard a small boat carrying 22,000 pounds of marijuana on a long trip to the United States. Defendant claims he had no knowledge of the illegal enterprise.	From the facts, can inferences be drawn that defendant was a party to the illegal enterprise?	Yes, see *United States v. Guerrero-Guerrero,* 38 CrL 2235, 776 F.2d 1071 (1st Cir. 1985)

federal courts place the burden of proof on the party challenging the inference that a defendant is sane, normal, and competent. Therefore, a defendant seeking to use the insanity defense under the laws of his or her state (see chapter 5) has the burden of proving that he or she is so mentally diseased or defective as to be unable to formulate the mental intent to commit the crime charged.

In 1981, John Hinckley attempted to kill the president of the United States. In a wild shooting spree in Washington, D.C., Hinckley seriously wounded the president and other persons.

In his trial in a federal court in Washington, Hinckley and his attorneys entered pleas of not guilty and not guilty by reason of mental disease and defect. At the time of the Hinckley case, federal courts were using a rule that the government had the burden of showing a defendant (such as Hinckley) to be sane and normal. In view of his wild, bizarre behavior, the U.S. government was unable to carry the burden of showing that Hinckley was sane and normal. As a result, a jury found Hinckley to be not guilty by reason of mental disease and defect.

Within a short time, the Congress of the United States passed a law changing the federal rule (the "Hinckley" rule), and now defendants in federal court have the burden of coming forward with sufficient evidence to prove that they were so mentally diseased or defective that they were unable to formulate the mental intent to commit the crime charged. (See chapter 5 for more material on this subject.)

Questions and Problems for Chapter 3

1. A New York police officer made a lawful stop of a speeding vehicle. Four men were in the car (two in the front seat and two in the rear). The officer smelled burnt marijuana coming from the vehicle and as he was standing next to the vehicle, the officer saw an envelope marked "Supergold" on the floor of the car between the two men in the front seat. The officer had probable cause to believe that the envelope contained marijuana. These facts would justify a conclusion (inference) as to which of the men were in possession of marijuana (all four? only two? only one?)? There would be authority to arrest (or cite) which of the men? Explain your answer. *New York v. Belton,* 453 U.S. 454, 101 S.Ct. 2860 (1981).

2. The defendant, James Jackson, admitted that he had shot and killed his friend, Mrs. Cole. Jackson testified that he was not drunk at the time of the shooting but that he had been "pretty high." He testified that Mrs. Cole had taken off some of her clothes and then attacked him with a knife when he had resisted her sexual advances. Jackson testified that he had fired warning shots and then reloaded the gun. When the victim attempted to take the gun from him, it "went off," killing her. Without seeking help for the victim, he drove her car to another state. No other person was at the scene of the shooting and defendant argues not only self-defense, but also that he was too intoxicated to form the specific intent necessary for conviction of first-degree murder.

A deputy sheriff also testified at the trial. He knew the defendant and Mrs. Cole and had seen them in a restaurant just before the shooting. Because Jackson appeared intoxicated, the sheriff offered to hold Jackson's revolver until Jackson sobered up. Jackson said that this was unnecessary because he and Mrs. Cole were about to engage in sexual activity.

Jackson waived his right to a jury trial and was tried before a judge. The judge found him guilty of first-degree murder. Was the evidence sufficient to support the conviction? Explain. *Jackson v. Virginia,* 443 U.S. 307, 99 S.Ct. 2781 (1979).

3. An Arizona police officer stopped a car for excessive speed. The three men in the car had difficulty speaking English. None of the men had identification, and it was discovered that the vehicle was stolen. Based on these facts, which of the men may be arrested for the crime of operating a motor vehicle without the owner's consent (only the driver? or all three men?)? Explain. *State v. Marquez,* 135 Ariz. 316, 660 P.2d 1243 (App. 1983).

4. Drug raids of "shooting galleries" are frequently made in the United States. An assortment of persons are sometimes found in such places when police enter under the authority of a search warrant. There could be derelicts and junkies, older persons who have been drug addicts for years, and younger persons. In some instances, the police are unable to determine who owns or rents the apartment or building. In other instances, ten or fifteen people may be in such an apartment and drugs may be laying around, including cocaine, Ts and blues, marijuana, etc. Is there sufficient evidence to arrest or charge a person: (a) who is not the owner of the apartment or home; (b) who has no drugs or other contraband on his or her person;

(c) who does not have an outstanding arrest warrant against him or her for other offenses; or (d) who was just hanging around and was present in a place where drugs have been seized? What statutes in your state would apply (if any)?

5. X shoplifts in W's store. W sees X shoplift and attempts to detain and recover the stolen property. X runs out of the store and down the street. After chasing X for a block, W has a heart attack and dies on the street. Can X be successfully charged with a homicide? (Review the criminal homicide statutes in your state.) Is this example any different than the *Nosis* case? (See case in this chapter.) In what ways?

6. "Tootie Pie" Cosby had in his possession a camera and zoom lens that had been stolen in a burglary a few days earlier. Cosby pawned the camera and lens that had been taken from an apartment in the complex where he lived. On this evidence, Cosby was charged with the burglary. He testified that he bought the camera from two men for $40. As he only had a $50 bill, he had to get change and the man who gave him the two $20 bills and a $10 bill testified that he provided the change for the $50 bill. Cosby also presented at his trial an alibi that he was in another town at the time of the burglary. Several witnesses corroborated this alibi, but there was some inconsistency in their testimony. The jury convicted Cosby and he was sentenced to twenty years imprisonment. Is there sufficient evidence (facts) to sustain and justify the burglary conviction? Explain. *Cosby v. Jones,* 682 F.2d 1373 (11th Cir., 1982).

7. In 1990, a young father had to make a quick stop at a store. Believing that he would be gone only a few minutes, the man left his keys in the unlocked car in which his six-month-old son was sleeping. When the man returned, he was shocked to find the car and his baby gone. When the police could not locate the vehicle, they requested assistance of local radio and television stations. Two hours later, the vehicle was found abandoned on a side street with the baby still sleeping.

What crime (or crimes) could the person who took the vehicle be charged with under the criminal code of your state? Could the person be charged with kidnapping or child abduction under the statutes of your state? If so, what scienter (knowledge) element would the state have to prove in this case? What defenses could probably be expected to the charges you have proposed?

Notes

1. *Powell v. Texas,* 392 U.S. 514, 535, 88 S.Ct. 2145 (1968).
2. *Morissette v. United States,* 342 U.S. at 251 (see chapter 7).
3. 444 U.S. 394, 100 S.Ct. 624, 26 CrL 3065 (1980).
4. 438 U.S. at 445, 98 S.Ct. at 2877 (1978).
5. 444 U.S. 394, 100 S.Ct. 624, 26 Cr.L. 3065 (1980).
6. See 22 Corpus Juris Secundum Criminal Law, Secs. 30–36.
7. 512 F.2d 1281 (5th Cir. 1975).
8. Smith and Hogan, *Criminal Law,* 3d ed. (London: Buttersworth, 1973).
9. *Liparota v. United States,* 471 U.S. 419, 105 S.Ct. 2084 (1985).
10. See the section on causation and intervening causes (pp. 246–267) in *Criminal Law,* by LaFave and Scott (St. Paul: West Pub. Co., 1972).
11. See *People v. Stevenson,* 416 Mich. 383, 331 N.W. 2d 143 (1982).
12. Blackstone, *Commentaries* 197.

13. The victim in the *Hefler* case was brain dead a short time after he was hit by the defendant's car. If a victim is brain dead, could the state go into court and have the person declared legally dead clearing the way to issuing criminal homicide charges? In such situations, the family of a victim are tempted "to pull the plug," which would also clear the way for criminal homicide charges. See chapter 13 for more material in this area.
14. See *Ker v. California,* 374 U.S. 23, 83 S.Ct. 1623 (1963), for an example of joint possession.
15. See Gardner and Manian, *Principle and Cases of the Law of Arrest, Search and Seizure* (New York: McGraw-Hill Book Co., 1974).
16. 394 N.W.2d 212 (Minn. 1986). Generally, the cases that go to trial are those cases where the evidence shows the defendant had a "trace" or "usable" amount in his or her possession and was also under the influence of the drug (had the drug in his or her body).
17. *Commonwealth v. Vogel,* 440 Pa. 1, 17, 268 A.2d 89, 102 (1970).
18. *Sumpter v. State,* 261 Ind. 471, 306 N.E.2d 95 (1974).

Chapter Four

CRIMINAL LIABILITY

This chapter concerns itself with the question of criminal liability and the problem of whom besides the person (or persons) who actually committed the crime should be charged and punished. Criminal participation in which there is criminal liability may be classified as follows:

1. Violations of the preliminary or anticipatory crimes (also known as "inchoate" crimes). These crimes are preparatory and by their nature lead to the committing of a more serious offense.
2. Parties to the principal offenses.
3. Postcrime offenses, crimes committed after the principal offense and related to that offense.
4. Offenses for which there is vicarious liability—that is, situations in which innocent parties (employers or corporations) may be held criminally liable for certain offenses of their employees, fellow employees, agents, etc.

A. PRELIMINARY, ANTICIPATORY, OR INCHOATE CRIMES

When Is a Crime Committed?

Not all crimes are planned in advance. Some crimes are committed impulsively, the decision to commit the crime being made on the spur of the moment or almost spontaneously with the commission of the offense.

Nor are all crimes completed. In some instances, the person (or persons) who has carefully planned to commit a crime decides, for one reason or another, not to. Crimes are also not completed because of events that prevent their completion.

A person who plans in his mind to commit a crime has not yet violated any law. He or she may even in some instances express vocally his intention to commit a crime without committing an offense. However, in some instances, such a person may be subject to arrest or to detention for expressing such intentions. The following examples illustrate this point.

EXAMPLE 1: X works at a home for senior citizens and is angry with his employer. After four or five beers at a tavern, he states that he is going to siphon gasoline out of his car and set fire to the home.

EXAMPLE 2: X, who has previously attempted to commit suicide, states that he is going home to kill his wife, his children, and himself.

EXAMPLE 3: X states that he is going to embezzle money from his employer, who is not paying him enough.

In Examples 1 and 2, X is threatening the life and the safety of others (and his own life in Example 2). Example 3 is a property offense in which lives and safety are not involved. Officers in different jurisdictions might handle these situations in different ways. Possible courses of action are:

The concept of criminal liability is ancient. Here, a colonial customs official receives the punishment of tar and feathering after a 1774 trial.

1. To take X into custody under the emergency detention laws of that jurisdiction, as he appears irresponsible and dangerous to himself or others (in Examples 1 and 2).
2. To arrest X for drunkenness or disorderly conduct if there is probable cause for such an arrest under the laws of that jurisdiction (in Examples 1 and 2).
3. To warn the intended victims and take protective steps to prevent X from carrying out his threats.

There are also some instances where the threat to commit a crime is a crime in itself.

EXAMPLE: X angrily tells Y, "I am going to kill you." If such language constitutes "fighting words" and is one step away from violence, an officer may arrest X or order him into a prosecutor's office, if such action is justified under the statutes of that jurisdiction (see the *Chaplinsky* "fighting words" rule in chapter 10).

EXAMPLE: 8 U.S.C.A. Section 871 makes it a federal offense to do the following: "(a) Whoever knowingly and willfully . . . makes any such threat (to take the life or to inflict bodily harm) against the President, President-elect, Vice President or other officer next in the order of succession to the office of President, or Vice-President-elect, shall be fined not more than $1,000 or imprisoned not more than five years, or both."

Because of the apparent need to prevent serious social harm before it occurs, courts long ago created the three separate and distinct common law crimes of solicitation, conspiracy, and attempt. Although these offenses were crimes in themselves, each of these acts is preliminary or anticipatory to another more serious crime that the offender has in mind.

In considering the preliminary offenses, the following questions always arise: Where and when does noncriminal conduct become criminal conduct by a further act of the suspect? Which of the preliminary offenses, if any, has been violated by the suspect? When does the commission of the principal offense begin so as to allow the state to charge either the preliminary offense or the principal offense? Convictions of both preliminary and principal offenses are, in most instances, forbidden by statute or the double jeopardy principle.

1. Solicitation or Incitement

By the early 1800s, English and American courts had recognized solicitation as a misdemeanor under the common law. Solicitation may be defined as an attempt to get another person to commit a crime. It may also be described as an attempt to conspire to commit a crime. The solicitation does not have to be successful. The crime of solicitation is committed even if the person solicited refuses to cooperate and repudiates the proposal. It is also immaterial, in most instances, whether payment or reward is offered and whether it is accepted or refused. Evidence of the offer of payment or reward, however, can be important in proving solicitation.

From a practical point of view, two things are necessary for the successful prosecution of a charge of solicitation:

1. The cooperation of the person who was solicited
2. Evidence that supports and sustains (corroborates) the testimony of the cooperating state witness

The following example illustrates this point. A man (A) whose name was in the newspaper because he went into bankruptcy called the police and stated that a stranger (B) had telephoned him and asked him if he would like to make some money. When A said yes, B told him that he wanted his wife killed and would pay A to do the job. A realized that he was talking to someone with severe mental or emotional problems and pretended to be interested but said that the job would have to be done by a professional killer. A said that he had a contact with such a man, and after B gave A his name and telephone number, A called the police.

At this point, the police had a weak case to take into court, as a denial by B could raise a degree of doubt. Law enforcement officers also realized that the story A told them could be a fabrication or a hoax. For these reasons, they had to investigate further. This is ordinarily done by using an undercover officer. (Students occasionally ask if this would be entrapment; the answer is no. See the section on entrapment in chapter 7.)

An undercover police officer telephoned B, pretending to be a hired killer from another city. A meeting was arranged and B again repeated his offer to pay to have his wife killed. When B paid money to the officer for the killing, the officer arrested B, who was charged with solicitation to commit murder under the statutes of that jurisdiction. The undercover officer was the complaining witness. His statements were corroborated by the money bearing B's fingerprints. Statements from A were also available as evidence.

In the circumstances previously set out, a prosecutor would be unable to charge B criminally with solicitation to commit murder if the state had abolished common law crimes and had neither a general solicitation statute nor a particularized statute making solicitation to commit murder a crime. Probably the only practical alternative left in such a jurisdiction would be either an emergency or civil detention action under the mental health statutes of that state.

The Model Penal Code Proposed Solicitation Statute

The present Federal Criminal Code (18 U.S.C.A. Section 2) and the proposed Federal Criminal Code make solicitation a crime. Section 5.02 of the Model Penal Code proposes a general solicitation statute, part of which is as follows:

> (1) *Definition of Solicitation.* A person is guilty of solicitation to commit a crime if with the purpose of promoting or facilitating its commission he commands, encourages or requests another person to engage in a specific conduct which would constitute such crime or an attempt to commit such crime or which would establish his complicity in its commission or attempted commission.

Although the Model Penal Code defines solicitation to include enticement to commit any crime (misdemeanor or felony), most states with a general solicitation statute limit solicitation to the solicitation of a felony.

All states make solicitation an important part of their prostitution and bribery statutes. Solicitation to commit prostitution and solicitation to commit bribery are by far the most common charges for prostitution and bribery throughout the United States. These crimes are generally charged under the bribery and prostitution statutes and not under the general solicitation statute of the state.

2. Conspiracy

The crime of conspiracy is the oldest of the preliminary crimes. It received some legislative recognition as early as 1292, but it was not until the early 1600s that the crime of conspiracy was developed into an offense of wide scope, capable of extensive application by the English Court of the Star Chamber. This court was created in the late 1500s to try certain high crimes without a jury. Because of the ruthless methods supposedly used, the court is sometimes referred to as the "infamous Star Chamber."

Modern critics of the crime of conspiracy sometimes recall the ancient unsavory use of the crime of conspiracy, as did former Justice Robert H. Jackson in his concurring opinion in *Krulewitch v. United States:*

> The crime comes down to us wrapped in vague but unpleasant connotations. It sounds historical undertones of treachery, secret plotting and violence on a scale that menaces social stability and the security of the state itself. "Privy conspiracy" ranks with sedition and rebellion in the Litany's prayer for deliverance. Conspiratorial movements do indeed lie back of the political assassination, the coup d'etat, the putsch, the revolution and seizure of power in modern times, as they have in all history.[1]

The federal government (18 U.S.C.A. Sec. 371) and probably all states have enacted statutes making conspiracy a crime in their jurisdictions. The reasoning behind such legislation generally is that when two or more persons plan a crime together (a) the extent of potential harm to the society is often increased con-siderably; (b) the possibility of the abandonment of the criminal plan is greatly reduced; (c) the chances of success in the criminal venture are greater than if only one individual were involved; and (d) their actions can be more difficult to detect than individual preparation to commit a crime.

The purpose, then, of criminal conspiracy statutes is to prevent and to punish criminal partnerships in crime and to stop, if possible, such criminal combinations of people before attempts to commit substantive crimes are made.

Although the statutes of each state define conspiracy within that state, the generally accepted common law definition of conspiracy is "a combination of two or more persons, by some concerted action, to accomplish some criminal or unlawful purpose, or to accomplish some purpose, not in itself criminal or un-lawful, by criminal or unlawful means."[2]

Conspiracy Today

Conspiracy used to be known as the "darling of the prosecutor's nursery."[3] How-ever, today the "new darling of the prosecutor's nursery" is the Federal RICO (Racketeer Influenced and Corrupt Organization Act) statute and the "little RI-COs" that have been enacted in many states. (See chapter 21 for a discussion of the RICO statutes.)

Conspiracy statutes have, in the past, been an important weapon in the fight against organized crime. In 1983, FBI Director William H. Webster testified that it was not until the 1980s that law enforcement agencies, prosecutors, and courts learned how to use RICO effectively. The RICO statutes have probably now become the most effective tool against organized crime, with conspiracy being used when needed.

Enforcement agencies responsible for the policing of business practices have used conspiracy charges in antitrust, price-fixing, and restraint-of-trade cases. The common denominator found in all conspiracy cases is the government's allega-tion that the defendants, as a group, conspired to violate one or more of the criminal laws of that jurisdiction.

The Requirement of "Two or More" Guilty Persons

As conspiracy was looked on as a partnership in crime, the traditional view was that the state must prove the involvement of "two or more" guilty persons. If A and B were charged with conspiracy to murder and the jury found A guilty and B not guilty, the traditional view is that the conviction against A could not stand. The reasoning for the dismissal of the charge and conviction against A is that A could not conspire by himself and there would have to be "two or more" guilty persons for his conviction to stand.

The National Advisory Committee Report on Organized Crime referred to the requirement of "two or more" as an "antique conspiracy law." The American Law Institute Model Penal Code rejected the "bilateral" requirement of "two or more" in favor of the "unilateral approach."

In 1961, Illinois adopted the "unilateral approach," stating that the "two or more" requirement was "too technical and overlooked the realities of trials which involve differences in juries, contingent availability of witnesses, the varying ability of different prosecutors and defense attorneys, etc."[4] Section 8–2(b) of the Illinois Criminal Code states:

> (b) Co-conspirators.
> It shall not be a defense to conspiracy that the person or persons with whom the accused is alleged to have conspired:
> 1. Has not been prosecuted or convicted, or
> 2. Has been convicted of a different offense, or
> 3. Is not amenable to justice, or
> 4. Has been acquitted, or
> 5. Lacked the capacity to commit an offense.

After using the "two or more" requirement for many years, the U.S. Court of Military Appeals, in 1983, held in *United States v. Garcia* that when two coconspirators are tried separately on a conspiracy charge, the acquittal of one does not mean that the other conspirator must also be acquitted. In pointing out that more than twenty-six states have adopted the Model Penal Code "unilateral approach," the court held:

> Our present system of judicial review is quite capable of considering the evidence against each and all the named conspirators, even when they are tried separately, and deciding the criminal responsibility of each without resort to a rule that must often result in a miscarriage of justice simply to avoid the possibility of a "wrong" verdict. . . . We do not now decide the question of whether inconsistent verdicts as to coconspirators in a *joint* trial may be treated separately.[5]

If One of the Two Parties Is Only Pretending to Have a Criminal Intent

If one of the two parties to a criminal plan is only pretending to go along with a criminal plan, when in fact he or she is an undercover police officer or a person cooperating with a law enforcement agency, conspiracy cannot be charged in states using the "two or more" requirement. However, in a state using the unilateral approach, conspiracy could be charged. The following case reflects what is now the majority rule in the United States:

STATE v. LAVARY
Superior Court of New Jersey (1977) 152 N.J.Super. 413, 377 A.2d 1255

The New Jersey court ruled that a defendant can be convicted of conspiracy even though the person she conspired with was actually an undercover police officer. In affirming the defendant's conviction for conspiracy to commit atrocious assault and battery and to commit mayhem on a police officer, the New Jersey appellate court held:

> *The relevant* Model Penal Code *section takes the approach that it is "immaterial to the guilt of a conspirator whose culpability has been established that the person or all of the persons with whom he conspired have not been or cannot be convicted." 305 Minn. 226, 232 N.W.2d 798.*

* * *

> *To hold otherwise here would mock justice, interfere with the interest of society in repressing crime, and lead to absurd results. This court finds, as evidenced by the proposed* New Jersey Penal Code, *that a unilateral approach to the crime of con-*

spiracy is appropriate and fully justified in New Jersey. This approach requires that the evaluation of guilt in New Jersey when conspiracy is charged be from the point of view of the individual actor. The court finds this interpretation fully consistent with modern New Jersey cases, not violative of any legislative directive and consistent with the increased danger and social harm inherent in the crime of conspiracy. The "intricacies and artificial distinctions" urged by defendant thwart rather than serve substantial justice and are hereby rejected. . . .

For the above reasons, the motion to dismiss the indictment or grant judgment notwithstanding the verdict is denied.

Husband and Wife as Coconspirators

Under the old common law, a husband and wife were one person, with the wife being subject to the control and discipline of the husband (see the discussion on the defense of duress and coercion in chapter 7). Because of this relationship, the common law rule held that *since* the husband and wife were one person, they could not conspire together and be charged as the two persons to a conspiracy.

This rule was adopted in the states, but in the few modern cases in which the issue has been presented before American courts, the courts have rejected the old common law rule. In the 1960 case of *United States v. Dege,*[6] the U.S. Supreme Court rejected the concept that a husband and wife are legally incapable of criminally conspiring with each other. In affirming the convictions of the husband and wife defendants for conspiring to illegally bring goods into the United States, the majority held:

> Considering that legitimate business enterprises between husband and wife have long been commonplace in our time, it would enthrone an unreality into a rule of law to suggest that man and wife are legally incapable of engaging in illicit enterprises and therefore, forsooth, do not engage in them.

This rule permits federal prosecutors to charge husband and wife with criminal conspiracy.

The Wharton Rule

Some crimes cannot be committed alone. Examples of such crimes are dueling, bigamy, gambling, adultery, and incest. Part of the justification for the creation of the crime of conspiracy is that the criminal agreement presents danger to the society beyond that inherent in the crime that is planned. In the 1850 case of *Shannon v. Commonwealth,*[7] the court threw out a prosecution for conspiracy to commit adultery, in which the man and woman were defendants, stating, "nothing is more ridiculous."

The Wharton Rule[8] holds that when the state charges a conspiracy to commit a crime that requires at least two people to commit, the state must charge three or more persons to sustain the conspiracy charge. Therefore, in jurisdictions that follow the Wharton Rule, in order to charge conspiracy to gamble the state must charge at least three persons.

In the 1935 case of *Gebardi v. United States,* the U.S. Supreme Court reversed the conviction of a man and a woman who were convicted of conspiring to violate the Mann Act by planning to transport the woman defendant from one state to another for the purpose of engaging in sexual intercourse with the male defendant. The Court stated "that where it is impossible under any circumstances to commit the substantive offense without co-operative action, the preliminary agreement between the same parties to commit the offense is not an indictable conspiracy either at common law ... or under the federal statute."[9]

Probably because of the organized crime problem in the Chicago area, Illinois is among the jurisdictions that have rejected the Wharton Rule. The Committee on the Revision of the Illinois Criminal Code Comments with respect to Section 8–2(a) of the Illinois Criminal Code are as follows:

> The Committee felt that the Wharton Rule fails to take into account the preventive aspect of prosecuting conspiracies, that is, to discourage the more dangerous criminal activity of several persons by punishing the preliminary agreement to engage in such activity. That the criminal activity is of such nature as to inevitably require more than one person in its accomplishment seems the more reason to punish the preliminary agreement to undertake it.[10]

Section 5.04 of the Model Penal Code rejects the Wharton Rule. Although the federal statute making gambling a crime (18 U.S.C.A. Sec. 1955) requires "five or more persons," this represents, as the U.S. Supreme Court points out, "a legislative attempt to merge the conspiracy and the substantive offense into a single crime."[11]

Objective of the Conspiracy

Common law conspiracy is defined as "a combination of two or more persons ... to accomplish some criminal or unlawful purpose." Under the common law, the unlawful act did not have to be criminal but could have been a tort or an act that violated public policy. The present general federal conspiracy statute (18 U.S.C.A. Sec. 371) prohibits not only conspiracy to commit a crime, but also any "offense against the United States, or to defraud the United States, or any agency thereof in any manner or for any purpose."

The tendency of modern conspiracy statutes is to limit the crime of conspiracy to criminal offenses. The proposed federal criminal code[12] (not yet enacted) limits the crime of conspiracy to "a crime or crimes." As the Federal Criminal Code is made up of more than 2,800 crimes, this gives considerable scope to future federal conspiracy charges.

3. Attempt

In states that have statutorized a general solicitation crime, solicitation is infrequently charged. Attempt, however, is the most frequently charged of the three preliminary crimes. This difference exists because it is difficult for law enforcement agencies not only to detect criminal solicitation (other than prostitution and bribery), but also to obtain sufficient evidence with which to charge. On the other hand, people who attempt to commit a crime often expose to witnesses and possible victims their criminal intent and purpose by their acts. The near victim of a crime and other witnesses are more willing to disclose to the police what they have seen and heard than are those who are solicited by a friend or acquaintance to commit a crime.

In defining an attempt, the New York Criminal Code provides that "a person is guilty of an attempt to commit a crime when, with intent to commit a crime, he engages in conduct which tends to effect the commission of such crime."[13]

But mere preparation to commit a crime is not an attempt. New York and other states require the state to show that the defendant performed acts that carried the "project forward within dangerous proximity of the criminal end to be attained."[14] Many states require an act amounting to a "substantial step" be shown as also required in Section 5.01 of the Model Penal Code.

Attempt, like the other preparatory crimes, has its origins in early English law. Attempt charges were reportedly used as early as the fourteenth century. The modern doctrine of attempt had been formulated before the ratification of the U.S. Constitution. Today, most states have enacted general attempt statutes that, with few exceptions, make the attempt to commit a felony or a misdemeanor a crime. Some states, however, limit the crime of attempt to felonies and only a few misdemeanors such as battery and misdemeanor theft.

What Acts by a Defendant Amount to an Attempt?

Courts and writers have spent a great deal of time with the most difficult problem in the area of attempt. When has a person who has an intent to commit a crime done enough to justify his or her arrest and conviction? Just how close to completing the crime must the defendant come before he or she can be successfully charged with attempt? Should the law emphasize what the defendant has done toward completing the crime or should the emphasis be on what remains to be done to complete the crime? The following case is used to illustrate:

YOUNG v. STATE
Court of Appeals of Maryland (1985) 303 Md. 298, 493 A.2d 352

After several banks in an area had been held up, police surveillance of banks was set up. A team of officers began following the defendant one afternoon where it appeared to them that he was "casing" banks. They observed him purchase a police scanner radio and clip it onto his belt. After driving past one bank several times, the defendant parked in the rear of the bank. As he walked hurriedly toward the front door of the bank, the police could see that the defendant had put on a blue knit stocking cap pulled down to the top of his sunglasses. He had also put on white gloves and a black eye-patch. His jacket collar was turned up. His right hand was in his jacket pocket and his left hand was in front of his face.

It was shortly after 2:00 P.M. and the bank had just closed. When the defendant tried to open the front door of the bank and realized it was locked, he ran back to his car with his left hand covering his face. The police stopped his car as he tried to leave the area. The defendant attempted to remove his jacket and the butt of a loaded .22 caliber revolver was seen sticking out of the right pocket. The defendant asked the police, "How much time (do) you get for attempted bank robbery?" After waiving his right to a jury, the defendant was convicted of attempted bank robbery and transporting a handgun. In holding that Young's conduct constituted a "substantial step" toward the crime of robbery, the Court affirmed holding:

* * *

> A criminal attempt requires specific intent.... The requisite intent need not be proved by direct evidence. It may be inferred as a matter of fact from the actor's conduct and the attendant circumstances.... Young concedes that "evidence is present ... from which it is possible to infer that [he] may have intended to commit a crime inside the bank...." He suggests, however, that this evidence is not "com-

pelling. . . ." We think that it is most compelling. We believe that it is more than legally sufficient to establish beyond a reasonable doubt that Young had the specific intent to commit an armed robbery as charged.

* * *

The determination of the overt act which is beyond mere preparation in furtherance of the commission of the intended crime is a most significant aspect of criminal attempts. If an attempt is to be a culpable offense serving as the basis for the furtherance of the important societal interests of crime prevention and the correction of those persons who have sufficiently manifested their dangerousness, the police must be able to ascertain with reasonable assurance when it is proper for them to intervene. It is not enough to say merely that there must be "some overt act beyond mere preparation in furtherance of the crime" as the general definition puts it. It is true that this definition is in line with the observation of Justice Holmes that [i]ntent to commit a crime is not itself criminal. There is no law against a man's intending to commit a murder the day after tomorrow. The law deals only with conduct. An attempt is an overt act. Oliver Wendell Holmes, The Common Law 65 (1923).

* * *

It is clear that the evidence which showed Young's conduct leading to his apprehension established that he performed the necessary overt act towards the commission of armed robbery, which was more than mere preparation. Even if we assume that all of Young's conduct before he approached the door of the Bank was mere preparation, on the evidence, the jury could properly find as a fact that when Young tried to open the bank door to enter the premises, that act constituted a "substantial step" toward the commission of the intended crime. It was strongly corroborative of his criminal intention.

One of the reasons why the substantial step approach has received such widespread favor is because it usually enables the police to intervene at an earlier stage than do the other approaches. In this case, however, the requisite overt act came near the end of the line. Indeed, it would qualify as the necessary act under any of the approaches—the proximity approach, the probable desistance approach or the equivocality approach. It clearly met the requirements of the substantial step approach. Since Young, as a matter of fact, could be found by the jury to have performed an overt act which was more than mere preparation, and was a substantial step towards the commission of the intended crime of armed robbery, it follows as a matter of law that he committed the offense of criminal attempt.

We think that the evidence . . . supported a rational inference . . . from which the jury could fairly be convinced, beyond a reasonable doubt, of Young's guilt of attempted armed robbery as charged. Therefore, the evidence was sufficient in law to sustain the conviction. We so hold.

* * *

(For a federal attempted bank robbery case where the court held that the "arrest was premature," see *United States v. Buffington*, 815 F.2d 1292 (9th Cir. 1987). In the *Buffington* case, the defendants were "casing" a bank and had disguises and weapons that could be used to rob the bank. They were arrested when one of the defendants entered a store near the bank and the other two defendants were leaning against their car facing the bank. The court held they made "no move toward the bank.")

Attempt under the Federal Criminal Code

"Although there is no comprehensive statutory definition of attempt in federal law, federal courts have rather uniformly adopted the standard set forth in Section 5.01 of the ... Model Penal Code ... that the requisite elements of attempt are:

1) an intent to engage in criminal conduct, and
2) conduct constituting a 'substantial step' towards the commission of the substantive offense which strongly corroborates the actor's criminal intent."

—United States v. Joyce,
693 F.2d 838 (8th Cir. 1982)

Criminal Attempt Requires a Showing of Specific Intent

In charging the crime of attempt (or the other preparatory crimes), the state must prove specific intent to commit the planned and intended crime. In doing so, the state must prove that the defendant intended to commit the intended crime and would have done so except that something occurred that prevented the act, or some fact came to the defendant's attention that caused a change of mind.

In the *Young* case, the bank door had just been locked and Young could not get into the bank. In a rape or mugging case, the screams of the victim and a person coming to her aid could cause the suspect to flee. The trier of fact (a jury or judge) must determine from the defendant's act, conduct, and the circumstances that existed what the mental intent and purpose of the defendant was.

Is Failure to Complete the Criminal Act an Essential Element of Attempt?

Can a person be charged with attempted burglary, robbery, or rape and be convicted even when the evidence showed that the completed crime was committed? In the 1965 case of *People v. English,*[15] the New York Court of Appeals held that a conviction for attempted rape based on conduct amounting to a completed rape was invalid. However, the New York Penal Code was amended in 1967 and Section 110.00 (attempt to commit a crime) now permits a conviction for an attempt to commit a crime even when the evidence shows that the crime was completed. In 1961, the Illinois legislature amended Section 8–4 of the Illinois Criminal Code so that it is no longer necessary in that state to show that the attempt failed. The majority rule in the United States is that failure to complete a crime is not an essential element of the crime of attempt.[16]

Attempt Cases Illustrating State and Federal Rulings

MERRITT v. COMMONWEALTH
Court of Appeals of Virginia (1935) 164 Va. 653, 180 S.E. 395

The defendant was convicted of attempted murder and sentenced to eight years in the penitentiary for pointing a loaded pistol at another man within range of the revolver. The Supreme Court of Virginia reversed, stating:

The intent is the purpose formed in a man's mind, and is usually proved by his conduct, sometimes by his statements; the necessary intent constituting one element in an attempt is the intent in fact, as distinguished from an intent in law. From the act alleged, the law infers a general evil intent, on the principle that a man intends the probable and necessary consequences of his act. The act charged here is an assault. In order to raise this assault to a more substantive crime, it must be done with a specific intent to take life. This intent cannot be inferred from the act alleged....

We cannot infer the specific intent to kill and murder from the allegation that the accused maliciously pointed the loaded pistol at Trull. From this allegation, a general evil purpose may be inferred, but not the specific design to kill.

PEOPLE v. PAYTON
Appellate Court of Illinois (1971) 2 Ill.App.3d 693, 276 N.E.2d 775

The defendant fired a gun twice at a woman's husband and missed by only 18 inches at 100 feet. He argued that he was only trying to scare the husband so that he would stay away from his estranged wife. (If a jury found that intent to kill existed, they could find the defendant guilty of attempted murder. If the jury found only intent to scare the husband, then the defendant could be convicted of a lesser offense. It would be very difficult to convict an expert marksman of attempted murder in this type of case.)

PEOPLE v. WELCH
Supreme Court of California (1972) 8 Cal.3d 106, 104 Cal.Rptr. 217, 501 P.2d 225

The fact that the defendant discontinued his efforts to rape a woman when she told him that she had gonorrhea did not prevent his conviction for attempted rape, since all the elements of the crimes were proved.

PEOPLE v. BINDER
Appellate Court of Illinois, First Division (1975) 18 Ill.App.3d 960, 310 N.E.2d 661, cert. denied, 420 U.S. 947, 95 S.Ct. 1329, 16 CrL 4190

During a burglary stakeout, police officers observed the defendant try the doorknob on the side door of a garage, hit the door with his shoulder in an attempt to open it, and attempt to lift the overhead door of the garage. Also admitted for use was evidence that the defendant admitted that he tried to gain entry into the garage. This was held to be sufficient evidence to support the conviction for attempted burglary. The U.S. Supreme Court refused *certiorari*.

UNITED STATES v. JOYCE
United States Court of Appeals, Eighth Circuit (1982) 693 F.2d 838

In a "reverse sting operation," an undercover police officer let it be known that he had cocaine to sell. The defendant arrived in St. Louis with $22,000 to purchase a pound of cocaine. The undercover officer gave the defendant a sealed and wrapped package that he said contained cocaine. Without opening the package, the defendant immediately gave it back to the officer. The officer refused to open the package until the defendant produced the purchase money. The defendant would not produce the money until the package was opened. The defendant left without making a purchase. The defendant's jury conviction of attempting to possess cocaine with intent to distribute was reversed as the court held there was insufficient evidence to establish that the defendant engaged in conduct amounting to a "substantial step" toward committing the crime of possession with intent to distribute.

Impossibility as a Defense to an Attempt Charge

In the 1983 case of *State v. Lopez,* the defendant was charged with attempt to traffic in a controlled substance when he tried to sell a substance he mistakenly believed to be cocaine. The New Mexico Supreme Court rejected the defense of "impossibility" and affirmed the defendant's conviction, holding that:

> The defendant should be treated in accordance with the facts as he believes them to be. In the present case ... Lopez demonstrated his readiness to violate the law.... When a defendant has done everything within his power to commit a crime, he has attempted to commit the crime.... Therefore, imposition of criminal liability is justified.[17]

In holding that a defendant can be convicted of attempt even when "completion is impossible," the New Mexico Supreme Court joined an increasing number of states that have rejected the distinctions between "legal" and "factual" impossibility.

Legal and factual impossibility can be defined and distinguished as follows:

1. In the defense of law known as *legal impossibility,* the completed act is not a crime even though the defendant intended to commit a crime. In the 1906 case of *People v. Jaffe,*[18] the goods received by the defendant, who believed that they were stolen, were not stolen property. The court held that the defendant could not be convicted of the attempt to receive stolen property. In the 1939 case of *State v. Taylor,*[19] the defendant bribed a person, believing him to be a juror, when in fact the person was not a juror. The court held that the defendant could not be convicted of attempt to bribe a juror. Legal impossibility is therefore a complete defense to an attempt charge (but not to a conspiracy or solicitation charge). The mental purpose (*mens rea*) to commit a crime exists, but the completed act is not a crime. This defense, however, is only available in those states that continue to allow the defense. An increasing number of states are rejecting the defense.

2. The defense of fact known as *factual impossibility,* or physical impossibility, deals with situations in which, because of some physical or factual factor or situation unknown to the defendant, the crime attempted cannot be completed. An example of factual impossibility is found in the 1869 case of *Kunkle v. State,*[20] in which the victim was out of the range of the weapon that the defendant used. In the 1966 case of *Osborn v. United States,*[21] the person who was offered a bribe by the defendant went to the police. The U.S. Supreme Court rejected the defense of impossibility, stating that "whatever continuing validity the doctrine of 'impossibility' with all of its subtleties, may continue to have in the law of criminal attempt, the body of the law is inapplicable here." When the criminal intent exists and the specific act that the defendant sought to complete is a crime, the defendant cannot argue impossibility just because he or she was unable to complete the crime. Factual impossibility is therefore not a defense to a charge of attempt.[22]

In addition to legal and factual impossibility, some courts also write of "inherent impossibility." The distinctions between these three forms of impossibility are sometimes difficult to determine. Court decisions vary considerably throughout the United States as to the application of the doctrine of impossibility. In 1967, the New York state legislature rejected impossibility defenses by the enactment of Section 110.10 of the New York Penal Code. The 1961 Committee Comment on the enactment of Section 8−4(b) of the Illinois Criminal Code is as follows:

> It is the intent of section 8−4(b) to exclude both factual and legal impossibilities as defenses to prosecution for attempt. However, inherent impossibility (attempts to kill by witchcraft such as repeatedly stabbing a cloth dummy made to represent the person intended to be killed) is not intended to be excluded as a defense.[23]

Section 5.01 of the Model Penal Code eliminates the defenses of legal, factual, and inherent impossibility but proposes that "(i)f the particular conduct charged ... is so inherently unlikely to result or culminate in the commission of a crime ... nor the actor presents a public danger ... the Court shall exercise its power ... to enter judgment and impose sentence for a crime of lower grade or degree, or, in extreme cases, may dismiss the prosecution."[24]

Renunciation or Abandonment of the Criminal Purpose (Withdrawal)

In attempt, conspiracy, and solicitation there is time for a person to change his or her mind and decide not to go ahead with the criminal project of completing the crime. The question of how far along the criminal enterprise had progressed and the reason for abandoning the project are important factors in determining whether the defense of abandonment should be accepted by a court.

Under the common law, abandonment would not be accepted as a defense if the defendant had performed required acts of the crime with criminal intent.[25] The status of this rule in the United States remains in doubt. Suppose a man places a ladder against the side of a dwelling, intending to enter and steal. At the last minute he changes his mind and walks away. Whether a man who voluntarily changed his mind under such circumstances could be convicted of attempted burglary might vary somewhat from state to state and from court to court. The question to be determined by a court or jury would be whether the conduct of the defendant before the abandonment amounted to attempted burglary. If the man discontinued his efforts to burglarize the dwelling because he heard someone coming or because he heard a dog barking inside the dwelling, his renunciation would not be considered voluntary.

Some of the states have abandonment and withdrawal statutes permitting the defense of abandonment under specific circumstances. Section 1001(3) of the proposed Federal Criminal Code provides that a voluntary and complete renunciation of the criminal effort is an affirmative defense to a charge of attempt. Section 5.01(4) of the Model Penal Code proposes the following withdrawal provision to a charge of criminal attempt:

> (4) *Renunciation of Criminal Purpose.* When the actor's conduct would otherwise constitute an attempt under Subsection (1)(b) or (1)(c) of this Section, it is an affirmative defense that he abandoned his effort to commit the crime or otherwise prevented its commission, under circumstances manifesting a complete and voluntary renunciation of his criminal purpose. The establishment of such defense does not, however, affect the liability of an accomplice who did not join in such abandonment or prevention.
>
> Within the meaning of this Article, renunciation of criminal purpose is not voluntary if it is motivated, in whole or in part, by circumstances, not present or apparent at the inception of the actor's course of conduct, which increase the probability of detection

Preliminary, Anticipatory (or Inchoate) Crimes

Crime	*The Crime Consists of Evidence Showing:*	*Other Aspects of the Crime*
Solicitation (the preparatory offense that is least often charged): The invitation (or urging) to commit a crime*	1. Requesting, encouraging, or commanding another person 2. to engage in a specific conduct that would constitute a crime (most states restrict general solicitation to felonies) 3. or attempt to commit such crime	As there is generally no requirement for an overt act, the crime is complete when the solicitation is made. If the request to commit a crime is accepted, the solicitee can also be a coconspirator or an aider and abettor to an attempted or completed crime.
Conspiracy (the oldest of the preparatory offenses): The criminal partnership	1. An agreement between two or more persons (more than half the states now follow the Model Penal Code and do not require "two or more" guilty persons. In these states, proof of guilt of one person is sufficient.) 2. with specific intent 3. to commit a crime 4. or to obtain a legal goal by criminal acts 5. (half the states require proof that one or more of the parties acted to effect the object of the conspiracy)	A conspiracy is punishable whether or not it succeeds in its objective (*United States v. Rabinowich,* 238 U.S. 78). In federal courts and some states, convictions for both conspiracy and the completed crime are held not to violate double jeopardy. (*Pereira v. United States,* 347 U.S. 1, 74 S.Ct. 358, and *Iannelli v. United States.* 420 U.S. 770, 95 S.Ct. 1284, 16 CrL 3127, 1975).
Attempt (the inchoate crime charged most often): An attempt often puts a possible victim in fear and apprehension. Many near victims can and do appear as witnesses in criminal trials.	1. That the defendant intended to commit the crime of which he or she is charged, and 2. that he or she did acts that (a) came within "dangerous proximity" of the criminal end or (b) amount to a "substantial step" (Sec. 5.01 Model Penal code) 3. and in some states, he or she would have committed the crime except for the intervention of another person or some other extraneous factor	The American Law Institute Model Penal Code recommends the broadening of criminal liability for the crime of attempt (see Sec. 5.01[2] for a discussion of these proposals).

*See *People v. Cole,* 91 Ill.2d 172, 435 N.E.2d 490 (1982), Review denied U.S. Supreme Court, 106 S.Ct. 409 (1985) where "solicitation by request" and "solicitation by encouragement" were held to be separate crimes in Illinois. The defendants were charged with both crimes having to do with the proposed murder of a single victim. A jury convicted the defendants of "solicitation by encouragement" but was unable to reach a verdict on "solicitation by request" and a mistrial was declared on that count. The courts affirmed the single count of solicitation to murder by encouragement" conviction and sentences.

or apprehension or which make more difficult the accomplishment of the criminal purpose. Renunciation is not complete if it is motivated by a decision to postpone the criminal conduct until a more advantageous time or to transfer the criminal effort to another but similar objective or victim.

In the 1985 case of *Young v. State,* 303 Md. 298, 493 A.2d 352 (presented in this section), Young argued that after he found the bank door locked, he abandoned his intent to rob the bank. The Court, however, found that he had already committed the crime of attempted bank robbery and quoted another case holding:

> We observed in *Wiley* that there was agreement among the text writers and the cases that if one who has intended to attempt a crime freely and voluntarily abandons the idea before it has progressed beyond mere preparation, he has not committed the crime of attempt; but a voluntary abandonment of an attempt which has proceeded beyond mere preparation into a direct act or acts in furtherance of the commission of the attempt does not (nullify), or forbid punishment for, the crime already committed. 237 Md. at 564, 207 A.2d 478.

* * *

B. Parties to the Principal Crime

Under the Common Law

The early common law recognized the different degrees of criminal participation in a completed crime. In the 1760s, there were more than two hundred crimes in England punishable by death.[26] The following four common law categories were used to determine the penalty that would be applied upon conviction:

1. A principal in the first degree was a person (or persons) who actually committed the crime.
2. A principal in the second degree was a person who was present at the commission of the crime, was not involved in the planning of the crime, but aided and abetted in the actual commission of the crime. This offender could not be tried under the common law until the actual perpetrator had been apprehended and convicted of the offense.
3. An accessory before the fact was a person who, knowing that a crime was to be committed, aided in the preparation for the crime but was not present at the time the crime was committed.
4. An accessory after the fact was a person who knew that the crime had been committed and gave aid or comfort to the person who committed the crime. Neither the accessory before the fact nor after the fact could be tried until after the conviction of the principal in the first degree.[27]

Criminal Liability in the United States Today

Today, most states[28] have done away with the four common law categories, and the majority of jurisdictions have by statute created only two categories of criminal liability:

1. All persons who knowingly are involved in or connected with the commission of a crime either before or during its commission are known as principals (or parties to the crime) regardless of their connection. This

category is a combination of the common law principle in the first and second degree and the accessory before the fact. The existing federal statute (Sec. 2 of Title 18) reflects the usual criminal liability used today in the various states. This section reads as follows:

Principals.

(a) Whoever commits an offense against the United States or aids, abets, counsels, commands, induces or procures its commission, is punishable as a principal.

(b) Whoever willfully causes an act to be done which if directly performed by him or another would be an offense against the United States, is punished as a principal.

2. The person or people who render aid to the criminal after he or she has committed the crime. Legislative bodies have statutorized criminal offenses in this category that were previously known to the common law as accessory after the fact. This category will be discussed in the section on postcrime offenses in this chapter.

Under the old common law, the degree of punishment varied considerably with the degree of criminal liability. As a principal in the first degree would receive the death penalty for more than two hundred offenses in England 150 years ago, the distinction between the principal in the first degree and the principal in the second degree was important under those circumstances. Today, probably all states make all principals (or parties to the crime) liable to the same degree of punishment.

The rule that neither the principal in the second degree nor the accessories before or after the fact could be forced to trial before the trial of the principal in the first degree has been abolished in most American jurisdictions. In states that have abolished the common law bar, any participant in a crime may be tried and convicted, even though the person who actually committed the crime has not been apprehended and tried or even identified.[29]

The Criminal Liability of Persons Involved in the Planning of a Crime

Mere knowledge of a contemplated crime or failure to disclose such information, without evidence of any further involvement in the crime, does not make a person liable as a party to that crime. However, the person who hires another to commit a crime or counsels, commands, induces, or procures the commission of the crime is punishable as a principal of the crime. Today, the "higher up" is regarded as more of a social menace than are the underlings. Under modern statutes, he or she can be punished just as severely as the person who actually committed the crime.

The mere association with persons who are planning or have committed a crime would not justify a conviction, but a person who consciously shares in any criminal act is liable whether or not there was an actual plan and conspiracy.[30]

If the circumstances show that there was a common design to commit an unlawful act to which all the parties assented, whatever is done in the furtherance of that design is the act of all the parties. To demonstrate a common design to commit a crime, it is necessary to show that there was an understanding between the parties. This does not mean that there has to be an expressed or formal agreement between the parties, but it does require that there be a meeting of the minds or a mutual understanding to accomplish a common criminal objective or to work together for a common criminal purpose.

Criminal Liability for a Completed Crime

Under the Old Common Law

Principal in the first degree —person who actually committed a crime

Principal in the second degree —person who was a conspirator to the crime and was present at the commission of the crime whether he or she gave any assistance at that time or not

Accessory before the fact —person who was a conspirator to a felony (ordered, counseled, encouraged, etc.) but was not present at the commission of the offense but hires, counsels, or otherwise procures another to commit a crime

Accessory after the fact —person who knew that a crime was committed and gave aid or comfort to the person who committed the crime

Under Present Statutes

All the following are equally liable:
1. The person who commits the crime
2. A party to crime as a conspirator who advises, hires, counsels, or otherwise procures another to commit a crime
3. A party to a crime who intentionally and knowingly aids or abets the person who committed the crime

Separate liability exists for the postcrime offenses, such as escape, refusal to aid an officer, obstructing, resisting, perjury, bribery, bail jumping, harboring a felon.

"What Either Did, All Did . . ." Accomplice Liability: Criminal Liability for the Conduct of Another

A person could be criminally liable for the conduct of another if he or she is a party to a conspiracy to commit a crime and hires, urges, counsels, or plans with another to commit a crime. A person is also liable for the conduct of another if he or she is an aider and abettor to a person who committed a crime.

Under the "common design" rule, when persons have a common design to do an unlawful act, whatever is done in furtherance of the design or criminal plan is the act of all. If there is a "common design," then what either of the parties did, all did. If one of the parties to an armed robbery wore a mask, then all of the parties wore a mask and are subject to the penalties of committing the crime of armed robbery while concealed (see *Curl v. State,* 40 Wis.2d 474, 162 N.W.2d 77 (1968)). The following case also illustrates:

WATTS v. BONNEVILLE
U.S. Court of Appeals, Ninth Circuit (1989) 879 F. 2d 685

Defendant Watts guarded the parents of a teenaged girl while his two friends raped the girl. Watts was convicted of two counts of rape in concert since he aided and abetted both rapes. In affirming the California convictions for these and other crimes, the Federal Court of Appeals held:

* * *

We hold that no violation of due process has occurred in this case. . . . The ancient and universally accepted principle of accomplice liability holds a defendant legally responsible for the unlawful conduct of others that he aids and abets. See generally

W. LaFave & A. Scott, Criminal Law § 6.6, at 575 (2d ed. 1986). California, applying this principle as embodied in its law, quite properly punished Watts for each of the two acts of rape in concert that he aided and abetted when he guarded the parents. Nothing in the Constitution prohibits this; indeed, in applying federal law, this court routinely has upheld convictions for multiple crimes aided and abetted by a single course of conduct. See, e.g., United States v. Rubier, 651 F.2d 628, 629, 631 n. 4 (9th Cir.) (per curiam) (upholding convictions for bank robbery and assault when the defendant aided and abetted the actual perpetrator of the two crimes by driving a getaway car), cert. denied, 454 U.S. 875, 102 S.Ct. 351, 70 L.Ed.2d 183 (1981). Although Watts stood guard only once, he enabled his accomplices to commit two rapes in concert. This is more culpable than enabling them to commit only one. Each rape was a separate wrongful act.

* * *

A common design is a spoken or unspoken conspiracy to commit an unlawful act. Any member of the conspiracy (plan) could be held liable as a principal for any offense committed in the furtherance of the plan or conspiracy while he or she is a member of it. Latecomers cannot be convicted as principals for offenses that were committed before they joined the conspiracy or after they withdrew from the conspiracy.[31]

A person could be liable for the criminal conduct of another as both a conspirator and an aider and abettor. Or, this person could be criminally liable only as a conspirator when, for example, he or she hires another to commit a crime and is not present at the scene of the crime. Or, a person could be liable only as an aider and abettor where he or she renders aid to a person who committed a crime without being involved in the planning of the crime.

Other Aider and Abettor Cases

UNITED STATES v. O'NEILL
United States Court of Appeals, Second Circuit (1983) 729 F.2d 1440, cert. denied, 464 U.S. 840, 104 S.Ct. 135, 34 CrL 4007

The fact that the defendants provided the following lawful goods and services to conspirators—fueled their plane, rented hangar space, stored ammunition and guns, falsely identified conspirators to outsiders, and offered to pay a security guard $20,000 to disappear while the plane was being loaded—was sufficient to affirm their conviction for aiding and abetting.

UNITED STATES v. BUTTS
United States Court of Appeals, Third Circuit (1983) 707 F.2d 1404, 33 CrL 2141

Postal inspectors had probable cause to arrest Butts and Passanante and followed them to their car, in which another man, Morgan, was sitting. In holding that the officers had no authority to arrest Morgan, the court stated:

. . . arresting authorities had no reason to believe that Morgan knew about or was involved in the scheme involving the stolen checks. Morgan might have been sitting in the car simply because he had some unrelated and wholly lawful business with Butts or Passanante. Mere presence at a given location cannot in and of itself constitute probable cause to arrest.

HALBERSTAM v. WELCH
United States Court of Appeals, District of Columbia Circuit (1983) 705 F.2d 472

A well-known physician, Dr. Halberstam, returned to his Washington, D.C., home one evening and came upon a burglar. The burglar, Bernard Welch, shot the doctor twice in the chest. The doctor tried driving himself to the hospital and on the way saw Welch. The doctor swerved the car and ran Welch down as Welch was walking on a sidewalk. The doctor died and Welch was taken into custody. A search of Welch's home by the police revealed $4 million worth of loot, which Welch said "was just peanuts." Over a five-year period, Welch and the woman he lived with, Linda Hamilton, had acquired a fortune from the many burglaries that Welch committed. Hamilton did not participate in the burglaries and was not charged criminally for any of the many crimes. However, the doctor's estate commenced a civil suit against both Welch and Hamilton and received a judgment of $5,715,188.05. The basis of liability was civil conspiracy and aiding and abetting.

It now seems that Hamilton could have also been charged criminally but was not because of the following reasons given by police officers at the civil trial (ftnt. 4, p. 476): (1) the police "did not realize the full extent of Hamilton's involvement with Welch's operations"; (2) "might have had difficulty charging Hamilton because of jurisdictional restrictions"; (3) "noted that all papers on transactions were in Hamilton's name and so concluded she helped sell the goods (gold, silver, furs, jewelry, antiques, etc.)."

RAEL v. CADENA
Supreme Court of New Mexico (1979) 93 N.M. 684, 604 P.2d 822

The defendant had not physically assisted in a battery but gave verbal encouragement to the assailant by yelling, "Kill him" and "Hit him more." In this *civil* action, the court found that liability did not require a finding of action in concert, nor even that the injury had directly resulted from the encouragement. Citing Restatement Section 876(b), the court held:

> *It is clear, however, that in the United States, civil liability for assault and battery is not limited to the direct perpetrator, but extends to any person who by any means aids or encourages the act.* Hargis v. Horrine, *230 Ark. 502, 323 S.W.2d 917 (1959);* Ayer v. Robinson, *163 Cal.App.2d 424, 329 P.2d 546 (1958);* Guilbeau v. Guilbeau, *326 So.2d 654 (La. App. 1976);* Duke v. Feldman, *245 Md. 454, 266 A.2d 345 (1967);* Brink v. Purnell, *162 Mich. 147, 127 N.W. 322 (1910); 6 Am.Jur.2d Assault and Battery § 128 (1963); 6A C.J.S. Assault and Battery § 11 (1975); Annot., 72 A.L.R.2d 1229 (1960). According to the Restatement: "[f]or harm resulting to a third person from the tortious conduct of another, one is subject to liability if he*

> * * *

> *(b) knows that the other's conduct constitutes a breach of duty and gives substantial assistance or encouragement to the other so to conduct himself."—Restatement (Second) of Torts § 876 (1979)*

CIVIL LAWSUIT AGAINST THE "PHIL DONAHUE SHOW"

Four months after her husband kidnapped her child, a Colorado woman learned that her husband had appeared on television on the "Phil Donahue Show" to talk about parental kidnapping and why and how he had kidnapped his child.

The show provided babysitting service, and when the mother of the child requested information and help from the show, the television company stood on their pledge of confidentiality to a news source. In a civil lawsuit against the company for aiding and abetting parental kidnapping, the mother of the child was awarded $5.9 million. The father was arrested in Tulsa, Oklahoma, on a fugitive warrant in 1983, and the child was returned to the mother.

Liability for Offenses Other than the Planned and Intended Crime

When the evidence shows that there is a common design to commit an unlawful act to which all the defendants agreed, whatever is done in the furtherance of the criminal plan is the act of all if it is a natural and probable consequence of the intended crime. If guns are carried and a shot is fired by one member of the group, that shot is fired by all the defendants and all of them must answer for the results.[32]

In *People v. Jones,*[33] the California courts held that an accused who knew that his codefendants were armed was responsible for all the consequences when a night watchman was killed in a robbery. The defendant in the *Jones* case was unarmed.

The definition of the natural and probable consequences of the intended crime will vary somewhat from jury to jury and court to court. The following example illustrates the problem:

EXAMPLE: X and Y conspire to burglarize a residence. X is the lookout and getaway driver while Y is in the house committing the burglary. Y commits the following additional crimes. Which of the following should X be charged with?

1. Y is surprised by the homeowner and, in his attempt to get away, kills the man.
2. Y is surprised by an eleven-year-old boy who lives in the house and needlessly kills the boy.
3. In addition to stealing, Y comes upon a woman in bed and rapes the woman.
4. After stealing from the house, Y sees a gallon of gasoline in the back hall of the house. He spills the gasoline around the house and burns it down.

Prosecutors could charge X with all the additional crimes, but whether X would be convicted would depend on whether the finder of fact determined that the additional acts were a natural and probable consequence of the burglary. It certainly could be argued in this case that X aided and assisted in all the crimes, because he was acting as lookout and the getaway driver. If X had hired Y to commit the burglary and X was not at the scene of the crime, his liability would be the same.

X's defense could be that some of the offenses are not the natural or probable consequence of the intended crime of burglary, and therefore he would not be criminally liable for those offenses. In all cases, X would be charged and convicted of the crime of burglary.

See the 1974 *Mumford v. Maryland*[34] case. In that case, a rape and murder occurred during a burglary. The defendant (a fifteen-year-old girl) stated that she was elsewhere on the premises when the rape and murder occurred and that she did not know these crimes were being committed. In reversing her conviction for first-degree murder (felony murder) and ordering a new trial, the court stated: "There must be a direct causal connection between the homicide and the felony. Something more than mere coincidence in time and place between the two must be shown; otherwise, the felony-murder rule will not be applicable."

Theories as to the Origins of the Crime that Are Used in Charging and Prosecuting

When two or more defendants are charged with a crime (or crimes), there are two ways in which the offense could have originated. One origin of the crime could be a conspiracy, in which the parties planned the crime together and had an explicit or implicit understanding and meeting of the minds to commit the crime. The fact of the agreement imposes criminal liability on all the conspirators when the crime is committed by one member of the conspiracy. Liability is also imposed on all if one person commits another crime that is the natural and probable consequence of the agreed-upon crime. This liability is under the "conspiracy theory."

If there was no prior agreement or mutual understanding as to a criminal purpose, the crime would then be considered a spontaneous and impulsive act by the person who committed it. If the other defendant rendered either verbal or actual assistance, knowing that a crime was being committed, he or she was then aiding and abetting in the commission of the crime and is liable as a principal under the "complicity theory."

When two or more persons plead not guilty to a crime or crimes that they are alleged to have committed, they do not disclose to the police and the prosecutor the details of the history and the origins of the crime, even if they did commit it. Therefore, the state must proceed with the information that is available on one theory or the other (and sometimes on both theories).

In the 1894 case of *State v. Tally*,[35] a group of men in one town set out to kill a particular person who lived in another town. The friends of the victim, hearing of the plot against him, attempted to warn him by sending him a telegram. Another person, a judge, who also disliked the potential victim, directed the telegraph operator to destroy the message, telling him that it was unimportant.

Criminal Liability for the Conduct of Another

A Person is Criminally Liable for the Conduct of Another if He or She

1. Has innocent people perform acts that, unknown to the innocent people, are crimes. *Example:* Having commercial movers take and carry away furniture or a piano that the person seeks to steal.
2. Knowingly becomes an aider and abettor to the crime of another. *Example:* Knowingly providing the means and transportation so that a person who has committed a crime may escape from the scene of the crime.
3. Conspires, hires, counsels, or otherwise procures another to commit a crime. Criminal liability when a "common design" extends to:
   a. the planned and intended crime (or crimes).
   b. crimes other than the planned and intended crime that are committed in the furtherance of the criminal plan, if such crimes are the natural and probable consequences of the intended crime.
4. If, as a supervisor, employer, corporate officer, etc., the person has:
   a. "a positive duty to . . . remedy violations . . . (and to) insure that violations will not occur." *United States v. Park,* 421 U.S. 658, 95 S.Ct. 1903 (1975).
   b. or, as required in *Vachon v. New Hampshire,* 414 U.S. 478, 94 S.Ct. 664 (1974), the person personally caused the forbidden act to be done.

The man was killed and the judge was held liable for the murder under the "complicity theory," since, although he was not involved in the plans to murder The victim, he did render aid and assistance. The perpetrators of the crime were not aware of the assistance given by the judge until after they had committed the crime.

In the 1964 case of *State v. Nutley,*[36] two deputy sheriffs stopped a car from another state because they observed a discrepancy in the license plates. As the officers walked up to the car, one of the occupants shot and killed one of the officers. In the gunfight that followed between the remaining officer and the occupants of the car (each of whom was armed), the officer was wounded. All three of the men in the car were convicted of first-degree murder and of attempted murder of the wounded officer. The Supreme Court of Wisconsin affirmed the convictions, stating that there was sufficient evidence to convict one of the defendants as the perpetrator of both crimes and the other defendants either under the "conspiracy theory" or under the "complicity theory." The court stated:

> It is not necessary that the aider and abettor enter into an agreement with the perpetrator to assist him in consummation of the crime. Nor is it necessary that the perpetrator be aware of the accomplice's efforts, in order to hold the accomplice liable for the substantive crime. . . .
>
> The rationale for the conspiracy theory recognizes that the fact of agreement materially reinforces the desire of the parties to carry out their portion of the division of criminal labor. Since each conspirator psychologically reinforces the conduct of the overt perpetrator, each is justly held responsible for his substantive crime.

C. POSTCRIME OFFENSES

Today all states and the federal government have enacted many statutes meant to assist officers in performing their duty of investigating crimes and apprehending criminals. Some statutes punish people who knowingly give police false information with the intent to mislead them. Other statutes are designed to permit the proper and efficient functioning of the courts and the criminal justice system. Some of these offenses existed under the common law, whereas others have been created in modern times. Examples are:

- Refusing to aid an officer while such officer is doing any act in his or her official capacity
- Obstructing or resisting an officer while such officer is doing any act in his or her official capacity
- Obstructing justice
- Compounding a crime: the making of an agreement (for a consideration) to withhold evidence of, or to abstain from prosecuting, a crime of which the accused has knowledge. The elements of this offense are:
  - a) the commission of a crime by another and the accused's knowledge of that crime.
  - b) an agreement or understanding to conceal, to withhold evidence of, or to abstain from prosecuting.

Scene of the Crime

A Person Who Was at the Scene of a Crime May Be Convicted for the Crime If the State Can Prove Beyond a Reasonable Doubt That:

1. He or she committed the crime, or
2. He or she intentionally aided and abetted the commission of the crime or that he or she was ready and willing to aid and abet the crime, and that the person who committed the crime knew this, or
3. He or she was a party to the conspiracy to commit the crime and advised, hired, counseled, or otherwise procured the person to commit the crime, or
4. Vicarious liability exists for the acts of an employee, subordinate, etc.

A Person Who Was Not at the Scene of a Crime May Be Convicted for the Crime If the State Can Prove Beyond a Reasonable Doubt That:

1. He or she was a party to the conspiracy to commit the crime and advised, hired, counseled, or otherwise procured the person to commit the crime, or
2. Vicarious liability exists for the acts of an employee, subordinate, etc.

---

    c) the receipt of a consideration (something of value, such as money or a promise). It has been held that it is not a crime for a victim to receive restitution, even when a wrongdoer hopes or thinks that the victim will drop the matter. (2 Wilkin, Crimes, Sec. 804, 1963)

- Misprision of a felony (failure to report or prosecute a known felon)
- Harboring or aiding felons
- Perjury
- Escape from custody
- Bribery of witnesses
- Bail jumping
- Communicating with jurors with intent to influence them

Are Material Witnesses Criminally Liable in Any Way?

A material witness is a witness who has material information regarding a crime. A person who was in a business place at the time of an armed robbery and observed the robbers and the crime would be a material witness.

    If the state cannot show probable cause that a material witness was a party to a crime, the material witness may not then be arrested. However, material witnesses may be reasonably detained to obtain their identity and to question them, as law enforcement officers have a legal duty and obligation to investigate criminal incidents.[37]

    Most material witnesses are cooperative and will honestly provide information that they have regarding a criminal incident. If it is shown that material witnesses intentionally provide false material information regarding a criminal incident to an investigating officer, the witness could be charged with obstructing and hindering a law enforcement officer in the performance of his or her duty. The following is an example of a cooperative witness:

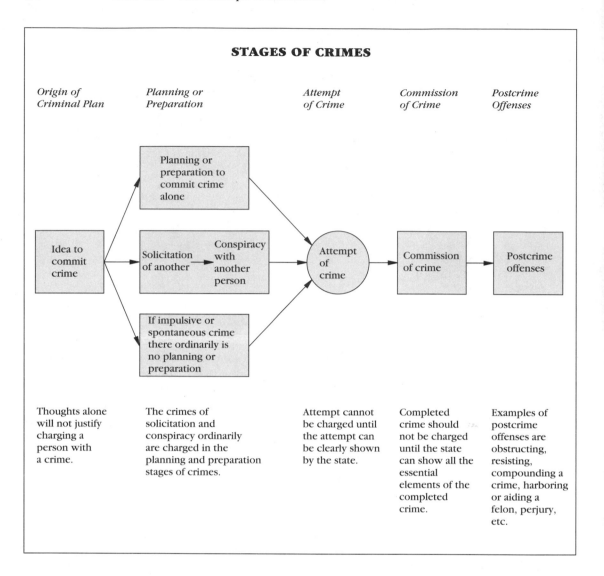

STAGES OF CRIMES

Origin of Criminal Plan — *Planning or Preparation* — *Attempt of Crime* — *Commission of Crime* — *Postcrime Offenses*

Planning or preparation to commit crime alone

Idea to commit crime

Solicitation of another — Conspiracy with another person — Attempt of crime — Commission of crime — Postcrime offenses

If impulsive or spontaneous crime there ordinarily is no planning or preparation

Thoughts alone will not justify charging a person with a crime.

The crimes of solicitation and conspiracy ordinarily are charged in the planning and preparation stages of crimes.

Attempt cannot be charged until the attempt can be clearly shown by the state.

Completed crime should not be charged until the state can show all the essential elements of the completed crime.

Examples of postcrime offenses are obstructing, resisting, compounding a crime, harboring or aiding a felon, perjury, etc.

EXAMPLE: After the assassination of the Rev. Martin Luther King, Jr., a witness was able to identify James Earl Ray as the man rushing down the steps of the hotel from which the shots came. As Ray was not apprehended until many months after the shooting, police were concerned for the safety of the witness who was an older man living on a small pension. The man was cooperative and moved into the county jail in Memphis to assure his safety. He was free to come and go but was accompanied by officers when he left the jail for a walk or to have a beer. Because of the inconvenience of providing guards every day, the state of Tennessee went into court and asked that bail be set to assure the appearance of this cooperative witness at the trial of James Earl Ray (if and when he was apprehended). Bail was set at $10,000 cash, and as the witness did not have this amount of cash, he could not meet bail. He was then held in jail without any freedom to leave. Lawyers challenged this procedure and the statute authorizing it as a violation of due process. As a result, an apartment was rented and the witness lived there with 24-hour-a-day police protection until Ray was apprehended and went to trial.

This example illustrates that unless there is probable cause to show that a witness has committed a crime, he or she cannot be held. If a witness is uncooperative, he or she may be brought before a grand jury, coroner's inquest, "John Doe" proceedings, or court and questioned under oath. Under such circumstances, a witness could be compelled to answer questions. If the witness takes the Fifth Amendment, she or he could be granted witness immunity and then would face jail or contempt for failure to answer.

D. Vicarious Liability

As discussed in chapter 3, some business, commercial, traffic, and health regulations are strict liability crimes. A strict liability offense forbids certain conduct or an omission and does not require the showing of any mental fault (*mens rea*). Proof that the person violated the statute is sufficient for a conviction.

Vicarious liability differs from strict liability. Vicarious liability punishes one person for the act of another (usually an employee). Forbidding the sale of alcoholic beverages to minors is an example of a law used throughout the United States. Two cases that were before state supreme courts illustrate the problem: the 1986 case of *State v. Guminga* (Minnesota),[38] and the 1983 case of *Davis v. City of Peachtree City* (Georgia).[39] In the *Guminga* case, a restaurant waitress was arrested when she served a minor an alcoholic beverage. The owner of the restaurant was not present at the time, but was also charged with a criminal offense for the incident at a later time.

The Supreme Courts of both Georgia and Minnesota reversed the convictions of employers charged when their employees had sold alcoholic beverages to minors in violation of criminal statutes. Both courts held that such convictions violated due process requirements with the Georgia Supreme Court stating:

* * *

In balancing this burden against the public's interest, we find that it cannot be justified under the due process clauses of the Georgia or United States Constitutions, regardless of Peachtree City's admittedly legitimate interests of deterring employers from allowing their employees to break the law and of facilitating the enforcement of these laws. This is especially true, when, as here, there are other, less onerous alternatives which sufficiently promote these interests. The Model Penal Code recommends that civil violations providing civil penalties such as fines or revocation of licenses be used for offenses for which the individual was not morally blameworthy and does not deserve the social condemnation "implicit in the concept 'crime'." Model Penal Code § 1.04(s), Comments, Tent. Draft No. 2, p. 7 (1954). The availability of such sanctions renders the use of criminal sanctions in vicarious liability cases unjustifiable. LaFave & Scott, supra, p. 228.

* * *

Employers (in cases such as the *Guminga* and *Davis* cases) can be punished under the civil law. They could be fined for selling liquor to minors. Their liquor or business licenses could be taken away if they continue to violate such laws. It is also a general practice of cities and states to make fines for second and third

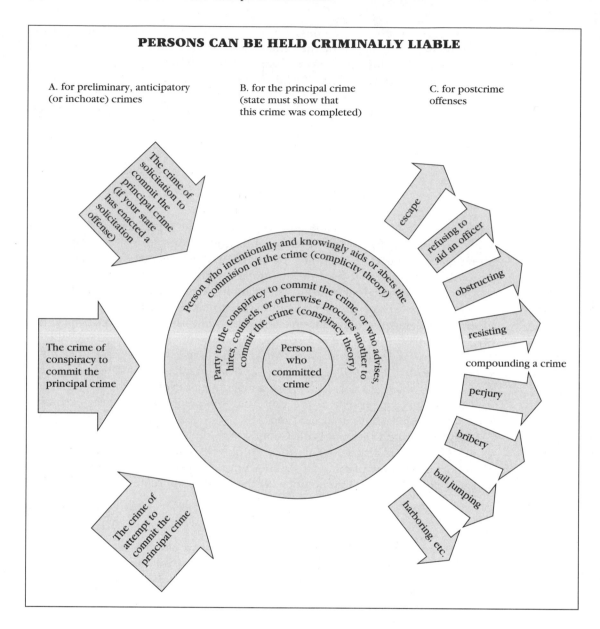

offenses increasingly higher for the additional offenses. The law in this area is further illustrated by two U.S. Supreme Court cases in the Questions and Problems at the end of this chapter.

Is Belonging to an Organization Involved in Illegal Activity Sufficient Alone to Sustain a Criminal Conviction?

The U.S. Supreme Court has repeatedly answered the question as to whether belonging to a gang or organization involved in illegal activity could alone justify criminal conviction. The Supreme Court again answered this question as follows in the 1984 case of *United States v. Abel,* 36 CrL 3003:

Vicarious Liability Distinguished from Strict Liability

Strict liability   Offenses are offenses that have no *mens rea* (guilty mind). For example, most states and cities have closing hours for taverns. Remaining open after hours is generally a strict liability offense. It does not require a showing of *mens rea* such as "intentionally," "knowingly," "recklessly," or "negligently." The law dispenses with the *mens rea* requirement and forbids remaining open after hours.

Vicarious liability   Imputes the criminal act of one person to another. Employers and bosses could be vicariously liable for the wrongful acts of their employees and agents. As "vicarious liability" makes one person liable for the acts of another, courts say that vicarious liability "dispenses with the requirement of the *actus reus* (forbidden act) and imputes the criminal act of one person to another." (*State v. Beaudry,* 365 N.W. 2d 593, 597, 1985)

It is settled law that the government may not convict an individual merely for belonging to an organization that advocates illegal activity. *Scales v. United States* 367 U.S. 203, 219−24 . . . *Brandenburg v. Ohio,* 395 U.S. 444 . . . Rather, the government must show that the individual knows of and personally accepts the tenets of the organization . . .

However, in the *Abel* case, the U.S. Supreme Court held that evidence of membership is admissible in criminal and civil trials if relevant and probative.

Therefore, if a street gang had twenty members and four of the members were apprehended selling drugs, only the four arrested members could be prosecuted unless the government could prove others in the gang had conspired and were part of an organization engaged in drug trafficking.

The arrest of the four members could be a very important phase of an ongoing investigation of the entire gang. The arrest of four members could provide any one or all of the following:

- probable cause to obtain search warrants for searches of other gang members, their vehicles, or residences and business places;
- probable cause to obtain wiretaps or conduct other electronic surveillance of gang activity;
- statements or confessions might be obtained from the arrested persons;
- because of the probability of a long prison term, one or more of the four might agree to testify and provide information against other members of the organization in return for concessions from the government.

Questions and Problems for Chapter 4

1. The defendant owned and operated the Head Shop in Manchester, New Hampshire. A fourteen-year-old girl walked into the shop and purchased for 25 cents a button inscribed "Copulation Not Masturbation." When the girl's parents saw the button, they became very angry and called the police. The defendant was convicted of contributing to the delinquency of a minor, which is a statutory offense in New Hampshire: "Anyone . . . who shall knowingly or wilfully encourage, aid, cause or abet or connive at, or who has knowingly or wilfully done any act

to produce, promote or contribute to the delinquency of (a) child may be punished." (Sec. 169.32, N.H. Rev. Stat. Ann.).

The defendant was convicted in a trial at which the girl was the only witness for the state. The fourteen-year-old girl did not testify that the defendant sold her the button or that she even saw him in the store at the time of the sale. She testified that she could not identify the person who sold her the button. The defendant admitted that he "controlled the premises on July 26 [the date of the sale]." Should the defendant's conviction be affirmed by the U.S. Supreme Court? Explain. *Dennis Vachon v. New Hampshire,* 414 U.S. 478, 94 S.Ct. 664 (1974).

2. Parks was the president of a retail food chain with 36,000 employees, 874 stores, and 16 warehouses. In 1970, federal inspectors advised officers of the corporation that unsanitary conditions were found in a warehouse. Twice in 1971, further unsanitary conditions were reported. In March of 1972, continued evidence of rodent activity and "rodent-contaminated lots of food items" was found. Despite the repeated warnings by the federal inspectors, the violations were not corrected. When the food corporation and Parks were charged with violations of the Federal Food, Drug and Cosmetic Act, the corporation pleaded guilty and Parks pleaded not guilty before a jury. The jury convicted Parks of a misdemeanor. Should the U.S. Supreme Court affirm Parks' conviction? Explain. *United States v. Parks,* 421 U.S. 658, 95 S.Ct. 1903 (1975).

3. The following situation occurred in Milwaukee: Two teenaged girls were walking toward a shopping center when a car containing two men in their twenties stopped. The men offered to give the girls a ride. When the girls refused, one of the men (the passenger) got out of the car and continued attempting to persuade the girls to ride with the men. When the man held one of the girls by her arm, she pulled away from him. The man then hit the girl a hard blow on her face, which sent her sprawling on the ground. The man immediately got back into the car and the driver quickly drove away. The other girl, however, observed the license of the vehicle and provided this information to the police when reporting the incident. When the investigating officers obtained the name and address of the owner of the vehicle, they went to that residence. The vehicle was parked in the driveway and a young man matching the description of the driver was identified as the owner of the vehicle. The

man at first denied being at the scene of the crime. But after he realized that the girls could identify him, he told the following story. The owner and driver of the car said that he picked up a hitchhiker about his age and that the two men had stopped to pick up the girls. After the battery occurred, the driver said he drove his passenger a short distance and then dropped him off. He stated that he did not know the man's name and had never seen him before. The police did not believe the man's story but is there anything they can do to obtain the identity of the man who sent the teenaged girl to a hospital with a very badly bruised face? Explain.

4. In 1984, CBS presented the television movie *The Lost Honor of Kathryn Beck,* which is based on a book and German movie. Marlo Thomas plays Beck, who picks up a stranger at a party and takes him home for the night. After the man leaves in the morning, police burst in, search the apartment, and take Beck to police headquarters for questioning. The man is a terrorist wanted for felonies, and the police believe that Beck knows his whereabouts and is not disclosing such information. Beck has disclosed all the information that she has, but a police officer threatens to "salt her away as a material witness for the rest of her life." Can Beck be arrested or detained for a long period of time based on the facts presented? Explain. If a detention is believed to be unreasonable or unlawful, could a Writ of Habeas Corpus be used to free a person such as Beck?

5. The defendant and two other men (Mr. Moore and Mr. Levy) entered a three-sided plexiglass bus shelter where a man sat waiting for a bus. The man did not try to leave but believed that his exit from the bus shelter was blocked by the defendant and Mr. Moore. Moore asked the man if he wanted to buy some cigarettes. When the man said he didn't, Moore then said, "Give us some change." When the man refused, the defendant repeated this demand four or five times in an increasingly loud voice. The defendant then reached into his coat pocket with his right hand, whereupon Moore said, "Put that gun away." Mr. Levy then said, "Come on, let's go." Levy then said to the man sitting on the bus shelter bench, "I don't want your money, I got lots of money." The three men left the bus shelter together and entered a restaurant across the street. A few minutes later, Moore returned and made "small talk" with the man in the bus shelter. When the police talked to the man waiting in the bus

shelter, he stated that he felt threatened by the encounter that lasted less than three minutes. The man also stated that none of the men ever touched him or raised a hand to him and at no time did the man attempt to leave the bus

shelter. Should the men be arrested for their conduct? Did a crime occur? What offense could be charged under the statutes of your state? *State v. Stewart,* 143 Wis.2d 28, 420 N.W.2d 44 (1988).

Notes

1. 336 U.S. 440, 445, 69 S.Ct. 716, 719 (1949).

2. *Commonwealth v. Hunt,* 45 Mass. (4 Metc.) 111, 123 (1842).

3. Judge Learned Hand, in the 1925 case of *Harrison v. United States,* 7 F.2d 259, 263 (2d Cir. 1925).

4. 1961 Committee Comments to Section 8–2 Conspiracy, Smith-Hurd Illinois Annotated Statutes.

5. 33 CrL 2404.

6. 364 U.S. 51, 80 S.Ct. 1589 (1960).

7. 14 Pa. 226, 227 (1850).

8. Named after the author who stated the rule in 2 F. Wharton, Criminal Law. sec. 1604 (12th ed., 1932).

9. 287 U.S. 112, 53 S.Ct. 35 (1932). Prosecution under the Mann Act is now limited to the commercial transportation and exploitation for prostitution and other immoral purposes in which women can be used. The Mann Act was formerly known as the "White Slave Act."

10. Committee Comment to Section 8–2 of the Illinois Criminal Code, p. 460. Smith-Hurd Illinois Annotated Statutes, Chapter 38.

11. *Iannelli* et al. *v. United States,* 420 U.S. 770, 95 S.Ct. 1284, 16 CrL 3127 (1975).

12. Sec. 1004.

13. Sec. 110.00, McKinney's Consolidated Laws of New York, Annotated, Book 39.

14. *People v. Ditchik,* 228 N.Y. 95, 41 N.E.2d 905 (1942).

15. 16 N.Y.2d 719, 262 N.Y.S.2d 104, 209 N.E.2d 722 (1965).

16. Sec. 663 of the California Penal Code also permits conviction of attempt when the evidence shows that the crime was completed. This section was enacted in 1872.

17. 100 N.M. 405, 671 P.2d 653, 33 CrL 2531 (1983).

18. 185 N.Y. 497, 78 N.E. 169 (1906).

19. 345 Mo. 325, 133 S.W.2d 336 (1939).

20. 32 Ind. 220 (1869).

21. 385 U.S. 323, 87 S.Ct. 429 (1966).

22. See also *United States v. Roman,* 356 F. Supp. 434, *aff'd,* CA 2 1973, 484 F.2d 1271, in which the defendants were transporting a suitcase containing heroin. Through the aid of an informer and unknown to the defendants, the contents of the suitcase were replaced with soap powder. The defendants were arrested when they attempted to sell the contents of the suitcase and were subsequently charged with attempted possession with intent to distribute. The

court concluded that since the objective acts of the defendants were criminal, factual impossibility would not be recognized as a defense. In *United States v. Berrigan,* 482 F.2d 171, 13 CrL 2361 (3d Cir. 1973), the defendants were charged with attempting to violate 18 U.S.C.A. Sec. 1791, which prohibits the smuggling of objects into or out of a federal prison. Since the evidence established that the warden had knowledge of the smuggling plan, and since lack of knowledge was a necessary element of the offense, the court held that the warden's knowledge precluded any conviction for attempt, since attempting to do that which is not a crime is not attempting to commit a crime.

In the 1976 case of *United States v. Oviedo,* 525 F.2d 881, 18 CrL 2411 (5th Cir. 1976), the defendant sold undercover agents a substance he thought was heroin but that was not heroin or a controlled substance. The U.S. Court of Appeals for the Fifth Circuit reversed the attempt conviction, holding that it could not conclude that the defendant's objective acts, apart from any direct or indirect evidence of his intent, indicated the defendant's conduct was criminal.

In the 1977 case of *People v. Dlugash,* 41 N.Y.2d 725, 395 N.Y.S.2d 419, 363 N.E.2d 1155, and in the case of *United States* ex rel. *Rangel v. Brierton,* 437 F.Supp. 908 (N.D. Ill. 1977), the courts held that the defendants could be found guilty of attempt to murder an intended victim already dead.

23. Committee Comments, p. 513, Chapter 38, Smith-Hurd Illinois Annotated Statutes.

24. Sec. 5.05 (2) Model Penal Code.

25. Sir James FitzJames Stephens, *A History of the Criminal Law of England,* (Macmillan & Co., 1883), vol 2, pp. 226–227.

26. See chapter 8 where Sir William Blackstone is quoted stating that more than 160 were felonies without the benefit of clergy.

27. In the 1980 case of *Standefer v. United States,* 447 U.S. 10, 100 S.Ct. 1999, 27 CrL 3143, the U.S. Supreme Court stated in footnote 9 that "four states—Maryland, North Carolina, Rhode Island and Tennessee—clearly retain the common-law bar."

28. See the 1978 case of *State v. Williamson,* 282 Md. 100, 382 A.2d 588, in which the Maryland court observes that Maryland is the only state that has not abolished the old common law doctrine of accessoryship. The court also notes that all of the English-speaking countries of the world have also made statutory changes. England changed the old common law doctrine as early as 1861.

29. In the 1980 case of *Standefer v. United States,* 447 U.S. 10, 100 S.Ct. 1999, 27 CrL 3143, the U.S. Supreme Court held that a defendant may be convicted of aiding and abetting the commission of a federal crime, even though the person who actually committed the crime had been acquitted of the offense.

30. *United Sates v. Sannicandro,* 434 F.2d 321 (9th Cir. 1970).

31. *Gradsky v. United States,* 376 F.2d 993 (5th Cir. 1967), *cert. denied,* 389 U.S. 908, 88 S.Ct. 224 (1967).

32. *People v. Bracey,* 110 Ill.App.2d 329, 249 N.E.2d 224 (1969).

33. 136 Cal.App. 722, 29 P.2d 902, 722 (1934).

34. 19 Md.App. 640, 313 A.2d 563 (1974).

35. 102 Ala. 25, 15 So. 722 (1894).

36. 24 Wis.2d 527, 129 N.W.2d 155 (1964).

37. Consider the following additional example: Police officers respond to an armed robbery call (tavern, business place, bank, hotel, etc.). The armed robbers have fled and radio bulletins are sent out describing the men and their vehicle. Police officers then seek to obtain identification of witnesses and further information. However, a customer who had a good look at the robbers will not identify himself stating he does not want to get involved. If the officers do not get information from the person as to name, address, etc., their superiors, the prosecutor, and defense lawyer are going to be very upset. The usual procedure is to bring the person to the police station for obstructing a law enforcement officer in the performance of his or her duty. At the station, the person is usually persuaded to cooperate and is released (no charges) with a warning.

38. *State v. Guminga,* 395 N.W.2d 344 (Minn. 1986).

39. 251 Ga. 219, 304 S.E.2d 701 (1983).

Chapter Five

CRIMINAL RESPONSIBILITY AND THE CAPACITY TO COMMIT A CRIME

A. Ancient Concepts of Criminal Responsibility

The law has undergone many changes over the centuries as to how criminal responsibility is determined and who has the capacity to commit a crime. At the time of the Norman Conquest of England (1066), for example, trial by ordeal and trial by battle were commonly used in the determination of criminal responsibility. A person who was of noble birth or titled could demand trial by battle if accused of a crime. If, in trial by battle, the suspect or accused came out second, it was then determined that he was guilty of the offense with which he was charged. However, the question of guilt or innocence could become moot, because the accused might be killed or badly injured.

In determining criminal responsibility in a trial by ordeal, the accused often would be required to take a pound weight of red-hot iron into his hands or to plunge his hand, up to the wrist, into boiling water. Ordeal by fire and ordeal by water were also used. Sir James Stephen described trial by ordeal in his *History of the Criminal Law of England,* published in 1883:

> It is unnecessary to give a minute account of the ceremonial of the ordeals. They were of various kinds. The general nature of all was the same. They were appeals to God to work a miracle in attestation of the innocence of the accused person. The handling of hot iron, plunging the hand or arm into boiling water unhurt, were the commonest. The ordeal of water was a very singular institution. Sinking was the sign of innocence, floating the sign of guilt. As any one would sink unless he understood how to float, and intentionally did so, it is difficult to see how anyone could ever be convicted by this means. Is it possible that this ordeal may have been an honourable form of suicide, like the Japanese happy despatch? In nearly every case the accused would sink. This would prove his innocence, indeed, but there would be no need to take him out. He would thus die honourably. If by accident he floated, he would be put to death disgracefully.[1]

Another form of superstition involved the concept that persons deliberately became witches or practiced witchcraft. Such persons were thought to be able to cause great social harm, such as crop failure, and to be able to cause serious injuries or bring illness and death to others. Witchcraft first became a crime under the Roman Empire. During the sixteenth, seventeenth, and eighteenth centuries, thousands of persons were tried and put to death because it was believed that they were either witches or practiced witchcraft. For example, Joan of Arc was charged as being a witch and condemned to death. She was burnt at a stake in France, in 1431.

Prosecution of such persons in the American colonies occurred in Massachusetts, Connecticut, and Virginia. These trials reached a high point in 1692, in Salem, Massachusetts, where 19 persons were executed as witches and 150 more were sent to prison. The Salem trials were the last American trials; the last English trial took place in 1712. In 1735, Scotland repealed all laws that made witchcraft a crime in that country.

Other Medieval Concepts

In the Middle Ages and later, animals were held criminally responsible for harm that they had done. They were tried in the same manner as human beings, except that domestic animals were taken before secular courts, whereas wild animals were required to face ecclesiastical (religious) courts. There were many animal trials at which horses, pigs, dogs, rats, and even roosters were accused of such crimes as murder, battery, and destruction of crops. Some people believed that animals who committed such offenses were possessed by demons; others believed that the devil himself took the form of an animal.

In 1499, a bear that had been killing people in a German village was captured and brought to trial. The attorney appointed to defend the bear was allowed to argue for days that the animal had the right to be judged by a jury of its peers (that is, other bears). However, the animal was tried and convicted by human beings. It was sentenced to dangle from the public gallows until relatives of its victims stoned the animal to death. In 1694, a mare was convicted of criminal homicide in France and was burned to death. The court found that the horse was possessed by demons. As late as 1712, an Austrian court sentenced a dog to a year in the marketplace pillory, where humans were also confined. The dog had bitten a man in the leg.

Today, no industrial nation would hold that an animal had the mental capacity to formulate criminal intent. An animal that killed or seriously injured a human being would probably be destroyed in recognition of the possibility that it might again attack humans. Criminal responsibility, if any exists, would attach not to the vicious animal, but to its owner.

B. Infancy as Affecting Criminal Responsibility

Under the civil law, an infant (child) is a person who has not yet reached the age of majority, whether that age is 18, 19, 20, or 21 as determined by the law of each jurisdiction. Although infants, with some exceptions, are not able to enter into contracts, make wills, or vote, the law as to a child's criminal responsibility for his or her acts differs from the law governing the child's civil capacity.

The question of the criminal responsibility of children came before the courts in the Middle Ages, and by the fourteenth century, the common law had determined that children under the age of seven did not have the capacity to commit a crime. By that time, seven was established as the "age of reason" under ecclesiastical law and also as the age of responsibility under Roman civil law. In establishing the age of seven as the lowest age of criminal responsibility, the common law reasoned that a child under the age of seven did not have the mental capacity to formulate the intent to commit a crime and that, therefore, for children under seven, the threat of punishment would not serve as a deterrent against crime.

Most states continue to maintain this common law rule in the form of a conclusive presumption.[2] The presumption is that children under the age of seven do not have the capacity to commit a crime. As the presumption is conclusive, evidence to the contrary may not be presented. Persons over the age of fourteen are inferred to be sane and capable of formulating the necessary mental frame of mind to commit a crime. Evidence showing otherwise, however, can be used to show incapacity.

Children between the ages of seven and fourteen are presumed to be without criminal capacity to commit a crime. This presumption, however, may be overcome by the presentation of evidence by the state showing that the child has the mental capacity and the ability to formulate the necessary criminal intent. British and American courts have held that the younger the child, the stronger must be the evidence of mental capacity. Testimony of doctors, psychiatrists, and other persons plus school records and reports are usually used to show that the child has physically, mentally, and emotionally reached an age of capacity at which he or she should be held responsible for his or her acts. The common law reasoning was that failure to punish particularly atrocious crimes committed by children between the ages of seven and fourteen would encourage other children to commit similar acts with no fear of punishment.

The Liability of Children Under State Statutes

All states have enacted statutes governing the jurisdiction of children's (juvenile) courts. These courts deal with children who are delinquent and in need of supervision or with children who are neglected and dependent. Delinquency is usually defined by statute as conduct by a child that, if committed by an adult, would be a violation of the criminal code of that state.

In the majority of states, children's courts have jurisdiction over persons under the age of eighteen. However other states set the children's court jurisdiction at an age above or below eighteen.

State statutes also generally provide that juvenile courts may waive jurisdiction to the adult courts of children at an age set by state statutes (14, 15, 16, or even younger). Such statutes often state that the waiver is to be made where public protection requires it, and the waiver is in the best interest of the child.

There have been many debates over the years as to what should be done with children who commit serious crimes. Should they remain in the juvenile system for treatment and be released at age eighteen or nineteen? Or should state statutes provide for some type of supervision until age twenty-one, or even as high as age twenty-five? Or should a child who has committed a serious crime be turned over to the adult system and sent to adult prison facilities?

Children have committed very serious crimes of violence such as murder, attempted murder, aggravated assault, rape, armed robbery, etc. Drug and alcohol addiction and drug peddling by children have become all too common. Crack addiction and dealing has brought with it a new level of violence that has shocked and surprised even criminal justice professionals.

C. THE INSANITY DEFENSE

No subject in criminal law has received as much attention and debate as the insanity defense. The questions of what degree of insanity, mental defect, or mental disease renders a person blameless for acts (or omissions) and what test or tests should be used in determining legal and moral liability have been debated for years.

A 1990 study done by Policy Research Associates of Delmar, New York, shows that now, as in the past, the insanity defense is not an easy way out for guilty defendants. Before the Hinckley shooting and after the Hinckley case, about 2 percent of defendants charged with serious crimes used the insanity plea. Success rates among those using the insanity defense varied throughout the

CRIME BY YOUTHS

The National Center for Juvenile Justice reports that the fastest growing areas in juvenile crimes were the youngest age groups. The following figures were compiled by the FBI (1985).

Crime Increases Per Age Group

12-year olds	38%	11-year olds	22%
13-year olds	37%	10-year olds	15%

Responsibility by Youths 15 Years Old and Younger		Responsibility by Youths 12 Years Old and Younger
381	Murder and Non-negligent Manslaughter	21
18,021	Aggravated Assult	3,545
13,899	Robberies	1,735
2,645	Rapes	436

Age Groups in Property and Violent Crimes

Arrest rate per 100,000 persons

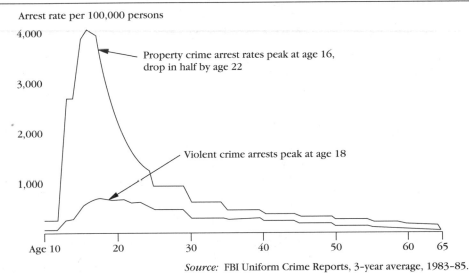

Property crime arrest rates peak at age 16, drop in half by age 22

Violent crime arrests peak at age 18

Source: FBI Uniform Crime Reports, 3-year average, 1983-85.

Reasons Given by Experts for Increase in Crime By Youths

- increased gang and drug activities
- increased use of hard drugs such as crack, which is highly addictive and available at low prices
- increased level of violence in society as a whole
- increased stress on families, particularly in poor urban areas
- Age groups where youths are impulsive and not likely to consider risks

United States from about 30 percent in most states to a high in a few places of 48 percent.[3]

The insanity plea is seldom used in minor charges; it is most often used in murder cases and for other serious felony charges in which, in most instances, the evidence is so conclusive that the defendant has no other defense available.

John Hinckley's shooting of President Reagan (and other persons), Mark Chapman's murder of John Lennon, and the Son-of-Sam crimes are examples of cases that have brought the insanity defense to the public's attention. In these

John Hinckley is subdued after the 1983 shooting of President Reagan and other persons in Washington, D.C.

cases, defense lawyers used the plea as a defensive tactic. It must be remembered that the state can also raise the issue of the sanity and competency of defendants. It is not uncommon for prosecutors to petition for a civil commitment to a mental hospital of a person who otherwise would be charged with a minor criminal violation.[4]

Stages in Criminal Proceedings When the Question of Insanity May Be Raised

The question of insanity, mental disease, or defect may be raised at separate stages of the criminal proceedings. A finding that the defendant is suffering from mental disease or defect will affect the proceeding differently, depending on which stage has been reached.

Insanity at the Time of the Criminal Incident.   If the defendant is found insane, mentally diseased, or defective at the time he or she committed the offense charged, then a judgment of not guilty because of insanity, mental disease, or defect is entered and the defendant may never again be tried for that offense. The disposition of the case is then governed by the laws of that jurisdiction. In most states, the defendant is committed to a state mental institution for the criminally insane and held there until he or she is found to be sane, at which time the person may be eligible for release under the conditions provided for by the statutes of that jurisdiction. The federal code [18 U.S.C.A. Sec. 4243(d)] places the burden on the defendant to show not only that he or she is sane but also that his or her release would not create a substantial risk of injury to the person or property of others.

Insanity (or Incompetency) at the Time of Trial.   A defendant who is insane, mentally diseased, or defective at the time of trial may not understand fully what is occurring and may not be of assistance to the defense attorney. When a court makes a finding that the defendant lacks competency to proceed with the trial, the proceedings must then be suspended and the defendant, in accordance with the statutes of that state, placed in an institution.

A defendant who has been found by a court to be incompetent to stand trial cannot be held indefinitely. In the 1972 case of *Jackson v. Indiana,*[5] the U.S. Supreme Court held that such defendants could not be held for longer than a "reasonable period of time" to determine whether they will regain their competency and capacity to stand trial. Some courts have held that a "reasonable period of time" is a period no longer than the maximum sentence for the crime or, at the longest, eighteen months. After this period of time, the state may either:

- try the defendant, if he or she is found competent and capable of standing trial
- dismiss the charges
- commence civil proceedings against the defendant for the purpose of committing him or her to a mental institution if the defendant remains incompetent and cannot be tried criminally.[6]

Insanity Just Prior to Execution.   Under the common law, if a person to be executed were found to be so disordered as not to understand the nature and purpose of the punishment about to be inflicted, the execution was stayed until such time as the person could understand what was about to occur. Blackstone, a great English writer and lawyer, stated that the reason for this rule was that if the condemned man were sane, he might offer some reason for the execution to be stayed. Probably all American jurisdictions that use the death penalty have adopted this rule, which was sustained by the majority of the U.S. Supreme Court in the 1958 case of Caritativo v. California.[7]

Insanity During Incarceration.   Within every prison population are persons who have used alcohol or drugs to excess or who have untreated venereal disease. These and other problems that manifest themselves while a prison term is being served can have a severe effect on the mental health of a prisoner and can result in his or her transfer to the mental ward of the prison hospital, in which the prisoner would serve the remainder of his or her term. If a mental disease, defect, or insanity exists at the time the prison term ends, civil proceedings could then be initiated for the purpose of commitment to a mental institution. One study indicated that six times as many convicts became mentally ill while serving prison terms as persons found not guilty because of insanity, mental disease, or defect.

The M'Naghten Case and the "Right and Wrong" Test

It was not until the 1800s that English and American courts considered the question of whether insanity, mental disease, and mental defect should be factors in determining the criminal responsibilities of persons charged with crimes. The "right and wrong" test, which became the most widely used test to determine the question of legal insanity in the United States, was developed in 1843 in the aftermath of the famous English murder case of *Rex v. M'Naghten,* House of Lords, 1843.[8]

Daniel M'Naghten lived in London in the 1840s and believed that the British Home Secretary, Sir Robert Peel, was the head of a conspiracy to kill him. (Peel was the widely recognized founder of the British police, who thus received the nickname "Bobbies.") In 1843, M'Naghten shot and killed Edward Drummond, private secretary to Peel, because he mistook Drummond for Peel. At his trial, the defense argued that M'Naghten was insane at the time of the shooting and that he should not be held responsible because his mental delusions had caused him to act as he did. The British jury agreed, and M'Naghten was found not guilty because of insanity.

The "right and wrong" test that emerged from the M'Naghten case became the prevailing standard and test for insanity in American courts. Under this test, the defendant is not legally responsible for his act if at the time he was "laboring under such a defect of reason, from diseases of the mind, as not to know the nature and quality of the act he was doing, or, if he did know it, that he did not know that what he was doing was wrong." The M'Naghten Rule established the burden of proof as follows:

> Every man is presumed to be sane and to possess a sufficient degree of reason to be responsible for his crimes, until the contrary be proved to (the jury's) satisfaction; and that to establish a defense on the ground of insanity, it must be clearly proved.

Other American Tests

Over the years, a few American jurisdictions adopted other tests than the M'Naghten right and wrong test. In 1871, the New Hampshire courts rejected the M'Naghten test and adopted the "New Hampshire test," but no other state has ever followed New Hampshire's lead.[9] In 1886, Alabama adopted the "irresistible impulse" test in *Parsons v. State.*[10] This test extended the M'Naghten Rule and held that, if it is found that the defendant had a mental disease that prevented him from controlling his conduct, even if he knew the difference between right and wrong, he should be found not guilty because of insanity. In practice, the "irresistible impulse" test often had the effect of freeing persons who had committed crimes of passion. An example of this is found in the novel *Anatomy of a Murder* by John Donaldson Voelker (under the alias Robert Traver). Voelker was a retired Supreme Court Justice of the state of Michigan when he wrote the story. Persons who have read the book or seen the movie know that in most states the issue before the court would have been that of self-defense or "heat-of-passion" manslaughter. Instead, the army officer in Voelker's story (based on an actual case) went free on the "irresistible impulse" defense.[11]

According to its critics, the principal fault of the M'Naghten test lies in its narrowness and its restricted application to only a small percentage of people who are mentally ill. In 1954, the "Durham product test" was adopted by the U.S. Court of Appeals for the District of Columbia in the case of *Durham v. United States.*[12] The court stated that "an accused is not criminally responsible if his unlawful act was the product of mental disease or defect." The Durham case established a test for insanity based on a substantial lack of mental capacity rather than a complete lack of capacity. It has been criticized on the grounds that it is too broad and places too much discretion in psychiatrists, rather than in the jury, for determining the legal issue of insanity. "Criminal responsibility is a legal not a medical question."[13]

The American Law Institute "Substantial Capacity" Test

About a year after the adoption of the Durham Rule by a few jurisdictions, the American Law Institute proposed still another test for determining criminal responsibility. In proposing the new rule, the following comment was made:

> No problem in the drafting of a penal code presents larger intrinsic difficulty than that of determining when individuals whose conduct would otherwise be criminal ought to be exculpated (freed of guilt) on the grounds that they were suffering from mental disease or defect when they acted as they did. What is involved specifically is the drawing of a line between the use of public agencies and public force to condemn the offender by conviction ... the problem is to discriminate between the cases where a punitive-correctional disposition is appropriate and those in which a medical-custodial disposition is the only kind that the law should allow.

The final draft of the American Law Institute "substantial capacity" test is found in Section 4.01 of the 1962 Model Penal Code and states:

1. A person is not responsible for criminal conduct if at the time of such conduct as a result of mental disease or defect he lacks substantial capacity either to appreciate the criminality (wrongfulness) of his conduct or to conform his conduct to the requirement of law.
2. As used in the Article, the terms mental disease or defect do not include an abnormality manifested only by repeated criminal or otherwise anti-social conduct.

The Model Penal Code Test (or the A.L.I. "substantial capacity" test) is now reported to have been adopted by about half the states.

While the M'Naghten test requires a defendant to show total mental impairment, there is less of a burden on defendants under the "substantial capacity" test. Under the "substantial capacity" test, even if a defendant "knew" what he or she had done, the defendant is permitted to attempt to show that he or she did not have the "substantial capacity to conform his or her conduct to the requirements of law" (lack of self-control).

President Nixon's Proposed Test

It is now generally accepted that states may write a wide variety of laws establishing tests for determining criminal responsibility. It is reported that two states—Montana and Idaho—have abolished the insanity defense. In 1973 former President Nixon made the following proposal, which was not enacted into law by the Congress of the United States:

> My new formulation would provide an insanity defense only if the defendant did not know what he was doing. ... The only question considered germane in a murder case, for example, would be whether the defendant knew whether he was pulling the trigger of a gun. Questions such as the existence of a mental disease or defect would be reserved for consideration at the time of sentencing.

The "Guilty but Mentally Ill" Verdict[14]

Michigan was the first of at least eight states to enact, in 1975, statutes creating the alternative verdict of "guilty but mentally ill." The new statute was passed after several Michigan defendants committed additional murders after being acquitted and released after using the insanity defense.

In Illinois, Thomas Vanda killed a girl when he was eighteen years old. While undergoing psychiatric treatment in Chicago, he was released and killed another girl. He was found not guilty because of insanity. When doctors concluded that his psychosis had disappeared, he was again released over objections from the trial judge and his own defense attorney. In 1978, when he was twenty-five years old, Thomas Vanda was again charged with murder. The third victim was a twenty-five-year-old woman.

Illinois enacted a "guilty but mentally ill" statute in 1981. Former Illinois Governor James R. Thompson described the new statutory procedure as follows:

> Under this procedure, when an insanity defense is raised, the court, if the evidence permits, may instruct the jury on the alternative verdict of guilty but mentally ill. When a person is not legally insane, he or she may be found guilty but mentally ill if, at the time of the offense, he or she suffered from a disorder of thought or mood that does not represent a condition amounting to insanity in the legal sense.
>
> When a guilty but mentally ill verdict is returned, the court may impose any sentence that could have been ordered for a conviction on the crime charged. However, the prison authorities must provide necessary psychiatric or psychological treatment to restore the offender to full capacity in an appropriate treatment setting. If the mental illness is cured, the offender must be returned to prison to serve out his or her sentence.
>
> Insanity determinations under existing law deal in absolutes; a defendant must be found totally sane or totally insane. This fails to reflect reality. It does not allow the jury to consider the degree of an individual's mental impairment, the quality of the impairment, or the context in which the impairment is operative. A mental impairment does not necessarily eradicate the state of mind required to make a person guilty

---

Insanity and Competency

A Defense of Insanity Is Recognized by All but Two States.

Two states—Montana and Idaho—have passed laws that abolish the insanity defense. In Idaho, however, psychiatric evidence is allowed on the issue of the intent to commit a crime.

In most states, a formal notice of an intent to rely on the insanity defense must be filed by defendants who wish to claim insanity as a defense. Such defendants enter a plea of not guilty at time of trial.

Competency to Stand Trial and the Insanity Defense Are Frequently Confused.

The issue of insanity refers to the defendant's mental state at the time of the crime while the issue of competency concerns the ability of the defendant to assist in the preparation of his of her defense or to understand the proceedings. For example, a defendant may be found competent to stand trial but be found not guilty by reason of insanity.

States Allowing a Verdict of Guilty but Mentally Ill.

In states in which this verdict is available, it is an alternative to (but does not preclude) a verdict of not guilty by reason of insanity.

Source: 1983 U.S. Department of Justice Report to the Nation on Crime.

of a crime, and the jury should be permitted to consider the gradations of a defendant's mental state.

The guilty but mentally ill verdict does not abolish the insanity defense. It simply recognizes that there are gradations in the degree of mental impairment; it provides accountability, promotes treatment, and eliminates the need to manipulate the system. Most importantly, it is designed to protect the public from violence inflicted by persons with mental ailments who previously slipped through the cracks in the criminal justice system.[15]

Opponents of the "guilty but mentally ill" verdict argue that it is nothing but a nice name for "guilty and going to prison." The Alliance for Mentally Ill oppose such legislation "because it would stigmatize insane offenders with a criminal conviction, compounding the handicaps already faced by those persons in obtaining employment and social acceptance."[16]

Many attacks have been made on the constitutionality of "guilty but mentally ill" statutes but such attacks have all failed.[17] Therefore, it is up to legislators and voters in each state to determine the type of laws they wish to have enacted. Most states have declined to adopt such statutes. It is reported that a "guilty but mentally ill" bill was defeated in California even though a "blue ribbon panel" recommended its enactment. However, Pennsylvania enacted a "guilty but mentally ill" law that was sustained by the Pennsylvania Supreme Court in the 1988 case of *Commonwealth v. Sohmer,* 43 CrL 2374.

Diminished Responsibility (or Capacity)

In 1957, the English Parliament introduced into law a new defense to the charge of murder known as "diminished responsibility." This defense is separate and distinct from the defense of insanity, in that partial forgiveness is possible, with a reduction of a charge from murder to manslaughter if an abnormal mental condition or mental disease is successfully shown to have existed at the time of the killing.

The English experience has shown that diminished responsibility has been pleaded with success in mercy-killing cases, as well as deserted-spouse or disappointed-lover cases when the killing occurred while the defendant was in a state of depression. Persons with chronic anxiety have also been able to use this new defense successfully. The English law was originally enacted because it was thought that defendants with mental conditions and abnormalities, such as those which would come under the M'Naghten test, would prefer a conviction for manslaughter rather than face the prospects of an indeterminate or possibly lifelong confinement in a mental institution under an "acquittal" on the grounds of insanity.

Some states, including California, adopted the use of the defense of "diminished responsibility."[18] In 1978, Dan White, a former San Francisco supervisor, concealed a gun and extra ammunition and entered City Hall, where he shot the mayor of San Francisco six times. White then reloaded the gun, sought out supervisor Harvey Milk (a leader of San Francisco's gay community), and executed him in the same manner.

As a defense to the charges of first-degree murder, White's attorney and a prominent psychiatrist presented a picture of a depressed defendant gorging himself on junk foods—Twinkies, Coca-Cola, chocolates—which depressed him further, causing him to consume even more junk foods. The jury accepted what is now called the "Twinkie Defense" and convicted White of two counts of manslaughter instead of murder.[19] The jury verdicts so enraged the San Francisco gay community that riots occurred protesting the results.

After five years in prison, Dan White was released in January 1984. His whereabouts were kept secret because of fear of retaliation from gays. In 1985, Dan white committed suicide, ending what San Francisco's then mayor Diane Feinstein stated was a tragic chapter in the city's history.

Can Compulsive Gambling Justify an Insanity Plea?

Defendants sometimes use the defense that they are compulsive gamblers against criminal charges such as theft, bank robbery, embezzlement, etc. They argue they would not have committed such crimes but were compelled to do so because of their gambling urges. For example, in the case of *United States v. Lynch,*[20] the defendant stole $7.5 million and unsuccessfully used compulsive gambling in an attempt to be found not guilty on his insanity plea.

Prosecutors argue that accepting compulsive gambling as an insanity defense could set a dangerous precedent. In any state that would allow such a defense, thieves could claim kleptomania as a defense; arsonists could claim pyromania; perjurers could claim pathologic lying; drunk drivers could claim alcoholism; and prostitutes could claim nymphomania.

In all of the reported cases, defendants seeking to be found not guilty because of insanity (compulsive gambling) have failed. The Federal Court of Appeals in the case of *United States v. Carmel*[21] reviewed prior cases as follows in refusing the defense:

* * *

United States v. Gould, 741 F.2d 45, 49−52 (4th Cir. 1984) (thesis that a compulsive gambler lacks the capacity to conform his conduct to the requirements of the law prohibiting entry of banks with intent to steal does not have substantial acceptance in the relevant scientific discipline); *United States v. Torniero,* 735 F.2d 725, 731−732 (2d Cir. 1984), certiorari denied, 469 U.S. 1110, 105 S.Ct. 788, 83 L.Ed.2d 782 (no showing of substantial acceptance among respected authorities in the mental health

---

Persons Incapable of Committing Crimes

The following persons are legally incapable of committing crimes and are therefore not responsible for their criminal acts in most states:

1) Children under the age of seven are presumed under the common law to be incapable of committing crimes because they have not reached the "age of reason."
2) Persons found to be insane (mentally diseased or defective) under the test used in that state.

Such persons could be institutionalized (or committed) under the laws of the state in which they reside.

profession that a compulsive gambler is unable to resist the impulse to steal); *United States v. Lewellyn,* 723 F.2d 615, 618–620 (8th Cir. 1983) (thesis that compulsive gamblers cannot conform their conduct to laws prohibiting embezzlement has not gained general acceptance in the fields of psychiatry and psychology).

* * *

A number of problems exist in such cases. First, does the defendant have a mental disorder that will come within the insanity test used in that state or court? Second, did the defendant lose all of the stolen or embezzled money gambling? There is always a chance that they have stolen funds stashed away in a secret account or hidden in a safe place. These cases generally involve large amounts of money taken from innocent victims.

D. THE REQUIREMENT OF COMPETENCY TO TRY A PERSON FOR A CRIMINAL CHARGE

A defendant must be competent (fit) before the government can force him or her to go to trial on criminal charges. This means that a defendant must have the ability to cooperate with his or her attorney and the ability to understand the charges and proceedings against him or her.

A translator or an attorney who can speak the language of a defendant would solve the problem of a defendant who does not understand English. Persons skilled in sign language could communicate for a deaf mute. But what about a defendant with an IQ (mental ability) of a five-year-old child, or a defendant who is spaced-out and in a semi-stupor because of excessive use of drugs or alcohol? If such persons do not understand the charges and proceedings against them, and cannot cooperate with the defense lawyers, they would be determined to be incompetent at that time. They could not be tried because they could not exercise their "rights under the Sixth and Fourteenth Amendments; his right to challenge jurors, to be informed of the nature and cause of the accusation, to confront the witnesses against him, to summon witnesses in his favor and to have the assistance of counsel."[22]

A person could be incompetent (and unfit) to stand trial for a short time (a few weeks or months). Or, a defendant could be permanently incompetent and a state could never force the person to go to trial on criminal charges. When a court makes a finding that a defendant lacks competency (is incompetent), the criminal proceedings must then be suspended. The defendant, in accordance with the statutes of that state, is placed in an institution.

If after a few weeks or months the defendant is found to be competent and fit to go to trial, criminal proceeding may again continue. But if a defendant is never going to become competent, can this person be held indefinitely in a mental institution by the state?

In the 1972 case of *Jackson v. Indiana,*[23] the U.S. Supreme Court held that such defendants could not be held for longer than a "reasonable period of time" to determine whether they will regain their competence and capacity to stand trial. Some courts have held that a "reasonable period of time" is a period no

Tests or Procedures Used to Determine Criminal Responsibility

Test or Procedure	Year When First Used	Type of Test	Extent of Use of Present Time
M'Naghten "right or wrong" test	1843	Based on ability of defendant to know the difference between right and wrong.	Used by practically all American courts until the 1970s. Now used by only half the state courts.
Model Penal Code "substantial capacity" test	1955	Did defendant have the "substantial capacity" to (a) distinguish between right and wrong, or (b) to conform his conduct to the requirements of law?	Used by many states, but California and the federal government returned to the M'Naghten test after using this test. See *U.S. v. Gould,* 801 F.2d 997 (1986) and *People v. Skinner,* 38 CrL 2002 (Calif. Sup. Ct., 1985). The Hinckley shooting and the Dan White shooting had much to do with these changes.
Diminished capacity defense	1957	*Only* partial forgiveness is possible if an abnormal mental or emotional condition is shown to have existed at the time of the crime (murder would be reduced to manslaughter).	Few states use this defense since the "Twinkie Defense" was used in the slaying of San Francisco Mayor Moscone and Harvey Milk. States are not constitutionally compelled to recognize doctrine of diminished capacity. *Muench v. Israel,* 33 CrL 2506, 715 F.2d 1124 (7th Cir. 1983).
"Guilty but mentally ill" alternative verdict and plea	1975	Defendant may be found "guilty but mentally ill" if all the following are found beyond a reasonable doubt; (a) defendant is guilty of offense, (b) defendant was mentally ill at time offense was committed, (c) defendant was not legally insane at time offense was committed.	Used in eight or more states with either the M'Naghten test or the "substantial capacity" test. States using "guilty but mentally ill" pleas are Michigan (1975), Indiana (1980), Illinois (1981), New Mexico, Alaska, Georgia, Kentucky, Delaware (1982), and Pennsylvania (1987).
Plea Bargaining		Such factors as emotional and mental conditions could be taken into consideration for plea bargaining.	Plea bargaining is used extensively in many state and federal courts (Hinckley offered to plea bargain and plead to lesser offenses but was turned down by the U.S. government).

Note: Tests that are no longer used in the United States include the "irresistible impulse" test and the "Durham product" test.

longer than the maximum sentence for the crime charged or, at the longest, eighteen months. After this period of time, the state may either:

- try the defendant, if he or she is found competent and capable of standing trial,
- dismiss the charges, or
- commence civil proceedings against the person for the purpose of committing him or her to a mental institution if he or she remains incompetent and cannot be tried criminally

Can Amnesia Be Grounds for Declaring a Defendant Incompetent?

Amnesia is the total or partial loss of memory regarding past experiences. Brain injury, disease, mental disorder, shock, and the excessive use of alcohol or drugs are some of the many factors that can cause amnesia. Although amnesia victims ordinarily have no difficulty comprehending the nature of the criminal proceedings against them, they would not necessarily remember the facts that occurred at the time of the alleged crime.

In the case of *Ex parte Thompson*,[24] the defendant could understand the crime charged and factual proceedings against her and could assist counsel in her defense. The court held that she was not rendered incompetent to stand trial by her alleged amnesia with respect to the commission of the alleged crime.

Courts generally have held that partial amnesia does not render a defendant incompetent to stand trial nor does it deny a defendant a fair trial. In the case of *Morrow v. State*,[25] the defendant was the driver of one of the vehicles in a bad two-car accident. The defendant's passenger was killed. The court held the defendant to be competent to stand trial, pointing out that the defendant was aware

---

Phases in the Criminal Trial of a Person* Who is Using the Defense of Insanity

Phase 1	*Phase II*	*Phase III*
If the defendant entered a not guilty plea, the first phase is a trial to determine whether the defendant committed the act (or acts) with which he or she is charged.	If found guilty, then the second phase is a hearing to determine whether the person is legally insane under the laws of that state.	If found not guilty because of mental disease or defect, the person is then committed under the laws of that state.
If found not guilty, this ends the proceedings and the defendant is free to leave.	If found to be sane (by a jury or judge), the defendant is then sentenced under the laws of that state for the crime (or crimes) defendant was convicted.	The usual commitment is to a state mental facility until a) the person is found sane, and b) the person is no longer a danger to society (see the laws of your state to determine the disposition used in your state.)

*A person must be competent to be tried for a criminal charge. A "competent" person is a person who understands the charges and proceedings against him or her and is able to assist in his or her defense. A person who is found to be not competent cannot be tried in a criminal or municipal court.

Is the Boss of a Large Mafia Family Faking Insanity?[26]

The New York Geneovese family has a long record of involvement in rackets going back to the 1930s. In 1988, it was estimated that the family had about two hundred sworn or "made" members and conservatively was producing more than a $100 million annually in illegal profits from the various rackets.

Law enforcement officers believe that Vincent (the Chin) Gigante has been the boss of the Geneovese family since he took over total control from Anthony (Fat Tony) Salerna in 1985 when Mr. Salerna was indicted as a member of the Mafia's commission, or ruling group.

Veteran law enforcement officers look upon Mr. Gigante as the most clever organized-crime figure they have observed and point out he has "his fingers in many, many pies." Mr. Gigante is a very wealthy man but is seen often dressed in old baggy trousers and work shoes. His lawyer states that he "has

been psychiatrically disabled" for twenty years and "it is inconceivable that he would be the leader of some organized-crime network."

Yet Mr. Gigante is seen being driven almost every night by top Mafia lieutenants and has a long criminal record associated with organized criminal activity. Law enforcement officers say he is "play acting" and an FBI agent states he is "setting up a defense in case he is ever arrested, and that is why he sometimes acts strangely in public." In 1973, he was charged with conspiracy to bribe police officers, but the charge was dropped when he presented a hospital report stating he was mentally unfit (incompetent) to stand trial.

Many former Mafia bosses are in prison and others have been indicted or retired. Is Mr. Gigante faking, or is he "mentally incompetent" as members of his family state he is?

of the trial events and was able to consult with and assist his lawyer. However, the defendant claimed not to remember the automobile accident because of head injuries. The court wrote:

* * *

The practical effects of expanding the definition of incompetency to include amnesia must be considered. Several courts have indicated that they were unwilling to hold that limited amnesia was an adequate ground for a determination of incompetency because the effect of such a holding would be to free, without trial, persons against whom prima facie criminal cases had been established. See, *State v. Johnson*, 536 P.2d 1035, 1036 (Ariz. 1975): *Commonwealth v. Price*, 218 A.2d 758, 763 (Pa. 1966). It has been noted that, if amnesia were held to render an accused incompetent then, if the amnesia were permanent, the accused would never be competent and could never be tried; at the same time, because limited amnesia cannot be considered a mental defect or disease, an amnesic accused could not be hospitalized or institutionalized. See, *Commonwealth v. Price*, 218 A.2d at 763. Thus permanent amnesia as to the circumstances of the crime charged would be a permanent bar to the imposition of criminal responsibility. This is especially significant in light of "the extreme difficulty—often impossibility—of distinguishing real from feigned amnesia." 71 Yale L.J. at 123. It has been noted that "an attempt to verify all but the most patently phoney claims of amnesia is at best a difficult and time-consuming task; at worst it is a hopeless one." Id. at 124.

Faking Insanity or Faking Incompetency

Every large American city has had criminal cases where a defendant has successfully faked either incompetency or insanity. The court in the case of *United States v. Carter*[27] stated that the defendant had "bamboozled the U.S. Attorney." Doctors

Defenses Not Otherwise Covered in this Text

Defense	*Description of Defense*	*Present Status*
Automatism (unconsciousness)	Automatism is a state in which a person is capable of action but is not conscious of what he or she is doing. This defense is statutorized in some states, including California. Held to be an affirmative defense separate from insanity defense. *Fulcher v. State,* 633 P.2d 142 (Wyo. 1981) 29 CrL 2556. The defendant in the 1984 case of *Polston v. State,* 685 P.2d 1, did not present enough evidence to raise the defense of automatism in Wyoming. The defendant was convicted of mayhem when he bit off two-thirds of his girlfriend's nose (she later married the defendant).	States adopting or statutorizing Sec. 2.01 Model Penal Code would hold as in *People v. Wilson,* 66 Cal.2d 749, 59 Cal.Rptr. 156, 427 P.2d 820 (1967). "Unconsciousness is a complete, not a partial defense to a criminal charge." See LaFave and Scott, *Criminal Law* (St. Paul: West Pub. Co., 1972), p. 337.
Premenstrual tension and syndrome	A form of emotional and physical distress that afflicts some women before their monthly periods. In certain cases, such stress is so severe that it seriously disrupts the women's lives. In 1982, Britain's Appeal Court held that it could not be used as a defense to a criminal charge but could be used in mitigation to lessen sentences.	No known American appellate case on the use of premenstrual syndrome as a defense in a criminal case.
Television intoxication	The 1978 case of *Zamora v. State,* 361 So.2d 776, 23 CrL 2490 (Fla. 1978), received national attention. Zamora was charged with first-degree murder, burglary, robbery, etc. His defense was that he was temporarily insane as a result of "involuntary subliminal television intoxication." The court proceedings were televised, and as Zamora was charged with the senseless slaying of an elderly woman, extensive coverage was given the case. Court held that insanity instructions were not necessary for the jury, as defense did not show insanity existed. A somewhat similar defense was used in a 1985 Kenosha, Wisconsin, murder case. A sixteen-year-old youth charged with shooting his stepfather blamed his obsession with the fantasy game Dungeons & Dragons. The jury took fifty-five minutes to find the young man was not suffering from a mental disease at the time of the slaying.	No other appellate case known. In 1978, Florida recognized a diminished capacity defense only when defendant's capacity was diminished to the point of inability to distinguish right from wrong. Defendant's attempt to come under this rule failed.

continued

Defenses Not Otherwise Covered in this Text (continued)

Defense	Description of Defense	Present Status
XYY chromosome defense	All persons have chromosomes. Some have either too few or too many, causing abnormalities. Some scientists believe that the abnormality of the supermale, or XYY in males, can cause such men to exhibit anti-social or criminal conduct. Not recognized as a defense unless the requirements of the insanity test of the state are met.	See LaFave and Scott, *Criminal Law* (St. Paul: West Pub. Co., 1972), pp. 332–337 for cases and material on this subject.
Cultural disorientation	Some immigrants to the United States bring with them cultural practices that are in conflict with our criminal codes. For example, some continue the ancient traditions of the medicinal use of opium, "capturing" of young brides, and the ritual slaughtering of animals. In 1985 when a young Japanese mother of two children learned that her husband was having an affair with another woman, she walked into the Pacific Ocean with her children to commit suicide (*oyako shinju*). She was saved but the children drowned.	The defendant in the 1986 case of *People v. Aphaylath,* 68 N.Y.2d 945, 510 N.Y.S.2d 83, 502 N.E.2d 998, killed his wife when she showed interest in an ex-boyfriend. The highest court in New York held that the trial court erred in not permitting testimony concerning the stress and disorientation the Laotian refugee of two years encountered. The defendant was permitted to attempt to establish the affirmative defense of extreme emotional disturbance for consideration by a judge or jury of conviction of a lesser degree of homicide.

later determined that the defendant was "without mental disorder." In the case of *Thompson v. Crawford,*[28] the defendant fooled psychiatrists and was later discovered. The Florida court vacated the judgment of acquittal and permitted the state of Florida to proceed again with criminal charges.

Doctors state that it is very difficult to fake insanity or incompetency if a thorough examination is given. The *Yale Law Journal* cited by the court in the case of *Morrow v. State* (described previously) points out "the extreme difficulty—almost impossibility—of distinguishing real from feigned amnesia."

E. The Criminal Responsibility of Corporations and the Capacity of Corporations to Commit Crimes

A corporation is a legal entity created under the laws of a state or the federal government. Since a corporation is not a living person and must act through human beings, any crime committed in the corporate name must be committed by a person or persons in control of the corporation's affairs or in the employment of the corporation.

Civil Laws Used by States to Obtain Public Order and Protect Public Health

Type of Law	*Examples*
"Sexually dangerous person" laws	The Illinois sexually dangerous person statute was tested before the U.S. Supreme Court in the 1986 case of *Allen v. Illinois,* 478 U.S. 364, 106 S.Ct. 2988. In such civil proceedings, the state can order a person who has committed a sex crime to submit to psychiatric examinations and treatment if appropriate (in addition to or while serving time for their crime). The Court held: "states must be free to develop a variety of solutions to problems and not be forced into a common, uniform mold."
Civil commitment to mental hospital and emergency mental detention laws	Such laws generally require that the state show the person was dangerous to himself or herself (attempted suicide) or others, or that the person was totally unable to take care of himself or herself. The mayor of New York City was astonished when experts told him that a homeless woman who defecated in her clothes did not qualify for institutionalization because she did not present an "imminent danger" to herself or others. In 1988, Laurie Dann walked into a Chicago suburban elementary school and opened fire with a handgun. After killing an eight-year-old child and wounding five other children, Dann later committed suicide. In view of her psychiatric problems, police said she was "a time bomb . . . ready to go off."

Sir William Blackstone wrote in his eighteenth-century Commentaries that "a corporation cannot commit treason or felony or other crime in its corporate capacity, though its members may in their distinct individual capacities."[29] Blackstone's statement reflected the early common law thinking that since a corporation had no mind of its own, it could not formulate a criminal intent, and since it had no body, it could not be imprisoned or executed. The early common law view was understandable because there were relatively few corporations in those days, and there were other ways of handling crimes that were committed in the names of corporations. The corporate officers (or employees) who committed the act (or acts) could be criminally charged. The corporation was civilly liable for the acts of its officers and employees and therefore civil suits for damages could be brought. And a corporation that had committed *ultra vires* acts (acts that are beyond the scope of the corporate charter or that violate the laws of the state) could have its corporate charter revoked by the state.

This old common law view changed as corporations became more numerous and as it became apparent that corporations should be made criminally responsible for some types of criminal acts. Today, corporations may be charged with many but not all crimes. It would be hard to imagine, for example, how a corporation could be charged and successfully convicted of rape. If a corporate employee, however, stole trade secrets from another, and his corporation, knowing of such theft, nevertheless used the stolen information for its benefit, the justification for charging the corporation with a criminal offense would be apparent.

Corporate criminal liability is a form of vicarious liability. That is, one person is punished for the act (or acts) of another. A corporation that is found to be criminally responsible for an act committed by even one employee of that corporation might be fined substantially for that offense. Through the fine, other employees and stockholders could suffer because of the vicarious liability of the corporation. In order to justify such criminal liability, there must be a showing that the corporation could have exercised control and precluded the act, or that there was authorization, consent, or knowledge of such act by persons in supervisory positions within the corporation.[30]

Crimes Committed by Corporations

Over the years, corporations have been charged with many different crimes. Corporations and persons can conspire in restraint of trade. For example, if all the bakers and car manufacturers were to meet and agree upon prices for which bread and cars would be sold in the United States, such agreements would be conspiracies in restraint of trade and violations of the Sherman Antitrust Act enacted by the U.S. Congress more than a hundred years ago. The Sherman act (15 U.S.C. sec. 1) provides in part:

> Every contract, combination in the form of trust or otherwise, or conspiracy, in restraint of trade or commerce among the several States, or with foreign nations, is hereby declared to be illegal. Every person who shall make any contract or engage in any combination or conspiracy hereby declared to be illegal shall be deemed guilty of a felony, and, on conviction thereof, shall be punished by a fine not exceeding one million dollars if a corporation, or if any other person, one hundred thousand dollars, or by imprisonment not exceeding three years, or by both said punishments, in the discretion of the court.

A few of the many charges brought against corporations in recent years are:

Corporation	Charge	Disposition
General Electric Corporation (1990)	Defrauding U.S. Army (overcharging)	Paid $16.1 million in criminal and civil penalties
Northrop Corporation (1990)	Military fraud (cruise missile and Harrier jet)	Paid $17 million in penalties
Eastern Airlines (1990)	Falsifying maintenance records	Large money fines
Ford Motor Corporation (1978)	Three counts of reckless homicide (deaths of three teenage girls in a Ford Pinto when Ford failed to recall and fix a gas tank problem in the Pinto)	Found not guilty by an Indiana jury but paid civil settlements of civil lawsuits.
Exxon Corporation (1990–91)	Exxon agreed to pay $100 million in criminal fines and $1 billion more in civil damages for the worst oil spill in America (11 million gallons of oil into Alaska's Prince William Sound in 1989).	After the plea bargain was announced, the Exxon chairman announced that the fines would "not have a significant effect upon our earnings." In 1991, the federal judge hearing the case would not accept the settlement, stating that the fines "do not adequately achieve deterrence." The case will either go to trial or a new settlement will be submitted to the trial judge.

More criminal and civil charges can be expected against corporations and persons where there is probable cause to believe environmental laws have been violated.

Questions and Problems for Chapter 5

1. In 1988, newspapers reported that a man charged with the attempted hijacking of an Air Canada plane was held to be incompetent by a San Francisco court. The newspaper reports further stated that the man was sent to a federal prison for up to four months of psychiatric examination. In such cases, what does "incompetent" mean? Is it the same as "not guilty because of mental disease or defect"? What will occur if (a) the man continues to be incompetent for years, or (b) a few months after being sent to the prison, the man is found competent? Explain.

2. Another 1988 newspaper article told of a New York cab driver who took a passenger to two banks and, after waiting, to another destination. The cab driver did not know that the man committed four robberies in the two banks and used the cab to escape. A few days later, after being informed of the robberies, the cab driver saw the man on the street in New York and held him until the police arrived. Why shouldn't the cab driver be charged as party to the crime of the robberies? How could four robberies occur with only two stops at different banks? Explain.

Notes

1. Sir James FitzJames Stephen, *A History of the Criminal Law of England* (Macmillan & Co., 1883), vol. 1, p. 73. See also the historical accounts of Joan of Arc. Joan was charged by the English as being a witch and was condemned to death. She was burnt at a stake in France, in 1431. England was at that time at war with France and Joan was a French national heroine leading French armed forces.

2. In the 1987 case of *In re Register,* 84 N.C. App. 336, 352 S.E.2d 889 (1987) a finding that a six-year-old girl was delinquent was set aside by the majority of the North Carolina Court of Appeals as the child was under the age of seven. The six-year-old took part in a burglary and the ransacking of a home. The majority of the court held that "At common law (the child could not be found guilty) because of irrebuttable presumption that she was doli incapax (incapable of criminal intent). . . ." A dissenting judge, however, wrote that the common law presumption "only shields a child from indictment and punishment for criminal offenses. . . . While the six- year-old in the instant case had an absolute defense to criminal prosecution, she could nevertheless be adjudicated delinquent in juvenile proceedings."

3. See the article "Insanity plea seldom used, seldom successful" in the 6/20/90 *Milwaukee Journal.*

4. In *Lynch v. Overholser,* 369 U.S. 705, 82 S.Ct. 1063 (1962) a municipal court refused to accept a former mental patient's plea of guilty to a minor check forgery charge. Instead, the court found the defendant not guilty by reason of insanity. As the defendant was a first offender, he would probably have not received a jail sentence. After the defendant served two years in a mental institution, the U.S. Supreme Court reversed the

trial court, holding that the trial court was not justified in committing the defendant to a mental institution on bare reasonable doubt concerning past sanity.

5. 406 U.S. 715, 92 S.Ct. 1845 (1972).

6. Justice Thurgood Marshall pointed out in his 1983 dissent in *White v. Estelle,* 459 U.S. 1118, 103 S.Ct. 757, 32 CrL 4149, that: "This Court has approved a test of incompetence which seeks to determine whether the defendant 'has sufficient present ability to consult with his lawyer with a reasonable degree of rational understanding—and whether he has a rational as well as factual understanding of the proceedings against him.' *Dusky v. United States,* 362 U.S. 402 (1960)." Many state statutes have adopted this standard as part of their code of criminal procedure.

7. *Caritativo v. People of State of California,* 357 U.S. 549, 551, 78 S.Ct. 1263, 1263 (1958).

8. 10 Cl. & F. 200, 8 Eng.Rep. 718.

9. For a discussion of the "New Hampshire test," see pp. 286–287 of *Criminal Law* by LaFave and Scott (St Paul: West Pub. Co., 1972).

10. 81 Ala. 577, 2 So. 854 (1887).

11. It is unethical for either a prosecutor or a defense lawyer to fabricate a situation in which a defendant appears to be insane and suffering from a mental disease or defect. In the novel *Anatomy of a Murder,* the defense lawyer delivers the famous "lecture" that lets his client (the defendant) become aware that the only way that he could avoid a murder conviction would be by faking "irresistible impulse," which defense was permitted in Michigan at that time. The defense lawyer (played by James Stewart in the movie) won his case by manipulating the system but lost his legal fee. In the movie and book, loss of the

legal fee seems to have been a just punishment for the improper conduct of the defense lawyer.

12. 94 U.S. App. D.C. 228, 214 F.2d 862 (1954).

13. *Sauer v. United States,* 241 F.2d 640, 648 (9th Cir. 1957).

14. In 1981, Connecticut enacted a statute (P.A. 81–301) creating the verdict of "guilty but not criminally responsible."

15. *The Journal of Criminal Law and Criminology* 73 (1982): 867–874 contains the entire text of former Governor Thompson's remarks as cochairman of the National Violent Crime Task Force. Governor Thompson stated that "the insanity defense has been described as the chronic scandal of American criminal law."

16. "The Insanity Defense: Ready for Reform?" *Wisconsin Bar Bulletin,* December 1982.

17. See *People v. McLeod,* 407 Mich. 632, 288 N.W.2d 909 (1980), *Taylor v. State,* 32 CrL 2150 (Ind. 1982), *Weismiller v. Lane,* 815 F.2d 1106 (7th Cir. 1987), *Keener v. State,* 254 Ga. 699, 334 S.E.2d 175 (1985).

18. Los Angeles Deputy District Attorney Dinko Bozanich was quoted as stating that "it (defense of "diminished capacity") works very, very often. All they have to do is paint the picture of a poor bastard, a social misfit, who could not possibly have premeditated." See "Insanity on Trial," *Newsweek,* May 8, 1978.

19. *People v. White,* 117 Cal.App.3d 270, 172 Cal.Rptr. 612 (1981).

20. 699 F.2d 839 (7th Cir. 1982).

21. 801 F.2d 997 (7th Cir. 1986).

22. *Parson v. Anderson,* 354 F.Supp. 1060, 1071 (E.D. Del.), affirmed 481 F.2d 94 (3d Cir. 1973).

23. 406 U.S. 715, 92 S.Ct. 1845 (1972). See also the book *Dummy* and the 1979 television movie. The book and the movie tell the story of Donald Lang, an eighteen-year-old black, totally illiterate, deaf mute. Lang could not talk, write, read lips, or understand sign language. In 1965, he was charged with the murder of a Chicago prostitute (Cook County criminal case #65–3421). Because he could not hear, speak, read, or write, he was declared incompetent to stand trial and was placed in a state mental hospital. After Lang was held for five years, the Illinois Supreme Court ordered him tried or released. Because witnesses were no longer available, he was released. In 1973, Lang was charged with killing another woman. After a conviction for the second murder, he was held to be incompetent and the conviction was reversed. He was found incompetent to stand trial but also not in need of hospitalization. Lang, however, continues to be held in Illinois institutions.

24. 364 So.2d 687, *review denied,* 25 CrL 4018 (Ala. 1978).

25. 47 Md. App. 296, 423 A.2d 251, 28 CrL 2335 (Md.Ct.SpecialApp., 1980).

26. See the New York Times article "Father Louis and The Chin: Gigante brothers attract a lot of attention in N.Y." 7/8/90. This article and other articles in newspapers and magazines tell of the Gigante brothers and their many activities.

27. 415 F.Supp. 15 (D.D.C. 1975).

28. 479 So.2d. 169, 38 CrL 2272 (Fla. 1985).

29. C. 18, sec. 12.

30. Section 2.07 of the Model Penal Code on "Liability of Corporations, Unincorporated Associations and Persons Acting, or Under a Duty to Act, in Their Behalf." See *State v. Christy Pontiac-GMC Inc.,* 354 N.W.2d 17 (Minn. 1984) for case citations on criminal charging of corporations.

Chapter Six

DEFENSES THAT SEEK TO JUSTIFY THE USE OF FORCE

No person, whether a law enforcement officer or a private person, may use force against another unless lawful authority exists justifying the use of force. If force is used, the person using the force should be able to come up with facts and reasons that legally justify the use of such force. The justification might be needed for an investigating law enforcement officer. Or an employer (or supervisor) may be asking "why?". If the matter went before a prosecutor (as serious matters generally do), the prosecutor has to be provided with facts that justify the use of force, or he or she may issue charges.[1] This chapter presents much of the law having to do with the use of force as it is generally applied in the United States.

A. SELF-DEFENSE AND THE DEFENSE OF OTHERS

Less than Deadly Force

A person may threaten or intentionally use force against another for the purpose of preventing or terminating what he or she reasonably believes to be an *unlawful* interference with his or her person. Force must be *necessary* under the circumstances, and the person may use only such force or threat thereof as is *reasonable* to prevent or to terminate the interference.

The key words in determining the lawfulness of force in self-defense or the defense of another are:

- *unlawful.* The force or interference used against the person must be *unlawful.*
- *necessary.* Force must be immediately *necessary* to protect the person or another from the use of *unlawful* force or interference by another.
- *reasonable.* The amount of force used in self-defense or defense of another must be *reasonable* under the circumstances that exist.

In determining what force is reasonable in self-defense, a court or a jury will take into account the size and age of the parties in relation to one another, the instruments or weapons used, and the aggressiveness of the assault made. Ordinarily, if fists were used in the attack and the parties were about the same size and strength, then fists and the strength of arms and body would be the maximum force that could be used in defense.

EXAMPLE: A man who is attacked by another man about the same size and strength in a fistfight would not ordinarily be justified in viciously hitting his assailant with a baseball bat.

EXAMPLE: A seventy-year-old, 100-pound woman becomes angry at a twenty-five-year-old, 200-pound man and begins to hit him with an umbrella. The man may defend himself by taking the umbrella away from the woman, but because he has such physical control of the situation, the amount of force that he would be justified in using would end there.

Coming to the Aid of Another

A person may come to the aid of another and use **necessary** and **reasonable** force to defend the other person against **unlawful** force or interference. The person coming to the assistance or defense of another must reasonably believe that the facts are such that the third person would be privileged to act in self-defense, and must reasonably believe that his or her intervention is necessary for the protection against unlawful force or interference.

In the case of *People v. Young,*[2] Young intervened in a street struggle between three men. Young argued that he came to the assistance of the younger man, believing in good faith that the two older men were unlawfully assaulting the younger man. Young injured the kneecap of one of the men and struck the other about the head with his fist.

The two injured men were police officers in plain clothes making an arrest of the younger man. In affirming Young's conviction for battery, the New York Court of Appeals rejected the argument that Young was privileged to use such force under the circumstances, holding: "The weight of authority holds ... that one who goes to the aid of a third person does so at his own peril."[3]

In the 1982 case of *Alexander v. State,*[4] the defendant, who was a prisoner, saw two guards subduing another prisoner. The defendant intervened, arguing that the two guards were violently attacking his friend and that the defendant acted to prevent injury.

At the defendant's trial for assaulting the guards, the judge instructed the jury that the defendant's right to defend the other prisoner was no greater than the prisoner's own right of self-defense. The defendant was therefore convicted.

A new trial was ordered by the Court of Appeals because Maryland had passed a "Good Samaritan" statute that changed the common law and encouraged persons to "get involved." This statute applied to all persons in Maryland and required that the jury determine whether the defendant believed that an unlawful assault was occurring and whether the defendant made a good faith attempt to defend his friend, the other prisoner.

The Use of Deadly Force in Self-defense or the Defense of Others

Deadly force is force that is likely to cause or is capable of causing death or serious bodily injury. Firing a weapon at a person is the use of deadly force, whether the intent is to kill or to wound.

All persons (including law enforcement officers) may use deadly force, if necessary, to prevent imminent death or great bodily harm to themselves or others. The following civil case illustrates this rule of law:

MULLINS v. PENCE
Court of Appeals of Louisiana (1974) 290 So.2d 803

When a belligerent customer in a bar refused to leave, the bartender called the police. Before the police arrived, the customer told the bartender that he was going to tear his arm off and beat him over the head with it. When the customer began climbing over the bar toward the bartender, the bartender pulled out a pistol and fired one shot into the customer (Mullins). When Mullins still did not retreat, the bartender (Pence) rapidly fired four more shots into Mullins. Mullins was six feet tall and weighed 215 pounds, whereas the bartender, a cripple, was five feet four inches tall and weighed 145 pounds. Mullins recovered and sued the bartender. In ruling in favor of the defendant bartender, the court quoted other Louisiana decisions, holding:

> *Of course, resort to the use of a dangerous weapon in order to repel a supposed attack upon defendant's person ... cannot be countenanced as justifiable save in exceptional cases where the actor's fear of the danger is not only genuine but is founded on facts which would be likely to produce similar emotions in men of reasonable prudence.*

* * *

> *The trial court in this case seemed especially impressed with the belligerence of the plaintiff, the large difference in size and strength of the two parties confronting each other, an overt act made by the plaintiff toward Pence coupled with threats of serious bodily harm against the defendant, and the impossibility of retreat by Pence. Regarding the fact that five shots were actually fired into appellant, the trial court believed that Pence was reasonable in his fear following the first shot that the appellant was continuing in his act of aggression against him. Therefore, like the firing of the first shot, the appellee's action in firing the next series of shots was reasonable. We find no error in the trial court's application of the law to the facts in this case. For the above reasons, the trial court's judgment is affirmed, all costs to be paid by plaintiff-appellant.*
> *Affirmed.*

Loss of the Privilege of Self-defense by the Wrongdoer or Aggressor

The general rule in the United States is that the wrongdoer or aggressor loses and may not claim the defense of self-defense. If the victim is using lawful force, the victim may assert the privilege of self-defense. The defense of self-defense may be used only when lawful force is used to defend against unlawful force or interference.

There are two situations, however, in which the aggressor or wrongdoer could regain his right and privilege of self-defense.

1. A wrongdoer (X) begins an encounter with the unlawful use of his fists or some nondeadly weapon. The victim, however, unlawfully uses deadly force, which, under the circumstances, is unnecessary and unreasonable. Now, X may use force in self-defense but is not privileged to resort to the use of force intended or likely to cause death unless he has exhausted (a) every means of escape (he has a duty to retreat) and (b) every means of avoiding death or great bodily harm to himself.
2. A wrongdoer may regain his right of self-defense if he or she withdraws in good faith from the fight and gives adequate notice to his victim as to his withdrawal. The wrongdoer has a duty to retreat, and his right to self-defense could be restored by retreating and giving notice (or attempting to).

The Privilege Not to Retreat, or the "Castle Doctrine"

A person who is violently assaulted in his own home by a trespasser or a person who has been invited into the home has no duty to retreat (or flee) but may stand

How Do Victims of Violent Crime Protect Themselves?

- Rape victims are more likely than other violent crime victims to use force, try a verbal response, or attract attention, and they are less likely than the others to do nothing to protect themselves.
- Robbery victims are the least likely to try to talk themselves out of being victimized and the most likely to do nothing.
- Assault victims are the least likely to attract attention and the most likely to attempt some form of nonviolent evasion.

- Compared with simple assault victims, aggravated assault victims are more likely to use a weapon, less likely to try to talk themselves out of the incident, and less likely to do nothing to defend themselves. The fact that weapons are used more frequently by victims of aggravated assault than by victims of any other violent crime leads to the suspicion that some of these victims may have played a part in causing the incident.

Victim Response*	Percentage of Victims Responding by Type of Crime*		
	Rape	**Robbery**	**Assault**
Weapons use			
Used or brandished gun or knife	3%	4%	4%
Physical force			
Used or tried physical force	29	22	23
Verbal response			
Threatened, argued, reasoned, etc. with offender	19	10	16
Attracting attention			
Tried to get help, attract attention, scare offender away	18	13	10
Nonviolent evasion			
Resisted without force, used evasive action	13	14	23
Other			
No self-protective actions	1	2	3
Total	100%	100%	100%
	1,206,755	8,484,516	36,269,845

*Victim self-protective responses are listed in the table in order of assertiveness. If victims indicated that they took more than one type of action, only the most assertive action was used in the analysis. Percentages may not sum to 100% because of rounding.

Source: BJS National Crime Survey 1979–85.

his ground and use such force as is necessary to defend himself.[5] The privilege not to retreat in one's home is known as the "castle doctrine."

The law has always recognized that a home is a person's castle and that the home is a special place of protection, security, and privacy that a person may lawfully protect from invasion.

A husband and wife have an equal right to be in their "castle," and neither has the legal right to eject the other. Because of this, some states hold that a "legal co-occupant" of a home, such as a husband or wife,[6] has a duty to retreat from the other instead of using deadly force. In the 1982 case of *State v. Bobbitt,*[7] a wife testified that she killed her husband in self-defense because he attacked her without provocation in their home. In affirming her conviction for manslaughter, the Supreme Court of Florida held that the jury was properly instructed that she had a duty to retreat before using deadly force. The court pointed out that fleeing would not leave her and others like her defenseless, since "a person placed in imminent danger of death or great bodily harm to himself by the wrongful attack of another has no duty to retreat if to do so would increase his own danger of death or great bodily harm."[8]

Battered Women Who Kill

The National Clearinghouse of the Defense of Battered Women states that every year 500 to 750 women kill men who abused them and "that our prisons are filled with women with long histories of abuse, linked to the crimes they're in prison for."[9] The Clearinghouse also estimates that a woman is abused in the United States every thirteen seconds.

These estimates show the high levels of anger, fear, hatred, and humiliation that exist in the households where such conditions prevail. Abused women (and those who allege they were abused) can be found in the prisons of every state serving sentences ranging from assault and battery to voluntary manslaughter and first-degree murder.

To lawfully use deadly force in self-defense, there must be a real (or reasonable) fear of imminent death or great bodily harm. If there is no immediate threat, then other alternatives are available to abused women, such as going to a shelter for battered persons or going to their family for help.

The problem of domestic homicides has existed for many years. It could involve the killing of a spouse or other member of a household. When credible witnesses are available who provide information showing that the killing was necessary in self-defense, criminal charges generally will not be issued.

If, however, there are no witnesses to the killing and the only person alive to describe what occurred is the person who caused the killing, there may be reasons to believe that the killing was not in self-defense.

Women charged with the killing of their spouses or "live-ins" often use the "battered woman syndrome" as a form of self-defense. If they and other witnesses testify as to a history of beatings and abuses inflicted on the woman by the deceased, expert witnesses can then generally testify as to the syndromes associated with prolonged beatings and abuses on victims. The Supreme Court of Kansas commented as follows in 1985 on the problem:[10]

> [T]here is no easy answer to why battered women stay with their abusive husbands. Quite likely emotional and financial dependency and fear are the primary reasons for remaining in the household. They feel incapable of reaching out for help and justifiably fear reprisals from their angry husbands if they leave or call the police. The abuse is so severe, for so long a time, and the threat of great bodily harm so constant, it creates a standard mental attitude in its victims. Battered women are terror-stricken people whose mental state is distorted and bears a marked resemblance to that of a hostage or a prisoner of war. The horrible beatings they are subjected to brainwash

them into believing there is nothing they can do. They live in constant fear of another eruption of violence. They become disturbed persons from the torture.

* * *

Many states now permit abused women charged with violence against their abusers to introduce evidence of their abuse, and its psychological effects, as part of their claim of self-defense. Women in prisons who were abused or who claim they were abused have appealed to state governors for clemency.

After reviewing the cases of more than one hundred women imprisoned in Ohio, Governor Richard F. Celeste granted clemency to twenty-six women in December 1990. Most were released from prison immediately, but a few had to finish a minimum term of two years for killing their abusers. In 1991, the Governor of Maryland commuted the prison sentences of eight women convicted of killing or assaulting men who abused them. Governors in other states are reviewing the cases of women serving sentences in their states. Further material on battered women who kill can be found in chapter 13 on Homicide.

B. THE USE OF FORCE IN THE DEFENSE OF PROPERTY

Less than Deadly Force in the Defense of Property

A person is privileged to threaten or intentionally use force to protect property that is lawfully in his or her custody or care. No force may be used if verbal requests to terminate and stop such interference are complied with.

The interference with the property must be *unlawful*. Force may be used only when *necessary* to terminate the interference, and the amount of force must be *reasonable* under the circumstances.

EXAMPLE: Y, a store employee, observes X snatch merchandise and run out of the store. Y may use *necessary* and *reasonable* force to prevent the *unlawful* taking of merchandise by X.

EXAMPLE: X snatches W's purse and runs off. Y, who observed the crime, would be justified in using necessary and reasonable force to recover the purse. Theft from the person (or robbery, if force is used) is a felony in most, if not all, states, which would authorize Y, in most states, to make a citizen's arrest. Force could also be used under these circumstances under the state law governing the use of force in making an arrest.

Deadly Force in the Defense of Property

Under the old common law used on the American frontier, deadly force was often used to protect property. A farmer who sought to prevent the theft of his horse, cattle, or farm equipment might use deadly force, if necessary, because law enforcement officers were seldom readily available.

Today, most, if not all, states forbid the use of deadly force in the defense of property. The reasons for the change in the law can be summarized as follows:

What Amount of Force May an Occupant of a Home Use Against a Person Illegally in the Home?

Probably all of us have heard noises in our home and went to check the source of the noise with the thought in mind that we might have an unwelcome stranger in our home. As half of burglaries in the United States occur during daylight hours, you could be a victim of one of the four million burglaries that occur every year in the United States in the middle of a day or night. What could you do if you were to come upon an intruder? Most burglars would attempt to flee. But maybe this burglar has been trapped, or maybe this person has violence on his mind. What are the rules of law governing these situations?

As the intruder's conduct is illegal, you may use the amount of force that is necessary and reasonable in self-defense, defense of another, or in defense of property. These rules are defined by the statutes of your state and have been discussed in this chapter. You have no legal obligation to retreat from an intruder in your residence, but this may be a wise way out if it is possible. This is a national problem and responses to it are occurring throughout the country. A few of the responses are described in the following material:

The Colorado "Make My Day Law" [a] Sections 18-1-704(3) of the Colorado Statutes became effective in 1986. It immediately became known as the "Make My Day Law" (Clint Eastwood's taunt to a felon in a movie). The backers of the law want it to be known as the "Homeowner's Protection Law" and point out that it is not a "license to kill" law. The law provides homeowners with immunity from prosecution for force used against a person making an unlawful entry into the home.

New York Times Newspaper article 8/20/88 entitled "Few Go to Jail for Using Unlicensed Guns in Self-defense." New York and about half of the states require a license or registration to have a gun in a home or business place. Some persons (maybe many people) have guns that are not licensed or registered. The newspaper article points out that few of the persons who use an unlicensed gun against an intruder in a home or business place are prosecuted in New York. The article also points out that it is a felony to have a loaded, unlicensed gun in a public place, and that this "is a different matter" than having an unlicensed gun in a home. The mandatory one-year sentence for having an unlicensed gun in a public place is enforced.

The California "Home Protection Bill of Rights" Section 198.5 of the California Penal Code permits a presumption that a person using deadly force on an intruder acted in reasonable fear of death or great bodily harm to him- or herself or a member of the household. (However, the presumption could be overcome with evidence showing otherwise.)

Milwaukee Journal article 8/21/88 entitled "No Charges are Likely in Slaying of Intruder." The article tells of a seventy-five-year-old man who awoke at 5 A.M. on hearing noises. When he went to his wife's bedroom, he saw a man standing in the room. The man had slit a screen and crawled in through the opening. The homeowner immediately shot the man, killing him. Wisconsin does not have statutes similar to the Colorado or California statutes, but the concepts found in the Colorado and California statutes could be used in deciding not to charge the homeowner.

---

[a] For cases on the Colorado statute see *People v. Guenther,* 740 P.2d 971 (Colo. 1987) and *Young v. District Court,* 740 P.2d 982 (Colo. 1987). Both cases were before the Colorado Supreme Court in 1987.

1. On the frontier, a horse and many other items of property were important for survival. Today, few items of property are vital to survival, as they can be replaced within a few days.

2. Today, many items of personal property (such as a car) are ordinarily insured against loss by theft. On the frontier, insurance was unknown and the loss of major or personal items could be a tragedy to a frontier family.

3. Today, thanks to modern communication and transportation, law enforcement agencies are readily available to assist persons confronted with theft.

The Use of Booby Traps to Protect Property

One cannot use deadly force to protect one's property. This rule applies whether the owner is present or uses a remote control device. Some jurisdictions, such as Oregon, Wisconsin, and England, go so far as to punish separately the mere setting of a spring gun.

EXAMPLE: A farmer who becomes exasperated because melons are being stolen from his melon patch is not justified in shooting the thieves with a shotgun. Neither can he set up a shotgun that is discharged when a thief brushes a wire attached to the trigger mechanism.

The common law in probably all states makes the user of such devices civilly liable for the wrongs that occur. The Restatement of Torts, Section 85, page 180, states:

> The value of human life and limb, not only to the individual concerned but also to society, so outweighs the interest of a possessor of land in excluding from it those whom he is not willing to admit thereto that a possessor of land has, as is stated in § 79, no privilege to use force intended or likely to cause death or serious harm against another whom the possessor sees about to enter his premises or meddle with his chattel, unless the intrusion threatens death or serious bodily harm to the occupiers or users of the premises. . . . A possessor of land cannot do indirectly and by a mechanical device that which, were he present, he could not do immediately and in person. Therefore, he cannot gain a privilege to install, for the purpose of protecting his land from intrusions harmless to the lives and limbs of the occupiers or users of it, a mechanical device whose only purpose is to inflict death or serious harm upon such as may intrude, by giving notice of his intention to inflict, by mechanical means and indirectly, harm which he could not, even after request, inflict directly were he present.

In 1990, the owner of a small machine tool shop in Denver, Colorado, rigged a shotgun booby trap after his business had been burglarized eight times in two years. A teenaged burglar was killed by the booby trap. The business owner was convicted of manslaughter. While the owner received probation, he was held civilly liable in a lawsuit. As the result of a damage award, he could lose his business, his home, and all his assets.[11]

After the Denver shooting, other Denver businesses put up signs on buildings stating that their premises were also booby-trapped. Police officers and firefighters became concerned for their safety and stated they would not enter such buildings until the buildings were determined to be safe. One building having such a sign (but no booby trap) was destroyed by fire when firefighters refused to enter.

Stun Guns, Mace and Other Products Marketed as Personal Protection Devices

Device	Description	For Private Use
Stun guns (electrical weapons)	Really not a gun as the device requires direct contact against a person to repel or incapacitate. More like a mini-cattle-prod that when activated gives off blue sparks and crackling noise, which hopefully will keep an attacker at bay. Powered by batteries and is about the size of a pocket radio. Releases electric shock of 35,000 to 50,000 volts, which penetrates clothing but takes several seconds of continued contact to really knock a person out. Manufacturer says shock does no lasting harm but does leave red marks on skin temporarily. Another device known as the "Taser" fires small darts connected to wires and is also a stun gun. The Taser is reported to be effective up to 12 to 15 feet. The Los Angeles Police Department has more than 500 Tasers that they have employed more than 700 times prior to early 1987. In the 1985 case of *Michenfelder v. Sumner,* 624 F.Supp. 457 at 463–64, the federal court held that Tasers and stun guns are more suitable than batons for use in prisons and they would inflict less discomfort than tear gas.	Illegal in a number of states and cities (Hawaii, Massachusetts, Michigan, New Jersey, New York City, Rhode Island, Washington, D.C., Wisconsin, and maybe others). Permits needed in other states.
Mace, tear gas, and other chemical sprays (chemical agents)	Like the stun gun, mace and other chemical sprays are marketed as defensive devices. Such devices seek to repel, but not kill, an attacker. Mace will burn the skin on contact and will irritate the eyes and nasal passages. As mace is ordinarily in a spray can, it can be sprayed toward an attacker without requiring personal contact with the person.	Some states forbid the sale or private possession of chemical sprays such as tear gas and mace. Other states permit citizens to carry mace and other sprays after they have completed a four- or eight-hour training course.

Stun guns and mace have been used as offensive weapons to commit crimes. However, the most frequent use for such devices has been the lawful use by law enforcement agencies.

C. The Use of Force in Making an Arrest

Less than Deadly Force in Making an Arrest

Force may not be used legally in making an arrest unless the arrest is a lawful, custodial arrest made in good faith. This does not mean that the arrested person must be found guilty of the charge; however, it does mean that probable cause (reasonable grounds to believe) must exist to authorize the arrest.

Connecticut police seek to maintain order during a 1981 KKK rally in Meriden, Connecticut. Under what circumstances may the police use force?

In most arrests, force is unnecessary because the person arrested complies with instructions and offers no resistance. If force should be necessary because of resistance or attempt to escape, the officer may use only such force as is reasonably believed necessary to:

1. detain the offender, make the arrest, and conduct lawful searches
2. overcome any resistance by the offender[12]
3. prevent an escape and retake the person if an escape occurs
4. protect the officer, others, and the prisoner, if necessary.

The tests used in determining whether excessive force was used by a law enforcement officer in making an arrest were established by the U.S. Supreme Court in the 1989 case of *Graham v. Connor,* 490 U.S. 386, 109 S.Ct. 1865. The U.S. Supreme Court held:

> . . . Today we make explicit what was implicit in *Garner's* analysis, and hold that *all* claims that law enforcement officers have used excessive force—deadly or not—in the course of an arrest, investigatory stop, or other "seizure" of a free citizen should be analyzed under the Fourth Amendment and its "reasonableness" standard, rather than under a "substantive due process" approach. Because the Fourth Amendment provides an explicit textual source of constitutional protection against this sort of physically intrusive governmental conduct, that Amendment, not the more generalized notion of "substantive due process," must be the guide for analyzing these claims.
>
> Determining whether the force used to effect a particular seizure is "reasonable" under the Fourth Amendment requires a careful balancing of " 'the nature and quality

"Brutality begins when resistance ends."—Police Chief Walker of Jackson, Mississippi.

of the intrusion on the individual's Fourth Amendment interests'" against the countervailing governmental interests at stake. *Id.,* at 8, 105 S.Ct., at 1699, quoting *United States v. Place,* 462 U.S. 696, 703, (1983). Our Fourth Amendment jurisprudence has long recognized that the right to make an arrest or investigatory stop necessarily carries with it the right to use some degree of physical coercion or threat thereof to effect it. Because "[t]he test of reasonableness under the Fourth Amendment is not capable of precise definition or mechanical application," *Bell v. Wolfish,* 441 U.S. 520, 559, (1979), however, its proper application requires careful attention to the facts and circumstances of each particular case, including the severity of the crime at issue, whether the suspect poses an immediate threat to the safety of the officers or others, and whether he is actively resisting arrest or attempting to evade arrest by flight. See *Tennessee v. Garner,* 471 U.S., at 8–9, 105 S.Ct., at 1699–1700 (the question is "whether the totality of the circumstances justifie[s] a particular sort of . . . seizure").

The "reasonableness" of a particular use of force must be judged from the perspective of a reasonable officer on the scene, rather than with the 20/20 vision of hindsight. The Fourth Amendment is not violated by an arrest based on probable cause, even though the wrong person is arrested, *Hill v. California,* 401 U.S. 797, (1971), nor by the mistaken execution of a valid search warrant on the wrong premises, *Maryland v. Garrison,* 480 U.S. 79, (1987). With respect to a claim of excessive force, the same standard of reasonableness at the moment applies: "Not every push or shove, even if it may later seem unnecessary in the peace of a judge's chambers," *Johnson v. Glick,* 481 F.2d, at 1033, violates the Fourth Amendment. The calculus of reasonableness must embody allowance for the fact that police officers are often forced to make split-second judgments—in circumstances that are tense, uncertain, and rapidly evolving—about the amount of force that is necessary in a particular situation.

* * *

Deadly Force by a Law Enforcement Officer in Making an Arrest

Deadly force is force that is likely to cause death or serious bodily injury. The law regarding the use of deadly force in making an arrest varies somewhat from state to state. Police department regulations also vary in the language used to regulate and instruct officers as to the use of deadly force. State laws and police regulations must conform, however, to the requirements established by the U.S. Supreme Court in the 1985 case of *Tennessee v. Garner:*

TENNESSEE v. GARNER
Supreme Court of the United States (1985) 471 U.S. 1, 105 S.Ct. 1694

* * *

At about 10:45 p.m. on October 3, 1974, Memphis Police Officers Elton Hymon and Leslie Wright were dispatched to answer a "prowler inside call." Upon arriving at the scene they saw a woman standing on her porch and gesturing toward the adjacent house. She told them she had heard glass breaking and that "they" or "someone" was breaking in next door. While Wright radioed the dispatcher to say that they were on the scene, Hymon went behind the house. He heard a door slam and saw someone run across the backyard. The fleeing suspect, Edward Garner, stopped at a six-foot-high chain link fence at the edge of the yard. With the aid of a flashlight, Hymon was able to see Garner's face and hands. He saw no sign of a weapon, and, though not certain, was "reasonably sure" and "figured" that Garner was unarmed.... He thought Garner was seventeen or eighteen years old and about 5'5" or 5'7" tall. While Garner was crouched at the base of the fence, Hymon called out "police, halt" and took a few steps toward him. Garner then began to climb over the fence. Convinced that if Garner made it over the fence he would elude capture, Hymon shot him. The bullet hit Garner in the back of the head. Garner was taken by ambulance to a hospital, where he died on the operating table. Ten dollars and a purse from the house were found on his body.

In using deadly force to prevent the escape, Hymon was acting under the authority of a Tennessee statute and pursuant to police department policy. The statute provides that "[i]f, after notice of the intention to arrest the defendant, he either flee or forcibly resist, the officer may use all the necessary means to effect the arrest." Tenn. Code Ann. § 40–7–108 (1982). The department policy was slightly more restrictive than the statute, but still allowed the use of deadly force in cases of burglary. The incident was reviewed by the Memphis Police Firearm's Review Board and presented to a grand jury. Neither took any action.

Garner's father then brought this action in the Federal District Court for the Western District of Tennessee, seeking damages under 42 U.S.C. § 1983 for asserted violations of Garner's constitutional rights. The complaint alleged that the shooting violated the Fourth, Fifth, Sixth, Eighth, and Fourteenth Amendments of the United States Constitution.

* * *

The federal Court of Appeals held

> *[T]he killing of a fleeing suspect is a "seizure" under the Fourth Amendment, and is therefore constitutional only if "reasonable." The Tennessee statute failed as applied to this case because it did not adequately limit the use of deadly force by distinguishing between felonies of different magnitudes—"the facts, as found, did not justify the use of deadly force under the Fourth Amendment." Officers cannot resort to deadly force unless they "have probable cause ... to believe that the suspect*

[has committed a felony and] poses a threat to the safety of the officers or a danger to the community if left at large."

The U.S. Supreme Court affirmed the Court of Appeals' conclusion that "the facts, as found, did not justify the use of deadly force" and further held:

* * *

While we agree that burglary is a serious crime, we cannot agree that it is so dangerous as automatically to justify the use of deadly force. The FBI classifies burglary as a "property" rather than a "violent" crime. See Federal Bureau of Investigation, Uniform Crime Reports, Crime in the United States 1 (1984). Although the armed burglar would present a different situation, the fact that an unarmed suspect has broken into a dwelling at night does not automatically mean he is physically dangerous. This case demonstrates as much.... In fact, the available statistics demonstrate that burglaries only rarely involve physical violence. During the 10-year period from 1973–1982, only 3.8% of all burglaries involved violent crime.

What Is an "Unreasonable Seizure" Today in the United States?

An "unreasonable seizure" would occur if deadly force were used by law enforcement officers or private persons under any of the following circumstances:

1. Deadly force may never be used to make the arrest or to prevent the escape of a person who has committed a misdemeanor.

EXAMPLE: Deadly force should not be used to catch a "prowler" seen in someone's backyard in the middle of the night or to halt a shoplifter who has taken a $75 item and cannot be apprehended in any other way.

2. Deadly force should never be used on mere suspicion.

EXAMPLE: In 1965, two New Orleans police officers fired at an automobile they were chasing because they suspected that the vehicle had been stolen. Mere suspicion does not justify the use of deadly force, and while "fleeing from an officer" is a felony in many instances, it would not justify the use of deadly force as it ordinarily is a nonviolent offense.[13]

EXAMPLE: Late on a hot summer night, a woman is heard screaming and a man runs out from between two houses and down the street. The man does not stop when ordered to stop by a police officer. The "rookie" officer (who is now a high ranking police officer) had the good sense not to shoot. When the man did stop, the officer found that the man was a boyfriend of the woman who got fresh with his girlfriend causing her to scream. The officer told that he woke up in a cold sweat a number of nights thinking what would have happened had he used his revolver in this situation.

3. Deadly force may never be used by law enforcement officers to arrest or prevent the escape of a person who has committed a nonviolent felony.

EXAMPLE: Deadly force cannot be used to apprehend and catch a burglar *(Tennessee v. Garner)*. Burglary is one of the most frequent felonies committed in the United States. Other nonviolent felonies include thefts (vehicles and other valuables), embezzlement, fraud, white-collar crimes, etc.

Current Controversy

Should States Legalize Shooting at Fleeing Burglars?

More than 3 million burglaries are committed in the United States every year, making burglary one of the most frequently committed felonies. As burglary is a nonviolent felony, shooting at a fleeing burglar in most states would result in criminal charges against the shooter. In addition, the shooter could lose his or her home, car, and all assets in a civil lawsuit.

In the 1988 case of *People v. Gilmore,* 203 Cal. App.3d 612, 249 Cal. Rptr. 914, 43 CrL 2373, Gilmore (a private citizen) cornered a man attempting to burglarize Gilmore's home. When the man ran, Gilmore fired four bullets in the direction of the fleeing burglar. One bullet ricocheted off the asphalt and a fragment of it struck the burglar in the back of the neck, killing him instantly. Gilmore was charged and convicted of manslaughter, but a California Court of Appeals reversed the conviction, distinguishing this case from *Tennessee v. Garner* in that:

1) The U.S. Supreme Court held in *Tennessee v. Garner* that shooting of the fleeing burglar by a police officer violated the Fourth Amendment. It is well established law that the Fourth Amendment applies only to government (police officers and other government officials) and does not apply to private citizens (Gilmore).

2) Homicide is deemed justified under California law "(w)hen necessarily committed in attempting, by lawful ways and means, to apprehend any person for any felony committed ..." (California Penal Code, Sec. 197(4)). Gilmore had ordered the man to "freeze" two or three times. The Court held that the felony "was a forcible and atrocious crime ... and the homicide was justified under (Sec. 197(4)) ...".

Should other states enact legislation following the precedent established in the California case of *People v. Gilmore?*

Arguments for following the Gilmore *case*

As the clearance rate for burglary is very low, it would not only deter burglary but would increase the number of burglary cases solved.

The system now not only victimizes persons like Gilmore by convicting them of a felony, but also makes them subject to a civil lawsuit where they could lose everything they have plus future earnings.

Arguments against following the Gilmore *case*

To legalize the shooting of a fleeing burglar is vigilantism and imposes the death penalty for a nonviolent offense. Allowing private persons to enforce the law is dangerous. With the increased use of firearms, innocent persons are going to be shot.

Occupants of homes have enough protection under present law. They should be limited in the use of deadly force to situations where there is a real and immediate threat of death or great bodily harm to themselves or others.

When seeking to apprehend a "fleeing felon," deadly force could lawfully be used in self-defense or the defense of another if the situation justifies such force. Deadly force could also be used when officers "have probable cause ... to believe that the suspect (has committed a felony and) poses a threat to the safety of the officers or a danger to the community if left at large." *Tennessee v. Garner.*

⚖ Does a Choke Hold Constitute Deadly Force?

In 1982, the choke-hold case of *Lyons v. City of Los Angeles* came before the U.S. Supreme Court. Lyons alleged that after a traffic stop, Los Angeles police officers rendered him unconscious and damaged his larynx by applying a choke hold (either the "bar-arm control" hold, the "carotid-artery control" hold, or both).

Lyons alleged that there had been seventeen deaths that were related to the use of the choke hold. As a result of the allegations, the Los Angeles chief of police prohibited the use of the bar-arm choke hold under any circumstances.[14] The federal district court in Los Angeles issued a preliminary injunction against the use of choke holds under circumstances in which there is no threat to life or of serious bodily injury. The U.S. Supreme Court held that federal courts did not have jurisdiction to grant the injunction that Lyons requested.

In 1983, at least twelve civil damage lawsuits were pending against the Los Angeles Police Department, alleging that persons were injured or died as a result of choke holds by officers. The plaintiff in the case of *Avery v. City of Los Angeles* (Sup.Ct., Los Angeles Co., 1983) received an award of $750,000 for injuries resulting from a choke hold. The family of a man who died as a result of a bar-arm choke hold received $500,000 in the case of *Nethery v. City of Chicago* (Cir.Ct., Cook Co., # 81 C2911, 1983).

An article entitled "Physiological Effects Resulting from Use of Neck Holds," in the July 1983 *FBI Law Enforcement Bulletin,* concludes:

> Because of the organs involved, neck holds must be considered potentially lethal whenever applied. Officers using this hold should have proper training in its use and effects. Police officers should have continual inservice training and practice in the use of the carotid sleeper. They should not use or be instructed in the use of the choke hold other than to demonstrate its potential lethal effect. Officers should recognize that death can result if the carotid sleeper is incorrectly applied.

Can Force Be Used to Resist an Unlawful Arrest?

Under the old common law, a person had a legal right to forcibly resist an unlawful arrest. This rule developed hundreds of years ago in England, when safeguards did not exist to protect a person from unlawful arrest. Today, many safeguards exist, and the old rule has been changed by court decisions and statutes in many states. California Penal Code, Section 834a, and Connecticut Statute, Section 53a–23, are examples of such statutes. The Connecticut statute is as follows: "A person is not justified in using physical force to resist an arrest by a reasonably identifiable police officer, whether such arrest is legal or illegal."

Some states, however, retain the old rule. The Maryland Court of Appeals held that "one illegally arrested may use any reasonable means to effect his escape, even to the extent of using force."[15]

In a 1983 case, the Supreme Judicial Court of Massachusetts held that if an officer uses "excessive or unnecessary force to subdue the arrestee," then "regardless of whether the arrest is lawful or unlawful, the arrestee may defend himself by employing such force as reasonably appears to be necessary." But the court held that:

> In the absence of excessive or unnecessary force by an arresting officer, a person may not use force to resist an arrest by one who he knows or has good reason to believe is an authorized police officer, engaged in the performance of his duties, regardless of whether the arrest was unlawful in the circumstances.[16]

Uses of Deadly Force and Less Than Deadly Force

Situation	Less than Deadly Force	Deadly Force
In self-defense or the defense of others	"The use of (reasonable) force upon or toward another person is justified when the actor (reasonably) believes that such force is immediately necessary for the purpose of protecting himself or herself (or another) against the use of unlawful force by such other person on the present occasion."[a]	"The use of deadly force is not justified ... unless such force is necessary to protect ... against death, serious bodily harm, kidnapping, or sexual intercourse compelled by force or threat."[b]
In the defense of property	"Only such degree of force or threat thereof may intentionally be used as the actor reasonably believes is necessary to prevent or terminate the interference."[c]	Under the old common law, deadly force could be used in the defense of property. All states now forbid the use of intentional deadly force in the defense of property.
To apprehend a person who has committed a crime	"When an officer is making or attempting to make an arrest for a criminal offense, he is acting for the protection of public interest and is permitted even a greater latitude than when he acts in self-defense, and he is not liable unless the means which he uses are clearly excessive."[d]	*Misdemeanor* NEVER *Fleeing Felon* Deadly force could be used when officers "have probable cause ... to believe that the suspect (has committed a felony and) poses a threat to the safety of the officers or a danger to the community if left at large." *Tennessee v. Garner*

The "proper application (of what is reasonable) requires careful attention to the facts and circumstances of each particular case, including the severity of the crime at issue, whether the suspect poses an immediate threat to the safety of the officers or others, and whether he is actively resisting arrest or attempting to evade arrest by flight." U.S. Supreme Court in *Graham v. Connor*

Situation	Less than Deadly Force	Deadly Force
To stop a person for investigative purposes when only a "reasonable suspicion" exists	Only reasonable force under the circumstances that then exist when necessary.	NEVER
Disciplining children (corporal punishment)	Only parents and other persons having a status of *in loco parentis* to a child may use reasonable force "reasonably believed to be necessary for (the child's) proper control, training, or education."[e] Other persons (strangers, neighbors, etc.) may not discipline a child.	NEVER

[a] Section 3.04(1) and 3.05(1) of the Model Penal Code.
[b] Section 3.04(2)(b) of the Model Penal Code.
[c] Section 939.49(1) of the Wisconsin Statutes.
[d] Restatement of Torts, Section 132(a).
[e] Restatement of Torts, Section 147(2), as quoted by the U.S. Supreme Court in *Ingraham v. Wright,* 429 U.S. 975, 97 S.Ct. 481, (1976).

Unlawful Force by Police

Founding Father James Madison warned in *The Federalist Papers* over two hundred years ago that "men are not angels." The truth of this statement was made apparent by two events that occurred in March 1991.

Late one night in Los Angeles, local residents heard the sounds of a motorist being stopped for speeding. Seventeen police officers were observed watching four other police officers beat and kick a prone, unarmed, black man. One resident videotaped the action. The videotape was presented to a Los Angeles television station and the scene was repeatedly shown throughout the United States. The images of uniformed officers beating a helpless man lying on the ground caused reactions of shock, disbelief, and anger.

In London, six Irish men jailed for sixteen years were released when the British government admitted that confessions obtained from the men were discredited because they were obtained by the use of illegal force. The arrests of the six men followed the 1974 bombings of two Birmingham pubs in which twenty-one people were killed. When the confessions and other evidence used to convict the six men were discredited, the men were released.

Pictures of the six men being released from prison in London and videotapes of the Los Angeles police beatings were seen throughout the world in newspapers and on television. Four of the Los Angeles officers were indicted on felony charges.

The City of Los Angeles acknowledged that in 1989 it had paid more than $6.3 million in jury awards and settlements in response to complaints of police brutality. The 1990 figure was reported to be more than $8 million in awards and settlements. (*New York Times* 3/15/91 article "Police Brutality Under Wide Review by US Justice Department.")

The president of the American Police Foundation commented, "I believe that there are more incidents of police use of force because of the volatility of the big cities, the violence, and the big guns the police are up against."

One month after the beating of the motorist by Los Angeles police officers, police chiefs from many American cities met in New York City for a one-day conference on police brutality.

Their host, New York City Police Commissioner Lee P. Brown, stated, "The problem of excessive force in American policing is real. It is, in part, related to the nature of the difficult challenge faced by the police in our urban centers. Regardless of its cause, it cannot be condoned and must be actively countered by police professionals."

The chiefs condemned the use of excessive force and stated they were outraged by the police beating of the Los Angeles motorist that was videotaped and seen nationally. They asked the federal government to develop a system for gathering information on the use of excessive police force and to pay for research in police use of force. (See the 4/17/91 *New York Times* article entitled "Police Chiefs Call for U.S. System to Gather Data on Excessive Force.")

D. Does the Use of Handcuffs Amount to Excessive or Unreasonable Force?[17]

When an Arrest Is Made

Courts have generally upheld the use of handcuffs when an arrest is made. In the 1983 case of *Healy v. City of Brentwood,* the Missouri Court of Appeals, in pointing out that there is always an element of danger in making an arrest, held:

When Private Persons Go Beyond The Law ("Vigilantism")

There are an increasing number of reports nationally of private persons going beyond the law in reacting to situations confronting them or their neighborhoods. Persons who violate the law run the risk of being charged criminally and also having a civil law suit filed against them for compensatory and punitive damages. The following incidents serve to illustrate:

Burning Out Crack Dealers: Two long-time residents of a Detroit neighborhood admitted to police in 1988 that they set fires to rid their neighborhood of crack dealers. The first time they torched a house being used to sell and distribute crack, firemen put the fire out before the house was extensively damaged. When the drug activity recommenced again a few days later, the two neighbors torched the house a second time but in a manner that gutted the house before firemen arrived. One of the men stated, "We just took the house out of commission. We have had no problems since then." Use of similar unlawful tactics against drug dealers have been reported in other cities throughout the USA.

Protecting Children from Pimps and Junkies: A Roman Catholic priest told of his efforts to protect children against pimps and junkies trying to recruit children for drugs and prostitution. Rev. Bruce Ritter tells of methods he used a number of years ago in his book, *Covenant House: Lifeline to the Street* (Doubleday, 1987). "I would hire some friends for $50 to break into their (junkies) apartment, steal their clothes, steal the furniture and remove the plumbing. I took over a dozen apartments that way." Father Ritter's book points out that he no longer breaks the law to protect children. He has opened shelters for children in New York, Houston, Fort Lauderdale, Toronto, and Guatemala, all under the name Covenant House.

Carrying Concealed Weapons: Every day in cities throughout the United States, private persons tell police officers, prosecutors, and judges why they violated the law by carrying a concealed weapon in their purse or pocket. "I needed it to protect myself," they say, or "I don't get off work until midnight and I live in an unsafe neighborhood." Reports also show that 60% of American homes have a weapon in the residence (lawful in many cities and counties).

Bernard Goetz and the New York Subway Shooting: After Bernard Goetz was robbed a second time in New York subways, he commenced to illegally carry a concealed gun.[a] In 1984, when Goetz believed that he was going to be violently attacked by four young men who approached him on a subway train, Goetz pulled out his pistol and shot each of the men. Two New York grand juries concluded that the shootings were justified, but Goetz was charged and convicted of the felony of illegally carrying a concealed pistol. Goetz was sentenced to one year in jail and five years probation. Goetz was sued for total of $63 million in civil lawsuits filed by three of the men.

The Guardian Angels and the Police: The Guardian Angels are a voluntary group of mostly young persons who conduct anticrime patrols. There have been very few instances where they have had difficulty with local police. In 1988, owners of restaurants in "Restaurant Row" located near the theater district in New York City invited the "Angels" to patrol their neighborhood. The restaurant owners said that business had declined because of crack trade in their neighborhood. In one incident in the following days, there was a wild street fight between a group of Guardian Angels and another group of men. A sixteen-year-old Guardian Angel from New Jersey was taken to a hospital with stab wounds in his chest and head. A day later, two members of the voluntary patrol group were arrested for menacing and harassing a man in the area. The police pointed out that mere suspicion to believe a person on the street is a drug dealer does not justify verbally harassing the person or asking that person to leave the neighborhood. A high ranking New York officer stated, "Even the police have no right to tell someone to get off the block." After the two incidents, the neighborhood became very peaceful, with the voluntary anticrime patrols continuing for some time.

---

[a] Goetz had applied for a permit to carry a pistol under New York law but his application was refused. There are a number of books and many articles written about Bernard Goetz and the subway shooting. One of them is entitled *A CRIME OF SELF-DEFENSE: Bernard Goetz and the Law on Trial* by law professor George Fletcher (New York: The Free Press, 1983).

> Police officers face serious risks every time they carry out an arrest. Sometimes the most inoffensive appearing individuals turn out to be uncharacteristically violent. A police officer who is proceeding to convey any prisoner to a police headquarters in a police vehicle should not be faced with a civil lawsuit because he takes the precaution to handcuff the prisoner to prevent her from causing trouble on the way to headquarters.[18]

Healy was arrested after a computer check showed that she had an outstanding warrant for an unpaid fine. She did not resist the arrest by a female police officer. It was later discovered that the fine had been paid and that a mistake had been made. The St. Louis County Police Department encouraged the use of handcuffs in all arrests.

When an Investigative Stop Is Made

Courts have held that when circumstances justify the use of handcuffs during an investigative stop, their use would be held reasonable. The Supreme Court of Washington sustained such use in the 1987 case of *State v. Wheeler* (737 P.2d 1005). It was also sustained in the case of *United States v. Bautista* (684 F.2d 1286) and by the Colorado Supreme Court in the 1983 case of *People v. Weeams* (33 CrL 2358). The Colorado Supreme Court cited *People v. Johnson,*[19] where police made an investigative stop in an attempt to apprehend armed robbers and murderers. The court held:

> The extended intrusion under the narrow circumstances of this case . . . is justified due to the fact that two armed robberies just occurred in a residential neighborhood, with the second robbery resulting in the death of one victim and serious injury to another. The suspects stopped by the police were reportedly armed with a sawed-off shotgun and other weapons, and the stop took place late at night in a deserted area.

Bernard Goetz (left) arrives at court before being sentenced to one year in jail and fined $5,000 in 1989 for the possession of an unlicensed gun. Members of the Guardian Angels (right), including leader Curtis Sliwa (far left) protect Goetz's apartment in 1984.

When weighed against the exigencies of the situation confronting the officers, it was not unreasonable to handcuff the defendant to ensure the safety of the officers.

In Transporting Mental Patients

Some mental patients are elderly; others are small or weak; still others are strong and capable of committing desperate and dangerous acts. The question whether all or some mental patients can be handcuffed was presented to the Attorney General of Wisconsin. His opinion, dated 5 November 1982, stated:

> Clearly, a police officer may use reasonable force to maintain custody over an individual facing an involuntary commitment hearing. But, if no force is necessary, then any force at all is unreasonable. Under the circumstances ... I equate the use of physical restraints with the use of physical force. Therefore, the automatic or universal use of handcuffs or other restraints amounts to an unreasonable use of force where no restraint is required.

Handcuffing all mental patients, whether weak or strong, would be unreasonable. Using handcuffs where there is a reason to be concerned for safety would be justified and reasonable.

E. DISCIPLINING CHILDREN

Use of Force by Parents

Under the old common law parents, and persons who take the place of parents *(in loco parentis),* have a natural right to the custody, care, and control of their children. They have a duty to provide food, clothing, shelter, and medical care to the children and to educate and discipline them. A parent or a person *in loco parentis* may use a reasonable amount of force in disciplining a child. However, if the force is excessive, the parent or person *in loco parentis* may be charged criminally. How much force or discipline is reasonable would be determined in view of the child's age and sex; the physical, emotional, and mental condition of the child; the child's conduct that prompted the punishment; the degree of the force used or the methods used to inflict the punishment; and the resulting injury or the effect that the punishment had on the child.

The question as to what amount of force is reasonable was presented to the Texas Court of Appeals (Houston) in the 1987 case of *Teubner v. State.*[20] The court held:

* * *

> Texas Penal Code section 9.61 permits the use of force against a child under a "reasonable belief" standard. However, force going beyond that which is necessary for discipline is prohibited. The question in this case is whether the appellants reasonably believed their use of force was necessary to discipline their child.
>
> From the evidence presented, no reasonable person could possibly believe the conduct was justifiable. The child was subjected to a savage beating with a leather belt on two successive nights. On the first night, Victoria Teubner took over the whipping when her husband tired himself. On the second night, they gagged their daughter to stifle her crying. The photographs admitted into evidence offer a grim record of the

effects of the beating. The appellants could not have reasonably believed that the degree of force used was necessary for disciplinary purposes. Appellants' second point of error is overruled.

***

Who Besides Parents May Discipline Children?

Besides the parents, any person taking the place of the parents and thus classified as *in loco parentis* may reasonably discipline a child in his or her care. This category includes legal guardians, foster parents, and public school teachers.

Because of the threats of lawsuits and pressure from anti-paddling groups, twenty states have forbidden corporal punishment in public schools within those states. In the thirty states that continue to permit corporal punishment, many school boards forbid or limit the use of corporal punishment of students within the school district. The common law remains the same, and in 1977 the U.S. Supreme Court held in the case of *Ingraham v. Wright* [21] that at common law, "a teacher may impose reasonable but not excessive force to discipline a child." The U.S. Supreme Court noted:

> Where the legislatures have not acted, the state courts have uniformly preserved the common law rule permitting teachers to use reasonable force in disciplining children in their charge.

Law enforcement officers, neighbors, and other adults who see children misbehave may not discipline a child (or children), although they may use reasonable force to prevent damage to property or injury to other persons or themselves. In chapter 10, reference is made to an actual incident in which a sixty-five-year-old man spanked an eight-year-old boy who made an obscene gesture to the man after the man reprimanded the boy for using vulgar language on a public street. The prosecutor did not charge the man with battery, as the boy's mother demanded, but the man was told that he had no right or privilege to discipline other people's children.

Reasonable force to maintain order (as distinguished from discipline) may be used by personnel on airplanes, ships, trains, or buses and by ushers for theaters,

---

Current Controversy

Should public school teachers be allowed to spank unruly students?

Is the old saying "Spare the rod and spoil the child" correct or incorrect? States and school boards can determine whether public school teachers are allowed to spank unruly students. Thirty states permit spanking in public schools, and the United States Supreme Court has refused to bar corporal punishment. The issue was again brought to the public attention by the following exchange:

For Spanking of Unruly Children

Mayor Sharon Pratt Dixon of Washington, D.C.: "I think that kind of authority needs to be restored starting at the earliest possible age. Young people respond to discipline."

Against Spanking in Public Schools

Washington, D.C., Teachers Union: "Violence begets violence."

What Private Persons May Do In Protecting Themselves and Others Against Crime

Private persons may take actions within the law in protecting themselves and others against criminal and unlawful acts.

Type of Action	Law Governing Action
Force in self-defense or the defense of others	Force in self-protection or protection of another may be used: a) when ***immediately necessary*** for protection, b) against ***unlawful*** force or conduct, c) and the amount of force is ***reasonable*** under the circumstances. See your State Statute (# _____) and this chapter.
Using force to protect property	State statutes often limit property that may be protected to your property, property of your family or employer, or where there is a legal duty to protect property. There must be: a) an ***unlawful*** interference with the property, b) the force must be ***necessary,*** and c) the amount of force must be ***reasonable*** under the existing circumstances. Deadly force may *NEVER* be used to defend only property, and there should be a prior request to desist as required by the Model Penal Code. See your State Statute (# _____) and this chapter.
Citizen arrest, detaining or holding a person seen committing a crime	As the law governing private person arrests, detentions, and holding in custody varies from state to state, consult your state statutes and your legal adviser. *Unlawful Conduct:* In 1988, a crowd attacked and killed a known drug dealer who had robbed a woman of $20 on a street in Harlem, New York.
Hundreds of neighborhood and community groups have come into existence in every state in a growing movement of citizens against crime and drugs.	Some of the many groups are: Citywide Anti-crime Coalitions, Block Watch organizations, Take Back the Night groups, Neighborhood Watch groups, MADD (Mothers Against Drunk Drivers), NFPDFY (National Federation of Parents for Drug-Free Youth), WAP (Women Against Pornography), SMART (Stop Marketing Alcohol on Radio and Television), Anti-Crack Patrols, Crime Stopper groups, which offer rewards for information and anonymous tips, and many other groups. *Questionable Tactic:* It was reported that private persons in New York would pretend to be drug buyers, and then, after receiving drugs, would make citizen's arrests. It was also reported that police generally did not try to stop this type of undercover buying and seizing of drugs.
Commencing a civil lawsuit or small claims action against offender (if known)	Most crimes give the victim the basis for filing a civil lawsuit or small claims action against the offender (if known). Burdens of proof are lower in civil courts. The problems are: (a) identifying the offender, and (b) being able to collect damages. Many states have statutes authorizing lawsuits against parents of juveniles who cause property damage or injury.

sporting events, and other public gatherings. A disorderly child or person may be ordered to leave if he or she is disturbing other persons or has failed to pay the fare or admission fee. The test, again, is that of reasonability. Did the provocation justify the action taken? Was the force reasonable under the circumstances? The Supreme Court of Minnesota held in 1885 that it was not reasonable to force a passenger off a moving train because he had not paid his fare.[22]

Questions and Problems for Chapter 6

Should the persons in the following actual cases be charged with a crime? Indicate what the charge should be (if any) in view of the laws of your jurisdiction and the material presented in this chapter. Give reasons for your answers, citing, wherever possible, statutes of your jurisdiction.

1. In Long Beach, California, a nineteen-year-old woman who was raped by two men invited them to a return date, at which time she killed one with a shotgun while the other man fled. The men had released the woman after raping her when she promised not to call the police and to agree to another meeting.

2. In Alexandria, Virginia, a sixty-two-year-old retired army colonel was awakened just after midnight by someone rattling the chain lock on his bedroom door. When the noise stopped, the colonel took a pistol and went into the hall to investigate. In the dim light, he saw two men coming toward him from another room. He fired at them and fatally wounded two burglars. When police officers arrived, they found that the burglars were not armed and had in their possession only a large screwdriver and money taken from the house.

3. In Massachusetts, a divorced woman got into a quarrel with her fiancé. He threatened to kill her and her two young children. She ran to the basement of her home, where her children were watching television, and obtained her former husband's rifle. Five minutes after the quarrel, her fiancé came down the steps and the woman shot and killed him. Her fiancé had no weapons in his possession. (*Commonwealth v. Shaffer,* 367 Mass. 508, 326 N.E.2d 880 [1975]).

4. In Tennessee, a man caught a window peeper looking into his sister's window at night. The window peeper ran away, although he was ordered by the man to stay where he was. The man shot and killed the fleeing window peeper, who was also an adult male.

5. In Wisconsin, an older man was shocked by the vulgar language of three small boys. When he reprimanded the boys for their language, the oldest boy, who was eight, made an obscene

gesture to the man with his finger, with words accompanying the gesture. The angry man chased the boy and gave the boy a spanking, which the man stated the boy deserved.

6. In Minnesota, the owner of a car chased a twenty-eight-year-old man who broke into his car and stole $150 in goods. The car owner shot the burglar in the foot, causing him to walk with a limp for the rest of his life. In Denver, Colorado, a store owner shot a fleeing burglar in the back, paralyzing him for life. The burglar, who was fourteen years old, was on a beer-drinking spree with other boys and broke into the store to obtain more beer to continue the party.

7. When a speeder would not stop, a high-speed chase took place. The motorist was clocked at 103 mph. Police lights and sirens did not stop the speeder and she was forced off the highway. One of the officers opened the car door and repeatedly requested her to get out of the car. The woman was forcibly pulled from the car when she refused the repeated requests. In a civil lawsuit, she asks for monetary relief because of alleged neck and back injuries received when she was "yanked" out of the car. What are the tests to determine whether the police used lawful force in removing the woman from the car? (*Clark v. Department of Public Safety,* 431 So.2d 83 [La. App. 1983]).

8. While having coffee in a crowded cafeteria, two students became involved in a heated argument. Student A (a very small man) angrily attacked Student B (a very large man). B easily defended himself and then grabbed A and forced him backward, knocking over four tables, many chairs, and many cups of coffee. A school security guard positioned himself between the two men in an attempt to stop the disturbance. B then charged the security guard to get at A and pushed

the security guard backward until other students assisted in subduing B. State who is at fault in this situation and what conduct was lawful. State the law that is applicable to this situation.

9. After the 1991 Gulf War, General Norman Schwarzkopf ("Stormin Norman") was interviewed at his Saudi Arabian headquarters for the ABC program "20/20." During the interview, Barbara Walters asked the general about returning Vietnam soldiers being spit upon by civilians and whether he had ever been spit on. General Schwarzkopf, who had served three tours of duty in the Vietnam theater, acknowledged that he had heard stories of returning military personnel being spit upon but emphatically stated that nobody had or was ever going to spit upon him.

If force can be used to prevent being spit upon, what are the legal limits of force that could be used? Could force be used to punish a person who attempted to spit on you?

Notes

1. When cases go before a criminal court, most states place the burden of proving there was no justification for the force (such as self-defense) upon the state. The U.S. Supreme Court pointed out in the 1987 case of *Martin v. Ohio*, 480 U.S. 228, 107 S.Ct. 1098 that only two states continue to follow the old common law "that affirmative defenses, including self-defense, were matters for the defendant to prove." Forty-eight states require "the prosecution to prove the absence of self-defense when it is properly raised by the defendant." Ohio and South Carolina continue to follow the old common law rule. The Supreme Court held that the rule used in Ohio and South Carolina is constitutional. The Court pointed out that "the Constitution (does not) require the prosecution to prove the sanity of a defendant who pleads not guilty by reason of insanity."

2. 11 N.Y.2d 274, 229 N.Y.S.2d 1, 183 N.E.2d 319 (1962).

3. Two dissenting judges urged that the case be sent back to the trial court for a determination as to whether the degree of force used by Young was reasonable under the circumstances.

4. 52 Md. App. 171, 447 A.2d 880, 31 CrL 2371 (1982).

5. Although there is no legal duty to retreat (flee) from a person who is larger and stronger, in most instances, retreat (if possible) would be practical and sensible.

6. Florida holds that a spouse must retreat (if practical) before using deadly force, but this rule does not apply to a "live-in" who was held to be an "invitee on the premises" as distinguished from a "legal co-occupant." This view is likely to change in view of the large number of nonmarried persons living together. Also, both parties in many instances contribute to the rent and utilities.

7. 415 So.2d 724, 31 CrL 2371 (Fla. 1982). See also *Rippie v. State*, 404 So.2d 160 (Fla. App. 1981), in which the Florida District Court of Appeal pointed out that "often when one party to an argument or fight leaves the room, the other party tends to calm down, become more rational and escalation of the dispute is avoided."

8. *Florida Standard Jury Instruction* (Crim.) 2d ed. p. 64. In the 1990 case of *State v. Herriges*, 155 Wis. 2d 297, 455 N.W.2d 635, the Wisconsin Court of Appeals reviewed the law as to the duty to retreat as follows:

* * *

Some states impose a duty to take reasonable measures to retreat as a limitation on the privilege of self-defense. See, e.g., Collier v. State, 49 Ala.App. 685, 275 So.2d 364, 367 (1973); Gainer v. State, 40 Md.App. 382, 391 A.2d 856, 860 (1978). The duty has often been modified by the rule that those assaulted in their own homes may stand their ground without losing the privilege of self-defense. Justice Cardozo's poignant explanation for the rule is set out in Gainer: "It is not now and never has been the law that a man assailed in his own dwelling is bound to retreat. If assailed there, he may stand his ground and resist the attack. He is under no duty to take to the fields and the highways, a fugitive from his own home. . . . Whither shall he flee, and how far, and when may he be permitted to return?" Gainer, 391 A.2d at 862.

The castle rule recognizes the importance of home as sanctuary but it is not without limits. The doctrine is for defensive and not offensive purposes. The rule is therefore almost invariably recited as requiring that the one seeking to invoke it be without fault. See, e.g., Annotation, Homicide: Duty to Retreat Where Assailant is Social Guest on Premises, 100 A.L.R.3d 532, 533, and cases cited therein; see also Conley v. State, 38 Ala.App. 618, 92 So.2d 7, 9 (1956); State v. Sales, 285 S.C. 113, 328 S.E.2d 619, 620 (1985); People v. Mroue, 111 Mich.App. 759, 315 N.W.2d 192, 194 (1981); see also 40 Am.Jur.2d Homicide sec. 167 (1968): "[W]hile a person assaulted in his own house is not bound to retreat, his right to invoke this doctrine depends upon his being without fault in bringing on the difficulty."

Wisconsin has no statutory duty requiring a reasonable attempt to retreat, although whether the opportunity to retreat was available is sometimes a circumstance for consideration in determining whether the defendant reasonably believed the amount of force used was necessary to prevent or terminate the interference. Wis.J I—Criminal 810. Our supreme court expressly abrogated the common law duty to retreat in Miller v. State, *139 Wis. 57, 76, 119 N.W. 850, 858 (1909). The legislature, however, requires reasonable effort to retreat before self-defense can be successfully asserted by one who acts to provoke an attack.*

* * *

9. See the 2/2/91 *New York Times* article "More States Study Clemency for Women Who Killed Abusers."

10. *State v. Hundley,* 236 Kan. 461, 693 P.2d 475 (1985).

11. See the New York Times article "Denver Machine Shop Owner Gets Probation in Booby Trap Slaying" 8/22/90 and the 12/29/89 article "Intruder Killed by Trap in House in Burglary-Prone Area of Mobile (Alabama)". Similar incidents have occurred in cities throughout the United States. See the 1971 case of *Katko v. Briney,* 183 N.W.2d 657 (Iowa) for a further discussion of civil liability and case citations on booby traps.

In the 1960s, a man rigged a handgun booby trap to protect his mountain cottage in Colorado. Weeks later when he returned to the cottage, he entered, forgetting the booby trap, and was shot in the chest. Fortunately, the wound was not fatal.

12. See the 1989 case of *Hammer v. Gross,* 884 F.2d 1200 (9th Cir.) which is a civil lawsuit by a drunk driver who resisted submitting to chemical testing needed to obtain evidence of intoxication. In holding that the conduct of the officers was not unreasonable, the Court held:

* * *

In fact, the "force" used by Officer Zatarain in this case was nothing more than the application of physical restraint required to conduct the blood extraction in a safe and efficient manner. As the Supreme Court recently observed, "Our Fourth Amendment jurisprudence has long recognized that the right to make an arrest or investigatory stop necessarily carries with it the right to use some degree of physical coercion or threat thereof to effect it." Graham, *109 S.Ct. at 1871. We think that jurisprudence also validates the particular application of force to effectuate the search and seizure which occurred in this case.*

The Graham *Court further noted that " 'Not every push or shove, even if it may later seem unnecessary in the peace of a judge's chambers,'* Johnson v. Glick, *481 F.2d at 1033, violates the Fourth Amendment." 109 S.Ct. at 1872. Although we, like the California Supreme Court, recognize that the forcible removal of a blood sample from a DUI suspect will virtually always be "unpleasant, undignified and*

undesirable," People v. Superior Court (Hawkins), *6 Cal.3d at 764, 100 Cal.Rptr. at 286, 493 P.2d at 1150, it will not always be—and was not in this case—unconstitutional.*

Because the amount of force applied was minimal, and did not exceed the amount necessary to effect the otherwise lawful search for and seizure of blood alcohol evidence which occurred in the circumstances of this case, we hold as a matter of law that Officer Zatarain's conduct was not "unreasonable" within the meaning of the Fourth Amendment. Having thus failed to establish that he was deprived of any right secured by the Fourth Amendment, Hammer's section 1983 claims against both the individual and municipal defendants must fall.

* * *

13. *Sauls v. Hutto and Ruppert,* 304 F.Supp. 124 (E.D. La. 1969).

14. In a 1987 seminar on "Critical Issues in the Use of Deadly Force," the International Association of the Chief's of Police Coordinator Of Deadly Force Training Project commented that "bad officers" use of the chokehold technique "rendered it unavailable to all of us." The speaker pointed out that the police needed a level of restraint below the use of a gun. "Now we have to use batons, which is why the injury rates are up." (see 42 CrL 2115 11/11/87).

15. *Diehl v. State,* 294 Md. 466, 451 A.2d 115 (1982), *review denied* 460 U.S. 1098, 103 S.Ct. 1798, 33 CrL 4018 (1983).

16. *Commonwealth v. Moreira,* 388 Mass. 596, 447 N.E.2d 1224, 33 CrL 2078 (1983).

17. In the 1988 case of *Robinette v. Barnes,* 854 F.2d 909 (6th Cir.) the Court of Appeals for the 6th Circuit held that the use of a properly trained police dog to make a felony arrest was reasonable and appropriate and did not constitute the use of deadly force even though the suspect died later from dog bites received during the arrest. The dog was trained to grab a suspect's arm or the closest part of the body if the arm was not available.

The dog found the suspect hiding under a car and his neck was the only part of his body that the dog could reach. The Court held that because "the evidence establishes that there is not a substantial risk that the use of a police dog to apprehend a criminal suspect could result in the suspect's death, we are hesitant to label 'unreasonable' a police practice which has proven useful in a variety of law enforcement situations."

18. 649 S.W.2d 916 (Mo. App. 1983).

19. 199 Colo. 68, 605 P.2d 46 (1980).

20. 742 S.W.2d 57 (Tex. App. 1987).

21. 430 U.S. 651, 97 S.Ct. 1401. The common law holds that besides the parents, any person taking the place of the parents *(in loco parentis)* may reasonably discipline a child in his or her care. This category includes legal guardians, foster parents, and school teachers.

22. *State v. Kinney,* 34 Minn. 311, 25 N.W. 705 (1885).

OTHER CRIMINAL DEFENSES

(continued on next page)

A. Criminal Defenses Generally

In criminal trials, the government must prove:

1. that the crime charged has been committed (proof of corpus delicti), and
2. that the defendant was a party to that crime, either
   a. having been the person who physically committed it, or
   b. as an aider and abettor (accomplice), or
   c. as a conspirator (accomplice).

The ultimate burden of proving that a defendant committed the offense charged is always on the prosecution in a criminal case. All defendants are presumed innocent until proven guilty through evidence and witnesses produced and presented by the state. However, defendants, when faced with evidence that will convict them, often enter a guilty plea in hopes of a more lenient sentence.

The level of proof required is usually "beyond a reasonable doubt." This level of proof is the highest the law requires in any case. It means that the finder of fact must be convinced of the defendant's guilt to a moral certitude. It does not mean that the evidence must show that the defendant is guilty beyond *any* doubt; it means that he or she must be proven guilty beyond any *reasonable* doubt.

Because of the constitutional assumption of innocence, our system is deemed an accusatorial process. The accuser must bear the entire burden of sustaining the charge through competent evidence. The defendant does not have to do anything. Even if the defendant is guilty, he or she may opt to have the prosecution prove its case. The defendant does not have to remain silent or inactive. He or she may assert a number of defenses and still take advantage of the legal assumption of innocence.

Asserting Defenses by Motions

Defenses are raised by motions before, during, or after trial. The various motions that might be brought by the defense, in addition to the claim of innocence, generally fall into three main categories:

1. The court does not have jurisdiction (a) over the defendant or (b) over the offense (see chapter 9, Criminal Jurisdiction).
2. Evidence to be used against the defendant was allegedly obtained in an improper or an illegal manner.
3. The accused was compelled, privileged, or entrapped into committing the offense.

The defendant may properly use defenses described in this chapter to justify his or her conduct.

Such motions may be classified as either procedural or substantive. *Procedural motions* attack the jurisdiction of the court by alleging that some formal defect has deprived the court of its authority to proceed (e.g., the complaint on which the charge is based is defective because it fails to allege a statutory element of the crime). These motions generally are "on the record," that is, no evidence is taken and the court is asked to review whatever is challenged on the record and determine if it is sufficient.

One of the defendants in the 1984 New Bedford tavern rape trial, John Cordiero, seeks to explain where he was during the criminal incident.

Substantive motions attack the manner in which evidence was obtained. The usual claim is that some portion of the evidence essential to a successful prosecution was obtained in an impermissible manner and must therefore be suppressed. One such motion is the charge that a defendant was not properly advised of his or her constitutional rights pursuant to the Miranda formula; the statement obtained from the defendant must thus be suppressed. Substantive motions usually require the taking of testimony by the court to determine whether or not the allegations raised by the motion are true.

Motions meant to attack the jurisdiction of the court or to suppress evidence are heard before the trial begins. The outcome of such motions could affect the continuation of the proceedings. The time and manner of the hearing of such motions are generally determined by the statutes or rules of evidence of a particular state. The court is generally given wide discretion to expand time limits in order to ensure that justice is done. Categories 1 and 2 above generally fall into the arena of substantive and procedural motions usually heard before trial.

Affirmative Defenses

The third category of motions may be placed under the heading of affirmative defenses. In an affirmative defense, the defendant, in effect, admits that he or she performed the acts charged but claims a lawful excuse for doing so and thus is not guilty of a crime. When the defense chooses an affirmative defense, the defense has the obligation to submit proof that the affirmative defense is viable. The prosecution has the ultimate burden of supplying sufficient evidence to find the defendant guilty beyond a reasonable doubt despite the affirmative defense claim. There is no shifting to the defense of the ultimate burden of proof—the defendant does not have to prove innocence but does bear the burden of persuading the

Defenses and Defensive Tactics in Criminal Cases

1. Entering a plea of not guilty and (a) remaining silent or (b) taking the witness stand on one's own behalf.
2. Entering a plea of not guilty because of mental disease or defect (with or without a plea of not guilty). See chapter 5 for this defense.
3. Challenging the jurisdiction of the trial court. See chapter 9 for different aspects of criminal jurisdiction.
4. Defense of infancy. See chapter 5.
5. Attack on the criminal statute (see chapter 1): (a) void-for-vagueness, (b) overbreadth, (c) status offense, (d) state cannot regulate the conduct that it seeks to regulate, (e) other constitutional grounds.
6. Motions to dismiss (a) because of insufficiency of complaint or indictment or (b) because of insufficiency of evidence at the preliminary hearing.
7. Motions to suppress (a) physical evidence, (b) admissions or confessions, (c) identification testimony or evidence.
8. Challenge to procedural irregularities.
9. Defense of immunity: (a) diplomatic immunity, (b) legislative immunity, (c) immunity granted by a court or legislative body (or prosecutor).
10. Defense of mistake or ignorance: (a) of fact, (b) of civil law, (c) of criminal law.
11. Defense of intoxication or drug condition: (a) involuntarily acquired, (b) voluntarily acquired.
12. The defense of duress, coercion, or compulsion: (a) where death results, (b) where the harm done is not death or serious injury.
13. Necessity as a defense: (a) where death results, (b) where the harm to be avoided is greater than the harm done.
14. Justification of the use of force: (a) in self-defense, (b) in the defense of property, (c) in arresting a person, (d) in arresting a person for a felony of violence, (e) by a law enforcement officer to make an investigative stop, (f) in disciplining children. See chapter 6.
15. Alibi as a defense.
16. The defense that the defendant was acting under the authority, direction, or advice of another.
17. The defense of double jeopardy.
18. *Collateral estoppel* and *res judicata* as a defense.
19. The defense of entrapment and frame-up.
20. Lapse of time as a defense: (a) the speedy trial defense, (b) statute of limitations as a defense.
21. Consent, contributory negligence, or condonation by the victim as a defense.

jury that his or her claim is true. In other words, the defendant is not required to put any evidence before the jury. If he or she chooses to do so, however, it is the defendant's responsibility, if the claim is to be effective, to give the jury some basis to believe that claim. The defense can do this by presenting evidence through its own witnesses, or by cross-examining the prosecution's witnesses and drawing support for the defense allegation from them. In a case in which the defendant is charged with theft, for example, the defense may claim entrapment. By use of cross-examination, the defense may show that the police actually set up a defendant and, when he had the stolen property in his possession, arrested him. Or the defense may wait until the prosecution has put in its case, and then show through defense witnesses how the defendant was entrapped. Ordinarily, the defense would attempt to lay the groundwork through cross-examination and then add evidence through defense witnesses to support the claim of entrapment. In any case, if the allegation is made, the responsibility of persuading the jury on the basis of the evidence falls on the defense. The prosecution must convince the jury that each element of the crime was committed by the defendant and that the claim of entrapment should not be accepted.

Motions attacking the jurisdiction of the court and those involving suppression of evidence because of the violation of some constitutional proscription or prosecutorial misconduct are not dealt with here. This chapter discusses those defenses that are generally considered affirmative defenses.

B. Immunity as a Defense

Diplomatic Immunity

By reason of their positions, foreign diplomats stationed in the United States are immune from arrest and criminal prosecution. Most foreign diplomats are located in Washington, D.C., or in New York (United Nations), whereas consular officials may be found in Chicago, San Francisco, and other cities. The *FBI law Enforcement Bulletin* published an article entitled "Procedures and Policies Relating to Diplomatic and Consular Officials" (August 1973), which stated:

> Diplomatic immunity, a principle of international law, is broadly defined as the freedom from local jurisdiction accorded to duly accredited diplomatic officers, their families, and servants. Diplomatic officers should not be arrested or detained for any offense, and foreign career consular officers should not be arrested or detained except for the commission of a grave crime. Family members of diplomatic officers, their servants, and employees of a diplomatic mission are entitled to the same immunities under current U.S. law (22 U.S.C.A. Sec. 252), if they are not nationals of or permanently resident in the receiving state.
>
> Associated with this personal diplomatic immunity is the inviolability enjoyed by the premises of the mission of the sending state and the private residence of a diplomatic agent, his property, papers, and correspondence.

* * *

Consular officers are consuls general, deputy consuls general, consuls, and vice consuls. They are also official representatives of foreign governments. Consular officers are required to be treated with due respect, and all appropriate steps are to be taken to prevent any attack on their person, freedom, or dignity. They are entitled to limited immunities.

In New York City alone, police issue more than 250,000 parking tickets yearly to illegally parked diplomatic vehicles. Few of the tickets are paid.

Frustration and anger over diplomatic immunity has grown in the United States because of such incidents as:

- the injuring and killing of persons in American cities by the automobiles of foreign diplomats, with generally no compensation for the wrongs done unless there is coverage by an American insurance company.
- occasional crimes being committed by family members of diplomats (in 1982, the son of the Brazilian ambassador shot a Washington, D.C., carpenter three times after drinking; in 1983, a relative of an Ethiopian delegate to the United Nations burglarized, sexually assaulted, and assaulted a nineteen-year-old New York art student). No criminal charges could be issued.
- diplomats and their families ignoring their bills, as they cannot be sued civilly.

In 1983, the wife of a Soviet diplomat attached to the Russian UN mission in New York was apprehended in Paramus, New Jersey, for shoplifting. As the woman did not have her diplomatic papers with her, she was held at the police station for fifteen minutes until her identity could be confirmed by telephone.

Legislative Immunity

Article I, Section 6 of the U.S. Constitution provides that U.S. senators and representatives "shall in all cases except treason, felony and breach of the peace, be privileged from arrest during their attendance at the sessions of their respective

---

Immunity as a Defense

Type of Immunity	Source	Extent	Public Purpose
Diplomatic	Historically, diplomats in a foreign country are not subject to the civil or criminal laws of that country. Therefore, foreign diplomats in the United States are not subject to federal or state civil or criminal laws.	Total	Diplomatic immunity, it is hoped, guarantees that American diplomats in foreign countries will not be arrested.
Legislative	Many states have similar constitutional provisions to that found in Art. I, Sec. 6 of the U.S. Constitution, which provides that U.S. senators and members of Congress "shall in all cases except treason, felony and breach of the peace, be privileged from arrest . . . at the sessions of their respective houses, and in going to and returning from the same."	Partial	Legislative immunity has existed since the birth of our republic. Its purpose was to prevent unnecessary harassment of legislators. As the question of legislative immunity seldom comes up, it is highly unlikely that the U.S. Constitution will be amended to change this form of immunity.
Witness*	Federal and state statutes authorize courts and legislative bodies to grant immunity in order to obtain testimony.	Specific types of crimes	This is sometimes the only way in which certain evidence and information can be obtained. A witness who has been granted immunity can no longer take the Fifth Amendment in refusing to answer, since his or her answers can no longer be used to incriminate him or her.**

*Witness immunity differs from testimonial privileges, such as husband–wife, physician–patient, lawyer–client, government–informant. A witness who has been granted immunity can be compelled to testify by jail threats. The person who has a privilege cannot be compelled to be put on a witness stand as a witness under most circumstances. The most widely used privilege is the privilege against self-incrimination, which is a constitutionally protected privilege.

**In 1987, the nation watched the nationally televised Iran-Contra Hearings being held before a U.S. Senate committee. Partial immunity was granted to Lieut. Col. Oliver L. North and Admiral John M. Poindexter. None of their statements before the Senate committee could be used against them, or as a basis for either investigation or further charges.

houses, and in going to and returning from the same." Probably most state constitutions extend the same or similar privileges to state legislators while the state legislature is in session. Representatives, senators, and state legislators thus have a limited degree of temporary immunity while their legislative bodies are in session. Charges, however, could be held until the legislative body adjourns.

Witness Immunity

Both the federal and state governments have enacted statutes that provide for the granting of immunity under specific circumstances. For instance, the Uniform Act for the Extradition of Witnesses provides that a person from another state who is summoned to testify under compulsion may be granted immunity from arrest for any pending criminal or civil wrong while in the state in response to such summons.

Many grants of immunity occur when a witness claims the Fifth Amendment privilege against self-incrimination. When this privilege is claimed, the court may be asked to grant the witness immunity. The witness can then be compelled to testify after immunity is granted as his or her statements cannot be used against the witness. As there is no self-incrimination, there is no Fifth Amendment violation.

A grant of immunity by one level of government also bars any other level from prosecuting the witness and from using his or her answers as the basis for criminal proceedings. Such grants of immunity apply only to the extent allowed by state or federal law. If the law of the jurisdiction provides "transactional" immunity, the person granted immunity may not be prosecuted for the offense about which he or she was compelled to testify. If the jurisdiction provides "use" immunity, only the testimony that was compelled may not be used against the witness. Any information that the authorities obtain through other means may be used to prosecute for the offense about which he or she was compelled to testify.

C. MISTAKE OR IGNORANCE OF FACT OR LAW AS A DEFENSE

Mistake or Ignorance of Fact[1]

A man walking out of a restaurant takes the wrong coat from the coatrack. A few minutes later, the true owner of the coat angrily complains to a police officer. The officer stops the man with the wrong coat blocks away and brings him back to the restaurant. Investigation shows that the man does have a coat similar to the coat that he walked away in. Is this a theft or has an honest mistake of fact been made?

The common law rule, statutorized in many states, is that an honest mistake or ignorance of fact is a defense if it negates the existence of a state of mind essential to the crime. Did the man take the coat with intent to deprive the owner of permanent possession of his coat? The following cases also illustrate this rule:

MORISSETTE v. UNITED STATES
Supreme Court of the United States (1952) 342 U.S. 246, 72 S.Ct. 240

The defendant had been deer hunting in northern Michigan on government property that had been used as a bombing range and was marked "Danger—Keep Out." However, the property was used extensively for hunting by people in the area. When the defendant failed to get a deer, he decided to salvage some of the spent bomb casings that had been lying around on the property for years. In broad daylight, he hauled out three truckloads and with much work realized a profit of $84. He was charged with and convicted of knowingly stealing and converting property of the United States. The trial judge would not allow the defense that the defendant believed that the property was abandoned, unwanted, and considered of no value to the government. After the trial court ruled that "this particular offense requires no element of criminal intent," the U.S. Supreme Court reversed the conviction, pointing out that criminal liability generally required an "evil-meaning mind (and) an evil-doing hand" and held:

> *Had the jury convicted on proper instructions it would be the end of the matter. But juries are not bound by what seems inescapable logic to judges. They might have concluded that the heaps of spent casings left in the hinterland to rust away presented an appearance of unwanted and abandoned junk, and that lack of any conscious deprivation of property or intentional injury was indicated by Morissette's good character, the openness of the taking, crushing and transporting of the casings, and the candor with which it was all admitted. They might have refused to brand Morissette as a thief. Had they done so, that too would have been the end of the matter.*

Reversed.

CROWN v. TOLSON
Queen's Bench Division (1889) 23 Q.B.D. 168

After the defendant was deserted by her husband, she was informed by persons she considered reliable that her husband had been lost at sea while on a ship bound from England to America. After waiting more than five years, during which time she believed herself a widow, she married again. Her first husband then reappeared and she was charged with bigamy.

The court held that she was not guilty of bigamy because she had believed, in good faith and on reasonable grounds, that her first husband was dead. The court stated:

> *At common law an honest and reasonable belief in the existence of circumstances, which, if true, would make the act for which a prisoner is indicted an innocent act has always been held to be a good defense.*

The following three examples are found in the New York Criminal Code Annotated Practice Commentary to Section 15.20, *Effect of ignorance or mistake upon liability.*[2]

> a) A police officer having a warrant for the arrest of A mistakenly arrests B, who resembles A, and holds him in a police station for an hour before ascertaining his mistake and releasing him. The officer is not guilty of "unlawful imprisonment" (sec. 135.05) because his mistake of fact "negatives a culpable mental state necessary for the commission of the offense," namely, "knowledge that the restriction is unlawful" (sec. 135.00(1)).
> b) M has sexual intercourse with F, a mentally ill woman whose condition is not always apparent and is not known to or realized by M. Although M would be guilty of third degree rape if he had realized F's condition . . . his unawareness thereof is, by statute, expressly made a defense to the charge (sec. 130.10).
> c) During a heated argument between A and B, B, a man with a reputation for violence and rumored to carry a pistol on occasion, suddenly places his hand in his bulging pocket, and A strikes him in the face, breaking his nose. Although B did not have a

pistol and was merely reaching for a cigarette, A is not guilty of assault . . . because his factual mistake was of a kind that supports a defense of justification (sec. 35.15 (1)).

Therefore, the question of whether the defendant made an honest mistake of fact or was ignorant of the true facts and conditions is a question that must be determined by the trier of fact, whether a jury or a judge. The accused must show that he or she was honestly mistaken and that his or her conduct was prompted by this mistake or ignorance.

Strict Liability Statutes and the Defense of Mistake or Ignorance of Fact

Some modern statutes impose strict liability and forbid a prohibited act regardless of the person's state of mind. Ignorance or mistake of fact may not ordinarily be used as a defense with such strict liability statutes. Even in situations in which a well-grounded mistake of fact exists, the law and courts deem it necessary for the common good to require persons to ascertain the true facts at their peril or face the consequences of the law.

Strict criminal liability has been imposed on persons who failed to have a license or to comply with regulations when trafficking in drugs or firearms. Such acts, however, are not innocent acts. Courts have held that persons engaged in such dangerous activities may be held to the highest standards of care enforced by strict criminal liability.[3]

Other areas in which strict liability offenses are used are sale of liquor to minors, food and drug handling, traffic law violations, and sale of misbranded articles. The Supreme Court of Wisconsin pointed out in *State v. Collova* that:

> The persons to whom the regulations are directed are generally in a position to exercise such high degree of care; they will be encouraged to do so by the imposition of strict penal liability, and the penalties usually involved are such as to make the occasional punishment of one who has done everything that could have been done to avoid the violation a reasonable price to pay for the public benefit of the high standard of care that has been induced.[4]

Many states have statutes that provide that mistake or ignorance as to the age of a minor is no defense. Such cases could involve "statutory rape," selling liquor to a minor, and so on. The following case illustrates:

PENNSYLVANIA v. ROBINSON
Supreme Court of Pennsylvania, (1981) 497 Pa. 49, 438 A.2d 964, *appeal dismissed* 457 U.S. 1101, 102 S.Ct. 2898, 31 CrL 4108 (1982)

The defendant was over eighteen years of age when he had sexual intercourse with a child under fourteen years of age in violation of Pennsylvania's "statutory rape" statute. The defendant argued that he made a reasonable mistake of fact as to the victim's age but was unable to use such a defense under Section 3102 of the Criminal Code, which states that "it is no defense that the actor did not know the age of the child, or reasonably believed the child to be the age of 14 years or older."

The Supreme Court of Pennsylvania held that the legislature may, in exercising its police power, pass a statute requiring that one eighteen years of age or older who engages in sexual intercourse with a child under eighteen years of age does so at his peril. The court ruled that due process does not require that a defendant be afforded the defense of mistake of age in "statutory rape" prosecutions. The U.S. Supreme Court dismissed the defendant's appeal.

Mistake or Ignorance of Criminal Law

The Latin maxim *Ignorantia legis neminem excusat* (Ignorance of the law excuses no one) may have caused Blackstone to change the phrase in his Commentaries (4 Bl. Comm. 27) to "Ignorance of the law which every one is bound to know, excuses no man." Blackstone's statement is a far better expression of the law, since courts will not allow a defendant who has committed an offense that is generally well known to the public to argue ignorance or mistake of that law. Serious offenses, such as murder, rape, robbery, and theft, are violations not only of the statutory law, but also of moral and ethical laws. Courts would not consider seriously a defense of mistake or ignorance of such laws. Nor would courts ordinarily permit a person charged with a traffic violation in the state in which he or she is licensed to drive to argue ignorance of the traffic laws of that state. It is presumed that the holder of a license knows the traffic laws when the license is received or renewed.

The requirement of filing a yearly federal income tax return is well known to the American public. The following case was before the U.S. Supreme Court in 1991:

CHEEKS v. UNITED STATES
Supreme Court of the United States (1991) _____ U.S. _____, 111 S. Ct. 604, 48 CrL 2071

Mr. Cheeks is an American Airline pilot who did not file federal income tax returns for six years. Mr. Cheeks argued that he did not "willfully" fail to file income tax returns because he and other persons belonging to a group believed that the federal income tax system was unconstitutional.

Mr. Cheeks argued that he honestly believed his failure to file was lawful. Because the Sixteenth Amendment authorizes the federal government to tax personal incomes and the federal income tax law has been challenged and found to be constitutional many times in the past years, the U.S. Supreme Court held that such a good faith belief could not be used as a defense to a criminal tax prosecution. In affirming the defendant's six convictions for willfully failing to file federal income tax returns, the Supreme Court stated:

* * *

The general rule that ignorance of the law or a mistake of law is no defense to criminal prosecution is deeply rooted in the American legal system. . . . Based on the notion that the law is definite and knowable, the common law presumed that every person knew the law. This common-law rule has been applied by the Court in numerous cases construing criminal statutes. . . .

The proliferation of statutes and regulations has sometimes made it difficult for the average citizen to know and comprehend the extent of the duties and obligations imposed by the tax laws. Congress has accordingly softened the impact of the common-law presumption by making specific intent to violate the law an element of certain federal criminal tax offenses. Thus, the Court almost 60 years ago interpreted the statutory term "willfully" as used in the federal criminal tax statutes as carving out an exception to the traditional rule. This special treatment of criminal tax offenses is largely due to the complexity of the tax laws. . . .

* * *

But what of the hundreds of criminal laws that are not well known? The President's Commission on Law Enforcement and Administration of Justice reported in 1966, in *The Challenge of Crime in a Free Society* (p. 18), that the federal government alone has defined more than 2,800 crimes and has observed that the offenses that state and local governments have defined are even more numerous. If a man with little experience and training were to violate an insurance regulation or security exchange regulation that the general public would not be expected to know, could he plead ignorance of these criminal laws? The accused, of course, would have the burden of showing an honest ignorance of such law in order for his defense to be accepted. The following cases illustrate the application and limits of this rule:

LAMBERT v. CALIFORNIA
Supreme Court of the United States (1957) 355 U.S. 225, 78 S.Ct. 240

The defendant was charged with and convicted of failing to register as required under a Los Angeles municipal ordinance that requires "any convicted person" who was in the city for longer than five days to register with local authorities. The defendant had been convicted of forgery and had lived in Los Angeles for longer than seven years without registering. In a 5-4 decision, the U.S. Supreme Court held that registration provision of the ordinance violated the due process requirement of the Fourteenth Amendment.

Justice William O. Douglas for the majority:

> *The rule that "ignorance of the law will not excuse"... is deep in our law, as is the principle that of all the powers of local government, the police power is "one of the least limitable."... On the other hand, due process places some limits on its exercise. Engrained in our concept of due process is the requirement of notice. Notice is sometimes essential so that the citizen has the chance to defend charges. Notice is required before property interests are disturbed, before assessments are made, before penalties are assessed. Notice is required in a myriad of situations where a penalty or forfeiture might be suffered for mere failure to act....*
>
> *This appellant on first becoming aware of her duty to register was given no opportunity to comply with the law and avoid its penalty, even though her default was entirely innocent.... Where a person did not know of the duty to register and where there was no proof of the probability of such knowledge, he may not be convicted consistently with due process. Were it otherwise, the evil would be as great as it is when the law is written too fine or in a language foreign to the community.*

(Authors' note: The better practice with laws or ordinances that are not generally known to the public is to notify persons of the law or ordinance and of their obligation to comply with the law or ordinance.)

UNITED STATES v. PETERSEN
U.S. Court of Appeals, Ninth Circuit (1975) 513 F.2d 1133

In the Petersen case, the jury sent the trial judge a note after three days of deliberation and numerous clarifications on intent–motive. The note asked, "Is ignorance of the law any excuse?" The judge wrote across the note, in what he termed a "bold hand," "ignorance of the law is not an[y] excuse." The Ninth Circuit criticized the judge's action.

The Ninth Circuit suggested that within the circumstances of that case, the judge's note about the ignorance of the law was misleading.

UNITED STATES v. SCHILLECI
U.S. Court of Appeals, Fifth Circuit (1977) 545 F.2d 519

Wiretapping without court authority and in violation of the Federal Criminal Code, 18 U.S.C. 371, 2511, is a felony. The defendant in this case was a police chief who was convicted of three counts of conspiracy to wiretap.

Two illegal wiretaps were installed on a telephone in a tavern without a court order. The chief was present during the planning, but he argues that he took no active role in the decisions. The U.S. Court of Appeals ordered a new trial, holding that while ignorance of the law does not constitute an "excuse" for a crime, the defendant police chief was entitled to a jury instruction that the jury could consider his lack of knowledge "as evidence bearing on the credibility of his claim that he was not a knowing participant in the conspiracy or an active aider and abettor."

UNITED STATES v. AGUILAR
U.S. Court of Appeals, Ninth Circuit (1989) 871 F.2d 1436

The defendants ran an "underground railroad," smuggling Central Americans into the United States in violation of federal law. It was held that the defendants were not entitled to defenses of "mistake of law" or First Amendment religious belief.

Mistake or Ignorance of Civil Law

Blackstone's maxim that "ignorance of the law which every one is bound to know, excuses no man" also applies to civil law. The volume and complexity of civil law has increased considerably in recent years. An honest mistake of civil law could cause an unintentional violation of the criminal law. Take the example of a man with little education and knowledge of the law whose wife tells him that she is going to divorce him. She has a lawyer commence a divorce action, but the action is dropped after the service of the first papers. Several years later, the man, who honestly believes that his wife has divorced him, remarries and discovers that he has unintentionally violated the criminal law of bigamy. Could he argue that his honest mistake of the civil law of divorce should be accepted as a defense to the charge of bigamy? The answer is yes, but the burden would be on him to show that his conduct was prompted by an honest mistake of civil law.

D. INTOXICATION OR DRUGGED CONDITION AS A DEFENSE

Self-induced, Voluntary Intoxication or Drugged Condition

Under the common law, drunkenness was not a defense, but as Blackstone noted in his Commentaries, it was an aggravation of the offense rather than an excuse for any criminal misbehavior. The highest court in New York reflected this rule when it held in 1894 that if "a man made himself voluntarily drunk it was no excuse for any crime he might commit while he was so, and he had to take the responsibility of his own voluntary act."[5]

Today, the general rule remains the same. A defendant who voluntarily becomes intoxicated or drugged has no defense because of his or her intoxicated or drugged condition. There is one exception, however, and that is for specific intent crimes. New York Statute Section 15.25 states this exception, recognized by many states.[6] This Statute provides that "intoxication is not, as such, a defense to a criminal charge; but in any prosecution for an offense, evidence of intoxication of the defendant may be offered by the defendant whenever it is relevant to negate an element of the crime charged." The following cases reflect the application of this rule:

PEOPLE v. GREEN
Appellate Court of Illinois (1969) 105 Ill.App.2d 345, 245 N.E.2d 506

An accused will not be convicted of murder but might be convicted of manslaughter if his voluntary intoxication was so extreme as to suspend entirely his power of reason rendering him incapable of any mental action unless intent to kill was formed before his intoxication.

COMMONWEALTH v. BRIDGE
Supreme Court of Pennsylvania (1981) 495 Pa. 568, 435 A.2d 151

The defendant was convicted of voluntary manslaughter and argued that voluntary intoxication negated his intent to kill. The court held the defendant's intoxication had nothing to do with the intent required for voluntary manslaughter, which is a homicide based on sudden provocation.

STATE v. CAMERON
Supreme Court of New Jersey (1986) 104 N.J. 42, 514 A.2d 1302

The Supreme Court of New Jersey held in 1986 that a defendant had to be "so prostrated as to render him incapable of purposeful or knowing conduct" in order to use intoxication to show he did not have the mental capacity necessary for the crime charged. The Supreme Court of Wisconsin held that the degree of intoxication had to be such that the defendant was "utterly incapable of forming the intent to kill."[7]

The drinking of alcoholic beverages or the use of drugs before the commission of the crime does not by itself establish intoxication or require the presentation of a jury instruction on intoxication. There must be a showing of intoxication so extreme that it would justify a jury finding that the defendant was incapable of formulating the necessary criminal state of mind. In such a case, the defendant may be convicted of a lesser included crime that does not require specific intent.

To use intoxication as a defensive tactic, the defendant has to admit he committed the crime but was too intoxicated to be able to formulate the necessary state of mind (he did the act but did not have a guilty mind). Fact finders (juries or judges) are not sympathetic to defendants who argue that they could function physically after using a large amount of alcohol and/or drugs but were incapable of formulating the necessary criminal state of mind. The defensive tactic is seldom successful.

Involuntary Intoxication or Drugged Condition

Involuntary intoxication or drugged condition is a defense if the trier of fact (the jury or judge) believes the defendant's story, supported by credible evidence, that (a) he or she did not voluntarily take the drug or intoxicant and was tricked or forced into taking such substance and (b) the alcohol or drug rendered the defendant incapable of distinguishing between right and wrong with regard to the alleged criminal act at the time the act was committed. This would mean that the defendant was unable to form criminal intent but was physically able to commit the crime.

Insanity or Abnormality of Mind Caused by Alcohol or Drugs

Mere addiction to drugs or alcohol does not in itself constitute insanity. However, the prolonged or excessive use of alcohol and drugs can cause insanity and such conditions as delirium tremens. The insanity rules of the jurisdiction, whether the M'Naghten Rule or the American Law Institute Rule, would be used to determine the defendant's plea of not guilty because of insanity. If a jury or judge found that the facts were such as to constitute temporary insanity, the defendant could be found not guilty because of insanity, but if the defendant were merely drunk or drugged, he or she should then be convicted.

In the 1978 case of *Commonwealth v. Sheehan*[8] the Massachusetts Supreme Judicial Court held that the "normal consequences of drug consumption" provide no basis for a claim that the defendant lacked criminal responsibility. The court noted that Massachusetts differs from most states because it does not recognize voluntary drunkenness as a factor negating specific intent.

Although the standards for determining insanity can vary somewhat from state to state, jury to jury, and court to court, alcohol and drugs affect different people in different ways. Weight, physical conditions, and individual factors can make a difference in the effect of the drug or alcohol. The strength and potency of drugs purchased on the street vary considerably and simply knowing the quantity consumed is not sufficient to measure its effect.

Use of Alcohol or Drugs to Build up Courage to Commit a Crime

If it were found that a person used alcohol or drugs to build up courage to commit a crime, the defense of intoxication could not be used successfully. In the 1963 English case of *Rex v. Gallagher,* A.C. 349 (House of Lords) Lord Denning stated:

> If a man, whilst sane and sober, forms an intention to kill ... and then gets himself drunk so as to give himself Dutch courage to do the killing ... he cannot rely on this self-induced drunkenness as a defence to a charge of murder, nor even as reducing it to manslaughter ... the wickedness of his mind before he got drunk is enough to condemn him, coupled with the act which he intended to do and did do.

A finding that an intent to commit a crime was formed before the requisite degree of intoxication was reached would defeat the defense of voluntary or involuntary intoxication or drugged condition. If it could be shown that the defendant was a habitual user of that particular drug or type of alcohol, it could then be argued that the defendant was well aware of the effect the drug or alcohol would ordinarily have on him or her.

E. Duress or Coercion (or Compulsion) as a Defense

In attempting to use the defense of duress or coercion, defendants must admit that they committed the offense charged but assert that they were forced to do so to avoid death or serious bodily injury to themselves or others. Defining duress and coercion in *People v. Sanders,* the court stated:

> In order for duress or fear produced by threats or menace to be a valid, legal excuse for doing anything, which otherwise would be criminal, the act must have been done

under such threats or menaces as show that the life of the person threatened or menaced was in danger, or that there was reasonable cause to believe and actual belief that there was such danger. The danger must not be one of future violence, but of present and immediate violence at the time of the commission of the forbidden act. The danger of death at some future time in the absence of danger of death at the time of the commission of the offense will not excuse. A person who aids and assists in the commission of the crime, or who commits a crime, is not relieved from criminality on account of fears excited by threats or menaces unless the danger be to life, nor unless that danger be present and immediate.[9]

A well-known case involving the defense of duress was that of Patricia Hearst. Hearst claimed that she was kidnapped, "brain-washed," and then forced to participate in the robbery of a California bank.[10] The question before the California jury was whether Hearst was forced to participate in the robbery (duress and coercion), or whether she freely and willingly took part in the robbery. After listening to the many witnesses who were in the bank, and viewing the bank videotape showing Hearst pointing a submachine gun at bank customers and employees, the jury found Patty Hearst guilty of bank robbery.

Duress or Coercion as Justification to Escape from Prison

In 1977, the Supreme Court of Delaware held that "intolerable conditions" were not justification for escape from prison because the defendants failed to give sufficient proof that such justification existed.[11] The court held that it was proper to employ the tests used by California courts in determining justification. The California tests, established in *People v. Lovercamp*,[12] hold that justification is available as a defense to the charge of escape from prison only when:

(1) The prisoner is faced with a specific threat of death, forcible sexual attack or substantial bodily injury in the immediate future;
(2) There is no time for a complaint to the authorities or there exists a history of futile complaints which make any result from such complaints illusory;
(3) There is no time or opportunity to resort to the courts;
(4) There is no evidence of force or violence used towards prison personnel or other "innocent" persons in the escape; and
(5) The prisoner immediately reports to the proper authorities when he has attained a position of safety from the immediate threat.

In 1980, the U.S. Supreme Court ruled as follows in the escape case of *United States v. Bailey*:

We therefore hold that, where a criminal defendant is charged with escape and claims that he is entitled to an instruction on the theory of duress or necessity, he must proffer evidence of a bona fide effort to surrender or return to custody as soon as the claimed duress or necessity had lost its coercive force. We have reviewed the evidence examined elaborately in the majority and dissenting opinions below, and find the case not even close, even under respondents' versions of the facts, as to whether they either surrendered or offered to surrender at their earliest possible opportunity. Since we have determined that this is an indispensable element of the defense of duress or necessity, respondents were not entitled to any instruction on such a theory. Vague and necessarily self-serving statements of defendants or witnesses as to future good intentions or ambiguous conduct simply do not support a finding of this element of the defense.[13]

The Defense of Duress in a Charge of Murder

Under the common law, the defense of duress was not available to a defendant in a murder or treason charge. Blackstone stated that the reason for this was that a man under duress "ought rather to die himself than escape by the murder of an innocent."[14] This apparently is the common law today in England and in more than half the American states. About twenty states define the defense of duress by statute, and most do not allow the defense in murder cases (or sometimes in other serious crimes). In a few states, however, if the defense of duress is believed by a jury (or court) in a murder charge, this may reduce the charge of first-degree murder to manslaughter.[15]

EXAMPLE: C has a gun and threatens to kill A unless A kills B. A believes that C will kill him, and to save his own life, A kills B. A would be charged with first-degree murder in most states, since the defense of duress would not be accepted. However, a few states would reduce the charge to manslaughter if duress and coercion could be proved. In all states, C would be charged with first-degree murder.

Coercion of Wives

Under the old common law, a woman who married lost practically all the few rights she had before marriage. A husband could discipline his wife with a stick no bigger than the thickness of his thumb. He controlled any property she may have owned or inherited. Courts were reluctant to grant her a divorce, and if they did, the husband would probably receive custody of the children unless he was unfit. Until the 1920s, neither married nor single women could vote in most states, and few well-paying jobs were available to women before World War II.

Because of the control a husband exerted over his wife, there was a common-law rebuttable presumption holding that if a wife committed a crime in her husband's presence, the husband had coerced her into committing the crime. To successfully charge the wife, the state had to present evidence that would overcome the presumption of coercion by the husband. With the emancipation of women in recent decades, this presumption of coercion by the husband has been abolished in most, if not all, states. A married woman today may use the defense of coercion, but like everyone else, she has the burden of proving that she would not have committed the crime charged were it not for the threat of imminent death or serious bodily harm to herself or to another person.

The Crime of Coercion

A person who forces (coerces) another to commit a crime can be charged and convicted of the crime committed in addition to other offenses. For example, a person who forced another to commit a murder could be charged and convicted of that murder.

But what can be done regarding a situation where a person is forced to commit an act that is not a crime? Some states have addressed this problem and have created the crime of coercion. For example, the State of New York has two degrees of coercion. Public Law 135.60 defines coercion as compelling a person to engage in conduct "which the latter has a legal right to abstain from engaging in." First degree coercion is punished as a Class D felony while second degree coercion is a Class A misdemeanor.

In 1990, a former New York school board president pleaded guilty to first degree coercion when evidence was obtained showing that he illegally pressured school administrators into giving jobs to his friends (cronyism). (*New York Times* 4/27/90, p. A13)

F. NECESSITY AS A DEFENSE[16]

A person who, because of necessity, performs an act that otherwise would constitute a crime may use the justification of necessity as a defense if the "harm or evil sought to be avoided by such conduct is greater than that sought to be prevented by the law defining the offense charged."[17]

EXAMPLE: An airplane crashes at night in an isolated area. As it is very cold and rescue is not likely until daylight, the survivors break into a summer cottage and use the food and blankets in the cottage to comfort the injured and to sustain themselves until help arrives.

In the example given, the necessity of breaking into the cottage is obvious. In 1986, the Eighth Circuit Federal Court of Appeals held regarding the defense of necessity:

> A vital element of any necessity defense is the lack of a reasonable alternative to violating the law; that is, the harm to be avoided must be so imminent that, absent the defendant's criminal acts, the harm is certain to occur. *United States v. Bailey,* 444 U.S. 394, 410, 100 S.Ct. 624, 634, 62 L.Ed.2d 575 (1980). As the Tenth Circuit has emphasized:
>
> "The defense of necessity does not arise from a 'choice' of several courses of action, it is instead based on a real emergency. It can be asserted only by a defendant who was confronted with such a crisis as a personal danger, a crisis which did not permit a selection from among several solutions, some of which did not involve criminal acts. It is obviously not a defense to charges arising from a typical protest."[18]

* * *

In the example given, the survivors would openly admit what they had done. The owner of the cottage would be assured of compensation for the damages. Law enforcement officers and the prosecutor would not consider criminal charges and the matter would not receive further attention. In the following cases, prosecutors did charge, even though defendants argued necessity to justify their conduct:

UNITED STATES v. KABAT
U.S. Court of Appeals, Eighth Circuit (1986) 797 F.2d 580

The defendants (priests and other persons) were nuclear protestors who cut their way into a missile site where they used a jackhammer to damage radar devices and concrete launches. In affirming their convictions for destruction of government property, sabotage, and other charges, the Court held:

> *The necessity defense was never intended to excuse criminal activity by those who disagree with the decisions and policies of the lawmaking branches of government:*

*in such cases the "greater harm" sought to be prevented would be the course of
action chosen by elected representatives, and a court in allowing the defense would
be making a negative political or policy judgment about that course of action.*

CLEVELAND v. MUNICIPALITY OF ANCHORAGE
Supreme Court of Alaska (1981) 631 P.2d 1073, 29 CrL 2475

Four defendants were charged with and convicted of trespassing when they refused to
leave an abortion clinic where they were attempting to disrupt abortions being performed
there. They argued the defense of necessity to prevent the "killing of unborn children."
The Supreme Court of Alaska held that the trial court was correct in refusing a jury
instruction on necessity.

(See chapter 12 for the law on abortions).

STATE v. OLSEN
Court of Appeals of Wisconsin (1980) 99 Wis.2d 572, 299 N.W.2d 632

The four defendants formed a line blocking a road being used for a shipment of nuclear
material, which defendants believed was unsafe. They would not move when a sheriff
requested them to move and were arrested and charged with disorderly conduct. As
defenses, the defendants argued "necessity," "self-defense," and "defense of others."[19] The
court held that none of these defenses was applicable to the defendants.

STATE v. MARLEY
Supreme Court of Hawaii (1973) 54 Hawaii 450, 509 P.2d 1095

The defendants were convicted of criminal trespass after they entered the offices of Hon-
eywell Corporation during the Vietnam War to protest and to stop the corporation's "war
crimes." The court held that the activities of the corporation were not unlawful. Therefore,
as the "harm" that defendants sought to stop was not unlawful and did not arise from a
natural source, the defendants could not use the defense of necessity.

Would Necessity Justify Carrying an Unlicensed Concealed Weapon in Violation of State Law?

States have held that a person acting reasonably in defense of himself or herself
in a serious emergency could use the defense of necessity successfully to a CCW
charge (the crime of carrying a concealed weapon). However, the threat to the
person would have to be immediate, substantial, and unavoidable.

In the 1986 case of *Commonwealth v. Lindsey,*[20] the defendant carried an
unlicensed concealed pistol in anticipation of a possible dangerous encounter.
Hours later a man threatened the defendant with a knife. The defendant pulled the
pistol and fired. The Supreme Judicial Court of Massachusetts pointed out that the
defendant was not responding to an immediate and serious threat at all times
when he possessed the weapon in public. The Court affirmed his conviction of
unlawfully carrying a firearm and his sentence to the mandatory one-year term.
The Court wrote:

* * *

Other jurisdictions have recognized that particular circumstances may justify possession or carrying of a firearm in apparent violation of statute so as to warrant a not

guilty finding. In States where self-defense or necessity is recognized by statute as a justification, the courts have acknowledged that the prohibitions of firearms statutes might be inapplicable to one acting reasonably in defense of himself in a serious emergency.... Even in the absence of a statute on self-defense or necessity, numerous courts have acknowledged the possibility that a person's conduct might be justified despite a showing of all the basic elements of unlawful possession. See *United States v. Gant,* 691 F.2d 1159, 1162–1165 (5th Cir. 1982) (defendant did not show necessary elements of the affirmative defense of justification); *State v. Walton,* 311 N.W.2d 113, 115–116 (Iowa 1981) (evidence did not raise a jury question on defense of necessity); *Medley v. State,* 52 Md.App. 225, 236, 448 A.2d 363 (1982) (same); *State v. Spaulding,* 296 N.W.2d 870, 877 (Minn. 1980) (jury adequately instructed on defense of necessity in felon's possession of a pistol). Cf. *People v. Almodovar,* 62 N.Y.2d 126, 130, 476 N.Y.S.2d 95, 464 N.E.2d 463 (1984) (a suddenly discovered weapon or one taken from an assailant would not constitute unlawful possession).

Each statement of the rule of necessity in these authorities includes, expressly or impliedly, the requirement that the threat to the defendant must be immediate, substantial, and unavoidable and that it arise in circumstances in which action in self-defense would have been warranted (i.e., the defendant had a reasonable apprehension of death or serious bodily injury). ... The cases in which courts have found the evidence to have presented a jury question on justification are relatively rare and involve situations in which the defendant came into possession of the weapon only in the midst of an emergency. See *United States v. Panter,* 688 F.2d 268 (5th Cir. 1982) (bartender, stabbed by a man with a knife, seized a gun while his assailant was on top of him); *People v. King, supra* (weapon handed to defendant as intruders attempted to force their way into an apartment). Cf. *Mungin v. State,* 458 So.2d 293 (Fla.Dist. Ct.App. 1984) (a prison inmate may temporarily possess a weapon taken from a would-be aggressor when it is used to defend against the imminent peril of death or serious bodily injury).

* * *

It is possible that the defendant is alive today only because he carried the gun that day for protection. Before the days of a one-year mandatory sentence, the special circumstances involving the accused could be reflected reasonably in the sentencing or dispositional aspect of the proceeding. That option is no longer available to the judicial branch of government in a case of this sort. Any relief that the defendant may warrant must come from one of the other branches of government.[21]

Judgment affirmed.

When Death Results from the Defendant's Attempt to Save Self or Others

Can a person kill an innocent person to save his or her life? This question came before courts in the following cases many years ago:

UNITED STATES v. HOLMES
U.S. Court of Appeals (1842) 26 Fed.Cas. 360

The defendant was a member of the crew of a ship that sank, leaving him and many others in an overcrowded lifeboat. Because the ship's mate feared that the boat would sink, he ordered the male passengers thrown overboard, leaving the women and the ship's crew. The defendant assisted in throwing sixteen of the men out of the boat to their deaths. A grand jury refused to indict him for murder, so he was charged with and convicted of manslaughter.

REX v. DUDLEY AND STEPHENS
Queen's Bench Division (1884) 14 Q.B.D. 273

The defendants and another man and a boy were shipwrecked and adrift in an open boat for eighteen days. After seven days without food or water, the defendants suggested that the men kill the boy, who was then very weak. When the other man refused, the defendants killed the boy and all the men fed on the boy's body. Four days later, they were rescued. The jury, by a special verdict, found that the men would probably have died within the four days had they not fed on the boy's body. The jury also found that the boy would probably have died before being rescued. However, the defendants were convicted of murder, with the sentence commuted to six months' imprisonment.

These two cases have been debated by judges, lawyers, and law students throughout the English-speaking world for years. Few persons urge that the doctrine of necessity be expanded to full forgiveness instead of the partial forgiveness of manslaughter used in both the cases given. In commenting on the problem, former U.S. Supreme Court Justice Benjamin N. Cardozo observed: "Where two or more are overtaken by a common disaster, there is no right on the part of one to save the lives of some, by killing of another. There is no rule of human jettison."[22]

The attitude of the British courts today is probably reflected by the 1971 case of *Southwark London Borough v. Williams:*

[T]he law regards with the deepest suspicion any remedies of self-help, and permits these remedies to be resorted to only in very special circumstances. The reason for such circumspection is clear—necessity can very easily become simply a mask for anarchy.[23]

Other Uses of the Defense of Necessity

Many different types of genuine emergencies can be justification for minor violations of the law. A man rushing a badly bleeding child to a hospital twenty miles away could, if the road conditions were good, exceed the speed limit. He would not be justified, however, in running down a pedestrian.

Arguments over whether extreme hunger justifies theft of food have to be resolved by looking at each incident separately. The man who had just spent all his money on gambling or whiskey would not be justified in stealing food. Nor would the man who broke into a fine restaurant because he did not like the food available to him at the Salvation Army or the Rescue Mission. The person who was directly responsible for creating an emergency would not be in as good a position to use the defense of necessity as would a person who had done nothing to cause the emergency.

The newspaper article, "Trespassing to Survive: Is It Justified?" appeared in the March 6, 1990 issue of *The New York Times.* On a bitter cold night, would a homeless person be justified in gaining access to a warm building when the wind chill was below zero? This is a common problem confronting police and building managers in large cities. Should trespass charges be issued or should other solutions be sought?

G. Alibi as a Criminal Defense

In using the defense of alibi, the defendant is asserting that he or she physically could not have committed the crime because at the time the crime was committed, he or she was at another place.

EXAMPLE: X is charged with robbery and has been identified by two witnesses and the victim as the man who robbed a liquor store. X uses the defense of alibi and argues that it was physically impossible for him to rob the store, since he was at his mother's home 100 miles away at the time of the robbery. His mother and his wife corroborate X's story, stating that they were there also.

Because an alibi can be easily fabricated, it must be carefully investigated. Many states have statutes requiring defendants who plan to use an alibi defense to serve notice on the prosecutor before trial. These statutes are meant to safeguard against the wrongful use of alibis, as they give law enforcement agencies and prosecutors necessary notice and time to investigate the merits of the proposed alibi.

Generally, suspects will immediately inform the police or the prosecutor as to whether they have an alibi. Investigations at this stage could cause the police and a prosecutor to conclude that the suspect is innocent. If a suspect does not speak up and waits until the criminal proceedings are well under way before any mention is made of an alibi, government officials are likely to be suspicious.

When a suspect has too good an alibi, investigating officers could become suspicious that the suspect had someone else commit the crime under investigation. In the U.S. Supreme Court case of *Illinois v. Escobedo*,[24] Chicago police knew that Danny Escobedo had a motive to kill his brother-in-law, and Danny's criminal record told them he had the means and capacity. Danny had warned his brother-in-law to stop beating his sister, and the killing occurred the day after another bad beating. Danny hired another man to do the shooting while he hung out for hours in a busy poolhall.

Alibi Notice Statutes

Alibi notice statutes require that defendants make disclosures regarding their cases. Such disclosure includes the place where the defendant claimed to have been at the time the crime was committed and the names and addresses of witnesses to the alibi, if known.

In the 1973 case of *Wardius v. Oregon*,[25] the U.S. Supreme Court held that when a defendant is compelled to disclose information regarding his or her case, the state must also make similar disclosures. The U.S. Supreme Court held:

> [In] the absence of a strong showing of state interests to the contrary, discovery must be a two-way street. The State may not insist that trials be run as a "search for truth" so far as defense witnesses are concerned, while maintaining "poker game" secrecy for its own witnesses. It is fundamentally unfair to require a defendant to divulge the details of his own case while at the same time subjecting him to the hazard of surprise concerning refutation of the very pieces of evidence which he disclosed to the State.

Alibi notice statutes now require disclosure by prosecutors as well as defendants.

Determining the Validity of Alibi Defenses

An alibi presented to and believed by a jury constitutes a complete defense to the crime charged. Even if the alibi raises only a reasonable doubt in the mind of a jury, it becomes a good defense because the jury cannot convict if a reasonable doubt exists. If only two or three of the jurors believe the alibi, a "hung" jury may result. The burden is not on the defendant to show that he or she was not at the scene of the crime, but is on the state to show beyond reasonable doubt that the defendant was at the scene and did commit the crime. Charges of perjury, solicitation to commit perjury, or subornation of perjury have resulted when it has been shown that alibi witnesses testified falsely or that attempts were made to persuade persons to testify falsely.

Failure to Give Notice of Alibi and Names of Alibi Witnesses

The U.S. Supreme Court noted in 1983 that thirty-five states have statutes that permit trial judges in those states to prohibit a defendant from introducing testimony of an undisclosed alibi witness unless proper notice is given as required by statute. The following case illustrates this rule:

TALIAFERRO v. MARYLAND
Supreme Court of the United States (1983) 461 U.S. 948, 103 S.Ct. 2114, 33 CrL 4063

Without giving prior notice of alibi and the name of the alibi witness, the defendant in this case attempted on the second day of trial to call an alibi witness. The trial judge refused to grant a delay, as requested by the prosecutor, and would not permit the witness to testify. Defendant's conviction was affirmed and the U.S. Supreme Court denied review of the case.

H. THE DEFENSE THAT THE DEFENDANT WAS ACTING UNDER THE AUTHORITY, DIRECTION, OR ADVICE OF ANOTHER *only if that person is a special person policemen, state judge*

A person who commits an act that is obviously criminal, such as arson or murder, and then attempts to use as a defense the fact that he or she was acting under the direction of a superior officer or on the advice of an attorney or another person would ordinarily be held fully liable for such an offense. The general rule is that one who performs a criminal act under the advice, direction, or order of another cannot use such a defense.

However, because there are hundreds of crimes not well known to the general public, the U.S. Supreme Court, in 1908, quoted with approval a jury instruction stating that when a person:

> [F]ully and honestly lays all the facts before his counsel, and in good faith and honestly follows such advice, relying upon it and believing it to be correct, and only intends that his acts shall be lawful, he could not be convicted of crime which involves wilful and unlawful intent; even if such advice were an inaccurate construction of the law. But, on the other hand, no man can wilfully and knowingly violate the law, and excuse himself from consequences thereof by pleading that he followed the advice of counsel.[26]

In the 1975 case of *Toomey v. Tolin,*[27] it was held that following the advice of a legal adviser was a complete defense for law enforcement officers involved in a civil suit for false arrest and malicious prosecution. Other cases are:[28]

COX v. LOUISIANA
Supreme Court of the United States (1965) 379 U.S. 559, 85 S.Ct. 476

Among other charges, the defendant was convicted of demonstrating "in or near" a courthouse in violation of a Louisiana law modeled after a 1949 federal statute. The U.S. Supreme Court reversed the conviction, stating:

> *The highest police officials of the city, in the presence of the Sheriff and Mayor, in effect, told the demonstrators that they could meet where they did, 101 feet from the courthouse steps, but could not meet closer to the courthouse. In effect, appellant was advised that a demonstration at the place it was held would not be one "near" the courthouse within the terms of the statute.*[29]

RALEY v. OHIO
Supreme Court of the United States (1959) 360 U.S. 423, 79 S.Ct. 1257

The U.S. Supreme Court held "that the Due Process Clause prevented conviction of persons for refusing to answer questions of a state investigating commission when they relied upon assurance of the commission, either express or implied, that they had a privilege under state law to refuse to answer, though in fact this privilege was not available to them." The Court stated that this "would be to sanction an indefensible sort of entrapment by the State—convicting a citizen for exercising a privilege which the State had clearly told him was available to him."

UNITED STATES v. CALLEY
U.S. Court of Military Appeals (1973) 22 U.S.M.C.A. 534

In a search and destroy operation during the Vietnam War, U.S. Army Lieutenant Calley led a platoon into the village of My-Lai. More than four hundred Vietnamese women, children, and old men were killed. Lt. Calley was charged with the murder of twenty-two infants, children, women, and old men. His defense was that he was acting under orders of his superior officers. His commanding officer testified that no such orders had been given. In affirming Lt. Calley's convictions, the Military Court of Appeals held:

> *[There is] ample evidence from which to find that Lieutenant Calley directed and personally participated in the intentional killing of men, women and children who were unarmed and in the custody of soldiers . . . [T]he uncontradicted evidence is that . . . they were offering no resistance. In his testimony, Calley admitted he was aware of the requirement that prisoners be treated with respect . . . he knew that the normal practice was to interrogate villagers, release those who could satisfactorily account for themselves and evacuate the suspect among them for further examination. . . .*
>
> *We turn to the contention that the [trial] judge erred in his submission of the defense of superior orders to the court: '(I)f you find that Lieutenant Calley received an order directing him to kill unresisting Vietnamese within his control . . . that order (as a matter of law) would be an illegal order. A determination that an order is illegal does not, of itself, assign criminal responsibility to the person following the order for acts done in compliance with it. . . . [such] acts of subordinate . . . are*

excused and impose no criminal liability upon him unless the superior's order is one which a man of ordinary sense and understanding would, under the circumstances, know to be unlawful, or if the order in question is actually known to the accused to be unlawful'....

... [W]hether Lieutenant Calley was the most ignorant person in the United States Army in Vietnam or the most intelligent, he must be presumed to know that he could not kill the people involved here ... [the order was] so palpably illegal that whatever conceptual difference there may be between a person of 'commonest understanding' and a person of 'common understanding,' that difference could not have had any impact on a court.

High ranking Nazi officers and officials were tried before an international court at Nuremberg, Germany, after World War II. Some of the Nazi defendants used the defense that they were following orders of superiors. The Nuremberg Court, made up of judges from the Allied nations, held that this defense was not available where the orders given violated commonly accepted standards of humanity. Many of the actions taken by Nazi defendants violated specific prohibitions contained in treaties and agreements, which were used in part to determine what "crimes against humanity" included.

Some of the Nazi defendants were executed while others received jail sentences. The Nuremberg trials are discussed further in chapter 9, since the jurisdiction for these trials was that the Nazi defendants violated the "Law of Nations" (Article I, Section 8 of the U.S. Constitution).

The Watergate Cases

In 1972 the burglary at the Watergate Hotel in Washington, D.C., set into motion events that led to the resignation of President Richard Nixon. Several important cases, criminal and civil, resulted from that burglary and related activities of President Nixon's supporters.

The burglary of the Democratic headquarters in the Watergate complex occurred to obtain Democratic plans. Another burglary occurred in the office of a private psychiatrist, Dr. Fielding, to obtain records of one of his patients, Daniel Ellsberg. Ellsberg had earlier released classified information (the "Pentagon Papers") that embarrassed President Nixon. John Ehrlichman, a top adviser for President Nixon, conspired with others to obtain Ellsberg's files through the burglary of Dr. Fielding's office. Ehrlichman was convicted and went to jail. His appeal of his conviction and sentence is found in *United States v. Ehrlichman,* 546 F.2d 910 (D.C. Cir., 1976).

Ehrlichman's defense was that the break-in was justified under the presidential authority to authorize a search for national security reasons, without first obtaining a judicial warrant. The Court of Appeals rejected that defense, saying that it wasn't clear that such authority was possessed by the president, but if it were, the president must personally (or through the Attorney General) and explicitly authorize the activity. Since President Nixon maintained he did not authorize the break-in, Ehrlichman's defense failed.

The Court also rejected Erhlichman's defense that he reasonably believed he had the authority to conduct the break-in, noting that "mistake of law" was not a defense in this case.

I. THE DEFENSE OF DOUBLE JEOPARDY

The Fifth Amendment of the U.S. Constitution provides that "no person . . . shall . . . for the same offense . . . be twice put in jeopardy of life or limb." In the 1978 case of *United States v. Scott,*[30] the U.S. Supreme Court, quoting other Supreme Court cases, held that the double jeopardy clause ensures:

> . . . [T]hat the State with all its resources and power should not be allowed to make repeated attempts to convict an individual for an alleged offense, thereby subjecting him to embarrassment, expense and ordeal and compelling him to live in a continuing state of anxiety and insecurity, as well as enhancing the possibility that even though innocent he may be found guilty.

Therefore, a person who has been acquitted by a judge or a jury may not be tried again, even if subsequent investigation reveals evidence that proves conclusively that the defendant is guilty. If the acquittal resulted from a finding of mental defect or illness at the time of the commission of the offense, the defendant cannot be retried even though sanity is recovered.

When Is a Defendant Placed in Jeopardy?

In the 1984 case of *Press-Enterprise Co. v. Superior Court,*[31] the U.S. Supreme Court pointed out that jeopardy attaches when a jury is sworn.[32] In a nonjury trial, the Court pointed out that jeopardy attaches when the first witness is sworn.[33]

Prosecution by Both State and Federal Governments

Since many crimes are crimes only against a state, only the state may prosecute. Some crimes, however, are offenses not only against the state, but also the federal government. The robbery of a federally insured bank or savings and loan association is an example.

The question of whether state and federal government may both prosecute for such offenses has come before the U.S. Supreme Court more than a dozen times. Justice Oliver Wendell Holmes, repeating the rule that both state and federal prosecution in such cases is not in violation of the Fifth Amendment, stated that the rule "is too plain to need more than a statement."[34] The reasoning is presented in the 1959 case of *Bartkus v. Illinois* as follows:

> Every citizen of the United States is also a citizen of a State or territory. He may be said to owe allegiance to two sovereigns, and may be liable to punishment for an infraction of the laws of either. The same act may be an offense or transgression of the law of both. That either or both may (if they see fit) punish such an offender cannot be doubted. Yet it cannot be truly averted that the offender has been twice punished for the same offense; but only that by one act he has committed two offenses, for each of which he is justly punishable. He could not plead the punishment by one in bar to a conviction by the other.[35]

In *Bartkus v. Illinois,* the defendant was tried in a federal court and acquitted of robbing a federally insured bank. He was then indicted by an Illinois grand jury and convicted on substantially the same evidence used in the federal court. The

Other Important U.S. Supreme Court Cases on Double Jeopardy

HEATH v. ALABAMA
Supreme Court of the United States (1985) 474 U.S. 82, 106 S.Ct. 433 (1985)

Heath hired two men in Georgia to kidnap his pregnant wife from their Alabama home and kill her. The murder then took place in Georgia. Both states convicted the defendant of murder. The Supreme Court affirmed both convictions under the "dual sovereignty" doctrine, holding it would be shocking to "deny a State its power to enforce its criminal laws because another State has won the race to the courthouse...."

BALL v. UNITED STATES
Supreme Court of the United States (1896) 163 U.S. 662, 672, 16 S.Ct. 1192

The court held:

"It is elementary in our law that a person can be tried a second time for an offense when his prior conviction for that same offense has been set aside by his appeal."

MISSOURI v. HUNTER
Supreme Court of the United States (1983) 459 U.S. 359, 103 S.Ct. 673

Although the double jeopardy clause forbids multiple punishment for the same offense, it does not forbid the imposition, at the same trial, of convictions and punishments for two or more offenses that are specifically intended by the legislature to carry separate punishments. In the *Hunter* case, the defendant's conviction and punishment for robbery and armed criminal action was affirmed even though the offenses constituted the same crime.

Therefore, a defendant may be charged and convicted of multiple crimes arising out of one criminal act if the state legislature intends it.

BLOCKBURGER v. UNITED STATES
Supreme Court of the United States (1932) 284 U.S. 299, 52 S.Ct. 180

The applicable rule is that where the same act or transaction constitutes a violation of two distinct statutory provisions, the test to be applied to determine whether there are two offenses or only one, is whether each provision requires proof of a fact which the other does not.

MORRIS v. MATHEWS
Supreme Court of the United States (1986) 106 S.Ct. 1032, 38 CrL 3153

The Supreme Court ruled that an appellate court need not reverse outright a defendant's conviction of a double jeopardy-barred offense. The appellate court can reduce the conviction to one of a lesser included nonbarred offense unless the defendant can demonstrate a "reasonable probability that he would not have been convicted of the non-jeopardy-barred offense ..." A new trial is not required unless the defendant can show "a probability sufficient to undermine confidence in the outcome.

NORTH CAROLINA v. PEARCE
Supreme Court of the United States (1969) 395 U.S. 711, 89 S.Ct. 2072

The Supreme Court held that

[T]he double jeopardy clause affords three distinct constitutional protections: (1) protection against a second prosecution for the same offense after acquittal; (2) protection against a second prosecution for the same offense after conviction; (3) protection against multiple punishments for the same offense.

Illinois court sentenced him to life imprisonment under the Illinois Habitual Criminal Statute. The U.S. Supreme Court affirmed the conviction, holding that the second trial did not violate the Fifth Amendment of the U.S. Constitution.

However, since *Bartkus v. Illinois,* many states, including Illinois, have passed legislation that forbids prosecution after there has been prosecution in another jurisdiction for the same crime. In such states, it is the law of the state, and not the double jeopardy clause, that forbids prosecution after prosecution in another jurisdiction.[36]

Other Important U.S. Supreme Court Cases on Double Jeopardy (continued)

SMALIS v. PENNSYLVANIA
Supreme Court of the United States (1986) 476 U.S. 140, 106 S.Ct. 1745

The Supreme Court held that the granting of a "demurrer was an acquittal under the Double Jeopardy Clause. . . ." A demurrer is a finding that as a matter of law the prosecution's evidence is insufficient to establish the factual guilt of a defendant. Further prosecution is forbidden.

GREEN v. UNITED STATES
Supreme Court of the United States (1957) 355 U.S. 184, 78 S.Ct. 221

[T]he law attaches particular significance to an acquittal. To permit a second trial after an acquittal, however mistaken the acquittal may have been, would present an unacceptably high risk that the Government, with its vastly superior resources, might wear down the defendant so that "even though innocent he may be found guilty."

LOCKHART v. NELSON
Supreme Court of the United States (1988) 488 U.S. 33, 109 S.Ct. 285, 44 CrL 3031

. . . It has long been settled . . . that the Double Jeopardy Clause's general prohibition against successive prosecutions does not prevent the government from retrying a defendant who succeeds in getting his first conviction set aside, through direct appeal or collateral attack, because of some error in the proceedings leading to conviction.

. . . This rule, which is a well-established part of our constitutional jurisprudence, . . . is necessary in order to ensure the "sound administration of justice."

The double jeopardy clause does not forbid retrial so long as the sum of the evidence, erroneously admitted or not, would have been sufficient to sustain a guilty verdict.

 Conviction of a Lesser Included Crime and Double Jeopardy

A lesser included crime is an offense, such as drunken driving, that is necessarily included in the greater offense of homicide by intoxicated use of a vehicle or vehicular manslaughter. The facts needed to prove the lesser offense are also essential elements of the greater offense.

In the 1990 case of *Grady v. Corbin*,[37] the U.S. Supreme Court answered the question as to whether a conviction for a lesser included crime would bar (prevent) charging and conviction for the greater offense.

Double Jeopardy and Lesser Included Offenses

Conviction of a lesser included offense would bar (forbid) charging or conviction of the greater offense. A lesser included offense could be:

- a traffic ticket,
- or a minor crime, or any offense that has one or more of the elements of the greater offense (See the U.S. Supreme Court cases of *Grady v. Corbin* and *Illinois v. Vitale.*)

Punishment that could also bar (forbid) an additional criminal or civil charge for the same conduct could be:

- a civil action that results in a punitive fine as distinguished from a fine that compensates for damages or loss (See the U.S. Supreme Court case of *United States v. Halper.*)

In that case, Thomas Corbin drove a vehicle in the State of New York while very intoxicated and struck two oncoming vehicles. As a result of the collision, one person died and another was seriously injured. Two uniform traffic tickets were issued to Corbin that night (one for the misdemeanor of drunken driving and the other for failing to keep to the right of the median). Corbin's lawyer did what defense lawyers throughout the United States have been doing. He got into the court as soon as possible to enter guilty pleas to the two lesser included offenses and then argued double jeopardy when the state charged Corbin with the greater criminal charges of vehicular manslaughter and other charges.

The U.S. Supreme Court held that "if the offenses have identical statutory elements or that one is a lesser included offense of the other, then ... the subsequent prosecution is barred." The U.S. Supreme Court concluded:

* * *

Drunk driving is a national tragedy. Prosecutors' offices are often overworked and may not always have the time to monitor seemingly minor cases as they wind through the judicial system. But these facts cannot excuse the need for scrupulous adherence to our constitutional principles. See *Santobello v. New York*, 404 U.S. 257, 260, 92 S.Ct. 495, 497, 30 L.Ed.2d 427 (1971) ("This record represents another example of an unfortunate lapse in orderly prosecutorial procedures, in part, no doubt, because of the enormous increase in the workload of the often understaffed prosecutor's offices. The heavy workload may well explain these episodes, but it does not excuse them"). With adequate preparation and foresight, the State could have prosecuted Corbin for the offenses charged in the traffic tickets and the subsequent indictment in a single proceeding, thereby avoiding this double jeopardy question. We have concluded that the Double Jeopardy Clause of the Fifth Amendment demands application of the standard announced today, but we are confident that with proper planning and attention prosecutors will be able to meet this standard and bring to justice those who make our Nation's roads unsafe.

The U.S. Supreme Court held in the drunken driving case of *Illinois v. Vitale*[38] that the traffic charge of failure to reduce speed is not a lesser included crime of drunken driving and involuntary manslaughter. The *Grady* Court distinguished the *Grady* case from the 1980 *Vitale* case as follows:

* * *

The facts and contentions raised here mirror almost exactly those raised in this Court 10 years ago in *Illinois v. Vitale*, 447 U.S. 410, 100 S.Ct. 2260, 65 L.Ed.2d 228 (1980). Like Thomas Corbin, John Vitale allegedly caused a fatal car accident. A police officer at the scene issued Vitale a traffic citation charging him with failure to reduce speed to avoid an accident in violation of § 11−601(a) of the Illinois Vehicle Code. Vitale was convicted of that offense and sentenced to pay a $15 fine. The day after his conviction, the State charged Vitale with two counts of involuntary manslaughter based on his reckless driving. Vitale argued that this subsequent prosecution was barred by the Double Jeopardy Clause.

This Court held that the second prosecution was not barred under the traditional *Blockburger* test because each offense "require[d] proof of a fact which the other [did] not." See *Blockburger*, 284 U.S., at 304, 52 S.Ct., at 182. Although involuntary manslaughter required proof of a death, failure to reduce speed did not. Likewise, failure to slow was not a statutory element of involuntary manslaughter. Thus, the subsequent prosecution survived the *Blockburger* test.

* * *

The "Jurisdictional Exception" to the Double Jeopardy Clause

Some states have adopted the "jurisdictional exception" to the double jeopardy clause, which was stated by U.S. Supreme Court Justice Brennan in his concurring opinion in *Ashe v. Swenson,* 397 U.S. 436, 90 S.Ct. 1189 (1970). However, the U.S. Supreme Court has neither explicitly accepted or rejected the exception to date.

The jurisdictional exception would exist (in states using the exception) if no single court has jurisdiction over all the alleged crimes. Jeopardy, therefore, could not extend to an offense beyond the jurisdiction of the court in which the accused is tried. Examples of states using the exception are:

New Mexico: The defendant was convicted of assault and battery in a justice of the peace court and was later convicted of rape in a state court. Because the justice of the peace did not have jurisdiction to hear the felony rape charge, it was held there was no violation of double jeopardy. *State v. Goodson,* 54 N.M. 184, 217 P.2d 262 (1950).

Pennsylvania: After a seventeen-year-old youth struck and killed a seven-year-old boy while driving a car, the youth was convicted of reckless driving and driving at an unsafe speed before a district judge. Juvenile authorities then filed charges in children's court alleging homicide by vehicle and aggravated assault. Because the district court did not have jurisdiction over the youth in the serious felony charges, the Superior Court of Pennsylvania held that there was no violation of double jeopardy under the "jurisdiction exception." *In the Matter of Jelbert Huff,* 399 Pa. Super. 574, 582 A.2d 1093 (1990).

In accidents involving death or serious injuries, great care must be exercised by law enforcement officers not to issue minor charges in cases where there is the possibility of more serious criminal charges being filed after the facts of the case are known. For a case applying the double jeopardy rule of *Grady v. Corbin,* see *Taylor v. Sherrill,* 166 Ariz. 359, 802 P.2d 1058, 48 CrL 1056 (App. 1990).

Can a Civil Conviction in Addition to a Criminal Conviction for the Same Conduct Violate Double Jeopardy?

Money fines are commonly used in civil actions. Some civil fines can be very large and very punitive. For example, Adolfo Sanchez was fined $232,000 in a civil action for attempting to bring twenty-nine pounds of marijuana into the United States without declaring the marijuana.

After Mr. Sanchez agreed to pay the $232,000 fine, criminal charges were then commenced against him in the case of *United States v. Sanchez,* 47 CrL 1026 S.D.Tex. (1990). The District Court dismissed the charges, citing the U.S. Supreme Court case of *United States v. Halper,*[39] which held that a civil penalty for the same acts amounts to double jeopardy if the civil penalty is punitive and not remedial, i.e., to collect damages.

In the *Halper* case, the defendant was convicted of sixty-five violations of the false-claim statute (Medicare fraud). The civil penalties against the defendant amounted to $130,000. The U.S. Supreme Court stated:

> . . . We therefore hold that under the Double Jeopardy Clause a defendant who already has been punished in a criminal prosecution may not be subjected to an additional civil sanction to the extent that the second sanction may not fairly be characterized as remedial, but only as a deterrent or retribution.

* * *

... What we announce now is a rule for the rare case, the case such as the one before us, where a fixed-penalty provision subjects a prolific but small-gauge offender to a sanction overwhelmingly disproportionate to the damages he has caused. The rule is one of reason: Where a defendant previously has sustained a criminal penalty and the civil penalty sought in the subsequent proceeding bears no rational relation to the goal of compensating the Government for its loss, but rather appears to qualify as "punishment" in the plain meaning of the word, then the defendant is entitled to an accounting of the Government's damages and costs to determine if the penalty sought in fact constitutes a second punishment. We must leave to the trial court the discretion to determine on the basis of such an accounting, the size of the civil sanction the Government may receive without crossing the line between remedy and punishment.

* * *

SIngle Offense or Multiple Offenses?

A defendant, seeking to kill, fires a handgun three times at the victim, missing each time. Should the defendant be charged with one count of attempted murder or three? In a "drug store" drug case where a defendant had large and small amounts of ten different illegal substances, what criminal charges should be issued? In a sexual assault case that went on for an hour with a variety of conduct, should multiple charges be issued?

Is a prosecutor justified in issuing (or seeking) multiple criminal charges in order to obtain a guilty plea in return for dropping one or two of the charges? Victims like this practice. Court calendars are kept smaller and it saves time.

The following old U.S. Supreme Court cases illustrate rulings on whether multiple charges or a single charge are justified. The specific wording of the criminal statute and the legislative intent in your state would generally govern.

Conduct	Ruling	Case
"Whether one who, in the same transaction, tears or cuts successively mail bags of the United States used in conveyance of the mails, with intent to rob or steal any such mail, is guilty of a single offense, or of additional offenses. . .?"	". . . it was the intent of the lawmakers to protect each and every bag. . . . Whenever any one mail bag is thus torn, cut, or injured, the offense is complete. . . ."	*Ebeling v. Morgan,* 237 U.S. 625, 35 S.Ct. 710 (1915)
Illegal sale of ten grains of morphine on a specific day; followed by a sale of eight grains on the following day; and additional morphine at a still later date.	". . . the first transaction resulting in a sale, had come to an end. The next sale was not the result of the original impulse, but of a fresh one—that is to say, of a new bargain."	*Blockburger v. United States,* 284 U.S. 299, 52 S.Ct. 180 (1932)
Cohabiting with more than one woman (old crime of bigamy or adultery).	"It is inherently, a continuous offense, having duration; and not an offense consisting of an isolated act."	*In re Snow,* 120 U.S. 274. 7 S.Ct. 556 (1887)

Res Judicata and Collateral Estoppel as Part of the Double Jeopardy Guarantee

If Smith has a lawsuit against Jones, Smith is entitled to his day in court. However, if Smith loses his case, the controversy between the two persons has then been adjudicated and Smith cannot continue to commence new lawsuits based on the same issue. Should Smith commence a new lawsuit on the same issue against Jones, the lawyer for Jones could use *res judicata* (the issue has been decided) as a defense.

Collateral estoppel, an extension of the doctrine of *res judicata,* forbids retrying of factual issues that have already been determined. The doctrines of *res judicata* and *collateral estoppel* apply not only to civil cases, but as early as 1916 were also made applicable to criminal cases by the U.S. Supreme Court.[40] The following cases illustrate the application of *res judicata* and *collateral estoppel* in criminal cases:

ASHE v. SWENSON
Supreme Court of the United States (1970) 397 U.S. 436, 90 S.Ct. 1189

In 1960, six men playing poker in the basement of a house were surprised and robbed by three or four masked gunmen. The defendant was arrested and charged with six counts of robbery but was first brought to trial on the charge of robbing only one of the poker players. The jury found Ashe not guilty, after being instructed that the theft of "any money" would sustain a conviction. Six weeks later, Ashe was tried for the robbery of another of the poker players and this time convicted. The appeal was from the conviction. In reversing the conviction, the U.S. Supreme Court stated:

> *The question is not whether Missouri could validly charge the petitioner with six separate offenses for the robbery of the six poker players. It is not whether he could have received a total of six punishments if he had been convicted in a single trial of robbing the six victims. It is simply whether, after a jury determined by its verdict that the petitioner was not one of the robbers, the State could constitutionally hale him before a new jury to litigate that issue again . . .*
>
> *In this case the State in its brief has frankly conceded that following the petitioner's acquittal, it treated the first trial as no more than a dry run for the second prosecution: "No doubt the prosecutor felt the state had a provable case on the first charge and, when he lost, he did what every good attorney would do—he refined his presentation in light of the turn of events at the first trial." But this is precisely what the constitutional guarantee forbids.*

STATE v. PROULX
Supreme Court of New Hampshire (1970) 110 N.H. 187, 263 A.2d 673

The defendant was charged with incest based on allegations that he had sexual intercourse with his daughter on four different specific days in 1967 and 1968. His entire defense was that no act of intercourse had taken place. After he was acquitted of these charges, the state then charged him with the rape of his daughter on four days different from those that figured in the first trial. The defendant argues that double jeopardy bars the second trial.

The Court held that the doctrine of *collateral estoppel,* not double jeopardy, barred the second prosecution.

> *Collateral estoppel which is an extension of the doctrine of res judicata bars relitigation of factual issues which have already been determined and, like the doctrine of double jeopardy, is designed to eliminate the expense, vexation, waste and possible inconsistent results of duplicatory litigation.*

| PEOPLE v. ALLEE
| Supreme Court of Colorado (1987) 740 P.2d 1

The defendant and his son were charged with assault on a police officer following a fight in the parking lot of a tavern. The defendant's son was tried first and was found not guilty (acquitted). At the defendant's trial, the defendant used the defense of collateral estoppel against the criminal charges of assault and resisting arrest. The Supreme Court of Colorado held:

* * *

"The doctrine of collateral estoppel 'means simply that when an issue of ultimate fact has once been determined by a valid and final judgement, that issue cannot again be litigated between the same parties in any future lawsuit.'" Wright v. People, *690 P.2d 1257, 1260 (Colo. 1984) (quoting* Ashe v. Swenson, *397 U.S. 436, 443, 90 S.Ct. 1189, 1194, 25 L.Ed.2d 469 (1970)). The doctrine was first developed in the context of civil litigation in order to promote judicial economy, conserve private resources, and protect parties from the prospect of vexatious litigation.*

* * *

We conclude that the acquittal of one defendant in a separate proceeding does not collaterally estop the People from prosecuting another defendant in a separate trial. The jury's acquittal of Ronnie Allee does not mean that the People will necessarily be unable to prove Dale Allee's guilt beyond a reasonable doubt. We see no persuasive reason to forbid the People from attempting to do so. . . .

J. ENTRAPMENT, FRAME-UP, AND "OUTRAGEOUS GOVERNMENT CONDUCT" AS DEFENSES

1. Entrapment

When the U.S. Supreme Court recognized entrapment as a defense for the first time, Justice Owen J. Roberts wrote in the 1932 case of *Sorrells v. United States* that "society is at war with the criminal classes, and courts have uniformly held that in waging this warfare, the forces of prevention and detection may use traps, decoys, and deception to obtain evidence of the commission of crime."[41] It has always been necessary for law enforcement agencies to determine whether offenses that would not ordinarily be reported to them by victims or witnesses are being committed within their jurisdiction.[42]

In investigating possible narcotics, gambling, prostitution, liquor violations, bribery, and sometimes other very serious felonies, it is necessary for law enforcement officials to set traps, make some inducements, and employ decoys to afford suspects an opportunity to commit the crime of which they are suspected. Officers and agents of the officers must often act in the capacity of willing victims. Some encouragement, some pretended willingness, some persuasion, some temptation, and some inducement may be made by law enforcement officers or their agents, but it is improper for officers to use excessive inducement, encouragement, or temptation, which is likely to cause persons to commit crimes they would not ordinarily be disposed to commit.

A defendant using the defense of entrapment most often admits that he or she has committed the crime but alleges that a law enforcement officer or an officer's

Marion Barry, former mayor of Washington D.C., used the entrapment defense as his defense after he was charged with fourteen crimes related to his alleged use of drugs.

agent has used improper methods to induce the act that would not have been done had it not been for the improper inducement or encouragement of the officer. In a frame-up defense, the defendant claims innocence and maintains that evidence was planted by the police. If it can be shown that the defendant was entrapped or framed, the result is a complete defense, and the charge must fall.

What Inducements Do Not Amount to Entrapment?

Courts throughout the United States have long recognized that it is proper for law enforcement officers (or their agents) to create ordinary opportunities for a person to commit an offense if the criminal intent or willingness originated in the mind of the defendant. The fact that the officer afforded the opportunity or the facility for the defendant to commit the crime in order to obtain evidence does not constitute entrapment. For example, a mere offer to purchase narcotics, obscene literature, or other contraband without further inducement is not entrapment. The tolerable degree of governmental participation in a criminal enterprise was defined by the U.S. Supreme Court *Russell* and *Hampton* cases.

What Inducements Are Improper and Do Amount to Entrapment?

Although law enforcement officers may create and present the usual and ordinary opportunities for a person to commit a crime, they may not use excessive urging, inducement, temptations, or solicitations to commit a crime. The 1932 *Sorrells* case and the 1958 *Sherman* case illustrate misconduct by persons representing the government. The Supreme Court quoted another court as follows in the *Sorrells* case:

The Four U.S. Supreme Cases Defining Entrapment

SORRELLS v. UNITED STATES
Supreme Court of the United States (1932) 287 U.S. 435, 53 S.Ct. 210

This is the first entrapment case to appear before the Supreme Court. A federal prohibition officer passed himself off as a tourist and became acquainted with Sorrells. After talking about the same army division they were in, the officer repeatedly asked the defendant to get him some illegal liquor. When Sorrells did, he was arrested and convicted. The Supreme Court reversed the conviction, holding:

> "[T]he Government cannot be permitted to contend that [a defendant] is guilty of a crime where government officials are the instigators of his conduct," id. at 452

SHERMAN v. UNITED STATES
Supreme Court of the United States (1958) 356 U.S. 369, 78 S.Ct. 819

A government informant and the defendant met in a doctor's office where they were both being treated for narcotics addiction. After several accidental meetings, the informant asked the defendant for a source of narcotics, stating that he was not responding to treatments. The defendant tried to avoid the issue but the informant continued to ask for narcotics, stating that he was suffering. In holding that the informant "not only enticed the defendant into carrying out an illegal sale but also to returning to the habit of use" and that this was entrapment, the Court reversed the conviction of the defendant.

UNITED STATES v. RUSSELL
Supreme Court of the United States (1973) 411 U.S. 423, 93 S.Ct. 1637

An undercover narcotic agent worked his way into a group manufacturing "speed" by offering to supply them with an essential ingredient that was difficult to obtain but necessary. After seeing the drug lab, the undercover agent was told the defendants had been producing the illegal drug for seven months. After the agent supplied the essential ingredient, the agent received half of the finished batch of "speed" in payment. A month later, another batch of "speed" was made and the agent obtained a search warrant. Defendant Russell's sole defense was entrapment. In holding that the participation of the narcotic agent was not entrapment, the Supreme Court stated:

The illicit manufacture of drugs is not a sporadic, isolated criminal incident, but a continuing, though illegal, business enterprise. In order to obtain convictions for illegally manufacturing drugs, the gathering of evidence of past unlawful conduct frequently proves to be an all but impossible task. Thus in drug-related offenses law enforcement personnel have turned to one of the only practicable means of detection: the infiltration of drug rings and a limited participation in their unlawful present practices. Such infiltration is a recognized and permissible means of apprehension; if that be so, then the supply of some item of value that the drug ring requires must, as a general rule, also be permissible. For an agent will not be taken into the confidence of the illegal entrepreneurs unless he has something of value to offer them. Law enforcement tactics such as this can hardly be said to violate "fundamental fairness" or "shocking to the universal sense of justice."

HAMPTON v. UNITED STATES
Supreme Court of the United States (1976) 425 U.S. 484, 96 S.Ct. 1646

An informer arranged two separate unlawful heroin sales by the defendant to undercover law enforcement officers. A government witness testified at the trial that the defendant supplied the heroin, but the defendant testified that he received the heroin that he sold to the agents from the informer. The defendant also claimed that he believed the substance to be a "non-narcotic counterfeit drug which would give the same reaction as heroin." The defendant requested that the jury be instructed that he be found not guilty if they found that the informer, acting as a government agent, supplied the heroin. However, the trial court would not give the instruction and the jury convicted the defendant despite his claims. On appeal to the U.S. Supreme Court, the defendant argued that the jury instruction should have been given, because when the government itself supplies narcotics, the defendant is a victim of illegal government entrapment. In affirming the defendant's conviction, the Court held that a successful entrapment defense required that the defendant not have the criminal intention until implanted by the government agent.

It is well settled that decoys may be used to entrap criminals, and to present opportunity to one intending or willing to commit crime. But decoys are not permissible to ensnare the innocent and law-abiding into the commission of crime. When the criminal design originates, not with the accused, but is conceived in the mind of the government officers, and the accused is by persuasion, deceitful representation, or inducement lured into the commission of a criminal act, the government is estopped by sound public policy from prosecution therefor.

Tests Used to Determine When a Defendant Is Predisposed to Commit the Crime

In the 1973 case of *United States v. Russell,* the U.S. Supreme Court stated that, "this Court's opinions in Sorrells v. United States . . . and Sherman v. United States . . . held that the principal element in the defense of entrapment was the defendant's predisposition to commit the crime." The Supreme Court also pointed out that the entrapment defense was not of a constitutional dimension, and that Congress or any of the state legislatures may address themselves to the problem and "adopt any substantive definition of the defense that it may desire." Some states already have defined entrapment by statute, and more may do so in the future. Most states, however, use common law definitions of the defense of entrapment.[43] The jury instruction given by the court in the *Russell* case states this definition:

> Where a person has the willingness and the readiness to break the law, the mere fact that the Government Agent provides what appears to be a favorable opportunity is not entrapment and the jury should acquit the defendant if it had a . . . reasonable doubt whether the defendant had the previous intent or purpose to commit the offense . . . and did so only because he was induced or persuaded by some officer or agent of the Government.[44]

Therefore, the circumstances and the extent of government encouragement or participation would have to be considered by the trier of fact or law in determining the issue of entrapment. Most states and the federal courts use the "origin-of-intent" test or the "inducement test" in determining whether the defendant was predisposed to commit the crime charged. Under this test, the defendant's past criminal record is important as to the issue of whether entrapment did or did not exist. Therefore, a defendant who had several narcotics convictions would find it more difficult to show that he was not predisposed to commit further narcotics offenses if entrapment was used as a defense to a narcotics charge. The state would find it more difficult to show predisposition if a defendant had no criminal record and earned his or her living in a manner that would not suggest that he or she was predisposed to commit the crime charged.

In the *Sorrells* and *Sherman* cases, minority concurring opinions were written urging the adoption of what is known as the "objective." This test differs from the origin-of-intent test primarily in the fact that the state cannot present the past record of the defendant with respect to the issue of whether entrapment did or did not exist. In the minority concurring opinion in *Sherman v. United States,* the minority justices stated:

> A test that looks to the character and predisposition of the defendant rather than the conduct of the police loses sight of the underlying reason for the defense of entrapment. No matter what the defendant's past record and present inclinations to criminality, or the depths to which he has sunk in the estimation of society, certain police conduct to ensnare him into further crime is not to be tolerated by an advanced society.

Entrapment Used as a Defense in the De Lorean and Barry Cases

They were "set up," but were they entrapped?

Entrapment is an affirmative defense that must be raised by a defendant. The defendant must produce evidence showing:

1. that the government initiated, suggested, or proposed the crime and
2. that the defendant was not predisposed to commit the crime.

If the defense successfully raises the issue of entrapment, one of the following two results will occur:

1. If entrapment is shown to have clearly occurred as a matter of law, the trial judge should dismiss the criminal charge (police misconduct could cause immediate dismissal).
2. If the defendant has raised a factual question as to whether entrapment occurred, the defendant is then entitled to a jury instruction on the issue, with the jury making the factual determination.

Former Car Maker John De Lorean

De Lorean's company was known to be in financial trouble and it was suspected that De Lorean was dealing in cocaine. After a series of videotaped meetings with undercover drug agents, De Lorean was charged with drug trafficking.

The issue of entrapment was raised in the five-month De Lorean trial ending in August 1984. Defense lawyers showed on lengthy cross-examination of government agents that potential evidence was destroyed, that investigative guidelines were violated, and that the agents failed to keep a proper rein on their paid informant. The agents admitted that they, not De Lorean, had been in charge during the drug transaction. When De Lorean backed out of the drug deal because of a lack of cash, it was government agents who called him back suggesting the use of collateral. When the government's chief prosecutor and the drug agents had drinks together, the defense presented the meeting as a boozy celebration of De Lorean's imminent arrest. Agents admitted that they speculated as to whether they would make the cover of *Time* magazine. De Lorean did not take the witness stand in his own defense, but the jury after seven days of deliberation found him not guilty of all eight criminal charges.

Former Mayor of Washington, D.C., Marion Barry

Because law enforcement officers had information that Mayor Barry was using drugs, an FBI sting operation was set up. A former girlfriend lured the mayor to a fashionable hotel where an 83-minute videotape was made showing the mayor smoking cocaine. Marion Barry was charged with fourteen crimes. After a ten-week trial, Mayor Barry was convicted of one misdemeanor (possession of cocaine) and sentenced to six months in jail and probation. Mr. Barry's chief lawyer stated, "We feel very lucky," referring to the jury accepting the entrapment defense and not convicting the mayor of any of the felony charges.

In judging the defendant's conduct, the jury must determine whether his or her immediate and ready compliance with the inducement of the officer should be construed as indicating a prior disposition to commit the offense. If the defendant did not immediately comply with the inducement or showed reluctance to commit the crime, the jury would have to determine whether the reluctance was due to fear of detection or whether there existed a genuine reluctance on the part of the defendant to commit the crime charged.

Have the Police "Cast Their Nets in Permissible Waters"?

The question of "whether the police have cast their nets in permissible waters" was raised in the *Sherman* case (Justice Frankfurter asking this question). The answer in that case and also in the *Sorrells* case was "no," the police were held to be using excessive inducements to tempt otherwise innocent persons. The question as to whether the police were fishing in "permissible waters" was also raised in the following 1985 Florida case:

CRUZ v. STATE
Supreme Court of Florida (1985) 465 So.2d 516, review denied 473 U.S. 905, 105 S.Ct. 3527

Police set up a "drunken bum decoy" where a police officer pretended to be drunk and smelled of alcohol. As the officer leaned against a building near an alleyway, $150 in currency could be seen sticking out of his rear pants pocket. Cruz came by with a woman, may have said something to the "bum," and continued down the street. Ten minutes later, Cruz came back and took the money without harming the decoy. Cruz was then arrested and convicted of grand theft.

The Supreme Court of Florida quashed (threw out) Cruz's conviction and established a two-part test to be used in the State of Florida (the test is found in note 45). The court held that:

The decoy situation did not involve the same modus operandi as any of the unsolved crimes which had occurred in the area. Police were not seeking a particular individual, nor were they aware of any prior criminal acts by the defendant.

* * *

[T]hat the police activity . . . constituted entrapment as a matter of law under the threshold test[45] adopted here.

In a similar Nevada "drunken bum decoy" case, the Supreme Court of Nevada also ruled that the defendant was entrapped. To target a specific person in Nevada, law enforcement officers must have reasonable suspicion to believe the person is predisposed to commit the crime (See *Washoe County Sheriff v. Hawkins,* 43 CrL 2053, 3/31/88 and *Shrader v. State,* 38 CrL 2069, 10/23/85).

Under the *Cruz* test used by Florida courts, promising a drug addict free drugs if he buys drugs for an informer was held to be entrapment as a matter of law (*Pezzella v. State,* 513 So.2d 1328 (Fla.App. 1987). But Pennsylvania does not use Florida's "objective" test and a defendant who made drug purchases for an undercover police officer was not "entrapped" when the officer allowed him to keep some drugs for his personal use. The Court pointed out that this is a com-

---

Using the Defense of Entrapment while at the Same Time Denying Committing the Crime: Can Inconsistent Defenses be Used?

The question before the U.S. Supreme Court in the 1988 case of *Mathews v. United States* was whether a defendant could use the defense of entrapment while at the same time denying he committed the crime (accepting a bribe). Many courts would not allow defendants to use entrapment along with a denial. In reviewing the cases, the Supreme Court pointed out that, historically, inconsistent defenses have been permitted where the evidence justifies it:

- In an 1896 murder case arising out of a gunfight in Indian Territory, the defense of self-defense was used along with an instruction on manslaughter. Killing in heat of passion is inconsistent with self-defense. *Stevenson v. United States,* 162 U.S. 313, 16 S.Ct. 839 (1896)

- In a 1970 rape case, the defendant was permitted to argue that the act did not take place and that the victim consented. *Johnson v. United States,* 426 F.2d 651 (D.C. Cir. 1970)

- State cases permitting homicide defendants to jury instructions on both accident and self-defense. 4 *Wharton* Sec. 545 p. 32

- In permitting the defense of entrapment to be used along with a denial of the crime charged, the U.S. Supreme Court held that they were "simply not persuaded by the Government's arguments that we should make the availability of an instruction on entrapment where the evidence justifies it subject to a requirement of consistency to which no other such defense is subject." *Mathews v. United States,* 485 U.S. 58, 108 S.Ct. 883 (1988)

As this issue is not a constitutional issue, some states continue to require defendants to be consistent in the use of the defense of entrapment. The Supreme Courts of both Arizona and Florida held in 1991 that they would continue using the old rule. (See *Wilson v. State (Florida)* 49 CrL 1030 and *State (Arizona) v. Soule,* 49 CrL 1031). Defendants in these states must admit all elements of the crime charged to use the defense of entrapment. Florida does allow a defendant to assert innocence and use entrapment, as Florida does not consider this to be inconsistent.

---

mon practice known as "skimming" and a "copping fee." Pennsylvania's highest court held the practice was not an improper inducement to commit the crime (*Commonwealth v. Delligatti,* 371 Pa. Super. 315, 538 A.2d 34 (1988).

2. "Outrageous Government Conduct"

A defendant who cannot claim entrapment may still be able to invoke the defense of "outrageous government conduct." The U.S. Supreme Court first raised the concept of outrageous police conduct in the 1973 case of *United States v. Russell* (presented in this unit) where the Court stated:

> [W]e may some day be presented with a situation in which the conduct of law enforcement agents is so outrageous that due process principles would absolutely bar the government from invoking judicial processes to obtain a conviction.... *Id.* at 431–32, 93 S.Ct. at 1642–43.

In the 1976 case of *Hampton v. United States,* Justice Powell stated that "police overinvolvement in crime would have to reach a demonstrable level of outrageousness before it could bar conviction."[46] Reference was also made to "outrageous violation of physical integrity, e.g., *Rochin v. California,* 342 U.S. 165."

The defendants in the Abscam trials (including seven U.S. congressmen and a U.S. senator) could have used the entrapment defense but instead some of them argued that the "methods used by government agents in developing the cases against them exceed an outer limit of fairness mandated by the Due Process Clause."[47] They argued that "the conduct of Abscam violated standards of due process because the Government's role in the investigation was excessive and fundamentally unfair."[48]

The court rejected the Abscam defendants' claims that due process was violated by the conduct of the government agents. It held that the evidence "reveals them [defendants] as unmistakably involved in a corrupt agreement to misuse public office for private gain," and that the "conduct of the investigation, though subject to some criticism, affords no basis for rejecting the convictions."[49]

Cases Where Convictions Were Set Aside Because of "Outrageous Government Conduct"

In the following cases, the defendants' convictions were set aside because of what courts ruled to be "outrageous government conduct":

GREENE v. UNITED STATES
Court of Appeals, Ninth Circuit (1971) 454 F.2d 783

After the defendants' arrest on former bootlegging charges, government agents contacted them and offered to buy all the alcohol they could produce. Agents supplied sugar at wholesale prices, urged defendants to produce, and acted as only customer for more than two and a half years. The Court held that the government was so enmeshed in the criminal activity that it was barred from prosecuting defendants.

COMMONWEALTH v. MATHEWS
Supreme Court of Pennsylvania (1985) 347 Pa.Super. 320, 500 A.2d 853

The intense police involvement included physically hauling property, encouragement, supplying money, and supplying not only a manual with formula but also a government chemist to instruct defendants on detailed steps of manufacture of methamphetamine. (For a similar ruling, scc *United States v. Twigg,* 588 F.2d 373, 3d Cir. 1978.)

UNITED STATES v. VALDOVINOS
U.S. District Court, Northern District of California (1984) 588 F.Supp. 551

The Court held that the INS (Immigration and Naturalization Service) created crimes by setting up a "cold line" (telephone) in Mexico advising Mexicans (still in Mexico) that it was appropriate to violate U.S. laws. The INS was seeking to identify the persons running smuggling rings.

Cases of Unusual Conduct Where Convictions Were Affirmed

Convictions were affirmed in the following cases where unusual means were used to obtain evidence against the defendants:

STATE v. TOOKES
Supreme Court of Hawaii (1985) 67 Hawaii 608, 699 P.2d 983

Fox, a civilian police volunteer, went all the way and had sex with women in Honolulu to obtain evidence that resulted in their prostitution convictions. The Supreme Court of Hawaii affirmed the convictions holding:

＊ ＊ ＊

While we question whether the actions of Fox and the police in this case comport with the ethical standards which law enforcement officials should be guided by, we cannot say that they constituted outrageous conduct in the constitutional sense. Neither are we able to find a due process violation because Fox's conduct, if undertaken by a police officer, would have violated an internal Department rule against engaging in sex with a prostitute in order to obtain evidence sufficient for a conviction. Admittedly, the police are not to be congratulated for having discovered a means to circumvent the rules promulgated as standards for their own conduct. There was no showing, however, that such a rule was compelled by law or the constitution. As such, the fact that an agent was used to avoid it seems a slim thread upon which to hang a holding of constitutional dimensions.

* * *

Other cases where courts ruled the same are: *Municipality of Anchorage v. Flanagan,* 649 P.2d 957, 32 CrL 2015 (Alaska CtApp 1982); *State v. Putnam,* 639 P.2d 858 (Wash. Ct.App. 1982).

UNITED STATES v. SIMPSON
U.S. Court of Appeals, Ninth Circuit (1987), 813 F.2d 1462 (42 CrL 4037)

FBI agents continued to use a known prostitute and heroin addict as an informer even after it was learned that she was regularly having sex with the principle suspect. After reviewing cases and holding that it was not "outrageous conduct," the court stated:

* * *

We recognize that many people in our society may find the deceptive use of sex in law enforcement to be morally offensive. Nonetheless, "in order to apprehend those engaged in serious crime, government agents may lawfully use methods that are neither appealing nor moral if judged by abstract norms of decency," Bogart, 783 F.2d at 1438.

* * *

Our Constitution leaves it to the political branches of government to decide whether to regulate law enforcement conduct which may "offend some fastidious squeamishness or private sentimentalism about combatting crime too energetically," Rochin, 342 U.S. at 172, 72 S.Ct. at 209, but which is not antithetical to fundamental notions of due process.

* * *

| UNITES STATES v. SMITH
| **United States Court of Appeals, Ninth Circuit (1986) 802 F.2d 1119**

In a cocaine delivery case, using the defendant's brother as an informer might be called a dirty trick, but the Court held it was not "outrageous conduct":

* * *

The government's conduct in this case, although close, did not cross over the line into a due process violation. The agents used Smith's own brother to solicit the drug transactions, but those two had not been very close in the past, and the agents had no indication that Smith was emotionally dependent on his brother.

3. The Frame-up Defense

In the 1983 case of *Moore v. United States,*[50] the defendant claimed that a police officer "planted" a gun on him when he was stopped and searched on a street in Washington, D.C. In most "frame-up" cases, defendants argue that they did not know that the drugs (or gun) were in their pocket, and that they did not know who placed the illegal object there. In the *Moore* case, however, the Court pointed out that "this is not a case in which appellant denied any knowledge of the source of the item allegedly seized. Nor is this a case in which appellant did not allege he was illegally searched by police."

In the *Moore* case, the defense argued that as the defendant was not carrying a concealed weapon, he should not be convicted of carrying a concealed weapon.

In a frame-up defense, if a law enforcement officer is accused of "planting" the illegal contraband (gun, drugs, etc.) the officer is accused of illegal acts. When a defendant claims that he did not know who placed the contraband in his pocket (or on his person) and that he does not know the source of the contraband, he is alleging that (a) he was framed by another person and (b) as he did not knowingly and intentionally possess the contraband, he should not be convicted, as an essential element of the crime of possession cannot be shown.

A form of frame-up that would not be a defense is illustrated by the following example:

EXAMPLE: A wife persuades her husband to commit a burglary and, while the burglary is in process, the wife calls the police, who apprehend the husband.

Although the husband has been "set-up" by the wife, he could not successfully use this as a defense to either entrapment or frame-up. The husband could be convicted of burglary and the wife would also probably be charged as a party to the crime of burglary.

K. The Right to a Speedy Trial as a Defense

The Sixth Amendment of the U.S. Constitution provides that "in all criminal prosecutions, the accused shall enjoy the right to a speedy and public trial." Most defendants charged with a serious crime do not ordinarily wish either a speedy or public trial, but unless the right to a speedy trial is waived with the consent of the trial court, the constitutional mandate of a speedy trial must be complied

Sting and Scam Operations

Defense lawyers have attacked sting operations as "witch hunts" and "cunning plots to destroy." After Abscam sent seven members of the U.S. Congress, including one senator, to prison, Abscam was attacked on the floor of the U.S. Congress. The FBI director came to the defense of Abscam (see footnote 49) in a 90-minute televised interview. Many sting and scam operations have been very successful. A few have not. The need for such operations was stated by Leon Jaworski (late Watergate special prosecutor) in his defense of Abscam: "To catch a crook, it is usually necessary to conduct undercover work involving stealth. It is not to be expected that any (Abscam defendants) would accept money at high noon on the front steps of the Capitol." Examples of some of the many sting and scam operations follow:

Abscam   In this undercover FBI sting operation, FBI agents dressed as Arab sheiks and paid bribes to U.S. congressmen and other high officials suspected of engaging in such conduct. As a result of Abscam, seven members of the U.S. Congress, including one senator, were indicted and convicted of a series of offenses.

Operation FIST   (Fugitive Investigative Strike Team) Arrest warrants are issued every year for thousands of persons who cannot be located. Many of these persons are arrested through scams by FIST. Letters and telephone calls tell fugitives they have won free trips, a day at the races, or that income tax refunds are waiting to be picked up. When the wanted persons show up to claim their "prize," they are arrested.

Operation Greylord*   Because of information that for "the right price, bagmen can fix the outcome of court cases in Chicago ranging from theft to divorce to traffic violations to murder,"† a massive Abscam-type probe was commenced. The purpose was to uncover crooked attorneys, judges, and court personnel. With the assistance of a judge from southern Illinois, convictions of sixty-nine persons, including twelve sitting or former judges, were obtained through 1988.

Tavern, Restaurant, and Liquor Store Stings   Conducted to determine whether state liquor laws are being violated, particularly by sale of liquor to minors (also used to determine whether food stamp violations are occurring).

Storefront Stings   In every state and large city, police have set up sting operations to apprehend people selling and dealing in stolen property. Storefronts and other business fronts are used. These frequently used sting operations recover property taken in thefts, burglaries, shoplifting, and robbery. The offenders seek to exchange the property for drugs or money.

Operation Corkscrew   In order to determine whether some Cleveland judges were accepting bribes, FBI agents, in an Abscam-type sting operation, paid $85,000 to a court bailiff who had presented himself as a bagman arranging bribes. They ignored one small detail—obtaining pictures of the judges who the bailiff stated were accepting bribes. More than a year later, the FBI agents discovered the bailiff had used imposters to act as judges. The bungled sting did not disclose any crooked judges, but the bailiff and the persons who had pocketed the $85,000 were charged with criminal offenses.

"Sting" of Municipalities   In 1987 an FBI agent pretending to be a salesman of steel products offered bribes to public officials in forty New York and New Jersey municipalities. Of the 106 occasions that bribes were offered to highway superintendents, purchasing directors, and other municipal officials, 105 of the officials accepted the bribes. The 106th official refused the bribe because the amount was not enough. U.S. Attorney Giuliani pointed out that the municipal bribery and kickback case was the largest in his recollection and stated that New York "is a much friendlier place to corrupt politicians, crooked businessmen and organized criminals." An old-time politician shook his head over the matter and stated, "Bribery has been a crime in New York for over 200 years."

Drug Stings   Many drug stings have been used over the past years directed at persons selling drugs, persons seeking to purchase drugs, or both offenders. The January 1988 issue of the FBI Law Enforcement Bulletin has an excellent article, "Drug Stings in Miami," written by the Miami chief of police. It tells of sting operations in Miami, particularly directed toward persons buying drugs openly on Miami streets.

Internal Revenue Stings   In addition to a giant computer network, undercover agents, and use of informants, the IRS employs broad and sophisticated sting operations. In such operations, false documentation and laundered government money is used to infiltrate and penetrate businesses suspected of tax fraud.

*"Greylord" is a reference to the wigs worn by British judges.
†Statement by Illinois Judge Lockwood who worked with the FBI to uncover corrupt lawyers and judges.

with. Some states have enacted statutory requirements that specify the time period in which a defendant must be tried.[51] These statutes do not necessarily incorporate constitutional standards and may use alternative remedies without violating the Sixth Amendment requirements.

In holding that right to a speedy trial commences when a person "is indicted, arrested, or otherwise officially accused," the U.S. Supreme Court held in *United States v. Marion* that:

> The protection of the Amendment is activated only when a criminal prosecution has begun and extends only to those persons who have been "accused" in the course of that prosecution. These provisions would seem to afford no protection to those not yet accused, nor would they seem to require the Government to discover, investigate, and accuse any person within any particular period of time.[52]

The Court stated that the purpose and "interests served by the Speedy Trial Clause" are as follows:

> Inordinate delay between an arrest, indictment, and trial may impair a defendant's ability to present an effective defense. But the major evils protected against by the speedy trial guarantee exist quite apart from actual or possible prejudice to an accused's defense. To legally arrest and detain, the Government must assert probable cause to believe the arrestee has committed a crime. Arrest is a public act that may seriously interfere with the defendant's liberty, whether he is free on bail or not, and that may disrupt his employment, drain his financial resources, curtail his associations, subject him to public obloquy, and create anxiety in him, his family and his friends.[53]

In 1982, the widely publicized case of *United States v. MacDonald*[54] came before the U.S. Supreme Court. In 1970, Captain MacDonald's pregnant wife and two small daughters were brutally murdered in their home on the military reservation at Fort Bragg, North Carolina.

MacDonald, a physician, told a bizarre story of ritualistic murder by four intruders high on drugs who clubbed MacDonald into unconsciousness.

Because physical evidence at the murder scene contradicted MacDonald's story, he was charged by the Army with the three murders on May 1, 1970. After hearing fifty-six witnesses, the Army dismissed the charges on October 23, 1970. However, the U.S. Justice Department picked up the investigation in 1972, and in January 1975, a federal grand jury indicted MacDonald with the three murders.

Tried Twice for Murder in 1964 and Charged Again in 1991

In 1963, Medgar Evers, a nationally known civil rights leader, was shot and killed outside his home in Mississippi. Byron de la Beckwith, a segregationist, was tried twice for the slaying in 1964. However, two all-white juries were unable to reach verdicts ("hung" juries).

The State of Mississippi wants to try Beckwith a third time and commenced extradition proceedings to extradite Beckwith from Tennessee where he was living in 1991. Appeals were filed by Beckwith's attorney in the Tennessee state courts and from there could go into the federal courts. One of the defenses will be that of violation of the "speedy trial" requirement. Mr. Beckwith is now more than seventy years old.

MacDonald's attorney argued that MacDonald's right to a speedy trial had been violated, but the trial judge denied the motion and MacDonald was convicted by a jury of two counts of second-degree murder and one count of first-degree murder. He was sentenced to three consecutive terms of life imprisonment. The U.S. Supreme Court affirmed his convictions, holding that there were no speedy trial violations and stating: "Once the charges instituted by the Army were dismissed, MacDonald was legally and constitutionally in the same posture as though no charges had been made. He was free to go about his affairs, to practice his profession, and to continue with his life."

⚬ L. Time (Statute of Limitations) as a Defense

The old English common law adopted the doctrine that "no lapse bars the King"; therefore, statutes limiting the time for criminal prosecutions are rare in England.

However, criminal statutes of limitations appeared in America as early as 1652. The federal government adopted time limits for the prosecution of most federal crimes in 1790, and the majority of the states have enacted statutes of limitations for most crimes. Only South Carolina and Wyoming have no statutes of limitations.[55]

The speedy trial requirements are constitutional mandates and therefore are imposed on all states. Statutes of limitations on criminal prosecutions are optional legislative enactments. Reasons given for limitations on criminal prosecutions are:

> A limitation statute is designed to protect individuals from having to defend themselves against charges when the basic facts may have become obscured by the passage of time and to minimize the danger of official punishment because of acts in the far-distant past.[56]

* * *

> The Speedy Trial Clause and the limitations statutes work in tandem to prevent pretrial delay: the statutory period insures against pre-accusation delays and the Sixth Amendment controls the post-indictment time span. . . . Both provisions shield defendants from endless anxiety about possible prosecution and from impairment of the ability to mount a defense. By encouraging speedy prosecution, they also afford society protection from unincarcerated offenders, and insure against a diminution of the deterrent value of immediate convictions, as well as the reduced capacity of the government to prove its case.[57]

Statutes of limitations generally permit a longer period for the prosecution of felonies than for the prosecution of misdemeanors. No time limit is generally paced on prosecution for murder. As discovery of some theft offenses could occur years after the theft, extensions of time are generally given based on the time of discovery of the offense.

The running of time under a criminal statute of limitation could be halted by:

- issuance of an arrest warrant or summons, an indictment, filing of information, or the commencement of prosecution
- statute requirement that the person must be a public resident of that state for the time to toll
- acts by the suspect to avoid or to frustrate legal proceedings against him or her.

M. Consent, Contributory Negligence, or Condonation by the Victim as a Defense

Consent as a Defense

Lack of consent by the victim is an essential element of some crimes. In a rape or theft case, the defense that the victim consented to sexual intercourse or to the taking of the property may be a defense to the criminal charge. In a charge of statutory rape, the defendant may not use the defense of consent because children under certain ages are deemed incapable of giving consent. Most crimes, such as murder, gambling, narcotics offenses, and prostitution, cannot be consented to by the persons involved because the enforcement of such offenses concerns announced public policy. These offenses are against the society rather than the individual and, even where there are victims involved, the consent of the victim would be no defense.

Consent is implied on a football field, in a boxing ring, and under other circumstances. A hard tackle on a football field or a knock-out punch in a boxing ring would not be batteries, since implied consent exists. Kissing a woman at a New Year's Eve party would not ordinarily be disorderly conduct or a battery, although a man who seized a strange woman on the street and kissed her could be charged with disorderly conduct and, in some instances, battery.

Many crimes are against the government, so the question arises whether a governmental official (such as a police officer) could consent to the offense. The answer is no, but the question comes up from time to time, usually having to do with the interpretation of the law. For example, see the U.S. Supreme Court case of *Cox v. Louisiana* in this chapter, in which the defendant was told by law enforcement officers that he and others could demonstrate no closer than 101 feet away from the courthouse. Was this consent to violate the law or was it an interpretation of the law forbidding demonstrating "near" the courthouse? The officers could not consent to the violation of the law, but they could interpret "near" for enforcement purposes.

Victim Contributory Negligence as a Defense to a Criminal Charge

Contributory negligence may be used as a defense in a civil suit, but it may not be used as a defense in a criminal action. A defendant who is charged with manslaughter or reckless homicide may not use as a defense the fact that the victim was negligent. This issue may be important with respect to whether the defendant's conduct was the proximate cause of the injury or death, and it may be important in determining whether the defendant was criminally negligent, but it may not be used as a defense in itself.

Condonation as a Defense

Condonation, or the forgiveness of the criminal act by the victim, is no defense. In *State v. Craig,*[58] the defendant's mother forgave his act of burning her barn. The barn was burned without her consent, which constituted arson. Condonation after the offense was not permitted as a defense.

Although restitution to compensate the victim for the harm and injury that occurred as a result of the crime is no bar to criminal prosecution, it certainly may be taken into consideration by the court in sentencing as an indication that the defendant recognizes the wrong and seeks to make amends.

Defenses Not Presented in this Chapter

"Blame the victim" defense   In rape, assault, and battery cases, defense lawyers will sometimes seek to blame the victim. The defense is also sometimes used in murder cases as the victim is not available to appear as a witness to present his or her story. The 1988 *Chambers* murder trial is an example. Hulking Robert Chambers (6'4") blamed a teenaged New York City girl for getting too rough during sex in Central Park. He reacted with violence, causing her death. In a 50-minute videotaped statement shown to the jury, Chambers stated the girl "freaked out" and hurt him during the sex, which caused him to strike out. The couple had left a fashionable New York bar to have sex in the park. Chambers was charged with murder but was permitted to plead manslaughter when the jury appeared deadlocked.

Other "blame the victim" tactics are: Would a decent women dress like that? She didn't wear a bra. (rape) Why didn't you lock your windows? (burglary) What were you doing alone in that part of town? (mugging or assault) Why did you leave valuables in plain view on the seat of your car? (theft from vehicle)

Truth as a defense   Truth can always be used as a defense to criminal or civil charges. In 1986, a San Diego man used truth as a defense to criminal tax fraud charges. He admitted in court to receiving $400,000 in unreported income from drug dealing. The jury believed his statements that he got out of the narcotics business in 1976 because of his fears of being caught. The defendant was acquitted because the five-year statute of limitations had run.

Patriotism as a defense   Patriotism has always been used as a defense. It was used by Lieut. Col. Oliver L. North who stated that "Everything I did was done in the best interests of the United States of America." Not only do prosecutors have great amounts of discretion, but juries can, and do, acquit defendants in disregard of instructions given them. During the Vietnam War, Lt. William Calley, Jr. was convicted of offenses relating to the My Lai massacre. He was originally sentenced to life in prison at hard labor. This was cut to twenty years, then to ten years, and eventually he served three years of house arrest.

"No personal gain and no profit defense"   In showing that the defendant did not personally benefit nor profit from the crime, defendants sometimes argue that the offense was done to benefit another person or the community. This defense is also called the "Robin Hood" defense if it is used as a variation of "rob the rich and give to the poor." As this defense is rarely successful, it is used primarily as a plea for a light sentence.

In 1991, police were seeking a New York lawyer, Steven Romer, who disappeared along with close to $25 million belonging to clients. Romer wrote to his clients saying, "Your money is no longer available, I am sorry to say. . . . I used your money to feed some hungry and poverty-stricken people." Weeks later, Romer turned himself in and was charged with felony theft.

Misidentification as a defense   The defendant could acknowledge that a crime was committed but argue the state has accused the wrong person. *Misidentification* as a defense differs from a *corpus delicti* defense where a defendant argues that no crime has been committed. The *corpus delicti* defense is used often in acquaintance rape cases where the defendant argues the woman consented to sex and therefore no crime has been committed (see chapter 18).

The "Groupie" Defense   Celebrities, who attract female fans, sometimes use the "groupie" defense to rape charges. Not only will they emphasize clothing the victim wore ("sleazy" pants, midriff blouses, miniskirts) but also in "blaming the victim," defense lawyers will seek newspaper publicity. News stories will quote the defense lawyer as stating the charges are utter nonsense, and one lawyer was quoted as saying his cross-examination of the victim would be "a brawl" and he would impeach the woman with "all kinds of things."

N. PRIVILEGE AS A DEFENSE

Should public officials and employees who act in good faith and in reasonable fulfillment of a duty of their public office have a defense of privilege under such circumstances? A few states have statutorized such a defense.

Probably because of the good sense and judgment of the parties involved, few cases have come into the courts. The following 1981 Wisconsin appellate case is one of them:

STATE v. SCHOENHEIDER
Court of Appeals of Wisconsin (1981) 104 Wis.2d 114, 310 N.W.2d 650

The defendant was the vice-president of a volunteer fire department. He testified that he was lying in bed when he heard sirens. After dressing quickly, he drove his car with flashing red lights to the scene of a traffic accident. In attempting to park his vehicle, he collided with the rear of a parked car.

A state trooper investigating the accident arrested the defendant after a field sobriety test. A breathalyzer showed 0.12 percent by weight of blood alcohol. Defendant was convicted of driving under the influence, despite his defense that he was acting in "good faith" in his capacity as a volunteer fire fighter. The court of appeals affirmed the conviction, holding that "the defendant had no apparent authority to engage in the conduct of driving while under the influence of an intoxicant."

Questions and Problems for Chapter 7

1. A friend of yours, C, received a speeding ticket for doing 60 in a 30 mile per hour zone. The only defense that C has is that the officer was in an unmarked vehicle. Can C successfully argue entrapment, frame-up, or "outrageous government conduct"? Explain.

2. The defendant was convicted of joyriding. After serving his term of imprisonment for that crime, he was then charged with auto theft based on the same conduct used for the joyriding (see the term *joyriding* in the key word index). Does the defendant have a defense to argue before the U.S. Supreme Court? How did the Court rule? Explain. *Brown v. Ohio,* 432 U.S. 161, 97 S.Ct. 2221 (1977).

3. A man with a reputation as a local criminal bragged in taverns that a local judge could be bribed. When the FBI heard this, they provided $300 to an informant to be used for an attempted pay-off. The money never reached the judge and it was believed that the man doing the bragging pocketed the money. Weeks later, the FBI again heard from another man that he could "deliver" the judge. The man and an undercover FBI agent met with the judge and after a series of meetings began payments of $1500 for the judge's

"protection." From December of 1980 through September 1981, monthly payments of $1500 or more for traffic problems and other "protection" services were made to the judge. The judge used the defenses of entrapment and "outrageous government conduct" to criminal charges brought against him. As predisposition is generally a question for a jury, would most juries convict or acquit the judge? State arguments for and against whether predisposition existed. Was the conduct of the FBI "outrageous government conduct"? *United States v. Hunt,* 749 F.2d 1078 (4th Cir. 1984), review denied, 472 U.S. 1018, 105 S.Ct. 3479, 37 CrL 4087 (1985).

4. U.S. Postal inspectors ran advertisements and then wrote letters to persons answering the ads. The postal inspectors' letters were designed to attract persons who might use the mail to distribute child pornography. The defendant responded to the ads and offered to share his child pornography collection in return for opportunities to copy material from the collections of others. The defendant had previously ordered child pornography from other sources and in his correspondence warned and advised persons to take steps to prevent

detection by postal inspectors. Was the defendant entrapped into violating postal laws? Did the postal inspectors engage in "outrageous conduct"? Explain. *Vacanti v. United States,* 840 F.2d 22 (9th Cir. 1988), unpublished, review denied by 488 U.S. 821, 42 CrL 4072, 109 S.Ct. 66 (1988) U.S. Supreme Court.

5. Ms. Ramirez was shoplifting in a store when an employee observed her. When Ramirez noticed the employee following her, she threw several glass figurines belonging to the store to the floor, breaking them. When the law enforcement officer arrived at the store, Ramirez resisted arrest. She was convicted of shoplifting, criminal damage to property, and resisting arrest. She argued violation of double jeopardy. Should the convictions stand? *State v. Ramirez,* 83 Wisc. 2d 150, 265 N.W.2d 274 (1978)

6. In 1989, television cameras were permitted in a jury room to film jury deliberations. A national PBS "Frontline" documentary was then made, and later the film was shown at a meeting of lawyers and judges of the Federal Seventh Circuit. The audience of more than two hundred, with twenty federal judges present, reacted to the hour-long film at times with laughter. The facts of the actual case are:

- The defendant, a good-natured man with a low IQ and marginal intelligence was talking to an investigator from a district attorney's office. The investigator knew that the defendant was an ex-con (had previously been convicted of a felony). The defendant said that after watching the television crime show "The Equalizer," he had decided to become a private detective and had purchased a handgun. This is a criminal violation, as ex-cons cannot own or possess handguns. The investigator suggested that the defendant go to his home to obtain the gun and bring it back to the place where the two men were talking. When the defendant returned with the gun, he was arrested and charged with the offense of possession of a gun by an ex-felon.

If you were the defendant's public defender, what defenses would you use? If you were one of the twelve jurors, what reasoning would you present to your fellow jurors (with television cameras focused on you)?

Notes

1. The fact that a law enforcement officer made an "honest mistake" as to an important fact in making an arrest would not necessarily invalidate the arrest. In the 1971 Supreme Court case of *Hill v. California,* 401 U.S. 797, 91 S.Ct. 1106, police made an "honest mistake" in arresting the wrong man. In the 1980 case of *United States v. Allen,* 629 F.2d 51, 27 CrL 2307 (D.C.Cir.) the appellate court held that "the case law establishes that an arrest based on actual assumptions later found erroneous may be valid if there is adequate basis in the record to determine the reasonableness of the officer's conduct in making the arrest."

The U.S. Supreme Court heard another "honest mistake" case in 1987. In the case of *Maryland v. Garrison,* 480 U.S. 79, 107 S.Ct. 1013, police officers obtained a search warrant for a search on the third floor of a building believing that there was only one apartment on that floor. Before they discovered that there were two apartments on that floor, police found heroin and drug paraphernalia in the apartment of another man (Garrison). The Supreme Court held that the evidence was lawfully obtained, adding another case to what is known as the "honest mistake" exception.

2. The three examples were prepared by Richard G. Denzer and Peter McQuillan in McKinney's Consolidated Laws of New York Annotated. Permission to use the examples was granted by West Publishing Company.

Another "mistake of law" case is the 1989 case of *United States v. Aquilar* et al. 871 F.2d 1436 (9th Cir. 1989). A 1990 "mistake of age" case is the case of *State v. Fan,* 445 N.W.2d 243 (Minn. App. 1989), review denied, 110 S.Ct. 1480, 46 CrL 3182 (1990).

3. *United States v. Freed,* 401 U.S. 601, 91 S.Ct. 1112 (1971).

4. 79 Wis.2d 473, 255 N.W.2d 581 (1977).

5. *People v. Leonardi,* 143 N.Y. 360, 38 N.E. 372 (Ct.App., 1894).

6. Other cases in which courts have recognized that a state of intoxication at the time of a killing may properly be considered in determining whether the accused acted with "premeditation" are *State v. Stasio,* 78 N.J. 467, 396 A.2d 1129, 24 CrL 2438 (1979); *People v. Garcia,* 398 Mich. 250, 247 N.W.2d 547 (1976); *Harris v. United States,* 375 A.2d 505 (D.C. App. 1977); *Commonwealth v. Sires,* 370 Mass. 541, 350 N.E.2d 460 (1976); *People v. Horn,* 12 Cal.3d 290, 115 Cal. Rptr. 516, 524 P.2d 1300 (1974); *Commonwealth v. Reid,* 432 Pa. 319, 247 A.2d 783 (1968); *State v. Tansimore,* 3 N.J. 516, 71 A.2d 169 (1950).

7. *State v. Hedstrom,* 108 Wis.2d 532, 322 N.W.2d 513 (App. 1982). Other self-induced (voluntary) intoxication cases are *Burns v. State,* 556 N.E.2d 955 (Ind. App. 1990) and *Pharo v. State,* 30 Ark. App. 94, 783 S.W. 2d 64 (1990).

8. 376 N.E.2d 1115, 383 N.E.2d 1115 (1978).

9. 82 Cal.App. 778, 785, 256 P. 251, 254 (1927).

10. The Hearst family is a very wealthy and prominent California family. The kidnapping of their college-age daughter received a great amount of national attention. Patricia Hearst was not seen or heard of until the bank robbery when she was recognized as one of the robbers. In 1988, a movie of Patty Hearst was produced and released.

11. *Johnson v. State,* 379 A.2d 1129 (Del. 1977).

12. 43 Cal.App.3d 823, 118 Cal.Rptr. 110 (1974).

13. 444 U.S. 394, 100 S.Ct. 624 (1980).

14. Blackstone Commentaries, iv, 30.

15. See Wisconsin Statute 939.46.

16. In the 1980 case of *Untied States v. Bailey,* 444 U.S. 394, 100 S.Ct. 624, the U.S. Supreme Court pointed out the distinctions between the defenses of duress and necessity as follows: "Common law historically distinguished between the defenses of duress and necessity. Duress was said to excuse criminal conduct where the actor was under an unlawful threat of imminent death or serious bodily injury, which threat caused the actor to engage in conduct violating the literal terms of the criminal law. While the defense of duress covered the situation where the coercion had its source in the actions of other human beings, the defense of necessity, or choice of evils, traditionally covered the situation where physical forces beyond the actor's control rendered illegal conduct the lesser of two evils. Thus, where A destroyed a dike because B threatened to kill him if he did not, A would argue that he acted under duress, whereas if A destroyed the dike in order to protect more valuable property from flooding, A could claim a defense of necessity. See generally LaFave & Scott 374–384.

"Modern cases have tended to blur the distinction between duress and necessity. In the court below, the majority discarded the labels 'duress' and 'necessity,' choosing instead to examine the policies underlying the traditional defenses. See 190 U.S.App.D.C., at 152, 585 F.2d, at 1097. In particular, the majority felt that the defenses were designed to spare a person from punishment if he acted 'under threats or conditions that a person of ordinary firmness would have been unable to resist,' or if he reasonably believed that criminal action 'was necessary to avoid a harm more serious than that sought to be prevented by the statute defining the offense.' *Id.,* at 152, 585 F.2d, at 1097–1098. The Model Penal Code redefines the defenses along similar lines. See Model Penal Code § 209 (duress) and § 3.02 (choice of evils)."

17. Model Penal Code, Sec. 3.02 (Justification Generally).

18. *United States v. Kabat,* 797 F.2d 580 (8th Cir. 1986).

19. Would "disorderly conduct" or "disorderly person" be the proper charge in your state? Did the defendants create a disorder by their nonviolent conduct? Or did their conduct tend to create an immediate public disorder? Would obstructing,

hindering, and failure to obey an order of a law enforcement officer be a better charge?

20. 396 Mass. 840, 489 N.E.2d 666 (1986).

21. Probably the defendant's best and fastest relief would be a pardon from the governor. With mandatory sentences, parole boards have no discretion and could not help the defendant even if they wanted to.

22. Selected Writings of Justice Cardozo, 390.

23. 2 All E.R. at p. 181 (1971).

24. 378 U.S. 478, 84 S.Ct. 1758 (1964). In reversing Escobedo's conviction, the Supreme Court stopped American police from using a procedure that has been used for many years by police in all democratic countries. English and European police continue to use the practice on occasion.

25. 412 U.S. 470, 93 S.Ct. 2208 (1973).

26. *Williamson v. United States,* 207 U.S. 425, 453, 28 S.Ct. 163, 173 (1908).

27. 311 So.2d 678 (Fla.App. 1975).

28. See Criminal Law by LaFave and Scott (West Publishing Co., 1972), p. 368 for a discussion of the defense.

29. The defense lawyer "missed the boat" on this case. He or she could have also had the statute declared invalid as being "void for vagueness." Everybody has to guess as to what is meant by "near." Modern statutes now forbid demonstrations "in" a courthouse or within 200 ft. or 300 ft. from a courthouse. Such statutes do not violate "void for vagueness" (see chapter 1).

30. 437 U.S. 82, 98 S.Ct. 2187 (1987).

31. 464 U.S. 501, 104 S.Ct. 819, 34 CrL 3019 (1984).

32. *Downum v. United States,* 372 U.S. 734, 83 S.Ct. 1033 (1963).

33. *Wade v. Hunter,* 336 U.S. 684, 69 S.Ct. 834 (1949).

34. *Westfall v. United States,* 274 U.S. 256, 47 S.Ct. 629 (1927).

35. 359 U.S. 121, 79 S.Ct. 676 (1959).

36. In 1978, Dan White was convicted of two counts of manslaughter by a California jury for the murders of San Francisco Mayor George Moscone and Supervisor Harvey Milk (scc "Twinkie Defense" in chapter 5). Believing that the manslaughter convictions were inadequate, the governor of California, Mayor Dianne Feinstein, and California congressmen urged the U.S. Department of Justice to try White on federal charges of violating his victims' civil rights. Although the Justice Department had done this in previous cases, it decided not to prosecute in the White case, stating that in this case, it would not be an appropriate application of the law.

Had Dan White been convicted in a federal court, the State of California could not proceed against him for the same conduct. The State of California, like some of the other states, has a statute (Section 654 of the Penal Code) that forbids punishing the same act twice. But the federal government does not have such a statute and it is therefore up to the discretion of the U.S. Department of Justice as to whether it will seek a criminal indictment.

The U.S. Justice Department did charge a former autoworker with a federal civil rights violation for killing an Asian American man with a baseball bat in a Detroit suburb. After plea bargaining, the Michigan trial court had fined the former autoworker and placed him on probation. In 1984, a federal jury found the man guilty of the civil rights violation. The offense can be punished by a maximum penalty of life in prison. (*United States v. Ebens,* 800 F.2d 1422 (6th Cir., 1986)).

37. ____ U.S. ____, 110 S.Ct. 2084, 47 CrL 2091 (1990). In the 1990 case of *Grady v. Corbin,* the U.S. Supreme Court stated their reason for not adopting the "same evidence" or "actual evidence" test as follows in footnote 12:

12. Terminology in the double jeopardy area has been confused at best. Commentators and judges alike have referred to the Blockburger *test as a "same evidence" test. See, e.g., Note, The Double Jeopardy Clause as a Bar to Reintroducing Evidence, 89 Yale L.J. 962, 965 (1980); Ashe, 397 U.S., at 448, 90 S.Ct., at 1196 (BRENNAN, J., concurring). This is a misnomer. The* Blockburger *test has nothing to do with the* evidence *presented at trial. It is concerned solely with the statutory elements of the offenses charged. A true "same evidence" or "actual evidence" test would prevent the government from introducing in a subsequent prosecution any evidence that was introduced in a preceding prosecution. It is in this sense that we discuss, and do not adopt, a "same evidence" or "actual evidence" test.*

38. 447 U.S. 410, 100 S.Ct. 2260 (1980).

39. 490 U.S. 435, 109 S.Ct. 1892, 45 CrL 3046 (1989).

40. See *United States v. Oppenheimer,* 242 U.S. 85, 37 S.Ct. 68 (1916).

41. 287 U.S. 435, 454, 53 S.Ct. 210, 217 (1932), separate opinion.

42. Entrapment was not an English common law defense and was first recognized by the U.S. Supreme Court in 1932. The English authors Clarkson and Keating, in their book *Criminal Law: Text and Materials* (London: Sweet & Maxwell, 1984), state that the English House of Lords "firmly rejected" the defense of entrapment in the 1980 *Sang* case. It is pointed out that English courts have no discretion in refusing to admit such evidence "as an exclusionary rule to this effect would amount to admitting the defense of entrapment via the back door." It is also reported that the English Law Commission has also rejected proposals for the introduction of a defense of entrapment into English law.

Entrapment can be used in England for the consideration of the mitigation of a criminal sentence. Clarkson and Keating conclude that a "defendant has an excuse, or at least a partial excuse" (see pages 317–18 of Clarkson and Keating text) if he or she can show police conduct that amounted to entrapment in arguing for a lenient sentence.

43. The Supreme Court of California established a new test for the defense of entrapment in the 1979 case of *California v. Barraza,* 23 Cal.3d 675, 153 Cal.Rptr. 459, 591 P.2d 947. Pointing out that the federal courts and all but seven states use the "origin-of-intent" (subjective) standard and test, the California Supreme Court established a test that focuses on the guilt of the particular defendant and asks whether he or she was predisposed to commit the crime charged.

44. See footnote 4 of *Russell v. United States.*

45.   * * *

To guide the trial courts, we propound the following threshold test of an entrapment defense: Entrapment has not occurred as a matter of law where police activity (1) has as its end the interruption of a specific ongoing criminal activity; and (2) utilizes means reasonably tailored to apprehend those involved in the ongoing criminal activity.

The first prong of this test addresses the problem of police "virtue testing," that is, police activity seeking to prosecute crime where no such crime exists but for the police activity engendering the crime. As Justice Roberts wrote in his separate opinion in Sorrells, *"Society is at war with the criminal classes," 287 U.S. at 453–54, 53 S.Ct. at 217. Police must fight this war, not engage in the manufacture of new hostilities.*

The second prong of the threshold test addresses the problem of inappropriate techniques. Considerations in deciding whether police activity is permissible under this prong include whether a government agent "induces or encourages another person to engage in conduct constituting such offense by either: (a) making knowingly false representations designed to induce the belief that such conduct is not prohibited; or (b) employing methods of persuasion or inducement which create a substantial risk that such an offense will be committed by persons other than those who are ready to commit it." Model Penal Code § 2.13 (1962).

Applying this test to the case before us, we find that the drunken bum decoy operation fails. In Cruz's motion to dismiss, one of the undisputed facts was that "none of the unsolved crimes occurring [sic] near this location involved the same modus operandi as the simulated situation created by the officers." Cruz, 426 So.2d at 1309. The record thus implies police were apparently attempting to interrupt some kind of ongoing criminal activity. However, the record does not show what specific activity was targeted. This lack of focus is sufficient for the scenario to fail the first prong of the test. However, even if the police were seeking to catch persons who had been "rolling" drunks in the area, the criminal scenario here, with $150 (paper-clipped to ensure more than $100 was taken, making the *offense a felony) enticingly protruding from the back pocket of a person seemingly incapable of noticing its removal, carries with it the "substantial risk that such an offense will be committed by persons other than those who are ready to commit it." Model Penal Code § 2.13. This sufficiently addresses the* Casper *court's proper recognition that entrapment has occurred where "the decoy simply provided the opportunity to commit a crime to anyone who succumbed to the lure of the bait." 417 So.2d at 265. This test also recognizes, as the* Cruz *court did, that the considerations inherent in our threshold test are not properly addressed in the context of the predisposition element of the second, subjective test.*

For the reasons discussed, we hold that the police activity in the instant case constituted entrapment as a matter of law under the threshold test adopted here. Accordingly, we quash the district court decision.

* * *

46. 425 U.S. at 495, n.7.
47. 705 F.2d at 619.
48. 692 F.2d at 836.
49. 692 F.2d at 860. Because of the criticism of the Abscam tactics, FBI Director Webster held a 90-minute interview to answer charges. He pointed out that Abscam began as an attempt to catch art thieves, not members of Congress. However, the Congressmen walked into the net. Director Webster said that "they found their way to us." He stated that "Abscam was purposely sleazy so that no one would stick around it, except someone who wanted to deal with sleazy people." When asked if the FBI would ever conduct another undercover investigation of Congressmen, Webster said, "The answer is, we will always follow our leads."
50. 468 A.2d 1342 (D.C. App. 1983).
51. The Federal Speedy Trial Act, 18 U.S.C. 3161 sets a 70-day limit, which begins to run with the date of indictment. Sec. 3161 (c) (1). See *Henderson v. United States,* 476 U.S. 321, 106 S.Ct. 1871 (1986).
52. 404 U.S. 307, 92 S.Ct. 455 (1971).
53. Id. at 320, 92 S.Ct. at 463.
54. 456 U.S. 1, 102 S.Ct. 1497 (1982).
55. "The Statute of Limitations in Criminal Law," 102 U.Pa.L.Rev. 630.
56. See *Toussie v. United States,* 397 U.S. 112, 114–115, 90 S.Ct. 858, 859–860 (1970).
57. *United States v. Levine,* 658 F.2d 113 (3d Cir. 1981).
58. 124 Kan. 340, 259 P. 802 (1927).

CRIMINAL PUNISHMENT

Punishment has always been part of all criminal offenses. The concepts of crime and punishment are inseparable. Criminal codes are called penal codes or penal laws in some states, indicating that violations of such laws are subject to punishment.

Crimes are classified in terms of their punishment. For example, Section 1.04 of the Model Penal Code states that an "offense . . . for which a sentence of . . . imprisonment is authorized, constitutes a crime." Section 1.04(2) of the Model Penal Code states that a "crime is a felony" if the maximum possible punishment "is [imprisonment] in excess of one year."

Many states, in seeking to provide for more uniform punishments, use a classification system for penalties. There may be five classes of felonies (Class A through Class E), with each class having a statutory punishment. Misdemeanors are usually classified from Class A through Class C.

A. PUNISHMENTS USED IN EARLY ENGLAND

The criminal punishments used two hundred years ago in England and Europe were severe. In England alone, more than two hundred offenses were punishable by death. Condemned criminals were usually hanged, although occasionally they were beheaded, quartered, or drawn (dragged along the ground at the tail of a horse). Burning continued until 1790 to be the punishment inflicted on women for treason, high or petty (which later included not only the murder by a wife of her husband, and the murder of a master or mistress by a servant, but also several offenses against the coin). In practice, women were strangled before they were burnt; this however, depended on the executioner. In one notorious case a woman was actually burnt alive for murdering her husband, the executioner being afraid to strangle her because he was caught by the fire.[1]

For lesser offenses, various forms of mutilations, such as cropping (clipping of the ears), blinding, amputation of the hand, and branding, were common. The whipping post and the pillory were often used, as were fines and imprisonment. The pillory is a frame erected on a post. The offender's head and hands are placed in the open holes and the top board is then moved into place, immobilizing the offender in a standing position.

Practices Used in England to Avoid Severe Penalties

Probably because of the severity of penalties, procedures developed in England by which severe penalties could be avoided. By usage and custom, the following came into practice:

1. "Benefit of Clergy."   In the 12th century, a controversy arose as to whether priests accused of felonies should be tried by the royal courts or the ecclesiastical courts. It was decided that the royal courts could try priests but could not put them to death for the first felony conviction. This privilege was known as the "benefit of clergy," and by the end of the Middle Ages, it was extended to all laypeople who could read.

Pillory and whipping post at the
Joliet (Illinois) Correctional
Center, late 1800s

The test to determine which laypeople could claim the privilege of "benefit of clergy" was their ability to recite the first verse of Psalm 51: "Have mercy upon me, O God, after Thy great goodness." This came to be known as the "neck verse" because it saved the accused from hanging. The only punishment that could then be inflicted was imprisonment for one year and having an "M" branded on the brawn of the left thumb to prevent claiming of the privilege again. For many years, only three crimes were excluded from "benefit of clergy" (high treason, highway robbery, and the willful burning of a house), but in 1769, Blackstone noted that "among the variety of actions which men are daily liable to commit no less than 160 have been declared by Act of Parliament to be felonies without benefit of clergy."[2]

2. The Law of Sanctuary and the Right of Asylum.   Sanctuary was very common in the Middle Ages. The place of sanctuary was generally a church or some other religious place. Criminals who were permitted to take refuge in a church or monastery could not be removed from it. A system developed in England where the refugee would take an oath of abjuration before a coroner, admit their guilt, and swear to leave the country for life to an agreed upon place (often the American colonies or Australia).

Sanctuary was abolished in England in 1623. It is reported, however, that a modified form of sanctuary continued in England for another century.[3] Sanctuary never became part of the legal system of the American colonies, nor the newly formed United States of America.

The United States, however, recognizes and grants a right of asylum to refugees from other countries where a "well-founded fear of persecution" can be shown. Over the last fifty years, the United States has granted asylum to thousands of refugees under various refugee acts of the federal government. Two famous refugee cases illustrate this practice:

- After the Soviet invasion of Hungary in 1956, the United States gave asylum to Joszef Cardinal Mindszenty in the American embassy in Budapest for fifteen years until the Soviets permitted the Cardinal to leave Hungary.
- In 1989, the U.S. embassy in Beijing, China, sheltered China's most prominent dissident, Fang Lizhi, and his wife for months until China permitted Fang Lizhi and his wife to leave China.

Transporting, smuggling or harboring aliens in violation of the Refugee Act of 1980 (Public Law 96–212)[4] is a criminal offense. The defendants in the case of *United States v. Aguilar et al.,* 871 F.2d 1436 (9th Cir. 1989) ran a "modern-day underground railroad" that smuggled Central American natives across the Mexican border with Arizona. The defendants in the *Aguilar* case were convicted of violations of the immigration laws (smuggling, transporting, and harboring aliens) arising from their participation in a "sanctuary movement."

Unlike the United States, Latin American countries have a long tradition of granting political sanctuary to persons within their countries. *The New York Times* newspaper (December 26, 1989) quoted Otto Reich, a former American ambassador to Venezuela who explained this tradition as follows: "Politics has been so unstable in Latin America that all politicians have feared they'd have to use the right of asylum, so they all allowed their political enemies to use it."

General Manuel Noriega requested asylum in the Vatican's embassy in Panama City in 1989. Asylum was granted in keeping with the Catholic Church's long tradition. Weeks later, Noriega became fearful that mobs of Panamanian citizens would storm the Papal Nunciature (as the Vatican embassy is called). General Noriega walked out of the Vatican embassy of his own free will and surrendered to American troops. He was then transported to the United States where in 1991 he is being held in Miami, Florida, for trial on criminal charges.

3. Transportation.   Persons convicted of crimes in England could be pardoned if they agreed to be transported to a colony (first America and then Australia) for a number of years—usually seven. The first convicts were sent abroad in 1655. By the time of the American Revolution, some two thousand convicts a year were being sent to the colonies. After the American Revolution, Australia became the principal place to which prisoners were sent under the condition of the pardon. Over the years, approximately 100,000 prisoners were sent to America, and an equal number sent to Australia.[5] Australia and other colonies objected strongly to the practice of transporting convicts, which was gradually abolished between 1853 and 1864. Penal servitude or imprisonment and hard labor on public works were substituted.[6]

Other penalties that could be imposed for treason or the conviction of a felony were forfeiture of property and corruption of blood. Forfeiture of land and property could be imposed on a person in addition to the death penalty. Corruption of blood affected the family of the defendant. There was no right of descent through a person whose blood was corrupted. This practice, abolished in England by the Forfeiture Act of 1870, was never used in the United States.

B. Punishments Used in Early America

Blackstone points out that English criminal law and punishments, before the American Revolution, were fairly civilized when compared with those of the rest of Europe. U.S. Supreme Court Justice Thurgood Marshall made the following observations in comparing capital punishment in the American colonies with its use in England:

> Capital punishment was not as common a penalty in the American Colonies. "The Capitall Lawes of New-England," dating from 1636, were drawn by the Massachusetts Bay Colony and are the first written expression of capital offenses known to exist in this country. These laws make the following crimes capital offenses: idolatry, witchcraft, blasphemy, murder, assault in sudden anger, sodomy, buggery, adultery, statutory rape, rape, manstealing, perjury in a capital trial, and rebellion. Each crime is accompanied by a reference to the Old Testament to indicate its source. It is not known with any certainty exactly when, or even if, these laws were enacted as drafted; and, if so, just how vigorously these laws were enforced. We do know that the other Colonies had a variety of laws that spanned the spectrum of severity.
>
> By the 18th century, the list of crimes became much less theocratic and much more secular. In the average colony, there were 12 capital crimes. This was far fewer than existed in England, and part of the reason was that there was a scarcity of labor in the Colonies.[7]

C. The Constitutional Limitation on Punishment

The Eighth Amendment of the U.S. Constitution, ratified in 1791 as part of the Bill of Rights, provides that "excessive bail shall not be required, nor excessive fines imposed, nor cruel and unusual punishments inflicted." Two members of Congress opposed passage of this amendment. One stated: "What is meant by the term excessive bail? Who are to be the judges? What is understood by excessive fines? It lies with the court to determine. No cruel and unusual punishment is to be inflicted; it is sometimes necessary to hang a man, villains often deserve whipping, and perhaps having their ears cut off; but are we in the future to be prevented from inflicting these punishments because they are cruel? If a more lenient mode of correcting vice and deterring others from the commission of it could be invented, it would be very prudent in the Legislature to adopt it; but until we have some security that this will be done, we ought not be restrained from making necessary laws by any declaration of this kind."[8]

Criminal Laws and Punishment

Through Criminal Laws, the Criminal Justice Systems Seeks:

- to protect society
- to deter persons from committing crimes
- to rehabilitate persons who have committed crimes
- to punish persons who have committed crimes

Sentences for Criminal Offenses Are Most Often Determined by the:

- seriousness of the crime
- harm to the victim or society
- need to deter others
- need to protect society
- need to maintain supervision over the offender
- possibility of rehabilitation
- past criminal record of offender

Justice William J. Brennan stated in 1972 that "the Cruel and Unusual Punishments Clause, like the other great clauses of the Constitution, is not susceptible of precise definition. Yet we know that the values and ideals it embodies are basic to our scheme of government. And we know also that the Clause imposes upon this Court the duty, when the issue is properly presented, to determine the constitutional validity of a challenged punishment, whatever that punishment may be."[9]

What Punishment Is Appropriate for a Particular Crime?

In the 1984 case of *Pulley v. Harris,* the U.S. Supreme Court defined the manner of evaluating the appropriateness of a punishment for a particular crime:

Traditionally, "proportionality" has been used with reference to an abstract evaluation of the appropriateness of a sentence for a particular crime. Looking to the gravity of the offense and the severity of the penalty, to sentences imposed for other crimes, and to sentencing practices in other jurisdictions, this Court has occasionally struck down

---

Cases That Illustrate the Constitutional Limitation on Punishment

WEEMS v. UNITED STATES
Supreme Court of the United States (1910) 217 U.S. 349, 30 S.Ct. 544

The Supreme Court held in 1910 that fifteen years at hard labor in ankle chains was excessive punishment for the crime of falsifying government records. This was the first time in the history of the Supreme Court that a legislatively established penalty was invalidated as being "cruel and unusual."

ROBINSON v. CALIFORNIA
Supreme Court of the United States (1962) 370 U.S. 660, 82 S.Ct. 1417

California enacted a law making narcotics addiction in itself a crime. The defendant received a ninety-day sentence for being a narcotics addict. The Court held that a state may not punish a person for being "mentally ill, or a leper, or . . . afflicted with a venereal disease," or for being addicted to narcotics. "Even one day in prison would be a cruel and unusual punishment for the 'crime' of having a common cold."

LOUISIANA EX REL. FRANCIS v. RESWEBER
Supreme Court of the United States (1947) 329 U.S. 459, 67 S.Ct. 374

Because of an accidental failure of equipment, the defendant was not executed in the first attempt. The Court held that there was no intention to inflict unnecessary pain, and even though the defendant had been subjected to a current of electricity, this did not prevent the state from executing him in the second attempt. In the 1972 case of *Furman v. Georgia,* the U.S. Supreme Courts stated that "had the failure been intentional, however, the punishment would have been, like torture, so degrading and indecent as to amount to a refusal to accord the criminal human status."

TROP v. DULLES
Supreme Court of the United States (1958) 356 U.S. 86, 78 S.Ct. 590

The citizenship of a convicted wartime deserter was taken away after he had already served three years at hard labor, forfeited all pay, and received a dishonorable discharge. In holding that the taking away of the citizenship of the defendant was a violation of the "cruel and unusual punishment" clause of the Eighth Amendment, the Court stated:

The basic concept underlying the (Clause) is nothing less than the dignity of man. While the State has the power to punish, the (Clause) stands to assure that this power be exercised within the limits of civilized standards.

continued

Cases That Illustrate the Consitutional Limitation on Punishment (continued)

WILKERSON v. UTAH
Supreme Court of the United States (1878) 99 U.S. 130, 25 L.Ed. 345

In this case, the Court upheld death by shooting, on the grounds that such was a common method of execution.

ROBERTS v. LOUISIANA
Supreme Court of the United States (1977) 431 U.S. 633, 97 S.Ct. 1993

The Supreme Court held that the fact that the murder victim was a police officer performing his regular duties may be regarded as an aggravating circumstance. The Court held that there is a special interest in affording protection to those public servants who regularly risk their lives in order to safeguard other persons and property. However, a Louisiana statute that provided for a mandatory sentence of death for the crime of first-degree murder of a police officer and that did not allow consideration for particularized mitigating factors was held unconstitutional. The Supreme Court held that such a statute invites "jurors to disregard their oaths and choose a verdict for a lesser offense whenever they feel the death penalty is inappropriate."

WOODSON v. NORTH CAROLINA
Supreme Court of the United States (1976) 428 U.S. 280, 96 S.Ct. 2978

In holding a North Carolina death penalty statute unconstitutional because it provided for an auto-

matic death penalty in all first-degree murder cases, the Court held that "the Eighth Amendment draws much of its meaning from 'the evolving standards of decency that mark the progress of a maturing society.'" The Court concluded that North Carolina's mandatory death penalty statute varied "markedly from contemporary standards."

COKER v. GEORGIA
Supreme Court of the United States (1977) 433 U.S. 584, 97 S.Ct. 2861

The defendant escaped from a Georgia prison where he had been serving sentences for murder, rape, kidnapping, and aggravated assault. While committing an armed robbery and another offense, he raped an adult woman. The defendant was convicted of rape, armed robbery, and other offenses and was sentenced to death on the rape charge. The U.S. Supreme Court reversed the sentence of death, holding:

> *That question, with respect to rape of an adult woman, is now before us. We have concluded that a sentence of death is grossly disproportionate and excessive punishment for the crime of rape and is therefore forbidden by the Eighth Amendment as cruel and unusual punishment.*

punishments as inherently disproportionate, and therefore cruel and unusual, when imposed for a particular crime or category of crime. See, *e.g., Solem v. Helm,* 463 U.S. 277 (1983); *Enmund v. Florida,* 458 U.S. 782 (1982); *Coker v. Georgia,* 433 U.S. 584 (1977). The death penalty is not in all cases a disproportionate penalty in this sense.[10]

D. Corporal Punishment

Corporal Punishment as Criminal Punishment

Corporal punishment was used as criminal punishment in the early history of the United States. Mutilations, such as cutting off ears and various types of branding, were discontinued many decades ago. Whipping, however, continued in some

American states into this century. The Eighth Circuit Court of Appeals observed that in 1968 only two states permitted the use of the strap as punishment. As a result of the Eighth Circuit Court's decision in the 1968 case of *Jackson v. Bishop,* whipping as a form of punishment was discontinued in the remaining two states. In the *Jackson* case, the Court held:

> We have no difficulty in reaching the conclusion that the use of the strap in the penitentiaries of Arkansas is punishment which, in this last third of the 20th century, runs afoul of the Eighth Amendment; that the strap's use, irrespective of any precautionary conditions which may be imposed, offends contemporary concepts of decency and human dignity and precepts of civilization which we profess to possess; and that it also violates those standards of good conscience and fundamental fairness enunciated by this court in the *Carey* and *Lee* cases.[11]

The Use of Corporal Punishment in Schools

In the 1977 case of *Ingraham v. Wright,* the U.S. Supreme Court held that:

> At common law a single principle has governed the use of corporal punishment since before the American Revolution: teachers may impose reasonable but not excessive force to discipline a child. . . . The prevalent rule in this country today privileges such force as a teacher or administrator "reasonably believes to be necessary for [the child's] proper control, training, or education." Restatement (Second) of Torts § 147(2); see *id.,* § 153(2) . . .
>
> Of the 23 States that have addressed the problem through legislation, 21 have authorized the moderate use of corporal punishment in public schools. Of these States only a few have elaborated on the common law test of reasonableness, typically providing for approval or notification of the child's parents, or for infliction of punishment only by the principal or in the presence of an adult witness. Only two States, Massachusetts and New Jersey, have prohibited all corporal punishment in their public schools. Where the legislatures have not acted, the state courts have uniformly preserved the common law rule permitting teachers to use reasonable force in disciplining children in their charge.

In holding that the Eighth Amendment "cruel and unusual punishment" clause is not applicable to the use of corporal punishment for disciplinary purposes in the public schools, the Court held:

> The schoolchild has little need for the protection of the Eighth Amendment. Though attendance may not always be voluntary, the public school remains an open institution. Except perhaps when very young, the child is not physically restrained from leaving school during school hours; and at the end of the school day, the child is invariably free to return home. Even while at school, the child brings with him the support of family and friends and is rarely apart from teachers and other pupils who may witness and protest any instances of mistreatment.
>
> The openness of the public school and its supervision by the community afford significant safeguards against the kinds of abuses from which the Eighth Amendment protects the prisoner. In virtually every community where corporal punishment is permitted in the schools, these safeguards are reinforced by the legal constraints of the common law. Public school teachers and administrators are privileged at common law to inflict only such corporal punishment as is reasonably necessary for the proper education and discipline of the child; any punishment going beyond the privilege may result in both civil and criminal liability. . . . As long as the schools are open to public scrutiny, there is no reason to believe that the common law constraints will not effectively remedy and deter excesses such as those alleged in this case.

Sentence Enhancement Statutes and Other Statutes Protecting the Criminal Justice Process

A small group of offenders commit the vast majority of violent crimes such as rapes, homicides, robberies, and aggravated assaults according to studies done by the U.S. Department of Justice. Probably all states have enacted the following as either "sentence enhancement" statutes or making the conduct an additional crime:

Statute Number in
Your State

- if the offender is a habitual criminal (repeater)   _____
- use of a dangerous weapon in committing the crime   _____
- use of bulletproof garment in committing crime   _____
- possession of a police scanner radio while committing crimes such as burglary, robbery, etc.   _____
- concealment of identity while committing crime (use of mask, etc.)   _____
- selling drugs on or within 1,000 feet of any private or public school building (the "school ground" statute of the Uniform Controlled Substance Act [sec. 40] provides that the penalty for the crime may be increased five years)   _____

Can a suspect (or witness) be charged with a crime for the following conduct?

- hinders or obstructs a law enforcement officer who is conducting a lawful investigation   _____
- attempts to bribe (or does bribe) an investigating officer, witness, judge, or juror   _____
- destroys or conceals evidence of a crime   _____
- refuses to aid an officer when requested or ordered to do so   _____
- refuses to identify himself or herself when a material witness to a serious crime   _____
- if in custody, escapes from custody (or assists a person in custody to escape)   _____
- knowingly harbors or aids a felon (state statutes often exempt parents and other family members)   _____
- obstructs justice by knowingly giving false information to an officer or court   _____
- compounds a crime by not prosecuting or not giving information to prosecute in return for something of value   _____

To provide additional protection, a misdemeanor battery may be charged as a felony if committed against:

- a law enforcement officer or fire fighter acting in an official capacity   _____
- a witness or juror   _____
- a public official or officer   _____
- or, by a prisoner against any person (prison guard, another prisoner, visitor, etc.)   _____

In addition to the above, there is an increased use of mandatory sentences. An example of mandatory sentence in your state is: _____

We conclude that when public school teachers or administrators impose disciplinary corporal punishment, the Eighth Amendment is inapplicable. The pertinent is consonant with the requirements of due process.

While many school boards and states forbid paddling in public schools, private schools for the most part are free to determine their own policies. In 1991, the mayor of Washington, D.C., Sharon Pratt Dixon, urged the adoption of "spanking" in the Washington, D.C., public schools.

E. CAPITAL PUNISHMENT

The death penalty was widely accepted at the time the U.S. Constitution and the Bill of Rights were ratified. The only reference to capital punishment in the Constitution is found in the Fifth Amendment, which reads: "No person shall be held to answer for a capital, or otherwise infamous crime, unless . . ."

In 1972, the Supreme Court handed down a decision in the death penalty cases of *Furman v. Georgia, Jackson v. Georgia,* and *Branch v. Texas.*[12] Each of the three defendants had been convicted and sentenced to death (Furman for murder, Jackson and Branch for rape). In a long, confusing decision with nine separate opinions and no true majority position, five of the justices held that in the three cases before them, the death penalty was cruel and unusual. Justices Marshall and Brennan concluded that the death penalty was totally impermissible. The Chief Justice and Justices Powell, Rehnquist, and Blackmun dissented in separate opinions.

The Position of the Majority in the *Furman* Case

The majority of five did not hold that capital punishment was in and of itself cruel and unusual. They held that the way in which the punishment was inflicted on the three defendants in the cases before the Court was cruel and unusual. They also argued that the death penalty was so seldom imposed[13] that it was no longer a deterrent to crime and that when it was imposed, it was imposed in a discriminatory fashion. Justice Marshall wrote: "It also is evident that the burden of capital punishment falls upon the poor, the ignorant, and the underprivileged members of minority groups who are least able to voice their complaints against capital punishment."[14]

Not only did each of the five majority justices file a separate opinion in the *Furman* case, but each of the four dissenting justices also wrote separate opinions.

The Death Penalty After *Furman v. Georgia*

The 5-4 decision of *Furman v. Georgia* invalidated the death penalty statutes of forty one states as well as legislation enacted by Congress. The U.S. Supreme Court pointed out that after *Furman v. Georgia:*

> In response to that decision, roughly two-thirds of the States promptly redrafted their capital sentencing statutes in an effort to limit jury discretion and avoid arbitrary and inconsistent results. All of the new statutes provide for automatic appeal of death sentences. Most, such as Georgia's require the reviewing court, to some extent at

least, to determine whether, considering both the crime and the defendant, the sentence is disproportionate to that imposed in similar cases. Not every State has adopted such a procedure. In some States, such as Florida, the appellate court performs proportionality review despite the absence of a statutory requirement; in others, such as California and Texas, it does not.[15]

In 1976, the U.S. Supreme Court reviewed the new death penalty statutes of Georgia,[16] Florida,[17] and Texas.[18] In the 1984 California death penalty case of *Pulley v. Harris,*[19] the U.S. Supreme Court quoted their 1976 *Jurek v. Texas* decision in affirming the death penalty procedure used by California:

> Texas' capital sentencing procedures, like those of Georgia and Florida, do not violate the Eighth and Fourteenth Amendments. By narrowing its definition of capital murder, Texas has essentially said that there must be at least one statutory aggravating circumstance in a first-degree murder case before a death sentence may even be considered. By authorizing the defense to bring before the jury at the separate sentencing hearing whatever mitigating circumstances relating to the individual defendant can be adduced, Texas has ensured that the sentencing jury will have adequate guidance to enable it to perform its sentencing function. By providing prompt judicial review of the jury's decision in a court with statewide jurisdiction, Texas has provided a means to promote the evenhanded, rational, and consistent imposition of death sentences under law. Because this system serves to assure that sentences of death will not be "wantonly" or "freakishly" imposed, it does not violate the Constitution.

Standards to Guide Sentencing Deliberations in Capital Punishment Cases

The death penalty differs from other penalties that may be imposed because of its severity and because it is irrevocable. In *Furman v. Georgia,* the U.S. Supreme Court held that the death penalty "could not be imposed under sentencing procedures that created a substantial risk that it would be inflicted in an arbitrary and capricious manner."[20]

In the 1976 case of *Gregg v. Georgia,*[21] the U.S. Supreme Court again held that the death penalty was not unconstitutionally "cruel and unusual" punishment. The Court pointed out that the use of the death penalty for murder "has a long history of acceptance both in the United States and in England" and that "it is apparent from the text of the Constitution that the existence of capital punishment was accepted by the Framers."

In the 1984 case of *Pulley v. Harris,* the U.S. Supreme Court reviewed the statutes and procedures used by California in considering the death penalty. Harris had deliberately and ruthlessly killed two teenage boys by gunfire in order to steal their car to use in a bank robbery. After killing the boys, Harris finished eating the hamburgers the boys had been eating. After considering California's statutory special circumstances,[22] the statutory list of relevant factors,[23] and the procedures used in California, the U.S. Supreme Court held:

> By requiring the jury to find at least one special circumstance beyond a reasonable doubt, the statute limits the death sentence to a small sub-class of capital-eligible cases. The statutory list of relevant factors, applied to defendants within sub-class, "provide[s] jury guidance and lessen[s] the chance of arbitrary application of the death penalty," *Harris v. Pulley,* 692 F.2d at 1194, "guarantee[ing] that the jury's discretion will be guided and its consideration deliberate," *id.,* at 1195. The jury's "discretion is suitably directed and limited so as to minimize the risk of wholly arbitrary and capricious action." *Gregg,* 428 U.S. at 189. Its decision is reviewed by the

Public Concern about Murderers Getting Off Easy

Polls show that the American public want murderers punished harshly. There is also much public concern about lifers getting out of prison early. Sentences that achieve both goals (harshness and no early release) are:

| The Death Penalty | Life Without Parole (or where parole eligibility is set at 20, 25, or 30 years) | Life Without Parole with Compensation to the Victim's Family |

Methods of Execution

In the early 1990s, there were more than 2,400 persons on death row in the thirty eight states using the death penalty. Twenty-three of these states have not executed prisoners since new death penalty statutes were enacted in the early 1970s.

Anti-death-penalty groups such as the American Civil Liberties Union point out that more humane methods to execute would undercut their opposition to the death penalty. Public opinion polls continue to show that more than 60 percent of the American public endorse the use of capital punishment in principle.

Earliest Methods

- *Sword or executor's axe* used until the late 1700s. The guillotine was used in France and believed to be more humane.
- *Burning at a stake* was used until the 1790s in Europe.
- *Firing squad* continues to be a method used in two states (Utah and Idaho)
- *Hanging* was a common method in England and the United States. However, if the rope is too long, it will decapitate the victim, while if it is too short, death occurs by strangulation. Botched cases have occurred. In 1702 a condemned British burglar, John Smith, swung for fifteen minutes. The crowd then called to the executioner to cut him down and release him. John became known as "half-hanged Smith."

Other Methods

- *Electric chair* While hundreds of executions have been carried out using the electric chair, problems of malfunctioning have occurred. In 1990 Florida's electric chair malfunctioned three times before executing Jesse Tafero. In 1989, it took Alabama's electric chair nineteen minutes to execute Horace F. Dunkins. After the Louisiana electric chair failed to execute Willie Francis after giving him a painful jolt in 1945, the matter was taken to the U.S. Supreme Court. It was held that a second attempt to execute Mr. Francis would not violate the constitutional prohibitions against cruel and unusual punishment or double jeopardy. 329 U.S. 459
- *Gas chamber* This method of execution has been criticized because it causes a slow, painful death.
- *Lethal injection* is called the modern method of choice and has withstood a challenge in the U.S. Supreme Court. The 1985 case of *Heckler v. Cheney,* 470 U.S. 821, 105 S.Ct. 1649, was brought to the Supreme Court by death row prisoners who argued that the drugs used had not been approved by the U.S. Food and Drug Administration. Death by injection is now used in more than eighteen states, but extreme pain can occur if the injection is into the muscle tissue rather than into a vein. Problems also occur if improper dosage of chemicals are given, or if chemicals are given in the wrong order. Lethal injections are commonly used to put animals away.

trial judge and the State Supreme Courts. On its face, this system, without any requirement or practice of comparative proportionality review, cannot be successfully challenged under *Furman* and our subsequent cases.

F. Imprisonment as a Punishment

Under early Roman law, imprisonment was illegal as punishment and was used for detention only.[24] Imprisonment is as old as the law of England, but only rarely did statutes in early England provide for imprisonment as punishment for crime. Nearly every English court had its own particular prison, and the right of keeping a goal (jail) in and for a particular district was given as a franchise the king granted to certain persons, just as he granted other rights connected with the administration of justice in England. In addition to the franchise prisons, there was the Fleet, the prison of the Star Chamber, and of the Court of Chancery.[25]

Because of the filthy, unsanitary conditions of the early English prisons and the corruption and brutality that arose from the franchise system, reform movements began in England as early as 1773. In that year, John Howard became sheriff of Bedfordshire. When he saw the disgraceful conditions in his jail, he proposed that salaried gaolers replace the franchise system. The condition of American prisons has also been the subject of many reform movements, and the use of prisons for the purpose of punishment has been subject to much debate.

The Supreme Court stated in 1970 that "[a] State has wide latitude in fixing the punishment for state crime."[26] But a filthy prison or brutality within the prison can be held to be a violation of the Eighth Amendment "cruel and unusual punishment" clause.[27] The following Supreme Court cases have to do with the use of imprisonment as a punishment.

WILLIAMS v. ILLINOIS
Supreme Court of the United States (1970) 399 U.S. 235, 90 S.Ct. 2018

The defendant was convicted of petty theft and received the maximum sentence provided by state law: one year imprisonment and a $500 fine. The judgment of the court also provided that if at the end of the one-year sentence, the defendant could not pay the fine, he would "work off" the fine at the rate of five dollars per day. This provision was permitted by state law. The defendant showed that he was without funds and petitioned to be released at the end of the year so that he could get a job and pay the fine and court costs. The Supreme Court of Illinois rejected the petition and the Surpreme Court of the United States reversed, stating:

> *The mere fact that an indigent in a particular case may be imprisoned for a longer time than a non-indigent convicted of the same offense does not, of course, give rise to a violation of the Equal Protection Clause. Sentencing judges are vested with wide discretion in the exceedingly difficult task of determining the appropriate punishment in the countless variety of situations that appear. The Constitution permits qualitative differences in meting out punishment and there is no requirement that two persons convicted of the same offense receive identical sentences.*

* * *

> *The State is not powerless to enforce judgments against those financially unable to pay a fine; indeed, a different result would amount to inverse discrimination since*

it would enable an indigent to avoid both the fine and imprisonment for nonpayment whereas other defendants must always suffer one or the other conviction.

It is unnecessary for us to canvass the numerous alternatives to which the State by legislative enactment—or judges within the scope of their authority—may resort in order to avoid imprisoning an indigent beyond the statutory maximum for involuntary nonpayment of a fine or court costs. Appellant has suggested several plans, some of which are already utilized in some States, while others resemble those proposed by various studies. The State is free to choose from among the variety of solutions already proposed and, of course, it may devise new ones.

* * *

We conclude that when the aggregate imprisonment exceeds the maximum period fixed by the statute and results directly from an involuntary nonpayment of a fine or court costs we are confronted with an impermissible discrimination that rests on ability to pay, and accordingly, we vacate the judgment (of the lower court).

TATE v. SHORT
Supreme Court of the United States (1971) 401 U.S. 395, 91 S.Ct. 668

The defendant accumulated fines of $425 on nine traffic offenses in Houston, Texas. The defendant showed that he was indigent, but he was required to satisfy the fines at the rate of five dollars per day by serving 85 days at a prison farm. In reversing the court order, the Supreme Court stated:

> *Our opinion in* Williams *stated the premise of this conclusion in saying that "the Equal Protection Clause of the fourteenth Amendment requires that the statutory ceiling placed on imprisonment for any substantive offense be the same for all defendants irrespective of their economic status." 399 U.S., at 244, 26 L.Ed.2d at 594. Since Texas has legislated a "fines only" policy for traffic offenses, that statutory ceiling cannot, consistently with the Equal Protection Clause, limit the punishment to payment of the fine if one is able to pay it, yet convert the fine into a prison term for an indigent defendant without the means to pay his fine. Imprisonment in such a case is not imposed to further any penal objective of the State. It is imposed to augment the State's revenues but obviously does not serve that purpose; the defendant cannot pay because he is indigent and his imprisonment, rather than aiding collection of the revenue, saddles the State with the cost of feeding and housing him for the period of his imprisonment.*
>
> *In footnote 19 of the* Williams *case, the Court stated: "We wish to make clear that nothing in our decision today precludes imprisonment for willful refusal to pay a fine or court costs. See Ex parte Smith, 97 Utah 280, 92 P.2d 1098 (1939)." Therefore, a person who has money or an income may be imprisoned for refusal to pay either a fine or court costs.*

The New Sentencing Guidelines

In the late 1980s the federal government and some of the states adopted comprehensive new sentencing guidelines. Congress stated the purpose for the new federal guidelines in 28 U.S.C.A. 991 (b):

1. effectuate the purposes of sentencing . . . (in brief, those purposes are just punishment, deterrence, incapacitation, and rehabilitation);
2. provide certainty and fairness in sentencing practices, by avoiding unwarranted sentencing disparities among offenders with similar characteristics convicted of

similar criminal conduct, while permitting sufficient judicial flexibility to take into account relevant aggravating or mitigating factors; and

3. reflect, to the extent practicable, advancement in knowledge of human behavior as related to the criminal justice process.

The new guidelines generally require longer minimum sentences and prohibit parole in the federal system, even for first offenders. Judges must sentence generally within the guidelines and are left with less discretion to modify a sentence. Persons convicted as low-level participators in drug trafficking (such as so-called "mules") receive ten-year mandatory sentences.

Some federal judges complained that the new law was defeating its purpose. In a dramatic protest, federal Judge J. Lawrence Irving resigned because he thought the federal sentencing guidelines were too harsh. He gave the following example of how the new guidelines would change the way certain defendants were treated. Under prior sentencing standards:

A 19-year-old man (no previous record) was convicted of possession and intent to distribute cocaine. Under the old law, the judge would give him a split sentence of six months in prison with five years probation. "The young man understood that if he violated probation he'd go back to prison to serve out the rest of his term."

The young man would do "his six months, and after that he remained free of drugs—we knew this because of regular testing. He completed his education, got married, had a child and became a productive, tax-paying member of society."

Under the new mandatory sentencing guidelines, Judge Irving pointed out, the defendant would have to be sentenced to twenty years in prison with no possibility of parole.

"That's heavy," said Judge Irving, "and that's my problem. I just can't do it anymore." (See *New York Times* 9/30/90 article "Criticizing Sentencing Rules, U.S. Judge Resigns" and Chicago Tribune article 10/14/90 "Drug War Chokes federal courts".)

America's Rate of Imprisonment Is Now Reported To Be the Highest in the World

In 1991, more than one million people were reported to be in jails and prisons in the United States either serving time or awaiting trial.[28] The rate of imprisonment in the United States is now the highest in the world, with South Africa having the second highest imprisonment rate and the Soviet Union ranking third in overall incarceration.

A study done by Sentencing Project, a private research group, was released in January 1991. The study pointed out that while the overall crime rate in the United States had fallen 3.5 percent in the period from 1980 to 1990, the population in the nation's prisons has doubled. Reasons given by the study for this increase and the high rate of imprisonment in the United States are:

- drug-related crime, the biggest cause of the increase
- increased use by federal and state government of mandatory minimum sentences
- more use of imprisonment and less use of alternative sentences
- tightened parole eligibility requirements
- a crime rate in the United States higher than in most other countries (The murder rate in the United States is at least seven times higher than in most European countries. There are six times as many robberies and three times as many rapes in the United States as in former West Germany.)
- an increasingly harsh public attitude in the United States toward lawbreakers

Alternatives to Traditional Punishment

With more than one million persons in jails and prisons in the United States, more than half the states (and some federal prisons) are under court orders to stop violations caused primarily by overcrowding. Recidivism rates are very high. Recidivism is often defined as rearrest and conviction within three years of a previous criminal conviction. As traditional punishments are not working well, alternatives are being used (or considered) generally in a mix with other forms of punishment.

Alternative	Description of Alternative	Probable Use
"Electronic shackles" (home arrest)	A device worn like an ankle (or wrist) bracelet that sends signals to a receiver. If the device is tampered with or if the wearer leaves home, the sheriff's office is automatically notified. Detainee is under "house arrest" or imprisoned at home.	Also used as a mixture of penalties tailored to the offender. Person must agree to "shackles" as condition of parole, probation, or work release program.
Community service sentences	Tasks such as bookkeeping, painting, carpentry, electrical work, plumbing, etc. for churches, charities, elderly persons, public places, and even the victim's property. Particularly applicable when defendant has a skill or profession.	Also used with a mixture of punishments tailored to offender. Person must agree to services as a condition of parole, probation, or work release.
Voluntary commitment to drug or alcohol treatment	Many crimes are related to serious drug or alcohol problems. Treatment programs are not effective unless participant cooperates fully.	Could be used in a mixture of punishments believed to achieve the best results. Defendants would "voluntarily" commit themselves as a condition of probation or parole.
Denver boot	The boot is a $275 device that locks on the front wheel of a vehicle and renders the car immobile until the driver pays fines owed and police remove the clamp. Generally not used until five or more parking or other tickets are unpaid. (See *Baker v. City of Iowa City*, 260 N.W.2d 427 (Iowa 1977) for case citations.)	Use of the boot frees law enforcement and court personnel for other tasks, cuts number of persons in jail, and brings in much needed funds. Use of the boot also increases the number of persons who voluntarily pay traffic and parking fines.
Shock Incarceration or Boot Camp	The National Institute of Justice commented as follows in their publication of June 1989: "Offenders sentenced to shock incarceration spend a relatively short period (90 to 180 days) in prison in a military style boot camp that provides a highly regimented program involving strict discipline, physical training, and hard labor resembling some aspects of military basic training. If they successfully complete the program, they are subsequently placed under community supervision. Housed separately from the regular inmates, either in an independent facility or in a separate housing unit within a larger facility, offenders spend about 6 hours a day at work and 2 to 3 hours in military drills and physical training."	Now used by half or more of the states to shock first offenders out of a life of crime and to reduce overcrowding of jails and prisons. Young persons convicted of nonviolent offenses "volunteer" for the short shock program to avoid serving a longer term of many years for offenses such as burglary.

continued

Alternatives to Traditional Punishment (continued)

Alternative	Description of Alternative	Probable Use
Antabuse	A chemical that makes a person ill if he or she drinks alcohol. Used when alcohol abuse is the root of the problems and cause of criminal conduct.	Person agrees to take "voluntarily" as condition of probation or parole, usually to avoid imprisonment.
"Chemical castration"	Use of a controversial drug, Dep-Provera, which does not eliminate sex drive but does diminish it. Possible side effects include fatigue, loss of hair, itching, headaches, weight gain, and symptoms resembling female menopause.	"Voluntary" use as a condition of probation or parole after some imprisonment or to avoid any imprisonment.
"Son of Sam" Legislative bills	Some persons who commit crimes receive considerable public attention and receive money from interviews, books, films, and other money-making ventures. The name "Son of Sam" was used by a bizarre, New York serial killer who received large sums of money for stories of his killings, causing the State of New York to enact the first "Son of Sam" statute. Another example, the proceeds of the book *In the Belly of the Beast,* which tells of the brutality of prison life, is being held under the "Son of Sam" law. The author, Jack Henry Abbott, so impressed Norman Mailer that he helped in obtaining a parole for Abbott. Abbott immediately killed again and is back in prison.	Such statutes give victims and the families of victims liens against such profits and monies. Such monies would be held in escrow until claims could be filed and verified. It was reported in 1987 that 42 states had such statutes. The federal "Son of Sam" statute is found in Title 18, Chapter 232.
Drunk driving restraint	A $350 or so device with a sensor that can measure the blood-alcohol level of a person seeking to start a car (or truck). The driver breathes into the mouthpiece for four seconds for the device to test blood alcohol levels.	Could be: (1) required by state law, (2) ordered by a court, or (3) installed by spouses, parents, or relatives of problem drinkers.

G. Fines as Punishment

"The fine is one of the oldest forms of punishment and is widely used in Western Europe as the sole sanction for the major portion of cases coming before the criminal courts. Sweden, England, and Germany all report that more than three-quarters of cases result in a fine. In the United States, recent studies for the National Institute of Justice have shown that although the fine is widely used, the amounts levied tend to be relatively small and are used in combination with other sanctions, notably probation."

This statement was made in the National Institute of Justice article, "Innovations in Collecting and Enforcing Fines" (August 1989). The article points out that because of the "poverty of most offenders, fines cannot be collected; they are difficult to enforce; and their use adds to the courts' administrative burdens." Methods of improving collection listed by the National Institute of Justice are:

- allowing offenders to pay their fines on an installment plan, which is usually worked out by a clerk taking into account the income of an offender and the amount due
- accepting credit cards for payment
- computerizing record keeping systems
- Telemarketing (use of the telephone to contact persons and remind them of payments due)
- Turning collection over to private collection agencies that can pursue debtors across state lines and often have access to data bases that allow them to track the movements of an offender. Collection agencies often routinely notify credit bureaus of delinquent accounts, a practice that is reported to be an important factor in recovering overdue fines.

H. FORFEITURE AS A PUNISHMENT

The concept and use of forfeiture goes back to early English law. Seizing the property that was used to commit a crime is a strong deterrent to crime. Seizing the profits of crime is also a deterrent in crimes committed for profit.

Forfeiture was first used in custom violations, such as smuggling. In addition to the traditional criminal punishments of death and fines, the economic sanction of forfeiture was imposed with seizure of ships, implements, and the goods being smuggled.

Forfeiture not only punished the wrongdoer by depriving them of ships (or boats), implements, and goods, but it also rewarded the king and government who benefited from the use and sale of these items.

The concept of forfeiture came to America with English common law. It was used over the years in various forms. During the period when beer and other alcoholic beverages were contraband (Prohibition), forfeiture was used extensively to deter and discourage the manufacture, sale, and use of illegal alcohol.

Federal statutes today authorize the forfeiture not only of contraband property, but also of instrumentalities used in narcotics, gambling, and untaxed alcohol and tobacco. For example, Section 55 of the Uniform Controlled Substance Act, which has been adopted by many states and the federal government, provides for forfeiture not only of controlled substances in violation of the law, but also of all raw material, all vehicles—"used, or intended for use"— weapons, records and books, all property, "including money" and profits. Section 55.5 of the act details forfeiture proceedings.[29]

An important part of the Federal Comprehensive Crime Control Act of 1984 was the forfeiture provisions meant to strike "at the heart of racketeering and the illicit drug industry." Backers called the forfeiture sections "long overdue" and Senator Daniel Moynihan stated on the Senate floor:

[f]or years, law enforcement agents have recognized that the threat of prison terms and fines do not deter crime lords, well insulated from the streets, from engaging in activities that net them millions of dollars in illegal profits. . . . Establish the prospect

Review of Sentencing

Sentencing authority is granted to the trial judge by the law defining the crime and by other statutes in the state or federal criminal code. The sentencing judge could be further guided by sentencing guidelines enacted by that state legislature. The following reviews may be made of imposed sentences:

Trial judge   On motion by the defense attorney, the trial judge will review his or her sentence of a particular defendant and may modify the sentence after hearing arguments presented by both the defense lawyer and the prosecutor.

Appellate courts   (including the U.S. Supreme Court and state supreme courts) On appeal, an appellate court could find that a particular sentence was not within the statutory authority of the trial judge to impose, or that the sentence violated the Eighth Amendment "cruel and unusual" clause. (See the 1915 case of *Weems v. United States* where the U.S. Supreme Court held that 15 years at hard labor in ankle chains was excessive punishment for the crime of falsifying government records.)

A state prisoner would ordinarily use a Writ of Habeas Corpus in attempting to get his/her case into the federal courts. To do this, there must be a showing of a violation of a right under the U.S. Constitution. Because there are very few violations (or errors) of this type, few Habeas Corpus hearings are granted.

State parole board or parole authorities (federal government is phasing out the use of parole) Parole authority is granted by statute of that state. State statutes might provide that eligibility for murder does not commence until after 16 years—or after 20 or 25 years. Whether the convicted person would be released on parole (and the conditions of parole) would then be determined by the parole board.

Pardoning power of the president of the United States and state governors   The power to pardon, grant amnesty, or commute a sentence by the president or a state governor is generally very broad. Such authority is constitutional with additional statutory power often also provided. Article II of the U.S. Constitution provides that the president "shall have Power to grant Reprieves and Pardons for Offenses against the United States, except in Case of Impeachment"[a]

[a]See the case of *Murphy v. Ford,* 390 F.Supp. 1372 (W.D. Mich. 1975), where a federal district court found that President Gerald R. Ford had the constitutional authority to grant a pardon to former President Richard M. Nixon before Nixon was charged with a crime.

of losing everything, and much of the profit motive which drives drug lords and organized crime bosses will be eliminated.

Under federal law today and under the provisions of the forfeiture statutes of many states, the following can now be seized under court order:

1. Instrumentalities of the crime (vehicles, water craft, etc. used in the commission of the crimes)
2. Profits of the crime (money from drug dealing, stolen goods, etc.)
3. Proceeds of the illegal acts (farms, yachts, cars, homes, other luxury goods purchased from profits of illegal acts)

The Internal Revenue Service can also seize under court order property of persons charged or convicted of crimes. As persons involved in marijuana, cocaine, and other narcotics often make huge profits without paying proper taxes, tax liens may be filed against them. Property belonging to such persons may be seized. Such property could include homes, furniture, cars, stereo equipment, video games, gems, and real estate.

A New Mexico judge demonstrates an "electronic handcuff" or "electronic watchdog" used to monitor the movements and whereabouts of some defendants placed on probation.

1. Career Criminals and the Repeat Offender

Priority as to law enforcement is most often determined by the crime itself. High priority is most often given when crimes involve injury or death, or when important aspects of public interest are involved.

Attention is focused on the person committing the crime rather than on the crime when it is determined that the person is a career criminal or a repeater (or a habitual criminal). The career criminal or repeater has received special attention and priority since studies done between 1975 and 1978 showed that in Washington, D.C., 7 percent of the criminals committed 24 percent of the crimes. By taking such persons off the street, the incidence of crimes can be considerably lessened.

Many cities and states have created career-criminal programs. Such programs ordinarily:

- operate under statutes providing additional and longer sentences for repeat offenders
- establish special career-criminal units in the offices of police and prosecutors that vigorously investigate frequently committed crimes (auto theft, for example) or crimes following patterns
- speed up prosecution of career criminals
- discourage plea bargaining, which would lessen prison terms, unless the suspect incriminates associates

---

A Small Group of Career Criminals Commit the Vast Majority of Crimes

Calling these persons who threaten society "superfelons," former Florida Governor Martinez commenced a 1988 crackdown stating:

> "In the last three years, over 11,000 new arrests were made of individuals aged 40 and younger who already had at least four felony arrests and served at least two prison terms . . .
> It is clear that a disproportionate amount of serious crime is committed by a relatively small number of repeat felony offenders. We must do something to break this chain of oppression . . . a chain that manacles the spirit of all law-abiding Floridians."

Estimates of Chronic Offender Crimes

- 61 percent of all homicides
- 76 percent of all rapes
- 73 percent of all robberies
- 65 percent of all aggravated assaults

Recidivism Facts

Chronic violent offenders start out and remain violent.

Prior criminal behavior is one of the best predictors of future criminality.

Most criminals engage in several types of crime:
- Repeat offenders tend to switch between misdemeanors and felonies and between violent and property crimes, often engaging in related types of crime, such as property and drug offenses.
- It appears that juveniles, even more than adults, are generalists. This may be due partly to the random, unplanned nature of much juvenile crime.

Source: U.S. Department of Justice Report to the Nation on Crime

---

This concentration of resources on career criminals and repeaters is justified, because these offenders commit such a high proportion of crimes. One crime that receives the attention of many career-criminal programs is auto theft. In the early 1970s, when teenage "joyriders" were responsible for stealing many cars, auto theft was a low-priority crime.

However, organized criminal groups moved into "chop-shop" operations and commenced stealing expensive cars in larger and larger numbers. This criminal operation is much more serious than the "joyrider" who illegally uses a vehicle for a period of time before abandoning or returning it. As car thefts were committed more and more by repeat offenders, the offense became a high-priority in many cities.

Two repeater (recidivist) cases have come before the U.S. Supreme Court in recent years. The 1980 Texas case of *Rummel v. Estelle* involved a defendant who received a life sentence under the Texas repeater statutes for three nonviolent crimes that netted the defendant a total of $230. The court affirmed the conviction and sentence, holding that the sentence did not violate the Eighth Amendment. The following case was decided by the U.S. Supreme Court:

SOLEM v. HELM
Supreme Court of the United States (1983) 463 U.S. 277, 103 S.Ct. 3001, 33 CrL 3220

Helm lived in South Dakota and had a serious problem with alcohol. By 1975, he had committed six nonviolent felonies. In 1979, he pleaded guilty to uttering (passing) a "no

Current Controversy: Seizing Legal Fees Under Forfeiture Laws (Settled at Federal Level But an Open Issue in Many States)

Until 1984, an offender could use money obtained as a result of his or her criminal activity to pay the fees of a criminal lawyer to fight the criminal charges. For example, a speaker before a criminal justice class was telling of how he defrauded two Milwaukee banks of over $1 million. Upon his arrest, the lawyer of his choice requested $70,000 "up front." The speaker stated that he wanted that particular lawyer and knowing "it was the bank's money," he paid the lawyer fee required. Today under federal law, prosecutors can seek a court order seizing such lawyer fees. Before 1984, the lawyer kept the money.

In the two 1989 cases of the *United States v. Monsanto* a) and *Caplin et al. v. United States,* b) the U.S. Supreme Court held that there were no statutory, constitutional, or ethical obstacles in federal cases to seizing lawyer fees under federal law. However, as many states have not enacted statutes for legal fee forfeiture, the issue is an open question in many states.

For: Lawyer Fees Are Subject to Forfeiture

The FBI Law Enforcement Bulletin article entitled "Forfeiture of Attorney's Fees" (April 1990) quoted the U.S. Supreme Court and commented:

"Whatever the full extent of the Sixth Amendment's protection of one's right to retain counsel of his choosing, that protection does not go beyond 'the individual's right to spend his own money to obtain the advice and assistance of . . . counsel.' A defendant has no Sixth Amendment right to spend another person's money for services rendered by an attorney, even if those funds are the only way that defendant will be able to retain the attorney of his choice. A robbery suspect, for example, has no Sixth Amendment right to use funds he has stolen from a bank to retain an attorney to defend him if he is apprehended."[b]

Like the robbery suspect, the drug trafficker with no legitimate funds is entitled to court-appointed counsel. He is not, however, entitled to use the government's money to pay the attorney of his own choosing.

Against: Legitimate Fees Should Not Be Seized

The American Bar Association filed an *Amicus Curiae* brief in the *Caplin* case claiming that defendants in complicated drug or racketeering cases would have ineffective lawyers if they had to rely on court-appointed attorneys. The Supreme Court rejected this argument because all defendants in criminal cases that were complicated would then be in a position to argue they had a right to an attorney of their own choice (see footnote 3 of the *Caplin* case). This argument is similar to the dissenting opinion in the *Monsanto* Court of Appeal decision, which concluded:

"Surely this statute not only intrudes upon individual's right to secure counsel of his choice. It shakes the very foundations of our criminal justice system.

Accordingly I dissent."

a) 491 U.S. 600, 109 S. Ct. 2657 (1989)
b) 491 U.S. 617, 109 S. Ct. 2646 (1989)

account" check for $100 (his seventh felony). Under the South Dakota recidivist statute, he was sentenced to life imprisonment. Unlike Texas, South Dakota statutes forbade parole in such cases. Murderers and rapists were eligible for parole in South Dakota, but Helm would never be eligible for parole. In holding that the sentence violated the Eighth Amendment, the Supreme Court held:

The Constitution requires us to examine Helm's sentence to determine if it is proportionate to his crime. Applying objective criteria, we find that Helm has received the penultimate sentence for relatively minor criminal conduct. He has been treated

Current Controversy: Should the Federal Government Run "Country Club" Prisons?

Every time a well-known person is sentenced to a federal minimum-security prison, the issue of federal "country-club" or "Club Feds" is debated. When millionaire-stock broker Ivan Boesky was sentenced to three years at the federal prison camp at Lompoc, California,* attention was again focused on whether federal minimum-security facilities are too soft and easy. The television program "60 Minutes" did a segment asking this.

Arguments Against the Present Federal Minimum-Security System

As there are no cells for inmates nor walls around the camps, they really are not prisons or jails. One observer stated that the only restriction he could see was the "Keep Off the Grass" signs.

The system neither punishes nor rehabilitates the two most common groups sent into the federal prison system ("white-collar" criminals and persons convicted of drug-related crimes).

Persons such as Ivan Boesky can do far more damage to society by their crimes than inmates in maximum security prisons who have committed crimes of violence. (Boesky was convicted of "inside trading," which shook the financial markets and Wall Street.)

Arguments For the Minimum-Security System

Boredom and lack of true freedom in the prison camp setting is adequate punishment even though it is not harsh.

Minimum-security camps on the average cost only half as much to operate as the more secure prisons. Population in the federal prisons is expected to nearly double to 87,000 by 1995. In the more secure federal prisons, annual costs per prisoner can amount to $30,000. The federal government now has 20 minimum-security prisons and is likely to rely more on this type of facility.

It is presumed that "white collar" prisoners do not mix well with violent prisoners. Some experts say that the camps are a necessity because sentencing a "white-collar" prisoner to a maximum security prison is (as one expert stated) "like sentencing the guy to death. He wouldn't last two days."

*In 1990 Lompoc federal prison camp was converted into a higher security federal prison. Lompoc was the most famous of the "country club" prisons because of the persons who served time there (Watergate's H. R. Halderman, inside trader Ivan Boesky, and San Diego Charger star Chuck Muncie).

more harshly than other criminals in the State who have committed more serious crimes. He has been treated more harshly than he would have been in any other jurisdiction, with the possible exception of a single State. We conclude that his sentence is significantly disproportionate to his crime, and is therefore prohibited by the Eighth Amendment.

Questions and Problems for Chapter 8

Are the sentences in the following cases (usually a well-known person) appropriate in achieving the goals of the criminal justice system?

Person	Offense Convicted Of	Sentence
1. Pete Rose (baseball player and manager)	Failed to report and pay income taxes on $354,968	Five months in jail/3 months at a halfway house/11,000 hours of community service/$50,000 fine

Person	Offense Convicted Of	Sentence
2. Leona Helmsley (hotel owner)	Failed to report and pay taxes on $1.8 million	Four years in prison and a fine of $7.1 million
3. Zsa Zsa Gabor (actress)	Slapped a motorcycle officer during a valid traffic stop in Beverly Hills, California	Three days in jail/120 hours of community service in a homeless shelter for women/$13,000 fine
4. Jim Bakker (former television minister)	Fraudulently raised $158 million from followers contributions and stole $3.7 million of that.	First sentence of 45 years in prison was set aside because the sentencing judge improperly said, "Those of us who do have a religion are sick of being saps for money-grubbing preachers and priests." The convictions of 24 fraud and conspiracy charges stand.
5. Marion S. Barry, Jr. (Mayor of Washington, D.C., for 12 years until 1990)	Charged with 14 drug charges but convicted of only one misdemeanor charge of possession of cocaine	Six months jail/1 year on probation/$5,000 fine and costs. In 1991 appealed the conviction and sentence to a higher court.
6. Three commercial airline pilots	Flew a Boeing 727 with 91 passengers while intoxicated from drinking the night before	Pilot— 16 months in prison/other two officers— 1 year in prison
7. Joseph Hazelwood (former captain of the oil tanker Exxon Valdez)	Was drinking the night his ship caused the biggest oil spill in the history of Alaska	Sentenced to scrub oil-soaked beaches in Alaska for 1,000 hours (25 weeks)
8. Arch A. Moore, Jr. (former governor of West Virginia)	Extortion, mail fraud, tax fraud, and obstruction of a grand jury	Five years and 10 months prison term/$170,000 fine
9. Ivan Boesky (former Wall Street trader and arbitrageur)	Inside trading and other frauds of corporate stocks on Wall Street (cooperated with government investigation of Wall Street to minimize sentence)	Three years prison term/$100 million fine and disgorgement (giving up the plunder and ill-gotten gain)
10. Michael R. Milken (former "junk bond" king of the Wall Street firm of Drexel, Burnham and Lambert)	Entered a guilty plea to six felony charges of Wall Street fraud in scandals revealed after the fall of Ivan Boesky	Ten years prison term/$600 million fines and disgorgement
11. Lawrence Singleton (raped a 15-year-old California hitchhiker and then hacked her forearms off in 1978. Released after serving 8 years of a 14-year sentence)	Moved to Florida after being run out of several California towns. Convicted in 1991 in Florida of petty theft ($3 hat) and obstructing an officer (lying to the police about his identification)	Sentenced in Florida to two years prison (maximum sentence under statute)
12. Robert P. Aquilar (former California federal judge)	Unlawfully disclosed information of a government wiretap in violation of statutes and then lied to federal agents investigating the matter	Six months in prison/1,000 hours community service/$2,000 fine

Notes

1. *A History of the Criminal Law of England* (3 volumes) by Sir James FitzJames Stephens, Judge of High Court of Justice, Queen's Bench Division, (England 1883), I: 477.

2. Blackstone's *Commentaries,* 4 Comm. 18.

3. *A History of the Criminal Law of England,* chapt. 13, pp. 491–492.

4. Refugees from Central America created considerable controversy in the 1980s. The Immigration and Naturalization Services (INS) had concluded that the refugees were fleeing from poverty in their countries and thus were not eligible for legal entry into the United States. In response, more than two hundred Protestant, Catholic, and Jewish congregations offered their churches and temples as sanctuaries to the refugees and generally asserted the refugees were fleeing from the persecution of their governments. In 1986, eleven church workers were tried in a federal criminal court in Tuscon, Arizona, on charges of smuggling, transporting, and harboring Central Americans.

Following the 1986 convictions in Tucson, former New Mexico Governor Tony Anaya declared the state of New Mexico a "state of sanctuary" for Central American refugees. An aide to the governor stated, "The governor is not calling on people to go out and break the law, but does urge New Mexicans not to cooperate with the INS and to thwart INS efforts to arrest and deport people from Central America who are in this state." A number of American cities made similar declarations.

In August 1988, A Lutheran minister was acquitted by a federal jury in New Mexico of charges of smuggling women from El Salvador into the United States. His defense was that he thought he could legally help the refugees under the proclamation of former-governor Tony Anaya declaring New Mexico to be a "state of sanctuary."

5. *A History of English Criminal Law and Its Administration,* Radzinowicz (London: Stevens Publications, 1948) and *Crime, Courts, and Probation,* Chute and Bell (New York: MacMillan, 1956).

6. It is interesting to note that "transportation" was used by a number of countries. The Roman Empire transported prisoners to Rumania; Russia transported hundreds of thousands of political prisoners to Siberia. In addition, the frontiers of the world have always been used as a refuge by people fleeing from the law or in political trouble.

7. *Furman v. Georgia,* 408 U.S. 238, 92 S.Ct. 2726 (1972).

8. I Annals of Congress, 782 (1789).

9. *Furman v. Georgia,* 408 U.S. 238 at 258, 92 S.Ct. 2726 at 2736.

10. *Pulley v. Harris,* 465 U.S. 37, 104 S.Ct. 871, 34 CrL 3027 (1984).

11. 404 F.2d 571. The Court gave the following reasons for holding whipping to be unconstitutional: "Our reasons for this conclusion include the following:

(1) We are not convinced that any rule or regulation as the use of the strap, however seriously or sincerely conceived and drawn, will successfully prevent abuse. The present record discloses misinterpretation and obvious overnarrow interpretation even of the newly adopted January 1966 rules. (2) Rules in this area seem often to go unobserved. Despite the January 1966 requirement that no inmate was to inflict punishment on another, the record is replete with instances where this very thing took place. (3) Regulations are easily circumvented. Although it was a long-standing requirement that a whipping was to be administered only when the prisoner was fully clothed, this record discloses instances of whipping upon the bare buttocks, and with consequent injury. (4) Corporal punishment is easily subject to abuse in the hands of the sadistic and the unscrupulous. (5) Where power to punish is granted to persons in lower levels of administrative authority, there is an inherent and natural difficulty in enforcing the limitations of that power. (6) There can be no argument that excessive whipping or an inappropriate manner of whipping or too great frequency of whipping or the use of studded or overlong straps all constitute cruel and unusual punishment. But if whipping were to be authorized, how does one, or any court, ascertain the point which would distinguish the permissible from that which is cruel and unusual? (7) Corporal punishment generates hate toward the keepers who punish and toward the system which permits it. It is degrading to the punisher and to the punished alike. It frustrates correctional rehabilitative goals. This record cries out with testimony to this effect from the expert penologists, from the inmates and from their keepers. (8) Whipping creates other penological problems and makes adjustment to society more difficult. (9) Public opinion is obviously adverse. Counsel concede that only two states still permit the use of the strap. Thus almost uniformally has it been abolished. It has been expressly outlawed by statute in a number of states. See for example, N.D.Cent. Code § 12-47-26 (1960); S.D. Code § 13.4715 (1939), and 48 states, including Arkansas, have constitutional provisions against cruel and unusual punishment. Ark.Const. art. 2, § 9.

We are not convinced contrarily by any suggestion that the state needs this tool for disciplinary purposes and is too poor to provide other accepted means of prisoner regulation. Humane considerations and constitutional requirements are not, in this day, to be measured or limited by dollar considerations or by the thickness of the prisoner's clothing."

12. 408 U.S. 238, 92 S.Ct. 2726 (1972).

13. In his article entitled "The Death Penalty: Its Relation to Murder and Suicide," Mr. Neithercutt points out that a person is more apt to be killed by lightning than to be executed. See *Journal of Contemporary Criminal Justice* 5 (December 1989): 199–219.

14. 408 U.S. at 366, 92 S.Ct. at 2791.

15. In the 1984 case of *Pulley v. Harris,* the Supreme Court defined and explained the use of "proportionality."

16. *Gregg v. Georgia,* 428 U.S. 153, 96 S.Ct. 2909 (1976).

17. *Proffit v. Florida,* 428 U.S. 242, 96 S.Ct. 2960 (1976).

18. *Jurek v. Texas,* 428 U.S. 262, 96 S.Ct. 2950 (1976).

19. 465 U.S. 37, 104 S.Ct. 871, 34 CrL 3027 (1984).

20. 408 U.S. 238, 92 S.Ct. 2726 (1972).

21. 428 U.S. 153, 96 S.Ct. 2929 (1976).

22. The Court summarizes California's "special circumstances" as follows: "Briefly, the statutory special circumstances are: 1) the murder was for profit; 2) the murder was perpetrated by an explosive; 3) the victim was a police officer killed in the line of duty; 4) the victim was a witness to a crime, killed to prevent his testifying in a criminal proceeding; 5) the murder was committed during the commission of robbery, kidnapping, rape, performance of a lewd or lascivious act on someone under 14, or burglary; 6) the murder involved torture; 7) the defendant had been previously convicted of first or second degree murder, or was convicted of more than one murder in the first or second degree in this proceeding. Cal. Penal Code Ann. § 190.2 (West 1977). These are greatly expanded in the current statute. See Cal. Penal Code Ann. § 190.2 (West Supp. 1990).

23. California's statute Sec. 190.3 does not separate aggravating and mitigating circumstances. The statute provides: "In determining the penalty the trier of fact shall take into account any of the following factors if relevant:

(a) The circumstances of the crime of which the defendant was convicted in the present proceeding and the existence of any special circumstances found to be true pursuant to § 190.1.

(b) The presence or absence of criminal activity by the defendant which involved the use or attempted use of force or violence or the expressed or implied threat to use force or violence.

(c) Whether or not the offense was committed while the defendant was under the influence of extreme mental or emotional disturbance.

(d) Whether or not the victim was a participant in the defendant's homicidal conduct or consented to the homicidal act.

(e) Whether or not the offense was committed under circumstances which the defendant reasonably believed to be a moral justification or extenuation for his conduct.

(f) Whether or not the defendant acted under extreme duress or under the substantial domination of another person.

(g) Whether or not at the time of the offense the capacity of the defendant to appreciate the criminality of conduct or to conform his conduct to the requirements of law was impaired as a result of mental disease or the effects of intoxication.

(h) The age of the defendant at the time of the crime.

(i) Whether or not the defendant was an accomplice to the offense and his participation in the commission of the offense was relatively minor.

(j) Any other circumstance which extenuates the gravity of the crime even though it is not a legal excuse for the crime."

24. *The Law of Criminal Corrections,* Rubin (St. Paul, Minn.: West Pub. Co., 1963).

25. England also had debtors' prisons in which persons who owed civil debts could be imprisoned until the civil debt was paid. England abolished the practice of debtors' prison in 1869. Such imprisonment would not be lawful under the U.S. Constitution and some state constitutions specifically forbid this form of imprisonment. Although most of the democratic world has abolished the practice, Hong Kong continues to allow creditors to put their debtors behind bars.

26. See the U.S. Bureau of Justice Statistics bulletin "Prisoners in 1989" and the *New York Times* article "Rate of U.S. Imprisonment Is Cited as Highest in World" (January 7, 1991), p. A14. The yearly cost of maintaining jails and prisons in the United States was estimated at $16 billion.

27. Other federal statutes having forfeiture provisions, are Controlled Substances Act, 21 U.S.C.A. §881; Organized Crime Control Act of 1970, 18 U.S.C.A. §§1963 and 1955(d); Copyrights Act, 17 U.S.C.A. §§506(b) and 509(a); and Child Protection Act of 1984, 18 U.S.C.A. §§2253 and 2254.

28. *Williams v. Illinois,* 399 U.S. 235, 90 S.Ct. 2018 (1970).

29. See the two volume *Prisoner's Rights* by Haft and Hermann, published by the Practising Law Institute (1972).

CRIMINAL JURISDICTION

The concept of jurisdiction has a number of aspects in criminal law. There must be jurisdiction (power and authority) to create a criminal law. Jurisdiction also has to do with the enforcement of criminal law. A city that hires a police force authorizes it to enforce the law. What is the extent of the jurisdiction of this authority? What is the authority of officers outside the municipality that employs them? Jurisdiction also has to do with the authority and power of a court to try a criminal case. Following are some of the questions this chapter deals with:

- Can a person be charged with and convicted of a crime that the state (or the federal government) does not have the jurisdiction to create?
- Can a person be tried by a court that does not have jurisdiction over the crime he or she is alleged to have committed?
- Can a person be tried for a crime before jurisdiction over his or her person is obtained (that is, before the person has been captured or has submitted voluntarily to the jurisdiction of the court)?
- If two American citizens were on the moon and one killed the other, would a court in the United States have jurisdiction and, if so, which court?
- What could be the authority for an officer to make an arrest outside his or her jurisdiction?

A. JURISDICTION TO LEGISLATE CRIMINAL LAWS

Most criminal laws enforced today come into existence by enactments of either state legislative bodies or the Congress of the United States. If these bodies are legislating within the scope of the power granted to them by their constitutions, they then have the jurisdiction and the power to create crimes. If they exceed their jurisdiction or their authority, the laws that they enact are invalid and persons cannot be tried and punished for violations of such laws. Note the following exaggerated example:

EXAMPLE: Citizens in State X do not like the Nevada law legalizing prostitution in some parts of that state nor do they approve of Nevada's gambling laws. Pressure is put on the legislators in State X, and laws are passed making it a criminal offense for citizens of State X to go to Nevada to gamble or patronize the houses of prostitution.

State X does not have the jurisdiction or the authority to enact such laws, any more than the state of New York could pass a law forbidding murder in California. The jurisdiction and the police power to legislate with respect to prostitution and gambling in Nevada rests primarily with the Nevada legislature, and the jurisdiction with respect to homicide in California is primarily within the jurisdiction of the California legislature.

B. JURISDICTION OVER THE OFFENSE CHARGED AND OVER THE PERSON

Jurisdiction over the Offense Charged

When a state or the federal government issues a criminal complaint and seeks to commence a criminal action, it must allege and prove that the court has jurisdiction not only over the offense (or offenses) charged, but also over the defendant's person. The Sixth Amendment of the U.S. Constitution provides that "in all criminal prosecutions, the accused shall enjoy the right to a speedy and public trial, by an impartial jury of the State and district wherein the crime shall have been committed, which district shall have been previously ascertained by law."

Therefore, a person charged with a crime has a right to demand that the criminal trial be held in the proper venue. *Venue* refers to the locality, particularly the county, in which the criminal act or acts charged are alleged to have occurred. In 22 Corpus Juris Secundum (Criminal Law), Section 173, the following statement is made: "Venue is not an element of the offense, and it has been said that persons obviously guilty of criminal acts cannot escape punishment through technical questions of venue." The following case illustrates the defense of lack of jurisdiction:

GARDNER v. STATE
Supreme Court of Arkansas (1978) 263 Ark. 739, 569 S.W.2d 74, review denied, 440 U.S. 911, 99 S.Ct. 1224, 24 CrL 4196

The defendant was convicted of raping a sixteen-year-old girl in the backseat of a car driven from Foreman, Arkansas, to Idabel, Oklahoma. On appeal, the defendant challenged the jurisdiction of the Arkansas courts, as the trip took the vehicle into Texas and then Oklahoma. The Supreme Court of Arkansas, in ruling that there was substantial evidence presented at the trial to conclude that the offense occurred in Arkansas, held:

> *It is not essential to a prosecution in this state that all the elements of the crime charged take place in Arkansas. It has been said that it is generally accepted that if the requisite elements of the crime are committed in different jurisdictions, any state in which an essential part of the crime is committed may take jurisdiction.*

As a moving vehicle can travel through two or more counties (or states) within a short time, most states have statutes that provide that if some acts material and essential to a crime occur in one county (or state) and some acts in another, the accused may be tried in either county (or state).

Venue and jurisdiction will not ordinarily be presumed in criminal cases but may be inferred from the evidence available in the case. For example, the body of a man who was shot is found. There are no eyewitnesses to the crime and there is no evidence showing that the body has been moved. From this evidence, probably all courts would conclude or infer that the crime occurred in the county and state in which the body was found.[1] The accused has a right to be tried in the county or state in which the crime occurred. Thus, if prosecution has been in one venue but evidence is discovered that reveals the venue lies elsewhere, the venue must be changed.

Venue and Jurisdiction

Venue   A defendant has a right to be tried in the place (venue) where the crime is alleged to have occurred.

Jurisdiction   Courts and police must show they have the authority and power (jurisdiction) to act. Florida courts and police do not have jurisdiction over a burglary that occurred in Seattle. The venue to try a defendant for a Seattle burglary would be Seattle, as only courts in Seattle would have jurisdiction to try the case.

Jurisdiction over the Person Charged with a Crime

Not only must the state show that the court has jurisdiction over the offense charged, but it must also show that jurisdiction over the person exists. The fact that the accused is physically present in the court is usually sufficient to show jurisdiction over the person.[2] American courts cannot try a defendant in absentia (that is, without the accused having a right to be present) because of the defendant's Sixth Amendment rights "to be informed of the nature and cause of the accusation; to be confronted with the witnesses against him." The state must therefore have the defendant lawfully in custody. Or, the defendant voluntarily appears and submits to the jurisdiction of the court.

In minor offenses, when it is permitted by the statutes of a jurisdiction (usually with the permission of the court), the defendant may request and be granted the privilege of not appearing personally. Under these circumstances, the defendant is represented by an attorney and usually enters a plea of guilty or no contest (again with the permission of the court).

As a general rule, once a court has acquired jurisdiction of the accused and the charge against him or her, this jurisdiction continues until final disposition or determination of the case is made in the manner prescribed by law. If the defendant "jumps bail" or fails to appear as ordered, the jurisdiction of the court continues and the defendant is then liable for other charges.

In 1973, the case of *Taylor v. United States*,[3] came before the Supreme Court. The defendant, who was charged with selling cocaine, failed to return to court after a luncheon recess during his trial. After waiting that day for the defendant to appear, the trial judge continued with the case. The jury found the defendant guilty after being instructed that they were to draw no inference from the defendant's absence. The U.S. Supreme Court affirmed the conviction of the defendant.

Limits of Criminal Jurisdiction

At common law, prosecution for a crime could be commenced at any time. However, most states and the federal government have, by statutes, imposed time limitations for arrests and prosecutions of practically all crimes in the United States. Misdemeanors usually have a shorter statute of limitations than do felonies, whereas probably no state has placed a time limit on first-degree murder. State statutes usually provide that the running of the statute of limitations is stopped by the issuance of warrants or summonses. Many states do not include the time in which the wanted person was not a public resident of that state.

Jurisdiction to Regulate Conduct

In regulating conduct, jurisdiction (authority) is needed:

- by legislative bodies to enact rules
- by law enforcement officers to enforce rules
- by prosecutors to prosecute alleged violations
- by courts to hear and try cases

Rights of an Accused

An accused has a right:

- to be under a valid statute or ordinance
- to be tried in a court having jurisdiction
- to be tried in the district (place) where the crime was committed
- to be present at his or her trial (unless right is waived)

Practically all persons are subject to the jurisdiction of the state or the nation in which they reside or voluntarily enter. Persons going into Canada to fish or vacationers traveling in Mexico subject themselves to the laws of those nations and are subject to criminal prosecutions if they violate criminal laws. The exceptions, pointed out in chapter 7 under "Immunity as a Defense," are persons with diplomatic passports and (under certain conditions) national and state legislators. All other persons (with a few additional exceptions) are subject to the criminal laws of the jurisdiction in which they commit a crime.

Forcible Abduction as a Means of Obtaining Jurisdiction over the Person of a Defendant

Many American courts follow a century-old doctrine, holding that the manner in which jurisdiction is obtained over the person of a defendant does not impair the power to charge and try a defendant. This doctrine, known as the Ker–Frisbie rule, originated in the following cases:*

KER v. ILLINOIS
Supreme Court of the United States (1886) 119 U.S. 436, 7 S.Ct. 225

The defendant, who resided in South America, was indicted by an Illinois grand jury for larceny and embezzlement. On the request of the governor of Illinois, the president of the United States issued a warrant authorizing a Pinkerton agent to take custody of Ker from authorities in Peru. The agent did not serve the warrant or request Peruvian authorities to surrender Ker to him. Instead, he forcibly abducted Ker and placed him aboard an Amer-

---

* Courts in the United States have held that the Uniform Criminal Extradition Act has changed the old common law. Bail bondsmen (or women) and law enforcement officers can now be sued civilly for violations in failing to comply with the Uniform Extradition Act in forcing a person to return to another state without that person's consent. For cases involving bail bond agents, see *Lopez v. New Mexico* (N.M. Ct. of App. 9/9/86), rev. denied U.S. Sup. Ct., 40 CrL 4173 (1987) and *Loftice v. Colorado* (Colo. Ct. of App. 9/1/88), rev. denied 490 U.S. 1047, 109 S.Ct. 1957, 45 CrL 4025 (1989).

ican ship. Ker was tried and convicted in Illinois. On appeal to the U.S. Supreme Court, it was held that Ker could be tried by the state of Illinois regardless of the methods used to obtain personal jurisdiction over him.[4]

FRISBEE v. COLLINS
Supreme Court of the United States (1952) 342 U.S. 519, 72 S.Ct. 509

A prisoner in a Michigan state prison complained in a habeas corpus petition to the federal courts that he had been kidnapped, handcuffed, and blackjacked in Chicago by Michigan law enforcement officers. He argued that his criminal conviction in Michigan violated due process and the Federal Kidnapping Act. The U.S. Supreme Court held that the Ker doctrine continued to be valid and that the Michigan courts had jurisdiction over the person of the defendant even if forcible abduction had been used. The Court held:

> *Due process of law is satisfied when one present in court is convicted of crime after being fairly apprised of charges against him and after a fair trial in accordance with constitutional procedural safeguards.*

The U.S. Supreme Court continued to reaffirm the Ker–Frisbie rule in recent years.[5] In 1982, the case of *State v. Monje*[6] came before the Wisconsin Supreme Court. In that case, a Wisconsin police officer went into Illinois and arrested Monje, who was wanted for armed robbery in Wisconsin. The officer, however, brought Monje back into Wisconsin without complying with the Uniform Criminal Extradition Act. In affirming the Ker–Frisbie rule, it was held that: "This court has recognized that there is nothing in the constitution which prohibits a person from being tried even though the extradition process is totally ignored in removing him from an asylum state."

C. NATION-TO-NATION JURISDICTION OVER CRIMES

Nations long ago realized that the world could not afford criminal jurisdictional gaps between nations. An alarming situation would exist, for example, if a person could commit a murder in the middle of the Atlantic or Pacific Ocean and no nation would have criminal jurisdiction. Because of this, the jurisdiction of each nation was extended to follow its ships over the high seas. The English common law gave jurisdiction to English courts over crimes committed on British ships and over crimes committed by British subjects on foreign ships.

Today, statutes in both England and the United States give each country jurisdiction over crimes committed not only on ships, but on aircraft controlled by each country. By virtue of the international convention ratified by the Tokyo Convention Act of 1967, the courts of any country in the world may try piracy (armed violence at sea committed on a surface ship or an aircraft), even though the piracy was not committed within that country's territorial waters.[7] In addition to piracy, international conventions of nations have sought the elimination of slave trading, war crimes, hijacking and sabotage of civil aircraft, genocide, and terrorism.

Because of the statutes giving many nations jurisdictions over crimes, situations could exist in which a number of nations have concurrent jurisdiction (that is, the same crime could be tried in the courts of two or three nations).

Seizing Fugitives in Foreign Countries

Prior to 1989, the FBI and DEA prohibited the overseas seizure and arrest of fugitives without the consent of the foreign government. Such overseas seizures were viewed as kidnapping.

Because of the increasing number of federal fugitives, including some terrorists, who live abroad, it was announced that this policy has been changed. On October 14, 1989, the *New York Times* ran a front page headline stating "US, in Shift, Declares Right to Seize Fugitives Overseas." The headline surprised even President Bush and his Secretary of State. A spokesperson for the administration later stated that the FBI's new powers "would be used sparingly, if at all."

Two foreign nationals awaiting criminal trials in the United States in 1991 are:

General Manuel Noriega—seized when U.S. armed forces overthrew his government in Panama (the new Panamanian government consented to his arrest and removal from the country).

Dr. Humberto Alvarez Machain—abducted from his medical offices in Guadalajara, Mexico, and flown to the United States to await trial for participation in the torture and killing of a U.S. drug enforcement agent in 1985. The Mexican government denounced the kidnapping as an example of "the law of the jungle" and arrested six persons for their participation.

EXAMPLE: An American airline flies from the United States to England. While the plane is on the ground in England, one American kills another American passenger aboard the aircraft. The person committing the crime could be tried by either Great Britain or the United States (or both nations). In view of the fact that only Americans were involved and that the incident occurred on an American plane, the British would probably waive jurisdiction to the United States and the accused would be extradited for trial before a federal court in the United States.

EXAMPLE: While a German ship is traveling from one American city to another on the Great Lakes, one crew member murders another crew member (neither man is American). If the ship were in American navigable waters at the time, the United States would have jurisdiction over the crime. One of the states may also have jurisdiction. Because Germany also has jurisdiction and Americans were not involved in the incident, jurisdiction would probably be waived to Germany.

Territorial Limitations as Affecting Criminal Jurisdiction

Each nation has established territorial limits in the oceans and the air space around it. The Law of the Sea Treaty permits every nation to declare up to twelve miles as its territorial sea.[8] The following cases illustrate that such territorial limitations do not curtail jurisdiction on American watercraft and aircraft throughout the world:

UNITED STATES v. LEE
Supreme Court of the United States (1927) 274 U.S. 559, 47 S.Ct. 746

During Prohibition (1920s), a Coast Guard crew saw the defendant's boat alongside a foreign ship in "Rum Row" (international waters where European ships sold liquor to

Americans). Later, the Coast Guard ship found the defendant's boat and observed seventy-one cases of illegal whiskey on the defendant's deck. The U.S. Supreme Court affirmed the seizure and the conviction of the defendant even though the seizure occurred beyond American territorial waters.

UNITED STATES v. LAYTON
U.S. District Court, District of Northern California (1981) 509 F. Supp. 212

Just before the killings and suicides at the People's Temple in Guyana, Congressman Leo Ryan was killed and other persons were wounded in a savage attack on them. The defendant, Larry Layton, was charged in the United States with the following crimes that occurred in South America: (a) conspiracy to murder a U.S. Congressman, (b) aiding and abetting his murder, (c) conspiracy to murder an internationally protected person, (d) aiding and abetting in this murder (these charges are under 18 U.S.C. Sec. 351 and Sec. 1117). The Court held that an "attack upon a member of Congress, wherever it occurs, equally threatens the free and proper functioning of government." The Court further stated:

> Courts have generally inferred such jurisdiction for two types of statutes: (1) statutes which represent an effort by the government to protect itself against obstructions and frauds; and (2) statutes where the vulnerability of the United States outside its own territory to the occurrence of the prohibited conduct is sufficient because of the nature of the offense to infer reasonably that Congress meant to reach those extraterritorial offenses.

UNITED STATES v. RICARDO
United States Court of Appeals, Fifth Circuit (1980) 619 F.2d 1124

The defendants were convicted of conspiracy to import marijuana into the United States. The entire conspiracy took place abroad, with no overt acts in the United States.

UNITED STATES v. CONROY
United States Court of Appeals, Fifth Circuit (1979) 589 F.2d 1258, 24 CrL 2509

The Court held that, given probable cause or as a matter of necessity, the Coast Guard has authority to search an American vessel in waters governed by another country. The defendant in this case ran with 7,000 pounds of marijuana into Haitian waters when he was approached by a Coast Guard vessel. After receiving permission from the Haitian government, the Coast Guard searched the defendant's vessel.

In 1980, the U.S. Congress passed a statute (21 U.S.C. 955a) giving the federal government criminal jurisdiction over all stateless vessels on the high seas that are engaged in the distribution of controlled substances (illegal drugs). A stateless vessel is a ship or boat not flying any national flag or flying the flags of two or more countries. If a vessel registered with a foreign country should engage in narcotic activity on the high seas, the United States has, in the past, requested permission of that country to board the vessel. Through these means, all ships, registered or not registered, can be boarded if there is probable cause to believe that the ship is involved in narcotic activity. The federal statute was tested and affirmed in the 1982 case of *United States v. Marino-Garcia.*[9]

In the following case, the Coast Guard suspected, but did not have probable cause to believe, that a foreign ship in international waters but within "customs waters" was transporting drugs. When the captain of the foreign ship would not give consent for the Coast Guard to board, consent was obtained from the country having jurisdiction over the ship (United Kingdom).

United States v. Davis
U.S. Court of Appeals Ninth Circuit, 905 F.2d 245 (1990), review denied U.S. Supreme Court____ U.S. ____ 111 S.Ct. 753 (1991)

Defendant Davis was the British captain of the British ship *Myth*, sailing from Hong Kong to San Francisco. When the *Myth* was thirty-five miles from California, a U.S. Coast Guard cutter radioed asking permission to board. Davis denied the request and, because the *Myth* was suspected of smuggling contraband, permission was requested from the United Kingdom by telex message.

After denying the Coast Guard permission to board, Davis announced that he was changing course to the Caribbean and when permission to board was obtained, the *Myth* was approximately one hundred miles west of the California coast. The boarding officer smelled marijuana in a cabin of the *Myth* and numerous bales of material were seen. The Coast Guard confiscated over 7,000 pounds of marijuana from the ship. Davis's conviction for possession of, and conspiracy to possess, marijuana on a vessel subject to the jurisdiction of the United States with intent to distribute was affirmed, with the Court holding:

* * *

Davis contends that the Coast Guard illegally stopped, boarded, and searched the Myth. *The Coast Guard acted under valid statutory authority pursuant to 14 U.S.C. § 89(a), which states:*

The Coast Guard may make inquiries, examinations, inspections, searches, seizures, and arrests upon the high seas and waters over which the United States has jurisdiction, for the prevention, detection, and suppression of violations of laws of the United States. For such purposes, . . . officers may go on board of any vessel subject to the jurisdiction, or to the operation of any law, of the United States, address inquiries to those on board, examine the ship's documents and papers, and examine, inspect, and search the vessel and use all necessary force to compel compliance.

As discussed above, the United States had jurisdiction over the Myth *because it was within the customs waters of the United States.*

Davis also contends that the search and seizure of the Myth *violates the fourth amendment. We hold that the protections of the fourth amendment do not extend to the search of the* Myth *on the high seas. See United States v. Verdugo–Urquidez, ____ U.S. ____, 110 S.Ct. 1056, 1061, 108 L.Ed.2d 222 (1990). Although* Verdugo–Urquidez *only held that the fourth amendment does not apply to searches and seizures of nonresident aliens in foreign countries, the analysis and language adopted by the Court creates no exception for searches of nonresident aliens on the high seas. (No indication that fourth amendment was intended to protect aliens in international waters).*

III. Conclusion

We find that Congress had the authority to enact the Maritime Drug Law Enforcement Act and that it is constitutionally applied to defendant. Furthermore, because the fourth amendment does not extend to the search of nonresident aliens on the high seas, no fourth amendment violation occurred in the search of the Myth. *Davis' convictions are AFFIRMED.*

American courts have approached jurisdictional problems in much the same way as have British courts over the years. In 1879, the British Criminal Code Commissioners asked and answered the following question: "A shot is fired in one place which wounds a man in another place, who dies in a third place. In which of these places is the crime committed?" In 1879, the answer was "in each of the three places." In 1970, the British Law Commission's Working Paper No. 29 asked the same question and gave the same answer.

By their "long-arm statutes," most states have extended criminal liability beyond their territorial jurisdiction. The following example illustrates:

EXAMPLE: X, who lives in Paris and has never been in the United States, wants Y, who lives in a city in your state, killed. X contacts a hired killer who lives in Chicago and contracts with him to have Y killed for $5,000. The hired gun goes to the city in which Y lives and kills him. The killer is apprehended and tells everything.

Under a long-arm statute, extradition proceedings may be commenced against X to bring him to your state to stand trial as a party to the crime of murder.

The Law of Nations

Article I, Section 8 of the U.S. Constitution provides that: "The Congress shall have Power . . . To define and punish Piracies and Felonies committed on the high Seas, and Offenses against the Law of Nations. . . .

After the Nazi defeat in 1945, the Allied Nations tried many of the surviving military and civilian Nazi leaders before an international tribunal at Nuremberg, Germany. Some of the defendants were executed; others received jail sentences.[10] Defense lawyers at the war crimes trials argued that the Nuremberg trials had no legal basis in international law and that the defendants were being charged under penal laws created after the act (ex post facto). The following are excerpts from the closing argument of Justice Robert H. Jackson, who represented the United States before the tribunal:

> No half-century ever witnessed slaughter on such a scale, such cruelties and inhumanities, such wholesale deportations of people into slavery, such annihilations of minorities. The terror of Torquemada pales before the Nazi inquisition. . . . Goaded by these facts, we have moved to redress the blight on the record on our era . . . we should not overlook the unique and emergent character of this body as an International Military Tribunal. It is no part of the constitutional mechanism of internal justice of any of the Signatory nations. Germany has unconditionally surrendered, but no peace treaty has been signed or agreed upon. The Allies are still technically in a state of war with Germany, although the enemy's political and military institutions have collapsed. As a Military Tribunal, it is a continuation of the war effort of the Allied Nations. As an International Tribunal, it is not bound by the procedural and substantive refinements of our respective judicial or constitutional systems, nor will its rulings introduce precedents into any country's internal civil system of justice. As an International Military Tribunal, it rises above the provincial and transient and seeks guidance not only from International Law but also from the basic principles of jurisprudence which are assumptions of civilization and which long have found embodiment in the codes of all nations.

D. CRIMINAL JURISDICTION OF THE FEDERAL GOVERNMENT

Federal crimes fall into the following three classes:

1. Crimes affecting interstate or international commerce, over which the U.S. Constitution gives Congress exclusive power. The Mann Act, the Dyer Act, the Lindbergh Act, and the Fugitive Felon Act are examples of this class of federal crimes.
2. Crimes committed in places beyond the jurisdiction of any state. These include crimes committed in the District of Columbia and crimes committed overseas by the military or on American-controlled ships or aircraft.
3. Crimes that interfere with the activities of the federal government.[11] As the scope of the activities of the federal government is broad, this category of federal crimes is broad. It includes fraud by use of the U.S. mails, robbery of federally insured banks or savings and loan associations, violation of the federal income tax laws, and attempt to overthrow the U.S. government.

Federal jurisdiction over homicide is exercised in the following situations:[12]

- within the special maritime and territorial jurisdiction
- when death results from sabotage, or certain cases of reckless or negligent destruction of "federal" transportation facilities
- when the victim is the president of the United States, the vice-president, or successors to the office[13]
- when the victim is engaged in performing federal functions
- when the victim was killed "on account of the performance of his official duties"
- when death occurs in connection with a federally punishable bank robbery
- when the homicide occurred during an offense defined by the Civil Rights Act of 1968 (18 U.S.C.A. Sec. 245)

Federal Enclaves and the Assimilative Crimes Act of 1948

Federal enclaves are federally owned and controlled lands that can be found in all states. Military installations, such as army posts, naval yards, air force bases, coast guard stations, and marine bases, are enclaves if they are within the borders of states. National parks and forest lands and federal buildings, such as post offices, federal court buildings, and federal office buildings, are also enclaves. The federal government owns almost one-fourth of the land in the continental United States and has exclusive jurisdiction over much of this land.

Before 1948, some of the enclaves had a degree of autonomy, which created some problems throughout the United States. These problems had to do with the sale of liquor and the fact that gambling was permitted on many military bases. For example, slot machines were (and still are) illegal in Illinois but were available for use at the Great Lakes Naval Training Station and at Fort Sheridan army base, located in the Chicago area. Congress had passed criminal laws dealing with a few serious crimes committed in enclaves, but there was not a complete criminal code for the enclaves.

Areas of Federal and State Jurisdiction

The Federal Government has Jurisdiction within the Following Three Limited Areas:

for the protection of:

1. interstate and international commerce
2. the activities and interests of the federal government
3. the rights of citizenship

In Maintaining Public Order and Public Safety, States have Broad Jurisdiction within Their Police Powers to:

1. provide for the safety of their people
2. provide for the health of their people
3. protect the morals of their people
4. "protect the well-being and tranquility of a community" by prohibiting "acts or things reasonably thought to bring evil or harm." (U.S. Supreme Court in *Kovacs v. Cooper*, 336 U.S. 77, 69 S.Ct. 448 [1949])

In 1948, Congress passed the Assimilative Crimes Act (18 U.S.C.A. Sec. 13), which incorporates, by reference, the state criminal law of the surrounding state in force at the time of the defendant's conduct. Therefore, if slot machines are illegal in the state of Illinois, they are also illegal on such federal enclaves as the Great Lakes Naval Training Station and Fort Sheridan, which are within the borders of the state of Illinois.[14] In the case of *United States v. Sharpnack*,[15] the U.S. Supreme Court held that the Assimilative Crimes Act was constitutional. In that case, the defendant, who was a civilian, was convicted of committing sex crimes involving two boys at the Randolph Air Force Base, a federal enclave in Texas. In affirming the conviction, the Court stated:

> There is no doubt that Congress may validly adopt a criminal code for each federal enclave. It certainly may do so by drafting new laws or by copying laws defining the criminal offenses in force throughout the State in which the enclave is situated. As a practical matter, it has to proceed largely on a wholesale basis. Its reason for adopting local laws is not so much because Congress has examined them individually as it is because the laws are already in force throughout the State in which the enclave is situated. The basic legislative decision made by Congress is its decision to conform the laws in the enclave to the local laws as to all offenses not punishable by any enactment of Congress. Whether Congress sets forth the assimilated laws in full or assimilates them by reference, the result is as definite and as ascertainable as are the state laws themselves.

⚑ Indian Tribes within the United States

In 1832, Chief Justice John Marshall stated, in *Worcester v. State of Georgia:* "The Indian nations have always been considered as distinct, independent, political communities, retaining their original natural rights, as the undisputed possessors of the soil, from time immemorial."[16]

In 1886, the U.S. Supreme Court stated, in *United States v. Kagama:*

> They [the Indian tribes] were, and always have been regarded as having a semi-independent position when they preserved their tribal relations; not as states, not as nations, not as possessed of the full attributes of sovereignty, but as a separate people, with the power of regulating their internal and social relations, and thus far not

---

Jurisdiction of Law Enforcement Officers

The jurisdiction of law enforcement officers:

- is limited to their municipality or county (in the case of deputy sheriffs) unless determined to be otherwise by state statute.
- may extend into other states, counties, or municipalities if authorized by hot (or fresh) pursuit statutes or common law authority. If an arrest is made in another state, the officer must comply with the Uniform Criminal Extradition Act and take the suspect before a judge in that state to commence extradition proceedings.

- may be extended to other counties or municipalities in their state under the authority of a state arrest or search warrant.
- may be supplemented by the statutory or common law authority to make a "citizen's arrest" in their state.
- Federal officers are not limited by city, county, and state borders.

---

brought under the laws of the Union or of the state within whose limits they reside. ... These Indian tribes are the wards of the nation. They owe no allegiance to the states, and receive from them no protection.[17]

In 1916, the Supreme Court stated, in *United States v. Quiver:*

> At an early period it became the settled policy of Congress to permit the personal and domestic relations to the Indians with each other to be regulated and offenses by one Indian against the person or property of another Indian to be dealt with, according to their tribal customs and laws.[18]

In 1977, the Supreme Court stated, in *United States v. Antelope,* that:

> In the present case we are dealing not with matters of tribal self-regulation, but with federal regulation of criminal conduct within Indian country implicating Indian interests. ... Federal regulation of Indian affairs is not based upon impermissible classifications. Rather, such regulation is rooted in the unique status of Indians as "a separate people" with their own political institutions. Federal regulation of Indian tribes, therefore, is governance of *once-sovereign political communities;* it is not to be viewed as legislation of a " 'racial' group consisting of 'Indians.' " *Morton v. Mancari,* 417 U.S., at 553 n. 24.[19]

Criminal Jurisdiction of Indian Tribal Courts

In 1975 and again in 1977, the U.S. Supreme Court held that:

> Indian tribes are unique aggregations possessing attributes of sovereignty over both their members and their territory, *Worcester v. Georgia,* 31 U.S. 6 Pet. 515, 557 (1832); they are "a separate people" possessing the power of regulating their internal and social relations. *United States v. Mazurie,* 419 U.S. 544, 557, 95 S.Ct. 710, 717 (1975).[20]

Indians living on reservations and within "Indian country" are subject to the jurisdictions of Indian tribal courts. The authority of Indian tribal courts to impose criminal penalties is limited by federal law (25 U.S.C. Sec. 1302[7]) to the petty misdemeanor ceilings of six months' imprisonment and a $500 fine.

Under the federal Major Crimes Act, U.S. federal courts have criminal jurisdiction for fourteen serious crimes committed by Indians on Indian reservations and within "Indian country."[21] In the 1973 case of *Keeble v. United States,*[22] the Supreme Court noted that the federal government has characterized the Major Crimes Act as "a carefully limited intrusion of federal power into the otherwise exclusive jurisdiction of the Indian tribes to punish Indians for crimes committed on Indian land."

Indians who leave "Indian country" and commit crimes in a state or another place are subject to the criminal jurisdiction of the state or place in which the crime was committed. However, the state has jurisdiction over offenses committed on Indian reservations or within "Indian country" by persons who are non-Indian.[23]

An Experiment in Self-Government

There are some 1.4 million Native American Indians in the United States, with slightly more than half of them living on reservations located mainly in the southwest. There are 310 recognized Indian tribes living on 285 reservations throughout the country, covering about 50 million acres located in thirty states.

In various treaties between the United States government and many of these Indian tribes, some signed more than 150 years ago, the tribes relinquished their rights to vast amounts of land in exchange for a "special relationship" with the federal government. Among other obligations, the federal government was required to provide the tribes such services as health and education. That "special relationship" exists today but is in the process of change.

The tribes are seeking, with the approval of the U.S. Congress, to eliminate their dependence on the Bureau of Indian Affairs, which together with the Tribal Councils has managed Indian affairs since 1824. Recent studies show that Indian reservations have received only about 11 cents out of every dollar appropriated to the BIA by Congress. An audit released in 1991 disclosed that the BIA could not account for $95 million, or nearly one-tenth of its budget, in the 1990 fiscal year. Because of the problems at the BIA, several members of Congress expressed their belief that federal funds should be sent directly to those tribes seeking to manage their own affairs.

To date, seven tribes are experimenting with additional self-government in order to become, in effect, separate nations within a nation. An additional twenty tribes are set to join this experiment by 1993.

This experiment in self-government is considered by many to be the most important step toward Native American self-determination in more than a century.[24]

E. THE MILITARY, MARTIAL, AND WAR POWER JURISDICTION OF THE FEDERAL GOVERNMENT

Article I, Section 8 of the U.S. Constitution provides (in part) that:

> The Congress shall have power ... To define and punish Piracies and Felonies committed on the high Seas, and Offenses against the Law of Nations; To declare War ... and make Rules concerning Captures on Land and Water; To raise and support Armies

... To provide and maintain a Navy; To make Rules for the Government and Regulation of the land and naval Forces; To provide for calling forth the Militia to execute the Laws of the Union, suppress Insurrections and repel Invasions ... To make all Laws which shall be necessary and proper for carrying into Execution the foregoing Powers, and all other Powers vested by this Constitution in the Government of the United States, or in any Department or Officer thereof.

Article II of the U.S. Constitution provides in part that:

Section 1. The executive Power shall be vested in a President of the United States of America.... Section 2. The President shall be Commander in Chief of the Army and Navy of the United States, and of the Militia of the several States, when called into the actual Service of the United States.

Jurisdiction of Military Courts

When a person enters the American military service, he or she becomes subject to the court-martial process for violations of the Uniform Code of Military Justice.[25] Over the years, hundreds of thousands of military personnel have been tried for many offenses, ranging from "military" crimes, such as desertion, unauthorized absences, willful disobedience of orders, and drunkenness on duty, to "civilian" crimes, such as rape, murder, and drug violations, that took place on leave.

From 1969 through 1987, American military courts did not have jurisdiction for offenses that were not "service connected" and were committed off-base or off-post. In 1987, military courts were given back the authority and jurisdiction they lost in 1967. The U.S. Supreme Court abandoned the "service connection" requirement that was established in the 1969 case of *O'Callahan v. Parker,* 395 U.S. 258, 89 S.Ct. 1683.

In the 1987 case of *Solorio v. United States,* 483 U.S. 435, 107 S.Ct. 2924, the Supreme Court held that the military justice system has jurisdiction to try a member of the armed service for *any* crimes committed (on or off-base) so long as the accused was a member of the military service at the time of the alleged offense. A review of *Solorio v. United States* follows:

SOLORIO v. UNITED STATES
Supreme Court of the United States (1987) 483 U.S. 435, 107 S.Ct. 2924

The defendant was a member of the Coast Guard stationed in Alaska when he sexually abused young daughters of fellow Coast Guard members. The abuses occurred over a period of two years until he was transferred to New York where he committed similar abuses while stationed there. All of the offenses were then discovered.

The Coast Guard does not have a "base" or "post" in Juneau, Alaska, and the defendant's crimes were committed in private residences. The defendant was convicted in a general court-martial and appealed, challenging the jurisdiction of the military court. In abandoning the service connection requirement of *O'Callahan v. Parker* and holding that military courts have jurisdiction over all offenses committed by service persons on or off-base, the Court held:

* * *

The notion that civil courts are "ill-equipped" to establish policies regarding matters of military concern is substantiated by experience under the service-connection

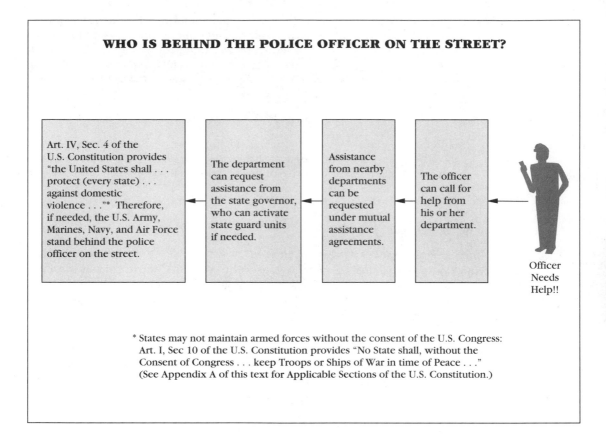

WHO IS BEHIND THE POLICE OFFICER ON THE STREET?

Art. IV, Sec. 4 of the U.S. Constitution provides "the United States shall . . . protect (every state) . . . against domestic violence . . ."* Therefore, if needed, the U.S. Army, Marines, Navy, and Air Force stand behind the police officer on the street.

The department can request assistance from the state governor, who can activate state guard units if needed.

Assistance from nearby departments can be requested under mutual assistance agreements.

The officer can call for help from his or her department.

Officer Needs Help!!

* States may not maintain armed forces without the consent of the U.S. Congress: Art. I, Sec 10 of the U.S. Constitution provides "No State shall, without the Consent of Congress . . . keep Troops or Ships of War in time of Peace . . ." (See Appendix A of this text for Applicable Sections of the U.S. Constitution.)

approach. In his O'Callahan *dissent, Justice Harlan forecasted that "the infinite permutations of possibly relevant factors are bound to create confusion and proliferate litigation over the [court-martial] jurisdiction issue." 395 U.S., at 284 . . .*

* * *

When considered together with the doubtful foundations of O'Callahan, the confusion wrought by the decision leads us to conclude that we should read clause 14 in accord with the plain meaning of its language as we did in the many years before O'Callahan *was decided. That case's novel approach to court-martial jurisdiction must bow "to the lessons of experience and force of better reasoning."* Burnet v. Coronado Oil & Gas Co., *285 U.S. 383 . . . We therefore hold that the requirements of the Constitution are not violated where, as here, a court-martial is convened to try a serviceman who was a member of the armed services at the time of the offense charged.*

Affirmed.

Crimes Committed by American Military Service Persons While Stationed in Foreign Countries

American military personnel are stationed in many countries throughout the world. If a service person commits a crime while off-base, off-duty, and in a foreign country, he or she is subject to the jurisdiction of the laws of that country. Under the status of forces agreement that many countries have with the United States, the military person could be tried by the courts in that foreign country.[26] However, in many instances the prosecutor in the foreign country will waive jurisdiction and turn the offender over to the American military authorities for trial before a military court.

Examples of crimes that American service personnel were charged with are 1983, *Plaster v. United States,*[27] murder of a West German taxidriver and desertion; 1974, *United States v. Newvine,*[28] murder of a Mexican prostitute; 1971, *Bell v. Clark,*[29] rape of a German woman.

Because foreign countries want a continued American military presence, they will often waive criminal jurisdiction. Military courts would then be the only courts with jurisdiction. Foreign prosecutors are aware that military punishment would probably be more severe than civilian punishment.

Trial of American Citizens by Foreign Courts

Americans who commit crimes in foreign countries are subject to prosecution before foreign courts, whether they are military personnel or tourists. American civilians have been sentenced to serve long prison terms in Turkey, Mexico, and other countries for narcotics violations. This is a grim reminder that sentences in some countries are quite severe.

When an American citizen commits a crime in a foreign country, generally only the foreign country has jurisdiction to try the crime. The exception to this would be in cases in which the crime was a violation of the U.S. criminal code (for example, the killing of Congressman Leo Ryan in Guyana, South America).

Martial Law and the Use of Military Forces in the Continental United States

In attempting to define martial law in 1946, the U.S. Supreme Court made the following statements in the case of *Duncan v. Kahanamoku:*

> The term "martial law" carries no precise meaning. The Constitution does not refer to "martial law" at all and no Act of Congress had defined the term. It has been employed in various ways by different people and at different times. By some it has been identified as "military law" limited to members of, and those connected with, the armed forces. Others have said that the term does not imply a system of established rules but denotes simply some kind of day to day expression of a General's will dictated by what he considers the imperious necessity of the moment. . . . In 1857 the confusion as to the meaning of the phrase was so great that the Attorney General in an official opinion had this to say about it: "The Common Law authorities and commentators afford no clue to what martial law, as understood in England, really is . . . . In this Country it is still worse." . . . What was true in 1857 remains true today.[30]

Military forces have been used many times in the history of our country to maintain public order and to enforce laws. In 1787, the year in which the Constitution was formulated, the governor of the Massachusetts colony used the militia to cope with Shay's Rebellion. Federal troops were sent by President Washington into Pennsylvania to suppress the Whiskey Rebellion of 1794. Federal troops were used by President Lincoln to prevent the withdrawal of the southern states from the Union and to maintain public order. Federal troops

General Jurisdiction Requirements

In order to charge a person with a crime, the state or federal government must:

- charge under a statute or ordinance that is constitutional on its face,
- charge in the county or place in which the crime is alleged to have occurred, and
- produce the person to be charged before the court that will try him or her.

Indians who commit crimes while *not* within their reservation or "Indian country" are subject to the jurisdiction of the state or government, just as non-Indians are. Indians who commit crimes while on their reservation or within "Indian country" can be tried (a) by their tribal court and punished by not more than six months' imprisonment and/or $500 fine (25 U.S.C. Sec. 1302[7]), or (b) before a U.S. federal court for the fourteen serious crimes under the Federal Major Crimes Act (18 U.S.C. Secs. 1153 and 3242).

Non-Indians charged with committing crimes against other non-Indians in "Indian country" are subject to prosecution under state law. *United States v. McBratney,* 104 U.S. (14 Otto) 621, 26 L.Ed. 869 (1881); *United States v. Antelope,* 430 U.S. 641, 97 S.Ct. 1395, 51 L.Ed.2d 701 (1977), footnote 2.

U.S. military personnel may be tried by a military court for all crimes they commit while they are in the military service, whether the offense was committed on or off a military base, ship, aircraft, etc.

Persons who commit crimes on federal enclaves can be tried before:

- a federal court, using the criminal code of the surrounding state under the Assimilative Crimes Act (18 U.S.C. Sec. 13)
- a military court, if the person was a member of the U.S. Armed Services.

remained in the South until the 1880s. During some of this time, martial law was in effect in the southern states in which federal troops remained.

Federal troops were used by President Eisenhower to secure compliance with Supreme Court school desegregation orders in Arkansas in 1957, and by President Kennedy in Mississippi in 1962 and in Alabama in 1963. In the twenty-nine-month period between January 1968 and the end of May 1970, National Guard troops were called up 324 times to cope with urban riots and disorders and unrest on college campuses.[31] In all the incidents in the 1950s, 1960s, and 1970s, troops and National Guard units provided assistance to civilian law enforcement agencies that had the primary responsibility for preserving public order. Persons arrested or taken into custody were brought before federal and state courts, where they were provided their constitutional rights.

In any street confrontation, law enforcement officers at the scene represent the authority of the state at that time and place. Should they need assistance, the resources of their department are available to them. If their department cannot handle the problem, other departments may be called on for assistance or personnel from the state may be requested. If the state does not have the resources to handle the situation, assistance may be requested from the federal government. The federal government is obligated under Article IV, Section 4 of the U.S. Constitution to commit such force as may be necessary to restore public order.[32]

May Civilians Be Tried by Military Courts?

The question of whether civilians may be tried by military courts has come before the U.S. Supreme Court in the following cases:

DUNCAN v. KAHANAMOKU
Supreme Court of the United States (1946) 327 U.S. 304, 66 S.Ct. 606

After the attack on Pearl Harbor in 1941, martial law was declared for the Territory of Hawaii by the territorial governor. Civil and criminal courts were forbidden to try cases and the military authorities took over the government of Hawaii. The Supreme Court reviewed two of the cases tried by military courts.

Petitioner in case No. 15 was a stockbroker convicted of embezzling stock eight months after Pearl Harbor. The offense was committed against another civilian. The military tribunal sentenced him to five years' imprisonment (later reduced to four).

Duncan (case No. 14) was a civilian shipfitter employed in the navy yard. He engaged in a brawl with two armed marine sentries at the yard and was sentenced to six months' imprisonment.

In reversing the convictions and ruling that "military tribunals have no such standing," the Court quoted the 1879 case of *Dow v. Johnson,*[33] stating:

> *The military should always be kept in subjection to the laws of the country to which it belongs, and that he is no friend of the Republic who advocates the contrary. The established principle of every free people is, that the law shall alone govern; and to it the military must always yield.*

KINSELLA v. UNITED STATES
Supreme Court of the United States (1960) 361 U.S. 234, 80 S.Ct. 297

Mrs. Dial was the wife of a soldier assigned to a tank battalion in Germany. The Dials and their three children lived in government housing quarters on a military base in Germany. Because of the death of one of their children, both of the Dials were charged with and convicted of involuntary manslaughter before a military court and both were sentenced to prison. Mrs. Dial challenged the jurisdiction of the court-martial to try her. The Court stated:

> *We therefore held that Mrs. Dial is protected by the specific provisions of Article III and the Fifth and Sixth Amendments and that her prosecution and conviction by court-martial are not constitutionally permissible.*

McELROY v. UNITED STATES EX REL. GUAGLIARDO
Supreme Court of the United States (1960) 361 U.S. 281, 80 S.Ct. 305

The Court, in applying the principles of *Kinsella,* held unconstitutional those provisions of the Uniform Code of Military Justice that subjected "persons . . . employed by . . . the armed forces outside the United States" to court-martial jurisdiction.

EX PARTE QUIRIN
Supreme Court of the United States (1942) 317 U.S. 1, 63 S.Ct. 1

The defendants were all Nazi spies who had received training at a sabotage school in Germany and then landed on beaches in Long Island and in Florida at night during World War II. While landing from submarines, they wore German marine infantry uniforms, which they buried before proceeding in civilian clothes to cities in the United States. The defendants were convicted in trials before military courts. The Supreme Court affirmed the convictions and the jurisdictions of the courts, stating:

> *By universal agreement and practice, the law of war draws a distinction between the armed forces and the peaceful populations of belligerent nations and also between those who are lawful and unlawful combatants. Lawful combatants are subject to capture and detention as prisoners of war by opposing military forces.*

Unlawful combatants are likewise subject to capture and detention, but in addition they are subject to trial and punishment by military tribunals for acts which render their belligerency unlawful. The spy who secretly and without uniform passes the military lines of a belligerent in time of war, seeking to gather military information and communicate it to the enemy, or an enemy combatant who without uniform comes secretly through the lines for the purpose of waging war by destruction of life or property, are familiar examples of belligerents who are generally deemed not to be entitled to the status of prisoners of war, but to be offenders against the law of war subject to trial and punishment by military tribunals . . . .

The rule, then, is that civilians may not be tried by military courts in the United States unless they are spies as described by the Supreme Court in *Ex Parte Quirin*. In 1957, a famous Russian spy, Colonel Abel, was captured in New York City. As it was not in time of war, Colonel Abel was tried before a federal district court in New York.[34]

Jurisdiction Arising from the General War Powers

Justice Oliver Wendell Holmes has been quoted as stating that when courts use the power of judicial review, they are not determining what the wisest and most prudent policy of government should have been or should be. The Constitution gives the power to determine public policy to the legislative and executive branches of government. In judicial review, the courts determine only whether the act or policy is within the lawful scope of authority granted by the Constitution of the United States. Courts should not be Monday-morning strategists, determining what the quarterback should have done in Saturday's game. Their function in judicial review is to determine only whether or not the "quarterback" acted within the rules.

In time of war or national emergency, the government uses its "war powers" to respond to the emergency. Former Chief Justice Charles E. Hughes wrote that the war power of the government is "the power to wage war successfully." Justice Felix Frankfurter wrote that "the validity of action under the war power must be judged wholly in the context of war. That action is not to be stigmatized as lawless because like action in times of peace would be lawless."[35] The question of the extent of the power of government to act in time of war was presented before the U.S. Supreme Court while World War II was still being fought.

KOREMATSU v. UNITED STATES
Supreme Court of the United States (1944) 323 U.S. 214, 65 S.Ct. 193

After the Japanese attack on Pearl Harbor in 1941, the president of the United States imposed a curfew and ordered all persons of Japanese ancestry in certain West Coast military areas to remain in their residences from 8 P.M. to 6 A.M. This action was sustained by the Supreme Court in the case of *Hirabayashi v. United States*.[36] In March of 1942, Congress enacted legislation authorizing the Executive Department to exclude persons of Japanese ancestry from military areas or zones designated by the Executive Department. Violation of such exclusionary order was made punishable by imprisonment for not more than one year. The defendant was convicted for violating the exclusion order. He was of Japanese ancestry and challenged the constitutionality of the law and the action taken. In sustaining the constitutionality of the law and the action of the Executive Department, the Court stated:

Like curfew, exclusion of those of Japanese origin was deemed necessary because of the presence of an unascertained number of disloyal members of the group, most of whom we have no doubt, were loyal to this country. It was because we could not reject the finding of the military authorities that is was impossible to bring about an immediate segregation of the disloyal from the loyal that we sustained the validity of the curfew order as applying to the whole group. In the instant case, temporary exclusion of the entire group was rested by the military on the same ground.... Approximately five thousand American citizens of Japanese ancestry refused to swear unqualified allegiance to the United States and to renounce allegiance to the Japanese Emperor, and several thousand evacuees requested repatriation to Japan.

We uphold the exclusion order as of the time it was made and when the petitioner violated it.... In doing so, we are not unmindful of the hardships imposed by it upon a large group of American citizens.... But hardships are part of war, and war is an aggregation of hardships. All citizens alike, both in and out of uniform, feel the impact of war in greater or lesser measure. Citizenship has its responsibilities as well as its privileges, and in time of war the burden is always heavier.

SUPPLEMENTARY READING FOR CHAPTER 9

Federal Crimes and Jurisdiction

by William J. Mulligan*

Introduction

The federal government, unlike the states, exercises no general police powers to regulate its citizenry. There is no federal criminal common law. Federal crimes are of statutory origin. They have not been passed down to us from the Magna Carta as interpreted by experience and reason.

Although our forebears could have provided in the Constitution that the Congress had a general police power exclusive, superior or coextensive with that of the states, they did not do so. Instead they limited the powers of Congress and retained to the states and people powers not otherwise conferred on the federal government. Such restrictive grant of power to the federal government was the result of philosophical and political concern of the drafters against a strong centralized government.

The philosophic and political background was explained by the Supreme Court in an early case upholding the validity of the White Slave Act.[37] In *Hoke v. United States*, 227 U.S. 308, 322, 33 S.Ct. 281, 283 (1913) the Court stated: "Our dual form of government has its perplexities, State and Nation having different spheres of jurisdiction . . . but it must be kept in mind that we are one people; and the powers reserved to the States and those conferred on the Nation are adapted

---

*William J. Mulligan is a former U.S. Attorney for the Eastern District of Wisconsin. Mr. Mulligan was assisted in the preparation of this article by Attorney David B. Bukey, also of the U.S. Attorney's office for the Eastern District of Wisconsin. The views expressed in this article do not necessarily reflect those of the U.S. Department of Justice.

to be exercised, whether independently or concurrently, to promote the general welfare, material, and moral." In regulating or prohibiting commerce among the states, Congress is equally free to support state legislative policy or to devise a policy of its own. The Supreme Court stated that Congress "may exercise this authority in aid of the policy of the State, if it sees fit to do so. It is equally clear that the policy of Congress acting independently of the States may induce legislation without reference to the particular policy or law of any given State. Acting within the authority conferred by the Constitution it is for Congress to determine what legislation will attain its purposes. The control of Congress over interstate commerce is not to be limited by the State laws."[38]

The limited scope of federal criminal law may amaze the present day observer who even casually examines and compares the federal and state criminal offenses. Quantitatively there exist more federal crimes than state offenses. Yet federal jurisdictional requirements limit areas of federal law enforcement.

Federal investigative and prosecutorial forces are restricted from entry into a matter of solely state concern. They may not enter into a matter unless a federal jurisdictional basis is established.

Jurisdictional Basis

Within the limited areas of federal jurisdiction, there are three primary bases of jurisdiction. They basically evolve from the nature and character of our federal system of government, i.e., a dual form of government with a national centralized government and its component states. Each of these primary bases is related to the nature and character of that government.

1. Protection of Federal Interest.   The centralized national government has an inherent interest in protecting itself, its operations and interests. Implicit in this basis is the government's right to protect its officials, personnel, agencies, property, or interests. Thus, the federal government may make criminal an assault upon or injury to the president, members of Congress, judges, U.S. attorneys and their assistants, and other federal agents.[39] It may make criminal the counterfeiting or forging of its currency, obligations and securities,[40] theft of its property,[41] theft from its mails,[42] fraud against the government or its agencies,[43] and fraud against its revenues.[44] The government can also uphold the integrity of its function and operations by prohibiting bribery of its officials,[45] conflicts of interest,[46] obstruction and interference with its judicial operations,[47] perjury in its courts or before a grand jury.[48] Similarly the government can prevent its services from being perverted to illicit ends, i.e., the use of the mails to defraud,[49] the use of the mails to extort,[50] the use of the mails to promote, manage, establish or carry on an illegal enterprise involving gambling, prostitution or narcotics.[51] Not only are the government's direct interests safeguarded, but the government's indirect interest in federally insured banks and savings and loan associations are protected. These include preventing the making of false statements to federal agencies or statements designed to defraud or mislead federal agencies.[52] The government's interests include the preservation of its navigable waters and the air in our environment.[53]

The federal government's interest in protecting its property has given rise to the area of assimilative crimes, i.e., the incorporation of state criminal laws in such areas as federal Indian and military reservations, federal enclaves and federal buildings.[54]

Federal Jurisdiction Cases

Cases Where Federal Jurisdiction Existed

United States v. Walton, 633 F.Supp. 1353 (D. Minn. 1986)

Local prostitution ring, but defendants accepted payments from customers with major credit cards over two-year period. Federal jurisdiction held under Travel Act, 18 U.S.C. Sec. 1952.[85]

United States v. Pecora, 693 F.2d 421 (5th Cir. 1982), review denied, 462 U.S. 1119, 103 S.Ct. 3087 (1983).

A single interstate telephone call was held to satisfy the Travel Act.

United States v. Eisner, 533 F.2d 987 (6th Cir. 1976), review denied, 429 U.S. 919, 97 S.Ct. 314 (1976), and *United States v. LeFaivre,* 507 F.2d 1288 (4th Cir. 1974)

Depositing or cashing an out-of-state check constituted the use of a facility in interstate commerce.

United States v. Raineri, 670 F.2d 702 (7th Cir. 1982), review denied, 459 U.S. 1035, 103 S.Ct. 446 (1982)

A single bank check crossing state lines as part of the regular clearing process was a sufficient basis for jurisdiction and "maintenance and regular use of (an out-of-state) bank account was significant enough to facilitate an illegal enterprise" in violation of the Travel Act. In this case, the defendant was a state circuit judge who was the owner of a nude bar featuring prostitution in the same county where defendant was a state judge.

United States v. Ebens, 800 F.2d 1422 (6th Cir. 1986)

The defendant killed Vincent Chin (an American of Chinese descent) and pleaded guilty to manslaughter in a Michigan court. The sentence was very lenient (probation and a fine of $3,720) and because of the public outrage, the federal government charged the defendant and his stepson of violating the civil rights of the deceased under 18 U.S.C.A. § 245(b) (2) (F). A twenty-five-year sentence was imposed after conviction.

United States v. Melia, 741 F.2d 70 (4th Cir. 1984), review denied, 37 CrL 4077 (1985).

Thieves stole $600,000 worth of jewelry in North Carolina, transported it to Ohio, and then to Melia's home in Connecticut. "Melia, a fence, knowing that the jewelry was stolen, received, concealed, and sold it in Connecticut." It was held that neither Melia's right to be tried where the crime was committed was violated, nor was his Sixth Amendment guarantee of a jury from the state where the crime was committed violated.

Cases Where Federal Jurisdiction did not Exist

United States v. Maze, 414 U.S. 395, 94 S.Ct. 645 (1974)

Maze stole his roommate's credit card and used it to charge meals and lodging as he traveled in several states. Held no federal jurisdiction under the mail fraud statute, 18 U.S.C.A. § 1341 (mailing of credit card invoices to credit card issuing bank in Kentucky).

United States v. Archer, 486 F.2d 670 (2d Cir. 1973)

Receiving a foreign telephone call by the defendant was an incidental occurrence and did not justify federal jurisdiction.

2. Protection of Commerce.   The Founders initially held a rather limited view of protecting the federal government's interest in foreign and interstate commerce. Through the years the commerce clause has been liberally construed and expanded to include any effect upon interstate commerce.[55] This has given the federal government much greater power of a general police nature. It has become the basis for statutes prohibiting interstate transportation of stolen motor vehicles,[56] controlled substances,[57] gun control,[58] theft from interstate shipment,[59] unlawful flight of a defendant, witness or prisoner to avoid prosecution, testimony or confinement,[60] hijacking of aircraft,[61] interstate transportation of pornography,[62] and extortion.[63]

3. Protection of Citizenship Rights.

The Thirteenth, Fourteenth and Fifteenth Amendments to the United States Constitution, adopted in 1866, 1868, and 1870, respectively, serve as the basis for a series of federal criminal statutes prohibiting deprivation of rights of persons. Thus, when two or more persons combine to deprive any person of his or her rights, there is a violation of the federal criminal code.[64] When any person, acting under color of state law, such as a police officer, denies a person of his or her rights, it is a felony.[65] The latter area includes such practices as police brutality. It is also unlawful for anyone to move in interstate or foreign commerce to avoid prosecution, custody, testimony, or confinement in connection with the damaging or destroying of any building, dwelling, synagogue, church, religious center, or educational institution, public or private.[66]

Dual Prosecution and Prosecutive Discretion

An examination of the areas of federal jurisdiction quickly demonstrates great overlapping with state criminal offenses. The robbery of a bank (whose deposits are insured by the Federal Deposit Insurance Corporation) is both a robbery punishable under state criminal laws and a federal crime punishable under 18 U.S.C.A. § 2113. Assuming the perpetrator is apprehended, should he be prosecuted by both state and federal authorities? Should the resources of both the state and federal criminal justice system be called into play? Should both the state and federal systems take the time and effort to prosecute the case? Should both the state and federal systems expend the funds necessary to pay witness fees, jury fees, and defense attorney fees? Generally, these questions are answered in the negative. In this era of crowded court calendars and limited budgets, such dual prosecutions would be improvident.

What then should determine whether the culprit is prosecuted in the state or federal system? Should it be simply the free enterprise system, i.e., that agency who has apprehended the villain?

In the case of a drug violation what are the determinative factors of state and federal prosecution? What type of drug is involved? What is the amount? What differences of proof are required by the different jurisdictions (e.g., which is most likely to uphold the search)? What is the past record of the defendant? What is the level of dealing—street level? Wholesaler? In which system is the defendant more likely to get an appropriate sentence?

These are some of the factors that must be weighed by the arresting officers and the prosecuting authorities in deciding whether to seek state or federal prosecution.

Although it has been held that prosecution by both state and federal authorities for offenses arising out of the same incident does not constitute double jeopardy,[67] there are some statutes which prohibit dual prosecution. For example, in the case of a theft or embezzlement from an interstate shipment of goods or chattels, Section 659 of Title 18, United States Code provides that a "judgment of conviction or acquittal on the merits under the laws of any state shall be a bar to any prosecution under this section for the same act or acts."

Authority of State Officer to Arrest for Federal Offense

In the typical situation where a state officer makes an arrest and federal prosecution follows, there is no problem because the state officer originally acted to enforce state law. Thus, he arrests a person for the robbery of a state bank whose deposits are insured by the Federal Deposit Insurance Corporation. This single occurrence of bank robbery constitutes both a state and federal crime. Here there is no question of the state officer's arrest power. The problem arises when there is an arrest by a state officer for a federal offense when there is no state offense.

A state officer possesses the authority to arrest for a federal crime under the command of a warrant. The authority is found in 18 U.S.C.A. § 3041, which provides in pertinent part:

> For any offense against the United States, the offender may, by any justice or judge of the United States, or by any United States Magistrate, or by any Chancellor, judge of a supreme or superior court, Chief or first judge of common pleas, mayor of a city, justice of the peace, or other magistrate, of any state where the offender may be found, and at the expense of the United States, be arrested and imprisoned or released as provided in Chapter 207 of this title, as the case may be, for trial before such court of the United States as by law has cognizance of the offense.

This statute has been construed as permitting local law enforcement officers to execute a warrant of arrest for a federal violation.[68]

The state and federal courts have held that state officers have the power to apprehend federal offenders without a warrant. Most cases that have given detailed consideration to this issue have found as the basis the "supremacy" clause of the federal constitution.[69] It has been specifically held that state officers have the power and *duty* to enforce federal criminal law.[70] It has also been recognized that a state officer is an ordinary citizen and therefore possesses the power of arrest of a private citizen.[71]

Searches by State Officers

At one time the United States Supreme Court ruled that evidence unreasonably obtained by state officers, who were not acting under a claim of federal authority, could be used in federal court since the Fourth Amendment was not directed to misconduct of such officials (the so-called "silver platter" doctrine).[72] The Supreme Court, however, in *Wolf v. Colorado*, 338 U.S. 25, 69 S.Ct. 1359 (1949) held that the Fourth Amendment by virtue of the Fourteenth Amendment prohibited unreasonable searches and seizures by state officers. In *Elkins v. United States,* 364 U.S. 206, 80 S.Ct. 1437 (1960), the silver platter doctrine was abolished when the Court declared that evidence obtained by state officers during a search which, if conducted by federal officers, would have violated the Fourth Amendment was inadmissible in a federal criminal trial even when there was no participation by federal officers in the search and seizure.

Federal-State Cooperation in Obtaining Confessions

Although federal and state cooperation in obtaining a confession is commendable, there are several pitfalls. It may not be the fruit of the poisonous tree of prior illegality.[73] Nor may it be obtained during a period of unnecessary delay which occurred by the cooperative efforts of state and federal officers in bringing the defendant before a magistrate as required by Rule 5, Federal Rules of Criminal Procedure.[74]

Federal Offenses of Particular Interest

In the multitude of federal offenses, some are of particular and frequent interest to state law enforcement officers. In part this is due to the frequency of occurrence of these offenses and the similarity to state offenses. In other cases, federal statutory provisions provide valuable assistance to state officers in the enforcement of state criminal law. Some of these federal offenses will be briefly discussed.

1. Interstate Transportation of Stolen Motor Vehicles ("Dyer Act").   Auto theft represents statistically a large area of criminal activity. Originally, this was a local matter and state offense. Increasingly, however, the vehicle is taken from one state to another and sometimes thereafter is concealed. Such activity places a burden on local law enforcement in investigating the occurrence, recovering the vehicle, and prosecuting the offense when large distances become involved. Under federal law it is unlawful for any person to transport a vehicle in interstate or foreign commerce knowing the vehicle to have been stolen or thereafter to conceal such a vehicle, 18 U.S.C.A. §§ 2312, 2313. As a matter of policy, federal efforts are normally concentrated on car theft rings, although efforts are frequently made to return car thieves, particularly juveniles.

2. Interstate Transportation of Stolen Property.   Two common areas of criminal activity are prohibited by 18 U.S.C.A. § 2314. First, it is unlawful for anyone to transport in interstate of foreign commerce any goods, wares, merchandise, securities, or money of the value of $5,000 or more, knowing the same to have been stolen, converted, or taken by fraud. Thus, stolen merchandise valued at $5,000 or more may not be taken to another state for disposition. Second, it is unlawful for anyone with fraudulent intent to transport in interstate or foreign commerce any falsely made, forged, altered, or counterfeit securities (which includes money orders and checks). There is no monetary requirement with respect to this latter offense.

3. Thefts and Embezzlement from Interstate Shipments.   The purview of federal criminal law relating to thefts and embezzlements from interstate or foreign shipments of freight or property is extensive. It is set forth in 18 U.S.C.A. § 659. It protects pipeline systems, railroad cars, wagons, motortrucks, other vehicles, tank or storage facilities, stations, station houses, platforms, depots, steamboats, vessels, wharves, aircraft, air terminals, airports, and baggage in the possession of common carriers. The federal protection is afforded even though the goods are at temporary rest until they reach their final destination.[75]

4. Mail Thefts.   The theft of letters, cards, packages, or matter from mail receptacles, mail boxes, or carriers violates 18 U.S.C.A. § 1708. Separate provisions apply to thefts by postal employees.[76] Frequently, this type of criminal activity is coupled with the obtaining, forging, and uttering of U.S. Treasury checks. The latter activities are prohibited by 18 U.S.C.A. § 495.

5. Bank Robbery and Related Crimes. Federal Reserve Banks, National Banks, and other banks, savings and loan associations, and credit unions, the deposits of which are insured by federal agencies, are protected from robbery, larceny, or burglary by 18 U.S.C.A. § 2113. There are some state banks and other financial institutions whose deposits are not insured and they are not afforded this federal protection.

6. Kidnapping. 18 U.S.C.A. § 1201 generally prohibits kidnapping or abduction of any person for reward or ransom, when willful interstate transportation of the victim or use of the special maritime or territorial jurisdiction of the United States is involved. The federal kidnapping statute provides for imprisonment up to life.

7. Wiretapping and Other Eavesdropping. In 1968 legislation was enacted making it a federal offense for anyone to intercept, endeavor to intercept, or procure any other person to intercept any wire or oral communication with limited exceptions.[77] The legislation also prohibited willfully using, endeavoring to use, or procuring another to use any electronic, mechanical, or other device in interstate transportation, or use of the special maritime cable or like connection used in wire communication, or when the device transmits communication by radio or interferes with the communication, or when the device has been transmitted by mail or transported in interstate commerce or is used on the premises of a business which affects interstate or foreign commerce or for obtaining information relating to such a business.[78] It is also unlawful to disclose or use the content of an illegal interception.[79] Manufacture, distribution, possession, and advertising of intercepting devices is also illegal.[80]

Statutory exceptions are limited to certain court ordered wiretaps (based on federal or state enabling laws), certain activities of communications common carriers and employees of the Federal Communications Commission, foreign intelligence, and national security matters.[81] An exception is also made in the case of a person acting under color of state law, e.g., a police officer, to intercept a wire or oral communication where he or she is a party to the communication or where one of the parties to the communication has given prior consent to the interception.[82] Persons not acting under color of law may intercept in similar circumstances unless the communication is intercepted for the purpose of committing any criminal or tortious act or for the purpose of committing any other injurious act.[83]

8. Gambling. Essentially gambling activities are regulated or prohibited by local and state legislation. Federal legislation, 18 U.S.C.A. § 1955, prohibits the conducting, financing, managing, supervising, directing, or owning of all or a part of an illegal gambling business in violation of state or local law, involving five or more persons who conduct, finance, manage, supervise, direct, or own all or part of such business which has been or remains in substantially continuous operation for a period in excess of thirty days or has a gross revenue of $2,000 in any single day. 18 U.S.C.A. § 1084 prohibits the interstate or foreign transmission by a wire communications facility of wagering information by one engaged in the business of betting or wagering. 18 U.S.C.A. § 1952 prohibits interstate or foreign travel or the use of the mails in aid of racketeering enterprises such as a business enterprise involving gambling. 18 U.S.C.A. § 1953 prohibits the interstate transportation of wagering paraphernalia. 18 U.S.C.A. § 1082 prohibits operation of a gambling establishment on a gambling ship.

9. Narcotics and Other Controlled Substances.   Federal criminal law involving drugs is basically concerned with two areas of enforcement: the importation of controlled substances into the United States from foreign countries and the distribution or possession with intent to distribute of controlled substances within the United States. 21 U.S.C.A. § 811 establishes six schedules of controlled substances which may also be supplemented or modified (within appropriate limits) from time to time by the Drug Enforcement Administration, on the authority of the Attorney General. Penalties for controlled substance offenses vary with the schedule of the controlled substance involved, and certain substances (such as heroin and cocaine) which are classified as "narcotic drugs" involve even stiffer penalties. Since most controlled substance offenses overlap with state jurisdiction, federal officials will often defer smaller cases to local authorities so that their efforts can be directed against the higher echelons of drug traffic. 21 U.S.C.A. §§ 846 and 963 establish specific controlled substance conspiracy statutes, which do not require proof of specific overt acts and which are penalized according to the type of substance involved.

10. Firearms.   The federal law regulating firearms is a complex series of statutes enacted by Congress, chiefly in 1968, as a compromise between those favoring stiffer gun control and those opposing any regulation in this area at all. The result is a law leaving the great bulk of firearms enforcement to state and local authorities, with regulations of dealers, restriction of certain types of dangerous weapons, and regulation of sales to certain specified types of individuals remaining for the federal government. The law applies to both licensed firearms dealers and also to individuals. 18 U.S.C.A. § 922 prohibits dealers from selling firearms to out-of-state residents, to minors, to convicted felons, to former mental patients, to persons under indictment, fugitives, or drug users and it is also illegal for such persons to purchase weapons. The law requires specific forms to be filled out by a dealer for each firearm sale, and requires certain information to be furnished by the transferee at that time. A common area of federal prosecution deals with the falsifying of such forms, for example, by convicted felons who attempt to purchase weapons. Another area of federal concern is unlicensed dealing in firearms, which also is made an offense under 18 U.S.C.A. § 922. Federal law provides for imprisonment up to ten years for the use or carrying of a firearm to commit a felony, punishable under the laws of the United States, in addition to such other sentence as the individual may receive. Under present firearms law it is not illegal to possess or receive most types of firearms; however, certain more dangerous weapons are *per se* illegal unless specific transfer taxes are paid and unless registered with the Secretary of the Treasury.[84] These include machine guns and sawed-off shotguns, the unlawful possession of which is a major area of federal prosecution.

11. Prostitution (the "Mann Act").   Prostitution activities are basically prohibited by state and local law. Federal concern in this area centers upon some interstate involvement. Thus, the White Slave Act, 18 U.S.C.A. § 2421 et seq. prohibits the interstate transportation of any woman or girl for purpose of prostitution, debauchery, or any other immoral purpose, or with the intent and purpose to induce, entice, or compel such woman or girl to become a prostitute or give herself up to debauchery or to engage in any other immoral practice. It is also unlawful to procure or obtain any ticket or tickets or any form of transportation or evidence of the right thereto, to be used by any woman or girl in interstate commerce in going to any place for the purpose of prostitution, debauchery, or any other immoral purpose. 18 U.S.C.A. § 1952 prohibits travel in interstate or foreign commerce or the use of the mails in aid of prostitution offenses in violation of state or federal law.

12. Unlawful Flight Statute.   The unlawful flight to avoid prosecution statute, 18 U.S.C.A. § 1073, or as it is sometimes referred to, the fugitive felon act, was basically enacted as a means of permitting federal investigative resources being used to locate state fugitives who may have fled from one state to another. The fugitive may either be a person seeking to avoid prosecution for a felony, a person seeking to avoid giving testimony in a felony case, or a person seeking to avoid custody or confinement on a felony matter. Although federal investigative agents may apprehend a person who has traveled in interstate commerce for such purposes, actual prosecution must be personally approved in writing by the Attorney General of the United States.

13. Conspiracy.   The federal conspiracy statute, 18 U.S.C.A. § 371, is one of the most widely sweeping tools available to any federal prosecutor and this is often either criticized or applauded, depending on whether the person talking is defending or prosecuting a conspiracy charge. The law makes it illegal for two persons to "combine or conspire" either to commit any offense against the laws of the United States or to defraud the government of the United States. With the vast number of "laws of the United States" on the books, this obviously covers a lot of territory. A conspiracy may be defined as an agreement followed by the commission of an "overt act." Under conspiracy law the actual substantive crime need not have been completed for the conspiracy charge to be sustained and the overt act need not be an act criminal in nature. Another reason for federal prosecutors' favoring conspiracy charges is the generally more liberal evidentiary rules in that area which typically permit more evidence of a hearsay nature to be admitted at trial. For all of these reasons, federal conspiracy prosecutions are often used in selective significant areas of concern such as organized crime, white-collar crime, and political corruption.

14. Racketeer Influenced and Corrupt Organizations ("RICO").   One of the most devastating weapons available to federal law enforcement is Chapter 96 of Title 18 United States Code, 18 U.S.C.A. § 1961 et seq. 18 U.S.C.A. § 1962 makes it unlawful for any person who has received any income derived, directly or indirectly, from a pattern of racketeering activity to use or invest, directly or indirectly, any part of such income, in acquisition of any enterprise which is engaged in, or the activities of which affect, interstate or foreign commerce. Purchases of stock on the open market are excepted if the person or members of his immediate family or accomplices after such purchase do not own 1 percent aggregate of the securities in a clan or do not have power to elect a director. It is also unlawful for any person through a pattern of racketeering activity to acquire or maintain, directly or indirectly, any interest in or control of any enterprise which is engaged in, or the activities of which affect, interstate or foreign commerce. It is also unlawful for anyone employed by or associated with such an enterprise to conduct or participate in the conduct of its affairs through a pattern of racketeering activity.

Racketeering activity is defined by 18 U.S.C.A. § 1961 to include state offenses involving murder, kidnapping, gambling, arson, robbery, bribery, extortion, or dealing in narcotics or dangerous drugs, which are punishable by imprisonment for more than one year or federal felony offenses involving bribery, sports bribery, counterfeiting, theft from interstate shipment, embezzlement from pension and welfare funds, extortionate credit transactions, transmission of gambling information, mail fraud, wire fraud, obstruction of justice, of criminal investigation, or of state or local law enforcement, relating to interference with commerce, robbery, or extortion, racketeering, interstate transportation of wagering paraphernalia, unlawful welfare fund payments, illegal gambling businesses, interstate transportation of stolen property, white slave traffic, certain labor law violations, bankruptcy fraud, securities fraud, or dealing in narcotics or other dangerous drugs.

A pattern of racketeering activity requires at least two acts of racketeering activity, one of which occurred after October 15, 1970, and the last of which occurred within ten years.

The statute, 18 U.S.C.A. §§ 1963 and 1964 provides, in addition to criminal penalties, for the forfeiture of the enterprise to the United States and permits treble damage awards to those victimized. It is also possible to enjoin the participants from again engaging in such prohibited activities.

15. Mail Fraud.   18 U.S.C.A. § 1341 prohibits the use of the mails as part of a scheme or artifice to defraud. The gist of the mail fraud offense is the use of the mails by a defendant, but usually this element can be established through introduction into evidence of some correspondence or other document sent through the mails at one point by a defendant or an agent. Traditionally the mail fraud statute has been aimed at con artists, dummy corporations, phony franchise schemes, and other frauds upon the general public. However, the law has recently been used against corrupt public officials as well.

Conclusion

Federal criminal statutes, although subject to limited jurisdictional basis, serve as an important force in complementing state and local law enforcement.

Questions and Problems for Chapter 9

Using the following choices, indicate which court has jurisdiction in situations 1 to 13.
a. Only a U.S. federal court would have jurisdiction
b. Only a military court or tribunal would have jurisdiction
c. Only your state courts or municipal courts would have jurisdiction
d. Two of the above courts would have jurisdiction (indicate which two)
e. None of the above courts would have jurisdiction
Give reasons for your answers.

1. A soldier on a weekend leave in your city gets drunk on Saturday night and breaks a store window. He is in civilian clothes.

2. A substantial amount of evidence becomes available to the sheriff's department in your county showing that the soldier in question No. 1

committed a burglary that Saturday afternoon. Which jurisdiction can prosecute?

3. The president of the United States is shot and killed while visiting your state.

4. The governor of a neighboring state is shot and killed in your state.

5. X, who lives in London, hires and pays Y, who lives in Mexico City, to go into your state and kill W. Y is apprehended after he kills W. Can Y be prosecuted, and where?

6. Can an arrest warrant for X be issued and X extradited to your state for prosecution? Where can he be tried?

7. M drives a car at high speed in your state while under the influence of alcohol. He is near your state border when he hits another vehicle. The impact carries both cars into a neighboring state, where the driver of the other car dies. The homicide charge against M would be in which court?

8. An American soldier with a weekend pass and in civilian clothes commits a felony in Mexico. The Mexican authorities state that they will waive their jurisdiction to try the soldier. Where can he be tried in the United States?

9. Same as No. 8 except that the man is a civilian. Can he be tried in the United States?

10. Where would a spy captured in time of peace in the United States be tried?

11. A German national who is illegally in the United States is apprehended committing a burglary in your jurisdiction.

12. A U.S. congressman kills his wife in your state and claims legislative immunity because Congress is in session.

13. A man has been arrested in your state. Reliable witnesses can testify the man went to a city in a nearby state and, after purchasing a large amount of cocaine, returned to your state with the cocaine.

Notes

1. See *Ford v. State,* 184 Tenn. 443, 201 S.W.2d 539 (1945) in which it was held that a presumption arises that the homicide occurred in the county in which the body was found.

2. If the accused were arrested while he was a witness extradited from another state to testify, or on a speedy trial conveyance, or while he was in court in response to a subpoena, he would then have grounds to challenge the court's jurisdiction over his person. See your legal adviser for the law in your state in regard to these exceptions.

3. 414 U.S. 17, 94 S.Ct. 194 (1973).

4. Ordinarily jurisdiction is obtained over a fugitive who has fled from a jurisdiction by means of extradition. The United States presently has over eighty extradition treaties in force with foreign countries. A compilation of these treaties can be found in 18 U.S.C.A. § 3181.

5. *Gerstein v. Pugh,* 420 U.S. 103, 119, 95 S.Ct. 854, 865 (1975); *United States v. Crews,* 445 U.S. 463, 474, 100 S.Ct. 1244, 1251 (1980); also see *Akins v. Hamlin,* 327 So.2d 59 (Fla. App. 1976).

6. 109 Wis.2d 138, 325 N.W.2d 695 (1982). In a case such as the *Monje* case, the officer should have taken Monje before an Illinois judge, who would determine whether probable cause existed to hold Monje. Extradition proceedings would then be commenced to return Monje to Wisconsin, where he had committed an armed robbery.

7. Article 19 of the Geneva Convention on the High Seas, 1958 states: "On the high seas, or in any other place outside the jurisdiction of any State, every State

may seize a pirate ship or aircraft, or a ship taken by piracy and under pirates, and arrest the persons and seize the property on board. The courts of the State which carried out the seizure may decide upon the penalties to be imposed, and may also determine the action to be taken with regard to the ships, aircraft or property, subject to the rights of third parties acting in good faith."

8. The Law of the Sea Treaty to which the United States is a party provides that every state has the right to declare up to twelve miles as the width of its territorial sea. "Innocent passage" in the territorial waters of a country is defined by the Law of the Sea Treaty as follows: "Passage is innocent so long as it is not prejudicial to the peace, good order or security of the coastal state."

9. 679 F.2d 1373 (11th Cir. 1982).

10. The movie *Judgment at Nuremberg* powerfully presents the legal questions and the dilemmas of the Nuremberg Trial. Can a state legislate beyond its borders under the "law of nations" authority?

11. If federal property is intentionally damaged or destroyed, the federal government ordinarily has jurisdiction over the matter. When state property is intentionally damaged or destroyed within that state, the state government has jurisdiction. What about a situation in which the property is internationally owned, such as the United Nations building in New York City? In the 1976 case of *People v. Weiner,* 85 Misc.2d 161, 378 N.Y.S.2d 966 (1976), the defendant was charged with criminal mischief for having sprayed red paint on the outside wall of the United Nations

headquarters. The New York Criminal Court held that the court had jurisdiction over the person of the defendant and the offense.

12. This material was presented in the Working Papers of the National Commission on Reform of Federal Criminal Laws, Vol. II, p. 832.

13. At the time of the assassination of President Kennedy, only the state of Texas had jurisdiction to try the homicide charges.

14. Indian reservations and "Indian country" are lands that belong to the Native American Indians. The United States government does not have title to such lands. Bingo is a big source of income for many Indian tribes. Whether slot machines and other forms of gambling would be permitted on Indian reservations and "Indian country" would be determined most often by whether state law and the state constitution permit such forms of gambling.

15. 355 U.S. 286, 78 S.Ct. 291 (1958).

16. 31 U.S. (6 Pet.) 515 (1832).

17. 118 U.S. 375, 6 S.Ct. 1109 (1886).

18. 241 U.S. 602, 36 S.Ct. 699 (1916).

19. 430 U.S. 641, 97 S.Ct. 1395, 21 CrL 3007 (1977). In the 1965 case of *Colliflower v. Garland,* 342 F.2d 369 (9th Cir.) an Indian woman was found guilty by an Indian tribal court in the Fort Belknap Indian Community (Montana) of failing to remove her cattle from another Indian's land. She was fined $25 or five days in jail for failing to obey the tribal court's order to remove her cattle. She elected to take the jail sentence, stating that she could not pay the fine. She sought a writ of habeas corpus in a federal district court, alleging that the tribal court had denied her Fifth Amendment rights under the U.S. Constitution. The federal court concluded that it was "without jurisdiction to issue a writ of habeas corpus" in her case. This ruling was appealed to the Circuit Court of Appeals. After reviewing some of the decisions cited above, the Court of Appeals held that the district court did have the jurisdiction to issue a writ of habeas corpus and hear the matter.

The Court held: "We do not pass upon the merits of Mrs. Colliflower's claims, because the district court did not reach them. It does not follow from our decision that the tribal court must comply with every constitutional restriction that is applicable to federal or state courts. Nor does it follow that the Fourteenth Amendment applies to tribal courts at all; some of the cases cited above indicate that it does not."

20. Supra, see footnote #14.

21. Title 18 U.S.C.A. § 1153 provides in pertinent part: Any Indian who commits against the person or property of another Indian or other person any of the following offenses, namely, murder, manslaughter, rape, carnal knowledge of any female, not his wife, who has not attained the age of sixteen years, assault with intent to commit rape, incest, assault with intent to kill, assault with a dangerous weapon, assault resulting in serious bodily injury, arson, burglary, robbery, and larceny within the Indian country, shall be subject to the same laws and penalties as all other persons committing any of the above offenses, within the exclusive jurisdiction of the United States."

22. 412 U.S. 205, 93 S.Ct. 1993 (1973).

23. In the 1978 case of *Oliphant v. Suquamish Indian Tribe,* 435 U.S. 191, 98 S.Ct. 1011, 22 CrL 3055 (1978), the U.S. Supreme Court held that an Indian tribal court could not try non-Indians unless it had been granted specific authority by the Congress of the United States.

In the 1990 case of *Duro v. Reina,* ___ U.S. ___, 110 S.Ct. 2053, 47 CrL 2119, the U.S. Supreme Court held that an Indian tribal court can exercise criminal jurisdiction only over members of its own tribe and not members of another tribe, even if the latter lives on the reservation covered by the tribal court and commit a crime thereon. (In this case it was murder.) The Court noted that the Bill of Rights does not apply in tribal courts. As members of a tribe consent to the jurisdiction of the tribal court by maintaining membership in the tribe, the fact that the Bill of Rights does not apply poses no problems. Nonmembers of a tribe do not grant such consent, even by living on the reservation controlled by the tribe.

24. See "7 Indian Tribes Seeking End to Shackles of Dependency," *The New York Times* (January 16, 1991); and a report about Native American Indians on the February 24, 1983, broadcast of the PBS program, "The MacNeil-Lehrer Report."

25. 10 U.S.C.A. Secs. 801–940 (Supp.v, 1970) amending 10 U.S.C.A. §§ 801–940 (1964).

26. The best known SOFA (status of forces agreement) is that with the NATO countries. The largest American military commitment has existed in these European countries since 1945 in a continuous effort to keep the peace.

27. 720 F.2d 340, 34 CrL 2154 (4th Cir.).

28. 14 CrL 2387.

29. 437 F.2d 200 (4th Cir. 1971).

30. 327 U.S. 304, 66 S.Ct. 606 (1946).

31. From the testimony of Major General Wilson, Chief of the National Guard Bureau, before the President's Commission on Campus Unrest, 116 Cong. Rec. 27,339.

32. 10 U.S.C.A. § 331 also provides: "Whenever there is an insurrection in any State against its government, the President may, upon the request of its legislature or of its governor if the legislature cannot be convened, call into federal service such of the militia of the other States, in the number requested by that State, and use such of the armed forces, as he considers necessary to suppress the insurrections."

33. 100 U.S. 158, 25 L.Ed. 632 (1879).

34. See *Abel v. United States,* 362 U.S. 217, 80 S.Ct. 683 (1960). The *Abel* case illustrates the fact that all persons, including spies and persons illegally in the United States, have all the rights under the U.S. Constitution. The Bill of Rights uses the terms persons and people. Officers must therefore give all persons *Miranda* warnings and receive a waiver if they seek to use any statements in evidence against such persons.

35. See Justice Frankfurter's concurring opinion in *Korematsu v. United States.*

36. 320 U.S. 81, 63 S.Ct. 1375 (1943).

37. The White Slave Act or "Mann Act" prohibits the interstate transportation of a woman for immoral purposes. 18 U.S.C.A. § 2421 et seq.

38. *United States v. Hill,* 248 U.S. 420, 425, 39 S.Ct. 143, 145 (1919).

39. 18 U.S.C.A. §§ 111, 1114.

40. 18 U.S.C.A. § 471 et seq.

41. 18 U.S.C.A. §§ 641, 2112.

42. 18 U.S.C.A. § 1708.

43. 18 U.S.C.A. §§ 286, 287, 371 & 1001.

44. Tax evasion and similar offenses. See 26 U.S.C.A. § 7201 et seq.

45. 18 U.S.C.A. § 201.

46. 18 U.S.C.A. §§ 205, 207, 208, 209.

47. 18 U.S.C.A. §§ 1503, 1504.

48. 18 U.S.C.A. §§ 1621, 1622, 1623.

49. 18 U.S.C.A. § 1341.

50. 18 U.S.C.A. § 876.

51. 18 U.S.C.A. § 1952.

52. 18 U.S.C.A. §§ 1005, 1006, 2113.

53. 18 U.S.C.A. §§ 407, 411; 42 U.S.C.A. § 1857 et seq.

54. 18 U.S.C.A. § 13.

55. *United States v. Hyde,* 448 F.2d 815, 836–837 (5th Cir. 1971), cert. denied 404 U.S. 1058, 92 S.Ct. 736 (1972).

56. 18 U.S.C.A. § 2312.

57. 21 U.S.C.A. § 811 et seq.

58. 18 U.S.C.A. ch. 44, § 921 et seq., 18 U.S.C.A. Appendix, §§ 1201, 1202.

59. 18 U.S.C.A. § 659.

60. 18 U.S.C.A. § 1073.

61. 49 U.S.C.A. § 1422(I) & (J).

62. 18 U.S.C.A. § 1462.

63. 18 U.S.C.A. § 1951.

64. 18 U.S.C.A. § 241.

65. 18 U.S.C.A. § 242.

66. 18 U.S.C.A. § 1074.

67. *Bartkus v. Illinois,* 359 U.S. 121, 79 S.Ct. 676 (1959); *Abbate v. United States,* 359 U.S. 187, 79 S.Ct. 666 (1959).

68. *Harris v. Superior Court of Sacramento County,* 51 Cal. App. 15, 196 P. 895 (1921); *Goulis v. Stone,* 246 Mass. 1, 140 N.E. 294 (1923).

69. *Marsh v. United States,* 29 F.2d 172 (2d Cir. 1928); other cases have found such authority without detailed consideration. *Theriault v. United States,* 401

F.2d 79 (8th Cir. 1968); *Davida v. United States,* 422 F.2d 528 (10th Cir. 1970).

70. *Henderson v. United States,* 237 F.2d 169, 175 (5th Cir. 1956).

71. *United States v. Montos,* 421 F.2d 215 (5th Cir. 1970).

72. *Weeks v. United States,* 232 U.S. 383, 34 S.Ct. 341 (1914).

73. *Harrison v. United States,* 392 U.S. 219, 221, 88 S.Ct. 2008, 2009 (1968); See also: *Wong Sun v. United States,* 371 U.S. 471, 488, 83 S.Ct. 407, 417 (1963).

74. *McNabb v. United States,* 318 U.S. 332, 63 S.Ct. 608 (1943); *Mallory v. United States,* 354 U.S. 449, 494–497, 77 S.Ct. 1356, ___ (1957).

75. *Sharp v. United States,* 280 Fed. 86 (5th Cir. 1922).

76. 18 U.S.C.A. §§ 1701, 1702, 1709.

77. 18 U.S.C.A. § 2511.

78. 18 U.S.C.A. § 2511.

79. 18 U.S.C.A. § 2511.

80. 18 U.S.C.A. § 2512.

81. 18 U.S.C.A. § 2511.

82. 18 U.S.C.A. § 2511.

83. 18 U.S.C.A. § 2511.

84. 26 U.S.C.A. §§ 5861 & 5871.

85. The Travel Act provides:

(a) Whoever travels in interstate . . . commerce or uses any facility in interstate . . . commerce, including the mail, with intent to . . .

(3) otherwise promote, manage, establish, carry on, or facilitate the promotion, management, establishment, or carrying on, of any unlawful activity,

and thereafter performs or attempts to perform any of the acts specified in subparagraphs (1), (2), and (3), shall be fined not more than $10,000 or imprisoned for not more than five years, or both.

(b) As used in this section 'unlawful activity' means (1) any business enterprise involving . . . prostitution offenses in violation of the laws of the State in which they are committed . . .

To convict (A) defendant for violating this statute . . . the prosecution had to prove that the defendant (1) with intent to promote a business enterprise involving illegal prostitution, (2) caused someone to travel in interstate commerce or use an interstate facility, and (3) the defendant thereafter promoted or attempted to promote the business enterprise . . .

Part Two

THE BALANCING OF CONSTITUTIONAL RIGHTS WITH THE NEED FOR PUBLIC ORDER

Chapter Ten

THE LIMITS OF
FREE SPEECH

A. BELIEF — SPEECH — ACTION

Belief

As thought and belief are not subject to control by government, persons may legally entertain any thoughts on any subject. Because thought and belief, by themselves, do not infringe on the rights of other persons, the right to believe is absolute. As persons may not be punished for what they think, thoughts about committing a crime are not, by themselves, punishable by the state.

Speech

Speech and other forms of communication, however, are not absolute rights, for they can seriously clash with the rights of others. For example, a man who calls another man's wife or mother the most vile and vulgar names he can think of may not assert that this is within his constitutional freedom of speech. The U.S. Supreme Court has stated that the right of freedom of speech and other forms of communication "implies the existence of an organized society maintaining public order without which liberty itself would be lost in the excess of unrestrained abuses."[1] The Court has also stated that "the line between speech unconditionally guaranteed and speech which may be regulated, suppressed or punished is finely drawn."[2]

Human communications take many forms. Pure speech includes words spoken on a face-to-face basis or through the media or radio, television, or recording devices. Written communication includes newspapers, books, and magazines as well as signs or symbols carried or displayed in public. A certain gesture with a finger, which would be interpreted by many as obscene, is certainly a form of communication. Picketing, protest marches, boycotts, and the like are also forms of communication. (These are discussed in chapter 11.)

Action

Speech is often the link between thought and action. Action, like speech, is not an absolute right, because it can interfere with the rights of others; a person has a right to swing his arm, but his right to swing his arm ends where another person's nose begins. Each state and the federal government have enacted criminal statutes forbidding certain conduct and, in some instances, requiring other conduct.

EXAMPLE: A man may believe that the 55-mile-per-hour speed limit "stinks." He may state this belief in any form of communication available to him because this communication would not ordinarily present any "clear and present danger" to other persons. However, when the man actually violates the speed limit by action, he may then be punished.

EXAMPLE: In an extreme case, a man may believe that he has the right to kill the president of the United States because he disagrees with his policies. However, because of the "clear and present danger" that communication of this thought presents, the man may be arrested and convicted under 18 U.S.C., Section 871(a) of the Federal Code if he knowingly and willfully threatens the life of the president or encourages other persons to do so.[3]

B. The "Clear and Present Danger" Test

The First Amendment of the U.S. Constitution provides that "Congress shall make no law . . . abridging the freedom of speech, or of the press." Does this mean that persons can say and communicate anything and everything without restriction by either state or local government?[4] The answer is "no," because under the old English common law and under the laws of the United States, there have always been restrictions on speech and communications within constitutional limitations.

Free speech is essential to a democracy. The "freedom to speak one's mind is not only an aspect of individual liberty—and thus a good unto itself—but also is essential to the common quest for truth and the vitality of society as a whole."[5]

The test used for government restriction of speech is the "clear and present danger" test. Local, state, or federal governments in the United States cannot forbid or suppress speech and punish the speaker unless the connection between the speech and an illegal harm is so close that the speech presents a "clear and present" danger. Justice Oliver Wendell Holmes announced the "clear and present danger" doctrine in the 1919 case of *Schenck v. United States:*

> The most stringent protection of free speech would not protect a man in falsely shouting "Fire" in a crowded theater, causing a panic. It would not even protect a man from an injunction against uttering words that may have all the effect of force. The question in every case is whether the words are used in such circumstances that are of such a nature as to create a clear and present danger that they will bring about the substantive evils that Congress has a right to protect. It is a question of proximity and degree. When a nation is at war many things that might be said in time of peace are such a hindrance to its efforts that their utterances will not be endured so long as men fight and that no court could regard them as protected by any constitutional right.[6]

Using Oliver Wendell Holmes's example, a person could go into a public park on a sunny day and stand in a large, open field yelling "fire." Bystanders might be curious or amused, but they would not panic and would not stampede, injuring one another. They would know that they were in no immediate danger as they could see and smell that there was no fire in the area. There would therefore be no "clear and present" danger that the person's speech would bring about a harm and a wrong that would concern society.

The balance of this chapter outlines the areas in which states restrict speech and communications by criminal and sometimes civil laws. As First Amendment rights are very important to all persons, the burden of proof, as usual in criminal law, is upon government to prove beyond a reasonable doubt.

C. The Insulting or "Fighting Word"

The "fighting word" test was first clearly presented by the U.S. Supreme Court in the 1942 case of *Chaplinsky v. New Hampshire.* The defendant in that case was

Former vice-president of the United States, Nelson Rockefeller, "responding in kind" (his words) to hecklers during an appearance for Senator Robert Dole (background). Could this gesture, under entirely different circumstances, ever amount to "fighting words"?

arrested when he said to a city marshal on a public sidewalk, "You are a god-damned racketeer" and "a damned fascist and the whole government of Roches-ter are fascist or agents of fascists." The U.S. Supreme Court affirmed Chaplinsky's conviction under a New Hampshire opprobrious language statute because the New Hampshire courts had limited the statute to "fighting words." The U.S. Supreme Court stated:

> It is well understood that the right of free speech is not absolute at all times and under all circumstances. There are certain well-defined and narrowly limited classes of speech, the prevention and punishment of which have never been thought to raise any Constitutional problem. These include the lewd and obscene, the profane, the libelous, and the insulting or "fighting" words—those which by their very utterance inflict injury or tend to incite an immediate breach of the peace. It has been well observed that such utterances are no essential part of any exposition of ideas, and are of such slight social value as a step to truth that any benefit that may be derived from them is clearly outweighed by the social interest in order and morality.[7]

In commenting on *Chaplinsky* in 1972, the U.S. Supreme Court, in *Gooding v. Wilson,*[8] quoted the Supreme Court of New Hampshire in *Chaplinsky* as follows:

> No words were forbidden except such as have a direct tendency to cause acts of violence by the person to whom, individually, the remark is addressed. . . .

The test is what men of common intelligence would understand would be words likely to cause an average addressee to fight. . . . Derisive and annoying words can be taken as coming within the purview of the statute . . . only when they have this characteristic of plainly tending to excite the addressee to a breach of the peace. . . .

The Statute, as construed, does no more than prohibit, the face-to-face words plainly likely to cause a breach of the peace by the addressee. 91 N.H. 310, 313, 320–321, 18 A.2d 754, 758, 762 (1941)

The Requirements for a "Fighting Word" Violation

The requirements for the "fighting word" violation are (a) that a valid criminal statute or ordinance exist in that jurisdiction which clearly and specifically prohibits such language likely to cause a breach of the peace by the person to whom it is addressed; (b) that such language is used and addressed to a person on a face-to-face basis and that the words and the manner in which they were used could cause the average person to respond with an act of violence.

The occasion, the manner, and the context in which the words were used do much to determine the offensiveness of the words. The words must be one step away from violence. The following examples illustrate two different situations:

EXAMPLE: Two old friends who have not seen each other for a long time meet in a tavern with only themselves, the bartender, and an off-duty police officer present. One man joyfully exclaims to the other, "Joe, you old X#%_____." The bystanders are amused, and Joe is not offended by the language.

EXAMPLE: A man walking down a street makes foul and insulting remarks to every girl and woman he meets, causing angry reactions. Persons complain to an officer, who hears him make such remarks.

In the first example, there would be no justification for an arrest, whereas in the second example, there would be ample justification for an arrest in jurisdictions having statutes or ordinances that forbid language or conduct tending to cause or provoke a disturbance or a breach of the peace.

Should the second example go to trial before a jury or judge, the burden on the state (or city) would be to prove (a) the language that the man used and the individual to whom the language was addressed, and (b) that the language had "a direct tendency to cause acts of violence by the person to whom, individually, the remark (was) addressed. . . ." *(Chaplinsky).*

"The test is what (persons) of common intelligence would understand would be words likely to cause an average (person) to fight" *(Chaplinsky).*

The First Limitation on the "Fighting Word" Doctrine

During the 1970s, the U.S. Supreme Court imposed two additional limitations on the "fighting word" doctrine. The first limitation was established in the 1970 case of *Cohen v. California.* In protest of the Vietnam War, Cohen wore a jacket bearing the words "Fuck the Draft" into the Los Angeles courthouse. In reversing Cohen's conviction for a "fighting word" violation, the U.S. Supreme Court held:

This court has . . . held that the States are free to ban the simple use, without a demonstration of additional justifying circumstances of so-called "fighting words," those personally abusive epithets which, when addressed to the ordinary citizen, are, as a matter of common knowledge, inherently likely to provoke violent reaction. While the four-letter word displayed by Cohen in relation to the draft is not uncommonly employed in a personally provocative fashion, in this instance it was clearly not "directed to the person of the hearer." Cantwell v. Connecticut, 310 U.S. 296, 309, 60 S.Ct. 900 (1940). No individual actually or likely to be present could reasonably have regarded the words on appellant's jacket as a direct personal insult. Nor do we have here an instance of the exercise of the State's police power to prevent a speaker from intentionally provoking a given group to hostile reaction. There is . . . no showing that anyone who saw Cohen was in fact violently aroused or that appellant intended such a result. . . .

Persons confronted with Cohen's jacket were in quite a different posture than, say, those subjected to the raucous emissions of sound trucks blaring outside their residences. Those in the Los Angeles courthouse could effectively avoid further bombardment of their sensibilities simply by averting their eyes. . . .

We have been shown no evidence that substantial numbers of citizens are standing ready to strike out physically at whoever may assault their sensibilities with (statements) like that uttered by Cohen. There may be some persons about with such lawless and violent proclivities, but that is an insufficient base upon which to erect, consistently with constitutional values, a governmental power to force persons who wish to ventilate their dissident views into avoiding particular forms of expression. . . .

Absent a more particularized and compelling reason for its actions, the State may not, consistently with the First and Fourteenth Amendments, make the simple public display here involved of this single four-letter expletive a criminal offense. Because this is the only arguably sustainable rationale for the conviction here at issue, the judgment below must be reversed.[9]

The *Cohen* case established two new concepts to be used in applying the "fighting word" doctrine:

1. The U.S. Supreme Court defended Cohen's use of the admittedly vulgar word "fuck." The Court refused to allow a state "to cleanse public debate to the point where it is grammatically palatable to the most squeamish among us" because the Court concluded that "one man's vulgarity is another's lyric."[10] This ruling makes it difficult to define any vulgar, profane, impolite, or other type of curses as "fighting words" in and of themselves.

2. The U.S. Supreme Court held in the *Cohen* case that people "in the Los Angeles courthouse could effectively avoid further bombardment of their sensibilities simply by averting their eyes." In the 1975 case of *Erznoznik v. City of Jacksonville,* the Supreme Court held that "the burden normally falls upon the viewer to avoid further bombardment of [his] sensibilities simply by averting [his] eyes."[11]

The following case illustrates the application of the principles found in the *Cohen* case:

VILLAGE OF SKOKIE v. NATIONAL SOCIALIST PARTY OF AMERICA
Supreme Court of Illinois (1978) 69 Ill.2d 605, 14 Ill.Dec. 890, 373 N.E.2d 21

Nazis sought to march and demonstrate peacefully in the village of Skokie, Illinois, where more than half the 70,000 population are of "Jewish religion or Jewish ancestry." The village of Skokie attempted to prevent the march and demonstration, urging that the swastika and the stormtrooper uniforms amounted to "fighting words." The Supreme

Court of Illinois ruled that the use of the swastika was entitled to First Amendment protection, holding:

> *The display of the swastika, as offensive to the principles of a free nation as the memories it recalls may be, is symbolic political speech intended to convey to the public the beliefs of those who display it. It does not, in our opinion, fall within the definition of "fighting words," and that doctrine cannot be used here to overcome the heavy presumption against the constitutional validity of a prior restraint.*
>
> *Nor can we find that the swastika, while not representing fighting words, is nevertheless so offensive and peace threatening to the public that its display can be enjoined. We do not doubt that the sight of this symbol is abhorrent to the Jewish citizens of Skokie, and that the survivors of the Nazi persecutions, tormented by their recollections, may have strong feelings regarding its display. Yet it is entirely clear that this factor does not justify enjoining defendants' speech.*

* * *

> *By placing the burden upon the viewer to avoid further bombardment, the Supreme Court has permitted speakers to justify the initial intrusion into the citizen's sensibilities.*
>
> *We accordingly, albeit reluctantly, conclude that the display of the swastika cannot be enjoined under the fighting-words exception to free speech, nor can anticipation of a hostile audience justify the prior restraint. Furthermore,* Cohen *and* Erznoznik *direct the citizens of Skokie that it is their burden to avoid the offensive symbol if they can do so without unreasonable inconvenience.*

The Second Limitation on the "Fighting Word" Doctrine

The second limitation to the "fighting word" doctrine resulted from the 1972 case of *Gooding v. Wilson.*[12] The new test appears to require the likelihood that "the person addressed would make an immediate violent response." Courts using this test would hold that evidence was necessary to show that the victim was aggravated to fight immediately, and that only being "insulting" is not sufficient for a "fighting word" conviction. Cases illustrating this limitation include:

ROSENFELD v. NEW JERSEY
Supreme Court of the United States (1972) 408 U.S. 901, 92 S.Ct. 2479

The defendant said "motherfucker" several times at a public school board meeting. Because the defendant's words were not directed toward any specific individual, and because physical violence on the part of the audience was unlikely, the U.S. Supreme Court vacated the defendant's conviction.

BROWN v. OKLAHOMA
Supreme Court of the United States (1972) 408 U.S. 914, 92 S.Ct. 2507

During a meeting at which no police officers were present, the defendant referred to police officers in general as "motherfucking fascist pigs" and to one officer in particular as that "black motherfucking pig." The Supreme Court vacated the defendant's conviction under a statute prohibiting obscene or lascivious language in a public place or in the presence of females.

DOWNS v. STATE
Court of Appeals of Maryland (1976) 278 Md. 610, 366 A.2d 41

In a crowded restaurant filled with a racially mixed crowd, the defendant stated in a loud voice to his friends that "all the goddamn policemen in this county are no fucking good, they're just after me" and "the fucking niggers in this county are no better than goddamn policemen." A state trooper who was in the restaurant went over to the defendant's table and told him that his talk was disruptive, and that he would be placed under arrest if he did not refrain from using such profane language. Downs replied, "You ain't bad enough to place me under arrest." When the trooper then arrested the defendant, a scuffle occurred. The defendant was charged with disorderly conduct ("fighting words"), resisting arrest, and assault and battery. On appeal, the Maryland Court of Appeals reversed the defendant's "fighting words" conviction, holding:[13]

> *We need not consider whether Downs' first remark, "All the goddamn policemen in this County are no fucking good, they're just after me," constituted "fighting" words because the state trooper, a possible addressee, was not aroused by the comment. We need only examine his second remark, "[T]he fucking niggers in this County are no better than goddamn policemen." Since* Cohen v. California . . . *apparently teaches that the use of the adjective "fucking" is not punishable in the absence of compelling reasons, the potentially punishable words are "[T]he niggers in this County are no better than goddamn policemen." This remark was made by Downs during a conversation with friends. There was no direct evidence that it was spoken to anyone other than the persons sitting in the booth with Downs. Even if there were, no evidence was adduced that anyone else, besides Trooper Taylor, heard this statement. Even if someone else did, there was no evidence that he or she was offended by it. And, even if someone were offended by it, there was no evidence that any person was so aroused as to respond in a violent manner. Thus, Downs' remarks were not the kind of personally abusive epithets which fall outside of the protection of the First Amendment under the rubric of "fighting" words. He engaged in protected speech. That his views might be offensive to someone who overheard him does not warrant a conviction for disorderly conduct.* Bachelar v. Maryland, *397 U.S. 564, 90 S.Ct. 1312, 25 L.Ed.2d 570 (1970). Accordingly, we hold that the trial judge erred in not granting Downs' motion for judgment of acquittal on the disorderly conduct charge, and that conviction must be reversed.*

(Note: Downs's convictions for resisting arrest and assault and battery were not reversed.)

CITY OF OAK PARK v. SMITH
Court of Appeals of Michigan (1977) 79 Mich.App. 757, 262 N.W.2d 900

When the defendant's careless driving almost caused an accident with an unmarked police car, the defendant gave the man in the other car "the finger," not knowing that he was a police officer. The Court of Appeals of Michigan reversed the defendant's conviction, holding that the gesture did not amount to a "fighting word" because the testimony of the officer "discloses that the officer, far from being aggravated to fight was only 'insulted.' " The Court, however, held the ordinance to be constitutional, stating:

> *In sustaining the Oak Park ordinance, this Court does not intend to condone or open the door to the gesture of "the finger" in all future occurrences. Defendant and the public are admonished that in other circumstances and conditions, such conduct is punishable under the ordinance. Given the right circumstances, the law may retaliate, not with its finger but with its long arm.*

Abusive Language Addressed to Law Enforcement Officers

The unanimous decision of *Chaplinsky v. New Hampshire* has been affirmed many times by the U.S. Supreme Court since the establishment of the "fighting word" doctrine in 1942. In the *Chaplinsky* case, the defendant was convicted for addressing insulting and fighting language to a law enforcement officer. Most state courts have also applied the "fighting word" doctrine in this manner. The Supreme Court of Wisconsin reflected this reasoning in the 1965 case of *Lane v. Collins,* holding that:

> The underlying reason for disorderly conduct statutes and ordinances proscribing abusive language is that such language tends to provoke retaliatory conduct on the part of the person to whom it is addressed that amounts to breach of the peace. . . . The fact that the abusive language is directed to a policeman or other law enforcement officer and is not overheard by others does not prevent it from being a violation of such statute or ordinance.[14]

However, before convicting for a "fighting word" violation addressed to a police officer, some courts have imposed one of the following requirements:

- Florida courts require that it must be shown either that such language "had no significance than to arouse (a) crowd into action against the police officer"[15] or that public interest, such as preventing "the possibility of a riot erupting resulting in injury to innocent bystanders,"[16] exists.
- In footnote #23 of the 1969 case of *Williams v. District of Columbia,* Federal Judge McGowan suggests that law enforcement officers caution persons and warn them before an arrest or "order in" for abusive language.[17]
- In the 1975 case of *Garvey v. State,* the Tennessee Court of Criminal Appeals stated that "a police officer trained to exercise a higher degree of restraint than the average citizen would not be expected to cause a breach of the peace."[18] The one word addressed to the officer in the *Garvey* case was "sooey," and the court held that there was "no direct face-to-face conduct." The defendant was driving by the police station; the officer was on the sidewalk.
- In the 1988 case of *Harrington v. Tulsa,*[19] the Court of Criminal Appeals of Oklahoma held that police officers must exercise a higher standard of restraint and that in the *Harrington* case the police officers were not "likely to cause a fight."

Most American courts, however, seem to follow the reasoning used by the Virginia Court of Appeals in the 1989 case of *Burgess v. City of Virginia Beach.*[20] In that case, after listening to defense arguments that law enforcement officers should exercise a higher degree of restraint than the average citizen, the Court said it "shudder(ed) to think of the verbal abuse that law enforcement officers would be subject to" should this position be adopted.

In 1991, the U.S. Supreme Court agreed to hear the case of *Buffkins v. City of Omaha,* 922 F.2d 465. When Buffkins angerly called a police officer an "asshole", she was arrested for disorderly conduct (fighting words). After she was found not guilty, she commenced a civil suit for false arrest and other allegations. The U.S. Court of Appeals for the 8th Circuit held that "Buffkins' speech directed at the officer did not constitute 'fighting words'." In deciding the case, the U.S.

"Fighting Words" Addressed to Law Enforcement Officers

A "fighting word" violation has not occurred if the officer is only insulted or offended by the words addressed to him or her. To convict for a "fighting word" violation, there must be evidence of a likelihood that "the person addressed would make an immediate violent response." Some courts have held that:

- law enforcement officers are "trained to exercise a higher degree of restraint than the average citizen," or that
- officers should give persons who have used "fighting words" in anger a warning not to use such language to the officer again.

To obtain a conviction in some jurisdictions, it must be shown that:

- the words "create a substantial risk of violence" (Washington, D.C.)
- the language "had no significance than to arouse [a] crowd into action against the police officer" (Florida), or
- the language creates "the possibility of a riot erupting, resulting in injury to innocent bystanders" (Florida).

Supreme Court may rule on the question as to whether law enforcement officers are required to exercise a higher degree of restraint than the average citizen when confronted with verbal abuse (see 49 CrL 3074).

Possible Problems in Going to Trial in a "Fighting Word" Case

Some "fighting word" cases are difficult to prove. Courts require that all essential elements be proved and the job of the defense lawyer is to call the trial court's attention to any failure by the state. Some of the fatal flaws or defects that could cause a court to find a defendant not guilty are:

- failure to show that the language was addressed to a specific person (or persons) and that such person was aggravated to fight (*Downs v. State*[21] and *City of Milwaukee v. George Carlin*[22])
- the distance between the speaker and the offended person might have been too far apart for an immediate violent reaction. This was a factor in the *City of Oak Park v. Smith*[23] and also in *In Re S.L.J.,*[24] where a small, fourteen-year-old child shouted "Fuck you pigs" to two police officers from a distance of 15 to 30 feet as she was going home after being told by the officers that it was past her curfew.
- failure to show that the language produced "or is likely to produce a clear and present danger of substantive evils" that a state may seek to prevent (*State v. Porter*[25])
- when the vulgar language is in response to improper or unlawful police conduct or speech. In the case of *Diehl v. Maryland,*[26] Diehl was a passenger in a car that was stopped for tire squealing. When the officer ordered Diehl to get back into the car, Diehl responded with obscenities and vulgarities. The Maryland Court of Appeals held that "the officer did not have any right to make this demand on Diehl. Only then did Diehl begin to address [Officer] Gavin. Diehl's communication expressed his outrage with this unlawful police conduct, it was addressed only to [Officer] Gavin."

Convictions in cases in which juveniles shout obscenities or berate police officers with vulgar speech seem to be particularly difficult to obtain. The Supreme Court of Minnesota ruled in the 1978 case of *In Re S.L.J.* (footnote 24) that: "While it is true that no ordered society would condone the vulgar language used by this 14-year-old child, and as the court found, her words were intended to, and did arouse resentment in the officers, the constitution requires more before a person can be convicted of mere speech."

The 1982 case of *State v. Montgomery*[27] is another example of a juvenile case occurring in Seattle, Washington. The officers stopped their squad car when they heard Montgomery screaming "fucking pigs, fucking pig asshole." The Appellate Court held:

> We find the behavior and language of the defendant reprehensible and disgraceful. He deserves censure and rebuke, and his conduct has degraded him in the eyes of society. However, the law requires that the individual's right to free expression take precedence over the interests of others to be undisturbed by crude language. The defendant's offensive language did not create probable cause to arrest him for disorderly conduct. The marijuana seized incident to that arrest must be suppressed. The judgment and sentence of the juvenile court is reversed.[28]

The Probable Cause Requirement

In some "fighting word" cases, ordinance citations are given to persons using "fighting word" language. In other cases, persons are told to appear at the office of a prosecutor on a given date and time. In other situations an arrest is made. To make an arrest, the law enforcement officer needs probable cause.

The U.S. Supreme Court pointed out in the 1979 case of *Michigan v. DeFillippo* that:

> The validity of the arrest does not depend on whether the suspect actually committed a crime; the mere fact that the suspect is later acquitted of the offense for which he is arrested is irrelevant to the validity of the arrest. We have made clear that the kinds and degree of proof and the procedural requirements necessary for a conviction are not prerequisites to a valid arrest.[29]

The July 1976 *FBI Bulletin* article entitled "Probable Cause: The Officer's Shield to Suits Under the Federal Civil Rights Act" states that: "The Civil liability of the police officer does not turn on whether the arrest was in fact legal, but whether he reasonably believed the arrest to be legal, an obviously lesser standard."

Handling Abusive Language

Some officers are assigned to duty that subjects them to more abusive language than the ordinary officer would be subjected to. Officers assigned to a radar traffic unit might receive occasional verbal abuse from motorists receiving traffic tickets. A Wisconsin officer who wrote out a good number of speeding tickets found an effective response to abusive language. He carried a small tape recorder in his pocket, and when a speeder's language became profane or abusive, he would say, "Hold it a minute sir (or ma'am) until I have my tape recorder going. I want to get all of this down." He would then hold the tape recorder close to the person. Even without batteries in the recorder, this would usually have the desired effect.

Another officer reported an equally effective tactic. He would say to his partner in a loud voice, "Get the names of the witnesses." Then, as his partner took out his pad and pencil and began taking down the names of the witnesses, the officer would turn to the person who had used the foul language and would ask, "Now do you want to repeat that?" This officer reported that he had used this tactic successfully a number of times, with no one taking him up on the request to repeat the abusive language. Other officers have attempted humor through such retorts as, "Do you eat with that dirty mouth?" However, this might well trigger an additional outburst, and the officer could be accused in court of taunting and thus encouraging such responses.

The Supreme Court of Minnesota recommended in the case of *In Re S.L.J.* that "the arrest of this child [fourteen-year-old girl who shouted obscenities at officers] under these circumstances appears to have been an overreaction by criminality; a preferable approach would have been to march her home to her parents for parental discipline."

Does Abusive Language Ever Justify a Battery?

The question is sometimes raised in criminal law classes as to whether the person called vile and abusive names may respond with physical retaliation against the name-caller. The answer is no. The child's singsong phrase, "Sticks and stones may break my bones but names will never hurt me," reflects a correct principle of the law. There is no doctrine of American law that states that words or gestures are sufficient provocation to justify an intentional battery. Nor are words or gestures justification for an intentional homicide, regardless of how insulting and abusive they are (see chapter 13).

However, whether the person would be charged with a battery would depend on (a) the type of battery committed, (b) the injury inflicted, (c) the words and gestures used, and (d) the degree of provocation. The following actual cases illustrate.

EXAMPLE: When a sixty-five-year-old man reprimanded an eight-year-old boy for the foul language the boy was using on a public street, the boy directed a vulgar gesture with the middle finger of his right hand to the man. The man chased the boy and, when he caught him, shook the boy by the shoulders and spanked him a few times on the seat of his pants. When the police would not order the man into the prosecutor's office, the boy's mother took the matter to a prosecutor. The man had no prior criminal record (even had a perfect driving record). The prosecutor refused to issue a battery complaint against the man, but warned him not to spank children who were not his own.

EXAMPLE: During an angry exchange of words in a restaurant in Washington, D.C., a thirty-five-year-old man called seventy-year-old Texas Congressman Henry Gonzalez a "communist." The police report stated that Gonzalez "nailed (the man) with his fist" causing a black eye and a cut over his eyebrow. Citations for disorderly conduct were issued to both men, and after pleading guilty they paid their fines. Congressman Gonzalez stated, "The word 'communist' is a fighting word."

In a few situations reported during the Vietnam War, antiwar activists taunted the survivors of men killed in Vietnam. Such taunts could be highly provocative and could produce violent reactions. The question of whether the person who committed a battery in such a situation would be charged would depend on what was done and the injury inflicted.

Can an Officer Provoke Abusive Language and Then Arrest for Disorderly Conduct?

Angry words are sometimes exchanged between law enforcement officers and private citizens. Arguments also sometimes occur in prosecutors' offices over charges that are to be issued against persons for conduct that prosecutors believe violates criminal codes. The U.S. Supreme Court repeated twice in 1988 that:

> As a general matter, we have indicated that in public debate our own citizens must tolerate insulting, and even outrageous, speech in order to provide "adequate 'breathing space' to the freedoms protected by the First Amendment." *Hustler Magazine, Inc. v. Falwell,* 485 U.S. 46, ___ 108 S.Ct. 876, 882, 99 L.Ed.2d 41 (1988). See also, e.g., *New York Times Co. v. Sullivan,* 376 U.S., at 270, 84 S.Ct., at 720.[30]

Law enforcement officers and prosecutors should not provoke abusive language and then expect to successfully issue charges. The following case illustrates:

LANE v. COLLINS
Supreme Court of Wisconsin (1965) 29 Wis.2d 66, 138 N.W.2d 264

A police officer had been dating a divorced woman, and the former husband objected. While on duty and in uniform, the officer stopped the former husband on the street and asked the man not to telephone him. The officer then taunted the ex-husband about the fact that the man had been convicted of nonsupport. The ex-husband called the officer a son-of-a-bitch and repeated the expression when the officer asked him to do so. The officer arrested the man and held him in custody for an hour and a half before releasing him on bail. When the city attorney refused to prosecute for disorderly conduct, the former husband began a civil suit against the officer and received a jury award of $1,500 for false imprisonment. In affirming the judgment, the Supreme Court of Wisconsin stated: "A police officer cannot provoke a person into a breach of the peace, such as directing abusive language to the police officer, and then arrest him without a warrant."[31]

Can Profane or Vulgar Language Be Made an Offense in Itself?

Cohen v. California has affected hundreds of cases every year. Before the *Cohen* case, it was not uncommon for vulgar or profane expressions to form the basis of a criminal prosecution. Vulgarity and profanity are concepts different than "fighting words." Communications may be vulgar and profane and not be "fighting words." The Supreme Court of Rhode Island reviewed "profanity" cases as follows in the case of *State v. Authelet.*[32]

> Several courts have ... determined that profanity may only be prohibited if it is considered within the category of fighting words. In *Tallman v. United States,* 465 F.2d 282 (7th Cir. 1972), the court held that unless the *Chaplinsky* test of fighting words was read into a statutory proscription against profanity, the statute would be unconstitutionally overbroad. Likewise, in *Williams v. District of Columbia,* 136 U.S.App.D.C. 56, 419 F.2d 638 (1969), the court reversed a conviction for the use of "profane language, indecent and obscene words." The court held that the only interests which the state could assert in forbidding profane or indecent language were those delineated in *Chaplinsky.* A third case, *Conchito v. City of Tulsa,* 521 P.2d 1384

(Okla. Crim. 1974), ruled that a city ordinance proscribing "profane or obscene language" was unconstitutionally broad on the ground that it was not limited in accordance with the Supreme Court's previous rulings. The court implicitly found that profanity could only be constitutionally punished if the penal statute was restricted to the proscription of fighting words. Finally, in *Reese v. State,* 17 Md.App. 73, 299 A.2d 848 (1973), the court held that the statutory phrase "profanely cursing, [or] swearing" was meant to restrict only such language as came within the category of fighting words.

We subscribe to the position taken by courts in *Tallman, Williams, Conchito,* and *Reese,* all *supra.* Although the Supreme Court has not specifically decided whether profanity may be independently proscribed, we feel that choosing to analyze profanity under the fighting words approach strikes the proper balance between the state's interest in maintaining order and an individual's right to free speech. While we do not condone the use of profanity in any context, neither can we countenance unwarranted state intrusions upon how a person comports or expresses himself. Of course, we would all perhaps wish that each person would conduct himself or herself in the most exemplary way possible, but failure to measure up to what society considers to be in good taste is not, and has never been, grounds for the imposition of criminal sanctions.

Speakers before crowds who are not addressing their remarks at specific individuals in the audience now have more latitude in what they say than ever before. However, the chairperson of a meeting continues to have the power to rule a vulgar person out of order. The manager or owner of a restaurant, tavern, or other private or public place continues to have the authority and responsibility to silence vulgar or profane persons. In the following case, the speaker used the following language:

STATE v. OLIVEIRA
Supreme Court of New Hampshire (1975) 115 N.H. 559, 347 A.2d 165

The defendant addressed a crowd during an intermission at a dance in the gymnasium of a community club. In talking about the club's need for additional funds and in urging persons to attend an upcoming city council meeting, the defendant used the words "fuck" and "fucking" a number of times. Police officers were present. After the dance was over and the hall nearly empty, the defendant was arrested and convicted of rude and disorderly conduct in a public place. In dismissing the complaint, the Supreme Court of New Hampshire held:

> *This is not a case involving "fighting words" admittedly subject to greater regulation by the State because of their inherent capacity to occasion a breach of the peace.* Chaplinsky v. New Hampshire, *315 U.S. 568, 62 S.Ct. 766, 86 L.Ed.1031 (1942). The defendant's references were not to persons present at the time.* Chaplinsky *and subsequent cases clearly indicate that the term "fighting words" is meant to apply to "face-to-face words plainly likely to cause a breach of the peace by the addressee."*

> * * *

> *The case does not involve words which, though not personally abusive, nevertheless occasion a "clear and present danger of riot, disorder . . . or other immediate threat to public safety, peace or order."* Cantwell v. Connecticut, *310 U.S. 296, 308, 60 S.Ct. 900, 84 L.Ed. 1213 (1940).*

* * *

However distasteful the language used by this defendant is to the average person, this case is controlled by Rosenfeld v. New Jersey, *408 U.S. 901, 92 S.Ct. 2479, 33 L.Ed.2d 321 (1972) and* Cohen v. California, *403 U.S. 15, 91 S.Ct. 1780, 29 L.Ed.2d 284 (1971) which require dismissal of this complaint.*

D. COMMUNICATIONS THAT ARE OBSCENE

Obscenity and "Fighting Words" Are Separate and Distinct Concepts that Are Not Constitutionally Protected

In the 1975 case of *City of Columbus v. Fraley*,[33] the defendant was arrested, tried, and convicted for using obscene language. The defendant had become "boisterous and loud" and called police officers "motherfuckers" and "pigs." The Ohio Court of Appeals affirmed the defendant's conviction, not because the words were obscene, but rather because they constituted "fighting words." The Ohio Supreme Court held that the words used by the defendant were not legally obscene, and that the process used denied the defendant due process of law, holding:

> Obscene expression and fighting words are separate and distinct exceptions to the freedom of speech protected by the First Amendment. Obscene expression, as indicated herein, must involve an appeal to a prurient interest in sex. Fighting words, on the other hand, are those words which "by their very utterance inflict injury or are likely to provoke the average person to an immediate retaliatory breach of the peace." *Cincinnati v. Karlan, supra,* 39 Ohio St.2d at 110, 314 N.E.2d at 164. In making a determination whether specific language constitutes fighting words, it is irrelevant that such words may also be legally obscene.

Legal Definition of Obscenity

Obscenity is not protected by the First Amendment and may be forbidden and regulated by government. Defining obscenity, however, has been the subject of many debates and court rulings. The U.S. Supreme court established the following tests and standards to define obscenity in the 1973 case of *Miller v. California*.[34]

- whether "the average person applying contemporary community standards" would find that the work, taken as a whole, appeals to the prurient interest (prurient interest would be appealing to the sexual interest, causing a person to become sexually aroused)
- whether the work or communication depicts or describes, in a patently offensive way, sexual conduct specifically defined by the applicable state law
- whether the work or communication, taken as a whole, lacks serious literary, artistic, political, or scientific value.

Obscene, Indecent, and Sexually Explicit Conduct

The U.S. Supreme Court has held that the following phrases are not obscene: "Fuck the Draft" (*Cohen v. California*), "Motherfucker Acquitted," "Up Against the Wall, Motherfucker," and "The Motherfuckers" (*Papish v. University of Missouri,* 93 S.Ct. 1197).

A communication (movie, picture, words, dance, etc.) can be sexually explicit without being obscene if the communication has serious "literary, artistic, political, or scientific value" (*Miller v. California*). Local standards in some communities might regard sexually explicit material as not obscene, while standards in other communities would. When a question of obscenity and local community standards is at issue, defense lawyers generally seek to empanel a jury made up of persons expressing a more tolerant notion of permissive conduct. The prosecution will seek a more conservative type. Presumably, out of this process will come a representative body of local opinion.

Contemporary community standards as determined by juries vary from community to community and from state to state. For example, in 1991 criminal charges were brought against rock groups who rapped (sang) sexually explicit songs in adult-only night clubs. Two juries in separate trials acquitted the two different groups in Broward County (Fort Lauderdale), Florida.

The same group rapping the same songs could be convicted in other cities by juries interpreting contemporary community standards for their community. After suffering two defeats in Broward County, the Florida prosecutor stated as to future prosecutions in Broward County that "I think the chances of success after these two verdicts are just nonexistent." The two Fort Lauderdale verdicts differed from the ruling of a U.S. district judge, who ruled in 1990 that the same material (the 2 Live Crew album "As Nasty As They Wanna Be") was obscene.

The costs of one of the Florida proceedings was estimated by local newspapers at $103,750. Jurors criticized the trials as a waste of time, and one Florida juror (a middle-aged woman) stated, "They should be sending fathers who don't pay child support and drug dealers to jail, not these people" ("Rock Group Not Guilty of Obscenity," *Fort Lauderdale Sun-Sentinel,* January 18, 1991).

In 1990, the Cincinnati art museum and its director were charged criminally with obscenity. In a 175-picture exhibition, five of the photographs showed sadomasochistic and homosexual acts, and two photographs were of nude and partly nude children. The defendants would not remove the offensive photographs and, for the first time, a museum and its director were charged with misdemeanor violations. After a two-week trial, the jury took two hours to acquit the defendants in the Cincinnati case. The Robert Mapplethorpe exhibit was shown in other American cities.

The U.S. Supreme Court dealt with the "dial-a-porn" issue in the following 1989 case:

SABLE COMMUNICATIONS v. FCC
Supreme Court of the United States (1989) 492 U.S. 115, 109 S.Ct. 2829, 45 CrL 3164

The $2-billion-a-year "dial-a-porn" industry in the United States sells sexually suggestive recorded messages for a fee on special telephone exchanges. The U.S. Supreme Court held that the federal government could ban obscene but not "indecent" messages. The government could seek to prevent children from being exposed to indecent telephone messages but could not prevent adults from access to material that has the protection of the First Amendment. The Supreme Court held:

* * *

> *There is no constitutional barrier under* Miller *to prohibiting communications that are obscene in some communities under local standards even though they are not obscene in others. If Sable's audience is comprised of different communities with different local standards, Sable ultimately bears the burden of complying with the prohibition on obscene messages.*
>
> *... the District Court concluded that while the government has a legitimate interest in protecting children from exposure to indecent dial-a-porn messages, § 223(b) (Section 223(b) of the Communications Act) was not sufficiently narrowly drawn to serve that purpose and thus violated the First Amendment. We agree.*
>
> *Sexual expression which is indecent but not obscene is protected by the First Amendment; and the government does not submit that the sale of such materials to adults could be criminalized solely because they are indecent. The government may, however, regulate the content of constitutionally protected speech in order to promote a compelling interest if it chooses the least restrictive means to further the articulated interest. We have recognized that there is a compelling interest in protecting the physical and psychological well-being of minors. This interest extends to shielding minors from the influence of literature that is not obscene by adult standards.... The government may serve this legitimate interest, but to withstand constitutional scrutiny, "it must do so by narrowly drawn regulations designed to serve those interests without unnecessarily interfering with First Amendment freedoms.* Hynes v. Mayor of Oradello, *425 U.S., at 620 ..."*
>
> *It is not enough to show that the government's ends are compelling; the means must be carefully tailored to achieve those ends.*

The "dial-a-porn" industry uses the "900" telephone number series for its business. Prior to May 1991, many long distance telephone companies facilitated the porn industry by billing and collecting their long-distance customers for calls made to the "dial-a-porn" numbers. This practice greatly helped the porn industry, since it did not have to bill customers directly but would receive payment when its customers paid their regular phone bills. By May 1991, however, AT&T, Sprint, and MCI (the three largest long distance companies) had ended this practice. (See the May 7, 1991, issue of the *Omaha World-Herald,* page 7.)

Nudity and Obscenity

In the 1981 case of *Schad v. Borough of Mount Ephraim,* the U.S. Supreme Court held:

> Entertainment, as well as political and ideological speech, is protected; motion pictures, programs broadcast by radio and television and live entertainment, such as musical and dramatic works, fall within the First Amendment guarantee.... Nor may an entertainment program be prohibited solely because it displays the nude human figure. "Nudity alone" does not place otherwise protected material outside the mantle of the First Amendment.... Furthermore, as the state courts in this case recognized, nude dancing is not without its First Amendment protections from official regulation.[35]

Although "nudity alone" is not obscenity and cannot be punished as obscenity, nudity may be regulated by a state or municipality:

"Fighting Word" Violations

Words (or other communication) may be offensive, profane, and vulgar ...

but not be "fighting words" (see *Cohen v. California,* in which the words "Fuck the draft" were offensive but not "fighting words").

Words may be insulting and even outrageous ...

but not be "fighting words" because there was no face-to-face confrontation, as in *Falwell v. Hustler Magazine.*

Words may make a person or an audience angry ...

and may be protected by the First Amendment and thus not be forbidden by government.

Words may be rude, impolite, and insulting ...

but may fall short of the "fighting word" violation.

If the person to whom the words are addressed is not angered by the words, ...

there is no "fighting word" violation.

If the person to whom the words are addressed is not likely to make an immediate violent response, ...

there is no "fighting word" violation.

Obscenity is a different concept than "fighting words." ...

To be obscene, the state must show as a matter of law that (a) the work taken as a whole appeals to the prurient (lustful) interest in sex; (b) "portrays sexual conduct in a patently offensive way"; (c) the work "taken as a whole does not have a serious literary, artistic, political or scientific value." *Miller v. California,* 413 U.S. 15, 93 S.Ct. 2607 (1973).

"Fighting words" and obscenity cause different reactions in persons. . . .

"Fighting words" cause persons to become very angry while obscenity appeals to the prurient interest (erotic interest), causing persons to become sexually aroused.

Graphic sex scenes on television or scenes that are sexually explicit ...

are not necessarily obscene.

Because it is absolutely disgusting ...

it is not necessarily obscene.

Nudity in itself is not obscene or lewd, ...

but a state or community may regulate (a) when nudity is in a place where liquor is sold (see *California v. LaRue,* 409 U.S. 109, 93 S.Ct. 390 [1972]) and (b) when public nudity is forbidden by a specific ordinance or law.

- in places in which alcohol is sold. Nudity may be totally forbidden or regulated as to the extent of the nudity. In *California v. LaRue,*[36] the U.S. Supreme Court pointed out that the Twenty-first Amendment gives states "broad sweep" of authority to regulate places in which alcohol is sold.[37]
- in public places in which nudity may be forbidden by specific statutes or ordinances.[38]

In the 1991 case of *Barnes v. Glen Theater,* ___ U.S. ___ , the U.S. Supreme Court sustained an Indiana law requiring that dancers in that state wear at least pasties and a G-string. In the 5–4 decision, the Court held that:

> Nude dancing of the kind sought to be performed here is expressive conduct within the outer perimeters of the First Amendment, though we view it as only marginally so . . .
>
> The perceived evil that Indiana seeks to address is not erotic dancing, but public nudity. The appearance of people, of all shapes, sizes and ages in the nude at a beach, for example, would convey little if any erotic messages, yet the state still seeks to prevent it. Public nudity is the evil the state seeks to prevent, whether or not it is combined with expressive activity.

E. Communications That Urge Unlawful Action (Inciting)

Inciting (urging) other persons to commit a crime or perform an unlawful act is a misdemeanor at common law. The offense of inciting is committed even though the other person does not commit the suggested crime. Speech or other forms of communication that urge unlawful conduct are not protected by the U.S. Constitution and may be forbidden by government. To be unlawful, however, the speech or other communication must be "directed to inciting or producing *imminent* lawless action and [must be] likely to incite or produce such action."[39]

In the 1987 Senate committee confirmation hearings of Judge Robert Bork's appointment to the U.S. Supreme Court, considerable time was spent discussing the "clear and present danger" test and its application to the *Brandenburg* and *Hess* cases that follow. Both cases hold that in the United States, the crime of incitement requires that "imminent lawless action" be urged.

TERMINIELLO v. CHICAGO
Supreme Court of the United States (1949) 337 U.S. 1, 69 S.Ct. 894

The defendant was a suspended Catholic priest associated with the Gerald L. K. Smith organization. He addressed a friendly audience of more than 800 persons in an auditorium in Chicago, while more than a thousand people gathered outside to protest the meeting. Disruptions occurred after the meeting, and the defendant was charged with and convicted of disorderly conduct for statements that he had made in his address. The jury was allowed to convict if it found that Terminiello's speech either stirred the public to anger or constituted "fighting words." Because only "fighting words" may have been forbidden, the Supreme Court reversed because it was "possible that the jury found that Terminiello's speech merely stirred the public to anger and yet had convicted him."

BRANDENBURG v. OHIO
Supreme Court of the United States (1969) 395 U.S. 444, 89 S.Ct. 1827

The defendant was a Ku Klux Klan leader who spoke at a KKK organizer's meeting to which the press and TV cameras were invited. At the meeting, on an Ohio farm, he said that "if our president, our Congress, our Supreme Court continue to suppress the white

Caucasian race, it's possible that there might have to be some revengeance taken." Some of the persons attending the meeting were hooded and some carried firearms. They gathered around a large wooden cross, which they burned. The defendant was convicted under the Ohio Criminal Syndicalism statute for "advocating . . . violence or unlawful methods of terrorism as a means of accomplishing industrial or political reform" and for "assembly with . . . persons . . . to teach or advocate the doctrine of criminal syndicalism." In holding that the defendant's statements did not urge "*imminent* lawless action" the Court reversed the defendant's conviction, holding:

> *constitutional guarantees of free speech and free press do not permit a State to forbid or proscribe advocacy of the use of force or of law violation except where such advocacy is directed to inciting or producing imminent lawless action and is likely to incite or produce such action. As we said in* Noto v. United States, *367 U.S. 290, 297−298, 6 L.Ed.2d 836, 841, 81 S.Ct. 1517 (1961), "the mere abstract teaching . . . of the moral propriety or even moral necessity for a resort to force and violence, is not the same as preparing a group for violent action and steeling it to such action." A statute which fails to draw this distinction impermissibly intrudes upon the freedoms guaranteed by the First and Fourteenth Amendments. It sweeps within its condemnation speech which our Constitution has immunized from governmental control.*

* * *

> *Accordingly, we are here confronted with a statute which, by its own words and as applied, purports to punish mere advocacy and to forbid, on pain of criminal punishment, assembly with others merely to advocate the described type of action. Such a statute falls within the condemnation of the First and Fourteenth Amendments. The contrary teaching of* Whitney v. California, *supra, cannot be supported, and that decision is therefore overruled.*
>
> *Reversed*

HESS v. INDIANA
Supreme Court of the United States (1973) 414 U.S. 105, 94 S.Ct. 326

During an antiwar demonstration on the campus of Indiana University, 100 to 150 demonstrators moved onto a public street and blocked the passage of vehicles. When the demonstrators did not respond to verbal directions to clear the street, the sheriff and his deputies began walking up the street, moving the demonstrators to the curbs on either side, where a large number of spectators had gathered. Hess was standing off the street with his back to the street as the sheriff passed him. The sheriff heard Hess say, "We'll take the fucking street later" or "We'll take the fucking street again." Hess was immediately arrested and charged with disorderly conduct.

The Indiana Supreme Court placed primary reliance on the trial court's finding that Hess's statement "was intended to incite further lawless action on the part of the crowd in the vicinity of the defendant and was likely to produce such action." In reversing the conviction, the U.S. Supreme Court held

1. That Hess's words could not be punished as obscene.
2. That Hess's words did not amount to "fighting words" under *Chaplinsky v. New Hampshire.*

> *Even if under other circumstances this language could be regarded as a personal insult, the evidence is undisputed that Hess' statement was not directed to any person or group in particular. Although the sheriff testified that he was offended by the language, he also stated that he did not interpret the expression as being directed*

personally at him, and the evidence is clear that appellant had his back to the sheriff at the time. Thus, under our decisions, the State could not punish this speech as "fighting words."

3. That there was no evidence to show that Hess's speech amounted to a public nuisance.

In addition, there was no evidence to indicate that Hess' speech amounted to a public nuisance in that privacy interests were being invaded. "The ability of government, consonant with the Constitution, to shut off discourse solely to protect others from hearing it is . . . dependent upon a showing that substantial privacy interests are being invaded in an essentially intolerable manner." Cohen v. California, 29 L.Ed.2d 284. The prosecution made no such showing in this case.

4. That Hess's words did not incite further lawless action on the part of the crowd in the vicinity and were not likely to produce such action.

At best, however, the statement could be taken as counsel for present moderation: at worst, it amounted to nothing more than advocacy of illegal action at some indefinite future time. This is not sufficient to permit the State to punish Hess' speech. Under our decisions, "the constitutional guarantees of free speech and free press do not permit a State to forbid or proscribe advocacy of the use of force or of law violation except where such advocacy is directed to inciting or producing imminent lawless action and is likely to incite or produce such action." [Emphasis added.] Brandenburg v. Ohio, 395 U.S. 444, 447, 23 L.Ed.2d 430, 89 S.Ct. 1827 (1969). See also Terminiello v. Chicago, 93 L.Ed. 1131. Since the uncontroverted evidence showed that Hess' statement was not directed to any person or group of persons, it cannot be said that he was advocating, in the normal sense, any action. And since there was no evidence, or rational inference from the import of the language, that his words were intended to produce, and likely to produce, imminent disorder, those words could not be punished by the State on the ground that they had "a tendency to lead to violence." 36 Ind.Dec., at 529, 297 N.E.2d, at 415.

Accordingly, the judgment of the Supreme Court of Indiana is reversed.

F. Verbal and Physical Obstruction

Obstructing an officer in the performance of his public duties was an offense at common law, punishable as a misdemeanor. Most (if not all) states have now statutorized this offense. However, state statutes vary considerably in defining the crime of obstruction. A few states limit the crime to "resisting." Other states use the words "resist," "obstruct," or "oppose," and still other states use "resist," "obstruct," or "abuse."[40]

Some states hold that verbal acts alone cannot constitute obstruction and that physical acts are also required. However, other states hold that verbal communication can amount to obstruction. The following cases illustrate some of the obstruction issues that have come before courts:

LYNN v. CITY OF NEW ORLEANS POLICE DEPT.
U.S. District Court, Eastern District of Louisiana (1983) (E.D.La.) 567 F.Supp. 761

Police investigating a traffic accident in New Orleans found that one of the drivers had left the scene without identifying himself. From the license of the fleeing car, police obtained an address. When Officer Clement was admitted to the apartment of the "hit and run" driver, he "was confronted by an antagonistic clamor and four people who had been drinking most of the day." After they continued to interfere with the police investigation, they were arrested. Jane Lynn filed this false arrest lawsuit which was dismissed, with the judge holding:

> *I conclude that under the circumstances Officer Clement had probable cause to arrest Jane Lynn for obstructing his investigation and resisting arrest. Knowing nothing about the hit-and-run offense, she apparently considers that her First Amendment rights permitted her to continue protesting his presence and her arrest. She exceeded her First Amendment rights in this case.*

STATE v. TAGES
Court of Appeals of Arizona (1969) 10 Ariz.App. 127, 457 P.2d 289

The defendant stated to officers who wanted to talk to her husband, "That is my husband. . . . If you want to talk to him, talk to him right here." And to her husband, "We don't even know they are cops. . . . Don't go anywhere, Honey, until he shows you a warrant for your arrest." The defendant was arrested for obstructing and interfering with the officer.

The Court of Appeals of Arizona reversed the conviction, holding that merely remonstrating with a police officer on behalf of another or criticizing the officer while he was performing a duty does not amount to obstruction or interference with the officer.

STATE v. MANNING
Superior Court of New Jersey (1977) 146 N.J.Super. 589, 370 A.2d 499

After a vehicle passed his squad car at a high rate of speed, a New Jersey trooper stopped the car. When the trooper detected an odor of alcohol, he asked the driver to step out so he could conduct tests to determine the driver's condition. When the driver and the trooper went to the rear of the car, the car's passenger (the defendant) also got out and joined them. "Despite the fact that the trooper three times requested defendant to get back into the car, defendant refused and said 'Lock me up.' " The defendant was convicted of interfering with a state trooper's performance of his duties. In affirming the conviction, the Superior Court of New Jersey held:

> *The trooper testified that he would have conducted a more formal and thorough investigation of the driver's condition had he been left alone by defendant and that defendant's actions interfered with his further investigation. The Municipal Court judge found as a fact that the trooper had to cut short his investigation because of defendant's actions. In affirming the conviction, the County Court judge found as a fact that defendant interfered with the lawful exercise of police duty by the trooper.*
>
> *On appeal it is defendant's contention that the investigation of the driver's condition had actually been concluded inasmuch as the trooper had already determined that the driver was not intoxicated. For that reason, defendant argues, there was no interference with the investigation. We disagree. The trooper was following routine procedures in attempting to interview the driver to determine whether he was under the influence of intoxicating liquors. It was perfectly reasonable for him to require that he be able to interrogate and observe the driver without any distraction from defendant. It was also in the interest of safety for defendant to remain in the car.*

PEOPLE v. COOKS
Superior Court, Appellate Department (1967) 58 Cal.Rptr. 550

The defendant was a bartender in a tavern. A uniformed police officer came into the bar searching for a suspect in a robbery that had occurred a short time before and saw a man

who resembled the suspect sitting at the bar. When the officer asked the man for identification, the defendant continued to tell the man not to show identification until the officer
"tells us what he wants in here." When the officer explained his purpose, the defendant
continued to tell the customer not to show identification. The defendant was arrested for
obstructing. In affirming the conviction, the Court held:

> *Defendant . . . deliberately and wilfully set about to delay and obstruct the police*
> *officer in his rightful attempt to question the suspect; and, defendant pointedly*
> *succeeded in his purpose. Such speech-conduct with respect to this front-line func-*
> *tion of the law is even less tolerable than a focused attempt to influence a particular*
> *court decision.*

STATE v. HARRIS
Circuit Court of Connecticut (1967) 4 Conn.Cir. 534, 236 A.2d 479

Police officers were arresting an intoxicated man when the defendant approached them. In
response to her question about what they were doing, they stated that the man was
intoxicated and would be released at six o'clock in the morning. The defendant did not
know the man but kept arguing with the policemen in a voice louder than conversational
tone. She was warned to leave on six separate occasions over a period of 15 minutes but
continued to use vile and profane language directed at the officers. When a vehicle arrived
to transport the intoxicated man, the woman was arrested for obstructing, as she had made
the officers' task more difficult. The conviction was affirmed.

G. DEFAMATION (LIBEL AND SLANDER)

As early as 1275, the English Parliament enacted a libel statute that forbade false
news and tales. The colonies and the original thirteen states undoubtedly all had
laws concerning libel and slander. Over the years, the laws of England and America developed into the libel, slander, and defamation laws of today.

Defamation is the offense of injuring the character or reputation of another
by oral or written communication of false statements. Defamation consists of the
twin offenses of libel and slander. Libel is generally a written offense, whereas
slander is generally an oral offense. Although most states probably have one or
more criminal defamation statutes, charges under these statutes are infrequent.
Most victims choose to rely primarily on the civil actions of libel and slander that
are available to them. Money awards can be obtained through the civil suits to
both compensate and punish. The burdens of proof are also lower in civil actions.

The *Chaplinsky* doctrine of "fighting words" is limited to words and gestures
and requires that there be a face-to-face confrontation involving words that are
one step away from violence and likely to provoke a public disorder. The law of
defamation requires that the communication be made to persons other than the
victim and that the victim's reputation be lowered in the esteem of any substantial
and respectable group. It is possible that words spoken could not only be "fighting words," but also the basis for civil libel and slander suits.

Immunity from Criminal and Civil Liability for Defamation

The doctrine of privilege in the law of defamation developed long ago, based on
the premise that if a person is acting in furtherance of a socially important

function, he or she should be encouraged and allowed to speak freely without the fear of a civil or criminal defamation action. Absolute immunity from criminal and civil liability for defamation is granted to the following:

1. Judges, jurors, and witnesses in civil and criminal actions for statements relevant and pertinent to the case. The statement could be made before or during the trial in any of the pleadings or affidavits or in open court. Perjury and contempt actions may be brought against witnesses if the need arises, but neither civil nor criminal defamation actions may be brought (see chapter 22 for the law of contempt).

2. Members of legislative bodies and witnesses before legislative committees that are performing a legislative function. A graphic example of the privilege as applied to witnesses can be found in the 1947 confrontation between Whitaker Chambers and Alger Hiss. Chambers, in testifying before the congressional committee on which Congressman Richard Nixon served, stated that Alger Hiss was a courier for the Communists. Hiss, who had held high governmental offices, challenged Chambers before the committee and told Chambers that if he made the statements out and away from the committee room, Hiss would sue him for libel and slander. Chambers repeated the statements outside of the committee rooms and Hiss did commence a libel and slander suit against him. The matter was resolved with Hiss ending up in jail on a perjury charge.[41]

3. Writers state that absolute immunity to civil and criminal defamation actions is enjoyed by high officers of the executive branches of government (the president, governors, and heads of important governmental agencies) who are acting within the scope of their authority. Lesser officials may enjoy a limited privilege. The extent of these privileges is uncertain because of the lack of modern cases testing the law in this area.

4. In 1884, the case of *Vogel v. Gruaz,*[42] was heard before the U.S. Supreme Court. An Illinois State attorney had testified concerning what the defendant had told him in regard to the plaintiff committing a crime. The statements were made in the State attorney's office and contributed to a judgment against the defendant for libel and slander. In reversing the judgment, the Court held:

> The free and unembarrassed administration of justice in respect to the criminal law, in which the public is concerned, is involved in a case like the present, in addition to the considerations which ordinarily apply in communication from client to counsel in matters of purely private concern. . . . Therefore, statements made within the scope of privileged communication [to one's attorney, doctor, minister, or spouse] may not be the basis for a criminal or civil defamation action.

U.S. Supreme Court cases dealing with the power of the state to regulate and punish (either criminally or civilly) defamation are:

NEW YORK TIMES CO. v. SULLIVAN
Supreme Court of the United States (1964) 376 U.S. 254, 84 S.Ct. 710

The plaintiff was a public official (police commissioner) who was awarded a judgment and money damages in a civil libel suit against the defendant newspaper for the false statements made by the newspaper in criticizing the official conduct of the plaintiff. The U.S. Supreme Court stated:

> In New York Times Co. v. Sullivan, *we hold that the Constitution limits state power, in a civil action brought by a public official for criticism of his official conduct, to an award of damages for a false statement made with "actual malice"—that is, with knowledge that it was false or with reckless disregard of whether it was false or not. The Court reversed the judgment against the defendant.*[43]

GARRISON v. LOUISIANA
Supreme Court of the United States (1964) 379 U.S. 64, 85 S.Ct. 209

The defendant, who was the district attorney of New Orleans, was convicted of criminal defamation when he criticized the judicial conduct of eight judges in New Orleans. He attributed the large backlog of pending criminal cases to their inefficiency, laziness, and excessive vacations. The Supreme Court reversed, stating:

> *We held in* New York Times *that a public official might be allowed the civil remedy only if he establishes that the utterance was false and that it was made with knowledge of its falsity or in reckless disregard of whether it was false or true. The reasons which led us to hold in* New York Times *apply with no less force merely because the remedy is criminal. The constitutional guarantees of freedom of expression compel application of the same standard to the criminal remedy. Truth may not be the subject of either civil or criminal sanctions where discussion of public affairs is concerned.*

The February 1974 issue of the *FBI Law Enforcement Bulletin* contains an article entitled "A Law Enforcement Officer Sues for Defamation."[44] After reviewing cases on defamation nationwide, the article concludes:

> Under the current state of the law, a public official faces a far more difficult situation than a private citizen with regard to obtaining recompense for defamatory publications. A law enforcement officer has been defined by case law as a public official. To succeed as a party plaintiff in a defamation proceeding he must therefore plead and move that the person publishing the defamation did so with a reckless disregard as to the truth or falsity of his statements.

H. SPOOFS, SATIRE, AND POLITICAL CARTOONS

Accusing a man of having sex with his mother is certainly one of the greatest insults possible. The reaction to this insult is usually immediate anger and violence. This is thus a classic example of what the law calls "fighting words," at least if spoken face-to-face. What if, however, the insult is spoken, or written, in jest? Consider the following well-known case.

Hustler magazine published a story that it presented as a parody, intended for comic effect to ridicule Rev. Jerry Falwell, a nationally known television evangelist and conservative minister. The author pretended to "interview" Mr. Falwell, who recounted that his first sexual experience occurred during a drunken rendezvous with his mother in an outhouse. The story contained additional outrageous material, with a small-print disclaimer at the bottom of the page stating "ad-parody—not to be taken seriously."

The Reverend Jerry Falwell (center), with his wife and lawyer, talks to reporters outside the U.S. Supreme Court building. The question before the Supreme Court was whether the "outrageous speech" against him by *Hustler* magazine and Larry Flynt could be punished criminally or civilly.

Mr. Falwell sued *Hustler* magazine and publisher Larry Flynt for libel, invasion of privacy, and intentional infliction of mental distress. The trial court dismissed the invasion of privacy claim, and the jury found against Mr. Falwell on the libel claim, reasoning that the story could not "reasonably be understood as describing actual facts about (Mr. Falwell) or actual events in which (he) participated." On the emotional distress claim, however, the jury awarded Mr. Falwell $100,000 in compensatory damages and $50,000 from each defendant as punitive damages. *Hustler* appealed.

The case ultimately reached the U.S. Supreme Court, which held, in a unanimous decision (8–0), against Mr. Falwell. The Court held that Mr. Falwell had no civil or criminal remedy for the wrong done to him, because to permit recovery on the emotional distress claim would conflict with the First Amendment rules governing libel of public figures.

The Supreme Court found that *Hustler's* article on Mr. Falwell was "gross and repugnant," but held that the "expressions involved in this case (are) not governed by an exception to the general First Amendment principle" established by the Court. In denying Rev. Falwell the "emotional distress" award, the Supreme Court held:

> We conclude that public figures and public officials may not recover for the tort of intentional infliction of emotional distress by reason of publications such as the one here at issue without showing in addition that the publication contains a false statement of fact which was made with "actual malice," i.e., with knowledge that the statement was false or with reckless disregard as to whether or not it was true. This is not merely a "blind application" of the *New York Times* standard . . . it reflects our

considered judgment that such a standard is necessary to give adequate "breathing space" to the freedoms protected by the First Amendment.

* * *

The *Hustler v. Falwell*[45] decision makes it much more difficult for a person (particularly a public figure) to successfully sue a magazine such as *Hustler* or a supermarket tabloid. Other cases of "monstrous jokes," sometimes called "the most insidious form of defamation,"[46] are:

PRING v. PENTHOUSE INTERN., LTD.
U.S. Court of Appeals (10th Cir. 1982) 695 F.2d 438

Penthouse published what it claimed to be a very funny story about a Miss Wyoming who was so expert at fellatio that she could actually make men levitate. At the time of the story, the plaintiff was a college student and Miss Wyoming. The story singled her out in other ways and caused such ridicule and turmoil in her life that she left the university and was unable to obtain a job in Wyoming. Like Rev. Jerry Falwell, she was unable to recover in a civil action and there was also no basis for criminal charges.

WALKO v. KEAN COLLEGE OF NEW JERSEY
Superior Court of New Jersey (1988) 235 N.J.Super. 139, 561 A.2d 680

A college newspaper ran a "spoof" ad stating "WHORELINE—Have a problem? Want to Rap? Call WHORELINE at 687–SEXY anytime for good phone sex," and then it listed the names of college administrators. One of the women listed brought this civil lawsuit against the college and the students who wrote and published the article. Like Rev. Jerry Falwell, she lost the civil lawsuit, with the court holding that a spoof or parody that is not action-able as defamation cannot form the basis of recovery for the tort of outrage (intentional infliction of emotional distress).

I. Unlawful Telephone Calls

Before 1966, few states had criminal laws dealing with abusive and obscene telephone calls. However, because of the increased volume of complaints received during the 1960s, all the states and the federal government have now enacted statutes making such telephone calls a criminal offense.[47]

Abusive phone calls include the deliberate obscene call, threats, the cruel hoax, bomb scares and threats of bombs, and the "silent" call, in which the person answering the telephone hears nothing or hears breathing on the other end of the line. Criminal charges may be issued in all the above cases if it is apparent that the call was deliberate and made with intent to harass, frighten, or abuse another person. However, charges should not be issued if it appears that the person has dialed the wrong number and simply does not explain the error. Other criminal uses of the telephone include situations in which the telephone is used to "case" the residence by persons planning a burglary (in this way, they are able to determine whether anyone is in the residence).

Apprehending persons making abusive and obscene telephone calls has been a difficult task in the past, but the job is now made easier by the development of devices by telephone companies. Two of these are:

- *The pen register,* which does not eavesdrop but does record the number called on the suspected line and the time of all calls. Neither the suspect nor the complaining party know that the pen register is being used. It is necessary to have sufficient information to reasonably suspect a particular person or telephone as the source of such calls.
- *The polarity trap,* which locks in the two telephones until the telephone company chooses to release the phones. This procedure is used when a person has been receiving regular abusive calls.

One-shot nuisance calls are virtually untraceable, unless the receiving telephone has equipment that records the caller's identification. However, the repeat caller stands a good chance of being apprehended by teams of police and telephone employees. The full cooperation of the victim is also needed.

J. Loud Noise and Loud Speech (Sometimes Called "Nuisance" Speech)

Probably all cities in the United States have ordinances forbidding loud noises and loud speech that (a) disturb other persons, or that (b) creates a clear and present danger of violence. States and cities may reasonably regulate the volume of speech, but they may not prohibit all loud speech.[48] The Supreme Court of California, in construing the terminology of a statute regarding "loud and unusual noise," held in *In Re Brown* that:

> The statute, however, cannot be interpreted consistent with the First Amendment and traditional views as making criminal all loud shouting or cheering which disturbs and is intended to disturb persons. When the word noise in the statute is properly construed consistent with the First Amendment and traditional views, it encompasses communications made in a loud manner only when there is *a clear and present danger of violence or when the communication is not intended as such but is merely a guise to disturb persons.* [*Id.* 108 Cal.Rptr. at 469, 510 P.2d at 1021.] [Emphasis supplied.][49]

Loud party noises in an apartment house or in a neighborhood could cause telephone calls to the police or could cause a fight among neighbors if it were the middle of the night. Such "noise" calls are common on weekends in the summer in all large cities. The noises under such circumstances are interfering with the rights of other persons. Notice and cautions are generally given before a citation is issued by the police.[50]

The U.S. Supreme Court ruled as follows on street noises in the case of *Kovacs v. Cooper:*

> City streets are recognized as a normal place for the exchange of ideas by speech or paper. But this does not mean the freedom is beyond all control. We think it is a permissible exercise of legislative discretion to bar sound trucks with broadcasts of public interest, amplified to a loud and raucous volume, from the public ways of municipalities. On the business streets of cities like Trenton, with its more than 125,000 people, such distractions would be dangerous to traffic at all hours useful for

the dissemination of information, and in the residential thoroughfares the quiet and tranquility so desirable for city dwellers would likewise be at the mercy of advocates of particular religious, social or political persuasions. We cannot believe that rights of free speech compel a municipality to allow such mechanical voice amplification on any of its streets.

The right of free speech is guaranteed every citizen that he may reach the minds of willing listeners and to do so there must be opportunity to win their attention. This is the phase of freedom of speech that is involved here. We do not think the Trenton ordinance abridges that freedom. It is an extravagant extension of due process to say that because of it a city cannot forbid talking on the streets through a loud speaker in a loud and raucous tone. Surely such an ordinance does not violate our people's "concept of ordered liberty" so as to require federal intervention to protect a citizen from the action of his own local government.[51]

K. SYMBOLIC SPEECH AND THE FIRST AMENDMENT

Symbols, along with gestures, conduct, and speech, have always been used to communicate between human beings. The symbol can be used alone, or can be used with other forms of communication. American courts have wrestled for years with the problem of which symbols should receive First Amendment protection as forms of nonverbal communication. For example, during World War II, the Nazi swastika would not have received First Amendment protection; today, it generally would, depending, of course, on the way in which it was used.

Uniforms and the manner in which people dress are forms of symbols. People communicate by their dress who they are, what their lifestyles are, and, to some extent, what they think and believe. Suppose that a police officer on duty in a squad car sees three men in Nazi uniforms walking down the street or sees a number of men dressed in the robes of the Ku Klux Klan. Is there any violation of the law by the manner in which these people are dressed? But suppose the men in Nazi uniforms are picketing with signs expressing anti-Jewish sentiments in front of a Jewish synagogue. Or suppose the Ku Kluxers are walking through a black neighborhood. Do these actions fall within the insulting or "fighting words" doctrine? Suppose the Ku Kluxers have hoods covering their faces as they walk down the street. Is this within their First Amendment rights? In all the examples given, would officers be authorized to stop the men and obtain their names, addresses, and an explanation of what they were doing?

Major symbolic speech cases that have come before the U.S. Supreme Court are:

WEST VIRGINIA BD. OF EDUC. v. BARNETTE
Supreme Court of the United States (1943) 319 U.S. 624, 63 S.Ct. 1178

The defendants were Jehovah's Witnesses who were prosecuted because their children would not salute the American flag while in school. The Court held that the compulsory flag salute and pledge of allegiance could not be enforced against Jehovah's Witnesses because to "sustain the compulsory flag salute, we are required to say that a Bill of Rights which guards the individual's right to speak his own mind, left open to public authorities to compel him to utter what is not in his mind." In recognizing that the flag is a symbol and that saluting the flag is a form of communication, the Court stated:

Verbal Offenses

Type of Verbal Offense	To Constitute the Verbal Offense, There Must Be
"fighting words"	1. insulting or abusive language 2. addressed to a person on a face-to-face basis 3. causing a likelihood that "the person addressed will make an immediate violent response"
obscenity	1. a communication that, taken as a whole, appeals to the prurient (lustful) interest in sex, 2. and portrays sexual conduct in a patently offensive way, 3. and the communication, taken as a whole, does not have serious literary, artistic, political, or scientific value.
urging unlawful conduct (inciting)	1. language or communication directed to inciting, producing, or urging 2. *imminent* lawless action or conduct, or 3. language or communication likely to incite or produce such unlawful conduct
obstruction of a law enforcement officer (or of justice)	1. deliberate and intentional language (or communication) that hinders, obstructs, delays, or makes more difficult 2. a law enforcement officer's effort to perform his official duties (the scienter element of knowledge by the defendant that he or she knew the person obstructed was a law enforcement officer is required) 3. some states require that the "interference would have to be, in part at least, physical in nature" (see the New York case of *People v. Case*)
defamation (libel and slander)	1. words or communication that are false and untrue 2. and injure the character and reputation of another person 3. defamation must be communicated to a third person ***When a public official is the victim, it must also be shown*** that the words or communications were uttered or published with a reckless disregard as to the truth or falsity of the statement. (See also the case of *Falwell v. Hustler Magazine* as Rev. Falwell is a public figure.)
abusive, obscene, or harassing telephone calls	1. evidence showing that the telephone call was deliberate, 2. and made with intent to harass, frighten, or abuse another person, 3. and any other requirement of the particular statute or ordinance
loud speech and loud noise	***Cities and States May:*** 1. forbid speech and noises meant by the volume to disturb others 2. and forbid noise and loud speech that create a clear and present danger of violence

There is no doubt that, in connection with the pledge, the flag salute is a form of utterance. Symbolism is a primitive but effective way of communicating ideas. The use of an emblem or flag to symbolize some system, idea, institution, or personality, is a short cut from mind to mind. Causes and nations, political parties, lodges and ecclesiastical groups seek to knit the loyalty of their followings to a flag or banner, a color or design. The State announces rank, function and authority through crowns and maces, uniforms and black robes; the church speaks through the Cross, the Crucifix, the altar and shrine and clerical raiment. Symbols of State often convey political ideas just as religious symbols are appropriate gestures of acceptance or respect; a salute, a bowed or bared head, a bended knee. A person gets from a symbol the meaning he puts into it, and what is one man's comfort and inspiration is another's jest and scorn.

STROMBERG v. CALIFORNIA
Supreme Court of the United States (1931) 283 U.S. 359, 51 S.Ct. 532

The Supreme Court reversed a conviction for the display of a red flag in a public place under a statute that punished such display of a red flag if it was used "as a sign, symbol or emblem of opposition to organized government." The Court, in holding that advocating violent overthrow of government may be punished but that advocating peaceful change within the law may not be, stated:

> *The right (of free speech) is not an absolute one and the State in the exercise of its police power may punish the abuse of this freedom. There is no question but that the State may thus provide for the punishment of those who indulge in utterances which incite to violence and crime and threaten the overthrow of organized government by unlawful means. There is no constitutional immunity for such conduct abhorrent to our institutions. . . .*
>
> *The maintenance of the opportunity for free political discussion to the end that government may be responsive to the will of the people and changes may be obtained by lawful means, an opportunity essential to the security of the Republic, is a fundamental principle of our constitutional system.*

TINKER v. DES MOINES INDEPENDENT COMMUNITY SCHOOL DIST.
Supreme Court of the United States (1969) 393 U.S. 503, 89 S.Ct. 733

The principal of a high school forbade the wearing of black armbands as an expression of objection to the Vietnam War. The U.S. Supreme Court held that: "The wearing of an armband . . . was closely akin to pure speech which, we have repeatedly held, is entitled to comprehensive protection under the First Amendment. . . . Students or teachers [do not] shed their constitutional rights to freedom of speech or expression at the schoolhouse gate." (In this case, the "speech" of the students did not disrupt classes or school.)

UNITED STATES v. O'BRIEN
Supreme Court of the United States (1968) 391 U.S. 367, 88 S.Ct. 1673

The Supreme Court sustained the federal law that made it an offense to destroy or burn a draft card, stating:

> *A government regulation is sufficiently justified if it is within the constitutional power of the government; if it furthers an important or substantial governmental interest; if the governmental interest is unrelated to the suppression of free expression; and if the incidental restriction on alleged First Amendment freedoms is no greater than is essential to the furtherance of that interest.*

L. Flag Burning as a Form of Expression Protected by the First Amendment

American flags have always been destroyed when they have become so torn and worn they can be of no further use. Such destruction of old flags is usually done with reverence and has never been forbidden by criminal statutes of any of the states.

Because the American flag is the symbol of America, and its symbolic meaning cherished by most Americans, protesters and demonstrators have often burned or otherwise defiled flags in an attempt to communicate political messages of anger, protest, frustration, or requests for change. Flag-burning is a way of focusing attention on their political message. Many states passed criminal statutes making the burning or defilement of American flags under such circumstances a crime. To what extent can states do this consistent with the First Amendment?

In the 1989 case of *Texas v. Johnson*,[52] the U.S. Supreme Court faced this question. The Court pointed out that the Texas flag desecration statute (like other flag protection laws) was enacted to protect the flag's symbolic meaning, and applied "only when a person's treatment of the flag communicates some message" (109 S.Ct. 2542). Because of this, in the *Johnson* case, and again in the 1990 flag burning case of *United States v. Eichman*,[53] the U.S. Supreme Court held that "the State's asserted interests could not justify the infringement on the demonstrator's First Amendment rights."

In the *Eichman* case, the government argued that flag-burning should be classified as a form of communication similar to obscenity, or "fighting words," and like these forms of expression be subjected to regulations by states. The Court's curt response to this argument was: "This we decline to do" (110 S.Ct. at 2407).

Therefore, after the rulings in the two cases, states may not punish flag-burners who are burning their own flags and not committing other offenses while they are doing so.

Flag-burners could be punished if they burned the flag of another person without the consent of that person (criminal damage to the property of another). They could also be charged with trespass if they climbed a government building to take down the flag flying over the building (check the trespass statute in your state or city). If the burning occurred in the middle of a busy traffic intersection, or in a city that had an ordinance forbidding burning without a proper permit, charges could be considered.

M. Balancing the Need for a Free Press with the Right to a Fair Trial

Can Newspaper and TV Publicity Jeopardize a Defendant's Right to a Fair Trial?

A free and unfettered press that seeks out and publishes the news is necessary to the functioning of a democracy. The people must be fully and adequately informed in order that they may intelligently discharge their responsibilities as citizens. On the other hand, we as a nation have long cherished the fundamental principles that a defendant in a criminal case shall be afforded all the safeguards of due process of law and shall be given a fair and impartial trial. These two principles come into conflict when newspapers and other communication media publish detailed information before a defendant has been tried.

In 1966, the case of *Sheppard v. Maxwell*[54] came before the U.S. Supreme Court. The defendant in that case, Sam Sheppard, was tried for and convicted of the brutal murder of his pregnant wife in their suburban Cleveland home. The question before the Court was whether the trial judge failed "to protect Sheppard sufficiently from the massive, pervasive and prejudicial publicity that attended his prosecution." In holding that the state trial judge "did not fulfill his duty to protect Sheppard from the inherently prejudicial publicity which saturated the community and (failed) to control disruptive influences in the courtroom," the Court quoted the Ohio Supreme Court as follows:

> Murder and mystery, society, sex and suspense were combined in this case in such a manner as to intrigue and captivate the public fancy to a degree perhaps unparalleled in recent annals. Throughout the preindictment investigation, the subsequent legal skirmishes and the nine-week trial, circulation-conscious editors catered to the insatiable interest of the American public in the bizarre.... In this atmosphere of a "Roman holiday" for the news media, Sam Sheppard stood trial for his life.

Questions and Problems for Chapter 10

Indicate whether the following speech and conduct should be charged as a criminal offense in your state. Explain your answer and state the offense (or offenses).

1. A large group of demonstrators was ordered by the police to leave an Air Force recruiting office located in a large office building. The demonstrators proceeded to leave peacefully, using elevators and stairs. However, just as an elevator door was closing a young woman demonstrator yelled, "Fuck the Air Force."(*City of Milwaukee v. Rosnick,* Case # 1-253981 [1972])

2. The defendant called "sooey" once as an officer was walking toward the police station and the defendant was driving past in a car. (*Garvey v. State,* 537 S.W.2d 709 [Tenn. App. 1975])

3. The defendant stated to a friend in a loud voice in a crowded restaurant that he "didn't want to play the fucking pin ball machine because they beat us for too much money last week." This language was offensive to an older couple, who complained to the police. (*Reese v. State,* 17 Md.App. 73, 299 A.2d 848 [1973])

4. If a city enacted an ordinance forbidding vehicle bumper stickers sporting phrases such as "Shit Happens," what type of attacks could be made on the constitutionality of such an ordinance? (See the 1991 case of *Cunningham v. State,* 260 Ga. 827, 400 S.E. 2d 916 (1991) where this issue was before the Georgia Supreme Court.)

5. Defendant and another man met "to speak out against abortion" and "to preach the gospel of Jesus Christ" in front of an abortion clinic. Their loud voices could be heard in business places and residential apartments that surrounded and were in the same building as the abortion clinic. Each of the men spoke without artificial amplification for an hour and a half during business hours. Residents and persons employed in the area complained to the police that they were disturbed by the loudness of the preaching. Police requested that the volume level of the speech be reduced, but the defendant continued "shouting in a loud voice." The defendant was then arrested and convicted of a statute that made it unlawful for anyone to "wilfully disturb any neighborhood in any city, town or county by loud and unseemly noises." Should the conviction stand? *Eanes v. Maryland* 518 Md. 436, 569 A.2d 604 (1990), review denied, ___ U.S. ___, 110 S.Ct. 3218, 47 CrL 3074 (1990)

6. The defendant (an adult man) asked an eleven-year-old girl, "Have you ever been laid?" The girl immediately walked away but wrote down the license number of the defendant's car. The girl's parent reported the incident to the police. (*Breaux v. State,* 230 Ga. 506, 197 S.E.2d 695 [1973])

7. A Wisconsin attorney was upsetting mental patients by his statements and would not leave a mental ward when requested to do so by attendants and police officers. The attorney was arrested when he stated that he would not leave unless arrested. (*State v. Elson,* 60 Wis.2d 54, 208 N.W.2d 363 [1973])

8. As the defendant was about to board a plane, he was asked by a security guard what was in a small sealed paper box. The defendant answered, "Nitroglycerine." A deputy sheriff was called and when the box was opened, it was found to

contain food items. (See the article "His Little Joke Bombs Out," in the *Milwaukee Journal*, 27 May 1979.)

9. On June 2, 1982, Larry Rodgers telephoned the Kansas City, Missouri, office of the FBI and reported that his wife had been kidnapped. The FBI spent more than 100 agent hours investigating the alleged kidnapping only to determine that Rodgers' wife had left him voluntarily. Two weeks later, Rodgers contacted the Kansas City office of the Secret Service and reported that his "estranged girlfriend" (actually his wife) was involved in a plot to assassinate the president. The Secret Service spent more than 150 hours of agent and clerical time investigating this threat and eventually located Rodgers' wife in Arizona. She stated that she left Kansas City to get away from her husband. Rodgers later confessed that he made the false reports to induce the federal agencies to locate his wife." (*United States v. Rodgers*, 466 U.S. 475, 104 S.Ct. 1942 [1984]) If Rodgers had made such false reports to law enforcement agencies in your state, would he be charged with one or more criminal offenses? If so, indicate the offense(s).

10. At about 10:45 P.M. on Christmas night, 1971, the defendant was walking home from work in a high-crime neighborhood. A police officer approached the defendant because he had been notified of a "suspicious man" in the neighborhood. The defendant was sixty-nine years old and had lived in the United States twenty years. When the officer asked him if he lived in the area, the defendant looked at him and walked away. The officer then stopped the defendant twice, but each time the defendant threw off the officer's arm and protested, "I don't tell you people anything." The defendant would not stay in the officer's presence and he would not answer any of the officer's questions. The defendant was charged and convicted of disorderly conduct and his conviction was appealed to the U.S. Supreme Court. Was the conduct of the defendant disorderly so as to justify the conviction? (*Norwell v. City of Cincinnati*, 414 U.S. 14, 94 S.Ct. 187 [1973]).

11. A city attorney refused to issue an ordinance citation against two juveniles who repeatedly shouted "Fuck you pig," "Get fucked, pig," "Fucking pig," "Oink, oink," and "Sooey" to a police officer in a squad car. Ten or fifteen people in and about an apartment complex for the elderly heard and observed the conduct of the young men. The officer took the juveniles into custody and, after the city attorney refused to issue a citation, wrote the following in a report:

> *During recruit training, the undersigned was taught that a police officer must tolerate verbal abuse and name-calling without legal recourse during the course of an arrest or when no one other than the officer is present and takes offense to such verbal treatment. However, he was also taught that when such conduct disturbs and offends other citizens, disorderly conduct charges can be brought against offender. Further, no signed complaint from a citizen is necessary, nor would identities be disclosed. Reasonable testimony as to circumstances and time of day, etc. is sufficient.*

Is the city attorney right, or is the officer correct? Could a citation be issued under these circumstances? What type of testimony would be necessary to support a citation for disorderly conduct?

12. After police officers arrested two of his friends, Mesarosh shouted at the officers,

> *"[L]ook at this s. .t going on right here. . . . I'll get you mother f. . . .rs, you son-of-a-bitches. . . . F .k you pigs. All you ever want to do is pick on us. . . . We're going to get your a. ., I'm going to see you in court."*

A crowd gathered in front of the pool hall, and other persons came out of businesses to watch the incident. Some other persons in the crowd may have been shouting at the officers, but no one attempted to interfere with the arrest. Was Mesarosh's speech protected by the First Amendment? *Mesarosh v. State*, 459 N.E.2d 426 (Ind.App. 1984).

Notes

1. *Cox v. New Hampshire*, 312 U.S. 569, 61 S.Ct. 762 (1941).

2. *Speiser v. Randall*, 357 U.S. 513, 78 S.Ct. 1332 (1958).

3. See *Watts v. United States*, 394 U.S. 705, 89 S.Ct. 1399 (1969).

4. A small group of persons, including the late U.S. Supreme Court Justice Hugo Black, have argued that gov-

ernment should not restrict speech or communication in any way. These "absolutists" (as they are called) argue that the First Amendment should be interpreted literally and that freedom of speech and communication be absolute rather than limited.

However, most justices and people in democratic societies have believed otherwise. There have always been restrictions on speech and communications in the United States within constitutional limitations.

5. The U.S. Supreme Court in the 1988 case of *Hustler Magazine v. Falwell* 485 U.S. 46, 108 S.Ct. 876, quoting *Boese Corp. v. Consumers Union of the United States,* 466 U.S. 485, 104 S.Ct. 1949 (1984).

6. 249 U.S. 47, 39 S.Ct. 247 (1919).

7. 315 U.S. 568, 571, 62 S.Ct. 766, 769.

8. 405 U.S. 518, 521, 92 S.Ct. 1103, 1105.

9. 403 U.S. 15, 91 S.Ct. 1780.

10. *Id.* at 25, 91 S.Ct. at 1788.

11. 422 U.S. 205, 95 S.Ct. 2268.

12. 405 U.S. 518, 92 S.Ct. 1103.

13. This case demonstrates that it is the owner or manager of the business who is obligated to maintain order in a situation such as this. The manager could have ordered Downs out (or to behave himself). If Downs refused, then the manager could request the assistance of a law enforcement officer. If persons were injured because a business failed to meet responsibilities (a fight could erupt because of Downs's language), civil liability would exist that might give rise to a lawsuit.

14. 29 Wis.2d 66, 138 N.W.2d 264 (1965).

15. *City of St. Petersburg v. Waller,* 261 So.2d 151 (Fla. 1972) in which the Florida Court of Appeals states the "defendant as a police car approached a group gathered at a corner, stepped into the street, thrust his amplified megaphone close to the window of the police car, and yelled 'pig.' This Court held that under the circumstances the language had no significance than to arouse the crowd into action against the police officer."

16. *Bradshaw v. State,* 286 So.2d 4 (Fla. 1973) in which the defendant used abusive and insulting language in the presence of 100 to 150 people when the possibility of a riot existed. See also *Phillips v. State,* 314 So.2d 619 (Fla. App. 1975) in which the defendant told the arresting officer "fuck you" twice before he was arrested. As none of the Florida extenuating circumstances existed, the Florida Court reversed holding: "It is our view that the use of the expletive was not such as to afford the arresting officer with substantial reason to believe the defendant was committing the misdemeanor of a breach of the peace in violation of F.S. 877.03, *supra.* . . . Thus, we reverse."

17. 136 U.S.App.D.C. 56, 419 F.2d 638 (1969). Judge McGowan stated:

A policeman's special powers and training and his constant exposure to situations where the norms of common speech are not distinguished by unvarying delicacy of expression, leave him less free to react as quickly as the private citizen to a purely verbal assault. On a situation where he is both the victim of the provocative words of abuse and the public official entrusted with a discretion to initiate through arrest the criminal process, the policeman may ordinarily at least be under a necessity to preface arrest by a warning. It would appear that there is no First Amendment right to engage in deliberate and continued baiting of policemen by verbal excesses which have no apparent purpose other than to provoke a violent reaction.

18. 537 S.W.2d 709 (Tenn. App.).

19. 763 P.2d 700 (Okl. Crim.).

20. 385 S.E.2d 59 (1989).

21. 278 Md. 610, 366 A.2d 41 (1976).

22. Milwaukee County Case # 1-264020. In 1972, George Carlin was arrested for disorderly conduct when he included in an hour-long show before thousands of young people and adults the seven words not allowed on television or radio. Carlin was acquitted in a trial when the city failed to show either (a) that Carlin caused a disturbance or breach of the peace or (b) that he angered his audience to the point that persons in the audience were "aggravated to fight." Most of the audience was amused by the presentation, which Carlin presented as humorous and not meant as "fighting words." However, several complaints were made to police officers because of the language.

23. 79 Mich.App. 757, 262 N.W.2d 900 (1977).

24. 263 N.W.2d 412 (Minn. 1978). The Supreme Court of Minnesota held that "with the words spoken in retreat from more than 15 feet away rather than eye to eye, there was no reasonable likelihood that they would tend to incite an immediate breach of the peace or to provoke violent reaction by an ordinary, reasonable person."

25. 384 A.2d 429 (Me. 1978).

26. 294 Md. 466, 451 A.2d 115 (1982), *review denied* 460 U.S. 1098, 103 S.Ct. 1798 (1983). Officer Gavin testified that Diehl said, "Fuck you, Gavin"; "I know my rights"; "You can't tell me what to do." After the arrest, he was alleged to have told Gavin he was "full of shit" and "a crazy son-of-a-bitch."

27. 31 Wash.App. 745, 644 P.2d 747.

28. Juvenile cases similar to *State v. Montgomery* are *State v. John W.,* 418 A.2d 1097 (Me. 1980), and *White v. State,* 330 So.2d 3 (Fla. 1976).

29. 443 U.S. 31, 99 S.Ct. 2627.

30. The U.S. Supreme Court in the 1988 case of *Boos v. Barry,* 485 U.S. 312, 108 S.Ct. 1157.

31. The angry words in the *Lane v. Collins* case had to do with the personal lives of the parties and had nothing to do with the official duties of the law enforcement officer. In the 1971 case of *Colten v. Commonwealth,* 467 S.W.2d 374 (Ky.), the defendant complained that the arresting officer had called him a "loudmouth." However, the defendant argued in his brief that he had the right to call policemen and their wives "pigs" as he had done. The Kentucky Court held that "the evidence warrants the conclusion that Colten was in fact a 'loudmouth.'"

32. 120 R.I. 42, 385 A.2d 642 (1978).

33. 41 Ohio St.2d 173, 324 N.E.2d 735 (1975).

34. 413 U.S. 15, 93 S.Ct. 2607 (1973).

35. 452 U.S. 61, 101 S.Ct. 2176.

36. 409 U.S. 109, 93 S.Ct. 390 (1972).

37. See *New York State Liquor Authority v. Bellanea,* 29 CrL 4104 (1981).

38. *Doe v. Indiana,* 28 CrL 4021 (1981).

39. The U.S. Supreme Court in *Brandenburg v. Ohio,* 395 U.S. 444, 89 S.Ct. 1827 (1969).

40. The Wisconsin Criminal Code defines obstructs as follows in Sec. 946.41(2)(b) *Resisting or Obstructing Officer:* (b) "Obstructs" includes without limitation knowingly giving false information to the officer with intent to mislead him in the performance of his duty including the service of any summons or civil process.

41. Books written by Whitaker Chambers, Alger Hiss, and Richard Nixon relating to this incident in greater detail from the point of view of each of the writers are available in public libraries.

42. 110 U.S. 311, 4 S.Ct. 12.

43. The quotation used is from the ruling by the U.S. Supreme Court in *Garrison v. Louisiana,* 379 U.S. 64, 85 S.Ct. 209 (1964).

44. For other defamation cases see *Gertz v. Robert Welch, Inc.,* 418 U.S. 323, 94 S.Ct. 2997 (1974); *Munn v. Burks,* 19 Or.App. 144, 526 P.2d 1040 (1974); and *Kerpelman v. Bricker,* 23 Md.App. 628, 329 A.2d 423 (1974).

45. 485 U.S. 46, 108 S. Ct. 876 (1988). The U.S. Supreme Court also stated in the case of *Falwell v. Hustler Magazine* that:

* * *

We recognized in Pacifica Foundation, that speech that is " 'vulgar,' 'offensive,' and 'shocking' " is "not entitled to absolute constitutional protection under all circumstances." 438 U.S., at 747 . . . In Chaplinsky v. New Hampshire, 315 U.S. 568 . . . we held that a state could lawfully punish an individual for the use of insulting " 'fighting' words—those which by their very utterance inflict injury or tend to incite an immediate breach of the peace." Id., at 571–572

. . . These limitations are but recognition of the observation in Dun & Bradstreet, Inc. v. Greenmoss Builders, Inc., *472 U.S. 749, 758 . . . that this Court has "long recognized that not all speech is of equal First Amendment importance." But the sort of expression involved in this case does not seem to us to be governed by any exception to the general First Amendment principles stated above.*

* * *

46. For an angry attack on rulings having to do with what the author calls "monstrous jokes," see the article "The Sale of the First Amendment" in the March 1989 issue of the *American Bar Association Journal.* The author was Ms. Pring's attorney. He tells how the article in *Penthouse* magazine impacted and changed the life of Ms. Pring.

47. The Consumer Credit Protection Act (Pub. Law 95–109 Stat. 877) prohibits debt collectors from "placing telephone calls without meaningful disclosure of the caller's identity"; from "engaging any person in telephone conversation repeatedly or continuously with intent to annoy, abuse, or harass any person at the called number"; and from us[ing] obscene or profane language or language the natural consequence of which is to abuse the hearer or reader. "

48. *Saia v. New York,* 334 U.S. 558, 560–562, 68 S.Ct. 1148, 1149–1151 (1948).

49. 9 Cal. 3d 612, 108 Cal.Rptr. 465, 510 P.2d 1017 (1973), *cert denied,* 416 U.S. 950, 94 S.Ct. 1959 (1974).

50. Many city ordinances define in decibels what volume is "too loud." An interesting twist on this is that air conditioners, construction equipment, and farm machinery, among other things, often run afoul of the definitions.

51. 336 U.S. 77, 69 S. Ct. 448 (1949).

52. 491 U.S. 397, 109 S. Ct. 2533.

53. ___ U.S. ___ , 110 S. Ct. 2404.

54. 384 U.S. 333, 86 S. Ct. 1507 (1966). See also the "fair trial-free press" case of *Press-Enterprise Co. v. Superior Court,* 478 U.S. 1, 106 S.Ct. 2735, 39 CrL 3253 (1986).

Chapter Eleven

Maintaining Public Order in Public and Private Places

A. Regulating the Use of Public and Private Places

Most private property (and some public property) is closed to the public. Private homes and apartments, for example, are not open to the public nor are offices of many governmental officials.

On the other hand, private property like shopping centers and retail stores is open to the public. In determining the regulations and controls that may be used in public places and in private places open to the public, courts have pointed out that the following must be considered: (a) the character and the normal use of the property, (b) the extent to which it is open to the public, and (c) the number and type of persons who use the facilities.[1] Applying these factors, it can be seen that the waiting room of a mayor's or governor's office could ordinarily accommodate a small number of protesters but could not accommodate hundreds of protesters. Nor could sidewalks used by many people accommodate large numbers of protesters without hindering and interfering with pedestrian traffic.

Balancing of Conflicting Rights and Needs

The U.S. Supreme Court has held that when private property is not generally open to the public, access to the property for the purposes of exercising First Amendment rights may be absolutely denied.[2]

In a rush for seats at a rock concert, nine young persons were killed and many others injured trying to get through these doors at Cincinnati's Riverfront Coliseum in 1979. Similar deaths also occurred at rock and rap concerts in Nashville (1985) and Salt Lake City (1991). The potential for such harm is one of the factors that must be balanced against the expression of personal rights.

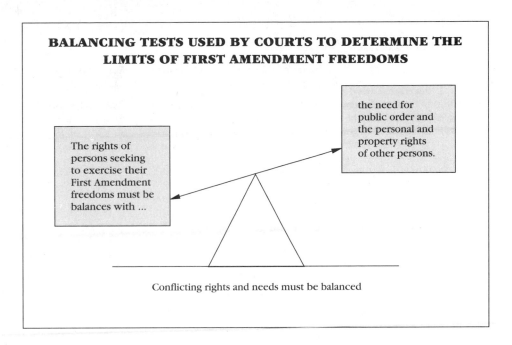

BALANCING TESTS USED BY COURTS TO DETERMINE THE LIMITS OF FIRST AMENDMENT FREEDOMS

The rights of persons seeking to exercise their First Amendment freedoms must be balances with ...

the need for public order and the personal and property rights of other persons.

Conflicting rights and needs must be balanced

Nor is there a general right to exercise First Amendment rights on public property and private property open to the public if this interferes with normal use of the property. As the U.S. Supreme Court pointed out (see note 1), making a speech in the reading room of a public library would interfere with the normal use of such a facility. However, students silently protesting the Vietnam War were held not to disrupt and disturb their high school classes by wearing black armbands.[3]

Therefore, both public and private places may be regulated for the normal use of the property.[4] Libraries, hospitals, and schools would have different regulations than basketball arenas, taverns, and gyms because of the different uses of such facilities.

Public and private places must be regulated by the persons in charge of such facilities because failure to provide ordinary care in protecting employees, customers, and other persons lawfully on their premises makes such businesses or public places liable for accidental negligence or intentional acts of third persons.

Cases Establishing Broad Rights of Access to Public Places

In 1972, the U.S. Supreme Court held:

> The right to use a public place for expressive activity may be restricted only for weighty reasons. Clearly, government has no power to restrict such activity because of its message. Our cases make equally clear, however, that reasonable "time, place and manner" regulations may be necessary to further significant governmental interests, and are permitted. For example, two parades cannot march on the same street simultaneously, and government may allow only one. A demonstration or parade on a large street during rush hour might put an intolerable burden on the essential flow of traffic, and for that reason could be prohibited. If overamplified loudspeakers assault the citizenry, government may turn them down. Subject to such reasonable regulation, however, peaceful demonstrations in public places are protected by the First

Types of Public and "Quasi-Public" Property

Property	Extent of Use by the Public and Social Protesters	Restrictions that May Be Placed on Use
Publicly owned streets, sidewalks, and parks	Are used extensively by the public and ordinarily will accommodate the exercise of most First Amendment rights.	Reasonable regulations may be imposed to assure public safety and order (for example, traffic regulations).
Government buildings, such as courthouses, and city halls	Are used for the business of government during business hours. Open to the public at these times so that the public may ordinarily come and go as they wish.	Greater restrictions may be imposed to assure the functioning of government or the regular use of the facilities by the public. Can accommodate only limited expressions of social protest.
Public hospitals, schools, libraries, etc.	Use of these public facilities is ordinarily limited to the specific function for which they are designed.	As these facilities need more order and tranquility than do other public buildings, there are generally more restrictions concerning use by the public.
Quasi-public facilities, such as shopping centers, stores, and other privately owned buildings or property to which the public has access	Many quasi-public facilities are as extensively used by the public as are public streets, sidewalks, and parks.	Private owners of quasi-public facilities have greater authority to regulate their property than does the government of public streets and parks (see the material in this chapter).
Public property whose access by the public is limited and restricted	Government may limit and restrict in a reasonable manner the access by the public to jails, executive offices (mayor, police chief, etc.), and other facilities that must be restricted to permit government to function effectively.	Such restrictions must be made in a reasonable and nondiscriminating manner.

Amendment. Of course, where demonstrations turn violent, they lose their protected quality as expression under the First Amendment.[5]

The importance of access to public places for expression has long been recognized by the courts. The Supreme Court of the United States held in 1951 that:

> Wherever the title of streets and parks may rest, they have immemorially been held in trust for use of the public and, time out of mind, have been used for purposes of assembly, communicating thoughts between citizens, and discussing public questions. Such use of the streets and public places has, from ancient times, been a part of the privileges, immunities, rights, and liberties of citizens.[6]

Some of the cases establishing this broad right of access to public places are:

EDWARDS v. SOUTH CAROLINA
Supreme Court of the United States (1963) 372 U.S. 229, 83 S.Ct. 680

The U.S. Supreme Court reversed the convictions of 187 students for breach of the peace. The students were conducting an orderly demonstration on the South Carolina State House grounds, carrying placards with such messages as "I am proud to be a Negro" and "Down with segregation."

BROWN v. LOUISIANA
Supreme Court of the United States (1966) 383 U.S. 131, 86 S.Ct. 719

TINKER v. DES MOINES SCHOOL DIST.
Supreme Court of the United States (1969) 393 U.S. 503, 89 S.Ct. 733

In the *Brown* case, the Supreme Court vacated convictions of five blacks for breach of the peace. The blacks sat or stood silently in a branch library that served only white persons. In the *Tinker* case, the Court held that a school could not discipline students for wearing black armbands in school in protest against the Vietnam War. In both cases, the defendants communicated political messages without disrupting the functions of either the library or the school.

UNITED STATES v. GRACE
Supreme Court of the United States (1983) 461 U.S. 171, 103 S.Ct. 1702

Mary Grace stood alone on the sidewalk in front of the U.S. Supreme Court with a sign containing the words of the First Amendment. Earlier, Thad Zywicki, also standing alone in front of the Supreme Court, had passed out leaflets to passersby. Both were told that all such expressive conduct on the grounds of the U.S. Supreme Court were forbidden by a federal statute (40 U.S.C.A. 13k), and that if they did not discontinue their activity and leave, they would be arrested. Both peacefully left the grounds, but Mr. Zywicki first protested "that he was denied a right that others were granted," referring to the newspaper vending machines located on the sidewalks. Both challenged the statute. In holding that public streets and sidewalks occupy a "special position in terms of First Amendment protection" and that the government's ability to restrict expressive activity "is very limited," the Supreme Court held the federal statute 40 U.S.C.A. 13k unconstitutional and void, further stating:

> *We do not denigrate the necessity to protect persons and property or to maintain proper order and decorum within the Supreme Court grounds, but we do question whether a total ban on carrying a flag, banner, or device on the public sidewalks substantially serves these purposes. There is no suggestion, for example, that appellees' activities in any way obstructed the sidewalks or access to the building, threatened injury to any person or property, or in any way interfered with the orderly administration of the building or other parts of the grounds. As we have said, the building's perimeter sidewalks are indistinguishable from other public sidewalks in the city that are normally open to the conduct that is at issue here and that § 13k forbids.*

BOOS v. BARRY
Supreme Court of the United States (1988) 485 U.S. 312, 108 S.Ct. 1157

Michael Boos and other persons wanted to carry signs critical of the governments of the Soviet Union and Nicaragua near the embassies of those governments in Washington, D.C. But the District of Columbia Code (section 22−1115) forbade such picketing within 500

Limits on Lawful Demonstrations and Other Conduct Protected by the First Amendment[15]

There Is No Constitutional Right to	Facts of the Case	Ruling of U.S. Supreme Court
Camp and sleep in national parks in downtown Washington, D.C. (the Mall and Lafayette Park)	Demonstrators argued that "without a permit to sleep, it would be difficult to get the poor and homeless to participate or to be present at all" in a demonstration to call attention to the plight of the homeless.	"[T]here is a substantial Governmental interest in conserving park property. ... [We are not going to] assign to the judiciary the authority to replace the Park Services as the manager of the Nation's parks. ..." *Clark v. Community for Creative Non-violence,* 468 U.S. 288, 104 S.Ct. 3065 (1984)
Destroy government property (burn draft card issued to person)	As a protest against the Vietnam War, O'Brien burnt his draft card in a public demonstration in violation of federal law. O'Brien wanted "to carry a message" of protest against the draft.	In affirming O'Brien's conviction, the Court noted that the draft card "furthers an important or substantial government interest ... unrelated to the suppression of free expression...." *U.S. v. O'Brien,* 397 U.S. 367, 88 S.Ct. 1673 (1968)
Trespass on government property in area closed to the general public	Demonstrators entered jail grounds through a driveway used only for purposes relating to jail business. They were arrested after they refused to leave after being requested to leave and warned.	"Nothing in the Constitution ... prevents Florida from even-handed enforcement of its general trespass statute. ... The State, no less than a private owner of property, has power to preserve the property under its control for the use to which it is lawfully dedicated. ..." *Adderley v. Florida,* 385 U.S. 39, 87 S.Ct. 242 (1966)

continued

feet of foreign embassies. Boos and others challenged the statute. In holding that part of the Code was unconstitutional, the Court stated:

> *[W]e conclude that the availability of alternatives such as § 112 amply demonstrates that the display clause is not crafted with sufficient precision to withstand First Amendment scrutiny. It may serve an interest in protecting the dignity of foreign missions, but it is not narrowly tailored; a less restrictive alternative is readily available.... Thus, even assuming for present purposes that the dignity interest is "compelling," we hold that the display clause of § 22–1115 is inconsistent with the First Amendment.*

Can There Be Limits and Restrictions on First Amendment Activities?

Persons lawfully present in a public place have a right to engage in peaceable and orderly conduct that is not incompatible with the place in question. That place might be a school,[7] a library,[8] a private lunch counter,[9] the grounds of a statehouse,[10] the grounds of the U.S. Capitol,[11] a bus terminal,[12] an airport,[13] or a welfare center.[14]

Limits on Lawful Demonstrations and Other Conduct Protected by the First Amendment continued

There Is No Constitutional Right to	*Facts of the Case*	*Ruling of U.S. Supreme Court*
Sell or solicit funds at a fairground, airport, etc. in violation of a rule limiting such conduct to fixed locations (booths, tables, etc.)	The Krishna religion (ISKCON) challenged such a regulation arguing that it violated its religious ritual of Sankirtan, which requires its members to go into public places to sell and distribute religious literature and to solicit donations for the support of the Krishna religion.	In holding that such activities, protected by the First Amendment, are subject to reasonable time, place, and manner restrictions the Supreme Court sustained such rule holding: [T]he rule does not exclude ISKCON from the fairgrounds, nor does it deny that organization the right to conduct any desired activity at some point within the forum. Its members may mingle with the crowd and orally propagate their views. The organization may also arrange for a booth and distribute and sell literature and solicit funds from that location on the fairgrounds itself. The Minnesota State Fair is a limited public forum in that it exists to provide a means for a great number of exhibitors temporarily to present their products or views, be they commercial, religious, or political, to a large number of people in an efficient fashion. Considering the limited functions of the Fair and the combined area within which it operates, we are unwilling to say that Rule 6.05 does not provide ISKCON and other organizations with an adequate means to sell and solicit on the fairgrounds. The First Amendment protects the right of every citizen to "reach the minds of willing listeners and to do so there must be opportunity to win their attention." *Kovacs v. Cooper,* 336 U.S. 77, 87, … Rule 6.05 does not unnecessarily limit that right within the fairgrounds. *Heffron v. Intern. Soc. for Krishna Consciousness,* 101 S.Ct. 2559 (1981) ("ISKCON")

First Amendment freedoms and the rights of expression in public places, however, are not absolute. They may be limited or restricted as illustrated by the U.S. Supreme Court cases in the following chart. When a city, state, or governmental agency restricts or limits conduct, there must be a showing that:

1. There is a significant governmental interest (or good reason) based upon the nature of the property, or from some other source.
2. However, the restriction or limitation can be no greater "than is essential to the furtherance of that (substantial) interest." *United States v. O'Brien* (see chart)

3. "The State, no less than a private owner of property, has the power to preserve the property under its control for the use to which it is lawfully dedicated." *Adderley v. Florida* (see chart)
4. Where there is communication (for example, yelling at a basketball game in a public arena as distinguished from yelling in a library or during a church service), the U.S. Supreme Court has said:

> "the crucial question is whether the manner of expression is basically incompatible with the normal activity of a particular place at a particular time." *Grayned v. City of Rockford*, 408 U.S. 104, 92 S.Ct. 2294 (1972)

In addition, such restrictions or limitations on freedom of expression:

- cannot be made because of its message (an unpopular political or religious, etc. message), and
- must be evenhanded enforcement applied to all persons and groups.

Residential Picketing[16]

Picketing is a form of communication protected by the First Amendment. Persons may picket city hall or the state capitol with messages. Strikers may picket their place of employment with signs telling the public why they are striking. All public places may be picketed, but may a law be passed forbidding the picketing of a private home? That was the issue presented to the U.S. Supreme Court in the following 1988 case:

FRISBY v. SCHULTZ
Supreme Court of the United States (1988) 487 U.S. 474, 108 S.Ct. 2495

The town of Brookfield, Wisconsin, (a suburb of Milwaukee) enacted an ordinance forbidding the picketing before or about any residence in the town. Sandra Schultz and others were strongly opposed to abortion and expressed their views on the subject by peaceful picketing on a public street outside the home of a doctor who performed abortions at two clinics in the area. The Supreme Court held that the ordinance was a valid limit of the First Amendment right to picket. Cities, towns, and villages may enact such ordinances:

1. If "alternative channels of communications" are left open. In this case, Ms. Schultz and other protestors could "enter such neighborhoods, alone or in groups, even marching. . . . They may go door-to-door to proselytize their views. They may distribute literature in this manner . . . or through the mails. They may contact residents by telephone, short of harassment."
2. If the ordinance is "narrowly tailored to serve a significant government interest." The Court held:

* * *

The type of focused picketing prohibited by the Brookfield ordinance is fundamentally different from more generally directed means of communication that may not be completely banned in residential areas. . . . Here, in contrast, the picketing is narrowly directed at the household, not the public. The type of picketers banned by the Brookfield ordinance generally do not seek to disseminate a message to the general public, but to intrude upon the targeted resident, and to do so in an especially offensive way. Moreover, even if some such picketers have a broader

Statutes and Ordinances Used to Maintain Public Order

"... where demonstrations turn violent, they lose their protected quality as expression under the First Amendment." U.S. Supreme Court in *Grayned v. City of Rockford*, 92 S.Ct. at 2303

Governments May Regulate Parades, Demonstrations, and Large Meetings of Groups of People in Public Places by:

1. requiring permits that state time, place, etc. (parade permits, permits to use parks, etc.)
2. enforcing existing ordinances and laws that deal with:

   - walking against traffic signals
   - jaywalking
   - blocking sidewalks, entrances to buildings, streets, etc.
   - disorderly conduct, loitering, unlawful assembly, etc.
   - forbidding loud and unnecessary noises

3. ordinances and laws forbidding picketing and demonstrations:

   - in or so many feet from a courthouse
   - on school grounds
   - in public buildings, etc.

"Suspicious" Persons or "Prowlers"

Persons near the scene of a crime or persons in an area late at night

- voluntary conversations with person
- loitering and prowling ordinances or statutes
- trespassing ordinances/statutes
- disorderly conduct/person statutes
- motor vehicle or traffic regulations

Disruptive Persons

Persons blocking sidewalks, passageways, roadways, or persons violating criminal law

- disorderly person/conduct or violation of other criminal statute or ordinance
- unlawful assembly law
- riot statutes

communicative purpose, their activity nonetheless inherently and offensively intrudes on residential privacy. The devastating effect of targeted picketing on the quiet enjoyment of the home is beyond doubt:

" 'To those inside ... the home becomes something less than a home when and while the picketing ... continue[s]. ... [The] tensions and pressures may be psychological, not physical, but they are not, for that reason, less inimical to family privacy and truely domestic tranquility.' " Carey, 447 U.S., at 478 (REHNQUIST, J., dissenting) (quoting Wauwatosa v. King, 49 Wis.2d 398, 411–412, 182 N.W.2d 530, 537 (1971)).

* * *

Because the picketing prohibited by the Brookfield ordinance is speech directed primarily at those who are presumptively unwilling to receive it, the State has a substantial and justifiable interest in banning it. The nature and scope of this interest make the ban narrowly tailored. The ordinance also leaves open ample alternative channels of communication and is content-neutral.

Regulation by Municipalities of Parades, Demonstrations, and Assemblies

Many municipalities require that groups obtain permits in advance for use of streets or parks. In this manner, municipalities can minimize those inconveniences that a parade or demonstration might cause other persons. Parades and demonstrations can be scheduled at times other than rush-hour traffic periods and so that sufficient law enforcement officers are in the area to handle traffic and other problems. The following cases illustrate situations that have come before courts:

WE'VE CARRIED THE RICH, ETC. v. CITY OF PHILADELPHIA
United States District Court (1976) 414 F.Supp. 611, 19 CrL 2273

The plaintiff coalition wanted to conduct a July 4th parade near the official bicentennial activities in Philadelphia. The Federal District Court affirmed the city's refusal to issue a permit because contact between the two groups might lead not only to confusion, but also to violence. The Federal Court held: "If anything is clear in the area of freedom of expression, it is that two parades cannot march on the same street simultaneously and the city may allow only one."

VIETNAM VETERANS AGAINST WAR v. MORTON
United States Court of Appeals, District of Columbia (1974) 164 U.S.App.D.C. 391, 506 F.2d 53

The Court held that the protest group had no constitutional right to camp and cook food on the Capital Mall in Washington, D.C., and that they were properly denied a permit.

NATIONAL SOCIALIST PARTY OF AMERICA v. VILLAGE OF SKOKIE
Supreme Court of the United States (1977) 434 U.S. 1327, 98 S.Ct. 14, 21 CrL 4088

(The 1978 decision of the Illinois Supreme Court of this case is presented in chapter 10). As a result of hearings in a series of courts, it was held that the Nazis must be issued a permit to parade in the largely Jewish suburb of Skokie, Illinois. The Nazis would be permitted to march in their storm trooper uniforms and to display swastikas.

Presence in Government Buildings or Offices as a Form of Protest

Municipalities, states, and the federal government may regulate the use of their buildings in a reasonable manner. The following cases illustrate such regulations:

ALONSO v. STATE
Supreme Court of Georgia (1973) 231 Ga. 444, 202 S.E.2d 37

The defendant and some 40 other students and faculty representatives went to the office of the president of the University of Georgia. After being informed that the president would not be in his office that day, they presented their petition on housing disputes to the president's assistant. After an hour, during which time they were milling around the offices, they were asked to leave. After they refused, the University Director of Public Safety asked secretaries in the office whether their work was being interrupted. When the secretaries stated that their work was being interrupted, the defendant and others were told that they must leave. After the defendants again refused, they were arrested for criminal trespass. In affirming the convictions, the Supreme Court of Georgia held:

> *The fact that appellants were on public property at the time they were requested to leave is immaterial. See Adderly v. Florida, 385 U.S. 39, 87 S.Ct. 242, 17 L.Ed.2d 149. It has been held many times, both here and in the United States Supreme Court, that the rights protected by the First Amendment to the United States Constitution, though fundamental, are not absolute, and must be tempered to a degree by the concepts of order and a healthy respect for the rights of other citizens. The constitutional attacks here made are without merit.*

When an Officer May Order a Person (or Persons) in Public Places to "Move On"

The First Amendment gives all persons the constitutional right "peaceably to assemble." Therefore, an officer may not without good and sufficient reasons having to do with public order or keeping the streets open for public use order a person to "move on" and then arrest him or her for failure to comply with the order. In previous cases, defendants were arrested when they refused to leave government offices or buildings. In the following cases, the defendants were in public places when ordered to "move on" by a law enforcement officer:

SHUTTLESWORTH v. BIRMINGHAM
Supreme Court of the United States (1965) 382 U.S. 87, 86 S.Ct. 211

The defendant, a civil rights leader, and ten or twelve companions were standing on a sidewalk outside a department store when Patrolman Byars of the Birmingham Police Department observed the group. After a minute or so, Byars walked up and told them they would have to move on and clear the sidewalk. Some, but not all, of the group began to disperse, and Byars repeated this request twice. In response to the second request, Shuttlesworth said, "You mean to say we can't stand here on the sidewalk?" After the third request he asked "Do you mean to tell me we can't stand here in front of this store?" By this time everybody in the group but Shuttlesworth had begun to walk away, and Patrolman Byars told him that he was under arrest. Shuttlesworth then responded, "Well, I will go into the store," and walked into the entrance of the adjacent department store. Byars followed and took him into custody just inside the store's entrance.

Noting the lack of any evidence showing that defendant Shuttlesworth actually did block or obstruct the sidewalk for the use of other persons and pedestrian traffic, the Supreme Court reversed the conviction, quoting the Alabama Court of Appeals on another case regarding the same ordinance as follows:

> *The ordinance, that court has ruled, "is directed at obstructing the free passage over, on or along a street or sidewalk by the manner in which a person accused stands, loiters or walks thereupon. Our decisions make it clear that the mere refusal to move on after a police officer's requesting that a person standing or loitering should do so is not enough to support the offense.... [T]here must also be a showing of the accused's blocking free passage." Middlebrooks v. City of Birmingham, 42 Ala.App. 525, 527, 170 So.2d 424, 426.*
>
> *There was thus no evidence whatever in the record to support the petitioner's conviction under this ordinance as it has been authoritatively construed by the Alabama Court of Appeals. It was a violation of due process to convict and punish him without evidence of his guilt.*

Obeying Lawful Police Orders

Failure to obey a lawful, valid police order is probably punished as an offense in all states. For example, Section 843.02 of the Florida Criminal Code forbids *resisting officer without violence:* "Whoever shall obstruct or oppose any such officer . . . in the execution of legal process or in the lawful execution of any legal duty . . . shall be guilty of a misdemeanor of the first degree."

A defense to the charge of refusal to obey a police order is an attack on the lawfulness of the order. If the order is not lawful, there would be no duty to obey. Another defense in all criminal cases would be conviction for a criminal charge that was never made (issuing the wrong criminal charge). The following cases illustrate:

Case	Facts of Case	Ruling
Gregory v. City of Chicago, Supreme Court of United States, 89 S.Ct. 946 (1969)	Comedian Dick Gregory was leading a peaceful and orderly demonstration to the home of the Chicago mayor. Police officers accompanied the marchers and things went very well until persons in a large crowd near the mayor's home began throwing rocks and eggs at the demonstrators. Tough, foul language was directed toward them. As the situation was dangerous and becoming riotous, the senior police officer asked and then ordered Gregory to discontinue the march and lead the demonstrators out of the area. After repeated refusals, Gregory and others were arrested for disorderly conduct (not the charge of refusal to obey a police officer) and fined $200. The U.S. Supreme Court reversed the convictions holding:	. . . (Dick Gregory and others) were convicted not for the manner in which they conducted their march but rather for their refusal to disperse when requested to do so by Chicago police. However reasonable the police request may have been and however laudable the police motives, petitioners were charged and convicted for holding a demonstration, not for a refusal to obey a police officer. As we said in *Garner v. Louisiana,* 368 U.S. 157, 164, 82 S.Ct. 248 (1961): "[I]t is as much a denial of due process to send an accused to prison following conviction for a charge that was never made as it is to convict him upon a charge for which there is no evidence to support that conviction."
Norwell v. City of Cincinnati, Supreme Court of United States, 94 S.Ct. 187 (1973)	The defendant, a sixty-nine-year-old man, was walking home from work about 10:45 P.M. on Christmas night in a high-crime neighborhood. A police officer approached the defendant because he had been notified of a "suspicious man" in the neighborhood. When the officer asked the defendant if he lived in the area, the defendant looked at him and walked on. The officer then stopped the defendant twice, but each time the defendant threw off the officer's arm and protested, "I don't tell you people anything." The defendant would not stay in the officer's presence and would not answer any of the officer's questions. The defendant was charged and convicted of disorderly conduct (not refusal to obey a police officer). The U.S. Supreme Court reversed the conviction holding:	Upon this record, we are convinced that petitioner was arrested and convicted merely because he verbally and negatively protested Officer Johnson's treatment of him. Surely, one is not to be punished for nonprovocatively voicing his objection to what he obviously felt was a highly questionable detention by a police officer. Regardless of what the motivation may have been behind the expression in this case, it is clear that there was no abusive language or fighting words. If there had been, we would have a different case. See *Chaplinsky v. New Hampshire,* 315 U.S. 568.

continued

Obeying Lawful Police Orders continued

Case	Facts of Case	Ruling
King v. City of Oak Creek, Supreme Court of Wisconsin, 436 N.W. 2d 285 (1989)	When a commercial airline crashed near an airport, the site was sealed off so that emergency equipment and personnel could assist the injured and dying. The defendant and other employees of a newspaper were repeatedly ordered to leave the area, but the defendant wanted to take pictures of the crash site and stated that he would not leave unless he was arrested. The defendant was arrested and convicted of disorderly conduct (not the charge of refusal to obey the police order). The Supreme Court of Wisconsin affirmed his conviction and $40 fine.	... The mere refusal to obey a police command does not ordinarily ... constitute disorderly conduct. Mere presence absent any conduct which tends to cause or provoke a disturbance does not constitute disorderly conduct. To hold without limitation that any violation of a police command, whether or not lawful, constitutes disorderly conduct would be patently violative of the fourteenth amendment. *See Gregory v. City of Chicago*, 394 U.S. 111 * * * ... We conclude that the appellant's repeated refusal to obey Detective White's reasonable order, combined with his continued penetration into a nonpublic restricted area in the presence of the general public, was conduct of a type which tends to cause or provoke a disturbance, under the circumstances as they then existed. Therefore, we affirm the decision of the circuit court finding the appellant guilty of disorderly conduct ...
Storey v. Georgia, Court of Appeals of Georgia, 351 S.E.2d 502, review denied. U.S.Sup.Ct., 41 CrL 4023 (1987)	The defendant and others disrupted the Georgia legislature by shouting opposition to the death penalty. They then refused to obey orders of police and security persons to leave the State Capitol building.	Convictions for disrupting the legislature and refusal to obey orders were affirmed and review was denied by the U.S. Supreme Court.
State v. Werstein, Supreme Court of Wisconsin, 211 N.W.2d 437 (1973)	Three women and one man protested against the military by refusing to leave the waiting area of an Armed Forces induction center. There was no evidence they interfered with or disrupted the functioning of the center. The Court did not believe that the staff of the center feared for their safety because of the presence of the group. The conviction of disorderly conduct was reversed.	The defendants were merely present. Mere presence absent any conduct which tends to cause or provoke a disturbance does not constitute disorderly conduct.
State v. Jaramillo, Supreme Court of New Mexico, 498 P.2d 687 (1972)	The defendants sat and lay on the floor in the governor's waiting room. They refused to leave when the office closed at 5:00 P.M. and refused to leave when the building closed at 6:00 P.M. They were convicted under the New Mexico "wrongful use of public property" statute.	The convictions were affirmed and the statute was held to be constitutional. The court stated: "There is no question but that a State may regulate the use and occupancy of public buildings."

BROWN v. LOUISIANA
Supreme Court of the United States (1966) 383 U.S. 131, 86 S.Ct. 719

Five black members of Congress of Racial Equality (CORE) were arrested when they refused to "move on" and leave a segregated reading room of a public library on the order of a sheriff. At the time of their arrest, the defendants were conducting themselves in a quiet and orderly manner. In reversing the convictions, the Supreme Court stated:

> *Petitioners cannot constitutionally be convicted merely because they did not comply with an order to leave the library. See* Shuttlesworth v. City of Birmingham. . . . *The statute itself reads in the conjunctive; it requires both the defined breach of peace and an order to move on. Without reference to the statute, it must be noted that petitioners' presence in the library was unquestionably lawful. It was a public facility, open to the public. Negroes could not be denied access since white persons were welcome. . . .*
>
> *Petitioners' deportment while in the library was unexceptionable. They were neither loud, boisterous, obstreperous, indecorous nor impolite. There is no claim that, apart from the continuation—for ten or fifteen minutes—of their presence itself, their conduct provided a basis for the order to leave, or for a charge of breach of the peace. . . .*
>
> *Here, there was no disturbance of others, no disruption of library activities, and no violation of any library regulations.*
>
> *A State or its instrumentality may, of course, regulate the use of its libraries or other public facilities. But it must do so in a reasonable and nondiscriminatory manner, equally applicable to all and administered with equality to all. It may not do so as to some and not as to all. It may not provide certain facilities for whites and others for Negroes. And it may not invoke regulations as to use—whether they are ad hoc or general—as a pretext for pursuing those engaged in lawful, constitutionally protected exercise of their fundamental rights.*

COLTEN v. COMMONWEALTH
Supreme Court of the United States (1972) 407 U.S. 104, 92 S.Ct. 1953

Law enforcement officers stopped a vehicle on a highway to issue a traffic ticket. The defendant also stopped his car and identified himself as a friend of the person receiving the ticket. When the defendant began to argue, he was asked to leave four or five times by one officer and three times by another officer. When he called the officers "pigs," he was arrested for disorderly conduct. (This case is also cited in chapter 10, as one of the officers called Colten a "loudmouth" in response to being called a "pig.") Colten appealed his disorderly conduct conviction to the U.S. Supreme Court, arguing that he had a right to remain at the scene when his friend was receiving a traffic ticket. In rejecting this argument, the Supreme Court held:[17]

> *Nor can we believe that Colten, although he was not trespassing or disobeying any traffic regulation himself, could not be required to move on. He had no constitutional right to observe the issuance of a traffic ticket or to engage the issuing officer in conversation at the time. The State has a legitimate interest in enforcing its traffic laws and its officers were entitled to enforce them free from possible interference or interruption from bystanders, even those claiming a third-party interest in the transaction. Here the police had cause for apprehension that a roadside strip, crowded with persons and automobiles, might expose the entourage, passing motorists, and police to the risk of accident. We cannot disagree with the finding below that the order to disperse was suited to the occasion. We thus see nothing unconstitutional in the manner in which the statute was applied.*

Unlawful Assemblies and Riots

Under the old common law, an unlawful assembly was a gathering of three or more persons for any unlawful purpose or under such circumstances as to endanger the public peace or cause alarm and apprehension.[18]

An unlawful assembly became a riot under the old common law when those assembled began to execute their enterprise by a breach of the peace. A riot was a tumultuous disturbance of the peace by three or more persons assembled with a common purpose to do an unlawful act. Riot was a misdemeanor at common law, with all persons who encouraged, promoted, or took part in it being criminally liable.

Many states have statutorized one or both of these common law crimes. The state of New York, for example, has enacted the following offenses:[19]

- Section 240.10 Unlawful assembly (class B misdemeanor)
- Section 240.08 Inciting to riot (class A misdemeanor)
- Section 240.06 Riot in the first degree (class E felony)
- Section 240.05 Riot in the second degree (class A misdemeanor)

The present Federal Riot Control Statute, Section 2102, Title 18, United States Code Annotated is as follows:

> (a) As used in this chapter, the term "riot" means a public disturbance involving (1) an act or acts of violence by one, or more persons part of an assemblage, of three or more persons, which act or acts shall constitute a clear and present danger of, or shall result in, damage or injury to the property of any other person or to the person of any other individual or (2) a threat or threats of the commission of an act or acts of violence by one or more persons part of an assemblage of three or more persons having, individually or collectively, the ability of immediate execution of such threat or threats, where the performance of the threatened act or acts of violence would constitute a clear and present danger of, or would result in, damage or injury to the property of any other person or, to the person of any other individual.

Disruption of Religious Services, Public and Private Meetings

Many types of meetings and religious services are conducted daily and weekly throughout the United States. Audiences have a right to hear a speaker, and persons attending religious services have a right not to be disturbed. The Supreme Court of the United States has stated: "Hecklers may be expelled from assemblies and religious worship may not be disturbed by those anxious to preach a doctrine of atheism. The right to speak one's mind would often be an empty privilege in a place and at a time beyond the protecting hand of the guardians of public order."[20]

In the 1966 case of *State v. Smith*,[21] the defendant was ordered to leave a city council meeting on urban redevelopment because of his disruptive conduct. When the defendant resisted a police officer's efforts to remove him, he was arrested for disorderly conduct. In affirming the defendant's conviction, the Supreme Court of New Jersey held:

> Government could not govern if its vital processes could thus be brought to a halt. . . . The chair must have the power to suppress a disturbance or the threat of one, and the power to quell a disturbance would be empty if its exercise could be met by still another disturbance designed to test the officer's judgment. 46 N.J. at 517, 218 A.2d at 150.

Other meetings and religious services cases include:

STATE v. ENCALADE
Court of Appeals of Louisiana (1987) 505 So.2d 87, appeal dismissed by U.S. Supreme Court, 42 CrL 4057 (1987)

Defendants and about one hundred members of the Fisherman and Concerned Citizens Association filled the Plaquemines Parish (county) council chambers and requested the council to address the issue of unemployment in the parish and to form an unemployment task force. The item was not listed on the council's posted agenda for the meeting. The defendants were told that the job task force issue would be the first order of business at the council's next scheduled meeting the following week. However, a defendant refused to relinquish the floor or to sit down, and insisted on being heard. Other members of the group began speaking out of turn, yelling, clapping, and singing. The uproar continued after two recesses in attempts to restore order. A deputy sheriff then informed the audience that anyone refusing to keep order would be arrested. Defendants who refused were escorted from the chamber, charged with disturbing the peace, and convicted. In affirming the convictions, the Louisiana Court of Appeals held:

> [W]e conclude that there is no constitutional right, federal or state, that permits a citizen to disrupt a lawful meeting of a governmental body by demanding that the body discuss an issue that is not on its scheduled agenda and refusing to relinquish the floor to allow the body to continue its orderly business. Free speech does not belong exclusively to the vociferous. Rules for conducting public meetings must be observed so that everyone is given a chance to speak and be heard. Sometimes, as in this case, a speaker must wait his turn. To permit defendants to commandeer the public meeting and force the parish council to address an issue at defendants' whim would infringe on the rights of other less strident citizens to assemble and conduct governmental business without disruption.

* * *

> Defendants' First Amendment rights do not allow them to seize the rostrum at a public meeting and voice their opinions in violation of the rights of other citizens who have previously scheduled business. To allow defendants to disrupt a public meeting whenever and wherever they please would result in anarchy and a disintegration of our entire government by law. Defendants violated the disturbing the peace statute, and trial court properly convicted them.
> Accordingly, the convictions are affirmed.

REYNOLDS v. TENNESSEE
Supreme Court of the United States (1974) 414 U.S. 1163, 94 S.Ct. 928

The U.S. Supreme Court refused certiorari, thus permitting the defendant's conviction in the lower court to stand. Part of Justice William O. Douglas' dissent is as follows:

> This case involves a demonstration occasioned by the appearance of President Nixon at the week-long Billy Graham East Tennessee Crusade being held at a football stadium in Knoxville. The petitioner, an ordained Methodist minister and a professor of religious studies, was convicted under a Tennessee statute which in relevant part proscribes "willfully disturb[ing] or disquiet[ing] any assemblage of persons met for religious worship . . . by noise, profane discourse, rude or indecent behavior, or any other acts." Disruption of the meeting is not an element of the crime under the statute, and the jury was instructed that "if you find from the evidence

that the defendants indulged in any indecent or improper conduct, so near the worshipping assembly, if you find there was a worshipping assembly present on this occasion, as to attract the notice and attention of persons who were present as a part of the assembly—then, under such a state of facts, if they exist, the defendants would be guilty, and this would be so, whether witnesses say they were disturbed or not."... No evidence was introduced at trial that the meeting was disrupted, in the sense that speakers were shouted down, or that petitioner's group prevented, or sought to prevent, the meeting from proceeding as planned. Nor did the state appellate courts make any such findings in affirming the conviction. Although there were findings that some members of the protest group engaged in obscene chants,[22] it is uncontested that petitioner did not. The undisturbed findings of the state court of criminal appeals were that petitioner "did not chant obscenities and that his intent was for a peaceful demonstration." Petitioner's contentions that the statute was unconstitutionally vague and overbroad were rejected by the state courts.

Disruption of Political Meetings

Some courts have held that more latitude and a greater opportunity to respond should be permitted at political meetings and demonstrations than would be allowed at religious services or other types of meetings. In the case of *City of Spokane v. McDonough*, the defendant shouted "Warmonger" once to the vice-president of the United States during a political speech by the vice-president. In reversing the defendant's conviction for disorderly conduct, the Court held:

> Shouting "Warmonger" but once—without more to indicate a further purpose or intention of breaking up the meeting or to deprive the speaker of his audience or to interfere with the rights of others to hear or the speaker to speak—did not amount to a disturbance of the peace, in fact or in law.[23]

The Supreme Court of California set aside the defendants' convictions for disturbing a lawful meeting in the 1970 case of *In re Kay*. The defendants clapped, shouted slogans, and waved a flag bearing the emblem of farm workers at an open-air meeting in a public park at which a congressman spoke. The Court held:

> After Congressman Tunney had given a portion of his speech, a comparatively small part of the total crowd, between 25 and 250 persons, engaged in rhythmical clapping and some shouting for about five or ten minutes. This demonstration did not affect the program. Congressman Tunney, who had been using a microphone, finished his speech despite the protest, pausing to assure those protesting that they had a right to do so and to urge them to be grateful that they live in a country whose Constitution protects their right to demonstrate in that manner. At no time did either the speaker or the police ask the protestors to be silent or to leave. Following the end of the protest and of the congressman's speech, the fireworks were shown. The police made no arrests during or immediately following the protest; the prosecution filed charges only some two weeks later.

* * *

Audience activities, such as heckling, interrupting, harsh questioning, and booing, even though they may be ... discourteous, can nonetheless advance the goals of the First Amendment. For many citizens such participation in public meetings, whether supportive or critical of the speaker, may constitute the only manner in which they can express their views to a large number of people; the Constitution does not require that the effective expression of ideas be restricted to rigid and predetermined patterns. . . .

In the instant case, the questioned conduct continued for only a few minutes, Congressman Tunney was able to complete his speech, and it does not appear that a large part of the audience could not hear his remarks. We conclude that the state failed to meet its burden of establishing a substantial impairment of the conduct of the meeting.

Finally, we do not believe that there was a sufficient showing that the defendants disturbed the meeting within the constitutionally permissible limits of the statutory term "disturb." Generally, if disturbances are occasioned by nonviolent exercise of free expression, section 403 will require that defendants be shown to have engaged in such conduct with knowledge, or under circumstances in which they should have known, that they were violating an applicable custom, usage, or rule of the meeting. In instances in which the appropriate standard of conduct lies in doubt, a warning and a request that defendants curtail their conduct, either by officials or law enforcement agents, should precede arrest or citation. If section 403 were not so interpreted, individuals would be forced to speculate as to what conduct might entail criminal sanctions and would "necessarily . . . 'steer far wider of the unlawful zone.' "[24]

Public Order in Restaurants, Taverns, and Other Business or Public Places

Such private places as restaurants, theaters, sporting facilities, and taverns are regulated to a large extent by the managers and owners of such facilities. A person using coarse and indecent language in a loud voice in a restaurant, for example, might be asked to leave by the manager or the owner. If he or she failed to leave and continued the disruptive conduct, it is likely that the police would be called. In most instances, the police would order the person to leave if he or she were not too intoxicated to drive. The person's disruptive language would not fall within the "fighting words" doctrine unless it were addressed to a specific person.

In 1977, the case of *Griego v. Wilson*[25] came before the Court of Appeals of New Mexico. Evidence showed that Griego became angry, abusive, and profane and used obscene gestures toward John Wilson and other employees of a lumber store. The employees cautioned Griego to stop and offered to refund his money. When the employees became fearful that Griego was about to attack an employee, they restrained him. In ruling that the employees used reasonable force under the circumstances, the Court held:[26]

> We hold that the proprietor of a business has the right to expel or restrain a person who by virtue of abusive conduct refuses to leave or persists in this abusive conduct after being cautioned, though that person was initially on the premises by express or implied invitation, so long as the expulsion or restraint is by reasonable force. See *Ramirez v. Chavez,* 71 Ariz. 239, 226 P.2d 143 (1951); *Penn v. Henderson,* 174 Or. 1, 146 P.2d 760 (1944); *Crouch v. Ringer,* 110 Wash. 612, 188 P. 782 (1920); *Austin v. Metropolitan Life Insurance Co. of New York,* 106 Wash. 371, 180 P. 134, 6 A.L.R. 1061 (1919); *Johanson v. Huntsman,* 60 Utah 402, 209 P.197 (1922). Annot. Right to Eject Customer from Store, 9 A.L.R. 379.

Civil Liability for Crimes Committed on Premises

Business firms and public organizations do not have an absolute obligation to prevent crimes on their premises, but they do have a duty to provide persons lawfully on their premises with adequate security and safeguards against foreseeable risks.

The Restatement of Torts (2nd) states that civil liability should be imposed:

> for physical harm caused by the accidental, negligent, or intentionally harmful acts of
> third persons . . . and by the failure of the possessor (of premises or land) to exercise
> reasonable care to a) discover that such acts are being done or are likely to be done,
> or b) give (an adequate) warning.

In the 1982 case of *Butler v. Acme Markets Inc.,*[27] the Supreme Court of New
Jersey upheld a jury finding of $3,600 for the sixty-year-old woman plaintiff. Ms.
Butler (the plaintiff) was a customer in the defendant's store and was mugged as
she was putting her purchases in her car in the store parking lot. Plaintiff was the
eighth person to be mugged in a year in the parking lot. The store posted no
warnings and hired one guard who primarily remained inside. The court held that
is was reasonable for a jury to conclude that "absent warnings, hiring one guard
who primarily remained inside the store was an insufficient response in light of
the known repeated history of attacks on the premises."

In December of 1979, eleven young persons died in a stampede to get seats
in a first-come, open seating concert of The Who in Cincinnati's Riverfront
Coliseum. Similar deaths of other young persons also occurred at rock and rap
concerts in Nashville (1985) and Salt Lake City (1991). Generally, criminal
charges are not filed in such cases if promoters are complying with crowd
control laws. However, many wrongful death and negligent injury lawsuits were
filed. Such tragedies should cause cities and states to enact stricter crowd
control laws.

B. Crowd Control (Maintaining Order at Public Events)

Most large public gatherings are orderly and there is little likelihood of disorder
and disruption. However, because there is always the possibility of pickpockets or
purse snatchers, law enforcement officers (or private security persons) are generally present just in case a problem arises.

When there are possibilities of disruptions, fights, or violence, concerned
parties are likely to inform law enforcement agencies of the gathering and request
the presence of police (or deputy sheriffs). Public political meetings and rallies
could attract persons of contrary views who could also attend with the intentions
of disrupting the meeting or staging counter rallies and obtaining media coverage
of such disruptions.

The Ku Klux Klan scheduled sixteen political rallies in Connecticut through
1984. Not only did the Connecticut State Police learn of the planned rallies, but
groups hostile to the KKK also became aware of these meetings. One group, the
International Committee Against Racism (INCAR), had a history of hostile con-
frontations not only with the Klan but also with the police.

To maintain order at the planned KKK rallies, the Connecticut police used as
many of the standard crowd control techniques as they could: increased police
presence, crowd separation (hostile group separations), pre-rally clearance of
sites, and attempts to locate the rallies at sites where the police could best
maintain order.

When the police heard from reliable sources that members of both groups
would be armed and ready to attack one another, the police obtained a state court
injunction forbidding the "carrying on one's person or in a motor vehicle, a

More than two hundred Klansmen exercised their right to demonstrate in College Park, Georgia, in 1987. This gathering, indicative of all KKK exercises, created extreme concern over public order. In 1990, the Supreme Court of Georgia upheld the Georgia statute making the public wearing of the KKK mask a criminal act.

firearm or other dangerous weapon" in the vicinity of the rally. Searches of persons seeking to attend the rally produced an assortment of weapons and instruments. A number of persons were injured at the rally.

No court order was obtained for the next demonstration although the crowds were much larger, with fifty police officers attempting to maintain order. Only twenty-one Klansmen showed up, but close to 2,000 spectators were present. Rocks and bottles were thrown by anti-Klan groups. Fistfights broke out and violence was urged by a person with a bull horn. Twenty policemen, six Klansmen, and one bystander were injured, most hit with rocks or bricks.

More than one hundred police officers were assigned to the next rally. Pat-down searches were conducted where persons "allegedly consented" to the searches. When the Klan arrived, escorted by the police, INCAR members commenced throwing rocks, bottles, and tin cans. The police halted the rally immediately and ordered the area cleared.

The Use of Magnetometers at Airports, Courthouses, and Political Meetings

As it was clear that there was going to be trouble at all of the remaining scheduled rallies, the police sought court orders forbidding weapons on a person or in a vehicle near or at the scene of a rally. Mass pat-down searches of persons entering rally sites were conducted with some searches of vehicles. In a 1987 decision, the U.S. Court of Appeals for the Second Circuit forbade pat-down searches without reasonable suspicion or probable cause. But the Court held that "general magnetometer (hand-held or stationary) searches at the sites of future Klan rallies . . .

without regard to standards of reasonable suspicion or probable cause" would not violate constitutional rights of persons wishing to attend rallies.[28] In comparing such searches to searches made at airports and courthouses, the court stated:

> It is true that the constitutional right to free speech is implicated here; but the constitutional right to interstate travel is also implicated in airport searches, as is the constitutional right to attend public trials in courtroom searches. The key factor in the cases allowing such searches was the perceived danger of violence, based upon the recent history at such locations, if firearms were brought into them. *See e.g., United States v. Edwards,* 498 F.2d 496, 500 (2d Cir. 1974) (airport search); *United States v. Albarado,* 495 F.2d 799, 806 (2d Cir. 1974) (airport search); *McMorris v. Alioto,* 567 F.2d 897, 899–900 (9th Cir. 1978) (courthouse search); and *Downing v. Kunzig,* 454 F.2d 1230, 1232–33 (6th Cir. 1972) (courthouse search).

In approving the use of the magnetometer, the Court quoted the *Albarado* case as follows:

> . . . passing through a magnetometer has none of the indignities involved in . . . a frisk. The use of the device does not annoy, frighten or humiliate those who pass through it. Not even the activation of the alarm is cause for concern, because such a large number of persons may activate it in so many ways. No stigma or suspicion is cast on one merely through the possession of some small metallic object. Nor is the magnetometer search done surreptitiously, without the knowledge of the person searched. Signs warn passengers of it, and the machine is obvious to the eye.

C. Handbills as a Form of Communication

By standing on a sidewalk of a busy street, a person may communicate with a large number of people by passing out handbills or leaflets. Handbills are an inexpensive means of communication used for many years; their message may be political, religious, social, or commercial.[29] Like pure speech, written communications, such as handbills, cannot urge violence or unlawful acts. They may not contain libel or use clearly obscene communications. They may not direct insulting or "fighting words" to the persons receiving the handbills.

The U.S. Supreme Court observed that "the unwilling listener is not like the passer-by who may be offered a pamphlet in the street but cannot be made to take it."[30] Many of the persons who do accept handbills will only glance at them and then dispose of the material. This, of course, creates a litter problem.

In the 1976 case of *People v. Remeny,* the New York Court of Appeals held:

> It is settled that an ordinance which prohibits the distribution of leaflets or handbills in all public places, at all times and under all circumstances cannot be considered a reasonable regulation of constitutionally protected speech. . . .
>
> If an ordinance absolutely prohibiting all distribution of handbills containing constitutionally protected statements on political, social and religious topics is invalid, then this ordinance relating to commercial speech, now also constitutionally protected, suffers from the same infirmity.
>
> The City of course has a legitimate interest in seeing that the exercise of the right does not contribute to the litter on the streets or otherwise violate the law. Thus they may enact reasonable regulations governing the time, place and circumstances of the distribution. But in our view they cannot enact an ordinance absolutely prohibiting all distribution of commercial handbills on city streets and call it a reasonable regulation of the

activity. Although we sympathize with the City's desire to eliminate litter from the streets, we have concluded that the ordinance, as presently worded, is unconstitutional.[31]

D. Door-to-Door Canvassing as a Form of Communication

Persons running for a political office or persons with a religious message are among those who frequently go from door to door. Door-to-door communication is also used by persons selling a product or a service. Door-to-door calls may be limited to verbal communication alone, or they may be combined (as they are in most instances) with the use of handbills.

Many ordinances and statutes have been passed regulating door-to-door canvassing. These ordinances have been designed to prevent crime, to reduce residents' fears about strangers wandering door to door, and to avoid harassment of dwellers who find it annoying to answer such calls. The U.S. Supreme Court stated in *Martin v. City of Struthers* that:

> Ordinances of the sort now before us may be aimed at the protection of the house-holders from annoyance, including intrusion upon the hours of rest, and at the prevention of crime. Constant callers, whether selling pots or distributing leaflets, may lessen the peaceful enjoyment of a home as much as a neighborhood glue factory or railroad yard which zoning ordinances may prohibit. . . . In addition, burglars frequently pose as canvassers, either in order that they may have a pretense to discover whether a house is empty and hence ripe for burglary, or for the purpose of spying out the premises in order that they may return later. Crime prevention may thus be the purpose of regulatory ordinances.[32]

In the *City of Struthers* case, the U.S. Supreme Court struck down a municipal ordinance that made it a crime for a solicitor or canvasser to knock on the front door of a resident's home or to ring the doorbell. The Court held that the manner in which the ordinance was written conflicted "with the freedoms of speech and press."

States and municipalities, however, do have the authority to regulate door-to-door canvassing. As door-to-door canvassing falls under the First Amendment, "government may regulate . . . only with narrow specificity."[33] The U.S. Supreme Court affirmed the right to regulate door-to-door canvassing in the 1976 case of *Hynes v. Mayor and Council of Borough of Oradel,* holding:

> There is, of course, no absolute right under the Federal Constitution to enter on the private premises of another and knock on a door for any purpose, and the police power permits reasonable regulation for public safety. We cannot say, and indeed appellants do not argue, that door-to-door canvassing and solicitation are immune from regulation under the State's police power, whether the purpose of the regulation is to protect from danger or to protect the peaceful enjoyment of the home.

Possible regulations of door-to-door canvassing could be: a) a requirement that payment and delivery of an item occur twenty-four or forty-eight hours after the initial call at the home; or b) a requirement that canvassers secure permits and be responsive to complaints; or c) an ordinance that forbids door-to-door sales without first obtaining an invitation to enter the premise.

E. Exercising First Amendment Freedoms in Shopping Centers and Other Privately Owned Property

Malls, shopping centers, and supermarkets are privately owned properties that are open to the public. Many shopping centers and supermarkets forbid demonstrations and the distribution of handbills on their property.

Whether First Amendment freedoms such as passing out handbills, picketing, etc. can occur in shopping centers and malls would be determined in most cases by the laws of each state and the state court decisions. For example, in the case of *PruneYard Shopping Center v. Robins,* 447 U.S. 74, 100 S.Ct. 2035 (1980), the California Supreme Court held that the California Constitution protects "speech and petitioning, reasonably exercised, in shopping centers even when the centers are privately owned." The U.S. Supreme Court held that neither property rights nor the First Amendment rights of the owners had been infringed by the decision of the California Supreme Court.

Other state supreme courts have held differently than the California Supreme Court. For example, in the 1987 case of *Jacobs v. Major,* 139 Wis.2d 492, 407 N.W.2d 832, the Wisconsin Supreme Court held that shopping centers and malls may restrict activities such as demonstrations and distribution of handbills on their property. In that case, the shopping center showed that it lost money because of demonstrations on its property. The Supreme Court of Wisconsin pointed out that the function of malls is to make money for its owners.

Some shopping centers and malls restrict political and religious communications on their property to booths or tables provided for such persons by the managers of the shopping centers.

F. Other Public Order Aspects of American Streets

The Homeless (Street People)

Private organizations have estimated the number of homeless in the United States at 500,000 to 600,000. After the 1990 census, the federal government estimated the number of homeless in the United States at 230,000.[34] Every city and county in the United States has to deal with the problem of homelessness and poverty in some form. The article "Police and the Homeless" in the November 1990 issue of the *FBI Law Enforcement Bulletin* points out that "the responsibility of dealing with the homeless on a day-to-day level ultimately falls on the police ...".

It is estimated that about a third of the homeless are only on the street for a short time due to unemployment, eviction, loss of a needed income, or because of a domestic fight or disagreement. Other persons are homeless because of severe alcohol or drug problems. A national organization providing services for the homeless estimates that as many as half of the homeless people are mentally ill or have emotional problems.

About 90 percent of the homeless are males, with women and children making up the balance. Most (about 97 percent) are single, while more than a third of the homeless are veterans. The average age of persons living on the street is about forty, but ages run from the very young to over seventy. More than half of the homeless are white, while blacks, the next largest group, make up a third of the total. Hispanics, native Americans, and other ethnic groups make up small percentages of the balance.

New York City has more homeless people and spends more on them than any other city in the United States. It is also reported that New York City faces the worst drug problem among the homeless. Reports of fights, robberies, theft, and the use of drugs cause some homeless persons to prefer to sleep in the streets rather than go to a homeless shelter.

Panhandling or Begging

Panhandling or begging has always occurred in large cities and elsewhere in the United States. The begging can be friendly and nonaggressive. It could be an impersonal, brief, verbal request for money. Or aggressive, nonfriendly means could be used seeking to obtain funds. Aggressive panhandling can be menacing and threatening. When Bernhard Goetz was approached in a New York subway by four youths, he viewed the aggressive panhandling as so menacing and threatening as to amount to a mugging. New York juries agreed that the young men were demanding money with an implied threat of the immediate use of force.

A belligerent, angry panhandler who follows a person refusing to give money would be using aggressive tactics. The language addressed to the passer-by could become foul and insulting. Placing hands on the person, touching, blocking, or shoving would be further aggressive acts that could cause the pedestrian to become concerned for his or her safety, to take protective action, or to react in anger.

The panhandler could have emotional or mental problems. Or the panhandler could be intoxicated or on drugs. The size and apparent strength of a panhandler as well as the tactics used would be factors. The number of persons in the panhandling group is also important. Street women sometimes are very aggressive, belligerent panhandlers who will occasionally try to extract money from police officers on patrol duty in the area.

Homeless people frequently panhandle for money. Most often the begging is done in a pathetic, impersonal manner, or sometimes a friendly appeal to generosity is used. College students are said to be the most likely group to make contributions. Older persons are more likely to believe that any money given will be used for alcohol or drugs.

Because of increasing complaints of aggressive panhandling in large American cities, new ordinances and laws against begging are being enacted. In 1987, Seattle, Washington, enacted an ordinance forbidding intimidation or obstruction of passers-by. The law particularly seeks to protect older persons and children from aggressive begging.

The City of New York began enforcing its ban on begging in the New York City subway system, and a lawsuit was filed challenging the enforcement. Lawyers for a group of homeless people argued that asking others for money was a form of free speech that the government could not prohibit. In November 1990 the U.S. Court of Appeals for the Second Circuit held that begging was essentially "conduct" and not speech, and that the free-speech protections that the U.S. Supreme Court has given to solicitors for organized charities did not apply to panhandlers. The U.S. Supreme Court denied review in the case, *Young v. New York City Transit Authority,* 903 F.2d 146 (2d Cir. 1990). Review denied by the U.S. Supreme Court, 11/26/90. The Court of Appeals stated:

* * *

...The New York City Subway System transports approximately 3,500,000 passengers on an average workday, operates twenty-four hours a day, seven days a week, and consists of 648 miles of track, 468 subway stations and over 6,000 subway cars. Many parts of the subway system are almost one hundred years old. In a timeworn routine of New York City life, each day a multitude descends the steep and long staircases and mechanical escalators to wait on narrow and crowded platforms bounded by dark tunnels and high power electrical rails.

In 1988, the TA (Transit Authority) initiated a lengthy study-process concerning "quality of life problems" experienced by riders in their use of the subway system. The study-process disclosed the fact that begging contributes to a public perception that the subway is fraught with hazard and danger. A research survey conducted by Peter Harris revealed that, in fact, two-thirds of the subway ridership have been intimidated into giving money to beggars. The survey also revealed that beggars are perceived to pervade the subway system, and that the ridership considers the presence of beggars as a significant problem.

As another aspect of the study-process, Detective Bernard Jacobs, a twenty-four year veteran of the Transit Authority Police and initiator of the Transit Police Crime Prevention Unit, met with numerous groups of citizens and passengers. He reported that "passengers almost always voice their concern and discomfort about the prevalence of panhandling" in the subway system. The passengers "feel harassed and intimidated by panhandlers." Moreover, "it is difficult from the police perspective to draw the fine line between panhandling and extortion." Many passengers have complained that demands for money by beggars and panhandlers include "unwanted touching, detaining, impeding and intimidating."

* * *

Professor George Kelling, the president of (a) consulting company and an expert with extensive national and international experience in social problems, concluded that behavior such as begging generates "high levels of fear in the passengers, thereby discouraging use of the system." In explaining the need for rules against begging in the subway, Kelling drew a distinction between ordinary city streets and the more constrictive New York City subway system. Open city streets allow pedestrians what sociologists term "fate-control", or the ability to avoid and move away from an intimidating person. To the contrary, subway riders enjoy considerably less fluidity of movement and ability to control what happens to them. Whether standing in the crush of riders in a speeding subway car, waiting among the pressing masses on a platform, or swarming with the throng through a maze of mezzanines, staircases and ramps, the rider feels "captive". As a result, Kelling concluded, "[i]n the subway environment, begging is inherently aggressive even if not patently so." In addition, Kelling concluded that begging not only intimidates passengers, but also "has the serious potential of creating an accident and injuring many people." As Kelling observed, the act of placing a cup before persons is often disruptive, startling and potentially dangerous.

* * *

The Kelling affidavit earmarks research indicating that the homeless in the subways are generally males afflicted with serious mental illness and suffering from alcohol and/or drug abuse. Moreover, the sad statistics reveal that during a ten month period in 1989, an average of six homeless persons per month died in the subway, including fifteen persons who were struck by trains. As a result, Kelling counselled that this "subset of the homeless" should not be encouraged to beg and panhandle in the system "for their own well-being."

* * *

... We are not unaware that the giving of alms has long been considered virtuous in our Western tradition. In antiquity the humanist and jurist, Cicero, said of Caesar: "Of all thy virtues none is more marvelous and graceful than charity." ... The district court itself stated that "[i]n early English common law, begging by those able to work was prohibited, but beggars who were unable to work were licensed and restricted to specific areas." Thus, while there can be no doubt that giving alms is virtuous, in the Western tradition there is also no doubt that the virtue is best served when it reflects an "ordered charity." It does not seem to us that the TA's regulation of solicitation and ban on begging are inconsistent with the concept.

Urinating in a Public Place

Since the first century when the Romans forbade the conduct, urinating in a public place has been an offense. Both European countries and municipalities throughout the United States also forbid such conduct.

However, the offense continues to be a problem. Persons use streets, sidewalks, public buildings, and subways as a toilet. Public officials point out that public urination creates a health hazard and is also very offensive to the general public. Not only is the sight of an adult urinating in a public place offensive, but the smell of urine can linger for some time.

The unavailability of public bathrooms presents a problem in some areas. Private businesses (restaurants, gasoline stations, etc.) can reserve their facilities for their customers and employees. Vandalism and crime has caused the closing of some public toilets. Clogging of toilets is the biggest problem, while in other instances, fixtures are torn off the wall or otherwise damaged. Public facilities are sometimes closed due to a lack of maintenance and cleaning funds.

Safety in toilets in some areas is a serious problem, as criminal assaults are sometimes committed against persons using toilet facilities. Because of purse snatchings, muggings, etc., outer doors to toilet facilities in some airports are kept open to minimize assaults and to minimize the use of restrooms for drug dealing and drug use. Toilet facilities in buildings open to the public are sometimes locked for the same reasons.

Persons charged with urinating in a public place sometimes complain that no toilet facilities were available in the area. Offenders could be persons who have had too much to drink, or are too lazy to seek out a toilet facility. Homeless persons are also sometimes cited as offenders.

Men, by far, are the principal offenders. Enforcement varies with the area of town. Conduct sometimes tolerated in run-down parts of town would not be tolerated in more fashionable areas with beautiful homes and nice shopping centers. In addition, homeowners can become very belligerent if strangers enter their property to urinate. A Milwaukee homeowner was convicted of manslaughter in 1988 because of such a confrontation. He came out of his home in the late afternoon to find a stranger urinating on his flowers. The homeowner angrily scolded the stranger for his conduct. The man responded with ugly language, which was overheard by the homeowner's children. In an overwhelming rage, the homeowner obtained a handgun and shot the stranger, killing him.

Curfews

The use of curfews goes back in history to the Middle Ages. It is reported that William the Conqueror imposed a curfew on the English people after his invasion of England in 1066. Bells were rung in England at 8:00 P.M. at which time fires were to be put out and persons were not to be on the street. This law appears to have been met with so much opposition that, in 1103, it was repealed. Both Blackstone and Shakespeare refer to the use of curfews in early England.

Today, many states and cities have emergency curfew laws, which could be put into effect in the event of an emergency (war, riots, snow emergency, or other wide-spread disasters such as an earthquake). However, a curfew law aimed at all citizens where there is no genuine emergency is not likely to be passed as such a law would not be constitutional. The U.S. Supreme Court has repeatedly pointed out that the "freedom to leave one's house and move about at will is of the very essence of a scheme of ordered liberty."[35]

Many states and municipalities have enacted curfew laws and ordinances requiring teenagers of a specific age to be off the public streets after the curfew time. Such laws and ordinances have been enacted after communities concluded that late-night activities lead teens into drinking, drugs, sex, fighting, vandalism, youth gang activities, and thefts.

According to newspaper reports,[36] curfew laws in Newark, Detroit, Camden, N.J., and Panora, Iowa, have withstood court challenges in recent years. A 1990 curfew law in Atlanta, Georgia, was enacted to curb crime and enforce good parenting. The law provides for parents or guardians of repeat offenders to be jailed up to sixty days and/or fined up to $1,000. Washington, D.C., enacted an area curfew law because of disorders and fighting directed at the police. The following juvenile curfew ordinance was sustained by three courts that reviewed the challenge to the law:

BYKOFSKY ET AL. v. BOROUGH OF MIDDLETOWN
U.S. District Court, Middle District of Pennsylvania (1975) 401 F.Supp. 1242; Affirmed Federal Court of Appeals, 535 F.2d 1245; Review denied 429 U.S. 964, 97 S.Ct. 394 (1976)

A mother and her twelve-year-old son challenged a curfew ordinance requiring minors under eighteen to be off the streets from 11:00 P.M. until 6:00 A.M. with many of the usual exceptions (accompanied by a legal guardian, on the sidewalk of their home or a next-door neighbor, or coming home from a school or religious activity, etc.) The courts sustained the curfew, with the Federal District Court holding:

* * *

> *The rights of locomotion, freedom of movement, to go where one pleases, and to use the public streets in a way that does not interfere with the personal liberty of others are basic values "implicit in the concept of ordered liberty" protected by the due process clause of the fourteenth amendment. United States v. Wheeler, 1920, 254 U.S. 281, 293. . . . One may be on the streets even though he is there merely for exercise, recreation, walking, standing, talking, socializing, or any other purpose that does not interfere with other persons' rights.*

No right is more sacred, or is more carefully guarded, by the liberty assurance of the due process clause than the right of every citizen to the possession and control of his own person, free from restraint or interference by the state. The makers of our Constitution conferred, as against the government, the right to be let alone—the most comprehensive of rights and the right most valued by civilized man. . . . Uninhibited movement is essential to freedom. . . .

However, personal freedoms are not absolute, and the liberty guaranteed by the due process clause implies absence of arbitrary interferences but not immunity from reasonable regulations. . . .

Thus, the question is whether the curfew ordinance is reasonable, with reasonableness being determined by weighing the legitimate interest of the state which the ordinance actually furthers against the competing liberty interests of the minor. This interest balancing-means test requires the court to weigh the governmental interests against the burden upon the minor's rights of freedom of movement and use of the public streets, and to examine the ordinance to insure that it in fact furthers the asserted governmental interests.

* * *

The court holds that the minor's interest in freedom of movement upon the streets during the nighttime curfew hours under circumstances other than those provided for in the numerous curfew exceptions is clearly outweighed by the governmental interests which the ordinance furthers. Hence the ordinance is a reasonable exercise by the Borough of its police power to advance and protect the safety and welfare of the general community and the minors who reside therein. The ordinance is a constitutionally permissible regulation of the minor's right to freedom of movement upon and use of the streets as guaranteed by the due process clause of the fourteenth amendment.

Compulsory School Attendance Laws and Truancy

All states are reported to have laws requiring parents to send their children to school until the age required in that state. Failure to comply with the compulsory attendance statute could result in a civil or criminal conviction of the parents as provided by the statutes of that state.

A student who is not attending school as required can be classified as a truant if the state statutes so provide. Truancy laws vary considerably from state to state. The California Supreme Court stated that a minor (ages six to eighteen) "must be enrolled in a compulsory full-time education program and must be in school during school hours or else he is subject to a section 48264 arrest (truancy arrest)."[37] Exceptions and definitions are found in the laws of probably all states. The following case was before the California Supreme Court:

IN RE JAMES D.
Supreme Court of California (1987) 43 Cal.3d 903, 239 Cal.Rptr. 663, 741 P.2d 161

Police officers observed the defendant walking on a sidewalk over a bridge during school hours. As the defendant appeared to be fifteen or sixteen years old, the officers decided to ask him why he was not in school in order to determine if he was truant. The officers questioned the defendant after he agreed to talk with the officers. The defendant appeared nervous and his voice was shaky. When he suddenly shoved his hand beneath his jacket, an officer asked the defendant to slowly remove his hand. A pat-down for weapons then disclosed a hard object. When the hard object was removed over the resistance of the defendant, a hairbrush and an envelope with LSD fell to the ground. In holding that the police action was proper and lawful if "reasonable suspicion" or consent existed, the California Supreme Court held:

* * *

Courts have long recognized the importance of education to both the individual and to society . . . and defendant does not question the propriety of the compulsory education laws (which, as noted, cover persons aged 6 to 18) as a legitimate means of achieving that objective. As noted above, the legislative scheme is directed toward reforming and returning the truant student to school, and not toward punishment or imposition of traditional criminal sanctions. We conclude that the governmental interest in enforcing its truancy laws in order to achieve its educational goal, is substantial.

* * *

Los Angeles Unified School District, we are told, has about one-half million students enrolled. . . . we find it "ludicrous to assume that law enforcement and school officials would have the slightest chance of intercepting those few students [actually] known by them to be truant." We therefore agree that a section 48264 detention for the purpose of investigating whether a person is a truant is, as a practical matter, the only effective means of identifying and locating truants and hence substantially advances the state's compulsory education goals.

Finally, on balance, we find the degree of interference with personal liberty occasioned by a "truancy detention" to be slight. Questioning must, of course, be strictly limited to the purpose of the stop. . . . As explained above, the sole purpose of a truancy "arrest" is to return the absent student to school as expeditiously as possible. Therefore, "[t]he 'arrest' that takes place under section 48264 is a severely limited type of arrest and may not be used as a pretext for investigating criminal matters." (Miguel G., supra, 111 Cal.App.3d at p. 349, 168 Cal.Rptr. 688) . . . Likewise, the sole purpose of a truancy detention is to investigate whether a particular person is a truant, and if he is in fact a truant, to place him under a section 48264 "arrest" in order to return him to school. We are unwilling to conclude that the limited and brief investigative detention outweighs the legitimate governmental interest here involved.

* * *

Hate Crimes

The term "hate crime" is used to describe crimes committed out of hatred for a person's race, religion, ethnic group, or sexual preference. For examples, gays and lesbians report that they are sometimes the object of hate crimes.

A hate crime could be prosecuted as a regular crime such as assault, criminal damage to property, battery, etc. Some states have statutes that increase the penalty for such offenses if it is shown the offense was committed because of religious, racial, ethnic, or sexual hatred. Some cities have enacted hate statutes ("bias-motivated disorderly conduct"). St. Paul, Minnesota, enacted the following ordinance in 1990:

[w]hoever places on public or private property a symbol, object, appellation, characterization or graffiti, including but not limited to, a burning cross or Nazi swastika,

Freedom to Dress as You Wish

Dressing as you wish is a constitutionally protected freedom that is not specifically stated in the U.S. Constitution. Like other freedoms, however, there are limitations upon it. Some of these limitations are:

- States and cities may (and do) forbid nudity or the exposure of a sex organ in a public place.
- Many jobs, occupations, and professions have dress requirements that must be complied with if a person wants to keep his or her job. In 1986, the U.S. Supreme Court affirmed the uniform requirement of the U.S. Air Force when an officer would not comply and was dropped from the service. *Goldman v. Weinberger,* 475 U.S. 503, 106 S.Ct. 1310.
- Wearing a bulletproof garment or concealing identity while committing a crime is punishable in many (if not all) states in addition to the crime committed.
- The Supreme Court of Georgia held in 1990 that wearing the mask and hood of the Ku Klux Klan can be punished as a crime. The Court held that the Klan's history of anonymous violence makes the mask a form of intimidation subject to government control. *State v. Miller,* ___ A. 2d ___.

One of the many dangers in picking up a prostitute is the possibility that the person dressed as a woman may be a man dressed in women's clothing. To minimize this type of dangerous trap, the City of Chicago passed an ordinance forbidding cross-dressing by men (the ordinance did not forbid women from wearing men's clothing in public). The defendants who were arrested argued they were male transsexuals "undergoing psychiatric therapy in preparation for a sex reassignment operation." The Supreme Court of Illinois sustained the ordinance but held that as the ordinance applied to the defendants, it was "an unconstitutional infringement of their liberty interest." The Court did not reach defendants' arguments of equal protection and vagueness violations. *City of Chicago v. Wilson,* 75 Ill. 2d 525, 27 Ill. App. 458, 389 N.E. 2d 522 (1978). See also the 1986 case of *D.C. v. City of St. Louis,* 795 F. 2d 652 (8th Cir. 1986) where "D.C." was arrested for cross-dressing. In a civil suit for the arrest, he was awarded only nominal damage (a few dollars) because of his inappropriate behavior in a public place.

which one knows or has reasonable grounds to know arouses anger, alarm, or resentment in others on the basis of race, color, creed, religion, or gender commits disorderly conduct and shall be guilty of a misdemeanor. (St. Paul, Minn.Leg.Code § 292.02)

This ordinance was challenged in the 1991 case of *In the Matter of the Welfare of R.A.V.,* 464 N.W.2d 507 (Minn). R.A.V. (a minor) burned a cross in the yard of a black family living in St. Paul. After holding that the ordinance was not overbroad and did not infringe upon constitutionally protected conduct, the Supreme Court of Minnesota held that the St. Paul ordinance did not violate free speech as was held in the "flag burning" U.S. Supreme Court case of *Texas v. Johnson* (see chapter 10). In holding the St. Paul ordinance to be valid, the Minnesota Supreme Court held:

* * *

Burning a cross in the yard of an African American family's home is deplorable conduct that the City of St. Paul may without question prohibit. The burning cross is itself an unmistakable symbol of violence and hatred based on virulent notions of

Other Problems of Cities

Vehicle "Cruising"   Vehicle congestion on city streets has been aggravated in many cities by "cruising" vehicles. Business places in cruising areas complain, emergency vehicles can be blocked and hampered, and other persons using the roads can be delayed and become annoyed. Laws limiting or forbidding cruising have been enacted by some cities and counties. In 1990, the U.S. Court of Appeals for the Third Circuit upheld the cruising law in the case of *Lutz v. City of York, Pennsylvania,* 899 F.2d 255. The Court pointed out that neither the right to speak nor the right to travel is absolute. Public streets, like public forums, must be subject to reasonable regulations to avoid "chaos." It was held that the city's significant safety and congestion problems justified the law, which was held to be "narrowly tailored."

"Fare Beaters"   Cities with subways and other cities with turnstiles and fare gates have the problem of persons using the transit system without paying their fare. The City of New York estimates that fare beating costs the subway system more than $80 million per year. Fare beating is done primarily by jumping over fare gates or running through without paying. Thousands of fare evaders are reported arrested, with the usual punishment being fines and community service (oftentimes, cleaning the subway). See "Fare Beaters in Subway Pay in the End, in Sweat," *The New York Times,* February 18, 1991.

Fake IDs   Stolen, counterfeited, or doctored ID cards have been called the multimillion-dollar migraine for police, merchants, and financial institutions. MasterCard alone puts its annual losses from false IDs at more than $100 million worldwide. Fake IDs are used by teenagers to gain admission to taverns and by professional criminals to commit forgery and other big-time crimes. Phony driver's licenses, fake state ID cards, phony employee cards, fake social security cards, and even fake hospital ID cards can be obtained in most cities.

racial supremacy. It is the responsibility, even the obligation, of diverse communities to confront such notions in whatever form they appear.

* * *

Unlike the flag desecration statute at issue in *Texas v. Johnson,* the challenged St. Paul ordinance does not on its face assume that any cross burning, irrespective of the particular context in which it occurs, is subject to prosecution. Rather, the ordinance censors only those displays that one knows or should know will create anger, alarm or resentment based on racial, ethnic, gender or religious bias. . . .

* * *

St. Paul's bias-motivated disorderly conduct ordinance is also constitutional to the extent it prohibits conduct that is "directed to inciting or producing imminent lawless action and is likely to incite or produce such action." *Brandenburg v. Ohio,* 395 U.S. at 447, 89 S.Ct. at 1829 (footnote omitted). Where the "anger, alarm or resentment" the ordinance speaks of rises to the level of "imminent lawless action," *id.* at 449, 89 S.Ct. at 1830, the City is permitted to intervene and censor the provocative conduct.

See Texas v. Johnson, 109 S.Ct. at 2542. Because the City's disorderly conduct ordinance is reasonably subject to an interpretation limiting its scope to such conduct as *Brandenburg* places outside first amendment protection, we conclude that it is not substantially overbroad.

* * *

In upholding the challenged ordinance against R.A.V.'s constitutional attack, we do not take lightly the first amendment issues that his attack raises. "If there is a bedrock principle underlying the First Amendment, it is that the Government may not prohibit the expression of an idea simply because society finds the idea itself offensive or disagreeable." *Texas v. Johnson,* 109 S.Ct. at 2544. "Resort to epithets or personal abuse," however, "is not in any proper sense communication of information or opinion safeguarded by the Constitution, and its punishment as a criminal act [raises] no question under that instrument." *Cantwell v. Connecticut,* 310 U.S. 296, 309–10, 60 S.Ct. 900, 905–06, 84 L.Ed. 1213 (1940). Although the St. Paul ordinance should have been more carefully drafted, it can be interpreted so as to reach only those expressions of hatred and resorts to bias-motivated personal abuse that the first amendment does not protect. So interpreted, the ordinance is a narrowly tailored means toward accomplishing the compelling governmental interest in protecting the community against bias-motivated threats to public safety and order, . . . and therefore is not prohibited by the first amendment.

* * *

In 1991, the U.S. Supreme Court granted review and will probably hear the case of *R.A.V. v. St. Paul, Minn.* (see 49 CrL 3071).

Questions and Problems for Chapter 11

1. A young woman at a Houston, Texas, concert had to go to the bathroom. However, upon arrival at the women's room, she found a long line of waiting women. She stated that she just could not wait and went into the men's room to use a toilet stall there. She was charged with violating a city ordinance that prohibits people from using restrooms intended for members of the opposite sex in a manner calculated to cause a disturbance. The arresting officer, a twenty-year veteran, testified at her jury trial that he had been unfazed by her presence in the men's room.

What defenses could the woman use before the jury? If her identification looked in order and she lived in the community, should she have been taken to a police station, causing her to miss half of the concert for which she stated she paid $125?

2. Cantwell stopped two men on the street. He received permission from them and played a phonograph record that attacked their religion and church. Both men became angry and

threatened to strike Cantwell unless he went away. Cantwell immediately left. He was charged with and convicted of violating the breach of the peace statute. Did the U.S. Supreme Court affirm the conviction? (*Cantwell v. Connecticut,* 310 U.S. 296, 60 S.Ct. 900 [1940]).

3. The defendant addressed a group of blacks who had assembled to protest alleged police brutality. The defendant commended the crowd for their good conduct and restraint and stated that he believed in nonviolent behavior. He then stated to the crowd, "Do your own thing." Was this sufficient to justify a conviction for the offense of inciting to riot? (*State v. Douglas,* 278 So.2d 485 [La. 1973]).

4. An off-duty police officer and his friend attended a city council meeting in their home city. They were both properly found to be out of order by the mayor who was presiding over the meeting. When it appeared they were going to continue to disrupt the meeting, they were

ordered by the mayor to leave. Although the off-duty officer would not leave, his friend did and urged the officer to do the same. The mayor then ordered the off-duty officer removed from the meeting by other police officers. The off-duty officer physically resisted removal from the meeting and was then arrested. He argued he had a constitutional right to attend the meeting and the mayor as chair of the meeting did not have the right to eject him. Who is right and who is wrong in this situation? Explain. Should the conviction be affirmed by the court of appeals? *Gigler v. City of Klamath Falls,* 21 Or.App. 753, 537 P.2d 121 (1975).

5. Were the following regulations of premises lawful and reasonable? (all are true situations)

- In Denver, Colorado, a husband and wife brought their own popcorn, hidden under their coats, into a movie theater. They would not leave when discovered and asked to leave. The police were called and the husband told a police officer he would have to be dragged out "kicking and screaming." The husband was taken to jail in handcuffs

and both parties were charged with creating a disturbance.

- Trustees in a half-way house would take detainees staying at the house for long walks in the area. The detainees were men from a maximum security prison who were to be released in the coming months. One group of eight detainees and two trustees entered a fashionable shopping mall as part of their daily walk. The presence of the group was noted immediately by the mall security force. A number of mall security persons and a city police officer approached the group of men (most were black). After inquiring as to their identity, the police officer told them that they *must* leave the mall, as their presence made the security persons nervous. Was this a proper "move-on" order by the officer?
- Was the procedure used by the corporate board in footnote 4 a lawful and reasonable regulation of the premises of that corporation?

Notes

1. In the case of *Grayned v. City of Rockford,* 408 U.S. 104, 92 S.Ct. 2294 (1972), the U.S. Supreme Court held that: "The nature of a place, 'the pattern of its normal activities, dictates the kinds of regulations of time, place, and manner that are reasonable.' Although a silent vigil may not unduly interfere with a public library, making a speech in the reading room almost certainly would. That same speech should be perfectly appropriate in a park. The crucial question is whether the manner of expression is basically incompatible with the normal activity of a particular place at a particular time. Our cases make clear that in assessing the reasonableness of regulation, we must weigh heavily the fact that communication is involved; the regulation must be narrowly tailored to further the State's legitimate interest. 'Access to [the streets, sidewalks, parks, and other similar public places] for the purpose of exercising [First Amendment rights] cannot constitutionally be denied broadly.' Free expression 'must not, in the guise of regulation, be abridged or denied.' "

2. See *Breard v. Alexandria,* 341 U.S. 622, 71 S.Ct. 920 (1951); *Hall v. Commonwealth,* 188 Va. 72, 49 S.E.2d 369 (1948); *appeal dismissed,* 335 U.S. 875, 69 S.Ct. 240.

3. *Tinker v. Des Moines Independent Community School Dist.,* 393 U.S. 503, 89 S.Ct. 733 (1969). See this case in chapter 10.

4. An example of controlling premises that startled the business world occurred in Milwaukee in 1983. Mr. Checota, the founder of a large corporation, had been the president and chairman of the board. Mr. Checota had hired retired Admiral Elmo Zumwalt (former U.S. Chief of Naval Operations) as president, but in 1979, Admiral Zumwalt quit his job as president because of a dispute but stayed on the board. While Mr. Checota was vacationing in Italy in 1983, the board voted him out of office. On Mr. Checota's return to work, he was informed that he had been "fired" and was told to leave the premises immediately "or be physically carried out by security guards." As numerous guards were nearby, Mr. Checota was not permitted to go to his office and obtain his personal belongings. Mr. Checota then enlisted former Secretary of State Alexander Haig and a proxy fight and lawsuit was commenced. Retired General Haig (and former NATO commander) was heading the attacking forces and retired Admiral Zumwalt was defending.

5. *Grayned v. City of Rockford,* 408 U.S. 104, 92 S.Ct. 2294 (1972).

6. *Kunz v. New York,* 340 U.S. 290, 72 S.Ct. 312 (1951).

7. *Tinker v. Des Moines Independent Community School District,* 393 U.S. 503, 512–513, 89 S.Ct. 733, 739–740 (1969). This paragraph is a modified version of a paragraph presented by U.S. Justice Marshall in his

concurring and dissenting opinion in the case of *U.S. v. Grace,* 461 U.S. at 185.

8. *Brown v. Louisiana,* 383 U.S. 131, 142, 86 S.Ct. 719, 724 (1966); *id.,* at 146, and n. 5 (Brennan, J., concurring in judgment).

9. *Garner v. Louisiana,* 368 U.S. 157, 201–202, 82 S.Ct. 248, 271–272 (1961) (Harlan, J., concurring in judgment).

10. *Edwards v. South Carolina,* 372 U.S. 229 (1963).

11. *Jeannette Rankin Brigade v. Chief of Capitol Police,* 342 F.Supp. 575 (D.D.C. 1972), summarily aff'd, 409 U.S. 972, 93 S.Ct. 311 (1972).

12. *Wolin v. Port of New York Authority,* 392 F.2d 83 (2d Cir. 1968), cert. denied, 393 U.S. 940, 89 S.Ct. 290 (1968).

13. *Chicago Area Military Project v. City of Chicago,* 508 F.2d 921 (7th Cir. 1975), cert. denied, 421 U.S. 992, 95 S.Ct. 1999 (1975); *Kuszynski v. City of Oakland,* 479 F.2d 1130 (9th Cir. 1973).

14. *Albany Welfare Rights Organization v. Wyman,* 493 F.2d 1319 (2d Cir. 1974), cert. denied, 419 U.S. 838, 95 S.Ct. 66 (1974).

15. Other U.S. Supreme Court cases illustrating limits on First Amendment freedoms are:
a) All political speeches can be prohibited on military bases based upon (a) "the historical power . . . to exclude civilians," and (b) "the tradition of a politically neutral military . . . under civilian control." *Greer v. Spock,* 424 U.S. 828, 96 S.Ct. 1211 (1976).
b) Because of his previous improper conduct on a military base, an order was issued forbidding Albertini from re-entering the base. Albertini violated the order and was arrested. The Supreme Court affirmed the conviction. *U.S. v. Albertini,* 472 U.S. 675, 105 S.Ct. 2897 (1985).
c) The Supreme Court upheld a city's decision not to accept paid political advertising for its transit system advertising space as the city did so "in order to minimize chance of abuse, the appearance of favoritism, and the risk of imposing upon a captive audience." *Lehman v. City of Shaker Heights,* 418 U.S. 298, 94 S.Ct. 2714 (1974).

16. Justice Hugo Black stated in the case of *Gregory v. City of Chicago* as to residential picketing:
Were the authority of government so trifling as to permit anyone with a complaint to have the vast power to do anything he pleased, wherever he pleased, and whenever he pleased, our customs and our habits of conduct, social, political, economic, ethical, and religious would all be wiped out. . . . And perhaps worse than all other changes, homes, the sacred retreat to which families repair for their privacy and their daily way of living, would have to have their doors thrown open to all who desired to convert the occupants to new views, new morals, and a new way of life. Men and women who hold public office would be compelled, simply because they did hold public office, to lose the comforts and privacy of an unpicketed home. I believe that our constitution, written for the ages, to endure except

as changed in the manner it provides, did not create a government with such monumental weakness.

17. See *Diehl v. Maryland,* 294 Md. 466, 451 A.2d 115, *review denied,* 460 U.S. 1098, 103 S.Ct. 1798, 33 CrL 4018 (1983), in which an officer made a traffic stop in an A&P parking lot for "tire squealing." Diehl was a passenger and got out of the car. The officer ordered Diehl to get back into the car. The Maryland Court of Appeals held "the officer did not have any right to make this demand on Diehl." To order a person to get into a car (or to get out of a car) on a traffic stop (civil violation), the officer must show a good and sufficient reason, such as concern for safety of the person, or of the officer, or the public. This requirement was not shown in the *Diehl* case. See also *Delaware v. Prouse,* 440 U.S. 648, 99 S.Ct. 1391 (1979).

18. Under the old common law, if a number of persons met together and suddenly quarreled and fought among themselves, this would constitute an affray. An "affray" differs from a riot in that an "affray" is not premeditated. Under the old common law, a riot required three or more persons, while an "affray" could consist of two or more.

19. Under New York statutes, four or more persons plus the person charged are needed for the crime of "unlawful assembly." To convict of any of the riot offenses, it must be shown that there were ten or more persons plus the person charged.

20. *Kovacs v. Cooper,* 336 U.S. 77, 69 S.Ct. 448 (1949).

21. 46 N.J. 510, 218 A.2d 147 (1966).

22. Among the chants that petitioner did *not* engage in were "bullshit, bullshit," during the president's speech, and "one, two, three, four, we don't want your fucking war." One isolated member of the group rose during a minister's prayer and screamed an obscenity.

23. 79 Wash.2d 351, 485 P.2d 449 (1971).

24. 1 Cal.3d 930, 83 Cal.Rptr. 686, 464 P.2d 142 (1970).

25. 91 N.M. 74, 570 P.2d 612 (1977).

26. *Griego v. Wilson* was a civil action for damages for injuries which the plaintiff alleged that he received at the hands of the store employees. The dismissal of the case by the trial court was affirmed by the Court of Appeals.

27. 89 N.J. 270, 445 A.2d 1141, 31 CrL 2222.

28. *Wilkinson v. Forst,* 832 F.2d 1330 (2d Cir. 1987).

29. Commercial messages include commercial advertising by firms or persons seeking to promote sales of their products or services. In the 1942 case of *Valentine v. Chrestensen,* 316 U.S. 52, 62 S.Ct. 920, the U.S. Supreme Court held that cities and states could absolutely forbid the distribution of commercial handbills in public places. However, in 1976 the U.S. Supreme Court reversed itself in *Virginia State Board of Pharmacy v. Virginia Citizens Consumer Council, Inc.,* 425 U.S. 748, 96 S.Ct. 1817, in which the Court held that "commercial speech, like other varieties, is protected."

30. *Kovacs v. Cooper,* 336 U.S. 77, 69 S.Ct. 448 (1949).

31. 40 N.Y.2d 527, 387 N.Y.S.2d 415, 355 N.E.2d 375, 19 CrL 2366 (1976).

32. 319 U.S. 141, 63 S.Ct. 862 (1943).

33. *NAACP v. Button,* 371 U.S. 415, 433, 83 S.Ct. 328, 338 (1963).

34. See the articles "For New York's Homeless, It's Life and Hope Among the Ruins," *New York Times* (December 31, 1990) p. 10; and "Federal Count of Homeless Is Far Below Other Figures," *New York Times* (April 12, 1991).

35. *Palka v. Connecticut,* 302 U.S. 319, 325, 58 S.Ct. 149, 151 (1937).

36. "Atlanta's Answer: Curfew Gets Teens Off the Streets," *Los Angeles Times* News Service and *Milwaukee Journal* (December 6, 1990).

37. *In re James,* 43 Cal. 3d 903, 239 Cal.Rptr. 663, 741 P.2d 161 (1987) quoting *In re Miguel G.,* 111 Cal. App. 3d 345, 168 Cal.Rptr. 688 (1980).

Chapter Twelve

THE LIMITS OF OTHER FREEDOMS

A. The Second Amendment Right to Bear Arms

"A well-regulated Militia, being necessary to the security of a free State, the right of the people to keep and bear Arms, shall not be infringed."

—Second Amendment of the U.S. Constitution

When the Second Amendment to the U.S. Constitution was ratified in 1791 as part of the Bill of Rights, the newly formed United States was a frontier nation with its 3 million or so people isolated from one another to a degree that is hard for us to imagine. There were no telephones, radios, or motor vehicles by which public officials and law enforcement officers could be summoned in an emergency. The few law enforcement officers could be found only in the towns and cities that were hours and sometimes days away from the farms and homes of many of the settlers.

Firearms were essential for survival, since most of the families depended on wild game as part of their subsistence. Guns were also needed for self-defense because organized law enforcement agencies were not within immediate call of most of the population. The American colonies were fearful of standing armies, since they had just thrown off the military control of Great Britain. The American Revolution had been fought by citizen part-time soldiers. Under the new Republic, the country had no need for a big army and looked on all able-bodied men as militia members who would be available in time of need, just as they had been in the 1770s. The "well-regulated Militia" to which the Second Amendment refers comprised the farmers and townspeople who had taken up arms against the British. Under those circumstances, the logic and meaning of the Second Amendment was apparent, since it stated a national need as basic as free speech and free religion to the newly formed democracy.

The Second Amendment Today

Today, the United States is made up of fifty states with more than 200 million people living primarily in crowded metropolitan areas. Instead of a militia made up principally of part-time citizen soldiers who bring their own weapons, we maintain huge federal military forces and National Guard units. As the country no longer needs the private arms of its citizens for defense, what is the meaning of the Second Amendment today?

Nations like England[1] and Japan strictly forbid the private possession and ownership of weapons. Other European countries have strict gun control laws. Compared with these nations, the United States exerts little control over the private ownership and possession of weapons. The United States has the highest per capita ownership of handguns in the world today. Estimates as to the number of firearms in the hands of private persons run from 30 million to 120 million, with an additional 2 million or more firearms being added each year in recent years. The United States is also the most lawless of the industrial nations of the world, with the highest homicide rate of that group.

The handgun has become not only the number one tool of serious crime in the United States, but a common instrument in suicide. Although some other countries have higher overall suicide rates than does the United States, our firearm suicide death rate is the highest in the world. There are more suicides by firearms in the United States than in all the other countries combined. It also follows that because of the presence of large numbers of firearms, the United States has the highest number of accidental shootings in the world.

The National and Individualist Interpretations of the Second Amendment

Unless the Second Amendment were to be changed by constitutional amendment, the power of the states to prohibit the private ownership and possession of handguns rests on the interpretation of the Second Amendment by the U.S. Supreme Court. There are currently two interpretations of the Second Amendment, the "individualist view" and the "national view." The individualist view interprets the Second Amendment broadly and is urged by those who oppose laws forbidding the possession of handguns or registration requirements. They argue that the maintenance of a militia was only one of the purposes of the Second Amendment, and that the amendment ensures the right of individuals to bear arms to protect themselves not only from dangerous intruders against their homes and property, but also against possible oppression by government itself. They point out that when the Second Amendment was ratified, Americans had just created a strong central government and that the citizens of those days feared a repetition of the many abuses that strong centralized governments had imposed.

The national view interprets the Second Amendment strictly and holds that this amendment was meant to provide for strong militias of private citizens. Persons who advocate the national view argue that as the need for the militia no longer exists, the right of individuals to keep and bear arms no longer exists because private weapons are no longer needed either for the national defense or for emergencies.[2]

The Fight Between American Chiefs of Police and the NRA Over Firearm Laws

The controversy over handgun control has been fought for many years. The assassination of a public figure always brings the controversy to the front pages of newspapers throughout the country. Debates raged anew with the killings of John F. Kennedy, Rev. Martin Luther King, and Robert F. Kennedy. When an attempt was made on President Gerald Ford's life, and after the wild shooting spree by John Hinckley in seeking to shoot Ronald Reagan, the issue of handgun control was again brought to the front pages and consequently to the public's attention.

Full-page ads are regularly run in newspapers and magazines by advocates of both sides of the issue. Some chiefs of police of large American cities accuse the National Rifle Association of "irrational positions and behavior" and ask, "How high does the pile of dead and maimed bodies have to get before America comes to its senses?"[3] The NRA, however, responds that it represents the best interest of America's hunters and sports enthusiasts.

Easy accessibility of handguns is one of the areas of controversy and is primarily a national issue to be determined by the Congress of the United States. If one state has strict handgun laws and its neighboring states have no barriers at all to prevent a person from purchasing a pistol, the efforts of a state with strict gun-control laws are largely nullified.

Possession by individuals is primarily an issue for each state and city. *Concealed possession* of a weapon unless licensed or authorized (CCW) is forbidden by the laws of all states and cities. *Open* (not concealed) *possession* of a firearm is forbidden by many cities and states unless specifically licensed or authorized.

In about half of the states, possession of a firearm in a home or business place is forbidden unless a license is obtained or the gun is registered. A few American cities forbid possession of guns in private and public places and will not issue licenses to private persons. Morton Grove, Illinois, was one of the first of these communities. Persons and groups urging handgun ownership became concerned that the example of the small suburb of Chicago (Morton Grove) could be the beginning of a nationwide campaign by local communities to take away what they regarded as the public's constitutional right to keep and bear arms. A lawsuit was commenced challenging the Morton Grove ordinance. After the challenge failed in the Illinois courts, Morton Grove was obligated to defend its ordinance in the federal courts. The result in the federal courts is presented in the following case:[4]

QUILICI v. VILLAGE OF MORTON GROVE
Court of Appeals of the United States, Seventh Circuit (1982) 695 F.2d 261, cert. denied 464 U.S. 863, 104 S.Ct. 194, 34 CrL 4004

The courts held that the Morton Grove ordinance that bans possession of operative handguns within the village did not violate state or federal constitutions. The U.S. Supreme Court refused further review of the Federal Court of Appeals' decision, which held:

> *According to its plain meaning, it seems clear that the right to bear arms is inextricably connected to the preservation of a militia. Illinois municipalities therefore have a constitutional right to ban ownership or sale of items determined to be dangerous.*

The *Morton Grove* decision again held what most American courts have been holding for years; that states may enact any laws they wish in regard to firearms. Local communities must act within state law, and because the Morton Grove ordinance did not violate either state law or the Illinois Constitution, it was a valid enactment.

However, because of the following reasons, few local communities have followed the Morton Grove example:

1988 Statements of Retired U.S. Supreme Court Justice Lewis F. Powell before the American Bar Association in Toronto, Canada

"It is not easy to understand why the Second Amendment, or the notion of liberty, should be viewed as creating a right to own and carry a weapon. . . . "

"During the Vietnam War, some 58,021 Americans were killed. During that same period in the United States, approximately 122,000 Americans were murdered. Of those, over 70,000 were killed by firearms. . . . "

Owning and carrying weapons "contributes so directly to the shocking number of murders in our country."

1. After losing the *Morton Grove* lawsuit, the NRA began efforts in state legislative bodies, and by 1990, thirty-nine states forbade cities and other communities from enacting most gun-control measures.[5]
2. With the increasing number of burglaries of private homes and business places, and the additional problem of armed robberies and rapes, more private persons now keep handguns and other weapons in homes and businesses for protection. Therefore, there is an increased number of persons who do not want local ordinances forbidding the possession of handguns in homes or business places. Some studies indicate that a burglar runs as high a risk of getting shot during a burglary as he does of going to jail.
3. Local communities that have enacted Morton Grove-type ordinances run into a problem of enforcing them. Violation of a law forbidding the possession of firearms usually comes to the attention of the police when a local homeowner or business person repels a burglar or robber using a forbidden firearm. This could mean prosecuting a person who has already been victimized by a crime. Prosecutors who prosecuted in such cases have found that they are likely to lose if the matter is taken before a jury of persons from the local community.

Federal Gun Legislation Since the 1930s

In the 1920s and 1930s, criminals began crossing state lines and using cars, automatic weapons, shotguns, and handguns to commit crimes. In reaction to this gang warfare and the assassination attempt against President Franklin D. Roosevelt (which resulted in the killing of the Mayor of Chicago), federal legislation was enacted.

The 1934 National Firearms Act (Public Law 73–474), forbids the interstate shipment of special weapons used by gangsters. It forbids the interstate shipment without a license of sawed-off shotguns, machine guns, and mufflers and silencers for guns. The 1938 Federal Firearms Act requires that firearms manufacturers, dealers, importers, and other persons engaged in firearms shipment across state lines be licensed by the federal government. The act also forbids the interstate shipment of all firearms to or by convicted felons, persons under indictment, and fugitives from justice.

The Gun Control Act of 1968 (Public Law 90–618) bans the interstate and mail order shipments of firearms to individuals and provides for the licensing of dealers, manufacturers, and importers. It requires the registration of "destructive devices" (cannons, antitank guns, bazookas, etc.). It bars the importation of cheap concealable foreign handguns, such as the six-dollar "Saturday Night Special," which killed Senator Robert Kennedy.

But in the late 1970s, the movement toward legislation that would further regulate the sale and possession of firearms stopped. The president of the International Chiefs of Police stated that the NRA "called for the repeal of all firearm laws, starting with the 1968 Gun Control Act." Police Chief Casey said that the NRA went off the "deep end" and resorted to "political extortion, strong-arm tactics, deception and misinformation to further their cause."

The National Rifle Association has 2.8 million members and more than $70 million in annual revenue. The NRA has been very skilled in pushing its legislative programs with members of Congress from both parties. In 1986, both Houses of

Handgun Crimes

The most frequent handgun crime in the United States is the carrying or possession of a handgun (concealed or otherwise) where such conduct is illegal in that state or city. "Each year an estimated 639,000 residents of the United States face an offender armed with a handgun," states the *Special Report on "Handgun Crime Victims"* by the U.S. Department of Justice Bureau of Justice Statistics. The report also states:

Offenders armed with handguns committed an average of 639,000 violent crimes each year between 1979 and 1987. These criminals used handguns to kill an average of 9,200 people each year and to wound 15,000; they injured approximately 76,000 victims a year in ways other than by shooting them.

In 87% of the nonfatal crimes involving handguns, the offender did not fire the weapon but used it to intimidate. Victims reported that the offender fired the gun but missed in 10% of the crimes involving handguns and wounded the victim in 2%.

Other major findings on the role of handguns in crime include the following:

- Young black urban males were the group most vulnerable to victimization by an offender armed with a handgun. Urban black men age 16 to 24 were victimized at a rate more than twice as high as the rate of urban white men and of urban black women of similar ages.
- Handgun crimes represented 10% of all violent crimes and 27% of all violent crimes by armed offenders that occurred during the period of 1979–87. Offenders with handguns commit-

ted about 7% of all rapes, 18% of all robberies, and 8% of all assaults (22% of aggravated assaults) during this period. Approximately 4 in every 10 victims of murder or nonnegligent manslaughter were killed by offenders with handguns.

- For violent crimes committed with a handgun, white offenders were responsible for 43% of the rapes, 22% of the robberies, and 58% of the aggravated assaults; blacks were responsible for 51% of the rapes, 67% of the robberies, and 35% of the assaults.
- A higher percentage of crimes by strangers involved handguns than did crimes by

Handguns and crime, 1979–87

	Average annual number
Handgun crimes	638,900
Murder	9,200
Rape	12,100
Robbery	210,000
Assault	407,600
Nonfatal handgun crimes	629,700
Victims injured	91,500
Shot	15,000
Other injury	76,400

Note: Detail may not add to total because of rounding.

acquaintances or relatives of victims. While 12% of all violent crimes by strangers were committed by offenders wielding handguns, 5% of violent crimes by acquaintances and 6% of violent crimes by relatives were committed with a handgun.

- Of victims injured but not killed by gunshot injuries, 28% were treated in emergency rooms and released, and 68% were hospitalized overnight or longer. About 21% of all victims of nonfatal gunshots were hospitalized for 3 weeks or more.
- Victims of handgun robberies were more apt than other robbery victims to lose property in the robbery. Eighty percent of handgun robberies were completed versus 61% of robberies not involving handguns.
- Victims of handgun crimes were much less likely to take self-protective measures such as fighting back, running away, or trying to dissuade the offender than were victims of other violent crimes. Fifty-five percent of handgun crime victims took self-protective measures, compared to 76% of victims of violent crimes with no handgun present.

Almost 42% of the violent crimes with a handgun present occurred on the street. Another 11% took place near a victim's home, including the sidewalk or yard. About 20% of the crimes, an average of over 127,000 every year, happened in a commercial establishment. A victim's home was the location for almost 13% of the crimes that involved a handgun.

Victims of handgun crimes were more likely than other violent crime victims to report the crime to the police. The higher likelihood of reporting a crime that involved a handgun existed whether an injury had occurred or not. Sixty-nine percent of handgun crimes were reported to law enforcement authorities, compared to 46% for all other violent crimes.

U.S. Department of Justice Office of Justice Programs Bureau of Justice Statistics

Congress gave overwhelming approval to legislation weakening the 1968 Gun Control Act. Many American chiefs of police stated publicly that the NRA got almost everything it wanted and commenced newspaper ads seeking to limit NRA political power.

Legislation Before the U.S. Congress

Bills and proposed legislation before the U.S. Congress regarding firearms are:

1. *The "Brady" Bill*—fewer than half of the states have laws requiring waiting periods for the purchase of firearms. The "Brady" Bill would require a national seven-day waiting period to allow police to run background checks. Not only would the waiting period allow a check for criminal and mental background, but it would prevent an angry person or a person who wanted to commit a crime from immediately obtaining a firearm. The bill is named after Sarah Brady who worked very hard for its passage. Sarah's husband, John, was shot along with President Reagan and other persons when John Hinckley purchased a $29 revolver to shoot the president. NRA officials previously backed such a bill but switched their position in the late 1970s, stating that such laws were ineffective, bothersome to honest citizens, and ignored by criminals. The Brady Bill was defeated in 1988, 1989, and 1990. In 1991, the bill was again before the U.S. Congress and passed by the House of Representatives. The U.S. Senate would then have to pass the bill to have it sent to the President.

2. *Federal judges asked the U.S. Congress in 1990 to enact legislation authorizing them to carry guns in court* because of the increasing number of threats against their lives.

3. *Regulating the interstate sale and traffic in toy guns that look very real*—In 1987, the New York City Police Department reported that it seized 1,416 toy guns used in criminal incidents.[6] When a mentally impaired man waved a fake pistol in a fast-food restaurant in Los Angeles, a deputy sheriff mistook the toy for a real gun and shot and killed the man.

4. *Plastic guns that escape detection by airport security devices*—Because plastic handguns are difficult (sometimes impossible) to detect by metal scanning equipment, legislation stopping the interstate shipment of plastic handguns has been sought. In 1987, forty-three persons were killed in California when a handgun was smuggled aboard a PSA airplane.

5. *Forbidding the sale of rapid-fire machine guns*—There are already 100,000 rapid-fire machine guns in private hands, and police report that the illegal sale of such guns is very brisk. In 1986, although Congress passed a law blocking the sale of machine guns, American chiefs of police report that the NRA is seeking to get that law repealed. The latest models of such guns (such as UZIs) are light and concealable. In 1985, an automatic weapon was used to gun down twenty-one women, children, and men in a McDonald's restaurant in California.

6. *"Cop-killer" and "fast" bullets*—"Cop-killer" bullets are armour-piercing bullets capable of going through bulletproof vests and garments worn by law enforcement officers. These bullets are also referred to as "fast" bullets because they travel at higher speed and velocity. Further legislation is sought regulating these bullets.

California Congressman Mel Levine holds up toy guns during a press conference. Levine introduced legislation in the U.S. Congress requiring distinct markings on toy guns.

7. *Tightening federal gun dealer license laws*—The New York *Times* reports that there are more than 230,000 licensed firearm dealers in the United States.[7] In 1991, there were 1,043 federally licensed firearms dealers in New York City, but only 77 of them were city-licensed dealers. Obtaining a federal firearm license is very easy. Once it has been obtained, unlimited firearms can be purchased from manufacturers by mail. It is reported that some federally licensed firearm dealers have criminal records and are in business to supply weapons to criminals.[8] The U.S. Congress has been requested to enact legislation requiring federal arms dealers to comply with local and state laws.

"Carrying a Concealed Weapon" Statutes and Ordinances

All states have criminal statutes making it a criminal offense to carry a concealed weapon. Probably all municipalities also have ordinances regulating such conduct. The reason for enacting such statutes and ordinances is stated in Illinois as follows: "The possession and use of weapons inherently dangerous to human life constitutes a sufficient hazard to society to call for prohibition unless there appears appropriate justification created by special circumstances."[9] The Illinois Committee also commented that deadly weapons statutes have been criticized "for having the effect of prohibiting the law abiding citizen from protecting himself, while at the same time failing to reach the criminal who habitually uses dangerous weapons for illegal ends."

In the Illinois case of *People v. McClendon,* the court held that:

Concealment and accessibility are essential elements of the crime of carrying a concealed weapon on or about the person and the weapon must be in such proximity of the accused as to be within his easy reach and under his control and must be suffi-ciently close to his person to be readily accessible for immediate use.[10]

In the California case of *People v. Prochnau,* it was held that "(t)o establish unlawful possession of a contraband object it must be shown that the defendant exercised dominion and control over the object with knowledge of its presence and contraband character, but that such matters may be established by circum-stantial evidence."[11]

Therefore, in order to convict for a CCW (carrying a concealed weapon) charge, the state or city must show:

1. that the instrument was a "dangerous weapon," "deadly weapon," or "weapon," as described by the statute or ordinance, and
2. that the weapon was concealed, and
3. that the weapon was within the defendant's "easy reach and under his control."

What Is a "Dangerous Weapon" or "Deadly Weapon"?

All states and cities hold that operational revolvers, rifles, and shotguns are "dan-gerous" or "deadly" weapons within the meaning of their statutes or ordinances. Firearms (by themselves), per se, have always been considered deadly and dan-gerous. In order to make rifles and shotguns concealable, persons about to com-mit a crime will sometimes "saw off" the barrel. Many states and cities make sawed-off rifles and shotguns contraband in themselves and forbid possession of such objects.

Other objects that could fall within the category of "dangerous" or "deadly" weapons could include switchblade knives, folding knives with blades that lock open, brass knuckles, saps, and other specially designed objects with little or no other use than to cause injury to another person.

The question of whether an unloaded gun is a "dangerous weapon" was presented to the U.S. Supreme Court in the 1986 case of *McLaughlin v. United States.*[12] In following the majority rule used for years in the United States, the Supreme Court held:

* * *

Three reasons, each independently sufficient, support the conclusion that an unloaded gun is a "dangerous weapon." First, a gun is an article that is typically and character-istically dangerous; the use for which it is manufactured and sold is a dangerous one,

---

Bumper Stickers Seen in the United States

The Second Amendment gives every person the right to own guns.

If guns are outlawed, only outlaws will have guns.

Guns don't kill, people kill.

My wife yes, my dog maybe, my gun never.

I carry my .357 Magnum three nights a week—you guess which three nights.

and the law reasonably may presume that such an article is always dangerous even though it may not be armed at a particular time or place. In addition, the display of a gun instills fear in the average citizen; as a consequence, it creates an immediate danger that a violent response will ensue. Finally, a gun can cause harm when used as a bludgeon.

* * *

Is a Defective or Broken Weapon a Firearm?

A firearm has been defined as "any weapon from which a shot is discharged by force of an explosive or a weapon which acts by force of gunpowder." Under this definition, a New York court held that a Very pistol, designed to fire warning flares, is a firearm within the meaning of the New York Penal Code.[13]

It has been held that when a broken spring does not totally impair the use of a revolver, and the hammer can be operated manually, the instrument is a firearm within the meaning of the New York Penal Code.[14]

In the 1983 case of *York v. State,*[15] the Maryland Court of Appeals affirmed the conviction of defendant for using a handgun in the commission of a crime of violence (robbery). The gun had been damaged and could not be fired unless the person firing the gun was strong or used two hands. At the trial, a police firearms expert testified that the gun could be made operable in about a minute's time by using a hammer and a screwdriver or a fingernail file. Not only was York convicted of the above crime, but he was also convicted of robbery with a dangerous and deadly weapon and battery.

In the 1968 California case of *People v. Jackson,*[16] the defendant had previously been convicted of a felony and was convicted of violating a California statute making it unlawful for ex-convicts to possess concealable firearms. The court reversed the conviction on the grounds that the pistol was not in operating condition, and could not have been made operable without the procurement of a replacement part. The court stated:

> We do not question the rule that "a deadly weapon does not cease to be such by becoming temporarily inefficient, nor is its essential character changed by dismemberment if the parts may be easily assembled so as to be effective." (*People v. Guyette,* 231 Cal.App.2d 460, 467, 41 Cal.Rptr. 875, 880). As far as the meager evidence in the case at bar shows, the gun could not be made operable without the procurement of a replacement part.
>
> The only evidence before the court was that the pistol was not in operating condition. It is true that the judge as trier of the facts came to the opposite conclusion, but upon what evidence he based this conclusion is not known. There is nothing in the record to substantiate it.
>
> It is not a violation to carry a pistol that is so broken or out of repair that it cannot be used to shoot with or cannot be fired. (*Farris v. State,* 64 Tex.Cr.R. 524, 144 S.W. 249; *People v. Simons,* 124 Misc. 28, 207 N.Y.S. 56, 58).
>
> A pistol which was incapable of being fired because it had a broken firing pin is not a pistol within the statute (*People v. Grillo* [1962] 11 N.Y.2d 841, 227 N.Y.S.2d 668, 182 N.E.2d 278) in the absence of showing that a workable firing pin was also in the possession of defendant and that a simple substitution of pins would have made the weapon operable. (*People v. Guyette, supra* 231 Cal.App.2d 460, 41 Cal.Rptr. 875).

What Is Within a Defendant's "Easy Reach and Under His Control"?

STATE v. MOLINS
District Court of Appeal of Florida (1982) 424 So.2d 29

The defendant placed a zippered canvas bag on a conveyor belt at an airport security checkpoint. A pistol was in the bag covered with other items. In affirming the defendant's conviction for carrying a concealed weapon, the court held:

> *For an accused to be found guilty of the offense of carrying a concealed firearm, the firearm must not only be hidden from the ordinary sight of another person, as here but must as well be "on or about the person,"* Ensor v. State, *403 So.2d 349, 354, 29 CrL 2304 (Fla. 1981). A firearm is considered "about the person" if it is "readily accessible" to him. . . . While it is true that in order for the defendant to gain access to the firearm in the present case, he would have had to unzip two containers, in our view the firearm was not any less accessible than one in a locked glove compartment of a vehicle which, according to* Ensor, *may be considered, in the words of the statute, "about the person."*

PEOPLE v. DUNN
Court of Appeal of California (1976) 61 Cal.App.3d Supp. 12, 132 Cal.Rptr. 921

In affirming the defendant's conviction for carrying a concealed weapon (handgun) in a suitcase, the court held:

> *We hold that the Legislature intended to proscribe the carrying of concealed weapons by both men and women and that a handgun concealed in a suitcase and carried by appellant is sufficiently "upon his person" to constitute a violation of section 12025.*

PEOPLE v. PUGACH
Court of Appeals of New York (1964) 15 N.Y.2d 65, 255 N.Y.S.2d 833, 204 N.E.2d 176

In affirming the defendant's conviction, the New York court saw no significance in "the fact that the loaded gun was found concealed in the brief case, rather than in a pocket of the defendant's clothing." The court held that a "loaded firearm concealed in the brief case carried in the hands of the defendant was in the language of the statute 'concealed upon his person.'"

STATE v. WILLIAMS
Supreme Court of Utah (1981) 636 P.2d 1092

In holding that the defendant was "carrying" the gun that was next to him in a partially unzipped satchel on the seat of his car, the Court stated:

> *The danger to others is just as great where the weapon is readily accessible as where carried on the person of the individual.*

STATE v. MORRISON
Court of Appeals of Oregon (1976) 25 Or.App. 609, 549 P.2d 1295

When a law enforcement officer stopped the defendant's car for a traffic violation, he saw and seized a stiletto that was partially showing on the vehicle floor by the side of the defendant's foot. The Court held that the defendant was "carrying" the stiletto, stating:

Does Your State Have Gun Control Laws Regulating the Following?

Forbidding Possession by

Statute #

- a minor? (pistol only?)
- a person convicted of a felony?   _____
- a person who is intoxicated?   _____
- a person who is committing a crime?   _____
- a person going into or who is in a public building?   _____
- other?   _____

Statutes Providing "Add-on" Prison Terms for

- committing a crime with use of (or threat of) dangerous weapon:
     misdemeanor?
     felony?   _____
- use of bulletproof garment while committing crime?   _____
- concealing identity while commiting crime:
     misdemeanor?   _____
     felony?   _____
- repeater or habitual criminal statute for person who has previously committed:
     misdemeanors?   _____
     felonies?   _____
- other?   _____

Forbidding Possession, Sale, Use, or Transportation of

- short-barreled rifle or shotgun ("sawed-off")?   _____
- machine gun?   _____
- bomb, hand grenade, shell, projectile?   _____
- switchblade knife?   _____
- silencer?   _____
- electric weapon (stun gun)?   _____
- mace, tear gas and/or other chemical sprays?   _____
- other?   _____

Forbidding the Following Conduct

Statute #

- carrying a concealed weapon (CCW)?   _____
- pointing a firearm at or toward another person?   _____
- discharging a firearm on the land of another?   _____
- discharging a firearm within a municipality?   _____
- discharging a firearm into a vehicle or building?   _____
- setting a spring gun (trap)?   _____
- selling or giving a pistol to a minor?   _____
- reckless use of a weapon?   _____
- possession or transportation of firearm in:
     a watercraft (motor boat)?   _____
     an aircraft?   _____
     a motor vehicle?   _____
- brandishing a firearm?   _____
- possession of an unlicensed gun in a home or business place?   _____
- other?   _____

Regulating Purchase and Use of Firearms

- persons excluded (insane, convicted of felony, etc.)?   _____
- waiting period for purchase of? waiting time?   _____
- instructional program on safe use of firearms?   _____
     children ordered to attend?   _____
- other?   _____

We think it obvious that the legislature intended to prohibit only such carrying as by its nature makes the instrument readily available for use as a weapon by a person who has its constructive possession. That ingredient of the offense is fulfilled by the circumstances of the case at bar.

When Is a Weapon Concealed?

The question of when a weapon is concealed has come before many courts in CCW cases. Does a weapon have to be so concealed that it gives absolutely no notice of its presence, or is a weapon concealed when it cannot be seen in ordinary observation? In the following 1981 decision, the Florida Supreme Court adopted the majority position in the United States that "a weapon need not be totally hidden from view to be 'concealed'":

ENSOR v. STATE
Supreme Court of Florida (1981) 403 So.2d 349, 29 CrL 2304

After police officers made a lawful traffic stop, a derringer was observed protruding from a floormat in the car. The gun was held to be "concealed" within the meaning of the state law and the defendant was convicted of CCW. The court affirmed the conviction, holding:

The majority of courts in other jurisdictions that have considered the issue have concluded that a weapon need not be totally hidden from view to be "concealed." See, e.g. Mularkey v. State, 230 N.W. 76 (Wis. 1930), People v. Williams, 39 Ill.App.3d 129, 350 N.E.2d 81 (1976), and Driggers v. State, 26 So. 512 (Ala. 1899).

We agree with the majority view and find that absolute invisibility is not a necessary element to a finding of concealment under section 790.001. The operative language of that section establishes a two-fold test. For a firearm to be concealed, it must be (1) on or about the person and (2) hidden from the ordinary sight of another person. The term "on or about the person" means physically on the person or readily accessible to him. This generally includes the interior of an automobile and the vehicle's glove compartment, whether or not locked. The term "ordinary sight of another person" means that casual and ordinary observation of another in the normal associations of life. Ordinary observation by a person other than a police officer does not generally include the floorboard of a vehicle, whether or not the weapon is wholly or partially visible. Further, the fact that a firearm is encased in a holster does not remove it from the application of section 790.001. A firearm encased in a holster and hidden under an automobile seat is no different than a traditionally concealed firearm in a shoulder holster under one's coat. Both appear to be outside the "ordinary sight of another person."

STATE v. TEAGUE
Supreme Court of Florida (1985) 475 So.2d 213

After a lawful stop of his car, the defendant was asked for his driver's license. When the defendant opened his car door to get his license, the officer saw the muzzle portion of a rifle lying uncovered on the front seat of the car. The car had tinted windows through which the firearm could not be seen in the "ordinary sight of another person." The Supreme Court of Florida decided that the rifle was not concealed, holding:[17]

That tinted motor vehicle windows by themselves do not make an otherwise legally carried firearm a concealed firearm under section 790.01(2).

B. THE FREE EXERCISE OF RELIGION

The Right to Believe or Not to Believe

In 1890, the U.S. Supreme Court defined the First Amendment freedom of religion as follows:

> The First Amendment was intended to allow every one under the jurisdiction of the United States to entertain such notions respecting his relations to his Maker and the duties they impose as may be approved by his judgment and conscience, and to exhibit his sentiments in such form of worship, as he may think proper, not injurious to the equal rights of others, and to prohibit legislation for the support of any religious tenets, or the modes of worship of any sect. The oppressive measures adopted, and the cruelties and punishments inflicted, by the governments of Europe for many ages, to compel parties to conform, in their religious beliefs and modes of worship, to the views of the most numerous sect, and the folly of attempting in that way to control the mental operations of persons, and enforce an outward conformity to a prescribed standard, led to the adoption of [this] amendment.[18]

Freedom to believe is absolute; freedom to act is not. The U.S. Supreme Court held in *Cantwell v. Connecticut* that:

> Freedom of conscience and freedom to adhere to such religious organization or form of worship as the individual may choose cannot be restricted by law. On the other hand, it safeguards the free exercise of the chosen form of religion. Thus the Amendment embraces two concepts,—freedom to believe and freedom to act. The first is absolute but, in the nature of things, the second cannot be. Conduct remains subject to regulation for the protection of society. The freedom to act must have appropriate definition to preserve the enforcement of that protection. In every case the power to regulate must be so exercised as not, in attaining a permissible end, unduly to infringe the protected freedom.

* * *

> Nothing we have said is intended even remotely to imply that, under the cloak of religion, persons may, with impunity, commit frauds upon the public. Certainly penal laws are available to punish such conduct. Even the exercise of religion may be at some slight inconvenience in order that the state may protect its citizens from injury. Without doubt a state may protect its citizens from fraudulent solicitation by requiring a stranger in the community, before permitting him publicly to solicit funds for any purpose, to establish his identity and his authority to act for the cause which he purports to represent. The state is likewise free to regulate the time and manner of solicitation generally, in the interest of public safety, peace, comfort or convenience.
>
> But to condition the solicitations of aid for the perpetuation of religious views or systems upon a license, the grant of which rests in the exercise of a determination by state authority as to what is a religious cause, is to lay a forbidden burden upon the exercise of liberty protected by the Constitution.

* * *

> In the realm of religious faith, and in that of political belief, sharp differences arise. In both fields the tenets of one man may seem the rankest error to his neighbor. To persuade others to his own point of view, the pleader, as we know, at times, resorts to exaggeration, to vilification of men who have been, or are, prominent in church or state, and even to false statement. But the people of this nation have ordained in the

NOTICE TO THE PUBLIC

Certain individuals and groups exercising their first amendment rights of free speech, expression, and religion, are distributing literature and soliciting donations in the airport. These activities are constitutionally protected. However, they are in no way encouraged, endorsed or connected with the Airport Management or Airlines.

Airports may post signs such as this, or they may assign and restrict solicitors to tables (see case of *Hefron v. Krishnas* (see the case in this section).

light of history, that, in spite of the probability of excesses and abuses, these liberties are, in the long view, essential to enlightened opinion and right conduct on the part of the citizens of a democracy.

The essential characteristic of these liberties, is, that under their shield many types of life, character, opinion and belief can develop unmolested and unobstructed. Nowhere is this shield more necessary than in our own country for a people composed of many races and many creeds. There are limits to the exercise of these liberties. The danger in these times from the coercive activities of those who in the delusion of racial or religious conceit would incite violence and breaches of the peace in order to deprive others of their equal right to the exercise of their liberties, is emphasized by events familiar to all. These and other transgressions of those limits the states appropriately may punish.[19]

Cases on Religious Freedom Rights

EMPLOYMENT DIVISION v. SMITH
Supreme Court of the United States (1990) ____ U.S. ____, 110 S.Ct. 1595

The use of peyote by Navajo Indians as a religious practice goes back as far as 1560. Some states have made an exception in their drug laws for sacramental peyote use. In *People v. Woody*, 394 P.2d 813, the Supreme Court of California held that it could continue in that state as a bona fide religious practice. However, the Supreme Court of North Carolina held to the contrary in *State v. Bullard*.[20] Section 115 of the Uniform Controlled Substance Act includes a provision permitting the exception.[21]

The State of Oregon did not permit the exception, and Smith challenged Oregon before the U.S. Supreme Court after he lost his job as a drug rehabilitation counselor for smoking peyote as a member of the Native American Church in a religious ceremony. In affirming the Oregon law the U.S. Supreme Court held:

* * *

Because respondents' ingestion of peyote was prohibited under Oregon law, and because that prohibition is constitutional, Oregon may, consistent with the Free Exercise Clause, deny respondents unemployment compensation when their dismissal results from use of the drug.

* * *

WISCONSIN v. YODER
Supreme Court of the United States (1972) 406 U.S. 205, 92 S.Ct. 1526

The defendants were convicted of a misdemeanor for violating the Wisconsin compulsory school attendance law, which requires parents to have their children attend school until age sixteen.[22] The defendants, who were of the Amish faith, took their children out of school after they had finished the eighth grade because they believed that secondary schooling exposed their children to worldly influences in terms of attitudes, goals, and values that were contrary to the religious development of an Amish child. The U.S. Supreme Court sustained the Wisconsin Supreme Court in reversing the convictions and holding that the compulsory school attendance law violated the rights of the Amish to practice their religion freely. Justice William O. Douglas, in dissenting, stated in part that "on this important and vital matter of education, I think the children should be entitled to be heard."

The Religious Beliefs of Parents and the Rights of Their Children

An adult may exercise freedom of religion in many ways. The adult may go to the church or synagogue of his or her choice, or may decide not to attend religious services. Certain foods or beverages may or may not be used. Religious beliefs may determine the manner and types of clothing worn. There are many different types of private religious schools in the United States that persons may attend if they wish.

An adult may also decide to refuse medical treatment or medication because of religious beliefs even though such a decision could endanger his or her life or cause death. Christian Scientists, Jehovah's Witnesses, and some of the fundamental Christian sects teach that conventional medical treatments should not be used. The Florida Court of Appeals (3d Dist.) stated the following in 1987:[26]

> It would appear that, generally speaking, the courts have held that a fully competent adult patient may refuse on religious or other grounds to receive a lifesaving blood transfusion, *Mercy Hospital, Inc. v. Jackson,* 62 Md.App. 409, 489, A.2d 1130 (Ct.Spec.App. 1985); *In re Brown,* 478 So.2d 1033 (Miss. 1985); *In re Brooks Estate,* 32 Ill.2d 361, 205 N.E.2d 435 (1965), even where the patient has minor children whom he supports, so long as these children will be adequately cared for in the event the patient dies. *In re Osborne,* 294 A.2d 372 (D.C.App. 1972) (cited with approval in *St. Mary's Hospital v. Ramsey,* 465 So.2d 666, 668 (Fla. 4th DCA 1985)). This result is, of course, different where the patient is not competent because of her medical condition to make a decision on the matter and is the mother of a minor child, *Application of the President and Directors of Georgetown College,* 331 F.2d

1000 (D.C.Cir.) (Wright, J.), *petition for reh'g denied,* 331 F.2d 1010 (D.C.Cir. 1964), or where the refusal to administer the blood transfusion would result in the death of the patient's unborn child, *Raleigh Fitkin-Paul Morgan Memorial Hospital,* 42 N.J. 421, 201 A.2d 537 (1964); *In re Application of Jamaica Hospital,* 128 Misc.2d 1006, 491 N.Y.S.2d 898 (Sup.Ct. 1985), or where the minor children involved would be abandoned in the event of the patient's death. *Application of Winthrop University Hospital,* 128 Misc.2d 804, 490 N.Y.S.2d 996 (Sup.Ct. 1985).

But where a child is critically ill or injured and in need of immediate medical attention, should parents be able to reject and refuse medical care for their children on religious or philosophical grounds? Surprisingly, over half of the states have statutes permitting a parent or parents to reject and refuse medical attention for their child on religious grounds.

One newspaper described the reaction of many persons in the medical community to these laws as "outrage." This is an understandable reaction where means are available to save the life of a baby or young child and parents can legally say "no" because of their religious beliefs. On the other hand, the parents most often are following a religious belief they are deeply convinced is right.

In 1988, the American Academy of Pediatrics urged the repeal of state laws that allow parents to refuse medical treatment for their children. The chairman of the academy's committee on bioethics stated:[27]

> Under these laws, religion can be an excuse for many things that otherwise would not be tolerated. In some instances, it blocks investigation, or intrusion or prosecution by responsible authorities.
>
> We have numerous laws designed to protect the health and welfare of children, but many children are not receiving equal protection under the law because of the religious beliefs of their parents. We hope we are beginning a process to change that.

Cults, Sects, and Nontraditional Churches in the United States

More than 70 percent of Americans are members of a church or synagogue. Most of the religious organizations in America are old, traditional churches and synagogues. Some churches (primarily Evangelical Christians) are served by television ministers. Only a small percentage of the thousands of churches can be classified as cults.[28]

Estimates of the membership in cults and sects in the United States range from 3 million to 8 million persons belonging to more than 3,000 groups. Some cults are small, whereas others have memberships in the hundreds of thousands.

There has been increased concern over cults since the shocking events that occurred in Jonestown, Guyana (South America), in 1978. Because of complaints that U.S. citizens were being detained against their will in the People's Temple located in Jonestown, Congressman Leo Ryan traveled to South America to investigate the complaints. As he was leaving the People's Temple, Congressman Ryan and his party were slaughtered in a barrage of gunfire. The ambush killing was followed by murders and the mass suicide of approximately 900 cult members living in the People's Temple.

Although some cults and sects are ordinary religious groups, others have given rise to reports concerning some of the following:

- strange religious practices
- brainwashing

- questionable practices used to detain members[29]
- incredible devotion to a cult leader
- cult leaders who live in extreme luxury and acquire considerable wealth from their followers
- in few instances, bizarre sexual acts, torture, and killings

Such behavior has caused an increased number of persons to view cults as the dark side of religion.

The *FBI Law Enforcement Bulletin* presented a three-part article entitled "Cults: A Conflict Between Religious Liberty and Involuntary Servitude?" commencing in the April 1982 issue. The June article concludes:

> With the increase in cult membership over the last 10 years, law enforcement investigations involving cult members is increasing. Whether these investigations will be routine, such as proselytizing activities on the street, or criminal, such as shoplifting or drug use, the cult member should be treated the same as any other person. A more serious problem arises when an officer encounters a "kidnapping" for deprogramming or receives a complaint involving cult coercion by a parent of a cult member.
>
> Clearly, the officer cannot proceed to release the deprogrammer after observing him with a hostage or let him retain a person kidnapped against his or her will. Nor can they invade the property of a cult to release a victim, unless there is evidence of imminent harm to the cult member.
>
> Practical considerations would come into play at every stage, which would require close coordination with the prosecution. Who should be charged with a crime? What type of charges could be filed? What if the "kidnappers" include a close relative? What jury is going to convict a 50-year-old father for kidnapping his 20-year-old son! And if the state cannot prosecute the father, is it just to charge the deprogrammer who was hired by the father to perform the actual kidnapping? What defenses does the law allow in the jurisdiction, and what charges should be given to the jury? Law enforcement officers may wish to consult their local prosecutors to determine whether any guidelines are in place or being contemplated in their jurisdictions to answer these questions.

The article recommends that the following conduct be made crimes: "misrepresentation in recruitment and in proselytizing activities, preventing a [cult] member from contacting individuals outside the organization, or preventing members from leaving the cult." Such legislation must be drafted so as to not interfere with individuals' rights to enter and participate in cults. But new legislation is needed, as the article points out, "to resolve the problem facing parents and law enforcement. The coercive acts of some cults in recruitment and proselytizing activities should not be unchallenged. Nor should some cults be allowed to hide behind the first amendment, while at the same time denying constitutional rights to some of their followers."

Court Cases Involving Cults

UNITED STATES v. HUBBARD
U.S. District Court, District of Columbia (1979) 493 F.Supp. 209

Nine members of the Church of Scientology were convicted of various offenses ranging from conspiracy to obstructing justice, stealing government property, burglary, bugging, harboring fugitives from justice, and perjury.

Conduct Not Protected by the Freedom of Religion Clause

"We have never held that an individual's religious beliefs excuse him from compliance with an otherwise valid law prohibiting conduct that the State is free to regulate." U.S. Supreme Court in the 1990 case of *Employment Division v. Smith,* 108 L.Ed.2d 876.

Conduct Not Protected	Case
Multiple marriages in violation of state polygamy laws (obsoleted crime of bigamy)	*Reynolds v. United States* Supreme Court of United States (1879) 98 U.S. 145, 25 L.Ed. 244
Handling poisonous snakes in a public place in violation of state law[23] as part of a religious ceremony	*State v. Massey* Supreme Court of North Carolina (1949) 229 N.C. 734, 51 S.E.2d 179
Requirements at airports, state fairs, etc. that religious, political, and other groups distribute or sell literature from booths provided for that purpose[24]	*Heffron v. International Society for Krishna Consciousness* Supreme Court of the United States (1981) 452 U.S. 640, 101 S.Ct. 2559
Using a mailbox to put religious, political, or other literature can be in violation of the federal postal statute 18 U.S.C. 1725. The Supreme Court held that a letter box is not a "soap box" and upheld the statute.	*Council of Greenburgh Civic Assn. v. U.S. Postal Service* Supreme Court of the United States (1981) 453 U.S. 917, 101 S.Ct. 3150
Violation of Sunday retail store closing law is not protected by First Amendment	*Braunfeld v. Brown* Supreme Court of the United States (1961) 366 U.S. 599, 81 S.Ct. 1144
Violation of child labor laws	*Prince v. Massachusetts* Supreme Court of United States (1944) 321 U.S. 158, 64 S.Ct. 438
Failure to comply with compulsory military service by defendants who conscientiously objected only to the Vietnam War	*Gillette v. United States* Supreme Court of the United States (1971) 401 U.S. 437, 91 S.Ct. 828
Air Force officer continued to wear his yarmulke (Jewish skullcap) after repeated orders to remove it. He was dropped from service. Affirmed for Air Force.	*Goldman v. Weinberger* Supreme Court of the United States (1986) 475 U.S. 503, 106 S.Ct. 1310
Illegal importation of aliens in violation of Immigration and Nationality Act 8 U.S.C.A. Sec. 1324	*United States v. Merkt* review denied, U.S. Supreme Court (5th Cir. 1987) 794 F.2d 950, 41 CrL 4001[25]
Members of the Old Order Amish who do not use motor vehicles and travel in horse-drawn buggies would not obey a state law requiring reflecting triangles on the rear of all slow-moving vehicles. Held not exempted from complying with this highway safety law.	*Minnesota v. Hershberger* Supreme Court of United States (1990) ___ U.S. ___, 110 S.Ct. 1918, vacating 444 N.W.2d 282
There was also no exemption on religious grounds from complying with required vehicle liability insurance. South Dakota law makes it a crime not to carry the insurance.	*South Dakota v. Cosgrove* Supreme Court of South Dakota (1989) 439 N.W.2d 119, review denied, ___ U.S. ___ 110 S.Ct. 140, 46 CrL 3008

The Freedom of Religion Clause could not be used as a defense for:

Destroying government property (760 F.2d 447); extortion and blackmail (515 F.2d 112); racketeering (695 F.2d 765, rev. den 460 U.S. 1092); refusal to testify before a grand jury (465 F.2d 802, see 409 U.S. 944); photographing of arrested person (848 F.2d 113); putting logging road through area sacred to Indian tribes (108 S.Ct. 1319); vaccination of children (25 S.Ct. 358); participating in social security system (102 S.Ct. 1051).

UNITED STATES v. MOON

U.S. Court of Appeals, Second Circuit (1983) 718 F.2d 1210 review denied by 466 U.S. 971, 104 S.Ct. 2344, 35 CrL 4042

The Rev. Sun Myung Moon, founder of the Unification Church, was convicted of failing to pay $162,000 in federal taxes. His conviction and sentence of eighteen months in prison with a $25,000 fine was affirmed by the federal appeals court and let stand by the U.S. Supreme Court. Nine major religious and civil liberties groups filed friend-of-the-court briefs on Moon's behalf.

The Unification Church headed by Rev. Moon claims to have 4 million followers in 137 countries, including 600,000 in Moon's native country, South Korea. The church has been criticized for exercising tight control over its followers, to the extent that Moon selects many marriage partners. Their mass weddings of hundreds of couples have received worldwide news coverage.

C. THE RIGHT OF PRIVACY

The Use and Distribution of Contraceptives

In the 1960s, some states had criminal laws regulating contraceptives. For example, in Wisconsin it was a criminal offense to sell or give a contraceptive, such as a condom, to an unmarried person. The fact that the law was generally ignored was demonstrated by a newspaper reporter who purchased condoms at more than a dozen drug stores, making it known that he was not married. Another man attempted to get arrested and challenge the law by handing out hundreds of condoms to students at the University of Wisconsin. However, no one would arrest him and the Wisconsin law remained unused until it was repealed.

Prosecutors in Connecticut, however, decided to issue a charge using a statute that made it a crime to use contraceptives. The defendants were operators of a Planned Parenthood clinic and were fined as accessories for promoting the use of contraceptives. When the case of *Griswold v. Connecticut*[30] was appealed to the U.S. Supreme Court, the Court recognized a constitutional right of privacy for the first time. The Court held that the marital relationship was within the "zone of privacy" created by the Bill of Rights. It was held that the Connecticut statute invaded the protected right of privacy and was therefore invalid.

The concept that the Bill of Rights creates a fundamental right of privacy was again stated by the U.S. Supreme Court a few years after *Griswold* in the 1969 case of *Stanley v. Georgia.*[31] In *Stanley,* the Court held that the right of privacy protects the right to possess and look at obscene films in one's home. In the 1972 case of *Eisenstadt v. Baird,*[32] the U.S. Supreme Court upheld the right of unmarried persons to use contraceptives. The last of the contraceptives cases presented to the U.S. Supreme Court follows:

CAREY v. POPULATION SERVICES INTERN.

Supreme Court of the United States (1977) 431 U.S. 678, 97 S.Ct. 2010

The U.S. Supreme Court voided a New York law that: (a) required that nonprescription contraceptives be sold by pharmacists only to persons age sixteen and over, (b) mandated that persons fifteen years and younger obtain contraceptives from doctors only, and (c) prohibited advertisements for contraceptives from display in drugstores.

Quoting *Eisenstadt v. Baird,* the Court held that "if the right of privacy means anything, it is the right of the individual, married or single, to be free from unwarranted governmental intrusion into matters so fundamentally affecting a person as the decision whether to bear or beget a child."

Holding that the New York law served no compelling state interest in denying minors a right of privacy enjoyed by adults, the Court held:

> *Although we take judicial notice, as did the District Court, 398 F.Supp., at 331–333, that with or without access to contraceptives, the incidence of sexual activity among minors is high, and the consequences of such activity are frequently devastating, the studies cited by appellees play no part in our decision. It is enough that we again confirm the principle that when a State, as here, burdens the exercise of a fundamental right, its attempt to justify that burden as a rational means for the accomplishment of some significant State policy requires more than a bare assertion, based on a conceded complete absence of supporting evidence, that the burden is connected to such a policy.*

The Abortion Question

Until 1973, abortion was a crime in most states, with only four states permitting abortion on demand by women. In 1973, the following cases of *Roe v. Wade* and *Doe v. Bolton* came before the U.S. Supreme Court. The rulings in these cases caused the abortion laws in thirty-one states to be unconstitutional and made revisions necessary in the abortion statutes of fifteen other states.

ROE v. WADE
Supreme Court of the United States (1973) 410 U.S. 113, 93 S.Ct. 705

DOE v. BOLTON
Supreme Court of the United States (1973) 410 U.S. 179, 93 S.Ct. 739

The women in both these cases ("Jane Roe" and "Mary Doe") had requested abortions when they were pregnant and, like thousands of other women, were turned down. Both women went to court to attack their state statutes on abortion. Before the Court was the question of the power of government to enact criminal laws forbidding and regulating abortion. When does the fetus have legal rights that obligate the state to protect its existence? In a long, complicated decision, the Court held that:

- *In the first three-month period, abortion "although not without risks, is now relatively safe" and "any interest of the state in protecting the woman from an inherently hazardous procedure . . . has largely disappeared." During this period, "the abortion decision and its effectuation must be left to the medical judgment of the pregnant woman's attending physician."*
- *After the first trimester, a state may "regulate the abortion procedure in ways that are reasonably related to maternal health."*
- *Only during the last ten weeks of pregnancy, when the fetus has developed enough to have a reasonable chance of survival on its own, does the state's "important and legitimate interest in potential life" outweigh the mother's individual rights. It is when the fetus becomes "viable," usually during the seventh month of pregnancy, that a state "may go so far as to proscribe (forbid) abortion . . . except when it is necessary to preserve the life or health of the mother." Justice Harry A. Blackmun, writing for the majority, held that a fetus is not a person under the Constitution and thus has no legal right to life. Antiabortionists strongly object to this last point, as they maintain that there is a "right to life."*

Abortion Practices in the United States Generally

It is reported that approximately 6 million pregnancies occur in the United States each year, and it is estimated that more than half of those pregnancies are unintended. Of the unintended pregnancies, it is reported that more than 1.5 million are terminated by abortion. In 1991, the National Surveys of Family Growth reported that about half of the abortions were performed before the ninth week of pregnancy, and less than 1 percent occurred after twenty weeks or more of pregnancy.

Since 1989, more states have regulated to protect the lives of "viable" fetuses[33] and in doing so "may proscribe (forbid) abortion except where it is necessary, in appropriate medical judgment, for the preservation of the life or health of the mother."[34] Abortion, however, remains highly controversial[35] and laws differ from state to state. Abortion practices are generally governed by the following:

1. As only a licensed physician may perform a legal abortion, any other person who engages in such acts may be charged with practicing medicine without a license.[36]
2. Licensed physicians (who do abortions) limit abortions to early in the pregnancy, because of the increased possibilities of:
   a. a civil malpractice suit
   b. criminal charges if the fetus is "born alive" and then destroyed
   c. disciplinary measures taken by the medical licensing board (such as loss of license)
   d. loss of hospital privileges for violating hospital rules and thereby making the hospital vulnerable to civil suit
   e. increased malpractice insurance premiums because of increased liability.

The 1989 Case of Webster v. Reproductive Health Services

In the 1989 case of *Webster v. Reproductive Health Services,*[37] the U.S. Supreme Court did not overrule the *Roe v. Wade* decision, but did "modify and narrow *Roe*." The Court held:

* * *

Stare decisis is a cornerstone of our legal system, but it has less power in constitutional cases, where, save for constitutional amendments, this Court is the only body able to make needed changes. . . . We have not refrained from reconsideration of a prior construction of the Constitution that has proved "unsound in principle and unworkable in practice." *Garcia v. San Antonio Metropolitan Transit Authority,* 469 U.S. 528, 546 (1985). . . . We think the *Roe* trimester framework falls into that category.

In the first place, the rigid *Roe* framework is hardly consistent with the notion of a Constitution cast in general terms, as ours is, and usually speaking in general principles, as ours does. The key elements of the *Roe* framework—trimesters and viability—are not found in the text of the Constitution or in any place else one would expect to find a constitutional principle. Since the bounds of the inquiry are essentially indeterminate, the result has been a web of legal rules that have become increasingly intricate, resembling a code of regulations rather than a body of constitutional doctrine. As Justice White has put it, the trimester framework has left this Court to serve as the country's "*ex officio* medical board with powers to approve or disapprove medical and operative practices and standards throughout the United States." *Planned Parenthood of Central Missouri v. Danforth,* 428 U.S., at 99 (opinion concurring in part and dissenting in part). Cf. *Garcia, supra,* at 547.

In the second place, we do not see why the State's interest in protecting potential human life should come into existence only at the point of viability, and that there should therefore be a rigid line allowing state regulation after viability but prohibiting it before viability. The dissenters in *Thornburgh,* writing in the context of the *Roe* trimester analysis, would have recognized this fact by positing against the "fundamental right" recognized in *Roe* the State's "compelling interest" in protecting potential human life throughout pregnancy. "[T]he State's interest, if compelling after viability, is equally compelling before viability." *Thornburgh,* 476 U.S., at 795 (White, J., dissenting); see *id.,* at 828 (O'Connor, J., dissenting) ("State has compelling interests in ensuring maternal health and in protecting potential human life, and these interests exist 'throughout pregnancy'") (citation omitted).

* * *

Because none of the challenged provisions of the Missouri Act properly before us conflict with the Constitution, the judgment of the Court of Appeals is

Reversed.

In holding that the State of Missouri abortion statute was not in "conflict with the (United States) Constitution" and was therefore valid and enforceable, the Court provided states with new authority to limit a woman's right to abortion. Provisions of the Missouri Act, with the U.S. Supreme Court's holding on each provision, are:

1. The Missouri legislature "found" that life begins at conception and that unborn children have protectable interest in life, health, and well-being (*Held:* does not regulate abortion or restrict the activities of health professionals in any concrete way).
2. Prohibits the use of public facilities or public employees to perform abortions that are not necessary to save the life of a mother (*Held:* to be consistent with Court's prior abortion rulings that states need not commit any resource to facilitating abortion).
3. Prohibits state fiscal officers from using public funds to encourage or counsel women to have nontherapeutic abortions (*Held:* does not apply to health professionals and therefore the challenge to this provision is moot).
4. Physicians are required to perform tests to determine fetal viability for any fetus believed to be at least twenty weeks gestational age (*Held:* does not unconstitutionally infringe on the right to abortion).

The ruling in the *Webster* case does not affect doctors' offices and clinics. Since most abortions are performed in doctors' offices and clinics, women in Missouri and elsewhere who can afford the cost can continue to obtain abortions.

The New Role of the State

Because *Roe v. Wade* has now been narrowed, giving each state the opportunity to enact legislation within the framework of the U.S. Constitution, new attention has been focused on state capitols. Governors and members of state legislatures are constantly urged by both pro-life groups and pro-choice groups to enact legislation within that state. Protest activity has increased. A spokesperson for an anti-abortion group stated in October 1990 that more than 50,000 arrests had been made at clinics across the country since the *Webster* decision.[38] The arrests are primarily for illegal trespass and disorderly conduct, with a small percentage of the arrests being for unlawful assembly and such offenses as criminal damage to property (criminal mischief).

D. The Privilege against Self-Incrimination

In 1986, the case of *State v. Roberts*[39] came before the Supreme Court of South Dakota. Roberts was a drug dealer and had been convicted of not paying a required tax on illegal drugs and not obtaining a dealer's license required to sell marijuana and other illegal substances.

If such criminal laws were constitutional, states could then require bank robbers to register and obtain a license before robbing a bank. Failure to register and obtain a bank robber's license would permit a state to charge that offense in addition to the charge of bank robbery.

Burglars and other criminals could also be required to register and obtain a license. If they registered, they would notify local police of their intent to commit crimes. If they did not register, they could be charged with additional offenses.

The South Dakota tax on illegal drugs failed and was declared unconstitutional because information of the illegal drugs was provided to law enforcement agencies. Today, twenty-three states have laws that impose taxes on illegal drugs ("stamp tax" laws).[40] A usual tax is $3.50 for a gram of marijuana and $200 for a gram of cocaine. The identity of the drug dealer is not available for law enforcement agencies if they pay tax on their illegal activities.

But few pay the taxes. After they are apprehended for illegal drug dealing, efforts are made by tax departments to collect taxes due. If the person dealing in illegal drugs has a savings or checking account, or other assets such as real estate or an expensive car, collection of the tax could be obtained. But in many instances, the person charged with illegal drug activity has no money and cannot even hire his or her own attorney for legal defense.

U.S. Supreme Court cases holding that tax laws violated the Fifth Amendment privilege against self-incrimination by disclosing tax information to law enforcement agencies are:

MARCHETTI v. UNITED STATES
Supreme Court of the United States (1968) 390 U.S. 39, 88 S.Ct. 697

GROSSO v. UNITED STATES
Supreme Court of the United States (1968) 390 U.S. 62, 88 S.Ct. 709

In the 1950s and 1960s, very few states had any type of lawful gambling. The amount of illegal gambling and betting was growing in the United States. To meet the problem, the U.S. Congress passed a law requiring that all gamblers register and pay a yearly occupational tax. As all gambling was illegal in most states, this presented a problem to a person engaged in the illegal activity of gambling. If the person registered, this person would be telling local officials he or she was violating the gambling laws of that state. If this person did not register and pay the wagering tax, he or she could be charged with an additional offense.

The defendants were convicted of violating the federal wagering tax statutes. The defendants argued that their statutory obligation to register and pay the occupational tax violated their Fifth Amendment privilege against self-incrimination. In reversing the convictions and holding that such laws "may not be employed to punish criminally those persons who have defended a failure to comply with their requirements with a proper assertion of the privilege against self-incrimination," the Court stated:

The issue before us is not whether the United States may tax activities which a State or Congress has declared unlawful. The Court has repeatedly indicated that the unlawfulness of an activity does not prevent its taxation, and nothing that follows is intended to limit or diminish the vitality of those cases. . . .

The issue is instead whether the methods employed by Congress in the federal wagering tax statutes are, in this situation, consistent with the limitations created by the privilege against self-incrimination guaranteed by the Fifth Amendment. We must for this purpose first examine the implications of these statutory provisions.

* * *

The terms of the wagering tax system make quite plain that Congress intended information obtained as a consequence of registration and payment of the occupational tax to be provided to interested prosecuting authorities.

* * *

(W)e can only conclude under the wagering tax system as presently written, that petitioner properly asserted the privilege against self-incrimination, and that his assertion should have provided a complete defense to this prosecution. This defense should have reached both the substantive counts for failure to register and to pay the occupational tax and the count for conspiracy to evade payment of the tax. We emphasize that we do not hold that these wagering tax provisions are as such constitutionally impermissible; we hold only that those who properly assert the constitutional privilege as to these provisions may not be criminally punished for failure to comply with their requirements. If, in different circumstances, a taxpayer is not confronted by substantial hazards of self-incrimination, or if he is otherwise outside the privilege's protection, nothing we decide today would shield him from the various penalties prescribed by the wagering tax statutes.

LEARY v. UNITED STATES
Supreme Court of the United States (1969) 395 U.S. 6, 89 S.Ct. 1532

The defendant was convicted of selling marijuana without paying the tax imposed by federal law on the drug. The Supreme Court reversed Leary's conviction holding that by registering and paying the tax, Leary would have subjected himself to possible incrimination, as the tax records could be supplied to other law enforcement agencies for criminal prosecutions.

Valid Registration and Disclosure Statutes

There are many registration and/or disclosure statutes in the United States. For example, federal and state personal income reporting statutes require all persons with reportable incomes to file income tax returns every year reporting and disclosing the amount and source of their income. Could a drug dealer who made $1 million in illegal drugs successfully attack these statutes as violating his Fifth Amendment right against self-incrimination?

The answer is "no," as the basic purpose of such statutes is to raise money so as to provide the basic and necessary services of state and federal government. Only incidently do the tax statutes sometimes incriminate a big-time drug dealer who does not successfully "launder" his illegal income so as to make it appear to be legitimate. The New York courts have stated the test to be used as follows:

> One may put the basic issue [this] way. If the purpose of the statute is to incriminate, it is no good. If its purpose is important to the regulation of lawful activity to protect the public from harm, especially to the person . . . and only the incidental effect is occasionally to inculpate, then the statute is good.[41]

The following cases illustrate other valid reporting or disclosure statutes used in the United States:

CALIFORNIA v. BEYERS
Supreme Court of the United States (1971) 402 U.S. 424, 91 S.Ct. 1535

All states have statutes that require drivers of motor vehicles who are involved in an accident to stop at the scene and give their names and addresses. These "hit and run" or "stop and report" statutes impose criminal penalties on motorists who fail to comply with the requirements of the statute. The defendant argued that the California "hit and run" statute violated his privilege against compulsory self-incrimination. In holding that "disclosure of name and address is an essentially neutral act," and that "there is no constitutional right to refuse to file an income tax return or to flee the scene of an accident in order to avoid the possibility of legal involvement," the Court sustained the legality of the California requirement, stating:

> *Driving an automobile, unlike gambling, is a lawful activity. Moreover, it is not a criminal offense under California law to be a driver "involved in an accident." An accident may be the fault of others; it may occur without any driver having been at fault. No empirical data are suggested in support of the conclusion that there is a relevant correlation between being a driver and criminal prosecution of drivers. So far as any available information instructs us, most accidents occur without creating criminal liability even if one or both of the drivers are guilty of negligence as a matter of tort law.*
>
> *The disclosure of inherently illegal activity is inherently risky. . . . But disclosures with respect to automobile accidents simply do not entail the kind of substantial risk of self-incrimination involved in* Marchetti, Grosso, *and* Haynes. *Furthermore, the statutory purpose is noncriminal and self-reporting is indispensable to its fulfillment.*

UNITED STATES v. LAUCHLI
Court of Appeals of the United States, Seventh Circuit (1971) 444 F.2d 1037

The defendant was convicted of fifteen violations of the National Firearms Act and the Gun Control Act. On one occasion, he illegally sold two Thompson submachine guns and ten silencers to an undercover officer. On another occasion, he sold ten Thompson submachine guns and fifteen barrels to the officer. When officers searched his home and business place under the authority of a search warrant, they found 461 submachine guns and two white phosphorus rifle grenades. In the case of *Haynes v. United States,*[42] the Supreme Court held in 1968 that the National Firearms Act violated the Fifth Amendment privilege against self-incrimination. Defendant Lauchli was convicted in 1971 under the amended National Firearms Act, which the court held did not violate the Fifth Amendment privilege against self-incrimination because (a) it is no longer directed to a selective group inherently suspect of criminal activities but applies to all possessors of firearms and (b) the government does not disclose the information that is provided by the person who is required to register.

Questions and Problems for Chapter 12

Are the following valid and lawful use of the police power of a state or city? Explain your answer.

1. A state law makes abortion a crime regardless of the stage of pregnancy at the time of abortion.

2. A municipality takes away the liquor license from a night club that featured nude entertainment.

3. A state statute permits the death penalty to be imposed in first-degree murder convictions at the discretion of the jury or judge.

4. A state law forbids the criticism of any public official in that state.

5. Citations and arrests were made when demonstrators violated red traffic lights as a means of social protest.

6. A state statute forbids the possession of a loaded revolver whether the gun is carried concealed or in open view.

7. A state statute forbids the sale of obscene material.

8. A state statute forbids the use or sale of contraceptives to anyone (married or unmarried).

9. A state law requires a motorist involved in an accident to stop and leave his or her name and address.

10. A statute forbids loitering in a public school building by persons who have no legitimate business in the building.

11. A state statute forbids the carrying or possession of a loaded rifle or shotgun in a motor vehicle on the public highways. (See *State v. Duranleau,* 128 Vt. 206, 260 A.2d 383 [1969].)

12. A state statute forbids the sale of firearms to anyone without an identification card issued by the local police department. (See *Burton v. Sills,* 53 N.J. 86, 248 A.2d 521 [1968].)

13. A chronic alcoholic was arrested when he was disorderly and broke a store window while intoxicated.

Notes

1. The right to carry arms was regulated in England as early as 1328 in the Statute of Northampton. The English Bill of Rights of 1688 denounced the discriminatory arming of persons and seemed to acknowledge the legislature's power to regulate. Carrying weapons was not an absolute right under the old common law. See *Burton v. Sills,* 53 N.J. 86, 248 A.2d 521 (1968).

2. A third group argues that the Second Amendment has nothing to do with private gun ownership, apart from militia consideration. Two hundred years ago, most families had a gun and it was beyond the comprehension of the Framers that gun ownership would be infringed except to "quell rebellion" or similar problem.

3. President of the International Chiefs of Police Joe Casey who is the chief of the Nashville Metropolitan Police Department in 1988. Chief Casey and other American chiefs of police repeatedly have accused the NRA of "going off the deep end."

4. See also the 1976 case of *Commonwealth v. Davis,* 369 Mass. 886, 343 N.E.2d 847, in which the defendant argued that he had a constitutional right to possess a sawed-off shotgun. The Supreme Judicial Court of Massachusetts held: "The Second Amendment of the Constitution of the United States declares: 'A well regulated Militia, being necessary to the security of a free State, the right of the people to keep and bear Arms, shall not be infringed.' This was adopted to quiet the fears of those who thought that the Congressional powers under article I, § 8, clauses 15 and 16, with regard to the State militias might have the effect of enervating or destroying those forces. The amendment is to be read as an assurance that the national government shall not so reduce the militias."

5. In 1988, the Florida state legislature went even further. They enacted a bill sweeping away all local gun ordinances including those forbidding carrying a gun in the open. They changed the state law requiring strict background checks for handgun permits so that

practically any adult could get a handgun permit. Under the old system, there had been 17,000 handgun permits statewide. With the new system, it is estimated that 200,000 licenses will be issued. The "Dodge City Loophole" was closed in 1988 and permitted carrying handguns in the open. But the liberal handgun licensing system will be harder to change.

6. See "Topic of the Times," *New York Times* (August 5, 1988).

7. See the editorial "For $60, A License to Kill," *New York Times* (August 7, 1988).

8. See "Guns, Guns, Everywhere—Strategies for Arms Control," *New York Times* (January 4, 1991).

9. Committee Comments (1961) to Article 24, Deadly Weapons, Smith-Hurd Illinois Annotated Statutes, chap. 38, p. 165.

10. 23 Ill.App.2d 10, 161 N.E.2d 584 (1959).

11. 251 Cal.App.2d 22, 59 Cal.Rptr. 265 (1967).

12. 476 U.S. 16, 106 S.Ct. 1677.

13. People on Complaint of *Altomari v. Evergood,* 74 N.Y.S.2d 12 (Mag.Ct. 1947).

14. *People v. Tardibuono,* 174 Misc. 305, 20 N.Y.S.12d 633 (1940).

15. 56 Md.App. 222, 467 A.2d 552, 34 CrL 2163 (1983).

16. 266 Cal.App.2d 341, 72 Cal.Rptr. 162 (1968).

17. Some states make the carrying of a weapon without a permit in a vehicle a crime. The Connecticut statute was challenged in the 1989 case of *State v. Mebane,* 17 Conn.App. 243, 551 A.2d 1268 (1989), review denied U.S. Supreme Court, 45 CrL 4078. The Connecticut statute provides in part:

> *"Any person who knowingly has, in any vehicle owned, operated or occupied by him, any weapon for which a proper permit has not been issued as provided in section 29–28 or section 53–206, or has not registered such weapon as required by section 53–202, as the case may be, shall be fined not more than one thousand dollars or imprisoned not more than five years or both. . . ."*

18. *Davis v. Beason,* 133 U.S. 333, 10 S.Ct. 299 (1890).

19. 310 U.S. 296, 60 S.Ct. 900 (1940).

20. 267 N.C. 599, 148 S.E.2d 565 (1966).

21. See *United States v. Kuch,* 288 F. Supp. 439 (D.D.C. 1968), in which the Court held that the Neo-American Church was not a religion so as to qualify for the exception. Their solemn motto was "Victory over Horseshit" and their church "catechism" stated: "We have the right to practice our religion, even if we are a bunch of filthy drunken bums."

22. See the 1987 case of *Waddell v. Michigan,* 483 U.S. 1002, 107 S.Ct. 3223 (MichCirCt, Berrigan City) where the appeal was dismissed by the U.S. Supreme Court, 41 CrL 4077 (6/24/87). A mother did not have a religious right to keep her six-year-old child out of school in violation of the state's compulsory education law.

23. According to the New Testament in Mark 16:16-18, "He that believeth and is baptized shall be saved . . . they shall speak with new tongues; they shall take up serpents; and if they drink any deadly thing, it shall not hurt them." In *State v. Massey,* the defendant was convicted of handling poisonous snakes in a religious ceremony, taking literally these words from the New Testament. The court ruled that the state law forbidding the handling of poisonous snakes was a valid use of the police power of the state of North Carolina and held that the public safety factor outweighed the right to religious freedom.

However, the practice of handling poisonous snakes continues to a limited extent in some southern Appalachian churches. In 1972, two young men who had successfully handled such snakes as copperheads further testified to their belief in Mark 16:16-18 by drinking a mixture of strychnine and water at an evening service. Both were dead by the next morning.

24. The Minnesota State Fair made distribution or sale of literature or merchandise away from a booth rented on the fairgrounds a misdemeanor, subject to arrest and expulsion from the fairgrounds. Booths were rented on a nondiscriminatory first-come, first-served basis. The Krishna religion argued that this regulation suppresses their religious practice of Sankirtan, which requires its members to go into public places to distribute or sell religious literature and to solicit donations for the support of their sect.

The U.S. Supreme Court held that the rule of the Minnesota State Fair did not violate First Amendment rights of the Hare Krishna sect. The fairgrounds consist of a relatively small area in view of the massive crowds of people and the enormous variety of goods, services, entertainment, etc. that is exhibited. The Court held that the state's interest in maintaining the orderly movement of the crowd is sufficient to impose the time, place, and manner restriction not only on the Hare Krishna sect, but also on the many other groups seeking to exercise their First Amendment rights.

25. See also the case of *United States v. Aguilar et al* 871 F.2d 1436 (9th Cir. 1989) where the defendants ran an "underground railroad" smuggling Central Americans into the United States in violation of federal law. It was held defendants were not entitled to defenses of "mistake of law" or First Amendment religious belief.

26. *Wons v. Public Health Trust of Dade County,* 500 So.2d 679 (Fla.App. 1987).

27. January 1988 issue of *Pediatrics,* Journal of the American Academy of Pediatrics.

28. See "Image of TV Ministers Took a Beating in 1987," *Los Angeles Times,* and *Milwaukee Journal* (December 26, 1987). The article points out that 92 percent of Americans agreed that "religious organizations should make full disclosure of the funds they receive and how (the funds) are spent."

29. Many civil lawsuits involving cults and sects have occurred throughout the United States. In Santa Ana, California, Robin George, a twenty-three-year-old woman, was awarded $32 million in 1983 against the Hare Krishna sect and their leaders for false

imprisonment, intentional emotional distress, libel, and wrongful death of George's father, who died during the search for his daughter. Robin George and her mother alleged that she was kidnapped and brainwashed by the Krishnas when Robin was fourteen years old. The damages have been reduced to $5 million and the case is before the U.S. Supreme Court.

In 1982, twenty-five-year-old Bill Eilers and his wife were abducted from a parking lot in Minnesota by five religious deprogrammers. His wife was successfully deprogrammed, but Eilers escaped and went back to the Disciples of the Lord Jesus Christ. His wife divorced him and has custody of their child. Eilers sued the deprogrammers for nearly $6 million. The jury awarded Eilers $10,000 in 1984 for his false imprisonment. Both sides claimed victory for the relatively small damage award.

30. 381 U.S. 479, 85 S.Ct. 1678 (1965).

31. 394 U.S. 557, 89 S.Ct. 1243 (1969).

32. 405 U.S. 438, 92 S.Ct. 1029 (1972).

33. A "viable" fetus is defined by the U.S. Supreme Court in *Colautti v. Franklin,* 439 U.S. 379, 99 S.Ct. 675 (1979) as follows: "In *Roe v. Wade,* the Court defined the term "viability" to signify the stage at which a fetus is "potentially able to live outside the mother's womb, albeit with artificial aid." This is the point at which the State's interest in protecting fetal life becomes sufficiently strong to permit it to "go so far as to proscribe abortion during that period, except when it is necessary to preserve the life or health of the mother. 410 U.S., at 163–164, 93 S.Ct. at 732."

34. The U.S. Supreme Court in *Planned Parenthood of Central Missouri v. Danforth,* 428 U.S. 52, 96 S.Ct. 2831 (1976).

35. An example of an abortion controversy is a U.S. Supreme Court ruling that any state law requiring parental consent for minors to have an abortion must ensure that parents do not have absolute (and possibly arbitrary) veto (443 U.S. 622, 99 S.Ct. 3035 [1979]).

36. In the case of *Connecticut v. Menillo,* 423 U.S. 9, 96 S.Ct. 170 (1975), the U.S. Supreme Court held that a state may prohibit abortions by nonphysicians.

37. 492 U.S. 490, 109 S.Ct. 3040, 45 CrL 3217, (1989).

38. See "Tactics of Protesters Taxing Legal System," *Milwaukee Journal* (October 21, 1990).

39. 384 N.W.2d 688 (S.D., 1986).

40. See "Wisconsin Collects Few Fines with Stamps for Drug Sales," *Milwaukee Journal* (February 18, 1991).

41. *People v. Samuel,* 29 N.Y.2d 252, 327 N.Y.S.2d 321, 277 N.E.2d 381 (1971). See also the *Marchetti* and the *Leary* cases where the U.S. Supreme Court established tests for determining whether registration or disclosure laws violate the Fifth Amendment.

42. 390 U.S. 85, 88 S.Ct. 722 (1968).

Part Three

CRIMES AGAINST THE PERSON

Chapter Thirteen

HOMICIDE

A. Homicide in General

Homicide, the killing of one human being by another, is not always criminal. Sir William Blackstone, a famous English lawyer, wrote in the eighteenth century that there were three kinds of homicide—justifiable, excusable, and felonious. He wrote that the first involved no guilt, the second involved little guilt, and the third was the highest crime that humans were capable of committing against the law of nature.

Justifiable homicide is defined in the common law as an intentional homicide committed under circumstances of necessity or duty without any evil intent and without any fault or blame on the person who commits the homicide. Justifiable homicide includes state executions, homicides by police officers in the performance of their legal duty, and self-defense when the person committing the homicide is not at fault.

Excusable homicide is the killing of a human being, either by misadventure or in self-defense, when there is some civil fault, error, or omission on the part of the person who commits the homicide. The degree of fault, however, is not enough to constitute a crime.

Criminal (or *felonious*) *homicide* occurs when a person unlawfully and knowingly, recklessly, or negligently causes the death of another human being. The common law and the states have divided criminal homicide into the crimes of murder, manslaughter, and negligent homicide.

This chapter deals with criminal homicide and the circumstances that give rise to specific charges. Criminal homicide encompasses a wide variety of acts. The acts and the intent with which they were committed determine whether the homicide is intentional or unintentional. Such determination is relevant because penalties are severer when the killing was intentional rather than a result of recklessness, negligence, or carelessness.

B. The Requirement of Proving *Corpus Delicti*

Corpus delicti means the body or substance of the crime (proof that a crime has been committed). *Corpus delicti* must be proved in all criminal charges. The state must show that a crime has actually been committed before it may convict a person of committing the crime. If the state cannot show that a crime was committed, it should not charge a person with a criminal offense.

Corpus delicti cannot be presumed and must be established by legal evidence. Mere hearsay or the showing that the defendant had a motive to commit a crime is not sufficient to prove *corpus delicti*. As a general rule, *corpus delicti* must be established beyond a reasonable doubt.[1] It may be established not only by direct and positive evidence, but also by circumstantial evidence. When *corpus delicti* is established by circumstantial evidence, the general rule is that the evidence must be so conclusive as to eliminate all reasonable doubt in showing that a crime was actually committed. If there is no evidence of the *corpus delicti*,

Twenty persons were fatally shot when an out-of-work security guard went berserk in a San Ysidro California McDonald's restaurant (1984). Such bizarre tragedies focus the nation's attention on criminal homicide.

the court may so properly hold. But whether the *corpus delicti* has been proven is a question of fact for a jury.[2]

The Supreme Court of Pennsylvania stated in the case of *Commonwealth v. Leslie* that in order to prove *corpus delicti* in a criminal homicide case, the state must show "that the person for whose death the prosecution was instituted is in fact dead and that the death occurred under circumstances indicating that it was criminally caused by someone."[3]

In the *Leslie* case, the state police officer who investigated a fire that destroyed a summer cottage found no evidence that the fire was a deliberate burning. However, he had a hunch that it was not accidental. Because Leslie's description was similar to the description of a person seen in the area at the time of the fire, the officer interviewed Leslie in prison when he heard that Leslie had been arrested on other charges. Leslie confessed that he had started the fire and the officer went back to the scene of the fire but could not uncover any evidence that the fire was not started accidentally. As there was no corroborating evidence supporting the confession, the Supreme Court of Pennsylvania reversed Leslie's conviction for arson.

Proving *Corpus Delicti* in "No Body" Cases

Thousands of persons disappear each year in the United States and cannot be accounted for. Most of these persons are living elsewhere and are not communicating with their families and friends. Some, however, are victims of murders and other crimes. A California Court of Appeal stated in the *Charles Manson* case that the "fact that a murderer may successfully dispose of the body of the victim does not entitle him to an acquittal. That is one form of success for which society has no reward."[4]

Ordinarily if there is no body, there is no case. But *corpus delicti* can be proved by circumstantial evidence, or by confessions that have been corroborated and affirmed by other evidence. In cases in which a body is never found, the state must carry the burden of proving *corpus delicti* (that the crime alleged by the state has occurred). The following two cases illustrate the rules:

PEOPLE v. LIPSKY
Court of Appeals of New York (1982) 57 N.Y.2d 560, 457 N.Y.S.2d 451, 443 N.E.2d 925

While the defendant was in custody on an assault charge in Utah, he confessed that he murdered a prostitute in Rochester, New York. The victim, Mary Robinson, had been reported missing, but her body had not been found. To corroborate the confession, the state showed that the victim's purse, sandals, wallet, glasses, identification card, and other personal effects were found in an apartment that the defendant had rented in New York within a week of her disappearance. Although the defendant had registered to go to college in New York, he left the state a week after the victim's disappearance and appeared emotionally overwrought. Then, while he was in prison in Utah, he wrote a poem indicating that he had killed another person. In affirming the defendant's conviction and holding that there was sufficient evidence to justify the jury's verdict of guilty, the Court held:

> *The evidence reviewed above, when read with defendant's confession, the poem he composed and his admissions to his two Provo co-workers, sufficiently establishes both Mary Robinson's death and defendant's strangulation of her as the cause of it to take the issues to the jury. More is not required.*

EPPERLY v. COMMONWEALTH
Supreme Court of Virginia (1982) 224 Va. 214, 294 S.E.2d 882

An eighteen-year-old college girl was last seen leaving a dance with the defendant. Her body was never found, but her blood-soaked clothes were. Her car was found, and there was evidence of a violent struggle at a house on Claytor Lake, where the defendant was seen after the dance. Dogtracking evidence corroborating some of the allegations made by the state was permitted to be used at the defendant's trial. The defendant also made incriminating statements. In affirming the defendant's convictions, the court held:

> *We think the evidence was sufficient to warrant the jury in finding, to the full assurance of moral certainty, that Gina Hall was dead as the result of the criminal act of another person. The jury was entitled to take into account, in this connection, her sudden disappearance, her character and personal relationships, her physical and mental health, the evidence of a violent struggle at the house on Claytor Lake, her hidden, blood-soaked clothing, and the defendant's incriminating statements — particularly his reference to "the body" before it was generally thought she was dead.*

"Body Without Proof of the Cause of Death" Cases

The body of the deceased is available in most criminal homicide cases. But if doctors are not able to testify specifically that the cause of death was due to an unlawful act, *corpus delicti* has not been proved. Unexplained deaths are unusual but not rare in medical history. If doctors are unable to determine the cause of death, or if they are uncertain and unable to state whether the death resulted from criminal acts or from natural causes, then a reasonable doubt may have been created.

The television series "Quincy" popularized the role of medical examiners and coroners in both determining the cause of death and obtaining evidence necessary to establish *corpus delicti*. A doctor's testimony that he or she "suspected" or had a "hunch" that the criminal act was the cause of death is not sufficient to prove *corpus delicti*. The following cases illustrate the *corpus delicti* requirement that proof of the cause of death must be established:

PEOPLE v. ARCHERD
Supreme Court of California (1970) 3 Cal.3d 615, 91 Cal.Rptr. 397, 477 P.2d 421

During the period from 1947 to 1966, the defendant married a series of women. After each woman took out a large insurance policy, she would die after being in a coma for a number of hours. It was suspected in each case that a massive injection of insulin was the cause of death. But it was not until 1967 that doctors were able to testify with certainty that the brain tissues of the victims showed this was true. The defendant was suspected of killing six women, but was charged and convicted of three deaths. A movie was made of the trial and conviction of the defendant, and a detailed account of the investigation can be found in the January 1969 *FBI Law Enforcement Bulletin,* in an article by Sheriff Pitchess, "Proof of Murder by Insulin—A Medico-Legal First."[5]

IN RE FLODSTROM
Supreme Court of California (1954) 134 Cal.2d 871, 277 P.2d 101, *proceeding dismissed* **45 Cal.2d 307, 288 P.2d 859 (1955).**

The court ordered the release of a mother despite the fact that she had confessed to smothering her baby. However, doctors could not determine whether the baby died of the mother's alleged criminal act or of natural causes. As there was no corroborating evidence to support the confession, the charges against the mother were dropped.

The "Born Alive" Requirement

Under the common law, the killing of a fetus (unborn baby) was not a homicide. As a fetus is not a "person" or a "human being," and as most criminal homicide statutes forbid only the killing of a "person" or "human being," these statutes do not include the killing of a fetus.

Most states follow the common law, which requires that if the state is charging the homicide of a newborn baby, it must show that the child was "born alive" and was living at the time it was killed. The testimony of a competent witness that he or she saw the living child or heard the baby cry would ordinarily be sufficient to prove "born alive." The 1989 case of *State v. Cornelius,* 152 Wis.2d 272, 448 N.W. 2d 434, and the 1980 case of *People v. Greer,* 79 Ill.2d 103, 37 Ill.Dec. 313, 402 N.E.2d 203, illustrate the rule.

However in civil law, most states recognize unborn viable (quickened) children as "persons" for the purposes of commencing civil lawsuits for wrongs. Noting this inconsistency, the Supreme Court of South Carolina in the case of

State v. Horne[6] also recognized a quickened fetus as a "person" in criminal cases, ruling:

* * *

> It would be grossly inconsistent for us to construe a viable fetus as a "person" for the purposes of imposing civil liability while refusing to give it a similar classification in the criminal context.
>
> This court has the right and the duty to develop the common law of South Carolina to better serve an ever-changing society as a whole. In this regard, the criminal law has been the subject of change. ... The fact this particular issue has not been raised or ruled on before does not mean we are prevented from declaring the common law as it should be. Therefore, we hold an action for homicide may be maintained in the future when the state can prove beyond a reasonable doubt the fetus involved was viable, i.e., able to live separate and apart from its mother without the aid of artificial support.

* * *

> From the date of this decision henceforth, the law of feticide shall apply in this state.

Before effective birth control and legal abortion, there were many more infant homicide cases than there are today. Because of the difficulty of obtaining proof that the child was born alive and then killed, many states long ago enacted statutes making the concealing of the death of an infant a crime. These cases usually came to the attention of the police when the corpse of an infant was found in a garbage pail or elsewhere. Probably most prosecutions in cases of this type were based on statutes making it an offense to conceal the death of a child, rather than on criminal homicide.

The Crime of Feticide

Whereas South Carolina created the crime of feticide by a court ruling changing the common law, nineteen states are reported creating the crime of "feticide" by legislation. Section 16-5-80(a) of the Georgia statutes provides that "a person commits the offense of feticide if he willfully kills an unborn child so far developed as to be ordinarily called 'quick' by any injury to the mother of such child that would be murder if it resulted in the death of such mother." The Georgia Supreme Court defined "quick" as that "time when the fetus is able to move in its mother's womb."[7]

California statutes now define murder as the "unlawful killing of a human being, or a fetus, with malice aforethought" (Title 8, Sec. 187). This statute makes the killing of a fetus in California "with malice aforethought," murder and changes the common law. This statute, however, does not make abortion murder in California as Section 187 does not apply when the "act was solicited, aided, abetted, or consented to by the mother of the fetus."

Proof that the Victim Was Still Alive at the Time of the Defendant's Unlawful Act

Because criminal homicide is the unlawful killing of a living human being, the state has the burden of showing that the victim was alive at the time of the unlawful act. All persons have a right to life, and whether they have ten minutes or ten years left to live makes no difference in the eyes of the law.

However, if the victim had already died of illness or other injuries at the time of the defendant's unlawful act, the crime of criminal homicide was not committed. In the 1973 murder trial of a New York doctor, the doctor was charged with causing the death of a dying cancer patient by injecting a lethal dose of potassium chloride. The patient was in a coma and was not expected to live longer than two days. During the twelve-day trial in New York City, the defense attorney argued that the deceased was already dead of natural causes when the injection was made. The state failed to show conclusively that the deceased was still alive at the time of the injection, and the jury acquitted the doctor of homicide.

Motive is no defense in a murder charge. Nor is it a defense to show that the victim wanted to die. The crime of murder has been committed if it is shown that the unlawful act that caused the death was done deliberately and with premeditation. Motive and consent by the victim may be considered by the judge in sentencing the defendant in those states in which the sentence is not mandatory.

There have been many euthanasia (mercy-killing) cases in the United States and in Europe over the years. The author of an article entitled "Euthanasia: None Dare Call it Murder"[8] points out that the victims of this type of homicide usually fall into three groups: (1) persons with painful and terminal diseases, such as cancer, who have only a short time to live; (2) mentally defective or retarded persons and old people suffering from senility (some of whom are kept alive by artificial medical means); and (3) infants and young children with gross mental or physical defects.

See the 1987 case of *State v. Forrest*[9] where the defendant was convicted of first-degree murder and sentenced to life imprisonment for the mercy killing of his terminally ill father who had a number of untreatable conditions. The state had no difficulty proving the victim was alive at the time of the wrongful acts causing his death.

When Is a Person Legally Dead?

Historically, death has been defined in terms of cessation of heart and respiratory functions.[10] Until the 1950s and 1960s, the heart was considered the body's most vital organ. Today, medical technology is able to keep the heart and other organs alive for transplantation to other persons. Medical science now recognizes that the body's real seat of life is the brain.

On the average day, more than six thousand Americans die. Doctors estimate that at least several hundred of these deaths occur after doctors, patients, and family members agree to withhold life-sustaining treatment and allow the inevitable to occur.

In a landmark ruling in this area of law, Justice Marie L. Garibaldi of the New Jersey Supreme Court wrote, "Death comes to everyone; however, in our society, due to great advances in medical knowledge and technology over the last few decades, death does not come suddenly or completely unexpectedly to most people."[11] The New Jersey Supreme Court held that the individual's right to refuse treatment must come before the interests of the state in keeping the individual alive.

After the medical profession defined death in terms of "brain death," courts and state legislative bodies have followed with changes in the legal definition of

The Right to Die

Every day in the United States, approximately six thousand persons die. In 1990, the American Hospital Association estimated that hundreds of the deaths are somehow timed or negotiated privately by the concerned parties agreeing not to start, or to withdraw, some form of life-support technology or treatment. For example, every year 12,000 of the 80,000 patients on artificial kidney machines decide to withdraw from the machine knowing that death will occur within two weeks.

The common law recognized that a competent person has a right to control his or her own body. In 1990, the U.S. Supreme Court pointed out that "a competent (person's) . . . constitutionally protected liberty interest in refusing unwanted medical treatment may be inferred from our prior decisions" (110 S. Ct. at 2851). Therefore, an adult who has his mental faculties could refuse medical treatment, medication, or an operation knowing that the refusal would cause his death.

While a competent adult can make such a decision, a child (minor) or an incompetent adult cannot. New medical technology developed during the 1970s and 1980s provided the means of saving the lives of many persons severely injured in accidents, heart attacks, strokes, and other medical emergencies. While many of these persons go on to live normal, healthy lives, others do not because their brains have been so severely damaged that they are partially or totally brain-dead.

Of the many court cases of brain-dead victims, two young women received a great amount of public attention. Nancy Cruzan received severe injuries in an auto accident and Karen Ann Quinlan was brain-dead because of a drug overdose. After years in vegetative states, the parents of both young women went into courts to obtain permission to withdraw life-support systems. In both cases, the parents carried the burden of showing that their incompetent daughters would not have wanted to go on living in vegetative states. *Quinlan* 70 N.J. 10, 355 A.2d 647 (1976) review denied 429 U.S. 922, 97 S.Ct. 319 and *Cruzan,* ___ U.S. ___ , 110 S. Ct. 2841 (1990).

In the 1990 *Cruzan* case, the U.S. Supreme Court held that states could establish standards such as the Missouri "clear and convincing" evidence requirement showing that Nancy Cruzan would have wanted to die. The State of Missouri, which was paying about $112,000 per year to keep Cruzan alive in a "persistent vegetative state," had opposed efforts by her parents to have life-support systems withdrawn. In a hearing after the Supreme Court's decision, a Missouri court heard new evidence presented by three of Cruzan's co-workers who testified that Nancy had stated she would never have wanted to live "like a vegetable." Cruzan's doctor testified that her existence was a "living hell." After eight years on life support systems, the feeding tube was removed and Nancy Cruzan died.

The Patient Self-Determination Act became effective in 1991. This act requires what is known as the "Miranda warnings" of medicine. Patients and their families in hospitals, nursing homes, and other healthcare facilities must be informed of their rights, and medical records must show whether a patient has rejected life support. Persons can make known their wishes as to medical treatment through:

a) Living Wills—More than forty states now have laws providing for living wills whereby persons can give specific written instructions as to the extent of medical procedures they wish.

b) Medical power of attorney (healthcare proxies or durable power of attorney for health care)—More than twenty states have laws that allow individuals to appoint someone they trust to make medical decisions for them when they are unable to do so. Such decisions would include if and how long life support systems would be used.

c) Use of both living wills and medical power of attorney; or other written or oral statements where persons express their wishes as to medical treatments or use of life-support systems.

States will continue to have an obligation to preserve life unless evidence is presented showing that a person wished to exercise his or her right to die. Medical science will continue to develop new and better ways of preserving life, but the individual will continue to be able to exercise his or her right to life . . . or right to die.

death. In 1981, the Supreme Court of Indiana pointed out that twenty-eight states have followed the "virtually universal acceptance [of 'brain death'] in the medical profession."[12] In defining death as the "permanent cessation of all brain functions," the Supreme Court of Indiana joined the other states in holding "that for purposes of the law of homicide proof of the death of the victim may be established by proof of the irreversible cessation of the victim's total brain functions. The trial court did not err in so instructing the jury." Massachusetts had also adopted this definition of death in the case of *Commonwealth v. Golston*.[13] The defendant had struck the thirty-four-year-old victim on the head with a baseball bat. Surgeons were required to remove a portion of the victim's skull to relieve pressure on his brain in an attempt to save his life. In affirming the defendant's conviction of first-degree murder, the Court stated:

> There was medical testimony that on August 25 only the part of the victim's brain responsible for the most primitive responses, the brain stem, was still to some degree working. On August 26, the remaining brain stem functions, such as responding to painful stimuli and gasping for air, had disappeared; the victim never again exhibited any signs that his brain stem or cortex was functioning. In the opinion of the responsible physician, the victim was then dead, having reached the stage of irreversible "brain death." This opinion was confirmed by an electroencephalogram on August 26 and by another on August 28. The removal of the respirator on August 31 was in accordance with good medical practice. An autopsy the next day revealed a brain without architecture, a decomposed, jelly-like mass, consistent with a brain dead for substantially more than two days. The medical examiner concluded that the victim had been dead since August 28.

In 1983, two California doctors were charged with murder and conspiracy to commit murder. After one of their patients had undergone major surgery, the patient had a serious heart attack. The patient was revived and immediately was placed on life-support equipment. However, the patient had suffered severe brain damage and was in a deep comatose state from which he was not likely to recover. The patient was not "dead" by either statutory or historic standards, as there was some "minimal brain activity."

When the family members were informed, they requested that all life-support equipment be removed from the patient. In holding that no crime was committed by the two doctors who ordered removal of the life-support system, the California Court of Appeal held in *Barber v. Superior Court* that:

> In summary we conclude that the petitioners' omission to continue treatment under the circumstances, though intentional and with knowledge that the patient would die, was not an unlawful failure to perform a legal duty. In view of our decision on that issue, it becomes unnecessary to deal with the further issue of whether petitioners' conduct was in fact the proximate cause of Mr. Herbert's ultimate death.[14]

C. The Causation Requirement

 ## Causation and Proximate Cause

Causation and proximate cause are discussed in chapter 3 of this text. Causation is an essential element of all crimes. The state must show that what the defendant did (or failed to do) was the direct and proximate cause of the harm that occurred. The following two examples illustrate the law of causation:

EXAMPLE 1: After loading a gun with live ammunition, X points the gun at Y and pulls the trigger. The firing pin comes down hard on the back of the live cartridge that X has placed in the chamber of the gun. The blow of the hammer detonates the primer in the cartridge and the primer detonates the powder in the cartridge. The powder burns so rapidly that hot gases immediately build up tremendous pressure in the chamber of the gun. This pressure forces the propellant (the bullet) out of the muzzle of the gun at a high rate of speed. Because of rifling in the barrel of the gun and the direction in which X is pointing the gun, the bullet travels through the air and strikes Y in the head, killing him immediately.

EXAMPLE 2: X goes into a bank with a handgun and points the gun at a bank clerk, declaring in a loud voice his intention to rob the bank. X does not know that the bank clerk has a bad heart and that the robbery will be too great a strain for him. The bank clerk has an immediate heart attack and dies before X leaves the bank.

As a jury can easily conclude in Example 1 that X intended the natural and probable consequences of his deliberate act, it would then find that X intended to kill Y. In Example 1, X's acts were the direct and proximate cause of Y's death. The chain of events that occurred after X pulled the trigger was expected and desired by X. Therefore, X can be held criminally responsible for Y's death.

In Example 2, it will be much harder to prove causation. But courts are now ruling that a "defendant takes his victim as he finds him" (see the 1987 Illinois Supreme Court case of *People v. Brackett* in chapter 3). This matter could go to a jury who could consider the age and general appearance of the victim in determining whether the death was the normal and expected result of pointing a gun at another person. The following cases further illustrate the causation requirement:

PEOPLE v. STEWART
Court of Appeals of New York (1976) 40 N.Y. 2d 692, 389 N.Y.S.2d 804, 358 N.E.2d 487

In a dispute over a former girlfriend, the defendant stabbed another man in the stomach with a knife. The victim was taken to a hospital, where surgery was performed. After the doctor successfully closed the stomach wound that was inflicted by the defendant, the doctor then commenced correcting a hernia that was discovered. The hernia was not related to the stab wound. While the doctor was working on the hernia, the patient went into a cardiac arrest (heart attack) and died. A doctor testified that the patient probably would have survived the stab wound if the hernia surgery had not been performed. Defendant was convicted of first-degree manslaughter and appealed. The Court of Appeals noted that although causation is frequently an issue in civil cases, it is rarely encountered in appellate criminal cases.[15] In reducing the manslaughter conviction to assault in the first degree, the Court held:

> The requirement . . . is that "the defendant's actions must be a sufficiently direct cause of the ensuing death before there can be any imposition of criminal liability." . . . Thus an "obscure or merely probable connection between an assault and death will, as in every case of alleged crime, require acquittal of the charge of any degree of homicide." . . . We have held that "direct" does not mean "immediate." The defendant may be held to have caused the death even though it does not immediately follow the injury. . . . Neither does "direct" mean "unaided" for the defendant will be held liable for the death although other factors, entering after the injury, have contributed to the fatal result. Thus if "felonious assault is operative as a cause of

death, the causal co-operation of erroneous surgical or medical treatment does not relieve the assailant from liability for homicide."

STATE v. DIXON
Supreme Court of Nebraska (1986) 222 Neb. 787, 387 N.W.2d 682

The defendant smashed his way into the home of an elderly woman to burglarize the house. In affirming the defendant's conviction for felony-murder, the Supreme Court of Nebraska held:

* * *

Dixon admitted to Detectives Circo and Wade that Jourdan was alive when he entered the house. The implosion of window glass and part of the wooden kitchen door would startle the most imperturbable individual. Seeing Dixon coming through the doorway into the kitchen probably would stir one to "stare" at him, visual fixation founded in fear intensified by Dixon's ripping the "cord out of the phone." All that unfolded before Susan Jourdan, 76 years old and living alone. What total terror likely seized and constricted Susan Jourdan's heart may be beyond another's comprehension. What the jury did understand was Dr. Roffman's explanation of the cause of Susan Jourdan's death, "emotional trauma of having her door kicked in and stimulating her heart to beat abnormally, causing her collapse and ultimate death."

The "Year-and-a-Day" Rule

The "Year-and-a-Day" rule is also discussed in chapter 3. The old common law rule stated that a person could not be convicted of a murder unless the victim died within a year and a day from the time of the wrongful act.

The Supreme Court of Michigan pointed out in 1982 that the "year-and-a-day" rule dates back to 1278 and that the "original rationale for the rule was probably tied to the inability of 13th Century medicine to prove the cause of death beyond a reasonable doubt after a prolonged period of time."[16]

The Michigan Supreme Court and other courts have abolished this rule. However, some courts continue to use it. The California legislature extended the time limits in amending the California Penal Code in 1969 providing that: "To make the killing either murder or manslaughter, it is requisite the party die within three years and a day after the stroke received or the cause of death administered" (Title 8, Sec. 194).

D. MURDER

The first murder to be reported in the American colonies occurred ten years after the Pilgrims landed at Plymouth Rock. In 1630, John Billington, one of the original band of 102 Pilgrims to come over on the *Mayflower,* fired his blunderbuss at a neighbor and killed the man at close range. John Billington was charged with the common law offense of murder under the English law and, after a prompt trial and conviction, was hanged.[17]

Types of Killings

Passionate (Rage) Killings

- Committed ordinarily by friends, acquaintances, or relatives of the deceased.
- Often committed in a terrible rage, in the heat of passion, or in an emotionally disturbed condition.
- Often committed with no effort made to commit the crime secretly; therefore, in many situations, witnesses observe the commission of the crime.
- Offender is often under the influence of alcohol or a drug at the time the crime is committed.
- Witnesses are often cooperative and can usually give the name or an accurate description of the offender.
- Offender is apt to make incriminating statements and is likely to be remorseful for what he or she has done. Because of remorse or because of the evidence, the offender will sometimes confess.
- This type of offense has a high clearance rate.
- Because many guns are available, arguments are settled with a gun instead of a fistfight.
- Often a "smoking gun" killing where the offender is seen with the "smoking gun" or is apprehended at or immediately after the crime.

Drug-related and Gang Killings

- Often over turf or gang rivalry or within a gang in fights for leadership or because of cheating, etc.
- Often deliberate and carefully planned.
- Killer often escapes scene and cannot be identified.
- Offender is seldom under the influence of alcohol or drugs at the time of the commission of the crime.

Drug-related and Gang Killings (continued)

- Witnesses are fearful and uncooperative and often are unable to provide helpful information.
- As there is no sorrow or remorse and the offender is likely to be knowledgeable about crime, there are seldom incriminating statements or confessions.
- Clearance rates for gang killings are probably the lowest for any type of crime.
- Sometimes a "known but flown" killing where it is known that the killing is a gang or drug-related killing.
- There has been a shocking increase in drug-related killings with victims often innocent persons.

Serial and Random Murders[19]

The number and brutality of serial and random murders increased dramatically in the United States in the 1970s and 1980s. A computer-based tracking system is being used to apprehend the murderers who strike again and again, sometimes moving from city to city, choosing strangers as victims, then moving on to kill again.

Sex as a Motive

Sex is the apparent motive of some random killings. Although many of the victims are women and children, a number of homosexual males are committing multiple murders of male victims. In the United States, more than 4,000 bodies are found each year that are never identified. Some of these murders are motiveless, whereas others appear to be brutal sexual attacks. More than 20,000 murder victims are identified each year in the United States.

continued

Under the common law there was only one degree of murder, and that was punishable by death. After the American Revolution, some state legislative bodies began creating other degrees of murder. They were probably motivated by a desire to separate murder to be punished by death from murder that they did not want to be punished by death.

By the year 1900, probably all the states had more than one degree of murder, with most states having two degrees and some having three degrees. At

Types of Killings continued

Murder by Arson

Fires are sometimes started in anger to retaliate. In 1990, a man confessed that he torched the Happy Land Social Club in New York City because he was run out after arguing with his former girlfriend. The fire killed 174 persons and others were injured. The fire at the Dupont Plaza Hotel in San Juan, Puerto Rico, killed 97 people and injured 150 more in 1987. Employees at the hotel had threatened to go out on strike that night. Three men confessed to starting the fire.

Killings Occurring in Attempts to Commit Other Crimes

About 15 percent of the murders in the United States occur during the commission (or attempts to commit) other crimes such as robbery, rape, burglary, arson, etc.

Mercy Killing (euthanasia)

A very small percentage of killings are mercy killings (euthanasia).

Prison Murders[20]

In the early 1980s, prison killings and other prison violence shocked the nation. The worst violence occurred at the federal penitentiary at Marion, Illinois, where 300 of the most dangerous inmates in the country are held. Because of the widespread inmate violence, a "permanent lockdown" was commenced in 1983. Inmates are confined to cells continuously, frequent body cavity searches are made, and shackles are used for discipline as part of the harsh security measures. Most Marion inmates are serving life terms because the death penalty is seldom used under federal law. In 1988, the severe measures were attacked in

the case of *Bruscino v. Carlson,* 43 CrL 1077. The court noted the "lockdown" is working as killings and violence have been almost stopped. Reasonable alternatives to the "lockdown" are not available, so the court held that there is no violation of inmates' rights.

Mass or Spree Slayings

Because of mental and psychological problems, single persons sometimes commit terribly bizarre crimes including mass killing. The worst bloody rampage occurred at a McDonald's restaurant in San Ysidro, California, where a dismissed security guard shot and killed twenty-one people, many of them children, in 1984. In 1966, after killing his wife and mother, a man climbed into a bell tower in Austin, Texas, and killed fourteen, wounding thirty-one others before he was killed. In 1986, a retired mail carrier killed fourteen workers in the Edmond, Oklahoma, post office before committing suicide. In 1983, thirteen Chinese-Americans were killed in a Seattle gambling club. In 1982, a man killed thirteen persons (most were family members) in Wilkes-Barre, Pennsylvania. A Hamilton, Ohio, man also killed thirteen family members in 1975. Ten persons were killed in New York City in 1984, and Richard Speck stabbed eight Chicago nurses to death after drinking heavily in a tavern in 1966.

Hate and Terrorist Murders

These murders are committed for specific reasons. The narcotic-related murder is generally a fight over drugs, or a "turf" dispute. Terrorists kill for political or "cause"-related reasons. "Hate" murders are motivated by religious, racial, or other hate reasons.

that time, the degree system was a useful and meaningful method of distinguishing murder that was punished by capital punishment and that which was not. With the decline in the use of the death penalty in this century and its virtual nonuse in the 1960s and 1970s, the utility of the degree system declined considerably. With the blurring of the distinction in the wording of state statutes and the shift in the philosophy of punishment in recent years, the value of the degree system has declined even further.

The degree system is still meaningful today when first-degree murder carries a mandatory life imprisonment sentence or the death penalty. The degree system is also used as part of plea bargaining when, if it is of advantage to the state, the defendant may be allowed to plead guilty to second-degree murder or to some other lesser offense if a reduction is appropriate.

Intent-to-Kill Murder

The unlawful, intentional killing of another human being is considered the most serious criminal offense. These killings range from cold and careful killings by a paid assassin to those that are the culminations of one spouse's rage and frustration toward the other. The weapon used to implement the murder can be anything from a firearm to one's bare hands. The type of weapon used or the manner in which the fatal blow is delivered is not necessarily significant. It is the specific intent to take the life of another human being that separates this crime from all other degrees of homicide. The type of weapon and the manner in which it is used, however, may give rise to the legal inference that a person intends the natural and probable consequences of his or her deliberate acts.

Murder at common law and as enacted by the statutes of many states as first-degree murder is defined as unlawful homicide with malice aforethought. The phrase "malice aforethought" signifies the mental state of a person who voluntarily, without legal excuse or justification, does an act that ordinarily will cause death or serious injury to another. Although the word "malice" ordinarily conveys the meaning of hatred, ill-will, or malevolence, it is not limited to those meanings in "malice aforethought" and can include such motives as a mercy killing, in which the homicide is committed to end the suffering of a loved one. "Aforethought" has been interpreted to mean that the malice must exist at the time of the homicidal act. Courts have held that if the design and intent to kill precede the killing for even a moment, the person can be convicted of first-degree murder.[18]

Other states have defined first-degree murder as causing "the death of another human being with intent to kill that person." The American Law Institute Model Penal Code uses the words "purposely" and "knowingly," whereas the proposed Federal Criminal Code uses the wording "intentionally or knowingly causes the death of another human being."

The Deadly-Weapon Doctrine

Although intentional killings are the most common of all murders, there is rarely direct evidence of the intent. The evidence most often available to the state is objective observations of the cause of death, for example, the defendant pointed a gun at the deceased and pulled the trigger, or the defendant plunged a knife into the body of the deceased. Witnesses who have heard the defendant express intention to kill the deceased are seldom available. The questions that then arise are whether such evidence is sufficient to support a finding that malice existed and whether there was an intent to kill.

The deadly-weapon doctrine is related to and is part of the inference that a person intends the natural and probable consequences of his or her deliberate acts. A loaded revolver is certainly a deadly weapon when aimed and fired at close range. Under such circumstances, a jury can easily infer an intent to kill, as the natural and probable consequences of this act would be death or serious bodily harm.

Homicide Investigations in 1980s Receiving National Attention

Product Tampering   In September 1982, seven persons in the Chicago area died from cyanide-laced Extra-Strength Tylenol capsules. The killer has not been apprehended. James W. Lewis was convicted in 1983 in a federal court for attempting to capitalize on the Tylenol killings and extort $1 million from the manufacturer of Tylenol. In 1984, Congress passed the Consumer Tampering Act. The first person convicted under this law was a Seattle woman who wanted to collect her husband's life insurance. She was convicted of killing her husband and an innocent woman who used Excedrin capsules that had been laced with cyanide. In 1991, cyanide was placed in Sudafed cold capsules causing the death of two persons in Washington State. This brought the death toll due to tampering over a nine-year period to twelve persons.

The Billionaire Boys Club   of California received extensive television and newspaper coverage. The jet-set, get-rich-fast conduct ended in convictions of two defendants for kidnapping and murder in 1988. Both were sentenced to life imprisonment without parole.

Lovers Killings   Teenage Jennifer Levin left a fashionable New York City tavern to have sex with 6'4" Robert Chambers in Central Park. He blamed her for getting rough during the sex and in "a frenzy," he killed her. Using the "blame the victim" defense, he was convicted of manslaughter. Jean Harris (former head mistress of a fashionable school) shot the author of the Scarsdale Diet books, Dr. Herman Tarnower, after she was jilted for other women. She was paroled in 1988.

Killers-for-hire   have been advertising their services in such magazines as *Soldier of Fortune*. A jury in Houston, Texas, awarded $9.3 million in damages to the family of a woman whose husband hired her killer through a classified advertisement in *Soldier of Fortune*. The killer advertised his services for "high-risk assignments." The jury found this phrase meant illegal activities and that the magazine owners knew this but continued to run the ads. The killer was also convicted of contract killings in Florida and is serving three life sentences. The woman's husband is on death row in Texas.

Repressed Memory   A thirty-year-old California woman suddenly recalled her father killing her playmate when she was ten years old. The jury believed that the memory had been repressed for twenty-one years until a glance from the woman's own daughter brought it back. The father, George Franklin, was sentenced to life imprisonment in 1991.

Collapse of Skywalks   In the Kansas City, Missouri, Hyatt Regency Hotel, 114 persons were killed and more than 300 were injured in July 1981. After a two-year investigation, a joint statement was made by the federal and state prosecutors that there was insufficient evidence to charge any person criminally. Manslaughter by culpable negligence was one of the possible charges.

Serial Killers   The problem of serial killers continues. See note 19 for serial killings that have received national attention.

Reward   The Swedish Police are running notices in American newspapers of a $8.2 million reward for information leading to the arrest of the killer of Swedish Prime Minister Olof Palme in 1986. The Prime Minister was gunned down in downtown Stockholm.

John Belushi Overdose Death   John Belushi died of acute heroin and cocaine poisoning. In a plea bargain, Cathy Evelyn Smith entered a guilty plea to involuntary manslaughter in 1986. Prosecutors accused her of injecting the fatal drugs that killed Belushi.

Determining what is a deadly weapon would depend on the object used and the circumstances that existed at the time of the homicide. A strong man who struck a year-old infant in the head several times with his fists could easily be found to have an intent to kill, and his fists, under these circumstances, would be considered deadly weapons. However, a man who was in a fistfight with another man just as strong and agile as he would not ordinarily be considered to have used a deadly weapon when he used his fists.

Therefore, in determining what a deadly weapon is, a jury would consider the instrument used, who used it, and how it was used. Some items are almost per se deadly weapons because of the potential harm they can cause. Other instruments, such as automobiles, would have to be viewed in light of their uses. The U.S. Supreme Court ruled in the 1895 case of *Allen v. United States*[21] that a lower court erred when it withdrew the question of self-defense from a jury on the ground that sticks and clubs were not deadly weapons. Sticks and clubs can be deadly weapons, depending on their size, who is using them, and how they are used.

The deadly-weapon doctrine is used in cases in which a killing occurred and in assault, battery, and attempt cases. The following case illustrates:

PEOPLE v. CARTER
Court of Appeals of New York (1981) 53 N.Y.2d 113, 440 N.Y.S.2d 607, 423 N.E.2d 30

While driving his car, the defendant and his girlfriend began to quarrel. The defendant became angry when his girlfriend got out of the car and walked away. The defendant caught her and viciously assaulted her, knocking her to the ground. While she lay helpless on the pavement, the defendant kicked and "stomped" on her head and face. The woman lapsed into a coma, and at the time of trial, a medical expert testified that, in his opinion, the victim would never come out of the coma. Defendant was charged with attempted murder and assault with a deadly weapon or dangerous instrument. The jury acquitted the defendant of attempted murder and convicted him of the felony assault. The Court of Appeals affirmed the conviction, holding that a jury could find that the pair of rubber boots the defendant was wearing could be a "dangerous instrument." Citing New York cases and cases from other states, the Court held:

> The object itself need not be inherently dangerous. It is the temporary use rather than the inherent vice of the object which brings it within the purview of the statute.
>
> The courts of this State have consistently adopted this use-oriented approach. In People v. Cwikla . . . for example, we noted our agreement with the Appellate Division that a common handkerchief with which a victim was gagged and which led to his asphyxiation was a "dangerous instrument" within the meaning of the Penal Law. In a like manner, leather boots used to kick a victim in the face . . . and a spatula used to inflict a cut . . . have been found to satisfy the statutory standard. Thus, although the rubber boots in issue are not inherently dangerous, we must determine whether the evidence in this case is sufficient to support the jury's conclusion that they were readily capable of causing serious physical injury in the way in which they were used.
>
> Here, there is evidence that the defendant used the rubber boots to stomp upon the head and face of his victim, causing her head to contact the pavement below with tremendous force. The jury apparently concluded that the pair of boots, when used in this fashion, was readily capable of causing serious physical injury and, thus, was a "dangerous instrument" within the meaning of subdivision 13 of section 10 of the Penal Law. On this record, we cannot say that such a conclusion was erroneous as a matter of law.

"Transferred Intent"

If a killer is a poor shot and misses the intended victim but hits and kills another person, he or she could argue there was not intent to kill that person. Or if there was a mistake of identity and the killer kills the wrong person, the same argument

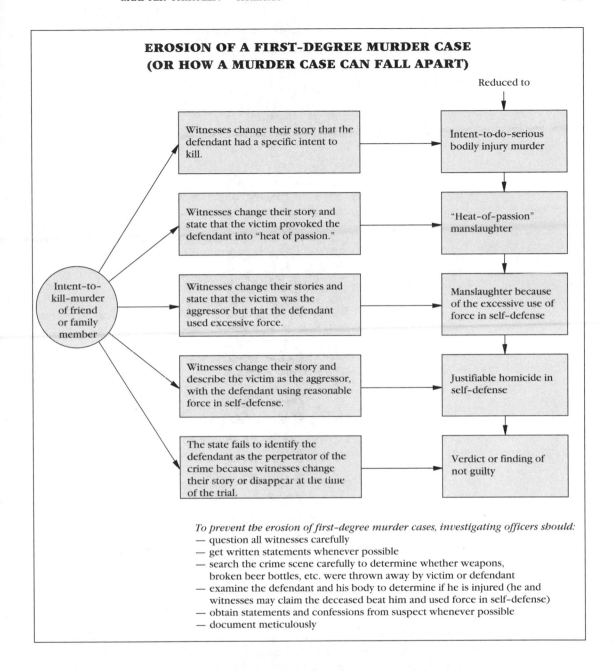

**EROSION OF A FIRST-DEGREE MURDER CASE
(OR HOW A MURDER CASE CAN FALL APART)**

Reduced to

| Intent-to-kill-murder of friend or family member | Witnesses change their story that the defendant had a specific intent to kill. | Intent-to-do-serious bodily injury murder |

Witnesses change their story and state that the victim provoked the defendant into "heat of passion." → "Heat-of-passion" manslaughter

Witnesses change their stories and state that the victim was the aggressor but that the defendant used excessive force. → Manslaughter because of the excessive use of force in self-defense

Witnesses change their story and describe the victim as the aggressor, with the defendant using reasonable force in self-defense. → Justifiable homicide in self-defense

The state fails to identify the defendant as the perpetrator of the crime because witnesses change their story or disappear at the time of the trial. → Verdict or finding of not guilty

To prevent the erosion of first-degree murder cases, investigating officers should:
— question all witnesses carefully
— get written statements whenever possible
— search the crime scene carefully to determine whether weapons, broken beer bottles, etc. were thrown away by victim or defendant
— examine the defendant and his body to determine if he is injured (he and witnesses may claim the deceased beat him and used force in self-defense)
— obtain statements and confessions from suspect whenever possible
— document meticulously

could be made. Defense lawyers have used these arguments for hundreds of years arguing that because there was no ill will and malice toward the victim killed by accident, the defendant should not be convicted of intent-to-kill murder but at the most, negligent or reckless homicide.

To accept such arguments would allow killers to benefit because of their poor marksmanship, or because they killed the wrong person in a mixup. The doctrine of "transferred intent" became part of the common law before the American Revolution and was stated in 1766 by Sir William Blackstone in 4 *Commentaries* 200–201. The following case states the rule:[22]

GLADDEN v. MARYLAND
Maryland Court of Special Appeals (1974) 20 Md.App. 492, 316 A.2d 319

In a dispute over a bad batch of heroin, Gladden emptied a revolver, firing wildly at the heroin pusher. He did not hit the man he was shooting at, but instead hit and killed an innocent twelve-year-old boy. The defendant appealed his conviction of intent-to-kill murder. In affirming the conviction, the court held:

* * *

The doctrine of "transferred intent" has long been recognized at common law. Sir Matthew Hale, in 1 History of the Pleas of the Crown (published posthumously in 1736), said, at 466: "To these may be added the cases abovementioned, viz. *if A. by malice forethought strikes at B. and missing him strikes C. whereof he dies, tho he never bore any malice to C. yet it is murder, and the law transfers the malice to the party slain; the like of poisoning."*

Forty years later, Sir William Blackstone, in 4 Commentaries *on the Laws of* England, *reiterated the common law rule according to Hale; at 200–201: "Thus if one shoots at A. and misses him, but kills B., this is murder; because of the previous felonious intent, which the law transfers from one to the other. The same is the case where one lays poison for A.; and B., against whom the prisoner had no malicious intent, takes it, and it kills him; this is likewise murder."*

* * *

The appellant contends that he should not have been convicted of murder, since he bore no malice toward the victim. He urges upon us that the common law doctrine of "transferred intent" should not be received into Maryland, although he acknowledges that this is the law in the overwhelming majority of common law jurisdictions. We have no difficulty in deciding that "transferred intent" is, and should be, a part of the common law of this State.

Intent-to-Do-Serious-Bodily-Harm Murder

The courts long ago decided that a death at the hands of one who intended to do only serious bodily harm was nevertheless murder. Under modern homicide stat-

---

Killings by Handguns

In 1990, New York City set another new record in criminal homicides of 2,245.* The total number of murders for the United States in 1990 was 23,600 (up 10 percent from 1989). The percentage of killings in New York City by handguns are as follows:

1960 — 19 percent

1970 — 48 percent

1980 — 56 percent

1990 — 69 percent

Sources: Uniform Crime Reports and New York City Police
*Included in this figure are the 87 deaths in the Happy Land Social Club (arson) and the 22 bystanders who were killed by bullets intended for someone else (ten of the bystanders were under age fifteen).

utes, such killing is not "intent-to-kill" murder but is usually considered a lesser degree of murder. The following old English cases illustrate this type of offense:

REX v. ERRINGTON
2 Lew.C.C. 148, 217 (1838)

The defendants covered a drunken man, who was sleeping, with straw on which they threw a shovel of hot cinders. The man was burned to death in the fire that resulted. The court instructed the jury that if it found that the defendants intended to do any serious harm to the deceased, the crime was murder under the common law; if the defendants' only intent was to play a joke or frighten the deceased, the crime was manslaughter.

HOLLOWAY CASE
79 Eng.Rep. 715 (K.B. 1628)

The defendant tied a boy to a horse's tail and hit the horse to make it run. The boy was killed. The defendant was convicted of murder even though it was found that there was no intent to kill.

Depraved-Mind or Depraved-Heart Murder

This classification, in some states called second-degree murder, is similar in some aspects to the "intent-to-do-serious-bodily-harm" murder. The primary difference is that in the "depraved-mind" murder, there is no specific intent to injure or harm. However, if the conduct of the defendant was so reckless as to create a high degree of risk of death, he or she would, in many instances, be found guilty of "depraved-heart" or "reckless conduct" murder.

The Supreme Court of California pointed out in the following case that "malice" may be implied where a person, knowing that his conduct endangers the life of another, deliberately continues to act in a manner that shows a conscious disregard for life:

PEOPLE v. WATSON
Supreme Court of California (1981) 30 Cal. 3d 290, 179 Cal.Rptr. 43, 637 P.2d 279

After drinking a large volume of beer in a bar, the defendant drove through a red light and avoided a collision with another car, late at night, only by skidding to a halt in the middle of the intersection. After the near collision, the defendant drove off at a high rate of speed (twice the 35 mph speed limit). On approaching another intersection, the defendant again applied his brakes, but he struck a Toyota sedan, killing the driver and her six-year-old daughter. Defendant's blood alcohol content one-half hour after the collision was .23 percent, which was twice the .10 percent then necessary to find a person legally intoxicated.

The issue before the Supreme Court of California was whether the defendant can be charged and forced to go to trial on two counts of second-degree murder instead of the usual charges of homicide by intoxicant use of a vehicle or of vehicular manslaughter. In holding that the conduct of the defendant was sufficient to support a probable cause finding of implied malice to justify charging and trying the defendant for second-degree murder, the court stated:[23]

> We have said that second degree murder based on implied malice has been committed when a person does "an act, the natural consequences of which are dangerous to life, which act was deliberately performed by a person who knows that his

Other Felony Murder Cases

Conduct	Finding	Case
Defendant kicked in door of elderly woman's home, tore telephone from wall and burglarized home.	"[E]motional trauma of having door kicked in and stimulating her heart to beat abnormally, causing her collapse and ultimate death."	*State v. Dixon* previously presented to illustrate proximate cause
Defendant tied up his victim during a robbery.	Medical testimony established the cause of victim's death as a heart attack "brought on by the emotional stress resulting from the action of the defendant."	*State v. Spates* Supreme Court of Connecticut, 176 Conn. 227, 405 A.2d 656 (1978)
Armed robberies (and one burglary) of victims who died of heart attacks after crimes (in burglary, victim exchanged gunfire with burglar).	Medical testimony that victims died of "cardiac arrest caused by . . . the stress of events before the victim's death."	*Durden v. State,* 250 Ga. 325, 297 S.E.2d 237 (1982), *People v. Stamp,* 2 Cal. App. 3d 203, 82 Cal.Rptr. 598 (1969), *Booker v. State,* 386 N.E.2d 1198 (Ind., 1979) *State v. Atkinson,* 298 N.C. 673, 259 S.E.2d 858 (1979)
Death of firefighters while fighting blazes started by defendants (deliberate arsons).	Felony murder convictions affirmed.	*State v. Leech,* 114 Wash. 2d 700, 790 P.2d 160 (1990), *People v. Zane,* 152 A.D.2d 976, 543 N.Y.S.2d 777 (1989), *Bethea v. Scully,* 834 F.2d 257, (2d Cir. 1987)
Two deputy sheriffs were killed when their helicopter crashed as they were chasing two teenagers believed to have committed a felony in Benton, Arkansas.	The teenagers were charged as adults with manslaughter under a state law permitting this charge when a death occurs while suspects are fleeing after commission of a felony	See "Fleeing Youths Are Charged After Deputies Die in Crash" *New York Times* (April 26, 1991)

continued

conduct endangers the life of another and who acts with conscious disregard for life." People v. Sedeno . . . Phrased in a different way, malice may be implied when defendant does an act with a high probability that it will result in death and does it with a base antisocial motive and with a wanton disregard for human life. . . .

Based upon our independent review of the record, we believe that there exists a rational ground for concluding that defendant's conduct was sufficiently wanton to hold him on a second degree murder charge.

STATE v. IBN OMAR-MUHAMMAD
Supreme Court of New Mexico (1985) 102 N.M. 274, 694 P.2d 922

In fleeing from arrest by law enforcement officers (a crime in itself), the defendant tried to run police officers off the road. He ran roadblocks at high rates of speed. He was charged with "depraved-mind" murder when he killed a man in fleeing from the police. It was held

Other Felony Murder Cases (continued)

Conduct	Finding	Case
The "Len Bias" law has been enacted in some states making the supplier of drugs that result in death liable for conviction of reckless homicide.	Supreme Court of California held felony murder conviction would stand only if furnishing drug has a "high probability" of resulting in death	*People v. Patterson* 46 CrL 1007 (Sup. Court of Calif., 1989)
Minutes after defendant was arrested in drug transaction, another defendant shot and killed a law enforcement officer.	"Case law makes it clear that a felon is liable for a homicide committed by co-felon during latter's attempt to escape from scene of felony."	*State v. Amaro* Florida Court of Appeals 436 So.2d 1056 (1983)
During an armed robbery, the victim shot and killed one of the robbers. Defendant was convicted of killing of other robber.	*Conviction reversed* "It is clearly majority view . . . the doctrine of felony murder does not extend to a killing . . . (by one other than) those associated with him in the unlawful enterprise. . . ."	*State v. Canola* Supreme Court of New Jersey 73 N.J. 206, 374 A.2d 20 (1977)
Two brothers planned and assisted the escape of their father and another man from an Arizona prison. When free, their father and the other convict kidnapped and robbed a family of four. The defendants watched while their father and the convict murdered the family with shotguns.	A survey of state felony murder laws and decisions indicates that a combination of factors may justify the death penalty even without a specific "intent to kill." Death penalty of two brothers remanded on other grounds.	*Tison v. Arizona* Supreme Court of United States 481 U.S. 137, 107 S.Ct. 1676 (1987)

that he was properly convicted of "depraved-mind" murder instead of the lesser offense of vehicle homicide because the defendant new the risk involved in his conduct.

Felony Murder

The felony murder rule came into existence in England many years ago. The rule states that if a death occurs while a defendant is committing or attempting to commit a felony, the defendant could be convicted not only of the felony (or attempt to commit the felony), but also of felony murder, even if the death were unintended.

The Supreme Judicial Court of Massachusetts and the drafters of the Model Penal Code point out that American courts have narrowed the scope of the felony murder rule by imposing one or more of the following limitations:

1. The felony that was attempted or committed must be one that is dangerous to life (or the state lists the felonies or requires the felony be *malum in se,* or a common law felony).
2. There must be a direct causal connection between the felony and the death that occurred.

3. The act that caused the death must have occurred while the felony was in progress.

England abolished the felony murder rule in 1957. The Supreme Judicial Court of Massachusetts pointed out in the 1982 case of *Commonwealth v. Matchett*[24] that some American courts have also abolished the rule.

WHITMAN v. PEOPLE
Supreme Court of Colorado (1966) 161 Colo. 110, 420 P.2d 416

PEOPLE v. FULLER
California Court of Appeals (1978) 86 Cal.App.3d 618, 150 Cal. Rptr. 515

In both of the above cases, the defendants were fleeing in vehicles after committing felonies (armed robbery and burglary). Both were traveling at high rates of speed in cities, to avoid apprehension. Whitman ran six stop signs and several red lights. Fuller almost collided head-on with another car while driving on the wrong side of the street. Both hit other vehicles, killing the drivers. The courts in both states held that the felony murder doctrine was applicable and the California court pointed out that Fuller "may also be prosecuted for ordinary second-degree murder." The Colorado Supreme Court held:

> *In the* Andrews *case, in commenting upon the statute which is the predecessor of the particular statute with which we are here concerned, we said: "There is no question, from the testimony, but that the defendants committed the homicide in an attempt to perpetrate the crime of robbery. That fact is undisputed. The element of malice does not enter into the crime of murder committed in such circumstances. The purpose of the statute was to make* every homicide committed in the perpetration or attempt to perpetrate certain felonies murder, *which may be punished by death, if the jury so determine, without regard to malice, deliberation, or premeditation. When, therefore, the proof was undisputed that the homicide was committed in an attempt to perpetrate a robbery which the defendants had conspired to commit, it was* not necessary to prove any facts from which malice, deliberation, or premeditation could be inferred." (Emphasis added.)

Classifications of Common Law Murder

Intent-to-Kill Murder   The most common murder, the intentional unlawful killing of another human being, is considered the most serious criminal offense. (The most frequent criminal homicide is that caused by drunk driving.)

Intent-to-do-serious-bodily-harm Murder   In this type of murder, it is found that the defendant intended to do serious bodily injury short of death, but his or her acts resulted in a killing.

Depraved-mind or Depraved-heart Murder When a death results from conduct that shows a wanton disregard for human life and when

there is a high probability that the conduct will result in death, the homicide can be classified as this type of murder.

Felony Murder   At common law, one who caused another's death while committing or attempting to commit a felony was guilty of felony murder. However, when the felony murder doctrine was created, there were only eight felonies and all were punishable by death. Because all states have many felonies, they generally limit the felony murder doctrine to felonies of violence.

* * *

The "perpetration of a robbery" does not come to an end the split second the victim surrenders his money to the gunman, and most certainly the "robbery" continues where, as in the instant case, the robbers are trying desperately to avoid arrest by police officers who are in extremely hot pursuit. In support of this, see Bizup v. People, *150 Colo. 214, 371 P.2d 786, where we stated that a robber's "escape with his ill-gotten gains was as important to the execution of the robbery as gaining possession of the property." Suffice it to say, in this regard, the facts and circumstances of the instant case clearly disclose that this was a murder committed in the perpetration of a robbery.*

E. Manslaughter

Definition

Manslaughter was defined by common law as a classification of criminal homicide that is less than murder. The common law divided manslaughter into the two categories: voluntary and involuntary. Most American jurisdictions have followed the common law classifications, but a few states have created three categories. For example, Section 192 of the California Penal Code creates the three classifications of voluntary, involuntary, and manslaughter in the driving of a vehicle. A few states have only one degree of manslaughter. A form of classification other than voluntary and involuntary manslaughter is that of identifying manslaughter by degrees (first, second, etc.)[25]

The penalties for manslaughter are less than those for murder. Two of the reasons given for the lesser penalties are:

1. The victim provoked the killing and by his or her unlawful conduct set into motion a chain of events that resulted in his or her death or,
2. The killings are not bad enough to be charged and punished as murder but are bad enough to be criminal.

Manslaughter is a crime that is generally considered to be separate and distinct from murder. Because the penalties are less severe than for murder, defense lawyers who are unable to obtain an acquittal for clients seek a conviction of manslaughter rather than murder.

Voluntary Manslaughter

The following 1984 example is used to illustrate voluntary manslaughter:

EXAMPLE: When Robert Lee Moody was eighteen years old, he killed his father with a shotgun and then went to a California police station to turn himself in, stating what he had done. The prosecutor charged Moody with voluntary manslaughter because of the reported conduct of the father: he had seduced his two teenage daughters, had begun fondling his eleven-year-old daughter, had forced his wife into prostitution to help pay for a pleasure boat, was a child- and wife-beater, had opened his older son's head with a screwdriver (son was committed to a mental hospital). After the trial court convicted Moody of voluntary manslaughter, the court received more than 700 letters, most of which urged a lenient sentence for

Moody. The sentence handed down in 1984 was five years of probation, with two of the years served in "Peace Corps-like" missionary work.[26]

In such cases as the *Moody* case, spouse beating, and other cases of shocking conduct, judges and juries have used manslaughter as an alternative to the severer penalties of murder. Although state criminal codes permit six to fifteen years' imprisonment for voluntary manslaughter, the judge in the *Moody* case imposed a lenient sentence because of the facts in the case.

In 1991, Christian Brando (son of actor Marlon Brando) received a six-year sentence for voluntary manslaughter in the shooting death of his half-sister's lover. He also received four more years for aggravating circumstances (use of a gun). Brando could be eligible for parole in four to five years.

Heat-of-Passion Voluntary Manslaughter

The usual type of voluntary manslaughter involves the intentional killing of another while the defendant has temporarily lost his normal self-control because of the conduct of the victim. To lower and reduce murder to manslaughter, courts hold that the following four requirements must exist:

1. There must be adequate provocation.
2. The killing must have been in a heat of passion (anger, rage, emotional disturbance).
3. There must have been no opportunity to cool off.
4. There must be a causal connection between the provocation, the rage, anger, and the fatal act.

What Is Sufficient and Adequate Provocation?   Sufficient provocation is the provocation that naturally and instantly produces in the mind of an ordinary person the highest degree of exasperation, rage, anger, sudden resentment, or terror. The provocation must be of such a nature and so great as to overcome or suspend an ordinary person's exercise of good judgment. The provocation must be such as to cause the person to act uncontrollably. The killing must occur immediately on the provocation and during the intense heat of passion. Only a few categories of provocation have been recognized by the law as legally sufficient and adequate to justify reduction of a murder charge to that of manslaughter.

In the United States, there is an almost uniform rule that words and gestures are never sufficient provocation to reduce a charge of murder to that of manslaughter. The U.S. Supreme Court stated in the 1895 case of *Allen v. United States* that "mere words alone do not excuse even a simple assault. Any words offered at the time [of the killing] do not reduce the grade of the killing from murder to manslaughter."[27]

In the 1991 case of *State v. Girouard,* the defendant got into an argument with his wife. She used taunting, angry words and he murdered her. The Maryland Court of Appeals held in 583 A. 2d 718 that words alone are not adequate provocation to reduce murder to manslaughter. The Court cited decisions from other states pointing out that other "jurisdictions overwhelmingly agree ... and hold that words alone are not adequate provocation." The Court also cited *Perkins on Criminal Law* at page 62 and 40. C.J.S. Homicide, Sec. 47 at 909 (1944).

CHAPTER THIRTEEN   Homicide

Examples of Manslaughter

Example of "Heat of Passion" Manslaughter

Defendant and his wife were separated. Defendant went to the home where the wife and child lived and found his wife having sexual intercourse with another man. Defendant shot and killed the other man and was convicted of first-degree murder. *Reversed to voluntary manslaughter.*

"Heat of passion" manslaughter because:

1. there was adequate provocation, that caused
2. extreme anger and rage ("In our opinion, the passions of any reasonable person would have been inflamed and intensely aroused by this sort of discovery. . . .")
3. there was no opportunity to cool off, and
4. there was a causal connection between the provocation, anger, and the fatal act.

State v. Thornton Supreme Court of Tennessee (1987) 730 S.W.2d 309

Example of "Wrongful Act" Manslaughter

A Wisconsin housewife heard noises in her yard one morning. She looked out a window to see two men hooking up the family boat and trailer to their car. Instead of calling the police, she got a handgun, commenced firing and killed one of the men.

The men were committing a felony in attempting to steal the boat, but Wisconsin's statutes (like all states) forbid the use of deadly force in the defense of property.

The woman was charged with "wrongful act" manslaughter and was also sued in a civil lawsuit for the wrongful death of the victim.

Example of "Imperfect Self-Defense" Manslaughter

Defendant and his brother became involved in a fight outside a Baltimore bar. When the defendant believed the other man had a knife, he pulled a handgun and fired, killing the other man. The victim did not have a knife. The trial court did not submit "imperfect self-defense" issue to jury. *Reversed for new trial.*

In a long decision tracing the history and cases on manslaughter, the court used the "honest but unreasonable belief" rule in holding: In sum, Faulkner produced evidence sufficient to generate a jury issue as to whether he had a subjectively honest by objectively unreasonable belief that he was in imminent danger of death or serious bodily injury, and the trial court should have granted his requested instruction on imperfect self defense.

State v. Faulkner Court of Appeals of Maryland, 301 Md. 482, 483 A.2d 759 (1984)

The Most Controversial Manslaughter Conviction

After losing his job as a San Francisco supervisor, Dan White sneaked a handgun into City Hall. He shot Mayor Moscone four times, reloaded the gun, and shot Supervisor Harvey Milk, a leader of the gay community, six times. Both men were killed. Using the defense of "diminished capacity" (see the "Twinkie" defense in chapter 5), White was convicted on two counts of voluntary manslaughter.

The maximum punishment for manslaughter in California at the time (1978) was a maximum term of four years. Angered by the low sentence, gays in San Francisco rioted and took over the downtown area, burning cars and breaking windows.

People v. White California Court of Appeals 117 Cal. App. 3d 270, 172 Cal.Rptr. 612 (1981)

Just as insulting words are not sufficient provocation, neither is failure to pay a debt. In the California case of *Morse v. People*,[28] the fact that the deceased victim welched on a gambling debt to the defendant and then had the audacity to try to "bum" cigarettes from him was held to be insufficient provocation.

The American rule that words and gestures are never sufficient provocation has been criticized as bringing about harsh results in some cases. However, if other provocation, such as a battery, accompanies the verbal provocation, then it might be held to be sufficient. In *People v. Rice*[29] the deceased slapped the defendant's child and a quarrel resulted. This was held to be sufficient provocation. A minor and technical battery accompanied with words was held in the 1928 Georgia case of *Lamp v. State*[30] to amount to a sufficient provocation to justify reducing the conviction from murder to manslaughter. But in *Commonwealth v. Cisneros,*[31] the Pennsylvania Supreme Court arrived at an opposite conclusion.

The Illinois court in *People v. Williams* held that "it is the defendant's state of mind at the time of the incident that is the critical element."[32] The following batteries were held to be sufficient provocations: a severe beating with a nightstick that fractured the defendant's jaw (*People v. Sain*, 384 Ill. 394, 51 N.E.2d 557 [1943]); throwing hot water into the defendant's face and partially blinding him (*People v. Rice*, 351 Ill. 604, 184 N.E. 894 [1933]); an attack with a knife in a fight in which several people were involved (*People v. Oritz*, 320 Ill. 205, 150 N.E. 708 [1926]); shoving and knocking the defendant into a rock pile (*State v. Ponce*, 124 W. Va. 126, 19 S.E.2d 221 [1942]).

There have been many American cases holding that when a married person finds his or her spouse in an act of adultery, this amounts to sufficient provocation if it causes a genuine heat of passion.[33] However, this rule may not apply if a girlfriend is caught "cheating" on her boyfriend (or vice versa).

Trespass, like battery, depends on the facts and circumstances in each particular case. A homeowner certainly would not have sufficient and adequate provocation to kill someone who walked across a lawn, yard, farm, or field in the middle of an afternoon. But snowmobilers who broke onto a farmer's land in Wisconsin and were circling the farmhouse at midnight caused a Wisconsin prosecutor to charge manslaughter when the farmer, in a terrible anger and rage, shot and killed one of the trespassers.

Heat of Passion and the Test of the Reasonable Person

The test of sufficiency or adequacy of provocation must be made in view of how the average or reasonable person would react to such provocation. Some persons have extraordinary self-control and could endure much provocation before an uncontrollable rage would cause them to use deadly force. Others have short tempers and fly into a rage with little provocation.

A jury cannot give any special consideration to a defendant who has an extraordinarily bad temper. If the provocation is such that it would not cause the average reasonable person to explode in a sudden outburst of rage, it is not adequate or sufficient provocation to reduce murder to manslaughter. California courts have quoted the 1917 case of *People v. Logan* as follows:

> The fundamental . . . inquiry is whether or not the defendant's reason was, at the time of his act, so disturbed or obscured by some passion—not necessarily fear and never of course the passion of revenge—to such an extent as would render *ordinary men of average disposition* liable to act rashly or without due deliberation and reflection, and from this passion rather than from judgment.[34] [Emphasis added.]

The defendant in the 1971 case of *Bateman v. State*[35] was convicted of two counts of murder in the second degree. He had found his wife being warmly hugged by a man whom the defendant had told to stay away from his wife. This occurred at a party of ten adults to which the defendant had not been invited. The Maryland Court of Special Appeals affirmed the trial court's refusal to give the "heat of passion" instruction to the jury. With respect to the question of the use of intoxicants, the court stated:

> Furthermore, it is still the well-settled law in Maryland that "voluntary intoxication will not reduce murder to manslaughter," *Chisley v. State,* 202 Md. 87, 106, 95 A.2d 577, but will be considered simply for purposes of lowering first-degree murder to second-degree murder.

The case of *Bedder v. Director of Public Prosecutions*[36] received considerable attention throughout the English-speaking world. The defendant, who knew that he was impotent, attempted to have sexual intercourse with a London prostitute in a quiet courtyard. She jeered when he was unsuccessful and attempted to get away from him. He tried to hold her, and she slapped him in the face and punched him in the stomach. When he grabbed her shoulders, she kicked him in the groin. He took a knife from his pocket and stabbed her twice, killing her. The House of Lords affirmed both the finding of the jury that there was not sufficient or adequate provocation and the following jury instruction given by the trial court:

> The reasonable person, the ordinary person, is the person you must consider when you are considering the effect which any acts, any conduct, any words, might have to justify the steps which were taken in response thereto, so that an unusually excitable or pugnacious individual, or a drunken one or a man who is sexually impotent is not entitled to rely on provocation which would not have led an ordinary person to have acted in the way which was in fact carried out.

Cooling of the Blood. "Cooling of the blood," also known as "cooling time" or "reasonable time to cool off," is a factor that must be considered when there is an interval between the provocation and the killing. Assume that after Y provokes X into a "heat of passion," X, who has lost his self-control, runs to get his gun. If it took X two minutes to get his gun, was this sufficient time for X to cool off? If it took X a half hour or an hour to obtain his gun, was this sufficient time for the heat of passion to cool off? These questions would have to be answered by a court and jury that would consider the type and degree of the provocation that caused the heat of passion.

"Imperfect" (Unlawful) Force in Self-defense Charged as Manslaughter

Homicide in "perfect" self-defense is either justifiable or excusable, and there is no criminal liability. "Perfect" self-defense requires that the killer not only subjectively believes that his conduct was necessary and reasonable, but that, by objective standards, it was lawful and complied with the requirements of the law.

In "imperfect" self-defense, the killer subjectively believes that his conduct was necessary. But if the killing was done with excessive or unnecessary force in self-defense, it is unlawful. An unnecessary killing in self-defense, in defense of another, or to prevent or terminate a felony of violence could be "imperfect."

The fact that a killing was "imperfect" would cause it to be reduced from murder to manslaughter because:

1. The deceased victim provoked the killing by his conduct (however, the killing was not legally justified).
2. As the killer believed that his or her conduct was lawful, there is no "malice."

In the 1983 case of *Faulkner v. State,* the Maryland Court of Special Appeals held that:

> Homicide in "perfect" self-defense is either justifiable or excusable and when established the killer is not culpable. . . . Perfect self-defense requires not only that the killer subjectively believed that his actions were necessary for his safety but, objectively, that a reasonable man would so consider them. Imperfect self-defense, however, requires no more than a subjective honest belief on the part of the killer that his actions were necessary for his safety, even though, on an objective appraisal by a reasonable man, they would not be found to be so. If established, the killer remains culpable and his actions are excused only to the extent that mitigation is invoked.
>
> The mitigating effect of imperfect self-defense is to negate malice. It therefore serves not only to reduce murder to manslaughter in the case of a felonious homicide but applies also to the felony of assault with intent to murder. It fatally erodes an assault with intent to murder charge. Since there is no crime of assault with intent to manslaughter, when malice is negated with respect to assault with intent to murder, the accused, if so charged, may be found guilty of simple assault and battery.[37]

Do Abused Women Have the Right to Kill?

To use deadly force in self-defense, there must be a fear of *imminent* death or great bodily harm. If the threat is not *imminent* (right now) and there are other options available to the person, deadly force is not legally justified.

Women using the "battered woman" defense have a number of problems. A few states will not permit evidence of the "battering" in their courts unless it is part of a defense seeking to show lawful self-defense. If the killing occurred at a time when there was no imminent threat or immediate fear of death or great bodily harm, courts will not permit a jury instruction on perfect or imperfect self-defense (see chapter 6). The following case illustrates this rule:

STATE v. NORMAN
Supreme Court of North Carolina (1989) 324 N.C. 253, 378 S.E.2d 8

John Norman and his wife had been married for twenty-five years and had five children. John seldom worked and forced his wife to prostitute herself to support him. Norman beat his wife "most every day" especially when he was drunk and when other persons were around to "show off." If his wife made less than the minimum of $100 per day in prostitution, he would beat her.

Norman made numerous threats on his wife's life. He would call her names and seek to humiliate her in many ways. An expert witness testified that after years of such treatment, Norman's wife "fits and exceeds the profile of an abused or battered spouse" and that Norman through "torture, degradation" had reduced her "to an animal level of existence, where all (her) behavior was marked purely by survival. . . ."

After a particularly horrible two days of drinking, beating, name-calling and acts seeking to humiliate his wife, Norman laid down to take a nap. His wife obtained a handgun and shot Norman three times in the head. The jury convicted Mrs. Norman of voluntary manslaughter after the trial judge refused to give the jury an instruction on perfect self-defense. Mrs. Norman appealed, arguing the trial judge errored in failing to give the "perfect" self-defense instruction to the jury.

The Supreme Court of North Carolina affirmed the conviction for voluntary manslaughter and the six-year sentence of imprisonment, holding:

* * *

Our law has recognized that self-preservation under such circumstances springs from a primal impulse and is an inherent right of natural law. . . .

The right to kill in self-defense is based on the necessity, real or reasonably apparent, of killing an unlawful aggressor to save oneself from imminent death or great bodily harm at his hands.

* * *

In North Carolina, a defendant is entitled to have the jury consider acquittal by reason of perfect *self-defense when the evidence, viewed in the light most favorable to the defendant, tends to show that at the time of the killing it appeared to the defendant and she believed it to be necessary to kill the decedent to save herself from imminent death or great bodily harm. . . .*

That belief must be reasonable, however, in that the circumstances as they appeared to the defendant would create such a belief in the mind of a person of ordinary firmness. Id. *Further, the defendant must not have been the initial aggressor provoking the fatal confrontation.* Id. *A killing in the proper exercise of the right of* perfect *self-defense is always completely justified in law and constitutes no legal wrong.*

* * *

The defendant in the present case was not entitled to a jury instruction on either perfect *or* imperfect *self-defense. The trial court was not required to instruct on either form of self-defense unless evidence was introduced tending to show that at the time of the killing the defendant reasonably believed herself to be confronted by circumstances which necessitated her killing her husband to save herself from imminent death or great bodily harm.* Id. *No such evidence was introduced in this case, and it would have been error for the trial court to instruct the jury on either* perfect *or* imperfect *self-defense.*

* * *

The evidence in this case did not tend to show that the defendant reasonably believed that she was confronted by a threat of imminent death or great bodily harm. The evidence tended to show that no harm was "imminent" or about to happen to the defendant when she shot her husband. The uncontroverted evidence was that her husband had been asleep for some time when she walked to her mother's house, returned with the pistol, fixed the pistol after it jammed and then shot her husband three times in the back of the head. The defendant was not faced with an instantaneous choice between killing her husband or being killed or seriously injured. . . .

* * *

Women in prison for voluntary manslaughter can petition the governors of their state for clemency. Newspaper stories tell of governors who are commuting sentences of abused women. For example, the former Ohio governor, Richard Celeste, after reviewing the records of more than one hundred women who were in Ohio prisons for killing or assaulting a spouse or male companion, granted clemency to twenty-five women during this last weeks in office in December 1990. Twenty-one of the women were released immediately. The remaining four were required to serve a minimum of two years in prison before release. One woman was in her twenties, was serving fifteen years to life, and had been in prison since she was sixteen. She was convicted of killing her father, who prison officials stated had been sexually molesting her. (See "More States Study Clemency for Women Who Killed Abusers," *The New York Times,* February 21, 1991.)

Involuntary Manslaughter

Involuntary manslaughter consists of two types: (1) criminal negligence manslaughter and (2) unlawful act manslaughter. An example of the criminal negligence manslaughter is the *Twilight Zone* helicopter accident case in which actor Vic Morrow and two children were killed in July 1982.

After a ten-month trial ending in 1987, movie director John Landis and four other persons were found not guilty of involuntary (negligence) manslaughter. Although the jury found the prosecutor did not prove a high degree of negligence necessary for a criminal conviction, the burden of proof in a civil negligence case would be that of ordinary negligence, which is a lesser burden of proof.[38]

Other workplace safety violations could be charged as criminal negligence or unlawful act manslaughter. In the 1989 Michigan case of *People v. Hegedus,* 432 Mich. 598, 443 N.W.2d 127, 45 CrL 2309, a supervisor was charged with manslaughter when an employee died of carbon monoxide poisoning while the employee was operating a company vehicle that had allegedly been negligently maintained. In Wisconsin, a construction company was convicted of two counts of homicide by reckless conduct because of failure to take safety measures after methane was detected in a tunnel three days before an explosion.[39]

The following case illustrates unlawful act manslaughter:

COMMONWEALTH v. KONZ
Superior Court of Pennsylvania (1979) 265 Pa.Super. 570, 402 A.2d 692

The Rev. David Konz was a diabetic and decided to withdraw from insulin and rely on his faith that God would heal him. However, he assured others that if his condition required it, he would resume taking insulin. When he arrived at the point where he needed insulin immediately, he went to the refrigerator but discovered his wife (the defendant) had hidden it. His attempt to leave the house was blocked. Mr. Konz was physically forced into the bedroom, where his wife and a friend talked to him. When he attempted to make a telephone call, his wife and the friend disconnected the telephone. In reinstating the conviction for involuntary manslaughter for the death of Mr. Konz, the Court held:

> *We hold that appellee Dorothy Konz, as wife of decedent, was under a duty to obtain medical aid for her diabetic husband when it became readily apparent that he was suffering the effects of lack of insulin, and in serious need of medical attention.*
>
> *The state of the law as to the duty owed by one spouse to obtain medical assistance for the other is not well-settled, with only a handful of cases addressing the issue. Indeed, our research uncovered no recent Pennsylvania case of import to the instant appeal. Nevertheless, a review of the case law from other jurisdictions discloses a duty of care, vague though it may be, arising from the spousal relationship.*

F. SUICIDE

At common law, suicide was considered to be self-murder and was a felony. Because the person who committed such a crime was beyond the reach of the law, the punishment was forfeiture of the deceased person's estate to the king and burial off the highway.

If the attempt to commit suicide failed, the person who made the attempt was guilty under common law of the misdemeanor of attempted suicide. If in the course of the attempt, the person killed another (for example, in a struggle for the gun), the person was guilty of murder under the doctrine of transferred intent or malice.

Today, attempted suicide is an offense in only a few states. Many states make aiding and assisting another to commit suicide a crime. The following "mutual suicide pact" case came before the California Supreme Court in 1983.

FORDEN v. JOSEPH G.
Supreme Court of California (1983) 34 Cal. 3d 429, 194 Cal.Rptr. 163, 667 P.2d 1176

Joseph G. (the minor defendant) drove a car containing himself and a friend over a 350-foot cliff in an attempt to carry out a mutual suicide pact. Joseph G. survived but his passenger was killed. The lower court held that the defendant should be charged with murder in the first degree. The Supreme Court of California ruled that he should be charged with aiding and abetting the deceased friend's suicide, holding:

Traditionally under the common law the survivor of a suicide pact was held to be guilty of murder.

* * *

Most states provide, either by statute or case law, criminal sanctions for aiding suicide, but few adopt the extreme common law position that such conduct is murder. Some jurisdictions instead classify aiding suicide as a unique type of manslaughter. But the predominant statutory scheme, and the one adopted in California, is to create a sui generis crime of aiding and abetting suicide.

* * *

In essence, it is actually a double attempted suicide, and therefore the rationale for not punishing those who attempt suicide would seem to apply.

The Crime of Assisting Another to Commit Suicide

The Hemlock Society is an organization that advocates a right to suicide and a right of persons to assist in the suicide of severely ill persons. Most states, however, have statutes that make aiding or assisting another to commit suicide a crime. For example, in California such assistance is punishable by up to five years in prison.

In 1990, the State of Michigan did not have a statute making assisting a suicide a crime. In June 1990, an Oregon woman suffering from Alzheimer's disease traveled to Michigan with her husband. A retired Michigan doctor, Dr. Jack Kevorkian, provided a suicide device he had made and assisted the fifty-four-year-old woman to commit suicide. Dr. Kevorkian was not charged with a crime, but he was put under a court order not to use the device again.

Changes (1970s–1980s) in the Pattern and Method of Suicide in the United States

Suicide is now the tenth leading cause of death in the United States, ranking just ahead of criminal homicide. Suicide is recognized as a rising and devastating public health problem. There are hundreds of suicide prevention centers and hot lines in the United States that have been helpful to troubled persons. It is estimated that close to a quarter of a million persons spend some time every year in hospitals and institutions under emergency detention statutes of state mental health laws after attempting suicide or threatening violence.

- There has been a 40 percent increase in the suicide rate among young people (particularly white males) aged 15 to 24, and suicide is now the third leading cause of death in this age group.
- Young adults aged 20 to 24 have approximately twice the number and rate of suicides as do adolescents aged 15 to 19.
- The ratio of male to female suicides in the age group 15 to 24 is now four to one.
- Dramatic changes in the method of suicide occurred by increased use of firearms and explosives replacing poisoning.

Source: Centers for Disease Control

Insanity, Self-Defense, and Manslaughter as Defenses to Murder Charges

Type of Defense	Degree of Liability	Tests Used to Determine Liability	Disposition of Person
Insanity Defense Finding of not guilty because of mental disease or defect	No criminal liability	(1) M'Naghten "right or wrong" test or (2) Model Penal Code "substantial capacity" test (see chapter 5)	Confined to state institution until released under the statutes or procedures of that state
Self-defense Finding that the killing was lawful in self-defense or in defense of another (or in some states, to prevent or to terminate a felony of violence)	No criminal liability	Was the killing necessary to avoid death or serious bodily harm? What is lawful under the laws of that state or jurisdiction?	Person is not charged, or if charged may use the defense before a jury or judge. If defense is proven, the defendant would be acquitted.
Manslaughter as a defense • Voluntary manslaughter • Heat-of-passion manslaughter • "Imperfect" use of force manslaughter • Criminal negligence • manslaughter • Unlawful act manslaughter	Defendant is convicted of manslaughter instead of murder (partial forgiveness).	(1) The victims provoked the killings by their unlawful conduct; or (2) the killings are not bad enough to be charged and punished as murder, but bad enough to be criminal; or (3) the killings violated a section of the manslaughter statute of that state (manslaughter is often the catch-all category of criminal homicide)	Defendant is sentenced for the crime of manslaughter.

Two months later, a California woman suffering from breast cancer came to Michigan, apparently to take advantage of the lack of a law forbidding the assisting of a suicide. In a Detroit area motel room, the woman committed suicide by taking sleeping pills and pulling a bag over her head. The death was reported to the police by the woman's seventy-two-year-old husband and her daughter, who were present at the time of the suicide. Stating that he was determined to keep Michigan from becoming a haven for assisted suicide, the county prosecutor charged the husband with murder. In May 1991, a Michigan jury, after deliberating for two hours, found the husband not guilty of second-degree murder.[40]

Questions and Problems for Chapter 13

1. A young married woman, Pamela Robbins, suffered from epilepsy and diabetes for many years. She required two daily injections of insulin along with other medication. Pamela and her husband, Robert, became deeply religious, "born again" Christians. They joined a group led by a minister who believed that if one had sufficient faith, God would cure all illnesses. During a religious meeting, Pamela had a revelation; she believed she was healed and resolved to stop taking all medication. She discontinued all medication and she and her husband prayed. He did all he could to ease her discomfort and attended to her every need. After her death, Robert Robbins was charged with criminal negligent homicide, and the minister was charged with "counseling, urging, suggesting and directing" that Pamela refrain from taking insulin or seeking medical assistance. Is there criminal liability for one or both of the defendants? (*People v. Robbins,* 83 A.D.2d 271, 443 N.Y.S.2d 1016 [1981]).

2. An elderly woman resisted a purse snatching near her home and was knocked to the pavement. The two purse snatchers escaped with $15 to $20 in the purse. The woman was taken to a hospital with a cut on the back of her head. Because a blood clot developed in her brain, surgery was performed. The woman remained in a coma, into which she had lapsed within hours of the purse snatching, and died six weeks after the incident. What criminal charges could be issued against the two men and what defenses to these charges would be used by a defense lawyer?

3. In 1984, a St. Paul, Minnesota, man admitted to police that he murdered his wife and buried her body in the snow. His defense attorney then advised him not to provide any further information. The man was arrested, and for weeks the police attempted to find the body of the woman. In order to obtain information as to the location of the body, the district attorney agreed to accept a plea to second-degree murder. Based on the plea bargain, the man disclosed the location of the body. The court, upon receiving the guilty plea, imposed a sentence of twenty-five years in prison, with parole eligibility in seventeen years.
- What are the factors that would cause a prosecuting attorney to make a plea bargain offer of second-degree murder instead of going for a conviction of first-degree murder in this case?
- What bargaining leverage does a defense attorney have in a situation such as this?
- Are the interests of the public and justice served by the outcome in this case?

4. In New York City in 1988, police officers were making what they called "a routine drug arrest" of three men. They had one man in custody when he suddenly broke loose, knocking the arm of one of the police officers who had his revolver in his hand. The gun discharged, killing one of the other police officers. Should the man, Joseph Barker, who attempted to escape be charged with a criminal homicide? If so, what would be the charge in your state? Explain.

5. Claude Hebert made homosexual advances to Stillman Wilbur. In a rage and frenzy, Wilbur killed Hebert. Is this a justifiable or excusable homicide, or should criminal charges be issued against Wilbur? Explain your answer and the defenses available to Wilbur, who admits the killing. *Mullaney v. Wilbur,* 421 U.S. 684, 95 S.Ct. 1881 (U.S. Sup. Court, 1975).

6. The defendant kidnapped a prominent Illinois businessman in a $1 million ransom attempt. The defendant then buried the businessman in a homemade plywood box with a plastic pipe rising from one end. Two days later, the box and the body of the victim were found under three feet of sand in a rural area. The box had been equipped with a jug

of water, candy bars, an unconnected battery-powered light, and the air pipe.

In charging the defendant with murder, the State argued the victim never had a chance. The prosecutor stated to the jury, "From the moment (defendant) put (the victim) in that box, he knew he would die." The defense lawyer called the victim's death "tragic but accidental" and pointed out that the victim was buried with candy bars and water. The prosecutor argued that defendant could not afford to let the victim live and the candy bars and water were not put in the box to keep the victim alive.

What inference and conclusions can the jury draw? Is there sufficient evidence to sustain a finding of specific intent to kill? Can the defendant be convicted of "intent to kill" murder? *State v. Edwards,* ___ N.E.2d ___ (Ill., 1988).

7. Two men (Lorenzo Owens and Kenneth Grice) had sex. After the sex, Grice told Owens that he had AIDS. In a rage, Owens killed Grice. Owens, who was nineteen years old and homeless, based his defense on "heat of passion." Explain the defense and state what has to be shown. If the defense was successful, what would Owens be convicted of in your state?

Notes

1. 23 Corpus Juris Secundum Criminal Law 917.

2. 23A Corpus Juris Secundum Criminal Law 1124.

3. 424 Pa. 331, 227 A.2d 900 (1967).

4. *People v. Manson,* 71 Cal.App.3d 1, 42, 139 Cal.Rptr. 275 (1977), *cert. denied,* 435 U.S. 953, 98 S.Ct. 1582 (1978).

5. In 1984, Clause von Bulow was tried on two counts of attempted murder of his wife. Mrs. von Bulow recovered from the first coma but the second injection of insulin caused an irreversible coma that she remained in for years. Children of Mrs. von Bulow suspected the "dapper Dane" (as newspapers called Mr. von Bulow) and stole critical evidence from him, which they turned over to the police. The police failed to get the search warrant necessary for the testing of the evidence. The case, involving wealthy jet-set persons, sex, and intrigue, received a great deal of national attention. See *Rhode Island v. von Bulow,* 475 A.2d 995, review denied, 469 U.S. 875, 105 S.Ct. 233 (1984).

6. *State v. Horne,* 282 S.C. 444, 319 S.E.2d 703 (1984).

7. *Brinkley v. State,* 253 Ga. 541, 322 S.E.2d 49 (1984). See also *Minnesota v. Merrill,* 274 N.W.2d 99 (Minn. 1978), review denied U.S. Supreme Court where the defendant was charged with first-degree murder of his girlfriend and the second degree murder of a twenty-eight-day embryo (no premeditation).

Most states require in a charge of murder of a fetus that the fetus be "quick." Minnesota does not, and the killing of any age fetus is covered by the Minnesota statute.

8. *The Journal of Criminal Law, Criminology and Police Science,* (1974) 60:351

9. *State v. Forrest,* 321 N.C. 186, 362 S.E.2d 252 (1987).

10. *Matter of Quinlan,* 70 N.J. 10, 355 A.2d 647, 656 (1976), review denied 429 U.S. 922, 97 S.Ct. 319.

11. *Matter of Conroy,* 98 N.J. 321, 486 A.2d 1209 (1985).

12. *Swafford v. State,* 421 N.E.2d 596 (Ind.)

13. 373 Mass. 249, 366 N.E.2d 744 (1977), review denied 434 U.S. 1039, 98 S.Ct. 777 (1978).

14. 147 Cal.App.3d 1006, 195 Cal.Rptr. 484 (1983).

15. The "speedy trial" requirement is one reason there are few causation cases. When a suspect is taken into custody for causing serious injury to another person, he or she must be taken before a court and charged or released. The issuing of charges would cause the "speedy trial" time to commence running, and the person's trial must commence within that time (seventy days in federal courts). If a victim is in critical condition, a knowledgeable defense attorney probably is not going to waive "speedy trial," as the lawyer wants his or her client to go to trial on the lesser charge. Murder charges can be issued if the victim dies before the case goes to trial. Once the case goes to trial on the lesser charge (or charges), double jeopardy would apply and the defendant cannot be charged with criminal homicide. (See chapter 7 for "speedy trial" and "double jeopardy" defenses.) Could such a condition be a factor in causing a family to "pull the plug" on a terminal case so that the suspect could be charged with murder?

16. *People v. Stevenson,* 416 Mich. 383, 331 N.W.2d 143 (Mich. 1982). See also *State v. Hefler,* 60 N.C. App. 460, 299 S.E.2d 456 (1983) *affirmed* 310 N.C. 135, 310 S.E.2d 310, 34 CrL 2374 (1984), in which the North Carolina court stated: "For the courts to remain judicially oblivious of these advances [in medical science] when considering whether to extend an ancient common law rule would be folly."

17. See *Bloodletters and Badmen: A Narrative Encyclopedia of American Criminals from the Pilgrims to the Present* by Jay Robert Nash (New York: M. Evans & Co., 1974).

18. In a case in which the defendant shot a fifteen-year-old gasoline service station attendant in the head, neck, and back six times, the Supreme Court of Minnesota held: "Extensive planning and calculated deliberation need not be shown by the prosecution

The requisite 'plan' to commit a first-degree murder can be formulated virtually instantaneously by a killer. . . . Moreover . . . premeditation can be inferred from either the number of gunshots fired into the victim . . . or the fact that a killer arms himself with a loaded gun in preparation . . ." (*State v. Newmann*, 262 N.W.2d 426, 22 CrL 2465 [Minn. 1978]).

19. Serial killings that have received national attention are: Seattle's "Green River" killer (still at large after killing forty-nine young women); New York "Zodiac killer" (still at large after four killings); Theodore Bundy (executed in Florida in 1988 after confessing to the killing of thirty-one women); Arthur Shawcross of New York (eleven women); Los Angeles "Hillside Strangler" (ten killings); John Wayne Gacy of Chicago (thirty-three young men and boys); Wayne Williams (Atlanta child killings); Wayne Eyler of Illinois (twenty-four young men).

20. See the article "More Prisons Using Iron Hand to Control Inmates," *The New York Times* (November 1, 1990). The article points out that prison administrations have taken control of prisons throughout the United States. New prisons have much better design and are much easier to control. Metal detector devices are used in some prisons to detect hidden weapons (usually homemade). Gangs are broken up before they cause trouble.

21. 157 U.S. 675, 15 S.Ct. 720.

22. See also *People v. Birreuta*, 162 Cal.App.3d 454, 208 Cal.Rptr. 635 (1984). Footnote 4 of the *Birreuta* case points out that *Perkins on Criminal Law* (2d ed., Foundation Press 1969, p. 822) states the "transferred intent" doctrine serves a useful purpose in the tort field but that it has no proper place in criminal law. Perkins states, "In the field of crime this concept has the vice of being a misleading half-truth, often given as an improper reason for a correct result, but incapable of strict application."

23. The Supreme Court of Oregon pointed out in *State v. Boone*, 294 Or. 630, 661 P.2d 917 (1983) that "other cases have inferred implied malice, often defined as depravity of mind and reckless and wanton disregard of human life, from the act of driving while intoxicated which causes death. *Jolly v. State*, 395 So.2d 1135 (Ala.Cr.App. 1981); *Hamilton v. Commonwealth*, 560 S.W.2d 539 (Ky. 1977): *Commonwealth v. Taylor*, 461 Pa. 557, 337 A.2d 545 (1975); *Edwards v. State*, 202 Tenn. 393, 304 S.W.2d 500 (1957); *Cockrell v. State*, 136 Tex.Cr.R. 218, 117 S.W.2d 1105 (1983); *State v.

Trott, 190 N.C. 674, 130 S.E. 627 (1925). These cases share many facts in common. While driving under the influence of intoxicants, the defendants drove erratically—speeding, swerving, running red lights, driving on the wrong side of the road. Such erratic driving, coupled with impairment of driving ability caused by intoxication, sufficed to indicate the implied malice necessary for second degree murder convictions."

24. 386 Mass. 492, 436 N.E.2d 400.

25. See the New York Penal Code Sec. 125.20.

26. See "Sentence by Public Opinion?" *Newsweek,* March 5, 1984.

27. 157 U.S. 675, 15 S.Ct. 720.

28. 70 Cal.2d 711, 76 Cal.Rptr. 391, 452 P.2d 607 (1969).

29. 351 Ill. 604, 184 N.E. 894 (1933).

30. 38 Ga. App. 36, 142 S.E. 202 (1928). In this case the deceased used profane and insulting language, with threats to cut the defendant's throat.

31. 381 Pa. 447, 113 A.2d 293 (1955).

32. 56 Ill.App.2d 159, 205 N.E.2d 749 (1965).

33. Texas, New Mexico, and Utah changed this common law ruling by statutes that provided that killings by husbands under these circumstances were justified homicides. Critics of these statutes argued that this permitted an "open shooting season" on paramours if they were caught by husbands in the act of adultery. Women's groups in these states angrily demanded that the statutes either be repealed or amended so as to give wives the same rights. It is reported that all three states have repealed these statutes and probably have gone back to the common law rule.

34. 175 Cal. 45, 164 P. 1121 (1917).

35. 10 Md.App. 630, 272 A.2d 64 (1971).

36. House of Lords, 2, All Eng. R 801 (1954).

37. 458 A.2d 81 and 483 A.2d 759 (1984).

38. A man was killed playing "Russian roulette" with two other men. The survivors were charged with and convicted of involuntary manslaughter. The court held that the game involved an unreasonable and high degree of risk of death. *Commonwealth v. Atencio,* 345 Mass. 627, 189 N.E.2d 223 (1963).

39. See "Healy Guilty in Deaths in '88 Sewer Tunnel Blast," *Milwaukee Journal,* December 29, 1990.

40. See "Michigan Charging Murder After a Second Assisted Suicide, *The New York Times,* August 26, 1990; and "Man Cleared of Murder in Aiding Wife's Suicide," *The New York Times,* May 11, 1991.

Chapter Fourteen

ASSAULT, BATTERY, AND OTHER CRIMES AGAINST THE PERSON

A. The Crime of Assault

Under common law, assault and battery were two separate crimes. Today, however, the term *assault and battery* is sometimes used to indicate one offense. As an assault is often an attempt to commit a battery, the California courts point out that an assault is an attempt to strike, whereas a battery is the successful attempt. A battery cannot be committed without assaulting a victim, but an assault can occur without committing a battery.

Most states have statutorized the old common law crime of assault. Included in the crime of assault are (a) an attempt to commit a battery in which no actual battery or physical injury resulted and/or (b) an intentional frightening (such as pointing a loaded gun at a person or menacing with a fist or knife). Generally, in an assault, the state must show apprehension or fear on the part of the victim if no blow, touching, or injury occurred.

In many states, the crime of assault also includes batteries. The state of New York does not have a crime of battery.[1] Therefore, in New York, a person who swings a knife at another with intent to cause serious physical injury is guilty of first-degree assault if he succeeds but is guilty only of attempted assault if he fails. (See New York Commentaries, Art. 120, p. 331.)

Section 240 of the California Penal Code (enacted in 1872) defines assault as "an unlawful attempt, coupled with a present ability, to commit a violent injury on the person of another."[2] Chapter 38, Section 12−1 of the Illinois Statutes provides that "a person commits an assault when, without lawful authority, he engages in conduct which places another in reasonable apprehension of receiving a battery."

In some states (including California), the lack of "present ability" to commit the injury (or battery) is a defense to an assault charge.[3] The defendant in the 1983 case of *People v. Fain*[4] used this defense. He argued that the rifle he pointed at three men was not loaded. However, one of the victims (Steen) testified that the defendant fired a shot from the gun during the incident and that the defendant struck two of the victims with the gun. In affirming the defendant's conviction, the Supreme Court of California held:

> Defendant testified that the gun was unloaded. . . . The jury, however, may not have believed defendant's testimony in this regard, as Steen had testified that at one point defendant had fired a round from the rifle.
>
> In any case, even an unloaded gun can be used as a club or bludgeon. . . . Defendant struck both Maestas and Steen with the gun, and approached sufficiently near Watkins to have the present ability to injure Watkins in the same manner.

Instead of requiring a showing of "present ability," other states require a showing of "apparent ability." In an assault with a dangerous weapon (gun), testimony of the victim that he or she reasonably believed the gun was loaded would be sufficient to show "apparent ability" to discharge the weapon. "Apparent ability" would be easier for the state to prove than "present ability", where the state would have to have specific proof the gun was loaded. Florida is one of the states requiring only "apparent ability" (Section 784.011).

Assault Under the Present Federal Criminal Code

Under the present Federal Criminal Code, the crime of assault also includes an actual battery; 18 U.S.C.A. Sec. 113(c) forbids "assault by striking, beating, or wounding." Therefore, the two common law aspects of assault are used, as well as a third aspect in which the crime of assault is committed by inflicting injury on another person. The following federal case illustrates:

UNITED STATES v. MASEL[5]
United States Circuit Court of Appeals, Seventh Circuit (1977) 563 F.2d 322, 22 CrL 2065

During a campaign for the presidency of the United States, the defendant became angry at U.S. Senator Henry Jackson and spat in his face. The defendant was charged with assaulting a member of the U.S. Congress and was convicted in a jury trial. The Federal Court of Appeals affirmed the defendant's conviction, holding:

> *Defendant would read the assault offense as confined to an attempt to commit a battery or an act putting another in reasonable apprehension of bodily harm. . . . The district court concluded that assault, in this statute, had a broader meaning. "Because the statute contemplates that personal injury may result from the 'assault,' it is clear that Congress intended to include 'battery' within the term 'assault.'" Accordingly, the district court instructed, in effect, that if the jury found a battery had been committed, defendant should be convicted of the charge of assault. . . . We find the reasoning of the district court persuasive. Moreover, comments in Senate debate suggest that battery as well as an unsuccessful attempt was thought of as constituting assault. . . . We also note that every battery must include or be the culmination of an assault (in the sense of attempt), U.S. v. Bell, 505 F.2d 539, 540 (7th Cir. 1974), citing Hawkins, Pleas of the Crown, c. 62, § 1 (6th ed. 1788). That being true, defendant, charged with assault, could not complain of an instruction which required proof that he had committed the battery which culminated it. Moreover, the court says, the instructions required the government to prove that the defendant willfully caused, by spitting, an offensive touching. "We think this is an adequate statement. . . . It is ancient doctrine that intentional spitting upon another is battery. . . . No more severe injury need be intended."*

Hands as "Dangerous Weapons"

As pointed out in chapter 13, the issue of what is a dangerous or deadly weapon is a question of fact for the fact finder (jury or judge). Just as it was held in New York that a common handkerchief can, under certain circumstances, be a deadly weapon, many courts have also held that hands can be dangerous or deadly weapons, even if the assailant has no training in martial arts or boxing.

The relative size and strength of the assailant as compared with the victim, the manner and duration of the assault, and the severity of the injuries are all facts that must be taken into consideration in determining whether hands are dangerous or deadly weapons. Fact finders (juries or judges) would surely find the hands of an adult man who punched a baby to be dangerous or deadly weapons under the circumstances.

The defendant in the 1982 case of *State v. Zangrilli*[6] broke his ex-wife's jaw in two places, grabbed her by the throat and strangled her until she could feel her "eyes bulge," dragged her through several rooms in her house, punched her

Violent Crime in the United States

- Violent crime is more likely to strike the young than the elderly.[a]
- Except for rape, violent crime is more likely to strike men than women.[a]
- Persons who live in central cities are more likely to be violent crime victims than persons who live in suburban or rural areas. Persons who live in cities of 250,000 to 499,999 population have the highest violent victimization rates.
- On average, 2.2 million victims are injured from violent crime each year; 1 million receive medical care; half a million are treated in an emergency room or hospital.
- Among those victims injured in rapes, robberies, and aggravated assaults in recent years, an estimated 22,870 received gunshot wounds each year, 76,930 received knife wounds, and 141,460 suffered broken bones or teeth knocked out.

- Of all violent crimes, 55% are committed by strangers, 32% by acquaintances, and 8% by relatives. In 1989 persons not known to the victim committed 3.2 million violent crimes.
- Nearly 25% of all violent crime incidents are committed by two or more offenders; 13% are committed by three or more offenders. Crimes committed by strangers are more likely to involve multiple offenders than are crimes by known persons.
- Of murder victims in 1989, 15% were killed by relatives, 39% by acquaintances, 13% by strangers, and 33% in circumstances where the relationship was not known.
- Among all female murder victims in 1989, 28% were killed by husbands or boyfriends. Five percent of male victims were killed by wives or girlfriends.

- Violent crimes are more likely to be cleared by arrest than other crimes. In 1989 the clearance rate was—
  68% for murder
  52% for forcible rape
  26% for robbery
  57% for aggravated assault.
- When prior conviction offenses are taken into account, an estimated 66% of state prison inmates in 1986 were found to have had a current or past conviction for a violent crime.
- Violent offenses are most likely to be handled by the states and localities. In 1988 there were an estimated 99,900 violent convictions in state courts, as compared to 2,241 in U.S. district courts. In state courts, violent offenses represented a larger proportion of all convictions (15%) than they did in U.S. district courts (5%).

[a]The elderly and women take more precautions to avoid being victims of crime than do young men.

Source: U.S. Department of Justice, 1991, "Violent Crime in the United States."

several times in the face and neck, and shoved her into a bathtub. The Supreme Court of Rhode Island affirmed his conviction of assault with a dangerous weapon, quoting the trial judge's holdings:

> The manner in which he used his hands on her throat constituted use of his hands in such a way that it could easily have led to her death.
> For that reason, I have concluded that his assault upon her was done with a dangerous weapon. As I say, hands are not per se dangerous weapons, but they are a means to produce death. And they were used, even though briefly, in a manner and in such circumstances as could be reasonably calculated to produce death.

A rubber-soled tennis shoe was held to be a dangerous weapon in the 1991 case of *State v. Munoz,* 575 So.2d 848 (La.App.). An eyewitness testified that the defendant kicked the victim so hard in the head that the victim's body was lifted off the ground. The attending physician also characterized the attack by the defendant as brutal.

B. Battery

In order for an offense to constitute assault, the victim must ordinarily be apprehensive of the impending harm or danger. This is not necessary in a battery. A blow from behind is a battery whether the victim is aware that it is coming or not. Battery is a crime that, like murder and manslaughter, is defined in terms of the conduct of the offender and also in terms of the harm done.

A battery is an unlawful striking; in many states, even a touching could be charged as a battery. Batteries can be committed with fists, feet, sticks, stones, or other objects used to inflict injury. Under some circumstances, dogs or other animals could be used to commit a battery if they are used to injure another person illegally.

All states that make battery a crime require that the act to commit a battery must be intentional (or must be done knowingly), as an accidental physical contact or injury is not a battery.

Street Fights and Public Brawls

Under the old common law, an affray was the offense of two or more persons fighting in a public place. Many street fights, tavern fights, and public brawls are matters of mutual combat where both parties want to settle a dispute by use of force. If a prosecutor concluded it was mutual combat, both parties are likely to be charged with disorderly conduct (or as disorderly persons). If the parties were charged with assault or battery, a long jury trial might then result when one or both of the parties used either the defense that the other party consented to the fight (mutual combat), or self-defense.

If one of the parties was the aggressor and wrongfully attacked the other party who then used force in self-defense, it would not then be mutual combat. In such a situation, the wrongdoer is the party who should be charged with either assault, battery, disorderly conduct, or a combination of these offenses.

Affrays differ from assaults and batteries in that the old offense of affray had to be committed in a public place. Assaults and batteries can be committed in either a private or a public place. Affrays also required two or more persons engaged in mutual combat, whereas an assault or a battery may be committed by one person on another.

A victim of an assault or battery can claim the privilege of self-defense, as necessary and reasonable force may be used to defend against an unlawful attack (see chapter 6 on defenses to the use of force). In an affray (fight in a public place), the combat generally is mutual, which would make it more difficult to assert self-defense or the defense of another.

Sexual Assault—Sexual Battery

More than twenty states have enacted sexual assault statutes to replace their old rape statutes. These statutes generally provide for three or four degrees of sexual assault. In addition to defining "sexual intercourse" broadly, these statutes also forbid and punish "offensive touching."

Before the enactment of the sexual assault statutes, offensive touching was ordinarily charged under the general assault statute, or as a battery, or as disorderly conduct. Although offensive touching may continue to be charged under the old statutes, the sexual assault statute is now available. However, under the sexual assault statutes, the offensive touching generally must be of an "intimate part" or "private part" of the body and for the purpose "of arousing or gratifying sexual desire of either party" (Section 213.4 Model Penal Code).

Most sexual assault or sexual abuse statutes include the buttocks as an "intimate part" or "private part." However the New York statute did not when the case of *People v. Thomas*[7] came before the Criminal Court of New York City in 1977. Thomas was charged with the offensive touching of the buttocks of a woman on a rush-hour train. On the complaint of the woman, the defendant had been arrested by a transit patrolman. The court affirmed the defendant's conviction, holding that the buttocks are an "intimate part" and that the defendant's intentional touching without consent violated the statute.

Sexual battery is charged in Illinois under a 1979 statute that provides that "a person commits battery if he intentionally or knowingly without legal justification and by any means . . . makes physical contact by an insulting or provoking nature with an individual."[8]

The rape charge in the 1983 case of *People v. Margiolas* was dropped because of lack of evidence of resistance. However, the defendant admitted that he unbuttoned the victim's blouse, despite her verbal as well as physical objections. The defendant was convicted of sexual battery in forcibly unbuttoning the blouse.[9] Under such a statute, a prosecutor with a weak case might also issue a sexual battery charge when it is apparent that the rape charge has defects that might be fatal. (See chapter 18 for more material on sexual assault and sexual battery statutes.)

Defenses to Assault or Battery Charges[10]

Defenses to an assault or battery charge could be as follows:

1. Self-defense
   - "perfect"—the force used was necessary and reasonable in self-defense, defense of another, or in the defense of property
   - "imperfect"—some force was necessary because of unlawful conduct but an excessive or unnecessary amount of force was used (defendant would be liable only for the amount of excessive or unnecessary force)
2. That the discipline of a child was reasonable in view of (a) the type of punishment inflicted and the manner in which it was inflicted, (b) the conduct of the child that brought about the punishment, and (c) the age, health, size, and sex of the child. This defense could *not* be used by persons other than:
   - parents, guardians, and those who act in the place of the parents who have the duty and obligation to educate, discipline, and train the child
   - teachers and school administrators as governed by state law, which was summarized by the U.S. Supreme Court as follows:

Of the ... States that have addressed the problem through legislation, (some) have authorized the moderate use of corporal punishment in public schools. Of these States only a few have elaborated on the common law test of reasonableness, typically providing for approval or notification of the child's parents, or for infliction of punishment only by the principal or in the presence of an adult witness. (Some states) have prohibited all corporal punishment in their public schools. Where the legislatures have not acted, the state courts have uniformly preserved the common law rule permitting teachers to use reasonable force in disciplining children in their charge.[11]

3. That the conduct is within the rules of the sport being played. A bone-jarring tackle in football or a hard right to the jaw in boxing is within the rules of those sports and would be consented to by persons engaged in those contests. Prosecutors have warned that violence outside of the rules of a sport is subject to criminal or civil prosecution.

4. Consent is a defense to "offensive touching" batteries and also "intent-to-injure" contacts if done within the rules of such body contact sports as boxing, ice hockey, and football. It is also a defense in "mutual combat" where both parties are found to mutually agree to settle a dispute in a fist fight or "brouhaha." (See *Faulkner v. State,* 54 Md.App. 113, 458 A.2d 81, (1983).)

5. Where the conduct is necessary and lawful:
   • in the accomplishment of a lawful arrest
   • when necessary to lawfully detain or hold a person in custody
   • when necessary to prevent an escape of a person lawfully in custody
   • when necessary to prevent a suicide
   • for any other reason when the conduct is privileged by the statutory or common law of that state

Other Physical Contact Without Consent

Pushing, pinching, biting, scratching, touching, kissing, punching, spitting, tackling, etc. are all forms of physical contact where the person initiating the contact could be acting in a friendly, joking, or loving manner, or the contact could be hostile, angry, or belligerent.

If such contact were intentional (not accidental) and done without any legal justification, it could cause a great amount of anger or concern by the person not consenting to such physical contact. If the physical contact were made in an obviously hostile or belligerent manner, the physical contact could provoke a verbal or physical reaction.

If it is shown that the conduct provoked or tended to provoke a disturbance or a disorder, the offender could be charged with disorderly conduct.

EXAMPLE: A strange man roughly grabs a woman or a girl in a public place and kisses and touches her in the presence of her husband, boyfriend, or other member of her family or friends. As such conduct is highly likely to cause a public disturbance or disorder, it can be charged as disorderly conduct (or disorderly person).

Defenses to a charge where touching or physical contact occurred could be that the touching was accidental. Implied consent could also easily be inferred where the touching was done to pull a victim away from danger. Or where mouth-to-mouth resuscitation was necessary to restore breathing to a victim of an accident, fire, etc. The defense of necessity could also be used if the physical contact was necessary to prevent and avoid a greater harm.

The Crimes of "Jostling" and "Menacing"

The crimes of "jostling" and "menacing" are both listed in *Moriarty's Police Law* (Butterworth Pub.), the handbook of British police officers. Jostling is listed under obstruction of public ways and would be pushing and shoving in a way that would obstruct and block the use of a public street, building, sidewalk, etc. Victims whose passage is blocked would likely react in anger and violence, which would cause the conduct to be charged as disorderly conduct (or disorderly person) in the United States.

Most cities and states have not passed jostling statutes. However, New York has done so in response to the pickpocketing problem that exists in crowded public places such as subways. The procedure used by most pickpockets is to bump or shove (or have a partner distract by bumping and shoving) to permit entry into a pocket or purse for the theft. Jostling is defined by PL 165.25 in New York as:

> In a public place, intentionally and unnecessarily:
> 1. Placing one's hand in the proximity of a person's pocket or handbag, OR
> 2. Jostling or crowding another person at a time when a third person's hand is in the proximity of such person's pocket or handbag.

Battery and assault statutes seek to protect persons from physical injury caused by the intentional conduct of others. To convict an offender of the completed offense, the state must show that the completed crime of battery or assault occurred. In many states, to convict someone of attempted battery or assault requires showing that the defendant came within dangerous proximity of committing the crime of battery or assault.

What about menacing or threatening an assault or battery? Such conduct could possibly be "fighting words" or other disorderly conduct if all of the requirements of those offenses can be shown (see chapter 10). The state of New York enacted the crime of menacing, which is defined as follows in Public Law 120.15 of New York:

> By physically menacing, intentionally placing or attempting to place another person in fear of imminent serious physical injury. (New York Class B misdemeanor)

Assault, Intimidation, or Threatening Airline Crew Members

The Federal Aviation Act of 1958 (49 U.S.C.A. Sec. 1472 (j)) forbids assault, intimidation, or threatening of a flight crew member, and punishes such conduct by imprisonment of up to twenty years.

In the 1991 case of *United States v. Tabacca,* 924 F.2d 906 (9th Cir.), the defendant continued to smoke a cigarette after airline flight attendants requested him to extinguish the cigarette. After very vulgar language to the attendant, Tabacca grabbed her arm "and jerked and twisted her arm, causing her to strike the bulkhead of the seat across the aisle."

The U.S. Court of Appeals for the Ninth Circuit held that such conduct was sufficient to justify a conviction, holding:

* * *

Looking to the particular circumstances of this case, Tabacca's actions come within a reasonable construction of § 1472(j). A person of ordinary intelligence could foresee that grabbing and shoving a flight attendant, coupled with a diatribe of profane remarks, are actions which could inhibit the performance of an attendant's duties.

* * *

Dangerous Dogs

Dogs are found in every American community as both pets and for security. Most dogs are well behaved and cause only minor problems. Probably all communities require that licenses be obtained yearly and a dog license fee be paid.

Criminal and civil liability exist for the negligent control of vicious dogs. State statutes and municipal ordinances impose duties upon persons to properly and safely control vicious animals within their care. A "vicious" animal is an animal with a demonstrated propensity, tendency, or disposition to attack, cause injury, or otherwise endanger the safety of a human being.

Because of the reputation of the pit bull terrier, some communities in the United States have enacted ordinances regarding this breed of dog. Such ordinance and statutes commonly provide that pit bulls are presumed to be vicious unless the owner of the dog can show otherwise. Other dogs and animals not specifically listed in statutes are judged under statutes and ordinances according to their past history (that is, whether they have bitten persons before; their possible aggressive training; and their temperament and personality).

Dogs could be used to deliberately cause injury or death to persons. When used in this manner, the animal would be an instrument just as a gun or a knife, and the person using the animal could be criminally charged for the harm done or the threat created.

C. FELONIOUS AND AGGRAVATED ASSAULTS AND BATTERIES

Misdemeanor assault and misdemeanor batteries are probably classified as class A or B misdemeanors in most states. The degree of these crimes and the penalties are increased with aggravating factors used by state legislatures. The Supreme Court of Oregon pointed out that the three factors used in Oregon are (1) the severity of the injury, (2) the use of a deadly or dangerous weapon, and (3) culpable mental state.[12] The presence of one or more of these aggravating factors could result in a felonious assault or battery. For example, when only minor injury occurred where hands were used, a misdemeanor assault or battery could be charged. However, in the 1982 *Zangrilli* case, the defendant almost caused the death of his ex-wife by strangling her with his hands. The Supreme Court of

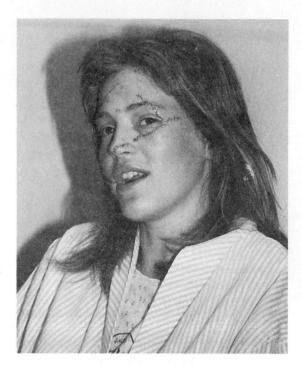

This New York model was attacked in 1986 by two assailants who slashed her face with a razor blade, causing wounds that required over one hundred stitches. Were aggravating factors present for a felonious conviction?

Rhode Island held that hands in the *Zangrilli* case were dangerous weapons and affirmed the felony conviction.

Mayhem

The common law offense of mayhem was the unlawful and violent depriving of the victim of full use of any functional member of the body (hand, arms, feet, eyes, legs, etc.) that would make the victim less able to defend himself or herself. State statutes have incorporated this concept in the form of maiming or mayhem statutes. Article 1166 of the Texas Penal Code provides that "whoever shall wilfully and maliciously cut off or otherwise deprive a person of the hand, arm, finger, toe, foot, leg, nose, or ear, or put out an eye or in any way deprive a person of any other member of his body shall be confined in the penitentiary not less than two nor more than ten years."[13]

Mental Culpability Increasing the Degree of the Crime

Probably all states have statutes making assaults and batteries felonies because of the seriousness of injuries or because dangerous or deadly weapons were used to commit the offense. Some statutes increase penalties and degree of crimes because of mental culpability.

The Oregon assault statute raises the offense from third- to second-degree assault if the crime is committed "under circumstances manifesting extreme indifference to the value of human life."[14] In holding that a jury must find not only recklessness, but also conduct that shows extreme indifference, the Oregon Supreme Court affirmed the defendant's conviction of assault in the second degree in the 1983 case of *State v. Boone,* holding:

Factors Used in Charging and Proving Attempted Murder

If the:	*"Intent to Kill" and "Attempt to Kill" Are More Likely to Be Charged:*	*A Lesser Offense Is Likely to Be Charged:*
• conduct of the defendant:	almost caused death or serious bodily harm to the victim	did not seriously threaten the safety of the victim
• weapon or instrument used:	was dangerous	is not ordinarily dangerous
• disposition and attitude of defendant:	showed extreme hostility, malice, and disregard for life	did not show an intent to kill or intent to cause serious harm
• conduct of the defendant:	constituted a "substantial step" toward causing death or serious bodily harm	did not come within "dangerous proximity" of killing or causing serious harm
• evidence showed that the defendant:	had a strong intent (or motive) to kill the victim	had little reason (or intent) to kill the victim

Unlawful Conduct with a Firearm or Other Dangerous Weapon

Because of the frequent unlawful use of firearms and other dangerous weapons, Section 2A2.2(b)(2) of the federal sentencing guidelines provides for increased sentences for the following unlawful conduct with a firearm or other dangerous weapons:

sentence increased
- possession (unlawful)
- displaying (unlawful)
- brandishing—"point(ing), wav(ing) about, or display(ing) in a threatening manner"
- pointing directly at victim
- pointing and verbally threatening to use weapon
- discharging (discharging could be with intent to frighten, intent to wound, or intent to kill. Attempted murder, assault with a deadly weapon, murder, and other serious offenses could be charged.)

See: *U.S. v. Johnson*, ___ F.2d ___ , 49 CrL 1140 (5th Cir. 1991) Armed robbery of three persons where handgun was pointed at persons and verbal threats made.
  U.S. v. De La Rosa, 911 F.2d 985 (5th Cir. 1990) In kidnapping, woman defendant waved gun at others and verbally threatened.
  U.S. v. Roberts, 898 F.2d 1465 (10th Cir. 1990) Knife used.

Witnesses testified that prior to the accident defendant was swerving across the road, tailgating so closely he almost hit the car in front of him and passing on a curve. The overwhelming weight of the evidence indicated that the accident occurred because defendant was across the center line in the oncoming lane of traffic. He sideswiped the first oncoming vehicle, bounced or swerved into his own lane and then swerved back across the center line into the second oncoming vehicle, causing serious injury to the passenger. Defendant had a blood alcohol content of .24 percent two hours after the accident. He was belligerent at the scene of the accident, threatening to hit the passenger of the first car he sideswiped. Because of his intoxication he was not only unable to assist the victim, but at one point interfered with the assistance. The degree of intoxication, defendant's erratic driving and his conduct at the scene of the accident are circumstances the jury could properly consider in determining whether defendant was extremely indifferent to the value of human life.

We hold that the circumstances which exist in this case suffice to establish defendant's extreme indifference to the value of human life.[15]

D. CHILD ABUSE AND NEGLECT

Child abuse, child neglect, and sexual abuse are serious problems throughout the United States. Estimates as to the number of children who die every year as the result of child abuse in the United States range from 2,000 to 5,000. The City of New York reports about 100 children die from child abuse each year.

Thousands of children in the United States suffer head injuries; broken bones from beatings; burns from cigarettes, stoves, hot liquids; ruptured internal organs (such as liver, spleen, kidney, and bowels) from blows to the abdomen; missing teeth; multiple scars; knife and gunshot wounds; and bruises and lacerations.

Persons who inflict such injuries on children may be charged with assault, battery, assault with a dangerous weapon, aggravated battery, and other offenses in the criminal code of the state in which the offense occurred. Criminal codes also have child abuse statutes and statutes forbidding the neglect of children. These statutes seek to protect children from injury and trauma inflicted on them by parents, stepfathers, paramours, relatives, baby-sitters, and other adults.

Parents and persons responsible for children have a duty to protect children and provide food, clothing, shelter, medical care, education, and a reasonable physical and moral environment for them. Child neglect is the failure to provide adequate food, clothing, shelter, sanitation, medical care, or supervision for a child.

The child abuse that generally appears in courts is physical abuse, such as deliberate injuries inflicted on children. Such injuries could result from excessive and unreasonable force used in disciplining children. The U.S. Supreme Court pointed out in *Ingraham v. Wright* that parents and persons taking the place of parents may use force "reasonably believed to be necessary for [the child's] proper control, training, or education."[16] What is reasonable is determined in view of the child's age and sex; the physical, emotional, and mental health of the child; and the conduct that prompted the punishment. Unfortunately, most children who are victims of abuse are under age five and are helpless in protecting themselves.

In response to the national problem, the following have occurred:

- *Mandatory reporting laws* have been enacted by all states requiring doctors, nurses, teachers, day-care workers, and other persons coming in contact with children to report suspected child abuse. But experts say there is still a tremendous amount of underreporting of abuse.
- *Increased authority to social workers* by some states to permit social workers to interview children without notifying their parents. Increased numbers of trained social workers are needed to handle growing case loads.
- *Education and help for parents* in the form of "hot lines" and shelters for battered spouses and children to prevent (if possible) situations leading to child abuse and neglect.

Child Abuse*

A crime that cuts across all walks of life and all social classes

Types of Child Abuse

Physical abuse	Possible source of the problem: • parent may be unable to distinguish between discipline and cruelty (or be unable to determine when one becomes the other) • may be the result of intoxication (drug or alcohol, or both) • may reflect severe stress because of such problems as unemployment, financial problems, etc. • any or all of the above combined. It is reported that the abused child often becomes an abusive parent.
Neglect	Children can be neglected (where parent has the ability to provide) • if adequate, proper food is not provided • if they are left alone or unsupervised for long periods of time • if clothing is dirty or not adequate for the weather • if medical, dental, or other physical needs are ignored • if child is not kept clean (poor hygiene, odors)
Sexual abuse (See chapters 18 and 19)	Under the law, children cannot consent to sexual acts. Sexual abuse occurs when a child is used for the sexual stimulation of an adult (or older child). The sexual abuse could include fondling, prolonged kissing, exhibitionism, and sex acts. Sexual abuse is reported to be the least reported of the abuses that are criminally prosecuted.
Emotional abuse and neglect (psychological)	Parents have a duty to love and emotionally care for their children. Constantly belittling, treating a child unequally, blaming the child for problems, emotionally neglecting the child, and failing to give children love and affection are forms of emotional abuse and neglect. Emotional abuse, alone or when combined with one or more of the other abuses, can have a devastating effect on a child.

*In 1990, the House Subcommittee on Health and Long-term Care on Aging reported that an estimated 1.5 million elderly Americans (5 percent of all older Americans) are abused each year, often by their own children. It was pointed out that older people often are ashamed to admit their families abuse them, or they fear reprisals if they complain. The report states that "Elder abuse has been virtually ignored by the Federal Government."

• *Increased awareness of the problems* by teachers, social workers, law enforcement officers, prosecutors, and courts.
• *Expert testimony* as to the "battered child syndrome" or "child battering profile" is permitted more frequently by courts in cases involving child abuse.
• *New criminal laws* such as the "homicide by abuse" statute enacted by the State of Washington, which makes child abuse resulting in death the equivalent of first-degree murder. Under this statute, prosecutors no longer have to prove premeditation or intent to kill for a conviction. Instead, the state must show that the defendant displayed "extreme indifference to human life." The writer of the bill stated, "Premeditation in child abuse cases is almost impossible to prove. This (law) gets around that oft-heard defense—'I didn't mean to kill the boy; I just wanted to discipline him.' " Other states are studying the new law.

Child neglect and child abuse is a continuing tragedy. This four-year-old weighing 14 pounds, 11 ounces was imprisoned by his parents in a playpen, with a set of bedsprings lashed to the top.

- *Recommendations*
    See "Deprived Children: A Judicial Response— 73 Recommendations" by the National Council of Juvenile and Family Court Judges.
    See also "Child Abuse: Prelude to Delinquency?" U.S. Department of Justice Office of Juvenile Justice, 1986.

Sexual abuse and sexual exploitation of children is discussed in chapter 18. Sexual abuse may be combined with physical abuse or child neglect. Abuse or neglect in any form may have a severe emotional and psychological effect on a child, causing behavioral problems that could have great impact on the child's life.

E. Offenses against the Liberty of a Person

Kidnapping

Kidnapping was a crime at old common law punishable by life imprisonment. All states and the federal government have enacted statutes making kidnapping a crime. The New Jersey jury instructions defining kidnapping are:

The elements of kidnapping are:
1) that the defendant unlawfully confined (the victim) for a substantial period; and
2) that the confinement was for the purpose of facilitation of the commission of another crime or to inflict bodily injury on or terrorize (the victim). (569 A.2d 1308 at 1313)

Motive or reason for kidnapping could be to obtain ransom or other valuables (such as in the kidnapping of twenty-six children in a school bus in Chowchilla, California, in 1976); to obtain a hostage for escape or other reasons; for the purposes of robbery, rape, murder, or other felony; to terrorize or blackmail; or for political reasons.

The question that has come before many courts is whether movements incident to the commission of such crimes as rape or robbery constitute kidnapping. According to California jury instruction # 652:

> To constitute the crime of simple kidnapping ... there must be a carrying, or otherwise forceful moving, for some distance of the person who, against his will, is stolen or taken into custody or control of another person, but the law does not require that the one thus stolen or taken be carried or moved a long distance or any particular distance.

In interpreting "some distance," the California courts have held that "movement across a room or from one room to another" is not sufficient movement to justify a kidnapping conviction.[17] The general rule seems to be that movement "merely incident to the commission of the robbery [or rape]" is not kidnapping.[18]

In 1982, the Supreme Court of Florida stated that there is a "definite trend" toward allowing a kidnapping conviction "where the purpose in confining or moving another person is to use that person as a hostage." In *Mobley v. State*,[19] the defendants were inmates in a jail. They took two guards and an attorney captive in the course of an escape attempt. In affirming the convictions of the defendants for kidnapping and other offenses, the Supreme Court held that the "confinement was not incidental to the attempted escape once [defendants] began using [the victims] as hostages and threatening physical harm."

In the 1983 case of *State v. Masino*,[20] the defendant dragged his victim from her car and down an embankment, out of sight from passersby, before sexually assaulting her. The Supreme Court of New Jersey affirmed the convictions of sexual assault and kidnapping.

In the 1990 case of *State v. LaFrance*, 117 N.J. 583, 569 A.2d 1308, the defendant was burglarizing a home in the early morning hours when he was confronted by the husband and wife. LaFrance pretended to have a gun and tied up the husband. After finishing his search for valuables, he then sexually assaulted the seven-month pregnant wife. After thirty minutes, the husband freed himself and overpowered the defendant. The Supreme Court of New Jersey affirmed the convictions of kidnapping, robbery, assault, sexual assault, and resisting arrest, stating:

* * *

> There are two basic kidnapping patterns. In one, the criminal seizes the victim and removes him or her to another place; in the other, the criminal confines the victim in the place where he or she is found. Were the latter not regarded as the moral equivalent of a kidnapping, the criminal might safely isolate a victim in the victim's "summer home in the mountains" and demand ransom with impunity. *See Commonwealth v. Hook*, 355 Pa.Super. 10, 13, 512 A.2d 718, 719 (1986) (quoting MPC § 212.1 comment (Tent. Draft No. 11, 1960) at 16).

> Just as obviously, however, not every movement or confinement of a victim is a kidnapping. The easiest illustrations are situations in which "the burglar puts the householder in the closet while he fills his sack with the silver," *see State v. Estes*, 418 A.2d 1108, 1113 (Me.1980), or in which the victim of a robbery is forced to open a

The Right of Government to Protect Children

Under early Roman law, children were considered to be the property of their father, who could discipline them as he saw fit: he could sell them, or even condemn them to death. This law changed slowly over the years and by the turn of this century, mothers were the primary custodians of their children when a divorce occurred. The concept of the "tender years presumption" held that only a mother has the nurturing qualities needed to love and care for a child through the early part of its life or the "tender years." The "tender years presumption" also changed, and today more than thirty states offer joint custody and shared parenting arrangements with parents who are divorced or have never married. Most criminal laws seek to protect all persons (children and adults alike). States seek to provide additional protection to children by the enactment of most (if not all) of the following statutes:

Laws Forbidding: *Statute # in Your State*

- child abuse   _____
- child neglect   _____
- abandonment of a child   _____
- contributing to the delinquency of a child   _____
- child snatching from the lawful custody of a guardian of the child _____
- exposing children to sexually harmful material   _____
- sexual exploitation of a child   _____
- "statutory rape" (children cannot consent to sexual intercourse or sexual contact)
    under age _____ is (crime) _____   _____
    under age _____ is (crime) _____   _____
    under age _____ is (crime) _____   _____
- "open house parties"   _____
- others   _____

Compulsory School Attendance Laws:

- imposing duty on parents until age ____   _____
- making student offense of skipping school truancy   _____
- authorizing police to take truant into custody   _____

Problem Areas

Problem: If a child needs medical attention, can parents use "spiritual healing" in keeping with their own religious beliefs instead of standard medical procedures?

Parents are protected from criminal charging in more than forty states by statutes permitting Christian Science and other religious parents to use "spiritual healing" instead of medical treatment.

The American Academy of Pediatrics urges pediatricians to work for repeal of such statutes, stating, "No statute should exist that permits or implies the denial of medical care necessary to prevent death or serious impairment to children can be supported on religious grounds."

Problem: As a good education is important to children, all states have compulsory school attendance laws. Parents who do not comply with such laws can ordinarily be charged with the crime of failing to send their child (or children) to school. Should parents be permitted to keep their children out of secondary school because of fear of worldly influences contrary to the attitudes, goals, and values of the religion of the parents?

See the U.S. Supreme Court ruling in the case of *Wisconsin v. Yoder,* 406 U.S. 205 (chapter 12).

* * *

safe in the home or go to the back of the store. *See State v. Dix,* 282 N.C. 490, 499, 193 S.E.2d 897, 902 (1973). Because courts sensed that these crimes should not be considered kidnapping, the problem became one of definition. In the absence of more precise statutes, courts supplied the necessary content.

* * *

...The Model Penal Code suggests requiring movement from home or place of business, or movement "a substantial distance" or confinement "for a substantial period in a place of isolation" as possible objective factors.... Our Code departs from the Model Penal Code in eliminating entirely any duration and danger requirements when a person restrains the liberty of another for the purpose of demanding ransom or holding the victim hostage. These crimes are so offensive to public morality that they stand in a separate category.

* * *

We repeat, as we did in *Masino,* that one is confined for a substantial period if that confinement "is criminally significant in the sense of being more than merely incidental to the underlying crime," and that determination is made with reference not only to the duration of the confinement, but also to the "enhanced risk of harm resulting from the [confinement] and isolation of the victim [or others]. That enhanced risk must not be trivial." 94 N.J. at 447, 466 A.2d 955.

* * *

The Crime of "Taking Hostage"

Because kidnapping requires a forcible movement of the victim "some distance" or a "substantial distance," some states have created the crime of "taking hostage." A movement of the victim is not required to prove this offense. In creating this new offense, the state legislature can require all the elements of the serious felony of kidnapping, except movement of the victim. They can require the state to prove "intent to use the person as a hostage."[21] As "taking hostage" is a serious offense, it can be made a class A or B felony. To encourage offenders to release victims unharmed, the offense can be reduced to a class B or C felony under such conditions.

False Imprisonment

Under the old common law, false imprisonment was also a crime that, like kidnapping, was punishable by life imprisonment. Many states have enacted statutes making false imprisonment a crime. The usual elements are:

1. The defendant must have confined or restrained the liberty or freedom of movement of another.
2. Such act must have been intentional and without the consent of the victim.
3. The defendant had no lawful authority to confine or restrain the movement of the victim.

False imprisonment differs from kidnapping in that, in kidnapping, the victim must be moved to another place. In false imprisonment, the confinement or

Offenses Against the Liberty of a Person

Offense	Usual Definition	Usual Motivation	Use of the Offense
False imprisonment	False imprisonment is the unlawful restraint of another and is committed when a person is detained unlawfully.	False imprisonment most often occurs today when employees of a retail store make an improper detention for shoplifting, or a law enforcement officer makes an illegal arrest.	False imprisonment charges are most often brought in civil suits in civil courts.
Kidnapping	Kidnapping is a false imprisonment that is aggravated by the movement or conveyance of the victim to another place.	• to obtain a hostage • to obtain ransom • for the purposes of rape, robbery, murder, etc. • to terrorize, blackmail, etc.	Kidnapping is one of the most serious crimes against a person's liberty and is punished severely.
"Taking hostage"	The criminal act of "taking hostage" is used to gain an advantage and compel others to comply with demands.	"Taking hostage" is a tactic often used as part of an escape attempt.	The crime of "taking hostage" does not require forcible movement of the victim "some distance."
Parental kidnapping or child snatching[a]	This crime is a kidnapping by a parent who has lost (or will lose) custody of the kidnapped child.	To harass; to retaliate against other spouse or use as leverage in determining support payments, etc.; or to maintain custody and control of the child.	This problem is serious in the United States. Some of the abducted children are never seen again by the other parent.
Abduction	The English enacted the first abduction statute in 1488. For many years, the crime forbade taking a female for any sexual purposes. Today, states have limited abduction to taking a child from the person having lawful custody of the child.	If the taking were by force, kidnapping would probably be charged. Abduction could be charged when a natural parent took a child in violation of a court order or when a victim was old enough to cooperate in the taking.	States using abduction as a crime have generally limited it to taking a child from a person having lawful custody.

continued

restraint may be at the place of the false arrest or unlawful detention of the victim. Under the old common law, it was also required that kidnapping be done secretly; this was not required for false imprisonment. However, the requirement of secretness for kidnapping has probably been eliminated by most state statutes.

Today, false imprisonment is seldom charged as a crime. Most false imprisonment actions are civil actions, in which it is alleged that there was a false arrest

Offenses Against the Liberty of a Person (continued)

Offense	Usual Definition	Usual Motivation	Use of the Offense
Slavery and involuntary servitude	The Thirteenth Amendment forbids "slavery . . . [and] involuntary servitude, except as a punishment for crime."	Two Michigan residents were convicted in 1984 of violations of civil rights and involuntary servitude of two mentally retarded men, who the federal prosecutor stated were held as slaves for at least 11 years.[b]	Slavery, serfage, peonage, debt bondage, and exploitation of children still exist in parts of the world.

[a]The National Incidence Studies on Missing, Abducted, Runaway, and Thrownaway Children in America estimated that in 1988 there were 345,100 family abductions in the United States. This was up sharply from previous estimates of 25,000 to 100,000 per year. (The child must be absent at least one night.) Of these children, it is estimated that 300 or 400 are snatched and taken to another country to keep the child from his or her rightful guardian in the United States. In 1988, the United States passed legislation (H.R. 3971) giving jurisdiction to the state or federal court of the aggrieved parent who can show by a preponderance of the evidence that the child has been wrongfully taken.

[b]In 1988, the convictions of the defendants from Michigan were affirmed by the U.S. Supreme Court, *United States v. Kozminski,* 487 U.S. 931, 43 CrL 3214. The Court defined "involuntary servitude":

***

Our precedents reveal that not all situations in which labor is compelled by physical coercion or force of law violate the Thirteenth Amendment. By its terms the Amendment excludes involuntary servitude imposed as legal punishment for a crime. Similarly, the Court has recognized that the prohibition against involuntary servitude does not prevent the State or Federal Governments from compelling their citizens, by threat of criminal sanction, to perform certain civic duties.

. . . Moreover, in *Robertson v. Baldwin,* the Court observed that the Thirteenth Amendment was not intended to apply to "exceptional" cases well established in the common law at the time of the Thirteenth Amendment, such as "the right of parents and guardians to the custody of their minor children or wards," *id.,* at 282, or laws preventing sailors who contracted to work on vessels from deserting their ships. *Id.,* at 288.

Putting aside such exceptional circumstances, none of which are present in this case, our precedents clearly define a Thirteenth Amendment prohibition of involuntary servitude enforced by the use or threatened use of physical or legal coercion. The guarantee of freedom from involuntary servitude has never been interpreted specifically to prohibit compulsion of labor by other means, such as psychological coercion.

or an improper restraint of the freedom of movement of the plaintiff. Many such civil suits originate from shoplifting incidents. To avoid such civil suits, it should be remembered that the freedom of movement of a person should not be restrained unless authority exists to make such a detention or arrest.

Parental Kidnapping or Child Snatching

"Child snatching" is the abduction of a child by one parent without the consent of the other parent. It could occur before the parents had commenced a divorce action, during the time in which a divorce action was pending, or after divorce judgment had been granted. Child snatching is also known as parental kidnapping, child abduction, or child stealing.

Thousands of children disappear each year as a result of parental kidnapping. Although the offending parent may state that he or she seeks to protect the child's welfare, other motives for child snatching are:

- retaliation against and harassment of the other spouse
- as a means to bargain for reduced child support or reduced division of property in the divorce settlement
- an attempt to bring about a reconciliation of the marriage

Children who are kidnapped by a parent experience changes that may lead to emotional damage. First, the child will probably be told that the parent who had custody is either dead or no longer loves the child. Second, in most instances, the child begins a lifestyle in which he or she grows up with only one parent. Third, the child is frequently exposed to life "on the run," as parental kidnapping is a felony in most states. The pain, fear, guilt, anger, and anxiety from these experiences can cause severe, irreparable psychological harm.

Most states are generally prepared to extradite the offending parent back to the state in which the offense was committed, if he or she can be located. Before the passage of the Uniform Child Custody Jurisdiction Act (UCCJA), a fleeing child-snatcher could run to another state, where residence would be established and a custody order would be sought from the courts of the new state. Under UCCJA, the home or resident state would continue to have jurisdiction.

Because the federal kidnapping statute (the "Lindbergh Act")[22] specifically excludes parents from its scope, a federal Parental Kidnapping Prevention Act was passed by Congress in 1981. This act facilitates interstate enforcement of custody and visitation determinations. The act also declares that the Fugitive Felon Act[23] applies in state felony parental kidnapping cases, giving the FBI jurisdiction when the child-snatcher crosses state lines.

The Missing Children Act[24]

Because of increasing concern for child kidnapping by strangers or parents, voluntary programs to fingerprint children for identification have commenced throughout the nation. The parents or legal guardians retain the fingerprint cards for use if the child, at a later date, gets lost or is missing.

In 1982, the Missing Children Act became law. The act requires the Attorney General to "acquire, collect and preserve any information which would assist in the location of any missing person (including children, unemancipated persons as defined by the laws of the place of residence) and provide confirmation as to any entry [into FBI records] for such a person to the parent, legal guardian or next of kin." The act thus gives parents, legal guardians, or next of kin access to the information in the FBI National Crime Information Center's (NCIC) missing person file.

The individual making the request is notified of the results of the check. If a record has not been entered, the person is instructed to contact local law enforcement authorities to determine whether the disappearance of the missing person meets the criteria for entry into the NCIC computer. Missing unemancipated minors is one of the four categories of records entered into the NCIC computer. Should a child of that description be found by another department, this information would be exchanged.

Missing Children in America

The U.S. Department of Health and Human Services estimates that over 1.5 million children disappear from their homes each year. Studies done as required by the Missing Children's Act enacted by the U.S. Congress in 1984 show that the missing children problem is really "a set of at least five very different, distinct problems."[a] These problems, which are reported to law enforcement agencies, are identified as follows:

Family Abductions where a family member took (or failed to return) a child in violation of custody rights or an agreement. In 1988, more than 345,100 family abductions were reported where a child was absent at least one night. Most of the missing children were under eleven years of age. About half of the abductions involved an unauthorized taking, while half were a failure to return a child after an authorized visit. Sexual abuse was reported in 1 percent of the cases, while neglect or abandonment of the child was a greater concern. The motive for taking the children was generally not love and concern for the children but revenge and retaliation. Family abductions were not limited to parents but also included other family members, lovers, and former live-ins. To deal with this growing problem, the Parental Kidnapping Act was passed by Congress in 1980.

Runaways Runaway age does not commence until nine and ten. Physical or sexual abuse in the home could cause the runaway. Home conditions could be deplorable, or the child could have become involved in crimes, drugs, sexual relations, or a gang (sometimes all). Most of the reported runaways return home after being missing for one night or more. Runaways from juvenile facilities tend to be more serious than household cases. Over half leave the state, one third are picked up by the police, and 10 percent are placed in jail.

Thrownaway Children are abandoned, deserted, told to leave the home, or not allowed to return to the house, or no effort is made to locate them. These children experience more violence within the family and more sexual and physical abuse away from the home. Shelters for runaway and thrownaway children report a high rate of exposure to AIDS and other diseases.

Lost Children are generally children so young that they cannot identify themselves or give a home address. However, older children could be lost in a rural or wooded area, causing extensive searches for the lost child. A "lost" child could be a runaway, a thrownaway child, or the victim of an abduction. Lost children in most cases are found and returned home.

A survey conducted by the U.S. Senate Subcommittee on Investigations shows that more than 85,000 children were missing in twenty-five of the largest American cities in 1981. Tragically, at the end of the year at least 7,000 of the cases remained unsolved. Law enforcement officers report that few stranger-abducted children are recovered alive. (See "Plight of the Children," *The Prosecutor Magazine* Vol. 16, No. 5 (1983). The entire issue is devoted to this subject.)

Abduction by Strangers or the Victims of Other Crimes Two to three hundred children are kidnapped by strangers every year in the United States. Criminal homicides of children average up to 147 per year. But it is also estimated that two to five thousand unidentified bodies are buried each year in the United States in John or Jane Doe graves, with approximately half of the unidentified being children. Strangers who steal children are broadly categorized by the Behavioral Science Department of the FBI Academy as follows:

- *The Pedophile.* The pedophile abducts a child primarily for sexual purposes. The Center for Child Advocacy and Protection states that such persons are generally young and middle-aged men who seek to control children rather than injure them. They will, however, murder children and perhaps make up the largest group in this category.
- *The "Serial" Killer* (see chapter 13). The killings of twenty-nine young blacks in Atlanta, after abduction, shocked the nation. Wayne Williams was convicted for the murders of two of the older victims.
- *The Psychotic.* The psychotic is usually a woman who has lost a baby or cannot conceive. To solve her problem, she abducts another family's child.
- *The Profiteer.* This person seeks to make money by stealing children. The child may be used by a baby adoption ring, pornographers, or, in rare instances, as a kidnapping for ransom.

[a] See the *National Incidence Studies on Missing, Abducted, Runaway, and Thrownaway Children in America* and *Parental Abduction Prosecutor's Handbook*, available at the National Center for Prosecution of Child Abuse, 1033 N. Fairfax St., Alexandria, VA 22314.

Missing, Abducted, Runaway, and Thrownaway Children in America

	Characteristics	1990 numbers
Family Abduction	• Taken in violation of custody or not returned after visit • Child concealed or transported out of state • Intent to permanently alter custody	354,100
Stranger Abduction	• Took, detained, or lured • Gone overnight, transported 50 or more miles, or killed • Intent to keep, or ransom	3,200–4,600
Runaways	• Gone one night, or gone longer and refused to return • Most runaways occurred in the summer and ran to friend or relative's home • Many came from a home with a step-parent or live-in partner	446,700 from home and 8,800 from juvenile facility and foster home
Thrownaways	• Told to leave, not allowed back, no effort made to recover runaway, or abandoned • No familiar and secure place to stay	127,100
Lost, Injured, Otherwise Missing	• Children who did not fit into any of the above categories • Children missing for a few minutes to overnight. Police were called.	428,200

Source: Office of Juvenile Justice and Delinquency Prevention, U.S. Department of Justice

The act does not confer on the FBI any new investigative jurisdiction. The FBI can enter parental kidnapping cases through the Fugitive Felony Act if the following conditions exist:

1. A state arrest warrant has been issued charging the parent with a felony violation.
2. There must be evidence of interstate flight.
3. A specific request for FBI assistance must be made by state authorities who agree to extradite and prosecute.
4. A U.S. attorney must authorize issuance of an unlawful flight warrant.

The National Center for Missing and Exploited Children coordinates efforts to recover missing children. A telephone hot line and other new facilities were established in 1984 to aid in these efforts.

False Arrest

The tort[25] of false imprisonment is sometimes called *false arrest.* False arrest is a wrongful arrest made either by a law enforcement officer or a private person. In a civil lawsuit (tort action) for false arrest, the plaintiff alleges that there was no authority or legal justification for the defendant to interfere with the plaintiff's freedom of movement.

Arresting, detaining, and holding a person in custody without authority is false imprisonment and gives the victim the basis for a civil lawsuit to recover for the false arrest and false imprisonment. The following illustrates:

EXAMPLE: Newspapers reported the arrest of two New York City Transit officers in 1988 as part of a false arrest scandal.

Officials became aware of the problem when a woman reported that while she was in a New York subway, she was "dumbfounded" when one of the officers told her that a man had sexually abused her and "maybe exposed himself" in the subway. The woman reported, "I didn't see anything and I told the officer so." The woman stated she did not want to press charges but charges were filed anyway. Police investigation concluded that the officers had made other "wrongful arrests."

Federal criminal charges were filed against the officers, which the federal prosecutor described as allegations of "false arrest" and that "false arrest is clearly a deprivation of civil rights." Civil lawsuits were also filed by the persons who alleged that they were wrongfully arrested by the police officer.

Shoplifting arrests and detentions are made every day in cities throughout the United States by law enforcement officers and private persons. If the laws of the state are complied with, the arrests and detentions are then lawful and legally justified. The following civil lawsuit for false arrest resulted from an arrest made in an Iowa shopping center:

CHILDREN v. BURTON
Supreme Court of Iowa (1983) 331 N.W.2d 673, Review denied 464 U.S. 848 104 S. Ct. 155 (1983)

Police in Charles City, Iowa, had been called a number of times to stores in a shopping mall where a man had been seen masturbating and indecently exposing himself. On a Sunday afternoon, a woman clerk, who had reported one of the previous incidents, saw a man she believed to be the "flasher" in a store. The police were called again and the man was pointed out to Officer Dunn. Before arresting the man (Peter Children), Officer Dunn asked the clerk (June Temple) "Are you sure it's him?" Temple replied, "Yes, yes, I'm sure." Children was then arrested and booked for indecent exposure. The criminal complaint against Children was dismissed about two months later and another man was arrested and convicted of the offenses. In a civil action against the police officers and Charles City, Children was awarded $1,250,000. The Supreme Court of Iowa reversed the judgment holding:

* * *

This is a false arrest case, not a malicious prosecution case.

* * *

A false arrest case involving the issue of probable cause turns on what the officer knew at the time of arrest, not what he learned later. Much of the evidence and argument Children presses upon us would go to a malicious prosecution claim but is not relevant on the liability *issue in a false arrest claim.*

* * *

A false arrest is one way of committing the tort of false imprisonment—restraining freedom of movement. Prosser, Law of Torts 42 *(4th ed. 1971) ("The action for the tort of false imprisonment, sometimes called false arrest, is another lineal descendant of the old action of trespass. It protects the personal interest in freedom from restraint of movement.") . . .*

* * *

The tort requires confinement of the person. Restatement (Second) of Torts § § 35(1)(b), 36 (1965). *If* liability *arose for false arrest in this case, it had to arise within the period commencing with the original arrest of Children and terminating with his release on recognizance. Before and after that period he was not confined.*

* * *

A. The essential elements of the tort of false arrest are (1) detention or restraint against one's will and (2) unlawfulness of the detention or restraint.

* * *

A peace officer in Iowa may make a warrantless arrest when he has reasonable ground for believing that an indictable public offense has been committed and has reasonable ground for believing that the person arrested has committed it.

* * *

When an officer acts with probable cause, he is protected even though the person arrested turns out to be innocent.

* * *

In dealing with civil damage actions for false arrest, courts apply a probable cause standard less demanding than the constitutional probable cause standard in criminal cases. If the officer acts in good faith and with reasonable belief that a crime has been committed and the person arrested committed it, his actions are justified and liability does not attach.

* * *

Officers confronted with situations such as this one must make a decision. They do not have the luxury of detached reflection before they act. Nor can they conduct extensive investigation and cross-examination out on the street, to see that all the legal elements of the crime are satisfied. They should be judged in the context of the real world in which they must function. We hold that this arrest was on probable cause.

Having lawfully arrested Children, Dunn had a right to process the arrest and arrange for bail. This he did with the help of Burton. Temple adhered to her iden-

tification but another of the clerks disagreed. The workup of the evidence in the case would obviously take time. That first evening was preliminary—taking the person into custody and arranging bail. These preliminaries took an hour and twenty minutes. We hold that this retention, following the lawful arrest, was also lawful.

We realize that Children suffered grievously from a mistake, but his claim founded on false arrest is untenable. On the liability issue, we cannot allow our attention to be diverted to events which happened after Children was released. The trial court should have sustained the motion for directed verdict or the subsequent motion for judgment notwithstanding verdict.

Reversed.

F. FAMILY VIOLENCE AND DISTURBANCES

A study conducted for the National Institute of Mental Health concluded that "physical violence occurs between family members more often than it occurs between other individuals or in any other setting except wars and riots."

The disturbance is often a quarrel between family members. It may have started with a few angry words, or it could have been a simmering dispute that exploded into violence. Destruction or damaging or taking of property may have occurred. One or both (or all) the parties may have been under the influence of alcohol or drugs. Job stress or unemployment may contribute to the situation.

Hitting, pushing, choking, wrestling combined with other abusive behavior may have occurred. Insulting and offending language is almost always used. Injuries range in severity from minor to critical and life threatening.

Both parties could be at fault or one party could be the agitator and the offender. The offender may have a prior record of violence and may be under a court order (divorce) or restraining order (criminal) forbidding such conduct. Or the offender may be on probation or parole and his domestic conduct may

---

Responses to Domestic Violence

The following are some of the responses available to violent family situations:

- arrest of the offending person (or persons)
  - if the state or city has a mandatory arrest law
  - or at the discretion of the officer (or under the policy of the officer's department)
- obtain a protective court order under the statutes of that state
- seek shelter for the victim (spouse, children, parent, etc.) under the shelter program available in that community
- divorce action and obtaining immediate (and also permanent) court orders that could:
  - protect
  - remove offending spouse from premise

  - forbid communication or contact by offending spouse
  - restrict visitation rights with children, and enforce other restrictions
- issue (or threaten to issue) a civil citation with a substantial money fine
- use of the emergency detention section of the state mental health act (if applicable) to place the offending party into custody for observation
- revocation of probation or parole if the offender has violated terms of a probation or parole agreement

violate the terms of his probation or parole. The offender's presence on the premises may be in violation of a court order or a condition of probation or parole. In addition to these violations, the offender may also be a trespasser.

Family units include not only the traditional family relationships, but also homosexuals and unwed heterosexual couples. The disturbance or violence could include not only adults, but also children within the family unit.

Past experience has demonstrated that "family trouble" calls can be dangerous for law enforcement officers. Approximately one-fifth of police deaths and almost one-third of assaults on officers occur in responding to family quarrels and domestic disputes in which a weapon is used.

In past years, unless serious injury occurred or a clear violation of a court order or probation (or parole) existed, an arrest would ordinarily not be made. Police officers would attempt to mediate the dispute. In counseling women, officers would sometimes ask: "Who will support you if he's locked up? Do you realize he could lose his job? Do you want to spend days in court? Why don't you kiss and make up? Why did you get him so worked up that he slugged you? Why do you want to make trouble? Think of what he'll do to you the next time."

Studies by the Police Foundation have shown that police arrests sharply reduce violence in the home. The police commissioner of New York City stated that because of this study and because of his own experience as a "cop on the street," he concluded that past police efforts to mediate have done little to stop what has been a growing problem. The commissioner stated that arresting violent members of a household would be more effective in protecting other family members and would help to safeguard police officers who are called to intervene in situations in which violence could occur.

Criminal charges could be, for example, assault, battery, disorderly conduct, trespass, criminal damage to property (if another person's property was damaged or destroyed), or reckless use of a weapon. In addition to spending time in jail, the offender could be placed under a restraining order or injunction in an attempt to prevent repeated violence or disturbances.

In past years, it was not uncommon for police departments to receive calls from women asking for protection from men who had threatened them or from wives who expected to be beaten by their husbands when they came home from a tavern. Threats to injure can be the basis of a criminal charge. If the threat was made over a telephone, the charge of unlawful use of a telephone may be made.

The battered woman problem has caused crisis counseling centers and shelters to be established throughout the United States to assist victims and their families. These centers provide shelter when needed, counseling, support, and emergency food and clothing. Location of the shelters are generally not disclosed to the public to avoid further confrontation by the victim with the offender.

Complaints of domestic violence are increasing in number throughout the United States. However, experts are uncertain whether there has been an actual increase in family violence. The violence may have existed for many years but for the most part gone unreported until recently, when victims have been encouraged to report such abuse.

When Do Police Have a Constitutional Duty to Protect Citizens in Domestic Violence Situations?

In the January 1991 issue of *FBI Law Enforcement Bulletin,* an article on domestic violence asked this question: "Domestic Violence: When Do Police Have a

Constitutional Duty to Protect?" Citing many cases dealing with this subject, the writer of the article concluded:

- ... as a general rule, police do not have a constitutionally imposed duty to protect citizens against domestic violence.
- As a matter of constitutional law, police have considerable discretion in deciding whether and when to make an arrest.
- ... the U.S. Supreme Court recently ... concluded that the Due Process Clause does not legally obligate law enforcement to protect an individual absent a custodial relationship.
- ... a constitutional duty to protect can arise where law enforcement action actually increases an individual's danger of, or vulnerability to, domestic violence.
- ... procedural due process claims against police for their failure to protect victims of domestic violence are likely to fail.

The Crime of Violation of a Court Order (or Court Injunction)

Many court orders (or injunctions) are issued every year in the United States. They are issued in divorce cases where one of the parties requests such an order (or orders). They are issued where there is serious harassment and the victim goes into a court for protection. The injunction could order a husband (or wife) or a boyfriend not to contact or harass his former spouse or live-in partner. The order could forbid the person against whom it is issued from going into or near the residence or the place of employment of the person the order seeks to protect. The order may forbid harassment, violence, or contact with a person or persons.

An increasing number of states are making the violation of such court orders (injunctions) crimes in themselves. This is because so many of these orders have been violated, because tragedies sometimes occur, and because there is no other practical way of enforcing such orders. Other statutes could also make a person who violates a court order subject to immediate arrest without the necessity of an arrest warrant or another court hearing.

When a court order is issued under these new laws, the person against whom it is issued is informed in the court order that any violation of the order could result in immediate arrest.

If a violation does occur, law enforcement officers are generally called by the person the court order seeks to protect. The person should be able to produce a copy of the order for the law enforcement officers. The order will generally show that it has been personally served on the defendant.

EXAMPLE: A court order is issued against a former live-in boyfriend ordering him (among other things) not to go near or into the place of employment of his former girlfriend. The police are called when the man enters the store or office that the order forbids him to enter. The police detain the man until they have viewed and read the copy of the court order. When it is clear that he has violated the order, the police then arrest the man and charge him with the crime of violation of the court order (injunction).

Questions and Problems for Chapter 14

1. When the doors of a subway train opened at Grand Central Station in New York, a young woman dragged a man off the train. As the twenty-seven-year-old woman punched the man and beat his head against a concrete wall, she accused him of fondling her body while on the

crowded subway train. He apologized while calling for the police. Both complained of the conduct of the other. The thirty-one-year-old man was charged with third-degree sexual abuse and the woman was issued a criminal summons for harassment (New York *Times* news article).

Assuming the accusations of the woman are correct, what amount and degree of force could she legally use against him (state the test used to determine how much force she could use)? Is the criminal charge and the citation that were issued appropriate? (Third-degree sexual abuse is "offensive touching" or "sexual contact" in New York under Public Law 130.55 and a Class B

Misdemeanor.) What would be appropriate (if any) charges in your state?

2. Baseball star Reggie Jackson was having lunch in a Milwaukee restaurant when he was spotted by a man at the bar who had been drinking. The man immediately went to Reggie Jackson's table, interrupted the conversation at the table, and insisted on an autograph. After an exchange of words, with the parties and witnesses differing as to what occurred, the man ended up on the floor with a broken jaw. Who is at fault? Which of the parties should be charged? Or should both of the parties be charged? With what offenses? Explain.

Notes

1. A few states (including Wisconsin) have not statutorized the common law crime of assault. Disorderly conduct and attempt to commit a battery are substituted for assault in charging.

2. See West's *Annotated California Codes,* Chap. 9, Sec. 240.

3. Probably all states have passed statutes that criminalize the conduct of pointing an unloaded gun at a victim who does not know if the gun is loaded or unloaded and becomes apprehensive and frightened. The New York crime of "menacing" (Sec. 120.15) by placing "or attempting to place another in fear of imminent serious physical injury" is an example of such criminal statutes.

4. 34 Cal. 3d 350, 193 Cal.Rptr. 890, 667 P.2d 694 (1983).

5. See also *United States v. Frizzi,* 491 F.2d 1231 (1st Cir. 1974), in which the defendant spat in the face of a mail carrier and then hit the carrier in the face when he demanded an apology. The Court affirmed the defendant's conviction of assaulting a federal officer in the performance of his duties.

6. 440 A.2d 710 (R.I. 1982). Other courts cited that have held that, depending on the circumstances, hands alone may be found to be a deadly weapon are *People v. Zankich,* 189 Cal.App.2d 54, 69–70, 11 Cal.Rptr. 115, 124–125 (1961); *Thomas v. State,* 237 Ga. 690, 691–692, 229 S.E.2d 458, 460 (1976); *State v. Heinz,* 223 Iowa 1241, 1259, 275 N.W. 10, 21 (1937); *Vogg v. Commonwealth,* 308 Ky. 212, 214 S.W.2d 86 (1948); *State v. Born,* 280 Minn. 306, 307–308, 159 N.W.2d 283, 284–285 (1968); *Pulliam v. State,* 298 So.2d 711 (Miss. 1974); *State v. Gardner,* 522 S.W.2d 323 (Mo. App. 1975); *Pettigrew v. State,* 430 P.2d 808, 812–13 (Okl. Cr. 1967); see generally, 33 A.L.R.3d 922 (1970); note, *The Fist or Teeth as a Dangerous Weapon,* 7 La.L.Rev. 584 (1974).

7. 91 Misc.2d 724, 398 N.Y.S.2d 821.

8. Chap. 38, para. 12–3(a)(2).

9. 117 Ill. App. 3d 363, 73 Ill. Dec. 17, 453 N.E.2d 842. The Illinois Appellate Court cited the following:

"Other instances of conduct held to be simple battery based solely on insulting or provoking physical contact [include]: *People v. Hamilton,* ... 401 N.E.2d 318 ... (where defendant reached around the female complainant and placed his hand over her mouth); *People v. Siler,* ... 406 N.E.2d 891 ... (where defendant lifted up complainant's dress during a confrontation having sexual overtones).

10. Also see chapter 6 on defenses to the use of force. A civil action of battery can occur in medical practice where there is a lack of consent. Patients have the right to weigh the risks that a particular treatment presents and to decide what course of action is to be followed. Therefore, treatment without consent in a nonemergency, or treatment that exceeds the consent given, is actionable as a civil battery. See *Prosser, The Law of Torts* 102, 103 (4th ed., 1971).

11. *Ingraham v. Wright,* 430 U.S. 651, 97 S.Ct. 1401 (1977). See also *People v. Donn Decaro,* 17 Ill.App.3d 553, 308 N.E.2d 196 (1974). See the New York *Times* article "Jailed for Paddling the Paddler" (November 13, 1987) where a mother received a six-month jail sentence for hitting a woman assistant principal who paddled her son in school. See also the *Newsweek* article "Paddling: Still a Sore Point" (June 22, 1987).

12. *State v. Boone,* 294 Or. 630, 661 P.2d 917 (1983).

13. Vernon's Penal Code of the State of Texas Annotated.

14. Oregon Stat. 163.175(1)(c).

15. 294 Or. 630, 661 P.2d 917 (1983).

16. 429 U.S. 975, 97 S.Ct. 481 (1976).

17. See *People v. Daniels,* 71 Cal.2d 1119, 80 Cal.Rptr. 897, 459 P.2d 225 (1969).

18. See *People v. Williams,* 2 Cal.3d 894, 88 Cal.Rptr. 208, 471 P.2d 1008 (1970).

19. 409 So.2d 1031 (Fla. 1982).

20. 94 N.J. 436, 466 A.2d 955 (1983).

21. Sec. 940.305 Wisconsin "taking hostage" felony.

22. 18 U.S.C.A. § 1201.

23. 18 U.S.C.A. § 1073.

24. In October, 1984, the President of the United States signed the "Missing Children's Assistance Act" (36 CrL 3063), which provides for the operation of a national toll-free telephone line for exchanging information on missing children through the national resource center and clearing house. The administrator of the program will "facilitate effective coordination among all federally funded programs relating to missing children." Section 406(a) of the Act provides that: "The Administrator is authorized to make grants to and enter into contracts with public agencies or nonprofit private organizations, or combinations thereof, for research, demonstration projects, or service programs designed—

"(1) to educate parents, children, and community agencies and organizations in ways to prevent the abduction and sexual exploitation of children;

"(2) to provide information to assist in the locating and return of missing children;

"(3) to aid communities in the collection of materials which would be useful to parents in assisting others in the identification of missing children;

"(4) to increase knowledge of and develop effective treatment pertaining to the psychological consequences, on both parents and children . . ."

25. A tort is a wrongful act for which the victim could commence a civil lawsuit. See chapter 1 for a discussion.

Part Four

CRIMES AGAINST PROPERTY

Chapter Fifteen

THEFT, ROBBERY, AND BURGLARY

A. General Property Law Concepts

A law student taking criminal law would also probably be taking courses in personal property law and real property law that would provide the necessary background for understanding criminal property law more thoroughly. The following concepts and principles are presented to acquaint the student who has not had courses in business law or property law with a few elementary property principles:

- Two important rights to property are (1) the right of ownership and (2) the right of possession of the property. A person may have the lawful possession of property but not necessarily be its owner. Possession of personal property is presumptive evidence of ownership if there is no evidence to the contrary. Possession accompanied by the exercise of the complete acts of ownership for a considerable period is strong evidence of the ownership of property.[1]

- Property ownership may be in the form of sole ownership. It may be in the form of joint ownership as between husband and wife, business partners, or friends or relatives. The property may be owned by a corporation or a business partnership. Property ownership may be vested in a governmental unit, such as a city, a state, a county, or the national government.

- There are many forms of lawful possession of property. The owner may have the possession of property or may permit another person to have lawful possession and use of the property. An employee or agent of the owner of the property may have possession. Bailees and pledgees also have the lawful possession of property that belongs to others. A bailment would exist, for example, when a man takes his car into a garage for repairs. The owner of the car retains title and ownership to the vehicle but gives possession to the garage so the repair work may be done on the vehicle. State statutes give the garage a right to a lien on the vehicle in the amount of the work that was done on the car. The garage then has a superior right of possession of the vehicle until the owner satisfies the amount lawfully due the garage. In many states, the owner of the property could be charged with theft if he intentionally and unlawfully took possession of such property from a pledgee or bailee who had a superior right of possession.

- A thief wrongfully deprives the true owner of the property of his lawful possession of the property. The unexplained or falsely explained possession of recently stolen property might give rise to an inference that the person had received the stolen property.[2] To prove theft, burglary, or robbery, there must be "other facts or circumstances indicating guilt."

- A thief cannot deprive the owner of property of the right of ownership and lawful possession of the property. For example, if X steals Y's $500 watch and sells the watch to A for $50, Y may demand from A the return of his watch and may go into a civil court in a "replevin action" to assert his right to the lawful ownership and possession of the watch.

- In most instances, an innocent purchaser of stolen goods takes only those ownership rights that the seller had. If the seller was a thief, then the buyer has only unlawful possession of the property. The ancient concept of

436

caveat emptor (let the buyer beware) puts a buyer on notice that if he or she purchases items without due care, the lawful owner of the property may assert his or her right to possession and ownership of the property. Under the old common law, with its severe penalties, it was dangerous to purchase anything from a stranger. The following 1990 case illustrates:

GREEK ORTHODOX CHURCH OF CYPRUS v. GOLDBERG ET AL.
United States Court of Appeals, Seventh Circuit (1990) 917 F.2d 278

Peg Goldberg, an art dealer, was in Europe on a buying trip. She "fell in love" with four early Christian mosaics that she was told were "found" in the rubble of an "extinct" church in northern Cyprus and were exported to Germany with the permission of the Cyprus government. Goldberg made some inquiries as to the mosaics and then borrowed money to purchase them for $1,080,000 (U.S.). After she shipped the mosaics to the United States, she was informed that the sixth-century mosaics had been stolen from the Greek Orthodox Church. Possession of the mosaics were awarded to the Church with the court concluding:

> . . . *when circumstances are as suspicious as those that faced Peg Goldberg, prospective purchasers would do best to do more than make a few last-minute phone calls. As testified to at trial, in a transaction like this, "All the red flags are up, all the red lights are on, all the sirens are blaring." . . . (quoting testimony of Dr. Vikan). In such cases, dealers can (and probably should) take steps such as a formal IFAR search; a documented authenticity check by disinterested experts; a full background search of the seller and his claim of title; insurance protection and a contingency sales contract; and the like. If Goldberg would have pursued such methods, perhaps she would have discovered in time what she has now discovered too late: the Church has a valid, superior and enforceable claim to these Byzantine treasures, which therefore must be returned to it.*

* * *

- If stolen money or negotiable securities have been passed by a thief to persons who receive the money in good faith and for valuable consideration, the money and the negotiable instruments cannot be recovered by the victims. In 1967, a man named Hanzl robbed a bank in Pennsylvania and obtained $18,500. Two days later, he paid the Internal Revenue Service $4,500 in back taxes. When Hanzl was arrested a week later, he disclosed what he had done with the money. A federal judge ruled that the $4,500 could not be recovered by the insurance company that covered the bank loss in the robbery. The court stated:

It is a rule of law that title to currency passes with delivery to the person who receives it in good faith and for valuable consideration. It seems clear that an obligation to pay income taxes constitutes a valid preexisting debt, and the transfer of currency in payment of that debt is for value. Thus, we hold that Hanzl's [the robber] obligation to pay income taxes constituted a valid debt, and his transfer of currency in payment of those taxes was for value.

* * *

It is absolutely necessary for commerce and business to continue that one who receives money, cashier's checks or money orders is not put on inquiry as to the source from which the funds have been derived. It is generally impossible or impractical to discover the source of money, and for this reason one who receives money in good faith for valuable consideration prevails over the victim.[3]

B. Larceny/Theft

A Modern Definition of the Crime of Stealing

Today, all states have defined the crime of stealing in terms of larceny or theft. The federal government alone has "well over 100 separate statutes now in Title 18 that deal with theft or some other theft-related activity."[4]

1. The Taking

Direct Taking

There are many types of direct taking. Some of those listed in the Uniform Crime Report are purse snatching, pocket picking, shoplifting, theft of bicycles, theft of motor vehicles, and theft of vehicle accessories. The Uniform Crime Report states that "the nature of larceny [theft] makes it an extremely difficult offense for law enforcement officers to solve. A lack of witnesses and the tremendous volume of these crimes work in the offender's favor."[5]

The state must show that there was a "taking" at least for a brief time and the defendant had control over the property "of another." The "taking" must be deliberate, with "intent to steal" (intent to permanently deprive the owner of possession).

The fact finder (whether a judge or a jury) decides whether the city or state has proved all of the essential elements of the crime of theft (or larceny). The following examples illustrate:

EXAMPLE: A stranger comes into your backyard and takes your $400 bike. A neighbor observes the taking and calls the police. The man and bike are stopped five miles from your house and the case goes to trial before your municipal court. There is no contest that there was a taking and carrying away of your bike without your consent. But the defendant (under oath) states that he was only "borrowing"

Theft and Larceny Can be Defined as:

a taking and carrying away	But many states expand these requirements to include "uses, transfers, conceals or retains possession of."
of personal property	All states have broadened this element to include "anything of value," "movable property," etc.
of another	See your state statutes with respect to what is property "of another."
without consent, and with intent to steal.	Which is the intent to permanently deprive the owner of the possession of property.

the bike and was going to return it after a little spin around the area. The fact finder would then have to determine whether there was an intent to steal or whether there was a "borrowing" with a genuine intent to return the bike to the owner. (Defendants who use such tactics find they rarely work.)

EXAMPLE: Same facts as above except it is your $4,000 car that is taken. The case goes to trial before your state court, but to avoid the defense of "borrowing," the charge is the criminal charge of "operating a vehicle without the owner's consent." States have created this crime to avoid the defense that the defendant did not intend to permanently deprive the owner of possession of his or her property.

The Taking of Lost and Mislaid Goods or Goods that Are Delivered by Mistake

Are finders keepers? Does a man who has lost his wallet containing $200 abandon his ownership and right of possession to the money and other valuables within the wallet? The answer is no. Finders may have possession of lost or mislaid property, but they do not have lawful ownership. Probably all states have statutes establishing the procedures to be used in handling lost and mislaid property. Persons who find valuables are obligated to comply with these statutes. Failure to comply with such statutes and ordinances would constitute a taking.

EXAMPLE: Chambermaids in a midwest Playboy Club found $107,690 stashed in two flight bags in a hotel room they were cleaning. Law enforcement officers questioned six men about the money, but no one claimed it. It is believed that the money was unclaimed because it was earnings from gambling or some other illegal activity. A jury held that the money was legally abandoned, and after legal fees, costs, etc., the balance was given to the finders.

EXAMPLE: In the 1982 U.S. Supreme Court case of *United States v. Johnson,*[6] the U.S. postal service delivered a check for $4,681.41 to the wrong address. Secret Service agents obtained arrest warrants for the defendants on information that they were attempting to negotiate the misdelivered U.S. Treasury check. Johnson was acquitted by a jury, but his codefendant, Dodd, was convicted of aiding and abetting the receipt of stolen property.

EXAMPLE: Every so often, a door on an armored truck is not closed properly and money bags fall out onto the street or highway. The finders are obligated to turn the money over to the owner. When a San Francisco armored truck was in an accident, over $700,000 was dumped on the street, causing a mad scramble for the money. Some persons voluntarily turned the money they picked up into Loomis Inc. Because a by-stander had jotted down license numbers of motorists picking up money, police were able to threaten jail if other persons did not turn money in to the owner.

EXAMPLE: Someone in the office of Lieut. Col. Oliver L. North made a mistake in providing the number of a secret Swiss bank account. The Sultan of Brunei intended to give $10 million to the Nicaraguan contras. However, the money was placed into the account of a Swiss businessman by mistake. The businessman immediately transferred the money to another account and by the time the mistake was discovered, the money had accrued $253,000 in interest. Criminal proceedings were immediately commenced and the money was returned. When this incident was disclosed at the televised Iran-contra hearings in 1987 before a

---

Sing-Song Phrases of Children

An Inaccurate Statement of Law	*An Accurate Statement of Law*
"Finders keepers, losers weepers."	"Sticks and stones will break my bones but names will never hurt me." (Neither battery nor homicide is ever justified because of name calling or insulting language.)

---

committee of the U.S. Senate, one of the senators drew a laugh when he said, "I'd hand-carry that $10 million to the bank."

EXAMPLE: In 1988, a Hartford, Connecticut, man spent the $44,000 that was mistakenly credited to his bank account. Under a plea bargain, the man pleaded guilty to larceny, was placed on probation, and ordered to repay the money.

Taking by Trick, Deception, or Fraud

Taking has been achieved by the use of many tricks, frauds, and deceptions. The owner of the property may be deceived by false representations that cause the owner to give up possession of the property. Con games would fall into this category. Modern theft and larceny statutes specifically define these forms of taking as elements of the crimes of theft and larceny.

Confidence games and schemes (con games) have been used for hundreds of years. It is reported that the "pigeon drop" was used more than a 1,000 years ago in China. The deception has always been the same. The con man (or woman) wins the confidence of the victim, talks fast enough to keep the victim confused while enough temptation is dangled to appeal to the victim. Unfortunately, a large percentage of the victims are elderly persons. Information on specific con games and schemes is presented in chapter 17.

"Phone-call" thefts are also very common in the United States. In 1987, the Federal Trade Commission (FTC), which monitors and investigates interstate telemarketing scams, reported that Americans lose nearly $1 billion each year in phony telemarketing schemes. The FTC reported that telephone swindlers are increasingly defrauding elderly persons in telephone frauds. The chance of victims recovering their money in con games and phone-call thefts, unfortunately, is very low.

The following cases illustrate only a few of the many ways used to commit theft by fraud:

HIXSON v. ARKANSAS
Court of Appeals of Arkansas (1979) 266 Ark. 778, 587 S.W.2d 70, *review denied*, 44 U.S. 1079, 100 S.Ct. 1030, 26 CrL 4201

Members of various churches make the mistake of paying the defendant in advance for church directories containing their pictures. A jury found that the defendant's promises were not "mere puffing" and when the defendant received the monies, he did not intend to carry out his promise to deliver the church directories in return for the money. The jury also found that the defendant knew that the promises were false and were made for the

Forms of Taking and Types of Theft

Shoplifting (retail theft) or price altering

- shoplifting—the most common form of theft in retail stores—is the taking by concealment to avoid payment for goods
- price altering avoids payment of the full price of an object by lowering the amount on the price tag

Taking by employee, bailee, or trustee

- employee theft of money and other objects causes large losses in business places
- embezzlement of funds or negotiable securities that are in the custody of employees, bailees, or trustees

Snatch and run

- where the taking is observed and the offender flees to avoid apprehension

Till tap

- thief opens cash register unobserved and takes cash and coins
- while store employee has cash drawer open, money is grabbed and the thief flees (snatch and run)

Taking by trick, deception, or fraud (stings and scams)

- con games and operations
- deceptions and tricks to obtain property illegally
- obtaining property by false pretense

Taking by force, or the threat of the use of force (robbery)

Taking during a burglary (trespass with intent to steal or commit a felony)

Taking by extortion (threats of future violence or threats to reveal embarrassing information—blackmail)

Taking from a person

- purse snatching (a form of snatch and run)
- pickpocketing
- rolling a drunk (taking from person incapacitated by alcohol, drugs, or other means)
- taking from a corpse

Taking of lost or mislaid goods or money

Taking of objects or money delivered by mistake

- Example: check for too much money is mailed to a person by mistake

Looting

- taking property from or near a building damaged, destroyed, or left unoccupied by tornado, fire, physical disaster, riot, bombing, earth-quake, etc.

Taking by failure to return a leased or rented object

- Example: failure to return a rented car or videotape within the time specified by state statutes or city ordinance

Taking by illegal entry into locked coin box

- vending machine, pay telephone, parking meter, etc.

Smash and run

- a store or other window is broken, and after snatching objects, the thief runs to avoid apprehension
- Women drivers waiting at stop lights are sometimes subjected to this tactic. The thief breaks the car window, takes the woman's purse from the front seat, and runs.[7]

Taking by illegally obtaining or using information

- such as in the "inside trading" scandals of 1987 and 1988 involving Ivan Boesky and others. See the 1987 U.S. Supreme Court case of *Carpenter v. United States,* 108 S.Ct. 316. One of the defendants in the case was the co-author of a *Wall Street Journal* column.

Taking by illegal use of a credit card or credit card number

Taking from a person with a superior right of possession

- persons may acquire a superior right of possession over the owner of property because of a bailment, pledge, or contract. State criminal codes may make taking from a person with a superior right of possession a crime.

Ordinary theft

- taking occurs observed or unobserved by owner or other persons purposes of depriving the owners of their money. The appellate court found there was sufficient evidence to sustain the jury findings.

| LAMBERT v. STATE
| **Supreme Court of Wisconsin (1976) 73 Wis.2d 590, 243 N.W.2d 524**

The defendant obtained substantial amounts of money from different women by promising to marry them. The Supreme Court of Wisconsin affirmed the convictions of the defendant for six charges of theft by fraud. (Broken promises are only punished in a minority of the states as theft by fraud. In the *Hixson* case, the defendant did not break a promise that he originally planned to keep. The jury found that when the defendant in the *Hixson* case made the statements, he knew that they were false and he made the "promises" with intent to deceive and to commit fraud.)

Theft and Larceny by a Bailee or Trustee

Because of their employment, businesses, or positions of trust, bailees, trustees, and other persons have possession and custody of valuable property belonging to others. The unauthorized use, concealment, transfer, or wrongful retaining of property that is in the possession of a bailee or trustee could amount to a taking and a theft or larceny under the laws of the jurisdiction in which the incident occurred.

Over 70 Percent of Felony Arrests Are for Property Offenses, Drug Violations, and Robbery

Most Serious Felony Arrest Charge	*Percent*
All offenses	100.0%
Violent offenses	21.3%
Murder	1.4
Rape	1.8
Robbery	8.0
Assault	7.9
Other	2.3
Property offenses	35.8%
Burglary	11.4
Theft	14.0
Other	10.4
Drug offenses	34.9%
Sale/trafficking	13.9
Other	21.0
Public-order offenses	8.0%
Driving-related	1.8
Other	6.2

Note: Data for the specific arrest charge were available for 99.2 percent of all cases.

Source: 1990 U.S. Department of Justice Bureau of Justice Statistics, *"Felony Defendants in Large Urban Counties 1988–89."*

2. The Carrying Away

Under the common law, there had to be a "carrying away" (asportation). This requirement was fulfilled by some movement of the property. The distance that the property had to be moved or "carried away" could be slight under the law.

The carrying away, in most cases, is done by the thief, although it can be done by an innocent third person, such as the one who purchased the property. Most states include the requirement of carrying away in their theft or larceny statutes; a few do not. Section 206.1 of the Model Penal Code uses the words "taking or exercising of unauthorized control." The following case illustrates the requirement of carrying away:

BERRY v. STATE
Supreme Court of Wisconsin (1979) 90 Wis.2d 316, 280 N.W.2d 204

An employee of a men's clothing store observed the defendant facing a wall in the lower level of the store and trying to force something under his coat and into his pants. When the

---

Sneak Theft Tactics

Stealing Blank Travelers Cheques

Normally, the gang is comprised of four or five members and may include a female, possibly with a small child. The gang's initial objective upon entering a financial institution is to determine where the cheques are stored, which is usually in a platform or customer service area. Once the storage area is known, some additional surveillance is required by the gang to determine the optimum striking time. Then, when the time is right, a member of the gang may purchase or pretend to purchase a small amount of cheques. And, as surveillance film taken during this stage will often show, the other gang members are positioned in various locations in the bank.

Since distraction is the key to masking the larceny, a coffee can full of coins dropped on a terrazzo floor, for example, will sufficiently occupy everyone's attention for the necessary time period. Other distracting techniques include gang members starting loud arguments between themselves or asking for the exchange of U.S. and foreign currency while speaking loudly in a foreign language. These techniques are especially effective in suburban areas where the modus operandi of such gangs may be unknown.

Salt Lake City Larceny

On May 30, 1987, two males entered the First Security Bank of Utah in Salt Lake City. Unfortunately, the foreign currency exchange and special service facilities were located in an alcove out of sight of the main banking floor. A newly trained teller on duty that day was approached by these two males, who began to wave foreign currency at her while speaking in a foreign language she did not understand. Somewhat flustered, she left her post to seek help from a supervisor in a back office, leaving her cage door ajar. When she returned with her supervisor, the men were gone, as were $65,000 in American Express travelers cheques and a quantity of official bank checks. The Salt Lake City Police were notified, and a call was placed to American Express.

(Because the FBI had distributed 50,000 flyers describing the modus operandi of this gang, they were apprehended a short time after the crime occurred.)

Source: "Sneak Thefts," *FBI Law Enforcement Bulletin,* December 1989.

employee approached the defendant, he saw a bulge under the parka and the trousers. When the defendant stated that there was nothing under the parka, the employee opened the parka and saw a brown leather coat that belonged to the store. In a tug of war, the employee pulled the leather coat out and away from the defendant. The defendant then pushed the employee and walked away quickly. A jury found the defendant guilty of attempted theft. The issue of whether there was a carrying away (asportation) was before the Supreme Court of Wisconsin. The court affirmed the conviction for attempted theft, holding:

> *The court of appeals determined that the defendant "took" the leather coat within the meaning of the statute when he moved the jacket from wherever he got it to his trousers. The court further determined that that movement and the acts of stuffing the jacket into his trousers and turning to face the clerk fulfilled the statutory requirement of "carrying away."*

* * *

> *The question is whether a jury could properly be convinced that the evidence did not support a finding that the defendant was guilty of "taking" and "carrying away" the leather jacket. We conclude that it could. It is clear that "asportation is a separate and necessary element of the crime of theft."*

* * *

> *The court of appeals, noting that any movement however slight has been held to satisfy their requirement, was of the opinion that there was sufficient proof of asportation in the present case.*
>
> *The asportation requirement should be considered in light of the statute's general purpose to proscribe the exercise of unauthorized control over the movable property of another. "Carrying away" must be given a practical, common-sense construction. While the asportation requirement may be satisfied by proof of the slightest movement, it is implicit in the statute that the movement must be a movement away from the area where the product was intended to be. A retail store owner selling clothing consents to having a potential purchaser, during business hours, take an item of clothing from a rack and into a nearby room for the purpose of trying it on. The part of the store in which Radtke first noticed the defendant was not restricted to authorized personnel; it was clearly accessible to customers. The defendant, when he had possession of the leather coat, did not evade the final point of purchase which, according to Radtke's testimony, was located at the opposite end of the lower level of the store. The test is not whether the court of appeals or this court is convinced that the defendant did not consummate the crime of theft by "taking away" the coat as charged in the information, but whether the jury acting reasonably could be convinced that the defendant did not consummate the crime of theft. While it is unnecessary to decide the issue in view of the disposition of the first issue, we conclude that under the circumstances of the present case the jury could have been so convinced.*

3. Personal Property

Under the old common law, only tangible personal property could be stolen. Real estate and items attached to the land could not be stolen. Such documents as stocks, bonds, checks, or promissory notes were not subject to theft, as they are intangible personal property.

All states and the federal government have broadened the original common law definition of property that can be stolen. Some modern criminal codes include any sort of property of value that can be moved. Illinois defines property subject to theft as "anything of value," including real estate, money, commercial instruments, tickets, written documents, etc.[8] Minnesota defines "property" to include documents and things growing on or affixed to land.[9] Section 223.2 of the Model Penal Code defines "Theft by Unlawful Taking or Disposition" as:

1. *Movable Property.* A person is guilty of theft if he takes, or exercises unlawful control over, movable property of another with purpose to deprive him thereof.
2. *Immovable Property.* A person is guilty of theft if he unlawfully transfers immovable property of another or any interest therein with purpose to benefit himself or another not entitled thereto.

Under modern statutes, not only personal property can be stolen, but also real estate and fixtures. Trees, crops, minerals, electricity, gas, and documents are all subject to theft. In the 1966 case of *United States v. Bottone,*[10] the Court pointed out that the content of a document is often much more important and valuable than the paper on which it is written.

In this age of computers, courts must consider whether information itself can be stolen. Situations occur when information is taken from the owner and used or sold to someone else. In the 1976 case of *United States v. DiGilio,*[11] the defendant copied FBI investigative records and sold them to persons who were subjects of the investigations. As the copies were made during office time, with a government machine and on government paper, the copies themselves were government property. However, the Third Circuit Court stated that it would not rest its decision on the "narrower ground that a technical larceny has been proved," but held that contents of the documents also had been stolen.[12]

In the 1982 case of *Moser v. State,*[13] the defendant was convicted of theft for tapping into a cable television line (theft of the signal). In the 1984 case of *State v. McGraw,*[14] the defendant, who was a municipal employee, was convicted of using the city's computer to conduct his private business. The Indiana Court of Appeals held that "computer services, leased or owned, are a part of our market economy in huge dollar amounts. Like cable television, computer services are 'anything of value.' . . . Thus computer services are property within the meaning of the definition of property subject to theft." However, in a similar case in Kings County, New York, the New York Criminal Court held that the New York statute was not intended to protect a computer used internally by an employee.[15]

Value of Property

If the property had no intrinsic value, it would be hard to sustain a prosecution for theft or larceny. A single sheet of paper worth a penny or less would have little intrinsic value. But if a signed promissory note for $1,000 were on the sheet of paper, the value of the paper would increase considerably. In charging theft or larceny, the state must introduce evidence showing the value of the property alleged to have been stolen.

The value of the property stolen, in most instances, determines whether the charge is a misdemeanor or felony. The value of the property must be determined by the court or jury. Statements by the owner concerning what he or she paid for the property, how long it was possessed, replacement cost, and its condition are admissible in determining value. Evidence of the value of comparable property in comparable condition is admissible to show the value of the property in issue. Experts and appraisers may, in some instances, be called into court to testify as to value (sentimental value can generally not be considered).

In the New York case of *People v. Harold,* the defendant was convicted of grand larceny for the theft of a water pump that had been purchased five days before the theft. However, the pump had been damaged before the theft by two men, Crego and Terpening, who had attempted to install the pump. In ordering a new trial, the court stated:

> The question presented by this appeal pertains to the value of the stolen pump.... Section 1305 of the former Penal Law, as first interpreted by this court in People v. Irrizari (5 N.Y.2d 142, 146, 182 N.Y.S.2d 361, 364, 156 N.E.2d 69, 71), states that the market value of a stolen item is to be measured by what the thief would have had to pay had he purchased the item instead of stealing it. Since we stated in *Irrizari* that the price for which an item is sold in a particular store is some evidence but not conclusive proof of its value when stolen from that store, it necessarily follows that the original cost of an item is not proof of its value some five days after the goods have left the store. In the instant case, the value of the pump must also be reduced to reflect the mechanical prowess of Crego and Terpening. Additionally, an allowance must be made for the fact that the pump, when taken, was no longer new.
>
> Many state statutes provide that "value" means the market value at the time of the theft or the cost to the victim of replacing the property within a reasonable time after the theft. The replacement value to a retail store would be the replacement cost to the store, and not the retail price of the item.[16]

If a coat with a price tag of $600 is stolen from a retail store, the value of the stolen property in most states would not be $600, but would be the replacement value of the coat to the store. The replacement value could be anywhere from $300 to $500 in most cases.

4. Property of Another

Difficulties in Identifying Property

In order to prove theft or larceny, the state must show that the property belonged to another. A showing that the property belonged to the city, a school, a corporation, or an individual would suffice. Since the consent of the owner would constitute a total defense in a theft or larceny charge, the owner (or a representative of the owner) must testify that the taking was without his or her consent. A showing that the owner did not consent to the conduct of the defendant is also necessary in criminal damage to property, in trespass, and in arson of either real property or personal property.

Some property is difficult for owners to identify. Diamonds and other valuable stones provide an example. Valuable stones may be easily identified by their settings, but once they are removed, it is difficult to distinguish them. The four "Cs" of the diamond business—cut, clarity, carat, and color—provide only the roughest means of identification. An owner's testimony, "That looks like my property, but I am not sure," is not sufficient identification. Because of the difficulty of identification, there have been situations in which police have been forced to return property to a known thief because of lack of evidence that the property was stolen.

This car was left overnight by its owner on a New York expressway. If the strippers who did their work to the vehicle were apprehended, could they successfully claim that they believed the vehicle to be abandoned property?

The stolen property must be identified by the introduction of evidence showing that there is no reasonable doubt as to its identity. For this reason, law enforcement agencies urge the marking of property in such ways that the identification marks cannot be easily removed or obliterated.

Abandoned Property and Other Problems in Proving "Property of Another"

If the property has been abandoned or if the owner of the property cannot be located, then theft or larceny cannot be proved.

Abandonment has been defined as the relinquishment or surrender of property or the rights to property. In 1952, the U.S. Supreme Court considered the case of *Morissette v. United States.*[17] Morissette was charged with the theft of scrap metal from an old bombing range. His defense was that he honestly thought that the property had been abandoned. Because the trial court would not allow the jury to determine whether the property had been abandoned or whether Morissette honestly, but mistakenly, believed that the property was abandoned, the conviction was reversed.

Wild animals, while in a wild state, are not the property of any person, even though they may be on the property of some person. A person who shoots and takes a wild deer could not be charged with theft, because the deer is not the property of another. However, the hunter could be charged with trespass or a firearms violation if he killed a wild animal on the land of another.

Many people hold property jointly with others. Suppose a business partner takes $1,000 out of the partnership checking account and uses it for his personal needs. Or suppose a wife runs off with another man and takes $500 out of a savings and loan account that is in the name of her husband and herself. Is this stealing the property "of another"? Whether this constitutes theft or larceny would be determined by the statutes of that jurisdiction in defining the property "of another."

The question of property "of another" came up in the Michigan case of *People v. Young.* In that case, the defendant took back from a prostitute the $10 he had paid the woman for her sexual services. In affirming the conviction for the crime of larceny from the person, the court stated:

> On appeal defendant Young's only argument is that his actions did not constitute a crime since the agreement he made to purchase sexual services was illegal and so his forcefully taking back the $10 was not a crime.
>
> We are not persuaded by that argument. The trial court did not enforce any contract legal or otherwise. The agreement had been completed and both parties had received the agreed-upon consideration. Defendant Young then forcefully took back the $10 which by that time belonged to the woman. Such action constituted the crime of larceny from a person. "Public policy requires that courts should lend active aid in punishing persons who obtain money or property from others by criminal means, and it is no defense that the complaining witness was himself engaged in an illegal transaction." 1 Gillespie, Michigan Criminal Law and Procedure (2d Ed.), § 29, p. 49.[18]

5. With Intent to Steal (or to Deprive the Owner Permanently of Possession)

To establish *corpus delicti* for a theft or larceny, there must be a showing that the property was taken and carried (or a showing of other conduct forbidden by the state's theft or larceny statute). There must also be a showing that the defendant was not given permission to take or use the property. If the property was taken from a business place, there could also be an additional showing that the property was not sold to a customer.[19] However, "proof of the corpus delicti does not require proof of the identity of the perpetrators of the crime, nor proof that the crime was committed by the defendant."[20]

"Borrowing" is not stealing. If A borrows B's book for a few hours, he would not be guilty of theft or larceny unless a jury or court found that there was an intent to deprive B of permanent possession of his book. If W loans Z his lawn mower and Z does not immediately return the mower, this would not be a theft or a larceny. The original taking was with W's consent. W's recourse would be to go to a civil court in a replevin action to recover the possession of his lawn mower.

If W saw his lawn mower sitting in Z's backyard and recovered possession of the mower, W would not have committed the crime of theft or larceny. However, if W took other items belonging to Z to compensate for money that Z owed him, this would be considered stealing in most jurisdictions.

Proving Intent to Steal

Theft or larceny requires a specific intent to deprive the owner of permanent possession of the property. The intent to steal may be proved by direct evidence or by circumstantial evidence. Generally, the fact finder (jury or judge) concludes and infers an intent to steal from the conduct and acts of the defendant. The following cases illustrate the issue of intent to steal:

CAR AND VEHICLE THEFT

The crime of car and vehicle theft has risen sharply in recent years. It formerly caused the largest property loss of any crime. The savings and loan scandal in the United States has now probably taken first place.

What happens to stolen cars and vehicles?
In 1989, 1.5 million vehicles were stolen and 2.9 million vehicles were illegally entered for valuables or accessories.

Chop-shop operations, in which professionals cut up the vehicle for parts. As nothing is left of the vehicle, the criminals are called "buzzards." Chop-shop operations are generally believed to be under the control of organized criminal groups.
Strippers who "strip" cars for some of the easily resalable parts: tires, wheels, doors, fenders, hoods, radios, stereos, spark plugs. Strippers are considered semiprofessionals; some are dope addicts who sell car parts to finance their habits. Stripped cars are generally recoved by owners.

Exported from the United States — The National Automobile Theft Bureau estimates that 200,000 vehicles are exported to other countries, where the vehicles or the parts sell at prices much higher than in the United States. (See "Motor Vehicle Theft Investigations" in the Sept. 1990 *FBI Law Enforcement Bulletin.*

Abandoned or Returned or Recovered
• after use by a "joy-rider" (once the biggest offender but now estimated to be responsible for 10 percent of missing cars)
• after being used for a crime
• after being abandoned by strippers
• after a breakdown or being damaged

Phony car thefts — Car owners hide or abandon their vehicles and then fasely report them stolen in hopes of collecting insurance. Estimates range from 15 percent to as high as 30 perecnt of reported thefts are phony.

Used on Streets and Highways of United States
• with original VIN numbers and different plates
• with identification numbers salvaged from similar model cars in junkyards ("salvage and switch" operations)

It is estimated that car theft and vehicle looting costs the American public $7 billion a year in out-of-pocket expenses, plus the costs of higher insurance and the additional cost of law enforcement expenses. The National Automobile Theft Bureau (a private group) suggests the following: 1. Lock your car to avoid car theft, 2. Do not leave valuables in plain view in the car, 3. Leave only the ignition key when parking in a commercial garage, 4. Park in well-lighted areas, 5. Close your garage door and lock it, 6. Do not leave your license or registration in the car.

MULLEN v. SIBLEY & COMPANY
Court of Appeals of New York (1980) 51 N.Y.2d 924, 434 N.Y.S.2d 982, 415 N.E.2d 971

Mr. Mullen was leaving a store with a shopping bag in which he had a tie rack that he had not paid for. He was stopped by a security guard at the door of the store and immediately admitted that he had not paid for the tie rack. He stated that he was about to pay for it and proceeded immediately to a checkout counter, where he tendered a $20 bill. While at the counter he was arrested and taken to a security office for questioning. He was then taken to a state police barracks, where he was photographed and fingerprinted. A jury found him not guilty of the petit larceny charge. The New York Court of Appeals held that probable cause to arrest by the security guard did not exist as a matter of law, and that this issue would have to be determined by a jury in this civil suit against the store.

PEOPLE v. JASO
Court of Appeals of California (1970) 4 Cal.App.3d 767, 84 Cal.Rptr. 567

The defendant was walking toward the parking lot and his car when he was stopped with unpaid merchandise in a shopping bag from a Sears store. The defendant stated that he left his wallet in the glove compartment of his car because he was wearing tight Levis. He stated that he was going to get his wallet and would pay for the merchandise, but when the security officer held him and would not let him go, he struggled with the security officer. Defendant was subdued and placed in handcuffs. A new trial was ordered after the defendant was convicted at the first trial. The Court of Appeals held that the trial court had failed to give the following California jury instruction:

> In the crime of [theft], there must exist in the mind of the perpetrator the specific intent to [take the property of another], and unless such intent so exists that crime is not committed. (CALJIC Instruction # 71.11.)
>
> The specific intent with which an act is done may be manifested by the circumstances surrounding its commission. But you may not find the defendant guilty of the offense charged in Count [II] unless the proved circumstances not only are consistent with the hypothesis that he had the specific intent to [take the property of another] but are irreconcilable with any other rational conclusion. (CALJIC Instruction # 27–A.)

6. Other Larceny/Theft Offenses

"Breaking Bulk"

The crime of "breaking bulk" is committed when a person takes a portion of goods that have been temporarily placed in his or her custody by the owner. This could be done by a warehouse employee or a common carrier in charge of transporting a shipment of goods.

EXAMPLE: Dock workers loading cases of beer into a railroad car remove many bottles from cases for their own consumption.

Some states have statutorized the common law crime of "breaking bulk" (or "breaking bale"). Other states have made the offense that of larceny or embezzlement; still others include it as "larceny by bailee."

Embezzlement

Embezzlement is another form of theft and larceny. In this offense, the thief has legal possession of property or negotiable instruments of another but uses, con-

New York City police officers tag evidence after a $20-million-a-year car theft and chop shop operation was broken up.

verts, or retains the property fraudulently. Some states list the various types of persons who might have lawful possession of property of another. The following examples illustrate:

- A cashier who occasionally takes a portion of the day's receipts and uses the money for his or her own use.
- A bank teller who falsifies accounts and takes money from the bank to finance a vacation.
- A stockbroker who sells stock belonging to a client and uses the money to invest in speculative stock. The stockbroker intends to return the stock to his client's portfolio before the client is aware that the stock is missing.

The statutes of many states provide that the crime of embezzlement can also be committed by state or local officials who have public funds in their possession. It is common to divide embezzlement into grand embezzlement (a felony) and petit embezzlement (a misdemeanor). As with larceny and theft, a series of small fraudulent conversions over a period of time that are part of a single scheme may be charged as one large embezzlement.

C. ROBBERY

Robbery is forcible stealing. It is one of the most frequent crimes of violence in the United States. The common law crime of robbery was defined before the early English courts had defined larceny. The usual elements incorporated into the modern statutory definition of robbery are:

- a taking and carrying away (only a slight movement of the property is needed)
- of the property of another
- with intent to steal
- from the person or from the presence of the victim
- by the use of force against the person or
- with the threat of the use of imminent force with the intent to compel the victim to acquiesce in the taking and carrying away of the property.

Strong-armed robbery, such as mugging and yoking (or simple robbery), is distinguished in probably all state statutes from the aggravated form of robbery, commonly called "armed robbery." Armed robbery carries penalties that are more severe than those for simple robbery. Some of the statutory distinctions used by various states in distinguishing between "armed robbery" and "simple robbery" are:

1. that the perpetrator was armed with a "dangerous" or "deadly" weapon
2. that the perpetrator intended to kill or wound if the victim resisted
3. that the perpetrator did actually inflict a bodily injury.[21]

Robbery, then, is the taking of property from a person or from the presence of a victim by the use of force or the threat of force. The crime of robbery creates a great deal of anxiety, because the victim is threatened not only with the use of force and violence, but with the loss of property.

The Chicago Police Department Training Bulletin[22] lists the following factors that favor a robber:

- He or she can carry out the crime swiftly.
- He or she will usually leave few clues that would lead to his or her arrest.
- The robbery is committed in such a short period that the victim and witnesses sometimes do not have sufficient time and composure to view the offender so as to furnish an accurate description to the police.
- The probability of interruption is limited because of the short time.

Distinguishing Robbery from Theft/Larceny

Robbery differs from theft/larceny because in charging the crime of robbery, it must be shown that:

- property was taken from the victim or taken from the presence of the victim
- the use of force or the threat of the use of force was used in the taking.

If there is no force or fear of the use of force, the crime of robbery has not been committed. The majority of American states and courts now hold that when an offender steals property without force or the threat of force but uses force (or the threat of force) to escape or to keep the property, the crime of robbery has been committed. The Florida Court of Appeals stated this position in the 1983 case of *Stufflebean v. State:*

> Our view of this case is supported by considerable authority. See *People v. Anderson,* 64 Cal.2d 633, 51 Cal.Rptr. 238, 414 P.2d 366 (1966) (if one who has stolen property from the person of another uses force or fear in removing the property from the

A Cambridge, Massachusetts, bank camera shows scenes of a bank robbery. In the left photo, a suspect holds a gun and orders customers to the ground. In the photo on the right, the second suspect climbs over the counter after taking less than $10,000.

owner's immediate presence, the crime of robbery has been committed); *People v. Kennedy,* 10 Ill.App.3d 519, 294 N.E.2d 788 (App.Ct. 1973) (while the taking may be without force the offense is robbery if the departure with the property is accomplished by use of force); *People v. Sanders,* 28 Mich.App. 274, 184 N.W.2d 269 (Ct.App. 1970) (woman who saw defendant run from her house with her purse and bag of money called for help; her grandson, who pursued defendant, gave up chase when defendant fired a gun); *Hermann v. State,* 239 Miss. 523, 123 So.2d 846 (1960) (defendant asked service station to fill up gas tank, then displayed a rifle in a threatening manner and drove away without paying); *State v. Bell,* 194 Neb. 554, 233 N.W.2d 920 (1975) (defendant took cash register from service station while attendant's back was turned, threw it into automobile and attempted to drive off; pursuing attendant stuck his hand through automobile window and was struck and pushed from moving vehicle). Three other states, Oregon, Maine and New York, have enacted statutes similar to the Florida statute which define as an act of robbery, the use of force to unlawfully retain property after a taking.

We hold that where an offender gains possession of property of another without force and with intent to deprive the true owner of its use, but the victim gives instant and uninterrupted protest or pursuit in an effort to thwart a taking, and the offender then assaults the victim in order to complete a taking of the property and make good an escape, the offense is robbery.[23]

However, in 1986 the Supreme Court of Florida reversed the position of the state and adopted the minority view in the following case:

ROYAL v. STATE
Supreme Court of Florida (1986) 490 So.2d 44

Petitioners Linda Gayle Royal and William Ellison were observed in a department store placing clothing in a plastic garbage bag. As petitioners proceeded past the cash register and toward the front door, they were intercepted by a store detective. Ellison pushed the detective aside. Petitioners left the store and were entering an automobile when the store detective and two other store employees attempted to deter them and recover the clothing. As one of the employees tried to grab the ignition key, Ellison struck him. When another employee began to struggle with Ellison, Royal pointed a pistol at the employee's head, causing all three employees to retreat. Both petitioners were convicted of robbery while carrying a deadly weapon. No evidence had been offered at trial to indicate that the pistol produced by Royal had been carried into the store.

Because they did not employ force prior to or while taking the store merchandise, we hold that petitioners cannot be properly convicted of robbery with a firearm under section 812.13. Under these facts, however, we find that petitioners could have been charged separately with theft, for the taking of the goods that occurred in the store; assault and battery, for the incident that occurred while petitioners were leaving the store; and aggravated assault, for the incident that occurred in the parking lot. . . . This record clearly establishes the petitioners' guilt of aggravated assault with a deadly weapon, which is a necessarily lesser included offense of robbery with a firearm.

The Requirement That Fear or Apprehension Exists If Actual Force Is Not Used

If actual force is not used on the victim, there then must exist a genuine fear or apprehension by the victim that force or violence will be used. There also must be a fear or apprehension that the perpetrator is capable of inflicting injury or violence.

This fear could be based on statements of the perpetrator that he or she has a weapon in pocket and will use it. In the 1985 case of *State v. Joyner,* 312 N.C. 779, 324 S.E.2d 841, the Supreme Court of North Carolina held that a defendant can be convicted of armed robbery even though the gun that he used in the crime was inoperable because of a missing firing pin.

In the following case, the Supreme Court of Louisiana stressed the reaction of the victim when he saw a toy pistol held up "in the air":

STATE v. BYRD
Supreme Court of Louisiana (1980) 385 So.2d 248

The Supreme Court of Louisiana reversed the attempted armed robbery conviction, holding that the toy pistol was not a "dangerous weapon" under the facts of this case. The court held:

Defendant ordered a single piece of fried chicken at the side window of a restaurant. When the employee rang up the sale on the cash register and asked for 57 cents, defendant produced a toy pistol from his pocket and held it up in the air, demanding all of the money in the register. The employee stated there was no money, and defendant grabbed the piece of chicken and began to walk away. However, the employee grabbed the chicken back and closed the window on defendant, who then left the window. . . . Numerous cases have developed the theory that the victim's potential reaction to an instrumentality not inherently dangerous can be considered by the jury in determining whether the instrumentality "in the manner used" is likely to produce great bodily harm and is therefore a "dangerous weapon." Under that theory the pertinent inquiry here is whether defendant's use of the toy pistol created a life endangering situation. . . . The undisputed facts in this record simply do not provide reasonable support for the apparent conclusion that the toy pistol in the manner used was likely to produce bodily harm. The actions of the victim and of the defendant refute the State's contention that the manner of use created the "highly charged" atmosphere described by the Court in State v. Levi, *250 So.2d 751*

(La. 1971). While defendant admitted he intended to rob the restaurant, he asserted he used the toy pistol so as not to hurt anyone. He did not threaten to harm, nor did he even refer to the toy pistol as a weapon. The victim testified that defendant did not point the toy pistol at him. Indeed, the victim's subjective reaction indicates he did not perceive any likelihood of great bodily harm. This is not to say that a toy pistol can under no circumstances be used as to create a life endangering situation which supports a guilty verdict of armed robbery.

Sudden Taking or Snatching

If a man snatches an item off a counter in a store and runs off with the item, the crime is stealing and not robbery. Purse snatching is ordinarily charged as theft from the person (which is probably a felony in all states that have enacted this crime). The general rule in the United States is that purse snatching does not ordinarily involve sufficient force to constitute robbery. However, if the victim resists and a struggle occurs, or if the victim in knocked down or assaulted, a jury or a court could find that the crime of robbery had occurred.

A few courts, however, have adopted the rule that the snatching of a purse without the use of any other force is sufficient to permit a jury verdict on the charge of robbery. The Supreme Judicial Court of Massachusetts adopted this rule in the 1972 case of *Commonwealth v. Jones.*[24] In affirming the defendant's conviction of unarmed robbery for a purse snatching, the court stated:

> The question whether the snatching or sudden taking of property constitutes robbery has arisen in other jurisdictions although not in Massachusetts. In Kentucky, the rule is that snatching, without more, involves the requisite element of force to permit a jury verdict on a charge of robbery. See *Jones v. Commonwealth,* 112 Ky. 689, 692–695, 66 S.W. 633; *Brown v. Commonwealth,* 135 Ky. 635, 640, 117 S.W. 281. According to the rule prevailing in most jurisdictions, however, snatching does not involve sufficient force to constitute robbery, unless the victim resists the taking or sustains physical injury, or unless the article taken is so attached to the victim's clothing as to afford resistance. . . .

Can Words be "Robbed" of Their Meaning?

In the parable of the good Samaritan, the King James version of the Bible (Luke 10:25–37) tells of the man who "fell among thieves, which stripped him of his raiment, wounded him . . . leaving him half dead."

Some newspaper stories also mistakenly report that "thieves beat the victim." However, other newspapers and other modern English Bibles correctly use words such as "robbers," "bandits," or "assailants" to describe criminals who use force to obtain valuables.

Another common misuse occurs when a person reports that "My apartment was robbed" when they mean to say, "My apartment was burglarized." A person could be robbed in his apartment if confronted with a person with a gun who takes valuables by the threat of the use of force. Most apartments, however, are burglarized when the occupants are not present.

A thief steals either secretly or by snatching and running. A robber uses (or threatens to use) force and takes from the presence of the victim, whereas a burglar trespasses with intent to steal or to commit a felony. The thief and burglar ordinarily do not want to confront the victim face to face. The robber does confront face to face.

We prefer the Kentucky rule on purse snatching. The majority jurisdiction rule, in looking to whether or not the victim resists, we think, wrongly emphasizes the victim's opportunity to defend himself over the willingness of the purse snatcher to use violence if necessary.

Convictions for More Than One Robbery Offense

Most (if not all) states will permit convictions for more than one robbery offense if property belonging to two or more victims is taken by the threat of force. For example, in *Ashe v. Swenson*,[25] the defendant was charged with six counts of armed robbery when six men playing poker were robbed of their wallets. As each man lost personal property, the six charges were justified.

However, where property of an employer is taken from more than one employee in a robbery (and no personal property is taken from an employee), courts differ as to whether more than one robbery charge would be justified. The following cases illustrate the different reasoning used:

STATE v. FAATEA
Supreme Court of Hawaii (1982) 648 P.2d 197

Robbery as an Aggravated Form of Theft The defendant robbed a Ramada Inn and took hotel money from five different hotel employees. The Supreme Court of Hawaii held that the defendant could only be convicted of one robbery, holding:

> [R]obbery is merely an aggravated form of theft ... there was but one act of theft here, from one owner ... each of the five employees named were (sic) simply custodians of the property for the benefit of their employer."

See footnote 26 for states following this rule.[26]

COMMONWEALTH v. LEVIA
Supreme Judicial Court of Massachusetts (1982) 385 Mass. 345, 431 N.E.2d 928

Robbery as an "Offense" Against the Person Assaulted While masked and armed, the defendant robbed a Cumberland Farms store taking money belonging to the store from two different employees. The Court affirmed defendant's conviction for two counts of masked armed robbery, holding:

> The "offense" is against the person assaulted, and not against the entity that owns or possesses the property taken. See Barringer v. United States, *399 F.2d 557 (D.C.Cir. 1968), cert. denied, 393 U.S. 1057, 89 S.Ct. 697, 21 L.Ed.2d 698 (1969)*; State v. Shoemake, *228 Kan. 572, 576–577, 618 P.2d 1201 (1980)*. So long as the victim of the assault has some protective concern with respect to the property taken, and the property is taken from his person or presence, then the defendant may be convicted and sentenced for a separate and distinct robbery as to that person.

The court rejected the "double jeopardy" argument made by the defense, holding that the "appropriate inquiry, then, is whether the Legislature intended that the putting in fear and taking from two individuals money belonging to a single entity would constitute one robbery or two, where the taking occurred during the course of a single episode."

Distinguishing Robbery from Extortion

Robbery and extortion (blackmail) are methods used to obtain money or property illegally. Extortion differs from robbery in that:

- There is a threat to inflict a future harm (extortion) rather than an immediate harm (robbery).
- The victim must comply immediately with the demands or the harm will result (robbery), rather than future compliance with demands or harm that could be threatened against third persons (extortion).
- Robbery must be committed in the presence of the victim, whereas extortion can be committed over a telephone or by use of the mail (such conduct, however, immediately makes the offense also a federal violation).

The harm that is threatened differs also. In robbery, immediate force is threatened or used against the owner or victim to compel the victim to acquiesce in the taking of the property. In extortion, the victim must pay the amount demanded to avoid:

- destruction of property. Bombing a restaurant or business place has been a standard practice of organized crime that could result in a serious loss of life and injuries if the restaurant or business place were open for business.
- kidnapping or injuries to the victim or his or her family or friends
- accusations of crime, etc.
- damaging the good name or business reputation of the victim or his or her family
- exposing a secret or failing of the victim or family

English textbooks point out that the term *blackmail* originated to describe the tribute paid Scottish chieftains by landowners to secure immunity from raids on their lands. In the early days of common law, blackmail seems to have been an offense included within the crime of robbery. Cases illustrating the crime of extortion are:

MOORE v. NEWELL
United States, Court of Appeals (Sixth Circuit, 1977) 548 F.2d 671

The defendant was convicted of extortion because he attempted to coerce a store to contribute to a charitable fund. Defendant threatened to close the store by picketing if a donation was not made.

UNITED STATES v. BALISTRIERI
U.S. District Court, Eastern District of Wisconsin (1984) 577 F.Supp. 1532

A witness testified that the defendant bragged that no one got into the vending business in Milwaukee without his permission. When an undercover FBI agent ("Conte") went into the vending business, the defendant declared that Conte was slated to be "hit." Conte made a deal with the defendant after which the defendant and his two lawyer sons were charged with attempted extortion and conspiracy to extort. All were convicted and also faced charges in Kansas City, Missouri, in 1985, of skimming about $2 million of unreported profits from Las Vegas casinos. Defendant was also convicted in 1983 of five felony gambling and tax charges.

PEOPLE v. DISCALA
Supreme Court of New York (1978) 45 N.Y.2d 38, 407 N.Y.S.2d 660, 379 N.E.2d 187

When a hospital administrator refused to use his influence to have criminal indictments dismissed (for offenses committed in the hospital), the defendant threatened the administrator in a telephone conversation, telling him that he could kill him or have him killed. The defendant's conviction of attempted coercion in the first degree was affirmed.

Home Invasion Robbery

Home invasion robbery occurs when a person is robbed in his or her home or apartment. Entry could be forced in strong-arm style, or it could be gained by pointing a weapon at the person opening the door. Entry could also be peaceful by the use of some hoax or pretense.

Elderly persons are particularly susceptible to home invasion robberies because they are likely to have valuables in their homes and often can be easily overpowered. Older persons also are often trusting and naive in allowing strangers into their home on a pretense. A theft from the home of an elderly person without the use or threat of force would be charged as theft and not robbery.

Ethnic gangs are reported to be increasingly using home invasion robbery against newly arrived refugees. Law enforcement officers on the West Coast have reported a "marked increase" in home invasion robberies. Vietnamese and other Asian gangs are intimidating and terrorizing refugees who have a lack of understanding or a lack of confidence in law enforcement. Violence and torture are used to force disclosure of where valuables are hidden in the home. Police estimate that as few as 30 percent of such crimes are reported. (See "For Vietnamese Refugees, An Epidemic of Gang Terror," *The New York Times,* April 8, 1991.)

When Does the Crime of Attempted Robbery Become the Crime of Robbery?

The crime of robbery has occurred when there has been a completed theft with the use of force or threat of the use of force. Therefore, if there has been a "taking" (caption) and "carrying away" (asportation) of property with intent to deprive the owner permanently of possession, there has been a theft. The following cases illustrate "takings" and "carrying away" in cases where it was held that the completed crimes of robbery had occurred:

PEOPLE v. MARTINEZ
Court of Appeals of California (1969) 274 Cal.App.2d 170, 79 Cal.Rptr. 18

The defendant argued that he should have been convicted of attempted robbery and not of the completed offense of robbery, because there was no showing of asportation or taking by the defendant. In affirming the defendant's conviction for the completed crime of the robbery, the court stated: "The evidence provided a reasonable inference that Currin [the victim], at gunpoint, had been forced to take the money from the cash box and place it in a paper sack." The court held that this act of the victim constituted asportation, stating: "Robbery does not necessarily entail the robber's manual possession of the loot. It is sufficient if he acquired dominion over it, though the distance of movement is very small and the property is moved by a person acting under the robber's control, including the victim."

PEOPLE v. ALEXANDER
Court of Appeals of Michigan (1969) 17 Mich.App. 30, 169 N.W.2d 190

The defendant, after ordering a gas station attendant to place money in a bag, was apprehended before he took physical possession of the money. The court held that the function

Examples of Different Theft Crimes

Theft   A man lays his ring on the edge of a sink while washing his hands. Another man takes the ring and runs off while the owner is not looking. (Felony if value is more than amount determined by state statute)

Theft from person   A ring is taken from a pocket by a pickpocket or taken in a purse by a purse snatcher. (Felony in most or all states regardless of value of ring)

Simple robbery (mugging)   A woman is accosted in an alley by a menacing robber who threatens to beat her if she does not give the thief the ring on her finger. (Felony regardless of value of ring if she gave up the ring out of fear)

Armed robbery   A woman is held at gunpoint by a robber who demands that she give him the ring on her finger. (Higher felony than "mugging")

of asportation was to demonstrate that the offense had passed the attempt stage and was a completed crime, and it affirmed the defendant's conviction for the completed crime of robbery.

| PEOPLE v. SMITH
| **Court of Appeals of Illinois (1971) 132 Ill.App.2d 657, 270 N.E.2d 136**

The defendant, while armed, forced a bartender to place money and whisky on the bar. The defendant chose to leave the items on the bar for a time and was arrested before he touched the property. The defendant's conviction for the completed crime of robbery was affirmed, with the court holding that the defendant had constructive possession of the property and that actual possession was not necessary to satisfy the requirement of the robbery statute.

D. Burglary

Burglary is among the most frequently committed major crimes in the United States, with more than 3.5 million burglaries committed every year. Because burglary is a crime of stealth and opportunity, the national clearance rate, as reported by the Uniform Crime Report, is low at approximately 15 percent (that is, arrests are made in only approximately 15 percent of the burglaries reported).

Burglary is a crime committed by both amateurs and professionals. It is committed against residences (homes and apartments) and nonresidences (offices, business places, etc.). It is committed not only at nighttime, but during the day.

Under the old common law, burglary was punished by death. Because of the severe penalty, burglary required a breaking under the common law. It was also limited to the dwelling house of another, in the nighttime, and with intent to commit a felony.

All states have modified and changed the definition of burglary in their jurisdictions, with the result that there are many different definitions of burglary in the United States.[27] The Uniform Crime Reporting Program defines burglary "as the unlawful entry of a structure to commit a felony or theft. The use of force to gain entry is not required to classify an offense as burglary."

Breaking

At common law, a "breaking" or a "breach" was required to constitute the crime of burglary. An entry through an open door or window without the consent of the person living in or controlling the building was not a "breaking." Many states have abolished the common law concept of "breaking," but it is used in a minority of jurisdictions.

Unlawful Entry into Premises

Because burglary is a form of trespass, there must be an unlawful entry into the premises. An entry could be made by inserting a hand or an arm (or even the tip of a screwdriver) into the premises. For example, suppose X threw a brick through a jewelry store window and then inserted his hand and arm through the broken window to obtain watches and rings that were in the window display. This would be an unlawful entry that would justify a conviction of X for burglary of the jewelry store.

Suppose that instead of using his arm, X inserted a cane and began removing watches and rings by hooking them with the cane. Would this be an entry so as to justify a conviction of burglary? Most courts would hold that this was an entry, since the cane was an extension of X's body inserted into the store to carry out his criminal purpose.[28]

In the 1983 case of *People v. Tingue,*[29] the defendant entered a New York church that was open at all hours so that the public could pray and meditate. However, instead of praying, the defendant stole the amplifier system from behind the altar rail and entered a room of the church not open to the public, where he attempted to force the lock of a safe. The defendant was charged with burglary. In his first trial, the state failed to "muster sufficient evidence" to prove unlawful entry and the case was dismissed. The state tried again and in the second trial obtained a conviction for burglary (the appellate court reversed the conviction, as double jeopardy forbade the second trial and conviction).

Any element of a crime may be proved by circumstantial evidence. In the U.S. Supreme Court case of *United States v. Edwards,*[30] someone had burglarized a U.S. post office using a pry bar on a window. The defendant had stolen property taken from the post office in his possession. Direct evidence of the break-in was not available, as there were no witnesses. However, crime lab tests showed paint and wood fragments on the defendant's clothing similar to the paint and wood on the post office window. As a jury held this evidence proved unlawful entry, the defendant's conviction was affirmed.

In the 1976 case of *State v. Tixier,*[31] police officers responded to a triggered burglar alarm within a minute. They found a small hole near the door-opening mechanism of a garage. The defendant was found hiding among tires stacked near the door. The piece of the door that had been removed was found near the defendant. It was concluded that the defendant had used an instrument to penetrate the building. In affirming the defendant's burglary conviction, the court held:

> Evidence of a break-in by use of an instrument which penetrates into the building is, in our opinion, evidence of entry into the building. The sufficiency of this evidence is not destroyed by a failure to prove that the instrument was used to steal something from the building or to commit another felony. Such proof is unnecessary because

burglary does not depend upon actions after the entry; the crime is complete when there is an unauthorized entry with the requisite intent.

In the 1978 case of *Champlin v. State,*[32] the defendant entered a hotel lobby open to the general public twenty-four hours a day and removed a television set and a cash register. Instead of charging the defendant with theft, a prosecutor charged the defendant with burglary. In reversing the conviction for burglary, the court pointed out that the defendant's conduct, although illegal, was not burglary, as the premises were open to the general public.

The Dwelling House of Another

A "dwelling house" is a place where people live and sleep. Under the old common law, unlawful entry and theft from a business place would not be a burglary, as a business place is not a "dwelling house." Hotel rooms and apartments are "dwelling houses," since people live and sleep in such places. A new building into which no one had yet moved has been held not to be a "dwelling house."[33]

All the states and the federal government have changed the old common law restricting burglary to only "dwelling houses." Today, virtually all buildings are contained within the scope of the crime of burglary (and some states, including California, also include vehicles). Many states punish the burglary of an inhabited building more severely than that of an uninhabited building. In the case of *People v. Lewis,*[34] the court held that the question "inhabited" or "uninhabited" turns not on the immediate presence or absence of people in the building, but rather on the character of the use of the building.

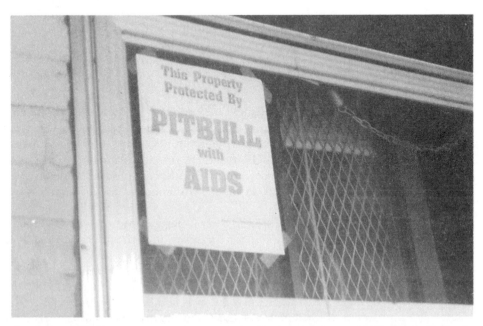

The threat of burglary in our society prompted college students to post this tongue-in-cheek warning.

Are outdoor telephone booths "buildings" within the meaning of burglary statutes? What about a telephone booth within a building? In past years, some courts have held that outdoor telephone booths are "buildings," so persons entering a booth with intent to steal from the coin container could be convicted of burglary. However, other courts have held otherwise. Today, most such cases would involve a charge of one or more of the following:

- theft/larceny
- entry into a locked coin box (or vending machine)
- criminal damage to property
- possession of a burglary tool

In 1975, the California Supreme Court held that a defendant could not be convicted of burglarizing his own home.[35] But sons or daughters who live away from home and do not have permission to enter the home of their parents may be convicted of burglary if all the other elements of burglary are proved. In the 1974 Indiana case of *Farno v. State*,[36] the Court of Appeals of Indiana affirmed the conviction of the defendant for the burglary of his mother's home. A restraining order had been issued prohibiting the defendant from visiting the home.

Nighttime

The old common law required that burglary be committed at night, which was defined as the time between sunset and sunrise. An entry into a dwelling house with an accompanying theft during the day could not be charged as a burglary under this definition. The defendant, however, could be charged with the separate crimes of trespass, stealing, and, depending on the circumstances, criminal damage to property. Today, about half the burglaries in the United States are committed during the day, and all jurisdictions recognize daylight burglaries. Some states impose severer penalties for nighttime burglaries.

With Intent to Commit a Felony

The common law element of burglary with "intent to commit a felony" has been broadened in all American jurisdictions. State laws vary in their intent requirement. Some provide that the intent necessary to convict for burglary must be to steal or commit a felony. Others provide that the intent must be to commit a crime (misdemeanor or felony). Other state statutes specify crimes, whereas still others require that an intent to commit a larceny or theft or other felony be shown.

Robbery and stealing are property crimes in which the state must show that there was a taking and carrying away. In theft and larceny, the state must show the value of the property taken, since this determines the classification of the crime. The value of the property taken in a robbery does not affect the classification of the robbery. A robbery is committed whether $2 or $2,000 is taken. If property is taken in a burglary or a felony is committed, such evidence is used to show the intent of the defendant to commit the crime of burglary. However, a person may be convicted of burglary even if there has been no theft or other felony committed. The state must show an intent to commit theft, or crime, or felony, as required by the statute of the jurisdiction.

Can You Correctly Answer the Following Questions?

1. If someone owed you $100 and had the money in his or her pocket, could you legally collect your $100 at gunpoint? (Could you recover a prized item belonging to you that was in the person's pocket?)
2. Can a person who points a gun at another person be convicted of attempted murder if this is the extent of the wrongful conduct? Explain your answer.
3. Could taking financial advantage of a girlfriend or boyfriend be a crime in some instances? When would a crime be committed?
4. Are the following sing-song phrases of children accurate statements of law?
   a) "Finders keepers, losers weepers."
   b) "Sticks and stones will break my bones but names will never hurt me."
5. Persons are sometimes heard to say "my home (or apartment) was robbed." Are they (usually) using the proper term?
6. Must there be a "breaking" for the crime of burglary to occur in your state?
7. What crime is committed most frequently? What felony is committed most frequently?
8. What is the most unreported crime? What felony is probably least often reported to a law enforcement agency?
9. How does purse-snatching differ from robbery (mugging)?

The answers to these questions are provided at the end of this chapter.

Proving Intent for Burglary When There Is No Evidence of Stealing or Any Other Crime

If a defendant is apprehended in a warehouse in the middle of the night with his arms filled with merchandise, there is usually no question concerning his intent in that particular situation. With respect to proving intent for burglary when there is no evidence of stealing or of any other crime, the Supreme Court of Illinois stated in the case of *People v. Johnson* that:

> Intent must ordinarily be proved circumstantially, by inferences drawn from conduct appraised in its factual environment. We are of the opinion that in the absence of inconsistent circumstances, proof of unlawful breaking and entry into a building which contains personal property that could be the subject of larceny gives rise to an inference that will sustain a conviction of burglary. Like other inferences, this one is grounded in human experience, which justifies the assumption that the unlawful entry was not purposeless, and, in the absence of other proof, indicates theft as the most likely purpose. This conclusion is supported by the decisions of other courts. (*Commonwealth v. Eppich* (1961), 342 Mass. 487, 174 N.E.2d 31; *State v. Hopkins* (1961), 11 Utah 2d 363, 359 P.2d 486; *Behel v. State* (1960), 40 Ala.App. 689, 122 So.2d 537; *Ex parte Seyfried* (1953), 74 Idaho 467, 264 P.2d 685; *People v. Les* (1939), 267 Mich. 648, 225 N.W. 407; *State v. Woodruff* (1929), 208 Iowa 236, 225 N.W. 254; *Bloch v. State* (1903), 161 Ind. 276, 68 N.E. 287; *People v. Soto (1879), 53 Cal. 415; cf. State v. Kennedy* (1962), 15 Wis.2d 600, 113 N.W.2d 372.)[37]

In the 1973 Pennsylvania case of *Commonwealth v. Muniem,*[38] the defendant, who had been found in an empty warehouse about noon, was convicted of burglary. The door was half open and the defendant was walking out when the police arrived. He was cooperative, did not run, and had nothing in possession. The owner testified that nothing was missing. The defendant stated that he had to

---

Intent to Steal in a Burglary Charge

The general rule of law is that intent to steal cannot be inferred from the single fact of an unlawful entry into a building. Additional circumstances must be considered, such as:

- type of entry—was it forcible?
- manner of entry—was there a breaking or splintering?
- place of entry—was it the rear or side of the building?
- type of building—did the building contain items that a thief would be interested in stealing?

- time of entry—was it the middle of the night or the middle of the day?
- conduct of the defendant when interrupted—did he or she attempt to hide or escape?

Source: This material is adapted from a chart originated by the Supreme Court of Wisconsin in the case of *State v. Barclay,* 54 Wis.2d 651, 196 N.W.2d 745 (1971).

---

go to the toilet and had looked for a lavatory in the empty building. The defendant was 33 years old, employed, married, and had no prior record. In reversing the conviction and ordering the defendant discharged, the court stated:

> In the instant case, the only evidence produced against the appellant is his presence, perhaps as a trespasser, in a vacant building in daylight at about noontime. When found by the police, he was walking to the open door by which he testified he entered the building. The owner of the building testified that nothing was missing and there was no evidence of a forceable entry, or possession of any burglary tools, other tools or anything else.
>
> Each case must stand on its own facts in determining whether the Commonwealth has sustained its burden of proof. At best, the evidence of the Commonwealth may give rise to suspicion and conjecture of guilt but most certainly does not have such volume and quality capable of reasonably and naturally justifying an inference of a willful and malicious entry into a building with the intent to commit a felony so as to overcome the presumption of innocence and establish guilt beyond a reasonable doubt of the crime of burglary.

Defendants often have explanations for why they entered the property of another. For example, the defendant in the case of *Commonwealth v. Muniem* stated that he made the entry into the warehouse because he had to go to the toilet. The trial court did not believe the defendant's explanation and convicted him on evidence that the Superior Court of Pennsylvania held to be insufficient. The Supreme Court of Illinois made the following statement concerning the testimony of defendants explaining their conduct:

> A person accused of a crime is not required to prove his innocence or even to testify in his defense. When he does so, however, his testimony must be considered and weighed according to the same rules which are applicable to the testimony of any other witness.[39]

The following cases illustrate some of the reasons put forward by defendants to explain why they were in buildings belonging to other persons:

Essential Elements of the Crime of Burglary

Burglary at Old Common Law	Burglary as Defined by Most States Today	Burglary in Your State Today
Breaking	(not required)	_____
Entry	same	_____
Dwelling of another	any building or dwelling	_____
Without consent of person in lawful possession	same	_____
In the nighttime	at any time	_____
With intent to commit a felony	with intent to steal or commit a felony	_____

- In the 1972 Nevada case of *Harris v. State*,[40] the defendant stated that he had been in the parking lot outside the pharmacy when the officers arrived, and that one of the officers forcibly dragged him into the building. When he tried to run out of the store, one of the police dogs butted him from the rear, knocking him into the box in which he was found hiding.
- In the 1971 Wisconsin case of *Strait v. State*,[41] the defendant stated that he broke a window in a restaurant at 4:00 A.M. and hid in the building because he was afraid of some teenagers he had seen in a car out on the street.
- In the 1966 Illinois case of *People v. Schneller*,[42] the defendant explained his presence in the Chicago Historical Museum after the museum was closed as follows: While he was visiting the museum in the afternoon, he observed a man and woman arguing. When he went to the aid of the woman, the man hit him and knocked him out. He did not remember anything until after the police placed him in custody (the defendant had a pistol, tools, and flashlight in his possession).

The trier of fact in all the aforementioned cases did not believe the stories of the defendants, in view of other evidence presented in each case. In all the cases, it was held that the defendant intended to steal and could therefore be convicted of the crime of burglary.

Proof of Burglary When Other Crimes Are Committed

As a trespass offense, burglary is most often committed by a defendant who steals or who has an intent to steal. Criminals, however, enter private premises for criminal purposes other than to steal. Offenders have entered the premises of others with intent to commit rape, arson, or other serious felonies. The charge of burglary is sometimes one of multiple serious charges against a defendant who went on a criminal rampage in a private home or business place. The charge of burglary also offers prosecutors an alternative charge when there is doubt whether the state can prove attempted rape, murder, arson, etc. If X broke into W's apartment with the intent to rape her but found that she was not home, X

Is the State Obligated to Show?

In Order to Charge	a. That There Was a Stealing (Taking and Carrying Away)?	b. The Value of the Property Taken?	c. Elements Other Than the Crime of Stealing?
Theft/Larceny	Yes	Yes	No
Robbery	Yes	Not necessary as long as the property was something of value	Yes, *a*) that the taking was by force or threat of force and *b*) that the taking was from the victim's person or presence
Burglary	No, only that there was an intent to steal or to commit a felony as required by the statutes of that state	Not necessary as long as the property was something of value (or there was an intent to steal)	Yes, there must be a showing of an unlawful entry (in some states a breaking) into a dwelling or building

could be charged with burglary if the state could prove his intent to commit a felony. The following cases illustrate various kinds of proof-supported convictions for burglary:

MITCHELL v. STATE
Court of Criminal Appeals of Oklahoma (1971) 489 P.2d 499

Evidence showed that at approximately 1:30 A.M. the defendant drove his fist through the screen door of a house and unlatched it after he tore the screen door off the facing. After gaining entry, he choked the 79-year-old woman who lived in the house. He demanded $25 from her and struck her in the face. He then discharged a firearm into the floor of the house. He left after an hour, demanding that the woman give him $100 by the following

In Most States, the Following Are the Essential Elements of:

Larceny/Theft	Burglary	Robbery
A taking and carrying away	Illegal entry or remaining (trespass)	A taking and carrying away
of the personal (or movable) property of another without consent	in a building or structure	of the property of another
with intent to steal (or permanently deprive the owner of possession).	with intent to steal, or intent to commit a felony (as specified by statute).	with intent to steal from the person or the presence of the victim by the use of force or the threat of the use of imminent force.

morning or he would come back and kill her. He received no money from the woman, who called the sheriff as soon as the defendant left. The conviction for first-degree burglary and the sentence of fifteen years imprisonment were affirmed by the Court of Criminal Appeals of Oklahoma.

STATE v. HANSON
Supreme Court of South Dakota (1974) 88 S.D. 48, 215 N.W.2d 130

The defendant was employed as an undercover narcotics agent by the Division of Criminal Investigation of the state of South Dakota. He admitted to participating in a burglary in which whiskey, cigarettes, and cash were taken but contended that he committed the crime to avoid "blowing his cover" as an undercover agent for the state. After the following jury instruction was given, the jury found him guilty of third-degree burglary. The Supreme Court of South Dakota affirmed the conviction.

In this case, the Defendant, David Hanson, has introduced evidence that he was acting as an undercover agent for the Division of Criminal Investigation and Law Enforcement Agency of Bon Homme County, State of South Dakota, thereby justifying his presence and participation in the alleged crime. Because of the introduction of such evidence, the State has the burden of proving beyond a reasonable doubt that the Defendant ... was not acting within the scope of his legal authority as an

---

Forms of Theft

Theft/Larceny

- ordinary theft (usually done secretly)
- snatch and run theft
- shoplifting
- theft from autos
- theft from buildings
- theft by fraud (con game)
- embezzlement
- theft by bailee
- fraud on innkeeper, restaurant
- "looting"—taking property from building that has been destroyed by disaster, riot, bombing, fire, tornado, etc.

Theft from the Person

- purse snatching
- pickpocketing
- "rolling a drunk" (taking valuables from an intoxicated person or person in stupor)
- taking valuables from injured, dead, or disabled persons

Robbery (Theft by Force or Threat of Force)

- mugging or yoking (strong-armed robbery)
- armed robbery
- robbery in which the victim is placed in apprehension that the criminal is armed with a dangerous weapon
- masked robbery (identity is concealed)
- purse snatching and pickpocketing in which such force is used against the person that it constitutes strong-armed robbery
- "home invasion" robbery

Burglary (Trespass with Intent to Steal or to Commit a Felony)

- ordinary burglary (some states punish burglary committed at night more severely)
- armed burglary
- burglary in which an occupant of the building is injured
- "break and run" burglary (breaking store window and running off with property)
- newspapers use the term "car burglary." Some states do have this crime. See *State v. Subin,* 536 A.2d 758 (N.J. 1988)

undercover agent. If the State fails to prove beyond a reasonable doubt that the Defendant . . . was not acting within the scope of his duties as an undercover agent, you shall find the Defendant not guilty.

Questions and Problems for Chapter 15

After reviewing the criminal property statutes of your state, select the correct answer for the questions from the following choices: The offense committed is:

    a. Stealing (theft or larceny)
    b. Robbery (indicate whether armed or unarmed)
    c. Burglary
    d. Attempt to commit one of the above (specify)
    e. None of the above (specify if another offense was committed)

1. X and Y, who are big men, tell a small clerk who is alone in a store that they will take what they want and she had better not interfere. They take merchandise and walk out of the store. Because of fear of injury, the woman clerk does nothing while the men are in the store.

2. An officer of a savings and loan association embezzles money from the association.

3. X obtains $500 from Y by threatening to reveal to Y's boss and wife that Y has a criminal record.

4. X breaks into a heroin pusher's car and takes $2,000 worth of heroin.

5. X breaks the window of a private club at night and steals $125 from an illegal slot machine the club has for gambling purposes.

6. X takes Y's automobile and uses it for two days. On the third day, he abandons the car on the city street, where it is found by the police on the fourth day.

7. X tells Y that he has an order for a certain type and color of car. Y steals the car and sells it to X, who also sells the car. What is the maximum charge that X can be charged with?

8. X purchases an automobile for $700 and pays for the car with a check on a bank in which he knowingly has no account.

9. X and Y ring the doorbell of a home at night. When the occupant answers, they demand money at gunpoint and take valuables from the persons in the house.

10. A married woman takes $400 from the joint checking account that she and her husband have and runs off with another man.

11. In a pigeon-drop scheme, X tricks an old man into giving X his life savings of $2,000.

12. X drives off from a filling station without paying for the $10 worth of gas that the attendant put in his car.

13. At gunpoint, X takes $4,000 worth of heroin from a heroin pusher.

14. X goes into a drug store and pretends that he has a gun in his pocket. The frightened clerk gives X money from the cash register on demand. X has no gun.

15. A woman makes a mistake in the family checking account and writes checks in excess of the money in the account. The additional funds are deposited as soon as the family is notified.

16. X breaks into a restaurant at 3:00 A.M. but is apprehended before he moves, disturbs, or steals anything in the restaurant.

17. X is apprehended attempting to fish money out of a bank night depository box with a fishline and hook. The incident occurred at midnight, when the streets were empty of people and traffic.

18. X took the wallet of a drunk when the man was too intoxicated to know what happened ("rolling a drunk").

19. The police are called to a tavern where X has bought a round of drinks for the whole house but does not have the $18 to pay for the drinks.

20. While a bank clerk was not watching, X reached into the bank cage and took a bundle of $5 bills. A guard saw X putting the money into his pocket.

21. X took an old bike that was placed in an alley for trash pick-up.

22. A business partner took $1,000 out of the business checking account without his partner's consent or knowledge and used the money for gambling.

23. X snatched a bag of money off a counter in a store and ran out.

24. X threw a brick through a jewelry store window and with a long stick was able to hook watches and rings worth more than $500.

25. A $10,000 check endorsed for deposit to a Miami bank disappeared in the mail. The defendant obtained possession of the check and deposited it to an account that he had opened at the bank. To make the deposit, the defendant had to alter the account number on the check to show the defendant's new account number at the bank. After the 20-day hold on the funds in his account, the defendant withdrew all the funds and closed the account. Has the defendant committed a crime? If so, what should he be charged with? Are there any defenses to the charge? *Bell v. United States,* 462 U.S. 356, 103 S.Ct. 2398 (1983).

26. A man walked into a Milwaukee fast food restaurant and handed a note to the seventeen-year-old clerk at the counter. The note read, "Hurry up. Give me the money." The man was carrying a paper bag. No other customers were in the restaurant and the clerk was very nervous. The man looked at her and said, "Hurry up." The clerk then scooped up $80 from the cash register. The man took the money and ran out of the restaurant.

Answers to Questions on Page 463

1. Possible charges could be assault with a deadly weapon, assault, pointing a gun at another, or disorderly conduct.

Charging robbery, armed robbery, or theft could run into some difficulties if the defense lawyer is aware of the law in that state. The old common law rule is that if the taker in good faith believes that he or she owns or is entitled to the possession of the property, a charge of robbery or theft will fail even if the money or property is taken at gunpoint.

However, some courts refuse to follow the old rule. In the 1970 case of *Edwards v. State,* 49 Wis.2d 105, 181 N.W.2d 383, the Wisconsin Supreme Court refused to follow the old rule and held that the person who collected a debt at gunpoint could be convicted of robbery in Wisconsin.

In the 1979 case of *People v. Robinson,* 25 CrL 2037, the Illinois Appellate Court held that the

minority view "simply makes more sense." The defendant in the *Robinson* case retook a gambling loss by use of the threat of deadly force. The Illinois court refused to substitute the "rule of the gun" for the "rule of reason" and, like the Wisconsin Supreme Court, refused to sanction an interpretation that permitted individuals to take the law into their own hands.

In 1987, the Court of Appeals of New York also held that force could not be used to recover money allegedly owed to a defendant. In the case of *People v. Reid,* 69 N.Y.2d 469, 515 N.Y.S.2d 450, 508 N.E.2d 661, the highest court in New York stated there may be some merit if the property was "specific chattel," but in the *Reid* case it was "the proceeds of crime."

2. Incidents where one person points a gun at another person unfortunately come into prosecutors' offices regularly. Pointing a gun at another person would justify an inference that "maybe" or "possibly" there was "mens rea" to kill. But the burden of proof imposed upon the state in criminal cases is that of proof beyond reasonable doubt. See the 1935 case of *Merritt v. Commonwealth* (chapter 12) where the Supreme Court of Virginia pointed out that pointing a gun alone will not justify an inference of intent to kill beyond a reasonable doubt.

See also your state criminal attempt statute, which in many states requires evidence that the defendant "unequivocally, under all the circumstances . . . formed the intent and would commit the crime except for the intervention of another person or some other extraneous factor." (Sec. 939.32(3) Wis.Stat.)

3. Yes, this type of a relationship leaves persons vulnerable to con games. See the material on confidence frauds in chapter 17. See also the section on **Taking by Trick, Deception, or Fraud** in this chapter.

4. "Finders keepers, loser weepers" is *not* a correct statement of the law. See the section on **The Taking of Lost and Mislaid Goods or Goods That Are Delivered by Mistake** in this chapter. As neither battery nor homicide is ever justified because of name-calling or insulting language, the second statement is a correct statement of law.

5. A robbery could occur in a home or apartment if the occupant was present and threatened with force. Most thefts from homes or apartments occur by burglary where the thief uses stealth

and opportunity to enter a building. Burglars seek to commit their crime without the knowledge of the occupant, while robbers confront the occupant.

6. It is reported that in about half the burglaries that occur in the United States there is no "breaking." A window or door is usually left unlocked or open or the burglar obtains a key in some way. All state statutes require "unlawful entry," which can be accomplished with or without breaking.

7. The crime committed most frequently in the United States is theft—petty theft, shoplifting, theft by employees, and felony theft. The felony committed most frequently is burglary (which in most instances is committed to steal and is a form of theft).

8. The most unreported crime is petty theft. If someone steals a 50-cent pen from your locker, or if a candy bar is stolen by an unknown person

from a store, neither you nor the store are likely to file a police report.

Probably the felony most unreported is sexual assault or rape. It is estimated that only about half of these felonies are reported. See the material on page 533 for reasons given by rape victims why they did or did not report an incident.

9. The robbery statute of your state requires that the state prove that force or the threat of the use of force (and apprehension) occurred when a defendant is charged with robbery. The burden upon the state is proof beyond reasonable doubt.

If a young man surprises a woman, snatches her purse, and runs away, can the state in most instances show that force was used? In most states, purse-snatching is a Class D felony (five-year felony) and does not require proof beyond reasonable doubt that force was threatened or used.

Notes

1. 22A Corpus Juris Secundum (Criminal Law) section 597.

2. 22A Corpus Juris Secundum (Criminal Law) section 597.

3. *Transamerica Ins. Co. v. Long,* 318 F.Supp. 156 (W.D.Pa.1970).

4. "Working Papers of the National Commission on Reform of Federal Criminal Laws," 2:913.

5. *State v. Jones,* 499 S.W.2d 236 (Mo.App. 1973).

6. 457 U.S. 537, 102 S.Ct. 2579.

7. The "bump" technique is also used. An expensive car with only a driver occupant is usually picked as the victim. While the victim is waiting at a stoplight, the victim's car is bumped intentionally. When the victim gets out of the car to view damages, one of the thieves distracts him or her while the other thief sneaks around to get into the victim's car. As the victim generally leaves the keys in the ignition, the thief drives off in the victim's car. The other thief jumps in his or her car and also speeds away, leaving the victim stranded.

8. Illinois Rev.Stat. Ch. 38 Sec. 15–1.

9. Minnesota Statut. Ann. Sec. 609.25.

10. 365 F.2d 389 (2d Cir. 1966).

11. 538 F.2d 972 (3d Cir. 1976).

12. Also see the 1978 case of *United States v. Lambert,* 446 F.Supp. 890, 22 CrL 2478 (D.Ct.) in which the defendant was convicted of the theft of computer-stored information that listed the names of informants and the status of government drug investigations conducted by the Drug Enforcement Administration.

13. 433 N.E.2d 68 (Ind.App. 1982).

14. 459 N.E.2d 61, 34 CrL 2390 (Ind.App.). See the 1985 case of *State v. McGraw,* 480 N.E.2d 552 (Ind.), where the court compared the use of an employer's computer resources "to a secretary's use of her employer's typewriter for outside purposes." The defendant was convicted of a felony for the "mere use of the personal computer 'library' assigned to him." In reversing the conviction, the court held that at most "the defendant could have been convicted of misdemeanor conversion, the definition of which omits the element of an 'intent to deprive.' "

15. *People v. Weg,* 113 Misc.2d 1017, 450 N.Y.S.2d 957 (1982).

16. 22 N.Y.2d 443, 293 N.Y.S.2d 96, 239 N.E.2d 727 (1968).

17. 342 U.S. 246, 72 S.Ct. 240 (1952). This case is also discussed in chapter 7.

18. 25 Mich.App. 371, 181 N.W.2d 551 (1970). In the 1983 case of *United States v. Perez,* 707 F.2d 359 (8th Cir. 1983) the defendant stole an exhibit of the government that was being used in a criminal case against him and others for the distribution of cocaine. The exhibit consisted of fifteen hundred-dollar bills. The Court of Appeals affirmed the conviction, holding: "We have little difficulty holding that here the United States had sufficient possession and control, if not actual title, to the property." The property had been seized when the defendants were arrested.

19. *People v. Brooks,* 154 Cal.App.2d 631, 316 P.2d 435 (1957).

20. *People v. Cobb,* 45 Cal.2d 158, 287 P.2d 752 (1955).

21. Many states also make "concealing identity" while committing a crime such as robbery conduct for which the degree of the crime and the penalty may be increased. The Supreme Court of Wisconsin has held that where one robber concealed his identity and the other did not, the second robber could be a party to the crime of "concealing identity." (*Vogel v. State,* 96 Wis.2d 372, 291 N.W.2d 838 [1980]).

22. Volume IX, No. 27, July 1, 1968.

23. 436 So.2d 244 (Fla.App.1983). See also *State v. Mirault,* 92 N.J. 492, 457 A.2d 455 (1983), in which a homeowner came home to find her house being burglarized. When the police officer arrived the defendant jumped on the officer and fought with him until other officers arrived. The New Jersey Supreme Court affirmed the convictions of burglary and robbery but merged the aggravated assault conviction into the robbery conviction.

24. 362 Mass. 83, 283 N.E.2d 840 (1972).

25. 397 U.S. 436, 90 S.Ct. 1189 (1970).

26. See *State v. Canty,* 469 F.2d 114 (D.C. Cir. 1972) (holding that the robbery of each of four bank tellers did not constitute a separate "taking" within the meaning of the federal bank robbery statute and therefore defendant could not be convicted on four counts of robbery based on a single incident); *People v. Nicks,* 23 Ill.App.3d 435, 319 N.E.2d 531 (1974) (holding that where the defendant robbed a store owner and two cashiers, separately, but all in one transaction, he could only be convicted of one count of armed robbery); *Rogers v. State,* 272 Ind. 65, 396 N.E.2d 348 (1979) (holding that the defendant was improperly convicted on two counts of robbery of a grocery store despite the fact that money was taken from two employees); *Williams v. State,* 271 Ind. 656, 395 N.E.2d 239 (1979) (holding that an individual who robs a business establishment, taking that business's money from four employees, can be convicted of only one count of armed robbery); *State v. Potter,* 285 N.C. 238, 204 S.E.2d 649 (1974) (holding that when the lives of all employees in a store are threatened and endangered by the use or threatened use of a firearm incident to the theft of their employer's money or property, a single robbery is committed); *State v. Whipple,* 156 N.J. Super. 46, 383 A.2d 445 (1978) (holding that the defendant's robbery of a liquor store and its owner constituted but a single transaction, which could not be fractionalized to enhance the defendant's punishment for a single crime). See also the 1980 case of *State v. Perkins,* 45 Or.App. 91, 607 P.2d 1202.

27. Florida's burglary statutes, adopted in 1975, provide that "burglary means entering or remaining in a structure or conveyance with the intent to commit an offense therein, unless the premises are at the time open to the public or the defendant is licensed or invited to enter or remain."

28. The New Mexico Court of Appeals held in the 1976 case of *State v. Tixier,* 89 N.M. 297, 551 P.2d 987, that: "A one-half inch penetration into the building is sufficient. Any penetration, however slight of the interior space is sufficient. The fact that the penetration is by an instrument is also sufficient. 2 Wharton's Criminal Law and Procedure (1957) § 421; Clark and Marshall, Crimes, 6th ed., § 13.04."

29. 31. 91 A.D.2d 166, 458 N.Y.S.2d 429.

30. 415 U.S. 800, 94 S.Ct. 1234 (1974).

31. See note 28.

32. 84 Wis.2d 621, 267 N.W.2d 295 (1978).

33. *Woods v. State,* 186 Miss. 463, 191 So. 283 (1939).

34. 274 Cal.App.2d 912, 79 Cal.Rptr. 650 (1969).

35. *People v. Gauze,* 15 Cal.3d 709, 125 Cal.Rptr. 773, 542 P.2d 1365 (1975).

36. 159 Ind.App. 627, 308 N.E.2d 724 (Ind.App. 1974).

37. 28 Ill.2d 441, 192 N.E.2d 864 (1963).

38. 225 Pa.Super. 311, 303 A.2d 528 (1973).

39. *People v. Urbana,* 18 Ill.2d 81, 163 N.E.2d 511 (1959).

40. 88 Nev. 385, 498 P.2d 373 (1972).

41. 41 Wis.2d 552, 164 N.W.2d 505 (1969).

42. 69 Ill.App. 2d 50, 216 N.E.2d 510 (1966).

Chapter Sixteen

SHOPLIFTING AND OTHER CRIMES AGAINST BUSINESSES AND CORPORATIONS

A. Shoplifting (Retail Theft)

Theft is generally the single biggest crime problem of any retail business. Shoplifting is the form of theft that occurs most frequently and probably causes the greatest losses. The *Economic Crime Digest* reported that shoplifting losses amounted to at least $16 billion a year nationwide. On the basis of this figure, shoplifting costs consumers more than a nickel on every dollar they spend in retail stores.

The crime of shoplifting, or retail theft, is a form of theft and larceny. Shoplifting has the same essential elements as theft and larceny: (a) a taking and carrying away (b) of the property of another (c) without consent, and (d) with intent to steal and permanently deprive the owner of possession of the property.

Taking and Carrying Away in Shoplifting

In modern self-service stores, customers are invited to examine merchandise on display. Garments may be taken to dressing rooms and tried on. Customers carry about merchandise either in their hands or in shopping carts provided by the store. The Court of Appeals of New York pointed out in the 1981 case of *People v. Olivo*[1] that stores therefore consent "to the customer's possession of the goods" for limited purposes.

Stores do not consent, however, to concealment of their merchandise by customers. The merchandise is offered for sale, and if the customer is not going

Due to the economic impact shoplifting has on business, signs such as this one are common sights in retail stores.

to purchase an object, he or she is obligated to return the merchandise to the display counter in good condition. If the customer is going to take the merchandise, there is a legal obligation to pay the purchase price. The New York Court of Appeals stated in the *Olivo* case:

> If the customer exercises dominion and control wholly inconsistent with the continued rights of the owner, and the other elements of the crime are present, a larceny has occurred. Such conduct on the part of a customer satisfies the "taking" element of the crime.

* * *

> A taking of property in the self-service store context can be established by evidence that a customer exercised control over merchandise wholly inconsistent with the store's continued rights. Quite simply, a customer who crosses the line between the limited right he or she has to deal with merchandise and the store owner's rights may be subject to prosecution for larceny. Such a rule should foster the legitimate interests and continued operation of self-service shops, a convenience which most members of the society enjoy.

In affirming the convictions of the three different defendants whose shoplifting cases had been consolidated on appeal, the New York Court of Appeals held:

> In *People v. Olivo,* defendant not only concealed goods in his clothing, but he did so in a particularly suspicious manner. And, when defendant was stopped, he was moving towards the door, just three feet short of exiting the store. It cannot be said as a matter of law that these circumstances failed to establish a taking.
>
> In *People v. Gasparik,* defendant removed the price tag and sensor device from a jacket, abandoned his own garment, put the jacket on and ultimately headed for the main floor of the store. Removal of the price tag and sensor device, and careful concealment of those items, is highly unusual and suspicious conduct for a shopper. Coupled with defendant's abandonment of his own coat and his attempt to leave the floor, those factors were sufficient to make out a prima facie case of a taking.
>
> In *People v. Spatzier,* defendant concealed a book in an attaché case. Unaware that he was being observed in an overhead mirror, defendant looked furtively up and down an aisle before secreting the book. In these circumstances, given the manner in which defendant concealed the book and his suspicious behavior, the evidence was not insufficient as a matter of law.

Must a Shoplifter Leave a Store to Be Guilty of the Offense?

The question of whether it is necessary to allow a shoplifter to leave a store in order to detain the person for shoplifting has been before many courts. The Criminal Court of the City of New York held in *People v. Britto:*

> There are a number of myths about the criminal law, comfortably shared and nourished by those in the street, the business community and sometimes, the courts. One of these is the belief that an observed shoplifter acts with impunity unless and until he or she leaves the store with the goods. So strong is this belief that the majority of store detectives are instructed to refrain from stopping the suspect anywhere inside the premises; although the likelihood of apprehension is thus enormously decreased.[2]

In the 1981 case of *People v. Olivo,* the New York Court of Appeals held:

> Case law from other jurisdictions seems unanimous in holding that a shoplifter need not leave the store to be guilty of larceny (e.g., *State v. Grant,* 135 Vt. 222, 373 A.2d 847; *Groomes v. United States,* 155 A.2d 73 [D.C.Mun.App.], *supra; People v. Baker,* 365 Ill. 328, 6 N.E.2d 665; *People v. Bradovich,* 305 Mich. 329, 9 N.W.2d 560; accord *People v. Britto,* 93 Misc.2d 151, 402 N.Y.S.2d 546, *supra*). This is because a shopper may treat merchandise in a manner inconsistent with the owner's continued rights—and in a manner not in accord with that of prospective purchaser—without actually walking out of the store. Indeed, depending upon the circumstances of each case, a variety of conduct may be sufficient to allow the trier of fact to find a taking. It would be well-nigh impossible, and unwise, to attempt to delineate all the situations which would establish a taking. But it is possible to identify some of the factors used in determining whether the evidence is sufficient to be submitted to the fact finder.
>
> In many cases, it will be particularly relevant that defendant concealed the goods under clothing or in a container (see, e.g., *People v. Baker,* 365 Ill. 328, 6 N.E.2d 665, *supra; People v. Bradovich,* 305 Mich. 329, 9 N.W.2d 560, *supra*). Such conduct is not generally expected in a self-service store and may in a proper case be deemed an exercise of dominion and control inconsistent with the store's continued rights. Other furtive or unusual behavior on the part of the defendant should also be weighed. Thus, if the defendant surveys the area while secreting the merchandise or abandoned his or her own property in exchange for the concealed good, this may evince larcenous rather than innocent behavior. Relevant too is the customer's proximity to or movement towards one of the store's exits. Certainly it is highly probative of guilt that the customer was in possession of secreted goods just a few short steps from the door or moving in that direction. Finally, possession of a known shoplifting device actually used to conceal merchandise, such as a specially designed outer garment or false bottom carrying case, would be all but decisive.
>
> Of course, in a particular case, any one or any combination of these factors may take on special significance. And there may be other considerations, not now identified, which should be examined. So long as it bears upon the principal issue—whether the shopper exercised control wholly inconsistent with the owner's continued rights— any attending circumstance is relevant and may be taken into account.[3]

In the 1984 case of *Lee v. State,*[4] the Court of Special Appeals of Maryland held:

* * *

> Although this is a case of first impression in Maryland, courts in other jurisdictions which have considered this issue appear to be unanimous in holding that a shoplifter need not leave the store to be guilty of larceny. . . . [the court cited cases from other states]

* * *

> In the instant case, Lee knowingly removed the bottle of liquor from the shelf and secreted it under his clothing. This act in itself meets the requirement of concealment. The fact that this concealment was brief or that Lee was detected before the goods were removed from the owner's premises is immaterial. The intent to deprive the owner of his property can be inferred from his furtive handling of the property. Lee not only placed the bottle in the waistband of his pants, but did so in a particularly suspicious manner by concealing the bottle such that it was hidden from the shop-owner's view. It cannot be so as a matter of law that these circumstances failed to

establish the elements of theft. Once a customer goes beyond the mere removal of goods from a shelf and crosses the threshold into the realm of behavior inconsistent with the owner's expectations, the circumstances may be such that a larcenous intent can be inferred.

Judgments Affirmed.

Costs To Be Paid By Appellant

The Requirement of Probable Cause Based on Personal Knowledge

Private security persons and retail store employees are often told, "If you have not seen it, it has not happened." Customers are not to be treated as shoplifters until there is hard firsthand information demonstrating that a shoplifting has occurred. The Criminal Court of New York emphasized the probable cause requirement in *People v. Britto:*

> It must be emphasized that this court's holding in no way lessens the burden of proof on the People in shoplifting cases. On the contrary, there is, and should be, a higher standard of proof upon the People in self-service situations than in other larceny cases, because the mere fact of possession may not be used to demonstrate larceny. This remains true even when such possession is accompanied by suspicious or equivocal actions, such as placing unpaid goods directly into the defendant's shopping bag (see, *Durphy v. United States,* 235 A.2d 326 [D.C.App.1967]). It is only when the trier of fact concludes, beyond a reasonable doubt, that defendant's actions were totally inconsistent with and clearly adverse to the owner's interests that a conviction may lie. If the facts are sufficient to support such a conclusion *before* the defendant leaves the store, the fact that he has not left is wholly irrelevant and should not absolve him from the consequences of his acts.[5]

The U.S. Supreme Court defined probable cause as "facts and circumstances within their knowledge and of which they had reasonable trustworthy information [that] were sufficient in themselves to warrant a man of reasonable caution in the belief"[6] that the suspect had committed a crime. The Supreme Judicial Court of Massachusetts held:

Self-Serve Stores

Customers are impliedly invited to:

- enter store
- view and handle merchandise
- try on clothing (if approved by store)
- carry merchandise in shopping cart, basket, or by hand (customer possession of goods for the limited purpose of bringing goods to a checkout counter)

There is no *invitation for customers to:*

- stay for long periods of time or to dress inappropriately ("no shoes—no shirt—no service" restrictions)
- intentionally conceal unpurchased merchandise
- furtive and unusual behavior by customer
- abandon his or her garments in exchange for property of store
- move toward one of store's exits with concealed merchandise
- possess known shoplifting device used to conceal merchandise (specially designed outer garment or a false bottomed carrying case)

Historically, the words "reasonable grounds" and "probable cause" have been given the same meaning by the courts.

* * *

The Oregon Supreme Court construed the meaning of the words "reasonable grounds" in its "shoplifting statute" as having the same meaning as they have in a statute authorizing arrest without a warrant and applied the probable cause standard to the facts before it.[7]

The following incident (and the problems at the end of this chapter) further illustrates the probable cause requirement:

EXAMPLE: On a hot July day, a woman customer stated to a clerk in a large food store, "I suspect that young man of shoplifting." She pointed at a young black man wearing a jogging suit. The clerk relayed the statement to the assistant manager of the store, who confronted the young man, accusing him in a voice overheard by other persons of shoplifting. The young man was detained and the police were called. Did probable cause exist to justify this action?

This incident resulted in a civil lawsuit, with a jury awarding the young man money damages for false imprisonment and defamation (slander). When the police arrived, they immediately realized probable cause did not exist from the facts known to the store employees. The woman customer was questioned by the police, but she had not seen a shoplifting occur and only "suspected" the offense.

The following 1989 case also illustrates the probable cause requirement:

MURRAY v. WAL-MART, INC. ET AL
United States Court of Appeals, Eighth Circuit (1989) 874 F.2d 555

Mary Murray was shopping in a Wal-Mart store with her daughter and grandchild. While leaving the store after purchasing over $100 in merchandise, she was stopped by a loss prevention employee who stated that he saw her place a bottle of cologne, valued at $5.87, inside her halter top.

Murray denied the shoplifting accusation and pulled down her halter top to show she was not concealing any merchandise. She was directed to accompany two store employees back into the store where the contents of her purse were emptied onto the floor, but concealed merchandise was not found. The local police were called and prosecution of Murray for shoplifting was requested. At the police station, a female officer conducted a search but found no concealed items.

The trial court awarded Murray $15,000 in actual damages, plus $10,000 in punitive damages for causing emotional distress by intentional and outrageous conduct, and attorney fees of $7,850. The Court of Appeals affirmed the awards, stating:

* * *

Wal-Mart has an established shoplifting policy which provides that (1) Wal-Mart employees should treat a suspected shoplifter with courtesy, (2) employees should let suspected shoplifters go when in doubt or when unable to find items on the person, and (3) store managers should check with the regional supervisor before prosecuting doubtful cases.

* * *

Murray argues that Wal-Mart had no probable cause to detain, arrest, or prosecute Murray for shoplifting or theft. While there may have been probable cause for the Wal-Mart employees to initially detain and confront Murray, we agree that no probable cause existed for further detention, or for arrest or prosecution. Probable cause to stop a customer does not necessarily give the merchant probable cause to prosecute . . .

* * *

Murray proved that there was no cologne in her halter top when she was initially confronted. At that point, the actions of the store employees were no longer "reasonable" so as to be afforded protection under the state statutes. In addition, the employees ignored Wal-Mart's own shoplifting policy. After the employees searched Murray's purse, probable cause became more elusive, and after she was thoroughly searched at the police station and no items were found on her person, Wal-Mart policy dictated that there should be no prosecution.

The district court found that Murray was searched without a warrant and without probable cause. The evidence is more than sufficient to support the court's finding of malicious prosecution.

* * *

Proving Intent to Steal in Shoplifting Cases

As pointed out in chapter 15, intent to steal and permanently deprive the owner of possession can be inferred and concluded by the fact finder based on the facts and evidence presented. The following case illustrates:

PEOPLE v. BRITTO
Criminal Court of the City of New York (1978) 93 Misc.2d 151, 402 N.Y.S.2d 546

A security supervisor in a supermarket observed the defendant placing paper towels and other items in a brown paper bag. Defendant then put six or seven ham steaks under his belt and walked past the checkout counter and registers without paying. The defendant was stopped while still in the store and asked for a receipt. Instead, the defendant handed the security officer the paper bag, stating "You got me—have the meat." Defendant was detained and the meat was recovered. The court held:

It seems clear that the People have presented enough evidence to permit a trier of fact to conclude that the defendant had exercised sufficient control over the goods to constitute a completed larceny. When one considers the realities of modern shopping, the wisdom of the Court of Appeals' decision to avoid slavish "adhere[nce] to the auxiliary common-law element of asportation" . . . is evident. In self-service stores, shoppers have a right to pick up, and often to move, merchandise for periods of time clearly long enough to satisfy asportation as required at common law. Yet no one would consider such possession felonious, for the self-service shopper is deemed to have conditional, or implied, possession until the merchandise is paid for. . . . However, when a defendant's actions are wholly inconsistent with that of a prospective purchaser, it is up to the trier of fact to decide whether at the time of acquiring possession and thereafter, the defendant possessed the requisite felonious intent.

Handling a Shoplifting Case

1. Make sure you have probable cause and a good solid case before you restrain the freedom of movement of a person for shoplifting. Probable cause (or "reasonable grounds to believe") must be based on personal knowledge (firsthand information) by you or another reliable adult employee. Remember: If you did not see it, it did not happen. When in doubt, let him go.

2. Observing a person concealing "something" or putting "something" in his or her pocket or purse is not sufficient to establish probable cause. The person may be putting a handkerchief or glasses back in a pocket. You must have "reasonable grounds to believe" (probable cause) that the object is unpaid merchandise and that the item belongs to the store. If you do not have probable cause, you may:

   • keep the person under observation
   • engage in voluntary conversation ("May I help you?" "Are you looking for something?" etc.)
   • ask the person what they put in their pocket, or whether they have a receipt for merchandise in their possession under circumstances in which there is no restraint of their freedom of movement.

3. After a person is observed shoplifting, the following options are available to store employees or a security officer.

   • Confront the person immediately and ask that he or she produce the item. *Always* ask if the person has a receipt showing that he or she paid for the item. Under these circumstances, you may seek only recovery of the item and deterrence, rather than prosecution in court.
   • You may be under instructions to allow the person to go beyond the last pay station (or in some cases, even out of the store). Under these circumstances, the person should be kept under surveillance.

If the person becomes aware of your surveillance, he or she may attempt to discard the shoplifted item or pass it onto another person. If you fail to observe the "discard" or "pass-on," you may then be unable to explain why the stolen property was not recovered. It if appears that the person may outrun you and other store employees, it may be wise to position yourself between the exit door and the person.

4. Shoplifting cases are handled by your local law enforcement agency (police or sheriff), prosecutor, and judge. It is advisable to consult a knowledgeable official to determine whether any specific standards are required, such as:

   • whether the local judge requires that the person observed shoplifting be allowed beyond the pay station (or out of the store) before being detained. (A young man in gym shoes who gets near a door or out of the store is going to outrun most store security people.)
   • whether cases will be prosecuted when:
     —the value of the merchandise stolen is small (what is the minimum for prosecution?)
     —the merchandise or item stolen has not been recovered
     —the offender is very young or very old
     —other factors are considered

5. Absolute defenses to civil suits are:
   • that the person either voluntarily stayed in the area, or that the restraint of movement was made in good faith on probable cause based on personal knowledge
   • that if any force was used, it was necessary and reasonable either:
     —in self-defense, or
     —to detain the person, and/or
     —to prevent the theft of the property

Thus when the instant defendant placed six or seven ham steaks under his belt and walked by the place where goods are paid for, his actions were not consistent with those of a prospective purchaser, and he was not acting within the implied invitation to conditional possession tendered by the supermarket owner.

Accordingly, the People have presented a prima facie case, and the defendant's motion to dismiss at the end of the People's case is denied.

The Crime of Obstructing (Hindering) in Shoplifting Cases

Because of the great number of traffic stops and shoplifting detentions, it is understandable why many obstructing cases are related to traffic violations and shoplifting. A person can obstruct and hinder a law enforcement officer in the performance of his or her duty by providing false information that delays and hinders the officer. The following 1990 case illustrates:

| STATE v. CALDWELL
| Court of Appeals of Wisconsin (1990) 154 Wis.2d 683, 454 N.W.2d 13

The defendant was detained for the shoplifting of two leather coats and was asked by a law enforcement officer for his name and date of birth (information necessary for the record and to enter the computer). Defendant gave the wrong name and wrong date of birth, which he later retracted. The defendant was convicted of obstructing an officer in the performance of his duty. In affirming the conviction, the Court of Appeals held:

* * *

The evidence established that Caldwell gave Officer Stern false information while Stern was investigating a retail theft. In reliance upon that information, Officer Stern requested that the false name and birth date be used in a record check. The lie actually hindered the officer in his attempt to identify a suspect in the reported theft. Identifying suspects is part of an officer's duty in an ongoing investigation. A jury could find that this hinderance and delay in identifying the suspect had the result of making more difficult the officer's duty because Officer Stern was required to take a step—requesting a check on false information—that he would not otherwise have had to take. Accord State v. Latimer, 9 Kan.App.2d 728, 687 P.2d 648, 653 (1984) (holding that a suspect carrying no identification who falsely identifies himself to an officer impedes an ongoing investigation and hinders the investigating officer in carrying out his duties).

* * *

B. Fraudulent Use of Credit Cards (or Numbers)

Credit cards are a means of extending short-term credit. The three parties ordinarily involved in a credit card transaction are (1) the issuer of the credit card, which could be a bank or an organization, such as Diner's Club, American Express, or Master Charge; (2) the credit card user, who is the holder of the card and the person purchasing the merchandise or service; and (3) the seller of the merchandise or provider of the services.

A person holding a valid credit card signs for the receipt of the goods and commits himself or herself to pay for the service or the property that has been received. The merchant or business organization supplying the goods or services is then reimbursed for the amount of the billing by the issuer of the credit card. The credit card issuer then bills the credit card holder.

Obtaining Credit Cards (or Numbers) for Fraudulent Use

The methods of obtaining credit cards for fraudulent use are many and varied. Burglars, robbers, and thieves seek credit cards because of their potential fraudulent use. Cards are stolen by pickpockets and purse snatchers. A prostitute might decide that stealing credit cards is more profitable than "turning tricks."

Personnel in a restaurant, retail store, or gas station might retain a card after a credit card transaction. Cards can be stolen from the mail or from an automobile or truck. Cards can be counterfeited or altered. They can be obtained through the corruption of employees of companies making cards or of postal employees.

Credit card numbers are also easy to obtain. A woman walked into a drugstore in Arlington, Virginia, and asked if she could have the used carbons from credit card transactions for a children's school project. The store set aside bundles of used carbon for her, but when complaints began coming in from customers as to unauthorized charges to their bills, the purpose of obtaining the carbons became apparent. The question "Do you want your carbons?" is now very common.

Credit Card and Debit Card Frauds

The rate of credit card and debit card crimes is increasing each year because:

- they are easy to carry out
- they are difficult, in some instances, to prosecute
- most offenders have little remorse, as the victim is generally a bank or large corporation (cardholder is generally liable for only the first $50 of the loss)

To Protect Against Unauthorized Credit or Debit Card Use

The following precautions should be taken:

- Make copies of each card you own (or have the card number and data), with the toll-free numbers of the firm issuing the card.
- Report lost and stolen cards immediately. By reporting within two days, or reporting an unauthorized withdrawal within two days of the finding, your penalty and loss cannot exceed $50 (no penalty or loss if bank decides not to charge you).
- Do not delay reporting a lost or stolen card because of a telephone call from a stranger stating that your cards have been found and will be returned promptly. The call may be a trick to give thieves time to run up charges on your cards.
- If you delay longer than two days in reporting a theft or fraud of cards, you can be charged up to $500 of the loss for each card.

- Debit cards are used on automatic-teller machines and authorize automatic withdrawals from your account (in some cities, debit cards may also be used as credit cards). With debit cards:
  - Do not carry your PIN number (personal identification number) with your debit card, as the loss of both provides immediate access to your account and funds.
  - Do not disclose to any person what your PIN number is, as this may be a scam that will allow a thief to steal every cent in your account. It is never necessary to identify yourself by your PIN.
- Failure to report an unauthorized withdrawal within sixty days of the mailing of your statement could make you liable for the entire loss. With debit cards, this loss could be the amount in your account plus the total loan that can be charged automatically to your card.

Credit Card Violations and Fraud

In addition to the many forms of theft of credit cards, knowingly receiving stolen credit cards is also a common illegal practice. Other violations are:

- use of a credit card without the cardholder's consent
- use of a revoked or canceled credit card
- knowing use of a counterfeit or altered card
- illegal use of a credit card number (or use of pretended number of a fictitious card)
- use of an expired credit card
- use of an illegally possessed card to negotiate a check
- receiving or possession of an illegally obtained card with intent to defraud
- delivery or sale of an illegally obtained credit card

Misusing a Credit Card Number

One of the most common illegal uses of credit card numbers is in fraudulent use of telephones. A labor union in Michigan received a telephone bill for about $321,000 and a woman in Bedford, New York, received a bill for $109,500. Similar situations are reported throughout the United States. As the long distance calls include global calls and the practice is persistent, it is believed that much fraud is committed by narcotic and organized criminal groups that do not want law enforcement and tax officials to trace such calls.

Is misuse of a credit card number, as opposed to the misuse of the card itself, a credit card fraud under federal statute 15 U.S.C.A. Sec. 1644(a)? In the 1982 case of *United States v. Callihan,*[8] the Ninth Circuit Court of Appeals held that it was not. However, in the 1983 case of *United States v. Bice-Bey,*[9] the Fourth Circuit Court of Appeals held that a defendant can be convicted of credit card fraud by misusing a credit card number. The court held that "the core element of a 'credit card' is the account number, not the piece of plastic."

The Increasing Problem of Credit Card Fraud

The average adult in the United States carries five to six credit cards. It is reported that almost 550 million cards are in use. With credit cards a part of everyday life, the possibilities for fraud will continue.

To reduce the opportunity for fraud, increased precautions are being taken. More investigators are being hired. Checks are being made before credit is extended, and verifications are made before shipments are sent out to determine whether the true cardholder placed the order. While losses are only a small fraction of a percent of total credit card sales, yearly losses in the United States are estimated between $100 and $300 million in credit card fraud.

C. CHECK VIOLATIONS

Worthless Checks (Checks that Bounce)

Most checks that bounce are the result of negligence, mistake, or bad bookkeeping. Persons writing NSF (nonsufficient funds) checks or ISF (insufficient funds) checks generally make the checks good within the period provided by the statutes of that state. For example, Florida statutes sec. 832.07 requires that a bad check be made good within seven days or a criminal prosecution may be commenced and the writer of the check is liable in a civil action for triple the amount of the check.

The problem of bad checks is very common in businesses, particularly in retail stores that cash hundreds of checks every week for their customers. Persons who have a bad check in their possession can obtain the assistance of their local prosecutor or law enforcement agency in collecting the money due them. A telephone call will generally provide the necessary information about the required procedure used in that city (or county) for handling a bad check complaint.

A check drawn on a nonexisting account or an account that has been closed is another matter. There is a strong inference that writing such a check reflects an intent to defraud under the criminal statutes of that state. No-such-account checks and worthless checks where the writer of the check has disappeared and cannot be found are viewed as criminal matters that should be handled immediately in hopes of recovering the lost funds.

Burglars and other thieves seek to steal blank checks when possible. Stolen blank checks can be forged and attempts to pass these forged instruments are a weekly problem for many businesses. Innocent persons sometimes accept worthless forged checks and become victims of theft.

The Crime of "Uttering"

The Supreme Court of Virginia defined the crime of "uttering" as:

> Under our bad-check statute, the gravamen of the offense is the intent to defraud, and the offense is complete when, with the requisite intent, a person utters a check he knows to be worthless. . . . A check is uttered when it is put into circulation; for example, when it is presented for payment. . . . The presentment is more than a request for payment; it constitutes an implied representation that the check is good. The statute itself dispenses with proof of an extrinsic representation.

* * *

> It need not be shown that the implied representation was relied upon or that anything was received in return for the check; indeed, the discovery by a payee that a check is worthless before a purchase transaction is completed does not preclude a conviction under the statute. . . . And, while we have stated that the statute is "specifically aimed to discourage the giving of bad checks for what purports to be a cash purchase," . . . such a purchase is not the only transaction proscribed; the statute clearly encompasses a worthless check given to obtain cash.[10]

The crime of uttering a forged instrument is most often committed when a person presents a forged instrument for payment. In the 1968 case of *England v. State*,[11] the defendant handed a forged check to a bank teller without saying anything. In affirming the defendant's conviction for uttering a forged instrument, the Supreme Court of Indiana held: "We conclude the offering of the check to the teller with no instructions, when this act is generally construed in the banking industry as a request to exchange said check for cash, is sufficient conduct to warrant the jury to believe that the appellant intended to cash a forged instrument."

Safeguards in Handling Checks

- Do not endorse checks in blank (with just your name), as the instrument then becomes a bearer instrument that can be cashed by any person obtaining possession.
- Do not sign blank checks, as any person obtaining possession of the checks could fill in the amount and cash the checks.
- In sending checks through the mail, make the checks payable to a specific person or corporation. Make bank deposits payable to "deposit only" or "for deposit to account number..."

In the 1989 case of *State v. Tolliver,* 149 Wis.2d 166, 440 N.W.2d 571 the defendant deposited a forged check into his own checking account through the use of an automated teller machine. A Wisconsin Court of Appeals affirmed his conviction for "uttering," holding that the defendant's act introduced the forged check "into the stream of financial commerce."

The Crime of Forgery

Documents and writing are important in the functioning of a modern society. The crimes of forgery and uttering are offenses created primarily to safeguard confidence in the genuineness of documents and writing. Forgery is committed when a person with an intent to defraud falsely makes or alters a writing or document. Forgery may be committed by:

- creating a wholly new false writing or document
- altering an existing document (raising the amount of a check would be an example)
- endorsing a check or other instrument with another person's name (example, X steals Y's check and cashes the check by endorsing Y's name on the back of the check)
- filling in blanks over a signature of another, either without authority or with unauthorized terms.

When a check is presented either for cash or in payment for goods, there is an implied representation that the check is good. A common business practice is to request a person presenting a check to either endorse or sign the check in the presence of the person who is about to honor the document. If the presenter of the check (the bearer) knows that the check is forged, he has committed the crime of uttering in presenting the forged document. If he or she signs a false name to the check, he or she has then committed the crime of forgery in the presence of the person who is about to honor the check.

Operation of Check-forging Rings

Check-forging rings operate in all large cities in the United States. In many instances, these rings obtain checks from business and industrial firms as a result of burglaries. By means of check-writing machines and typewriters, the stolen checks are then forged to appear as payroll checks.

The checks are often forged using names found on stolen identification cards and papers. Such identification can be obtained by purse snatching and pickpocketing. The thief looks for a victim with the same general appearance as the person who will utter (pass) the check. With a good set of identification cards and with checks that have all the appearances of payroll checks, the check-forging ring goes to work.

To minimize the possibilities of being apprehended, professional criminals will often recruit other persons to commit the actual uttering and passing of the checks. This can be done by selling the checks made out in whatever amount and name the person wishes. Or, the criminal transaction can be done under an agreement to share the criminal loot.

If a criminal is apprehended while attempting to pass a forged check, he or she is likely to attempt to destroy the evidence of the crime. This might be done by eating the check or destroying it in some other way. Should the offender be successful, he or she could then be charged with the offense of destroying (or attempting to destroy) evidence of a crime.

Passing Forged Checks and Other Counterfeit Securities in Interstate Commerce

In the 1930s, the U.S. Congress became concerned about the use of fraudulent securities in interstate commerce. The Congress amended the National Stolen Property Act (58 Stat. 1178) by also forbidding "falsely made, forged, altered or counterfeit securities" to be used and passed in interstate commerce. The U.S. Supreme Court recognized the "general intent" and "broad purpose" of Congress was to "curb the type of trafficking in fraudulent securities that often depends for its success on the exploitation of interstate commerce." *Moskal v. United States,* 111 S.Ct. at 466

The National Stolen Property Act, therefore, not only makes it unlawful to transport stolen property in interstate commerce but also fraudulent securities (which incudes forged or "falsely made" checks). The following U.S. Supreme Court cases illustrate the enforcement of law:

UNITED STATES v. SHERIDAN
Supreme Court of the United States (1946) 329 U.S. 379, 67 S.Ct. 332

The defendant was convicted under the National Stolen Property Act for cashing checks at a Michigan bank, drawn on a Missouri account, with a forged signature. The Supreme Court held:

> *Drawing the [forged] check upon an out-of-state bank, knowing it must be sent there for presentation, is an obviously facile way to delay and often defeat apprehension, conviction and restoration of the ill-gotten gain. There are sound reasons therefore why Congress would wish not to exclude such persons [from the statute's reach], among them the very ease with which they may escape the state's grasp.*

MCELROY v. UNITED STATES
Supreme Court of the United States (1982) 455 U.S. 642, 102 S.Ct. 1332

The defendant used blank checks that had been stolen in Ohio to buy a car and a boat in Pennsylvania. The Supreme Court held that the defendant circulated fraudulent security in violation of the National Stolen Property Act and that Congress's general purpose was "to combat interstate fraud."

Check "Kiting"

Check "kiting" can be compared to a "shell game" at a carnival, in that manipulations are used in both to deceive. The most common reason for the deception in check kiting is to create a false bank balance from which to draw and run off with money that does not belong to the person. The U.S. Supreme Court used the following example to explain a check kiting scheme in the 1982 case of *Williams v. United States:*

> The check kiter opens an account at Bank A with a nominal deposit. He then writes a check on that account for a large sum, such as $50,000. The check kiter then opens an account at Bank B and deposits the $50,000 check from Bank A in that account. At the time of deposit, the check is not supported by sufficient funds in the account at Bank A. However, Bank B, unaware of this fact, gives the check kiter immediate credit on his account at Bank B. During the several-day period that the check on Bank A is being processed for collection ... the check kiter writes a $50,000 check on his account at Bank B and deposits it into his account at Bank A. At the time of the deposit of that check, Bank A gives the check kiter immediate credit on his account there, and on the basis of that grant of credit pays the original $50,000 check when it is presented for collection.
>
> By repeating this scheme, or some variation of it, the check kiter can use the $50,000 credit originally given by Bank B as an interest-free loan for an extended period of time. In effect, the check kiter can take advantage of the several-day period required for the transmittal, processing, and payment of checks from accounts in different banks.[12]

Another variety of check kiting is presented in *United States v. Payne,*[13] in which used-car dealers exchanged checks for fictitious sales of automobiles between themselves. They then used the immediate credit received to operate their businesses. The same nonexistent automobile was sold seven or eight times a week for a four-month period. The court concluded that:

> Payne and Fountain successfully managed a kite for four months with a float that rose to $178,000. They obtained that credit, advance, loan, only by falsely representing the worthless checks as worth their face value. 18 U.S.C. § 1014 makes their misrepresentation a federal offense when the injured bank is insured by the FDIC.

In 1985, the stock brokerage firm of E. F. Hutton & Co. pleaded guilty to 2,000 felony counts of check kiting (federal mail and wire fraud). E. F. Hutton agreed to pay a $2 million fine and also to make restitution to the many banks cheated by their scheme. Investigations headed by former U.S. Attorney General Griffin Bell showed that there were three techniques used by some of the top E. F. Hutton managers to obtain maximum illegal interests on huge sums of money.

After pleading guilty to massive check kiting charges in 1985, federal prosecutors sought criminal indictments against E. F. Hutton in 1987 for allegedly helping organized-crime figures launder hundred of thousands of dollars illegally (see chapter 20 for material on the crime of money laundering).

Prison "Kiting"

Thousands of very clever persons are serving time in prisons in the United States. Some of these persons continue to commit crimes while they are behind bars. For example, the defendant in the U.S. Supreme Court case of *Mathis v. United*

States[14] filed for a federal tax refund even though he had been in prison for a long time, paid no federal taxes, had no income during that time, and had no refund owing.

Prison officials have taken measures to prevent mail "kiting" frauds originating from inside prisons and jails. Such frauds are generally aimed at businesses, although individuals can also be victimized. The term *kiting* is used in prisons to include the forbidden practice of sending or giving the material to be mailed in the frauds scheme to another person with instructions to have it forwarded to the intended victims. See the 1988 case of *Lucas v. Scully*[15] where it was held that prison kiting can be the basis for disciplinary action.

D. Computer Crimes

In the 1950s, a reformed bank robber named Willie Sutton was sometimes asked on talk shows why he robbed banks. His response was, "That's where the money is."

Today, computers are where the money is. It is estimated that over $400 billion is transferred every day through commercial and governmental computers. Our society is becoming increasingly cashless through credit cards and paperless through computers.

In 1977, a governmental committee[16] estimated the average loss in a computer crime at $430,000, compared with a $19,000 average where accounting was done manually. The average "take" in a street holdup is about $38, while the "take" in the usual bank robbery is about $5,000.

Computer crime is reported to be at a "staggering level."[17] There is much concern as to computer crime that has been committed and remains undetected. Estimates as to the risk of detection and risk of prosecution were given as only 1 in 22,000.[18] Computer crime has been called the "crime of the future" and home computers, the "burglar tool of the electronic age." These accusations may be exaggerations, but they do reflect the concern for the rising rate of computer crime in the United States.

Crimes that may be committed with computers are:

1. *Theft of funds*[19]
   a. By an outsider (or insider) who, by using a telephone and the necessary passwords from a remote terminal, could make the unauthorized transfer of millions of dollars to a designated account
   b. By an insider who would falsify claims in an insurance company (such as medical insurance) and the computer would process and mail out checks paying such claims
2. *Theft of information or data.* Computer data banks hold many different types of information worth billions of dollars (lists of customers, employees, banking information, consumer records, business plans, etc.). Two examples cited in chapter 15 are theft of FBI investigative records[20] and the theft of the names of Drug Enforcement Administration informants and status of drug investigation cases.[21]
3. *Theft of services.* If an authorized or unauthorized person uses a system for unauthorized purposes, such misuse could be charged as theft in many states (see chapter 15 for examples).

4. *Electronic break-ins.* In 1983, a group of young "hackers" (ages fifteen to twenty-two) from Milwaukee, with nothing more than home computers and a modem (a device that links a computer to a telephone), were able to "call up" computers connected by a giant network known as GTE Telenet. They were able to guess some passwords and learn others by intercepting calls of legitimate computer users. In this manner, they penetrated dozens of computer systems, including Los Alamos and the New York Sloan-Kettering Cancer Center. In the cancer center, computer memory containing accounting information was erased in part and new user accounts were installed.

FBI Director William S. Sessions was quoted in an article entitled "Computer Crimes: An Escalating Crime Trend" in the February 1991 issue of the *FBI Law Enforcement Bulletin* as stating:

> . . . just as American communities are threatened with drugs and violent crime, this Nation's computer networks are threatened as well. They are threatened by thieves robbing banks electronically; they are threatened by vandals spreading computer viruses; and they are even threatened by spies breaking into U.S. military systems.
>
> White-collar crimes in general—and computer crime in particular—are often difficult to detect and even more difficult to prosecute because many times they leave no witnesses to question and no physical evidence to analyze. And, because computer technology is such a rapidly evolving field, law enforcement has not yet developed a clear-cut definition of computer crime. Nevertheless, two manifestations of computer crime are obvious: The first is crime in which the computer is the vehicle or tool of the criminal, and second, crime in which the computer and the information stored in it are the targets of the criminal.

Computers as Crime Tools

When criminals use computers as their tools, the crimes they engineer are essentially traditional crimes, such as embezzlement, fraud, and theft, perpetrated by nontraditional means. The criminal uses a computer as an instrument, like the forger's pen or the terrorist's bomb.

The vast majority of computer-related crimes that the FBI investigates falls into the category of using the computer as a tool. For instance, if a team of FBI Agents in one of its 56 field offices uncovers information that a disgruntled employee is tapping into a bank's computer to transfer funds illegally, those Agents will probably open up a bank fraud and embezzlement case and proceed from there.

Computers as Crime Targets

But what about the emerging crime trend that is unique to computers—in which the computer is the target? This type of crime occurs when a computer and the information it stores are the targets of a criminal act committed either internally by employees or externally by criminals. The external threat usually involves the use of telecommunications to gain unauthorized access to the computer system.

In its investigations, the FBI has determined three groups of individuals involved in the external threat. The first, and the largest, group consists of individuals who break into a computer just to see if they can do it—without stealing or destroying data. The next group breaks into computer systems to destroy, disrupt, alter, or interrupt the system. Their actions amount to malicious mischief because they do not attack the system for financial gain, which is the motive of the last group. This group constitutes a serious threat to businesses and national security for these individuals are professionals who use specialized skills to steal information, manipulate data, or cause loss of service to the computer system.

The New Computer Crime Statutes and New Problems of the 1990s

Many states and the federal government have enacted new "computer crime" statutes. Generally these statutes provide that unauthorized access to a computer, or destruction or alteration and changing of data can be charged as a felony.

Personal computer users have become very sophisticated and are able to penetrate many different types of computer systems. In 1988, it was disclosed publicly that persons increasingly have penetrated the telephone systems of the United States.[22] Telephone companies use computer-controlled switches for electro-mechanical call-routing equipment. Persons with proper training and equipment can illegally connect their personal computers to the telephone network. For years, they have made free long-distance phone calls. They can eavesdrop on the telephone calls of others. They can add calls and charges to other persons' or corporations' bills. They can alter or destroy data. They can disrupt telephone calls to a person, corporation, or an entire switching office.

This technology is available to terrorists, organized-crime groups, and others who might use it to their advantage or to disrupt communications in parts of the United States. Another problem appearing in the late 1980s is vandalism called "trojan horses" or viruses. Programs that appear to be useful instead are electronic terrorists in that they erase or scramble data stored in computers. See the *New York Times* article entitled "Computer Users Fall Victim To a New Breed of Vandals" (May 19, 1987).

An article on page one of the April 21, 1991, issue of the *New York Times* was entitled "Dutch Computer Rogues Tap U.S. Systems With Impunity." The article told of Dutch computer hackers who had been "openly defying" the laws of the United States by breaking into American computer systems.

As computer networks can be penetrated from anywhere in the world by telephone calls, hackers operating from "hacker havens" have been entering computer systems for just the cost of a telephone call. It appeared the Dutch hackers were college students who had accessed American military, space, intelligence, and university computer systems. It was reported the Dutch hackers did not penetrate the most secure government computer systems, nor did they cause damage to the systems they trespassed and penetrated.

Desktop Forgery and Other Abilities of Computers, Printers, and Copiers

Personal computers, printers, and copiers have a growing ability to reproduce authentic looking reproductions of documents. Counterfeiters, forgers, and other illegal users have been taking advantage of these techniques to reproduce or alter many types of documents.

Some of the many documents that have been counterfeited or copied include checks, stock certificates, bonds, gift certificates, airline tickets, identification cards, college transcripts, and letters of recommendation.

Not only are computers used to alter and change documents, but full-color copiers are now available for the easy reproduction of documents. Experts point out that the laser printer now replaces the old counterfeiter's engraving plate. Counterfeiters no longer need the services of a professional engraver; instead they can use desktop publishing equipment.

National attention was called to the illegal use of computers at an international conference on AIDS in San Francisco in 1990. Hundreds of protesters drowned out the speech of the secretary of Health and Human Services. The protesters had gained entrance into the convention hall by using computer-generated false badges.

Questions and Problems for Chapter 16

In view of the information (evidence) available in problems #1 through #12, indicate which of the following courses of action may be taken by a store employee or a security person:

1. As the store employee has probable cause, a detention may be made by the person until the police arrive.
2. As less than probable cause exists, the store should not restrain the freedom of movement of the person but may:
   a. engage in a voluntary conversation with the person, or
   b. keep the person under observation (surveillance)
3. There is no legal authority or justification to do either of the above.

1. A well-dressed woman was looking at merchandise in a drugstore. After she left the store without purchasing anything, a clerk observed that only six items were on the shelf of the seven previously observed on the shelf. (*Crase v. Highland Village Value Plus Pharmacy,* 176 Ind.App. 47, 374 N.E.2d 58 [1978]).

2. Would it make any difference in Problem #1 if the woman were poorly dressed, or very young, or very old?

3. A man was leaving a department store with a shopping bag. In the bag was a tie rack that he had not paid for. He was stopped at the door of the store by a security guard. The man immediately admitted that he had not paid for the tie rack. Stating that he would pay for it, he went to a checkout counter and tendered a $20 bill. (*Mullen v. Sibley & Company,* 51 N.Y.2d 924, 434 N.Y.S.2d 982, 415 N.E.2d 971 [1980]).

4. A man was observed walking briskly up and down the aisles of a Sears store. The man was then observed backing his car up to a portable building used to display merchandise. The man took a lawn mower from the building and put it in the trunk of his car. The man would not produce a sales receipt for the mower. When the man was asked to get out of his car, he broke and ran away. (*Tinsley v. State,* 461 S.W.2d 605 [Texas Ct.App. 1970]).

5. A woman was waiting in a checkout line in a drugstore. The cashier saw a wrapping bow on the counter in front of the woman. The bow had all the appearances of bows that were on sale in the store. A few minutes later, the bow was not on the counter. When the woman paid for other items, the cashier asked if she had anything else to pay for. The woman did not pay for the bow, and as she walked away from the store she was asked if she had anything in her purse for which payment had not been made. The woman answered no. (*Kon v. Skaggs Drug Center, Inc.,* 115 Ariz. 121, 563 P.2d 920 [App. 1977]).

6. A man was seen leaving a men's clothing store with a bulge under his overcoat. A security officer who had arrested the man for shoplifting on two prior occasions followed the man to a barber shop. When the man sat down in the barber shop, the security officer returned to the clothing store, where he determined that a man's leather coat was missing. The security officer started back to the barber shop and saw the man on the street. The officer identified himself and asked for the coat. The man gave the officer the coat and then ran away. When the officer followed, the man threatened him with a knife. (*State v. Gonzales,* 24 Wash.App. 437, 604 P.2d 168 [1979]).

7. Police warned the manager of a Woolworth store to be on the lookout for three teenage girls believed to be shoplifting (two dark-haired and one blonde). When girls matching this description were observed in the store, it was determined that two hair pieces were missing. A clerk stated that the girls were near the hair piece counter. (*Meadows v. F. W. Woolworth Co.,* 254 F.Supp. 907 [N.D.Fla. 1966]).

8. A store clerk saw a woman place a sticker on a tube of suntan lotion, reducing the price from $1.99 to $1.12. The woman then paid the lower price at the checkout counter and commenced to leave the store. (*Dube v. Schwegmann Bros.*

Giant Supermarkets, 384 So.2d 1019 [La. App. 1980]).

9. An assistant security manager identified herself to a woman leaving a K-Mart store and asked the woman to show her a receipt for the scarf in the loop of the handle of the woman's purse. The woman stated, "Oh, I must have forgot to pay for it." The woman was then asked to go to the store office, where she was asked to show identification. When the guard asked, "You come all the way from North Riverside to steal at K-Mart?" the woman responded, "Sure, why not?" The woman signed a report stating that she "was wandering around in the store, took the price [tag] off the scarf and put the scarf on her purse." (*People v. Raitano,* 81 Ill. App. 3d 373, 36 Ill. Dec. 597, 401 N.E.2d 278 [Ill.Ct.App. 1980]).

10. A woman was leaving a department store when an antishoplifting device sounded. (*Sears, Roebuck & Co. v. Young,* 384 So.2d 69 [Miss. 1980], and *Clark v. Rubenstein, Inc.,* 326 So.2d 497 [La. 1976]).

11. A security guard observed two women stuffing a pantsuit into a shopping bag. The women were not in the pantsuit department at the time. The women were then seen leaving the store. When the guard attempted to place the younger woman under arrest, a skirmish broke out. (*Jones v. Montgomery Ward,* 49 Or. App. 231, 619 P.2d 907 [1980]).

12. A security employee at a large shopping mall saw a man "carrying a large garbage bag" and "walking very fast" toward an exit.

At that time I just seen [sic] how fast he was going, and I was curious that he was carrying a large garbage bag, so I followed him down and right as he was going out the exit, I asked him, "I don't believe we sell any garbage bags in here, why do you have a garbage bag?" And he told me it wasn't his bag, it didn't belong to him. So I said, "Well, if it don't [sic] belong to you, I'll take the bag." At that time I asked him if he would come along and be checked out, and he said fine, and we went and I took him in to Richard Bennett's, asked him if I could look in the bag. He said fine. I seen [sic] tags and all that in—and notified Wauwatosa Police on it.

There was stolen clothing in the garbage bag, but the security employee had not seen the man take any of the items. *State v. Lee,* 157 Wis.2d 126, 458 N.W.2d 562 (App. 1990)

Notes

1. 52 N.Y.2d 309, 438 N.Y.S.2d 242, 420 N.E.2d 40.

2. 93 Misc.2d 151, 402 N.Y.S.2d 546 (1978).

3. 438 N.Y.S. at 246. See also the case of *Berry v. State,* in chapter 15, in which the Supreme Court of Wisconsin affirmed the conviction of the defendant for attempted theft when the defendant was apprehended for shoplifting before he left a men's clothing store.

4. 59 Md.App. 28, 474 A.2d 537.

5. 402 N.Y.S.2d at 548.

6. *Carroll v. United States,* 267 U.S. 132, 45 S.Ct. 280 (1925).

7. *Coblyn v. Kennedy's Inc.,* 359 Mass. 319, 268 N.E.2d 860 (1971).

8. 666 F.2d 422 (9th Cir. 1982).

9. 701 F.2d 1086 (4th Cir. 1983).

10. *Warren v. Commonwealth,* 219 Va. 416, 247 S.E.2d 692 (1978).

11. 249 Ind. 446, 233 N.E.2d 168.

12. 458 U.S. 279, 102 S.Ct. 3088 (1982).

13. 602 F.2d 1215 (5th Cir. 1979), *review denied,* 445 U.S. 903, 100 S.Ct. 1079 26 CrL 4209 (1980).

14. 391 U.S. 1, 88 S.Ct. 1503 (1968).

15. 71 N.Y.2d 399, 526 N.Y.S.2d 927, 521 N.E.2d 1070 (1988).

16. Committee on Government Operations, "Staff Study of Computer Security in Federal Programs" (Washington, D.C.: Government Printing Office, 1977).

17. Committee Report, note 13 and LEAA Newsletter, January 1980.

18. Committee Report, note 13.

19. The Equity Funding fraud of the late 1970s, which resulted in losses of over $100 million, was done with the use of computers. Also in a computer fraud, Jack Benny, Liza Minnelli, and another man lost $925,000.

20. *United States v. DiGilio,* 538 F.2d 972 (3d Cir. 1976).

21. 22 CrL 2478.

22. See "Computer 'Hackers' Seen as Peril to Security of the Phone System," *The New York Times* (July 22, 1988).

Chapter Seventeen

FRAUD AND OTHER PROPERTY CRIMES

A. Fraud and Fraudulent Practices

Fraud consists of deceitful means or acts used to cheat a person, corporation, or governmental agency. Theft by fraud or larceny by fraud is often the criminal charge used, as fraud can be a form of theft and larceny. Fraud is always intentional, as distinguished from negligence. The following material illustrates the wide range of deception, fraud, and corruption that occurs at all levels of society.

Fraud and Corruption in Government

Fraud against government is as old as government itself. Reports of fraud and corruption date back to biblical times and throughout early civilizations. As the U.S. government today is spending $1.4 trillion per year in its total budget, it is not surprising that it has serious fraud and corruption problems. The General Accounting Office reported in 1978:

> Opportunity for defrauding the government is virtually limitless because of the number, variety, and value of federal programs.... The involvement of so much money, and so many people and institutions makes the federal programs vulnerable to fraud.

Losses through fraud and corruption occur in many ways, but the following three areas account for most fraud losses in the federal government:

- *contract fraud:* In the procurement of arms and military supplies, the federal government spends over $290 billion yearly. The Pentagon contract frauds of 1988–90 shocked the nation. The selling of inside information on contract bids was much more widespread than experts believed possible. Other fraudulent practices in contract fraud include "bid-rigging," "bribes," and "kickbacks." These practices could occur in federal procurement contracts, state and local government contracts, or in corporate contracting for supplies and services.
- *program frauds:* Billions of dollars are dispersed every year in programs such as Medicaid, Medicare, food stamps, small business loans, subsidy programs, HUD, social security, and various aid programs. Programs at state and local government levels include welfare. Welfare frauds include "ghost eligibles" and also persons taking welfare payments who are not entitled to the assistance. The defendant in the 1987 case of *State v. Micheaux*[1] obtained welfare payments knowing he was not entitled to receive welfare. In affirming the conviction, the Supreme Court of Kansas held that welfare fraud was an independent crime in Kansas in the same general category as theft offenses and carrying the same penalties.
- *fraud by public officials:* includes "bribes," "kickbacks," and other types of fraud. Fraud and corruption by public officials could be charged as theft or larceny, misconduct in public office, bribery, etc. Abscam and other sting operations have uncovered such dishonesty.

Great Public Scandals of the 1980s and 1990s

The Savings & Loan Scandal will cause the largest losses in the history of this country. The U.S. Justice Department reported to Congress in 1991 that 403 convictions had been obtained for fraud in savings and loan losses to that date. The report stated that 507 institutions had been victimized. American taxpayers could lose as much as $500 billion over a forty-year period (part criminal and part bad management). Charles Keating of the California Lincoln Savings & Loan and Don R. Dixon of the Texas Vernon Savings & Loan were officers in firms that could each cause losses to American taxpayers of over one billion dollars.

Wall Street Scandals Criminal charges of "inside trading" and other fraud has resulted in prison sentences for Ivan Boesky, Michael R. Milken, and more than ten other persons who were once prominent on Wall Street.

U.S. Military Contract Frauds Twenty-five of the one hundred largest Pentagon contractors have been found guilty of fraud. Boeing, Gruman, and Teledyne made payoffs to obtain confidential Pentagon documents. Contractors who overcharged the government were Rockwell, GTE, General Electric (Matsco division), and Emerson Electric. Fairchild Industries and Northrup falsified test results or failed to test. Harris Corporation was convicted of contract kickbacks.

The Iran-Contra Scandal of the 1980s Five persons were found guilty of criminal charges involving arms dealing and lying to the Congress of the United States. Oliver North's convictions were overturned by a Court of Appeals.

The Scandals of the TV Preachers Evangelical television ministers received national attention in a series of scandals. Jim Bakker of the PTL Network was convicted after a six-week trial of defrauding his followers out of $159 million. He offered promises of lifetime vacations that he could not provide and used $3.7 million for his opulent lifestyle, which included a fleet of Rolls Royces and an air-conditioned doghouse. Bakker's forty-five-year prison term was set aside in 1991 for another sentencing hearing.

Legislative Scandals In the Abscam operation, evidence was obtained to indict and convict seven members of the U.S. Congress, including one senator (see chapter 7). The matter of the "Keating Five" was before the Senate Ethics Committee in 1991. At the state level, South Carolina and Arizona lawmakers are being investigated for criminal violations.

Detroit Chief of Police In 1991, the Detroit chief of police, William L. Hart, was indicted and charged with stealing $2.6 million from a police undercover operation fund.

The HUD Scandal Huge losses of money in the Housing and Urban Development agency caused the U.S. Congress to order investigations of irregularities. Criminal indictments might be sought in the future. Former Congressman Jack Kemp became the new director of the agency after its reorganization.

Consumer Fraud

Consumer fraud consists of fraudulent promotions, dishonest business practices, and fraudulent schemes directed at buyers of products and services. Consumer frauds range from small money losses to losses of hundreds and thousands of dollars. The elderly are often targets of consumer frauds because of their vulnerability and trust in statements made by persons seeking to defraud them.

Among the most frequent consumer complaints are complaints of fraud in home improvement and repair, auto repairs, door-to-door sales, fraudulent insurance pitches, health and medical aids, land sales schemes, unlawful and deceptive charitable solicitations, and unsolicited merchandise.

Door-to-door selling can be deceptive if deceptive contract terms are used, if poor-quality merchandise is used deliberately, if nondelivery of goods ordered occurs, or if pressure selling and scare tactics are used. Generally, such victimizing occurs with uninvited sellers.

Deceptive selling practices include the "bait and switch" practice of deceptive advertising and sales.[2] The technique of "bushing" occurs when the selling price of an item is increased above that originally quoted to the purchaser. The increase occurs after the purchaser, in good faith, makes a down payment with money or a trade-in and before acceptance of a purchase order by the seller.

Charitable solicitations are fraudulent if the collectors plan to use the money for their own use or if there is no cause or organization. Fraud to obtain money also occurs if the collector falsely asserts that he or she is associated with a charity or religious group. Misrepresentation as to the use of the contribution could also be fraudulent, depending on the representations.[3]

Phony billing schemes include sending out invoices and billings for merchandise, supplies, or services that were never ordered or supplied. Substantial amounts of money have been lost through carelessness and failure to recognize the scheme. Other phony billing schemes include selling "phony" advertisement or directory advertising; the publication may not exist or the ad is not run.

Fraudulent Insurance Claims

Fraudulent insurance claims can occur with any type of insurance. The claim could be for a burglary loss of property when no burglary occurred, or for property that was not stolen. It could be for a fraudulent damage claim or for the loss of property in a robbery that is a false claim. Arson for profit is the crime of arson committed to present a false insurance claim.

Medical and health insurance fraud occurs when a person uses someone else's ID card for medical care. It can occur when medical records or receipts are falsified and used to receive insurance payment. Billing for service that has not been rendered is also a fraud.

Insurance claims for damages to automobiles or injuries in phony car accidents are common forms of fraud. Insurance companies believe that they pay out millions of dollars every year in false claims. Insurance companies estimate that insurance fraud takes about ten cents from every insurance premium dollar paid.

The article "Automobile Insurance Fraud Pays . . . and Pays Well" in the March 1986 issue of the *FBI Law Enforcement Bulletin* affirms the fact that auto insurance fraud is a big business. The article tells of the largest auto insurance fraud in the history of New York State, which was broken up in the mid-1980s.

Although motor vehicle insurance fraud occurs in every major city in the United States, California is identified as the crime capital of the country for this type of offense. Common forms of this type of fraud in California include the following:

- the "squat": a bump from behind involving two vehicles participating in the fraud
- the "swoop and squat": one vehicle swerves into another lane and strikes a vehicle from the rear
- the "rideout": a perpetrator seeks out an expensive car driven by a person of apparent wealth and rams the vehicle

Avoiding Cons: Don'ts and Do's

The Don'ts

1. Don't trust anyone who proposes a deal "too good to pass up." It probably is too good to be true.
2. Don't stop and talk with anyone who flashes a wad or roll of money. This is bait that con artists use to draw victims.
3. Don't be too good a listener with strangers, and don't fall for any extravagant hard luck story, no matter how convincing it may sound. Some con men work hard at gaining sympathy and confidence.
4. Don't ever put up any "good faith" money for anything and never pay cash for any promised service or product.
5. Don't invest money into any business scheme or adventure without first investigating the credentials and legitimacy of the person or company representing it.

The Do's

1. Do take con games and confidence schemes seriously. Con artists are career criminals who prey on other people's willingness to help and on their inherent nature to trust.
2. Do be aware of the ploys con artists use. It can be something as simple as, "You look like you can be trusted" or "Do you want to make some money?" It may be anything that could draw a person into a conversation with them.
3. Do trust instincts and insights. If your "inner" voice tells you that something is "fishy," listen to it, it probably is!
4. Do read and watch news media reports on suspected confidence schemes being operated in your area. Familiarizing yourself with con artist activities is the best way to avoid being victimized.
5. Do report a scam, or an attempted scam, to the police. Your report of the incident may lead to the subsequent arrest and conviction of the con artists and thus prevent others from getting "stung."

This material is taken from the article by this title in the June 1986 issue of *FBI Law Enforcement Bulletin*. The article was written by Officer Ronald J. Heintzman of Portland, Oregon.

Both personal injury and damages to vehicles are ordinarily claimed in this type of fraud. With the assistance of crooked lawyers and doctors, claims can be made for considerable amounts of money. Insurance executives estimate that if this type of fraud could be eliminated, insurance premiums could be lowered by up to 8 percent.

The "Con Game" as a Form of Fraud

"Con games," or confidence games, obtain their names because the swindle depends on gaining the victim's confidence. Most con men or women believe that there is a little bit of larceny in everyone. By selecting the right victim and applying the right techniques to gain the confidence of the victim, the con artist goes to work.

The "short con" operation generally is limited to the money that the victim has at the time. Examples of "short con" games are card games where fraud is used, handkerchief switch, and dropped pocketbook or wallet. The famous "pigeon drop" is a "short con" game that usually involves all or a good portion of someone's life savings.

The "big con" operation usually takes a considerable length of time to accomplish. The confidence of the intended victim must be gained. The stage must be set and the victim lured into believing that he or she can make a quick profit. The "take" in the "big con" operation is generally larger than the "take" in a "small con" operation.

The *Chicago Police Department Training Bulletin* makes the following observations about con games:

> Confidence men are successful in their operations because many people are eager for the opportunity to make some "easy" money. When people have the opportunity to realize a quick profit, they fail to inquire too diligently into the legality of the transaction.
>
> Victims are often reluctant to report the crime to police due to the publicity or embarrassment that may follow. The confidence man knows that his victim or "mark" may complain to the police. In most cases, however, he firmly believes that the victim will not complain. The fact that the victim can be "conned" out of making a complaint is an integral part of all confidence schemes. The con man usually feels he is safe, because the victim has entered into collusion with him to obtain money from someone else. The embarrassment of having to admit he was taken usually precludes a victim from notifying police authorities. Another part of the operation in favor of the con man is that the victim and the con man are friends up to the "break-away." The lapse of time that passes before the victim realizes that he has been "taken" usually gives the con man ample time to make good his disappearance.
>
> In many instances, the intended victim is permitted to profit by dishonest means (this operation is known as the "convincer"). Then, he is induced to make a large investment and is "fleeced." The victim in these swindles is usually referred to as the "mark," "egg," "sucker," "boob," "chump," and other similar names.[4]

Parts of the excellent *FBI Law Enforcement Bulletin* article "Confidence Schemes and Con Games" are presented to describe some of the common con games and schemes.

Pyramid Schemes

"Pay $105 — Recruit two other investors — And you will make $46,700 profit."

More than 28,000 people in 21 states and Canada were cheated out of more than $1 million dollars when they fell for this pyramid scheme in 1989 and 1990. FBI agents pointed out that the victims "were just ordinary people." The names used for the scheme, which was run out of Charlotte, N.C., were "Circles of Light Church," "The Woman Man God Program," "Winners Marketing Group," "Creative Solutions," and the "WMG Program." Payments of $46,700 were made to some persons throughout the scheme to keep enthusiasm up.

In recent years a number of states have enacted statutes making pyramid promotional schemes illegal. Other states have older statutes in their criminal codes forbidding pyramid schemes. The Court of Special Appeals of Maryland defined the forbidden practice as follows in 1986:[5]

* * *

> Pyramiding is a type of multi-level marketing operation which theoretically serves as a method of distributing a company's products to the public. Annot., 54 A.L.R.3d 217, 219 (1973). Participants in the operation are spread out over various distribution levels through which products are resold until they reach the consumer. However, because "one profits merely by being a link in the product distribution chain, the emphasis is on recruiting more investor-distributors rather than on retailing

products." Note, *Pyramid Schemes: Dare to be Regulated,* 61 Georgetown L.J. 1257, 1259 (1973).

A participant's recruitment of others into the pyramid operation results in creation of that participant's "downline," consisting of those persons recruited by the participant himself and by the participant's recruits. The downline is created by recruiting a preestablished number of individuals into the first level of the operation, each of whom then recruits an equal number of additional persons. The original participant moves up to the next level of the operation each time the bottom level of recruits in his downline is completed, with the process ideally continuing until the original participant's downline reaches a maximum figure determined by the number of levels in the pyramid. A participant may earn commissions from the sale of products to the distributors within his downline, but commissions are also received from entry fees paid by new recruits into one's downline.

The type of pyramid operation with which § 233D is concerned is one in which a participant's compensation is "derived primarily" from the participant's recruitment of others into the operation rather than from the sale of goods or services. With that consideration in mind, we now review the evidence in this case.

* * *

A former Detroit deputy police chief was convicted in 1991 of forty fraud and tax violations in running a pyramid scheme. The Internal Revenue Service stated that the three men running the pyramid scheme made no investments but did return $13 million to investors from 1983 through 1986, while pocketing $4 million profit on which they paid no taxes. (See "Ex-Deputy Police Chief in Detroit Is Convicted in a Pyramid Scheme," *The New York Times,* January 6, 1991.)

Stock Market and Financial Market Frauds

The stock markets and financial markets of the United States and other industrial democratic countries are very important to their economic development in creating jobs and providing for economic security. Among the crimes created to protect these vital activities is the crime of "inside trading." Persons obtaining "inside" information as to the plans of large corporations can oftentimes make huge profits by "inside trading" on information that is often bought illegally.

A series of "inside trading" scandals caused great concern and alarm in the late 1980s. Among the Wall Street speculators who went to prison were Ivan Boesky and Michael Milken. Milken received ten years in prison, three years probation, and agreed to pay $600 million in penalties. Boesky received a sentence of three years in a federal prison, paid $100 million in penalties, and agreed to work with the government in apprehending other offenders. Boesky made the covers of both *Time* and *Newsweek.* The *Time* cover story was "Wall Street Scam: Making Millions with *Your* Money: (Investor 'Ivan the Terrible' Boesky)."[6]

In 1991, federal banking regulators filed a $6 billion lawsuit against Michael Milken and others, including Charles H. Keating formerly of the Lincoln Savings & Loan Association. The government contended in their complaint that the defendants had participated in fraudulent schemes that led to huge losses from their "junk bond" investments.

In addition to the 403 people convicted of savings & loan frauds up to 1991, it was reported in a March 21, 1991, *New York Times* article, "Putting Lawyers

Confidence Schemes and Con Games—Old Games with New Players

Con Games

Three Card Monte is a widely known trick derived from a game known by different names, i.e., "three sea shells," "find the lady," or "three-card shuffle." Basically, it is a card game played with three cards, usually a picture card and two number cards. (By slight-of-hand movement of the cards, the victim is cheated of his or her money.)

The Coin Game is another form of scam employed by con artists. The object is to toss a coin against the wall, betting against your opponent. The one whose coin lands closest to the wall after landing and coming to a stop wins! The game appears to be an even-chance proposition. But, beware of the weighted coin. Weighted coins give the con artist the best odds at landing his or her coin closest to the wall on almost every toss.

The Pigeon Drop is one of the oldest confidence schemes in existence, said to have originated in China more than 1,000 years ago. The victim is approached by a con artist who initiates friendly conversation in an attempt to gain the victim's trust and confidence. A second con artist then enters the scene, claiming to have found a large sum of money. After some discussion and great acting on the part of the con artists, the victim is offered to split the found fortune. The money is to be divided later. The catch, though, is that the victim is required to put up some "good faith" money during the interim. The victim is given the money to hold for safekeeping, but not before envelopes are switched by a sleight-of-hand act. Later, the victim discovers that the envelop contains nothing more than worthless pieces of paper.

Dice are one of the most ancient gambling instruments known to man and are commonly used by the con artist on the street, since they are small and easily concealed.

Confidence Schemes

In *The Jamaican Boy Scam,* a con artist, using a phony foreign accent, approaches a victim asking for help. He tells the victim that he is a stranger in town and doesn't know anyone he can trust. The con man displays a huge roll of money, asking the victim to hold it for him, though not until the victim puts his money

There is little skillful play in dice games other than knowing the odds in various bets and not placing bets when the odds are unfavorable. However, unknown to the player, a "slick" con artist can gain a decided odds advantage in these games by using certain cheating and control techniques. With practice, these control and cheating techniques appear very natural and are difficult to detect by the unsuspecting and untrained player.

The Shell Game is perceived by a player as a game of chance. However, the operator has total control of the game, with no chance of the player winning. The game is played by the operator showing three shells (or bottle caps) under which an object (pea) can be concealed. The pea is made of flexible, soft, pliable material, frequently a woman's makeup sponge. The game consists of the operator placing the pea under one of the shells and moving the pea from shell to shell by quick movement of the hands. The player then wagers money, which the operator usually matches, to guess which shell conceals the pea. If the shell chosen by the player does hide the pea, the player wins; if not, the operator wins.

Currency Cons are initiated by a victim being approached by a stranger holding a $10 bill and asking for two $5 bills. Only after the change is given does the victim realize that he was given a $1 dollar bill instead of a $10 bill.

The con artist clipped the corners from four $10 bills and pasted them to the corners of a single dollar. Holding the bill in his hand, the con man covers the written denomination on the currency with his thumb. The con man easily exchanges the four partially mutilated $10 bills for new ones at a bank. He now has four "fresh" bills to use in pulling another scam.

together with the con's money as a "show" of real trust. The con artist then offers to demonstrate a safer way for the victim to carry the money. Wrapping the money in a handkerchief and placing it down the front waistband of his pants, the con explains that people in his country carry their valuables in this fashion, so

continued

Confidence Schemes and Con Games—Old Games with New Players (continued)

as to thwart a potential pickpocket. The hand-kerchief is then given back to the victim, but not before a switch has been made. Using a ruse to separate himself from the victim, the con man disappears. Opening the handker-chief, the victim discovers that it contains play money!

The Double Shot or *Phony Cop Scam* consists of repeated hits on the same victim. After be-ing flimflammed once by a con man, the victim is contacted by associates of the first con man. Posing as police officers, they tell the victim that he or she had been swindled by the first con, who is now attempting to get the rest of the victim's money. The phony cops tell the victim to withdraw all remaining money from the bank and turn it over to them for safekeep-ing, until the con artist is caught. The con men may even go as far as to drive the victim to a real police station, while one of them goes inside to supposedly deliver the money to a superior. The victim is fleeced out of every last dime he or she owns.

With *The Begger or Sympathy Con,* con artists may approach victims on a busy street, in a restaurant, or wherever, giving a bad luck story and asking for help and money. Though a variety of ruses may be used, the most profit-able con appears to be the "help me feed my starving children" scam. Also called the "silent con" because he rarely speaks, the con artist will prepare a cardboard sign which he holds while standing or sitting on a public sidewalk. The sign may indicate that he is not lazy, but that he can't find a job and has three children at home to feed. The con man may even go as far as to include photographs of children (not his own), along with some cleverly thought out hard-luck slogan. Putting on a great acting performance, the con man appears embar-rassed and distraught by lowering his head and looking away from passersby. In the right loca-tion, this sympathy con can net hundreds of dollars in a matter of hours.

In *The Bank Examiner Ploy,* a con artist pos-ing as a bank examiner, an auditor, or even an FBI agent, contacts the victim to solicit his or her help in apprehending a "dishonest" bank teller. The victim is asked to withdraw money from the bank and turn it over to an official from the bank who will contact him or her later. The victim is often offered a substantial reward when the "dishonest" teller is arrested and convicted and is sworn to secrecy about the "undercover" investigation. The victim turns the money over to the phony bank offi-cial and never sees it again.

The Merchandise Swindle, also known as the "weighted box" scam, entails the con artist contacting a victim on the street or parking lot and offering to sell a particular item, such as a radio or television set. The con man shows boxes of the same article, all wrapped and sealed. He tells the victim that his uncle has just sold his business and is liquidating all re-maining inventory at "rock bottom" prices. Too good a deal to pass up, the victim pays the con man, later realizing what he bought at "rock bottom" price. The victim is the proud owner of a box of rocks.

In *The Home Repair Con,* the con artist poses as a home repairman, offering to perform a free inspection. The con man wears an official-looking work uniform, bearing some fictitious company logo, and often presents some form of false identification. He suggests a list of needed home repairs at a good deal, if the vic-tim is willing to make, in advance, a "small" down payment. The victim pays, an appoint-ment for the work is made, and the con man leaves, never to return.

The Store Clerk Con   is usually committed during the busiest shopping time of the year, when people become more and more frus-trated with the long wait to reach the check-out counter. A sharply dressed man or woman wearing a store nameplate will approach cus-tomers who are waiting in line, show sympa-thy for the long wait, and offer to take the pur-chase to the cashier to speed things up. The store clerk tells the customer to remain in place and that he or she will be right back with the purchase and any change. The store clerk disappears into the crowd, and so does the money.

Because of the con artist's uncanny ability to adapt quickly to changing times and socio-economic situations, the list of con games and confidence schemes is never ending.

Citizens should be warned to be on guard against con artist activities. See the box entitled Avoid-ing Cons: Don'ts and Do's for important information.

After pleading guilty to one count of "inside trading," Ivan Boesky leaves the Federal Court building. Millions of dollars were lost in Wall Street frauds that Boesky confessed to committing.

Under Scrutiny," that more than 1,400 investigations were being conducted against lawyers, accountants, officers, directors, and other persons associated with failed banks and savings associations.

The chairman of the U.S. House Judiciary Subcommittee on Criminal Justice wrote that about "half of the recent bank failures and one-quarter of the thrift failures ... involved criminal activity by insiders, few of whom, according to a Congressional survey, were adequately punished."[7]

Rolling Back Odometers and "Title Washing" Schemes

Rolling back the miles on used cars and "title washing" are frauds that cost the American public hundreds of millions of dollars every year. As odometer mileage figures are entered on the titles of used cars and trucks, "title washing" is used to fraudulently alter titles.

A dishonest car or truck dealer who rolls back mileage on a vehicle must then fraudulently alter the title to reflect the new rolled-back mileage. The forged vehicle title is then sent to a state motor vehicle department to have a new title issued. The title has now been "washed" and the fraud is more difficult to uncover. The following 1990 U.S. Supreme Court case concerned interstate "title washing":

MOSKAL v. UNITED STATES
Supreme Court of the United States (1990) ___ U.S. ___ , 111 S. Ct. 461

Odometers on two used cars were rolled back 30,000 miles on each car. The titles for the cars were fraudulently altered to reflect the new mileage. The altered titles were then sent from Pennsylvania to Virginia where an accomplice submitted them to Virginia authorities who, unaware of the false mileage figures, issued Virginia titles. The "washed" titles were then sent to Pennsylvania where they were used in the sale of the vehicles to unsuspecting buyers. Defendant Moskal's role in this scheme was forwarding the altered titles to Virginia and receiving the "washed" titles when they returned. He was convicted under the National Stolen Property Act, 53 U.S.C. 1178, which also forbids the knowing transportation of falsely made, forged, altered, or counterfeited securities in interstate commerce. In affirming his conviction, the Supreme Court held:

* * *

We think that "title washing" operations are a perfect example of the "further frauds" that Congress sought to halt in enacting § 2314. As Moskal concedes, his title-washing scheme is a clear instance of fraud involving securities. And as the facts of this case demonstrate, title washes involve precisely the sort of fraudulent activities that are dispersed among several States in order to elude state detection.

* * *

B. Counterfeiting of Money and Commercial Products

Counterfeiting of Currency and Coins

Counterfeiting of currency and coins is a serious federal offense because it could have a severe economic impact on society. The history of counterfeiting in the United States can be summarized as follows:

- *Until and during the Civil War,* counterfeiting was a serious problem, as thousands of different legal bills were being printed by more than 1,500 state banks. It is estimated that as much as one-third of the currency used during the Civil War was counterfeit. Counterfeiting was easy during that period.
- *Establishment of a single national currency* in 1863 and creation of the U.S. Secret Service immediately made counterfeiting difficult. Counterfeiting the new currency required highly skilled persons with highly sophisticated equipment. The diligent efforts of the Secret Service made the pooling of the necessary material and equipment plus the necessary highly trained skills difficult. Counterfeiting and alteration of currency were kept at a minimum over the years.
- *Today,* sophisticated color copiers allow what law enforcement officers call "casual counterfeiters" to print thousands of crude bills. But the principal problem is professional craftsmen, many of whom live in foreign countries and are producing counterfeit money that is difficult to detect. In a six-month period from late 1987 until early 1988, the Secret Service, which has jurisdiction over and responsibility for counterfeiting, seized $40.6 million in phoney currency. However, the Secret Service estimated that $3.8 million in counterfeit bills slipped into circulation during that period.

Because of the counterfeiting problem, new currency is being prepared to replace the present currency used in the United States. Some of the new bills will go into circulation late in 1988, but it will be at least five years before the old currency is completely replaced. Law enforcement officers point out that meanwhile, color copiers and their technology will be getting better and better.

Counterfeiting of Commercial Products

Designer jeans, compact discs, videotapes of movies, electronic components, computers, books, circuit relays, and drugs are counterfeited and sold extensively in the United States. Many of the counterfeit products are manufactured in foreign countries where they are also sold under the well-known label. Usually, the counterfeit product is a cheap or inferior copy of the real thing. However, the phony label deceives many dealers and consumers who believe that they are buying the name brand product.

Importation, manufacture, or sale of a counterfeit product in the United States could result in (a) prosecution under the criminal code of a state, which would probably treat the offense as a misdemeanor; (b) civil suit and sanctions in federal or state civil courts; or (c) federal prosecution under the mail fraud statute (18 U.S.C. Section 1341), the wire fraud statute (18 U.S.C. Section 1343), the Food, Drug and Cosmetic Act (21 U.S.C. Sections 301, 321, etc.), or other federal statutes.

Counterfeiting of consumer and commercial goods and products is increasing in the United States and in other countries. American businesses and consumers who have been cheated by counterfeit products are requesting that the U.S. Congress pass additional legislation to cope with the problem.

C. The Crime of Trafficking in Stolen Goods ("Receiving Stolen Property")

The crimes of trafficking in stolen goods are defined by the statutes of each state and ordinarily include (a) receiving (a single act), (b) concealing and possessing (continuing acts), and, in some states, (c) buying and transferring. In determining the statute of limitations for these offenses, the Supreme Court of Minnesota held in the 1981 case of *State v. Lawrence:*

> The crime commonly known as "receiving stolen property," when used in a shorthand sense, is a misnomer, since it includes a number of different legal concepts in addition to and separate from receiving. The offense includes not only receiving, but concealing; . . . it includes buying; and . . . it also includes possessing and transferring. The issue here is whether any of these terms may be deemed continuing in nature. The two most likely descriptions of defendant's conduct are possession and concealment. Does either, or both, apply? In answering this question we should keep in mind that a crime is not continuing in nature if not clearly so indicated by the legislature. . . .
>
> Both possessing and concealing are distinguishable from receiving in that the latter connotes a single act. Behind possessing and concealing, however, is the notion that property is being kept from someone in violation of a duty to return and this duty to return continues. One of the reasons for including possessing and concealing as crimes is to be able to prosecute even though the time has run out on receiving. Surely this serves the purpose of the statute, which is to deter trafficking in stolen goods.

* * *

We hold, therefore, that either concealing or possessing stolen goods is a continuing offense for the purpose of the statute of limitations. We hold this defendant may not assert the statute of limitations as a bar where he kept the goods he stole in his house and garage, thereby not only possessing the goods but making their discovery more difficult for the owner.[8]

To convict of trafficking in stolen goods, it is ordinarily required that the state prove:

- that the property involved was stolen property
- that the defendant received, concealed, possessed, purchased, or transferred the property as forbidden by the statutes of that state
- that the defendant knew the property was stolen.

"Stolen" means that the property was obtained as a result of a theft, burglary, robbery, or any other form of theft crime, such as shoplifting or obtaining property by deception.

The "Fence" and "Fencing" Stolen Property

A "fence" is a person who traffics in stolen property (receiving, concealing, possessing, buying, transferring, etc.). A fence acts as a middleman and pays the thief for stolen property, which the fence in turn attempts to merchandise at a profit to himself or herself. The compensation paid by the fence to the thief is usually a small fraction of the value of the goods. The report of the President's Commission on Law Enforcement and Administration of Justice makes the following observations regarding fencing in the United States:

Nearly all professional theft is undertaken with the aim of selling the goods thereafter. Although the thief himself may retail his stolen merchandise, he probably will prefer to sell to a fence. He thereby increases his safety by reducing the risk that he will be arrested with the goods in his possession, or that they will be stolen in turn from him. He also avoids the dangers associated with the disposal process itself. In addition, large quantities of goods which may be perishable or otherwise quickly lose their value, or for which there is a specialized demand, will require a division of labor and level of organization beyond the capacity of an individual thief operating as his own retailer. The professional thief thus needs a "middleman" in the same way and for some of the same reasons as the farmer, manufacturer, or other producer.

* * *

Some fences engage in fencing as a supplement to their legitimate businesses, often on a more or less regular basis. The consultants learned of clothing and appliance dealers who regularly serve as outlets for stolen goods. The major outlets for stolen jewels in one of the cities studied were reported to be legitimate jewelry merchants. Other fences deal primarily or wholly in stolen goods, and are therefore professional criminals themselves.

Some narcotics pushers act as fences, taking stolen goods instead of cash for narcotics. While dealing with addicts is generally regarded as more dangerous than dealing with nonaddicts, it is also more profitable. The addict in need of a "fix" does not bargain well.

Little research has been done on fencing, despite its central role in professional crime. More information is needed about the nature of the market for illicit goods and the extent to which demand for various types of goods affects the incidence of theft. More should also be learned about the relationship of legitimate and illegitimate markets. Little is known about the pattern of distribution of stolen goods. When stolen automobiles are excluded, only a very small proportion of the total amount of goods stolen is returned to its owners. The redistribution of goods through theft and resale might constitute a significant subsidy to certain groups in our society; its curtailment might have significant side effects which should be explored. Finally, it would be desirable to have more information about the organization and operation of large-scale fencing operations, to aid in the development of better methods of law enforcement.[9]

Fences are hard to apprehend because they often operate behind the fronts of legitimate businesses, such as service stations, beauty salons, junkyards, jewelry stores, and taverns. Salesmen for the fence may work on factory assembly lines and in other industrial plants. People who cannot resist a bargain become an easy target for the fence and his salesmen.

Law enforcement officials are well aware that if they can put fences out of business or prevent them from operating profitably, they will minimize burglaries, shoplifting, and robberies in their jurisdictions. If there is no outlet for stolen goods, the incentive to steal is lessened considerably. One way of developing cases against fences has been through burglars who face trials with overwhelming evidence against them. Motivations that have caused burglars to testify against a fence are:

- to get even with a fence who has cheated on them
- to give up a life of crime
- to lessen the stiff prison term that they face.

When Property Loses Its Character as Stolen Goods

UNITED STATES v. MONASTERSKI
United States Court of Appeals, Sixth Circuit (1977) 567 F.2d 677, 22 CrL 2357

Three juveniles were caught attempting to steal tires from a railroad boxcar. The juveniles cooperated with FBI agents and delivered some of the tires to the defendant, whom they identified as their prospective fence. The defendant was convicted of receiving stolen property (the tires). In reversing the defendant's conviction, the Sixth Circuit held that once the thieves were caught, the tires lost their character as stolen goods and could no longer support the defendant's conviction. The court further held:[10]

> *In accord with the common law rule, one cannot be convicted of receiving stolen goods when actual physical possession of the stolen goods has been recovered by their owner or his agent before delivery to the intended receiver. We further hold, also in accord with the common law rule, that the term "agent" means any person with a right to possession or control over the goods.*

D. POSSESSION OF BURGLARY TOOLS

Probably all states have statutes making the possession of burglary tools a criminal offense.[11] The usual elements of this crime are:

- that the defendant had a device or implement in his or her possession
- that such device or implement was suitable or capable of being used in committing burglary[12]

- that the defendant intended to use such device or implement to break into a building, dwelling, or depository with the intent to steal.

Like the crime of receiving stolen property, possession of burglarious tools is also difficult to prove. The difficult element to prove in receiving stolen property is knowledge by the defendant that the property was stolen. In possession of burglarious tools, the difficult element is intent by the defendant to use such device or implement to break into a building, dwelling, or depository with the intent to steal. Possession of ordinary work tools will not ordinarily be sufficient to justify a conviction for possession of burglarious tools. There must be additional evidence of intent to use such tools for burglarious purposes.

Cases in which most convictions have been obtained can be divided into the following categories:

- The defendant was apprehended committing or attempting to commit a burglary.
- The defendant was observed under suspicious circumstances and attempted to throw away (or did rid self of) the tool.
- The defendant was in the possession of a specifically designed or adapted tool under circumstances in which a judge or jury could infer the tool's use for an illegal purpose of entry.

E. Destroying or Damaging the Property of Another

No American city, town, or village escapes the physical and psychological disfigurement caused by vandalism to public and private property. Vandalism is a serious problem in most public transport systems, costing millions of dollars in large cities. Schools are often hit hard, with broken windows, break-ins, broken property, and spray paint used on walls.

Veteran law enforcement officers observe that vandalism (criminal damage to property) occurs in cycles. In the summertime, public parks are hit. Benches are piled up, debris is thrown into lagoons, and beaches are littered. If buildings are left vacant, they sometimes are vandalized to the point where they must be razed. Criminal damage to private property varies considerably and is a constant source of citizen complaint to law enforcement agencies. The types and categories of vandalism, including some of the reasons such acts are committed, are presented in the Categories of Vandalism box (this chapter).

In 1990, an eighteen-year-old man was charged with more than twenty misdemeanor counts of vandalism and trespassing for painting "Chaka" on walls, buildings, and traffic signs and signals in the Los Angeles area. The city attorney said that the "extent of the property damage makes this the worst case of graffiti vandalism we have seen in Los Angeles or heard of anywhere else in the nation (by a single individual)." It was estimated that damages caused by the graffiti vandalism would be $500,000 or more.

Destroying and Damaging (Criminal Mischief)

Destroying and damaging can be perpetrated in many ways, depending on the physical characteristics of the property involved. Windows, glass doors, and street

---

When Damage to Property Is Not Criminal

- When the damage was not done intentionally (many states also make reckless damage to property a crime in order to include damages caused by such persons as shoplifters who resist detention and arrest. Such damages in a store could be extensive.)
- When the property belongs to the defendant (the damage must be done "to the property of another" to be criminal)

- When the damage was done with the consent of the owner
- When the property was abandoned (not the property "of another") or when the owner of the property cannot be located or determined

---

lights can be damaged and destroyed by rocks or hard objects. Aerosol paint can disfigure a beautiful building, wall, or landscape in a short time. A sharp object can scrape the paint on an automobile or puncture a tire. A twist of the hand can bend or break a car antenna. Because of the terrible human danger presented by fire and the harm it can cause to property, intentional damage by fire is charged as arson in all states.

Physical Property

Persons are not ordinarily charged with theft of buildings and real property. However, criminal damage to buildings is a common criminal charge. Buildings and real estate may be easily damaged by vandalism. Grave markers, flowers, trees, shrubbery, and other property attached to the land are often also damaged deliberately. Crops, vegetables, and fruit may be the subject of theft and may also be subject to vandalism, as they may be intentionally damaged or destroyed.

Property Belonging to Another

In charging criminal damage to property, there must be a showing that the property belonged to another person and that the owner did not consent to having the property damaged or destroyed. Persons may damage or destroy their own property if they do so in a manner that does not disrupt public order or present a threat to public safety or health.

Police officers are sometimes called into a home in which the husband has destroyed an item of property, such as the television set. If the set belongs to the man and he has paid for it out of his wages, then no criminal offense ordinarily has been committed. But if the man has broken a number of windows in the house deliberately, and the family is renting the house, the property of another has been damaged or destroyed.

The Requirement That the Act of Destroying or Damaging Be Intentional or Reckless

Cases often come into prosecutors' offices in which shoplifters, in their efforts to avoid being taken into custody, have broken something in a store as they were

These cars received criminal damage while parked near the route of the 1986 New York Mets World Championship parade.

running or as they bumped into a display and knocked merchandise down. If the statute or ordinance of that jurisdiction requires that the damaging or destroying be "intentional," the shoplifter may not then be charged with criminal damage to property. However, if the statute or ordinance reads that the damaging or destroying be "recklessly" done, the shoplifter may be charged if the state can show that the conduct was "reckless." In either case, the shoplifter is civilly liable for the damage caused. Courts will sometimes, as a condition of their sentences, require that the shoplifter (or any other person damaging property) make compensation for the damage or work to repair damage caused.

F. Arson

One of the first concerns of a fire investigator is the fire's origin. Fires can be classified by their causes as accidental fires, natural fires (caused without human intervention), arson, (fires of incendiary origin), and fires of unknown origin.

Many fires are started accidentally, as when children play with matches or when persons are careless with cigarettes, cigars, or pipe ashes. Some fires are of natural origin and occur without human intervention. These fires occur because of spontaneous combustion, defective heating units, faulty electrical appliances or wiring, and the like.

Arson is the deliberate, willful, and malicious burning of a building or personal property by a person. Arson is the easiest of the major crimes to commit, the most difficult to detect, and the hardest to prove in court.

Categories of Vandalism (Criminal Mischief or Criminal Damage to Property)

Type of Vandalism	*Purpose and Effects of Vandalism*
Vandalism to acquire property	Damage to vending machines, telephone coin boxes, etc. to obtain money; damages to motor vehicles, homes, and other buildings to obtain parts, fixtures, or other objects.
Sign vandalism	Damaging or removing highway signs or other signs to obtain souvenirs or as a prank. As the removal or damage to highway signs has caused accidents, injuries, and deaths, statutes such as Section 86.192 of the Wisconsin Statutes specifically forbid and punish as a misdemeanor.
Tactical or protest vandalism	Property damage to call attention to a grievance or to bring about a change. This might involve damage to a jail cell or to a prison mess hall, or damage to military or construction equipment.
Ideological vandalism	Vandalism to express political and ideological ideas. This is often done through signs pasted or nailed on buildings, walls, posts, etc. Greater damage is done when spray paint is used. Such vandalism is a serious threat to public safety when arson or explosives are used.
Revenge vandalism	Vandalism as an act of revenge against a person, business, or governmental unit. Revenge could be the act of a student against a school, or the act of an employee against his or her employer.
Play vandalism	Breaking windows or street lamps as part of a play activity of a gang or group would be play vandalism. Seeing who can throw rocks the furthest or the highest might be the test of play vandalism.
Graffiti	Graffiti is also called "harmless vandalism" and consists of words or names placed on walls, bridges, sidewalks, stairs, and other objects.
Rage or frustration vandalism	Criminal damage to property done in a rage or as an expression of frustration would be referred to as malicious vandalism. This type of vandalism is often directed at an institution or some group or class.

It is estimated that arson kills 500 to 1,000 persons every year in the United States, in addition to injuring thousands of others. More than a billion dollars in property damages occur every year plus the loss of millions of dollars in jobs and in property taxes to local governments. Arson also causes fire insurance rates to increase significantly, passing the costs of arson on to the general public.

Motives for Arson

If it can be shown that a fire was of incendiary origin and is indeed arson, the next questions are why and who. Why a person would commit arson is important, because there usually is a motive that causes a person to burn a

The problem of arsonists who torch vacant buildings concerns the entire nation. Here, a St. Louis community group offers a reward for information that leads to the arrest and conviction of arsonists.

building or personal property deliberately. Some of the common motives for arson are:

- *For profit.* For example: (a) Persons who are in serious financial trouble will sometimes burn their own buildings or personal property in order to collect insurance money. (b) Owners of property who no longer want the property and cannot sell it. (c) Business owners who are in financial trouble and seek to dispose of obsolete merchandise, or who want to move to a new business location.[13]
- *For revenge or out of anger.* "Spite" fires are started to retaliate against a former boss or a wife who has commenced a divorce action, or in anger over a failed love affair.
- *For political motives,* committed by political extremists or radical groups.
- *For destruction of evidence of other crimes,* such as murder, burglary, theft, or embezzlement.

Motive is important in the investigation of arson cases, because the person who might benefit from the crime is then identified as a possible suspect. When no motive for arson is apparent, the fire investigator may then suspect that the fire was set by a pyromaniac or as an act of vandalism.

The pyromaniac, or "firebug," may be a pathological fire setter who has been in trouble before. A desire for sexual excitement often motivates the pyromaniac to start a fire. Police officers should be suspicious of intoxicated persons in a crowd watching a fire. Some firebugs are able to control themselves unless they have been drinking or taking drugs. If their inhibitions are lowered, they acquire enough false courage to set a fire. Often they stay in the area to watch the fire.[14]

Arson as vandalism is often committed by juvenile thrill seekers. There is seldom a reason for this type of crime. Experienced fire investigators point out that if the fire was set in a part of a building readily accessible to the public and the "plant" was simple, the odds are great that the fire was set by a person who did not have a rational motive. A "plant" is the means of starting a fire; simple plants could be newspapers or some rubbish ignited with a match.

Essential Elements of the Crime of Arson

All states have enacted statutes that define arson. In general, most statutes require that the state prove the following elements:

- That there was a fire and that some part of the building or personal property was damaged by the fire. Mere blackening, discoloration, or blistering of the paint or parts of a building is not sufficient to prove arson of a building.[15] When the fire has not burned an actual part of a building or personal property the offense should be charged as attempted arson.
- That the fire was of incendiary origin and was willfully and intentionally set. This is the required proof of *corpus delicti* (that a crime was in fact committed). For a fire inspector to testify in court that he or she "suspected" arson or that the fire was of "unknown origin" is insufficient to prove *corpus delicti.*[16] An expert witness is usually required to testify specifically that arson did occur. The witness must then be able to support his or her statement with specific evidence.

Halloween "Trick or Treat"?

For many years, more crimes have been committed on Halloween than on other days, and for that reason law enforcement agencies all over the United States are on the alert each October. Many of the offenses are harmless (but annoying), such as dumping over garbage containers, soaping windows, and moving objects from one place to another.

On an average day in Detroit, Michigan, sixty fires are reported in the city. An arson spree began in the early 1980s during the Halloween period. The worst year was 1984 when 816 fires were reported during the last three days of October. Public awareness, community programs, and action by public officials cut the number of fires on Halloween night to 223 in 1989 and 281 in 1990.

Other forms of "wilding" also increase on Halloween night. Some wilding results in property damage. Unfortunately, some result in injury and even death. In New York City, young men in Halloween masks waving knives, bats, lead pipes, and a cleaver attacked groups of homeless persons while yelling "trick or treat." Nine homeless men were beaten and cut and one was killed. Five young men were arrested and charged in the Halloween rampage against the homeless people.

Essential Elements of the Crime of Arson

To Prove the Crime of Arson, the State Must Prove Beyond a Reasonable Doubt That:

1) there was a fire, and the witnesses for the state must testify as to:
   a. date and time of the fire
   b. how the fire department or the police department received the alarm
   c. nature of the alarm (whether there was a series of alarms indicating the seriousness of the fire)
   d. identity of person giving alarm
   e. information given by person
2) that some part of a building or property was actually damaged and burnt by the fire (Blackening, discoloration, or blistering of paint is not the completed crime of arson. Nor is the burning of a carpet or floor covering.) If the completed crime of arson cannot be proved, the state should then consider charging attempted arson or another lesser offense.
3) that the fire was of incendiary origin and that it was willfully and intentionally set. For a fire investigator to testify that he or she suspected arson would not be sufficient to prove the *corpus delicti* of the crime.

- That the accused committed or was party to the crime of arson charged. Like all other crimes, the evidence required to convict a person of arson is proof beyond a reasonable doubt.

The "Torch"

If the investigation of a fire shows that it was of incendiary origin and was indeed arson, a natural suspect would be the person receiving the fire insurance, unless other motives can be shown for the crime. As arson for profit is common, further investigation must be conducted concerning the finances of the property owner. Serious financial difficulties or inability to sell the property can raise further suspicions, as these conditions could be motives for arson.

Arson for hate and spite must also be considered, along with the possibility that the crime was committed by a professional "torch" (an arsonist for hire). There are a number of professional arson rings operating throughout the United States. By hiring a "torch," the person seeking to commit arson for hate or profit would (a) have the crime of arson committed in a more "professional" manner and (b) allow himself or herself an opportunity to establish whereabouts elsewhere at the time the crime is committed. Attempting to hire a "torch" (solicitation to commit arson) is in itself a felony in most states. As arson is one of the more serious felonies of violence, such an offense is viewed as a serious threat to both property and life.

Evidence Obtained at the Scene of the Fire

Persons who are among the first to be at the scene of a fire may obtain information that could be valuable to investigating officers. Such persons should observe:

- the color of the smoke and flames, which might provide valuable information as to whether the fire is of incendiary origin and is arson. Gasoline and other chemicals burn with different colored flames and smoke.
- the size of the fire

- the speed at which it travels
- the number of separate fires
- weather conditions at the time of the fire
- persons in the area at the time and the license number (if possible) of any vehicle leaving the scene.

The U.S. Supreme Court placed restrictions on the extent of investigation that can be carried out at the scene of a fire by firefighters or law enforcement agencies. In *Michigan v. Tyler,*[17] the Court ruled that investigators may not remain on the scene of a burned building indefinitely or search indiscriminately. The rules made applicable to the firefighters and investigating officers allow them to remain on the scene without a warrant only for a reasonable time. A reasonable length of time is determined by the size of the building, the contents thereof, the extent and intensity of the fire, the time of day or night the fire occurs, and other such factors. Once the reasonable time has expired, if the fire officials wish to reenter the burned building to determine whether a code violation caused the fire, consent or an administrative search warrant must be obtained. The Court further pointed out that even with an administrative search warrant, if probable cause that a crime has been committed is uncovered during the administrative search, the administrative search must stop and a search warrant must be obtained under the criminal procedure.

G. TRESPASS

In its broad sense, the word *trespass* means an unlawful act against a person, property, or right of another. For example, court decisions today continue to speak of the trespassory taking of property, meaning that the property was wrongfully taken. Murder, assault, and battery are trespassory acts because they are wrongful and unlawful acts that violate the rights of other persons.

However, in its usual and more common use, the word trespass refers to a wrongful intrusion on the land or into the premises of another person. All states have statutes that reflect this usual and common concept of the offense, and when newspapers use the word *trespass,* they are usually using the word in this limited sense.

A variety of trespass statutes can be found in criminal codes and municipal ordinances. The trespass to land statutes make the unlawful entry on land (when the land has been posted or the person notified to stay off) a criminal offense if the entry or the remaining on the land is without the consent of the owner or the person in lawful possession. Trespass to dwelling statutes and ordinances forbid the entry into homes and residences unless it is with the consent of an occupant.

Other trespass statutes and ordinances forbid entry into specific places, such as schools with classes in session, unless the person has legitimate business or is a parent. Trespass statutes generally have a section dealing with entry and also a section pertaining to "failure to depart." (Also see trespass cases and material in chapter 11.) The following cases illustrate the application of trespass statutes in various jurisdictions throughout the United States.[18]

COMMONWEALTH v. MARKUM

Superior Court of Pennsylvania (1988) 373 Pa. Suppr. 341, 541 A.2d 347, review denied 489 U.S. 1080, 109 S. Ct. 1533 (1989)

Defendants pushed their way into a Philadelphia abortion clinic, destroyed machines and equipment, and refused to leave. Police had to carry them from the scene. In holding that "justification" (see chapter 7) was not a valid defense for them, the Court affirmed their convictions for trespassing, holding:

* * *

Were we free to pick and choose which laws we wished to obey, the result would be a society of strife and chaos. Therefore, even the legislature had not made a clear choice regarding abortion, the justification defense would be unavailable because abortion is lawful by virtue of the United States Constitution. Certainly, justification may not be asserted as a grounds for interference with a person's right to free speech even though that right has not been legislatively approved. Free speech has been constitutionally approved, as has a woman's right to abortion. Democracy allows the citizenry to protest laws of which they disapprove. But they must nonetheless obey such laws or face the legal consequences. To allow the defense of justification to those who willingly and intentionally break the law would encourage criminality cloaked in the guise of conscience.

* * *

(For similar cases, see 784 S. W. 2d 193, 537 NYS 2d 734, 738 NYS 2d 149, 498 A. 2d 806, and 501 A. 2d 226.)

PEOPLE v. DORNER

Supreme Court (Kings County) (1982) 458 N.Y.S.2d 982

During school hours, the defendant was on the fourth floor of a high school and attempted to pass himself off as a student in the school. When it was discovered that the defendant had been suspended from the high school and was unlawfully in the school, he was arrested for trespass. A search disclosed that the defendant was carrying a concealed weapon. In denying the motion to suppress the evidence obtained through the search, the court held:

A person walking through a school building under these circumstances could reasonably expect that he would be asked to account for his presence to school personnel. As recognized in People v. Scott D., *34 N.Y.2d 483, 486–487, 358 N.Y.S.2d 403: "A school is a special kind of place in which serious and dangerous wrongdoing is intolerable. Youngsters in a school, for their own sake, as well as that of their age peers in the school, may not be treated with the same circumspection required outside the school or to which self-sufficient adults are entitled."*

* * *

Since Police Officer Moore had probable cause to arrest defendant, that arrest was lawful and, therefore, the police officer had the right to search defendant as an incident to a lawful arrest.

PEOPLE v. SPENCER
Appellate Court of Illinois (1971) 131 Ill.App.2d 551, 268 N.E.2d 192

The defendant, a Chicago high school teacher, was given a letter of dismissal by his principal while the defendant sat at his classroom desk. The teacher was asked to leave and report to a central administrative office. The defendant refused to leave after repeated warnings that he would be arrested if he did not. He was convicted of a criminal trespass to land statute that provided that a person who remained on the land of another after receiving notice from the owner or occupant to depart is guilty of criminal trespass. The defendant argued that, as his entry into the building was lawful, he had not committed a trespass. The appellate court affirmed his conviction and $25 fine, holding that remaining on the land after he had been ordered to leave violated the statute.

STATE v. CARRIKER
Court of Appeals of Ohio (1964) 5 OhioApp.2d 255, 214 N.E.2d 809

The defendant would not leave the premises of a business corporation when ordered to do so by officials of the firm in the presence of police officers. He was convicted of criminal trespass but argued that since his entry on the property was lawful he could not be convicted of criminal trespass. In affirming his conviction, the court stated:

> *In substance the defendant urges in the present case that an unlawful entry is indispensable to a conviction under the terms of the statute, and that the status of a business invitee cannot be changed to that of a trespasser. If this be so, the subject statute employs considerable unnecessary verbiage, and its practical application could lead to bizarre results. For a mild example, in comparison with the facts of the present case, is a businessman helpless against the will of a customer who refuses to leave his store after closing hours? Or for a somewhat harsher example, may a business invitee who, like the defendant in the instant case, admits that he had no intention of making a purchase, use the business premises of another for his own gain with complete immunity after his invitation has been revoked?*
>
> *In our opinion, the trespass statute is not so impotent as suggested by the defendant. It not only provides that the entry upon the premises of another without lawful authority is an offense, but it also provides that remaining upon the premises of another without legal authority after being notified to leave is a misdemeanor.*

STAHL v. STATE
Oklahoma Court of Appeals (1983) 665 P.2d 839, review denied 464 U.S. 1069, 104 S.Ct. 973 (1984)

Demonstrators entered a nuclear power plant closed to the public. The defendants were newspersons who entered along with the demonstrators despite previous warnings, signs posted on the fence, and loudspeaker warnings. The newspersons were arrested along with the demonstrators and appealed their convictions. In affirming their convictions, the court held:

* * *

> *The First Amendment does not shield newspersons from liability for torts and crimes committed in the course of news-gathering....*

* * *

> *Further, the First Amendment does not guarantee the press a constitutional right of special access not available to the public generally.... Moreover, this property is not*

a traditional public forum such as public streets, sidewalks, and parks, and there is no constitutional guarantee of access:

[T]he First Amendment does not guarantee access to property simply because it is owned or controlled by the government. In *Greer v. Spock,* 424 U.S. 828, 96 S.Ct. 1211, 47 L.Ed.2d 505 (1976), the Court cited approvingly from its earlier opinion in *Adderley v. Florida,* 385 U.S. 39, 87 S.Ct. 242, 17 L.Ed.2d 149 (1966) wherein it explained that 'The State, no less than a private owner of property, has power to preserve the property under its control for the use to which it is lawfully dedicated.' 424 U.S. 828, 836, 96 S.Ct. 1211, 1216, 47 L.Ed.2d 505.

U.S. Postal Service v. Council of Greenburgh Civil Associations, *453 U.S. 114, 129– 130, 101 S.Ct. 2676, 2685, 69 L.Ed.2d 517 (1981).*

H. Landlord-Tenant Disputes

The police are sometimes called when disputes arise between landlords and tenants. Although some disputes between landlords and tenants should be reported to a law enforcement agency, most are not police matters. The officers responding to the calls (or the dispatcher) must therefore determine whether the complaint involves a civil or criminal matter. The parties most likely to call the police (or a sheriff department) in "civil matters" are persons who have neither the money to hire a private lawyer nor the sophistication to distinguish between civil and criminal matters. They turn to the police because they need help and cannot think of anyone else who can help them.

Landlords' Complaints

Studies show that the following reasons cause landlords to call a law enforcement agency for assistance:

- Tenant has destroyed property.
- Landlord's property or the property of another tenant stolen by a tenant.
- Tenant refuses to pay rent.
- Tenant allows garbage to accumulate.
- Tenant refuses to allow the landlord to inspect or enter the premises.
- Tenant keeps pets or animals, in violation of the lease or rental agreement.

The deliberate destruction of property is a criminal offense. But accidental destruction of property, failure to care for the property properly, and the permitting of property to deteriorate rapidly are civil matters. Theft of property, whether it be the landlord's or another tenant's, is a criminal matter. Refusal to pay rent can be aggravating to a landlord who may be hard pressed for money, but this is a civil matter.

The accumulation of garbage, or other sanitation problems, should be referred to the health or sanitation departments of the jurisdiction. Refusal to permit the landlord to enter at reasonable times is also a civil matter, as is the presence of pets or domestic animals in violation of the lease or the rental agreement.

Landlords sometimes report their suspicions that tenants are engaged in criminal activities, but unless there is sufficient evidence that amounts to probable cause, neither a search warrant nor an arrest would be justified. Such suspicions, if based on evidence, could justify referring the matter to the vice squad or to the detective bureau for further investigation.

Tenants' Complaints

Some of the complaints that tenants have made to law enforcement agencies include:

- Landlord has trespassed by entering the tenant's apartment or building without the consent of the tenant.
- Landlord has seized property of the tenant.
- Property of the tenant was stolen by the landlord.
- Landlord locked the tenant out of the premises (this is usually accompanied by a lock-in of the tenant's possessions).
- Landlord failed to provide sufficient heat (or the premises are too hot).
- Electric, water, or gas services were cut off by the landlord.

Landlords may enter the premises of a tenant if an emergency exists, such as a broken water pipe or the smell of smoke. The lease or the rental agreement may provide for entry into the tenant's premises by the landlord under specifically prescribed circumstances. However, an unauthorized entry by a landlord could possibly be charged as a trespass if it could be shown that the entry was made for an unlawful purpose or to harass the tenant. Most of the complaints by tenants, like those of landlords, are civil matters that must be settled peacefully between the parties or, if necessary, can be taken into a civil court.

I. Complaints from Restaurants, Innkeepers, Cab Drivers, and Other Service Suppliers

Law enforcement agencies receive a considerable number of complaints from restaurants, innkeepers, cab drivers, and other service suppliers about customers who cannot or will not pay the amount they owe for services received. Officers who handle such calls must be aware of the statutes and ordinances of their jurisdiction, because some of these matters have been made criminal offenses. Officers should also be aware of the general orders of their departments, which should state departmental procedures to be used in handling such complaints.

As a general rule, officers should make reasonable efforts to settle these matters without resorting to an "order-in" or an arrest. Officers tell of situations in which a customer agreed to leave his wristwatch as a pledge with a restaurant manager until he paid the amount owed. Gasoline and other merchandise may be taken back by the merchant or service station attendants if it is not paid for, but the services of a restaurant, innkeeper, or cab driver cannot be returned.

The ability of a police officer as an adjudicator, peacemaker, and arbitrator is really put to the test in some of the street situations with which he or she is confronted in this area. If the officer cannot settle the matter between the parties, he or she may issue an ordinance citation, request that the parties appear in the city or district attorney's office, or, when necessary, make an arrest.

J. Product Tampering

Since 1982 product tampering has cost the lives of 12 persons in the United States. The offense of poisoning over-the-counter drugs and food products was described by a high federal official as "an insidious and terrible crime. It is a form of terrorism not unlike planting a bomb in some public place to gain media attention, notoriety, or some sick sense of control over human life."[19]

During a one-year period in 1986, the Federal Food and Drug Administration was involved in nearly 1,700 cases of actual tampering or hoaxes. The FBI investigated more than 300 of these incidents. Although it is rare that a product is actually contaminated or poisoned, crimes related to product tampering include:

- *Extortion:* After seven persons died in the Chicago area in 1982 from cyanide-laced Extra-Strength Tylenol, James Lewis tried to use the killings in attempting to extort $1 million from the manufacturer of Tylenol. Lewis was convicted in a federal court in 1983.
- *Threats to tamper and/or threats to allege tampering:* another form of extortion in attempts to obtain money from manufacturers who incur huge costs and loss of market and sales in tampering cases.
- *Attempts to create the basis of a civil lawsuit:* faking tampering cases to make it appear that a person in a family has been the victim of random tampering.
- *Covering up a murder by attempting to make it appear that the victim was killed by random tampering:* A Seattle woman was convicted in 1988 under the 1984 Federal Consumer Tampering Act. She laced Excedrin capsules with cyanide to kill her husband and collect $176,000 in life insurance. Then she planted other cyanide-laced Excedrin capsules in stores to make it appear that her husband was the victim of a random killer. Unfortunately, an innocent victim also died from the poison. The Seattle woman was convicted of two counts of homicide under the Consumer Tampering Act and three other counts of placing cyanide in three other Excedrin bottles.

Product tampering cases have received national attention:

- 1982 Cyanide was placed in Extra-Strength Tylenol in Chicago—seven killed
- 1986 Cyanide was placed in Extra-Strength Tylenol in Yonkers—one killed
- 1986 Rat poison was placed in Contac in Orlando or Houston—no deaths
- 1986 Cyanide was placed in Extra-Strength Excedrin in Washington state—wife of one of two victims convicted
- 1991 Cyanide was placed in Sudafed in Washington state—two killed

Experts point out that persons who tamper with products are similar to persons who commit other crimes. In some of the cases their motive is to make money by extortion or, as a con artist, to fake and deceive to make money. Revenge against a company, product, or person could be a motive. Greed, anger, and hatred motivate most crimes as it does product tampering. At the present time, mental illness and terrorism have fortunately only played a small role among those involved in the criminal act of product tampering.

The crime receives a great deal of attention and concern because all societies are very vulnerable to such acts. Millions of dollars have been invested to "tamper-proof" packages. Most consumers are well aware of the remote problem that the product that they purchase may have been tampered with in a way that could seriously hurt them or someone in their family. It is hoped that product tampering will diminish as a crime just as aircraft hijacking did in the middle and late seventies.

Questions and Problems for Chapter 17

1. Herbert North, a salesman, was using a telephone in the Seattle airport. He saw a wallet in the telephone booth that he assumed someone had left behind. There was $10 in the wallet but no identification. He took the $10 and left the wallet.

As North was walking out of the front door of the airport, he was arrested, handcuffed, and held in jail until the next day. North was one of twenty people caught that day in a police sting operation designed to curtail thefts at the airport.

Could North "take and carry away" the $10 he found ("finders keepers, losers weepers")? Had the police "cast their nets in permissible waters"? (See chapter 7.) *North v. Port of Seattle,* Circuit Court, King County (Wash., 1983)

2. A California sheriff's department learned from a telephone call that a footlocker containing a large number of vials and bottles had been found in a remote area. Investigation showed that the vials and bottles had been taken in a recent burglary of a drugstore. Officers kept the footlocker under surveillance until the defendant arrived at the scene. He was heard to express relief that the "stuff" was still there and then began to bury the footlocker. Can the defendant be charged with the burglary on this information? If not, what could he be charged with? State reasons. (*People v. Schroeder,* 264 Cal.App.2d 217, 70 Cal.Rptr. 491 [1968]).

3. A nationally known football player was approached by a man who stated that he was a great fan of the player. The man said that he wanted to show his appreciation and offered to sell the player an expensive automobile with only a few thousand miles at less than one-fourth the retail price. The player agreed; the vehicle was delivered; cash was paid for the vehicle. The player was told that he would receive the title to the car in a short time through the mail, but he never received the title. The vehicle was determined to be stolen and the true owner demanded that the vehicle be returned to him. May the owner recover the vehicle? Has the football player committed a criminal offense? How would this matter be settled?

4. A burglar apprehended in the act with burglarized goods fears a long prison sentence. He agrees to cooperate and the stolen goods are returned to him. The burglar sells the goods to his regular fence. The fence is arrested and charged with receiving stolen goods. Is the arrest and the charge of receiving stolen property valid? Would it stand up in court? State your reasons.

5. A wife who suspected her husband of associating with another woman saw his Mercedes Benz parked in front of the residence of the other woman. The angry wife threw a bottle through the window of the Mercedes Benz. If this occurred in your state, could the wife be charged with criminal damage to property (or criminal mischief) when the angry husband demands that she be charged criminally? Explain your answer after reading the criminal statute of your state. *People v. Kahanic,* 196 Cal. App. 3d 461, 241 Cal.Rptr. 722 (1987).

6. In the state of Washington, defendant Clark was given permission to use Dennis Noll's car to run some errands and return at noon. Instead he drove the car to Colorado, hundreds of miles away.

   a. If Clark were apprehended days later driving Noll's car, what would Clark likely be charged with in your state?

   b. If Clark abandoned Noll's car in Colorado after his trip, what would he likely be charged with in your state? Explain. *State v. Clark,* 96 Wash.2d 686, 638 P.2d 572 (1982).

Notes

1. 242 Kan. 192, 747 P.2d 784 (1987).

2. "Bait and switch" schemes usually consist of an attractive bargain that is offered at an eye-catching low price. The bargain is the "bait" to lure customers into the store. The "switch" to get the customer to buy a higher-priced item is done by knocking the quality of the advertised item, or stating that it has been sold out or that it is not available on the premises.

3. See the 1987 article entitled, "I know it when I see it: Mail-Order Ministry Tax Fraud and the Problem of a Constitutionally Acceptable Definition of Religion." in *American Criminal Law Review,* Vol. 25, No. 1 (1987).

4. Vol. 10, No. 39 (1969).

5. *Schrader v. State,* 69 Md.App. 377, 517 A.2d 1139 (1986).

6. Also see the 1981 case of *Carpenter v. United States,* 484 U.S. 19, 108 S.Ct. 316. Mr. Winans was a former reporter for the *Wall Street Journal* and wrote a column on stocks in that paper. Winans and others were convicted of profiting by trading on advance knowledge of stocks that were going to be touted (praised) and stocks to be downgraded in future columns. This enabled the "insiders" to take advantage of the predictable impact on the prices of these stocks.

7. See "Don't Water Down the Antifraud Law" by Congressman John Conyers Jr., *The New York Times* December 27, 1987. See also the U.S. Supreme Court case of *United States v. Maze,* 414 U.S. 395, 94 S. Ct. 645 where former Chief Justice Burger stated in dissent that:

> *The criminal mail fraud statute must remain strong to be able to cope with the new varieties of fraud that the ever-inventive American "con artist" is sure to develop. Abuses in franchising and the growing scandals from pyramid sales schemes are but some of the threats to the financial security of our citizenry that the Federal Government must be ever alert to combat. Comment, Multi-Level or Pyramid Sales Systems: Fraud or Free Enterprise, 18 S. D. L. Rev. 358 (1973).*

8. 312 N.W.2d 251 (Minn. 1981).

9. Task Force Report, "Crime and Its Impact—An Assessment," p. 99.

10. Instead of charging "receiving stolen property," the criminal charge in a case such as this should be "conspiracy to receive stolen property," "solicitation to receive stolen property," "attempt to receive stolen property," depending on which offense would best suit the situation and the laws of that particular state.

11. The English refer to this offense as "Going Equipped for Stealing." See *Moriarity's Police Law,* 21st ed. (London: Butterworths).

12. See 33 A.L.R.3d 798 (1970).

13. Arson for "indirect" profit is a more difficult crime to solve, as there is often no apparent connection between the fire setter and the target. The "indirect" profit could be (a) a business person who burns out a competitor to increase his or her own business; (b) tenants seeking to break a lease, or landlords seeking to get the tenant out, collect insurance, and use the property for other or more profitable use; (c) neighbors who burn a property to prevent an occupancy that might decrease property value; (d) prospective buyers who want the land but not the buildings.

14. In some instances, pyromaniacs are detected by studying photos of crowds who go to fires. If the same face shows up repeatedly at a series of fires, this might indicate a person committing arson because of emotional or mental problems. The pyromaniac sometimes remains at the scene after starting a fire, and there have been situations in which pyromaniacs have been hailed as heroes for saving lives at fires they started.

15. If the completed crime of arson cannot be proved beyond a reasonable doubt, the state may then consider charging attempt to commit arson (or in an appropriate situation, conspiracy to commit arson).

16. See the case of *Hughes v. State,* 6 Md.App. 389, 251 A.2d 373 (1969) in which the court pointed out that mere presence of the accused at the scene of a fire is not proof beyond reasonable doubt that the fire was willfully and maliciously set. In *Hughes v. State,* a fire chief testified that he could not determine the cause of the fire. The court reversed the defendant's conviction, holding that the evidence was legally insufficient to establish the *corpus delicti* of the crime of arson.

17. 436 U.S. 499, 98 S.Ct. 1942 (1978).

18. See chapter 11 for additional trespass cases and problems.

19. Dr. Frank E. Young, Commissioner, Food and Drug Administration. See the article "Product Tampering" in the April 1988 issue of the *FBI Law Enforcement Bulletin.*

Part Five

SEX CRIMES

Chapter Eighteen

RAPE AND RELATED SEX CRIMES

A. Sex Crimes in General

Sexual relations (nonmarital) become a crime in the United States if:

- there is a lack of consent
- they are with a child
- they are with a mentally deficient person (person incapable of legally consenting)
- they are performed in public
- they are performed for profit (prostitution)

Sex crimes occur often in the United States. The term sex crime includes a broad classification of offenses that range from serious offenses to nuisance offenses and private offenses between consenting adults.

The enforcement and definition of the more serious offenses is generally uniform throughout the United States, but the enforcement of lesser offenses varies considerably from state to state and somewhat from community to community within each state. To illustrate the wide range of sexual offenses, the following classifications are used:

1. Sexually motivated crimes in which violence is used or threatened.
   - murders of lust or sexual perversion
   - forcible, violent rapes
   - sadistically motivated offenses in which sexual excitement is derived from inflicting pain or injury on other persons
   - kidnapping or abduction when violence is threatened or used
   - forceful and violent sexual attacks on children
   - pyromania (a persistent impulse to set fires, in many cases accompanied by a desire to derive sexual excitement from watching a building burn)
   - pedophilia (committed by mentally ill persons who lust for children, are capable of kidnapping them, and, after using them sexually, are capable of killing them)
2. Offenses against children and mentally defective or deficient adults in which violence is not used or threatened.
   - "statutory rape" or sexual intercourse with a child
   - sexual intercourse with a person known to be mentally deficient or defective
   - abduction or "enticement" when force is not used or threatened
   - incest in which force or threat of force is not used but the victim is not legally capable of consenting to act
   - child pornography (exploitation and exhibition of children for financial and sexual purposes)
3. Offenses that violate the right of privacy
   - "offensive touching" of the person of another (see the case of *People v. Thomas* in chapter 14, in which the defendant offensively touched the buttocks of a woman on a rush-hour train in New York City)
   - window peeping (form of voyeurism)
4. Commercial offenses that are profit oriented

- prostitution (male and female)
- pimping and pandering
- sexual perversion
- sale of obscene material or presentation of obscene acts or films
- abortion violations

5. Offenses that are not physically dangerous but are against public policy
   - forms of voyeurism
   - public nudity forbidden by a specific statute or ordinance
   - sexual acts in public places
   - public nudity such as:
     —college and fraternal-type "streaking"
     —"mooning" (displaying the derriere from such places as a moving vehicle)
     —nonhumorous exposure to women and children ("flasher")
   - obscenity not done for profit
   - nuisances and other public indecencies

6. Private offenses between consenting adults (in states that have such statutes)
   - fornication
   - seduction
   - adultery
   - bigamy
   - incest (sexual intercourse between persons related within the degree in which marriage is prohibited)
   - homosexual relations

B. Forcible Rape of Women and Girls

Rape is one of the most underreported crimes. The crime is one of degradation as well as violence, and fear of reprisal and embarrassment contributes to the victim's hesitation to report it. Those who do report it must confront the trauma of the encounter with the police, the investigation of the crime and the ordeal of trial.[1]

Many reasons are given for not reporting rape. If the victim knows her assailant (which is often the case in a nonreported rape), she may not report the crime because of fear of retaliation or because she does not want to get the man in trouble. The "after-the-date" rape victim may have the same feelings. The rape victim who has never seen her assailant before may believe that the police will not be able to solve the crime and therefore conclude that the trouble and embarrassment of reporting the crime would be useless. Other women may either distrust the police or dislike the prospect of having to relate their shocking experiences to male police officers. Many law enforcement agencies now have female officers available for women who find it easier to tell such matters to another woman.

Capacity to Commit Forcible Rape

Vaginal rape is the most common form of rape, with women and girls being the victims not only to rape, but also to sexual assaults and batteries. Women of any age or status may be the victims of rape, including prostitutes.[2]

Under the old common law, a husband could not rape his wife. This concept was probably adopted by all states. A husband could be charged with assault or battery if he used considerable force to compel his wife to have sexual intercourse with him against her will. However, the new sexual assault laws that many states have adopted since 1970 have changed this concept. State statutes in many states now permit husbands to be charged with the rape of their wives under the conditions established by the statutes of the state in which the rape is committed.

Under both the old rape laws and the new sexual assault laws, a husband can be charged as a party to the crime of rape (either as a principal or as an aider and abettor) if he assisted, hired, encouraged, or procured another man to rape his wife. Although it is very rare that one woman rapes another woman, there are a few appellate cases where a woman was convicted as a party to the crime of the rape of another woman after it was proved the woman hired, encouraged, assisted, or procured a man to rape the victim.[3]

In the Missouri case of *State v. Drope*,[4] the defendant and four other men tied the defendant's wife to a bed, and while the defendant held a gun to her head, each of the men had sexual intercourse with the woman. The Supreme Court of Missouri affirmed the defendant's conviction as a principal to the crime of the rape of his wife.

In the 1981 case of *State v. Thomas*,[5] the defendant was found guilty of two counts of first-degree criminal sexual conduct when he forced a woman, at gunpoint, to perform fellatio on her husband. The defendant then forced the woman to perform fellatio on himself. The Supreme Court of Tennessee affirmed the two convictions, holding that a "defendant who forces an innocent party to commit armed robbery, burglary, rape, incest, etc. is guilty as the only principal, even though the defendant does not commit the crime with his own hand." (See chapter 4 on criminal liability.)

The Burden of Proof in a Sexual Assault or Rape Case

In all criminal cases, the state has the burden of proving all essential elements of the crime beyond reasonable doubt. In a sexual assault or rape case, the state must prove beyond reasonable doubt that:

- the crime of sexual assault (or rape) did occur (proof of *corpus delicti*). If both adults consented to a sex act, then the crime of rape did not occur.
- that the defendant was the person who committed the crime. When the offender is a stranger, identification often becomes a critical issue because of recall problems, look-alike problems, and the excitement and trauma of the situation.
- that the sex act was done "without consent" and "against the will" (these terms being synonymous in the law of rape[6]).

The Importance of Corroborative Evidence in a Rape Case

If the clothes of a woman complaining of rape look in order, and she appears as though she has just come from a beauty shop, observers are going to question whether a rape has occurred. Corroborating (affirming) her statements is very important. The woman should be immediately taken to a medical professional for observation, treatment, and the preservation of evidence of the crime of rape.

The defense attorney in the Big Dan's rape trial argues details in the case. The highly charged emotional element involved in the crime of rape, along with the complicated legal issues, brings national attention to such trials.

Statistics show that in as many as 30 percent to 40 percent of the cases that come into the offices of prosecutors in large cities, felony rape charges are not issued. Lack of corroborating evidence is probably the principal reason. Statements of the complaining witness can be corroborated and affirmed by the following:

- scratches, bruises, injuries, torn clothing, blood stains from either the victim or the suspect
- witnesses who heard screams or the sounds of a struggle, or observed either party before, during, or immediately after the assault
- colored photographs of bruises, black and blue marks, lacerations, cuts, scratches, or other injuries to either party as these injuries will disappear within a few days through the healing process
- blood, semen, saliva, nail scrapings taken from the victim or suspect, as well as pubic and head hair obtained at the scene of crime and from the bodies of the victim and suspect. Such genetic material could result in a positive DNA identification as to the identity of the offender.
- weapons or instruments that may have been used to force the victim to submit to the assault
- buttons, torn clothing, items that victim or suspect may have lost in the struggle
- soiled or stained clothing of the suspect and victim that contains blood, seminal stains, or other evidence of the crime
- fingerprints found at the scene of the sexual assault or elsewhere that can be used to corroborate or to identify the suspect

Sexual Assault Cases that Received National Attention

"Wilding" in New York City Central Park
More than thirty youths on a "wilding" spree randomly attacked people in the park. They brutally beat and raped a woman jogger and then left her to die naked in a wooded area. She was found hours later. Six of the youths were convicted of rape but acquitted of attempted murder.

Athletes Who Rape   Studies show that college and high school athletes are involved in a disproportionately high number of rapes. See "When Athletic Aggression Turns Into Sexual Assault" *The New York Times,* June 3, 1990. The article tells of incidents throughout the United States.

New Bedford, Massachusetts   Six men were charged with raping a twenty-two-year-old woman who went into a bar to buy cigarettes and stayed for a quick drink. The woman was raped on a barroom pool table while other men in the bar cheered.

Rape of Woman with Forty-Six Personalities   A Wisconsin jury found that a twenty-nine-year-old man knew of the mental illness of a twenty-seven-year-old woman and manipulated a personality named Jennifer to have sex. The woman's real self said she had no idea she had sex until other personalities revealed it to her. The conviction under a state law forbidding sexual contact with mentally ill persons was reversed on other grounds. *State v. Peterson,* ___, Wis.2d ___ , N.W.2d ___ (1990).

Wisconsin   The police, prosecutor, and defense lawyer all have a responsibility to make sure that blood, semen, hair, etc. obtained in a rape case is tested. No one tested semen obtained in the rape and kidnap of a fifteen-year-old girl. She identified the defendant as the rapist and he served eight and a half years of a sixty-year prison term before someone had the semen tested. The test showed the wrong man was in prison. After release, the man received $500,000 in settlement of a lawsuit against his defense lawyer and $85,260 from the state to compensate for his time in prison.

Akron, Ohio   A physician charged with sixty counts of raping and terrorizing women received prison terms totaling 665 years. Under Ohio law, the doctor technically will be eligible for parole in nine and a half years, but it is unlikely that he will be released that soon.

Madison, Wisconsin   A Wisconsin judge, in 1982, sentenced a man to three years' probation for fondling (sexual assault) the five-year-old daughter of his girlfriend. The judge commented on the record that the little girl was "an unusual, sexually promiscuous young lady." These comments caused voters to petition for the judge's recall, which resulted in his defeat in the following election.

The Controversal Case of Tawana Brawley
Brawley, a black teenager, was missing for four days and when found was smeared with dog feces and wrapped in a trash bag. She told of being raped by white men. Was this a hoax to explain her absence? A New York grand jury found there was no sexual assault and issued a 170-page report. The book *Outrage* (Bantam Books, 1990) also comes to this conclusion.

- observations by doctors and nurses and samples of fluids from vagina, rectum, or oral cavity showing that forcible intercourse had occurred.

The physical evidence collected and preserved by investigating officers could provide strong or conclusive evidence of guilt. On the other hand, lack of physical evidence could result in a weak case. In the 1990 trial of one of the young men accused of raping a woman jogger in New York City's Central Park, members of the jury pointed out that it was the physical evidence that caused them to convict. (See "Physical Evidence Decided Jogger Trial, Jurors Said," *The New York Times,* December 13, 1990.) Six young men on a "wilding" spree that almost killed the woman jogger were convicted of the attack.

The Serial Rapist

Following are the conclusions to the article "The Criminal Behavior of the Serial Rapist" found in the February 1990 issue of the *FBI Law Enforcement Bulletin:*

The research concerning serial rapists' behavior during and following the commission of the crimes has determined that:

- The majority of the rapes were premeditated
- The "con" approach was used most often in initiating contact with the victim
- A threatening presence and verbal threats were used to maintain control over the victim
- Minimal or no force was used in the majority of instances
- The victims physically, passively or verbally resisted the rapists in slightly over 50% of the offenses
- The most common offender reaction to resistance was to verbally threaten the victim
- Slightly over one-third of the offenders experienced a sexual dysfunction, and the preferred sexual acts were vaginal rape and forced fellatio

- Low levels of pleasure were reported by the rapists from the sexual acts
- The rapists tended not to be concerned with precautionary measures to protect their identities
- Approximately one-third of the rapists had consumed alcohol prior to the crime and slightly less reported using some other drug.

The most common post-offense behavior reported by the rapists were feelings of remorse and guilt, following the case in the media and an increase in alcohol and drug consumption.

These characteristics, although not generally applicable to every rapist, can be helpful in learning more about offenders, their behaviors and the heinous crime of rape.

In 1991, a woman reported to the Palm Beach, Florida, police that she had been raped by a nephew of Senator Edward Kennedy at the Kennedy Palm Beach estate. She had been invited to the Kennedy home after meeting the Kennedy party at a local nightclub.

While the New York Central Park incident was a violent attack by strangers upon a woman jogger, the Palm Beach alleged incident concerned acquaintances. Physical evidence is critical in both types of cases. Senator Kennedy's nephew voluntarily gave samples of his blood and hair to Palm Beach police. The police talked to witnesses and inspected the scene of the alleged incident (days after the incident). (See "Kennedy Nephew Gives Blood to Police," *The New York Times,* April 8, 1991.)

After the physical evidence obtained in the Palm Beach case implicated William Kennedy Smith, he was charged with one count of sexual battery (rape in Florida) and a misdemeanor charge of battery. The thirty-year-old nephew of Senator Ted Kennedy denied the allegations made in the nine-page police affidavit.

Proving that the Victim's Fear of Imminent Death or Serious Bodily Injury Was Genuine and Real

If little or no actual force was used, the state must then show that the victim's resistance was overcome by the threat of the use of force and that a genuine and real belief existed that imminent force would be used. The California courts have held that: "While generally the woman has the power to determine for herself the extent to which she feels she can safely resist ... her conduct must always be measured against the degree of force manifested and each case must be resolved on all of the circumstances present."[7]

The Maryland Court of Appeals pointed out in 1981[8] that the "vast majority of jurisdictions have required that the victim's fear be reasonably grounded in order to obviate the need for either proof of actual force on the part of the assailant or physical resistance on the part of the victim."[9] Pointing out that the reasonableness of a victim's apprehension of fear was plainly a question of fact for a jury to determine, the Maryland Court of Appeals held:

> It was for the jury to observe the witnesses and their demeanor, and to judge their credibility and weigh their testimony. Quite obviously, the jury disbelieved Rusk [defendant] and believed Pat's [victim] testimony.

* * *

> Just where persuasion ends and force begins in cases like the present is essentially a factual issue, to be resolved in light of the controlling legal precepts. That threats of force need not be made in any particular manner in order to put a person in fear of bodily harm is well established. . . . Indeed, conduct, rather than words, may convey the threat.

* * *

> That a victim did not scream out for help or attempt to escape, while bearing on the question of consent, is unnecessary where she is restrained by fear of violence.

From "Utmost Resistance" to New Rape Statutes that Eliminate Resistance as a Requirement

The Supreme Court of California observed in 1986 that the law originally demanded "utmost resistance" from a woman in order to prove that the crime of rape had occurred.[10] Not only did the woman have to resist to the "utmost" of her physical capacity, but it also had to be shown that the "resistance must not have ceased throughout the assault." The former rape statute of the state of Wisconsin (former section 940.01) required "utmost resistance" by a woman until the middle 1970s.

Courts and states have moved away from what the Supreme Court of California has properly called the "primitive rule" of utmost resistance. The modified rule was stated by the Supreme Court of California in the case of *People v. McIlvain*[11] as follows:

> A woman who is assaulted need not resist to the point of risking being beaten into insensibility. If she resists to the point where further resistance would be useless or, . . . until her resistance is overcome by force or violence, submission thereafter is not consent.

However, some courts using the new modified test continued to require proof of resistance and would reverse rape convictions where little or no resistance by the woman was shown. Convictions were reversed because the "evidence [was] insufficient to show any real resistance"; and "where protest by the female was 'feeble' "; and "when resistance was absent"; or was of "such equivocal character as to indicate consent."[12]

1991 Report on Rape

- Rape and attempted rape are relatively rare crimes compared to robbery and assault, amounting to less than 3 percent of all violent crime measured by the NCS (National Crime Survey).
- Almost two-thirds of rapes occurred at night. Completed rapes were more likely than attempted rapes to occur at night, particularly between midnight and 6 A.M.
- Most rapes occurred at home. Four in ten completed rapes took place at the victim's home; 2 in 10 occurred at or near a friend's home, and 2 in 10, on the street.
- About 3 in 10 attempted rapes took place at home; 2 in 10 attempted rapes occurred on the street, and about 1 in 10, at a friend's house.
- Black women were significantly more likely to be raped than white women, although a larger number of white women than the total of black, American Indian, Aleut, Eskimo, Asian, and Pacific Islander women were raped each year.
- Women age 16 to 24 were 3 times more likely to be raped than other women. This age pattern was similar for black and white women.
- Women who were separated or divorced or who had never married were 9 times more likely to be raped than those who were married or widowed.
- Nonstranger rape usually occurred in the victim's home (48 percent) or in or near a friend's home (24 percent). About 3 in 10 rapes by strangers occurred on the street; about 2 in 10, at the victim's home.

- Among women of different residential localities, central city residents were the most likely to be raped; those who lived outside the metropolitan area were the least likely.
- Women who rented were more likely than those who owned their own homes to be raped.
- Rape is largely a crime of the older offender. In almost three-fourths of all rapes, the offenders were age 21 or older.
- Of all attempted or completed rapes, 53 percent were reported to the police. Completed rapes and stranger rapes were reported more frequently than attempted rapes and those in which the offender and victim knew each other.
- The presence of a weapon increased the likelihood of the crime being reported to the police. Approximately 7 in 10 rapes were reported when the offender had had a weapon, and fewer than 5 in 10 when the rapist had been unarmed.
- In attempted or completed rapes with one victim and one offender, victims tended to be about the same age as their offenders. More than 6 in 10 of the victims of an offender under age 21 were age 19 or younger. About 3 in 10 victims were age 19 or younger when the offender was between age 21 and 29, and about 6 in 10 of the victims were age 20 to 34. When the offender was 30 or older, 2 in 10 victims were under age 21, and almost 6 in 10 were age 25 or older.
- Most rape victims (about 8 in 10) tried to protect themselves. Those using self-

protection were less likely to be victims of a completed rape than those not taking a self-protective measure.
- When victims were attacked and were thereby put at risk of injury, victims who tried to protect themselves were more likely to be injured (58 percent) than were those who took no measure (46 percent).
- Thirty percent of rape victims were threatened either with a weapon or verbally. About 45 percent of the victims of rape attempts were threatened; 55 percent were attacked. By definition, a completed rape is considered an attack.
- When rape victims knew their offenders, they were about as likely to be injured as victims of strangers. Just over a quarter of victims received medical care, whether or not the victim knew the offender.
- Rapes committed by strangers were more likely to be reported to the police than rapes by nonstrangers.
- Rapes from which physical injury resulted were more likely to be reported to the police than rapes without injury.
- Women raped by someone whom they knew cited, among other specific reasons for not reporting to the police, fear of reprisal (22 percent) and belief that the police would be inefficient (17 percent).
- The opinion that the rape was a personal or private matter was the most common reason for not reporting given by women victimized by someone they knew.

Source: 1991 Bureau of Justice Statistics Report, "Female Victims of Violent Crime."

In the late 1970s and early 1980s, the legislatures of many states did away completely with the requirement of proof that the victim physically resisted her attacker. Although the government must continue to prove the crime of rape beyond a reasonable doubt, resistance is no longer an essential element of the crime in the states making the change. California is one of the states that dropped the requirement of resistance. The 1980 change in the California statutes was tested before the California Supreme Court in the 1986 case of *People v. Barnes,*[13] where a San Francisco woman did not physically resist. In holding that the defendant was properly convicted by a San Francisco jury, the Supreme Court held:

* * *

Marsha testified she engaged in sexual intercourse with appellant because she felt if she refused, he would become physically violent. She based this assessment on appellant's actions and words, including his statements that she was about to "see the bad side" of him and that he could throw her out if he wanted.

* * *

In light of the totality of these circumstances, the jury, having observed the witnesses and their demeanor, could reasonably have concluded that Marsha's fear of physical violence from appellant if she did not submit to sexual intercourse was genuine and reasonable. Under these facts, a reasonable juror could have found that Marsha's subsequent compliance with appellant's urgent insistence on coitus was induced either by force, fear, or both, and, in any case, fell short of a consensual act. . . .

Additionally, Marsha several times communicated her unwillingness to stay and have sexual intercourse with appellant. Appellant should have realized that his threatening conduct, combined with Marsha's rejection of his sexual advances and repeated requests to leave, created a situation where he was able to overcome rather than respect her will. That appellant may have deluded himself into believing her eventual submission represented a consensual act could have been rejected by a rational trier of fact as an unreasonable response to Marsha's conduct. Therefore, the jury's rejection of appellant's defense that he reasonably believed she consented was proper given the totality of these circumstances.

* * *

Applying these principles, it cannot be said that Marsha's testimony is inherently improbable. She testified she returned to the room because she felt she could not leave without appellant's aid. The jury may well have concluded her return was a reasonable response, especially since it was cold outside and at that point the situation had not so grossly deteriorated.

* * *

Marsha also explained that she pretended to be a willing partner and to invite appellant to her house in an attempt to extricate herself from the situation. She testified that she engaged in sexual intercourse to avoid physical violence. A reasonable juror could have concluded that her subsequent act of exchanging kisses was part of a similar effort to avoid physical violence by simulating reciprocation. . . . Marsha was not required to display either active or passive resistance in order to save her testimony from inherent improbability, or to "develop corroborative evidence." (*People v. Salazar, supra,* 144 Cal.App.3d at p. 807, 193 Cal.Rptr. 1.)

Finally, the fact that Marsha fell asleep after sexual intercourse was of little consequence. Her failure to stay alert and awake was at least susceptible of the conclusion that she was physically exhausted after having spent almost two hours attempting to extricate herself from an escalating and potentially dangerous situation. Moreover, the jury could have reasonably concluded that in Marsha's judgment, the danger of physical violence had passed with the violation of her physical integrity and that, therefore, she could temporarily relax. Although the record is not clear, it appears that any slumber to which she succumbed lasted but a brief period of time—perhaps only minutes.

When she awoke, she renewed her efforts to leave by cajoling appellant into letting her out of the gate. Thereafter, she called Kaiser Hospital and reported to the sexual trauma center for an examination. At most, her falling asleep was an unusual circumstance and does not render the entirety of her testimony inherently improbable. . . .

Under these circumstances, this court holds that the evidence was sufficient to sustain appellant's conviction of rape. The false imprisonment conviction must also be affirmed, as its commission was attendant to the rape.

* * *

Defense Used in Forcible Rape Cases Where the Defendant Is an Acquaintance

Close to one-half of the forcible rapes that are reported are committed by friends, acquaintances, or relatives. The "after-the-date" rape (or "dates who rape") case can be particularly difficult to prove unless evidence of actual physical violence exists. Because of the friendly and sometimes close relationship that existed between the parties, the man can often convincingly argue:

Yes, the parties had sex, but:

she consented	and her conduct shows she consented (after all, she invited me up to her apartment, or she came up to my apartment late at night).
I honestly thought she consented	"It is a defense to a charge of forcible rape that the defendant entertained a reasonable and good faith belief that the female person voluntarily consented to engage in sexual intercourse" (*California Jury Instruction* 10.23).[14]
she never did say "no"	And I thought that because she didn't say no, she was consenting.
she consented, then changed her mind during the sex	and did not clearly communicate her change of mind.
the manner in which the woman dressed was sexy and provocative and her conduct (such as placing her hand on the defendant's upper thigh)	which led the defendant on, and she did not object until things got out of hand (a well-known professional football player was acquitted in a 1987 rape trial using this defense).

she consented, but later developed guilt feelings and regretted what she did

but before and during the sex, she consented. (This defense is sometimes used with the "groupie defense." Athletes and performers charged with rape often use the "groupie defense" arguing that the victim pursued and pestered them.)

Convictions for Lesser or Other Offenses When the Rape Case Is "Weak"

A rape case can be classified as a "weak" case if there is a lack of corroborating evidence; if the woman is an ineffective witness; or becomes so upset that she cannot testify effectively; or if the woman's conduct had been such that it could be interpreted as giving consent to the sex. Other factors that should also be considered are the effectiveness and persuasive abilities of the defense lawyer, and type of witness that the defendant might be.

In anticipating such problems, prosecutors could file a number of charges, including lesser charges to fall back on. Examples of such charges are:

- *Sexual battery or sexual assault.* For example, see the 1983 case of *People v. Margiolas,* in which the rape charge was dropped owing to lack of evidence of resistance, and the defendant was convicted of a misdemeanor "sexual battery," as he admitted that he forcibly unbuttoned the woman's blouse despite her verbal as well as physical objections.[15]
- *"Statutory rape,"* where the victim is underage. In the 1981 case of *Michael M. v. Superior Court of Sonoma County (California),*[16] a forcible rape of a sixteen and a half-year-old girl was committed by the defendant, who was then seventeen and a half years old. Because the state was unable to present proof sufficient to obtain a conviction for forcible rape, the defendant was charged with and convicted of "statutory rape." The U.S. Supreme Court affirmed the conviction. The California prosecutor stated in his brief that the "statutory rape" statute "is commonly employed in situations involving force, prostitution, pornography, coercion due to status relationships, and the state's interest in these situations is apparent." Justice John Paul Stevens dissented, stating:

  I cannot accept the State's argument that the constitutionality of the discriminatory rule can be saved by an assumption that prosecutors will commonly invoke this statute only in cases that actually involve a forcible rape, but one that cannot be established by proof beyond a reasonable doubt. That assumption implies that a State has a legitimate interest in convicting a defendant on evidence that is constitutionally insufficient. Of course, the State may create a lesser-included offense that would authorize punishment of the more guilty party, but surely the interest in obtaining convictions on inadequate proof cannot justify a statute that punishes one who is equally or less guilty than his partner.[17]

- *Sodomy and/or Kidnapping.* Sodomy (or "sexual perversion" or "an abominable and detestable crime against nature") does not require a showing of the use of force for conviction. The following case illustrates:

Classifications of Rape

Type of Rape	Definition	Most Common Defense Used
Forcible rape by a stranger	A 1991 report by the Bureau of Justice Statistics* showed that about half of the reported forcible rapes occurred between strangers.	Victim or other witnesses have identified the wrong man (mistaken identification).
Forcible rape by an acquaintance, friend or relative	Many of these offenses are not reported to law enforcement agencies. The "after-the-date" rape is particularly hard to prosecute unless substantial evidence is available.	Victim consented to the sexual act.
Nonforcible rape in which the victim is under age of consent	All states have laws that protect infants and children from sexual seduction by adults. Such statutory rape or SIWAC (sexual intercourse with a child) laws punish as a major crime such sexual intercourse (or sexual conduct) when committed with a child.	Sex act did not occur or that the defendant made an honest mistake as to the child's age (not permitted as a defense in most states).
Nonforcible rape in which the victim was mentally defective or diseased and incapable of giving consent	This type of criminal statute seeks to protect persons who are mentally incompetent and incapable of giving consent to sexual acts. The offense requires that the state show that the defendant knew of mental incapacity of the victim.\nA Wisconsin man was convicted of having sex with a woman who doctors say has forty-six personalities. When the conviction was overturned, prosecutors decided not to retry the case because of the stress on the woman.	Defendant denies that he knew of the mental incapacity of the victim or that any sex act occurred.
Nonforcible rape in which the victim is unconscious	Such statutes seek to protect persons who are unconscious (the defendant is aware of this condition). Some statutes also forbid sexual intercourse with a person known to be in a stupor. Such stupor could be caused by alcohol or drugs.	Defendant asserts that the person was conscious and consented or that no sex act occurred.
Sexual intercourse by deception	Such statutes punish sexual intercourse in which the victim is deceived into thinking that the act is a marital act. For example, a phony wedding is staged by the defendant. (This type of statute is now seldom enacted.)	No deception or sexual act occurred.
Sexual intercourse obtained by threats other than threats of violence, which would be forcible rape	In the few states that have enacted a statute such as this, the threat might be to disclose information that the victim did not want disclosed. Today, job-related sexual harassment is remedied through civil proceedings or in other ways.	No threat was made or implied or no sexual act occurred.

*Report NCJ–126826 entitled "Female Victims of Violent Crime."

To Obtain Sex, a Phony Cop Threatened Arrest and Jail—Is this Rape?

The Massachusetts Supreme Judicial held that the phony cop was properly indicted for rape by comparing "force" in robbery with that used in rape. Massachusetts courts have held that in robbery "actual force is applied to the body, constructive force is by threatening words or gestures and operate on the mind" (324 Mass. 467) and whether "actual or constructive force is employed, the degree of force is immaterial so long as it is sufficient to obtain the victim's property against his will" (362 Mass. 87). The Supreme Judicial Court held in the case of *Commonwealth v. Caracciola*, 409 Mass. 648, 569 N.E.2d 744, 49 CrL 1074 (1991) that:

> Applying the statutory language to the evidence presented, we conclude there was evidence of force and constraint of the victim's will. The evidence indicates that the defendant wore a gun; that he ordered the victim into his car; that he named a number of police officers; that he gave her a false name; and that he told her he was a police officer, and would imprison her if she did not obey him. The defendant made the complainant beg him not to "lock her up." The facts indicate that the woman was "petrified" by the defendant's threats that he would "lock her up." The issue whether, in light of the circumstances, the victim's obedience or submission to the defendant's threats was by force and against her will is for the petit jury.

STATE v. SANTOS
Supreme Court of Rhode Island (1980) 122 R.I. 799, 413 A.2d 58

The victim met the defendant at a tavern where they talked and danced for three hours until closing time. After having a cup of coffee at a nearby restaurant, the woman testified that the defendant grabbed her and would not let her go. The defendant told her to get into his car and stated that he had a knife, which he would use if he had to. The woman was driven to a secluded area, where the defendant first had sexual intercourse and then anal intercourse with her. The woman stated that she was too afraid to resist other than to push the defendant away. The defendant asked that she not complain that she had been raped, as two other women had previously done so. The jury acquitted the defendant of rape and kidnapping but convicted him of transporting for immoral purposes and committing an abominable and detestable crime against nature (anal intercourse). The Supreme Court of Rhode Island affirmed the convictions.

- *Burglary* is defined as an unlawful entry into a building or dwelling with intent to commit an offense (in some states a "felony") or intent to steal. The following case is not a forcible rape case but illustrates how the crime of burglary may be charged:

CLADD v. STATE
Supreme Court of Florida (1981) 398 So.2d 442

The defendant was separated from his wife (no legal action commenced). One morning he used a crowbar to break into her apartment, in which he had no possessory interest. He struck the woman and attempted to throw her over a second-floor stair railing. The next morning he attempted to break into the apartment again but left as the police arrived. The defendant was convicted of burglary and attempted burglary. In affirming the convictions, the Supreme Court of Florida held:

Since burglary is an invasion of the possessory property of another, where the premises are in the sole possession of the wife, the husband can be guilty of burglary if he makes a nonconsensual entry into her premises with intent to commit an offense, the same as he can be guilty of larceny of his wife's separate property.

The Effect of Delay in Reporting

After a sexual assault, the victim is many times confused and fearful of her assailant returning. This could result in a delay in reporting the assault to the authorities. Such delay can seriously weaken the possibilities of a conviction. Not only does the delay raise the question of credibility concerning the allegations of the victim, but it also substantially diminishes the possibility of obtaining physical evidence concerning the offense. Even if such physical evidence is found, the intervening period of time weakens the probative value of the evidence, since it raises the possibility that the evidence found came from a source other than the assailant.

False Reporting

The FBI Uniform Crime Reports state that "a national average of 15% of all forcible rapes reported to police were determined by our investigations to be unfounded. In other words, the police established that no forcible rape offense or attempt occurred."

It should be noted, however, that sexual assault is not the only offense subject to false reporting. About the same percentage of burglaries and auto thefts are also falsely reported primarily for the purpose of obtaining insurance money. Armed robberies of single-employee businesses are sometimes falsely reported to the financial benefit of that employee; and one can only speculate about the number of homes, businesses, and other buildings that are destroyed in "accidental" fires.

Rape Shield Laws

Many states have passed rape shield laws that limit the extent to which a defense lawyer can inquire into the details of a rape victim's sex life and practice. These laws were passed to protect victims of rape and to encourage women to report rape and cooperate in prosecuting offenders.

The National Organization for Women (NOW) urges that neither specific acts of prior sexual conduct nor evidence of the previous general reputation of the victim for unchastity should be admitted.

All courts permit defense lawyers to ask the victim whether she has ever had sexual relations with the defendant. If she answers no, this would then generally close the door to further questions. However, if the woman answers yes, then further questions may be asked as to the sexual relationship.

Other exceptions that could be made a part of a state's rape shield law could be:

- evidence that the woman (or accuser) has made false allegations of sexual assault in the past, or
- questions as to the source or origins of semen, pregnancy, or disease that were not linked to the defendant.

In 1990, the State of New York strengthened the state's rape shield law in part because of angry public reaction to the conduct of defense lawyers when women commence civil lawsuits. Marla Hanson, a former New York model, sued a landlord who hired other men to attack her and slash her face with razors. The defense lawyer insinuated with his questioning that she was "a racist, a prostitute and a slut." (See "New York Limits Trial Talk on Sex," *The New York Times*, July 30, 1990.)

In the 1984 case of *State v. Vaughn*,[18] the defendant was convicted of raping a fifteen-year-old runaway. Evidence was permitted showing that she had slept several nights in a bed with the defendant and two other women and had had sex with the defendant. The Supreme Court of Louisiana held that it was proper to forbid evidence that the girl had sex with another man after she left the defendant and before the rape.

The case of *State v. Colbath*, 130 N.H. 316, 540 A. 2d 1212 (1988), received additional attention because the decision was written by Justice David H. Souter before he was appointed to the U.S. Supreme Court. The question before the Supreme Court of New Hampshire in this case was whether the conduct of the woman who complained of the rape should have been admitted into evidence for the jury to consider. Just before the alleged rape, the parties were in a tavern where the woman was sexually provocative toward several men, including the defendant. The defendant testified that he had engaged in "feeling the [woman's] breasts [and] bottom [and that she had been] rubbing his crotch." The woman and the defendant then left the tavern and went to the defendant's trailer where they had sex. The woman said it was forcible and the defendant stated it was with consent. In holding that the evidence should have been admitted under the New Hampshire rape shield law for consideration by the jury, Justice Souter wrote:

* * *

In this case ... the jury could have taken evidence of the complainant's openly sexually provocative behavior toward a group of men as evidence of her probable attitude toward an individual within the group. Evidence that the publicly inviting acts occurred closely in time to the alleged sexual assault by one such man could have been viewed as indicating the complainant's likely attitude at the time of the sexual activity in question.

* * *

The Defense that the Woman Was a Prostitute

Victims in practically all rape cases are women or children. The defense that a woman is (or has been known as) a prostitute might suggest that a prostitute cannot be raped. This is not true. Prostitutes can be raped. They do not consent to sexual acts with everyone.

In recent years, an increasing number of defendants charged with rape have used the defense that the victim was a prostitute. These defendants allege there was a fight over the price or that the woman agreed to the price and then there was an argument over something and the woman subsequently made up the rape accusation to get even with the man. The following case is used to illustrate:

HARRIS v. STATE
Supreme Court of Georgia (1987) 257 Ga. 666, 362 S.E.2d 211

The victim was awakened by the defendant early in the morning as she was sleeping with her two-year-old daughter. The defendant had a large knife that he used to threaten the life of the victim and her child if she did not "make love to him." During the intercourse, the victim's finger was cut. Traces of her blood were found on the defendant's clothing after he was apprehended. A niece of the victim had been awakened by the noises, left the house, and went to a neighbor for help. The defendant was apprehended in the neighborhood. The defendant acknowledged on the witness stand that he had intercourse with the woman but he insisted that it was with her consent. The defendant contended the woman was a prostitute and he was at her home to negotiate a price for sex. The trial judge refused to admit evidence of the woman's prior sexual history under Georgia's Rape Shield Statute. The Rape Shield Statute was held to be constitutional. In affirming the defendant's conviction for rape, the Georgia Supreme Court held:

* * *

> "Rape 'is highly reprehensible, both in a moral sense and in its almost total contempt for the personal integrity and autonomy of the female victim ... Short of homicide, it is the "ultimate violation of self." '[cit.]" Warren v. State, supra at 155, 336 S.E.2d 221. Women who have already been victimized do not wish to be placed in the position of having their past "self" exposed when it serves no purpose but to "chill" the reporting of a crime. ·
>
> Contrary to the position of the appellant, if a victim is a prostitute, then it does not mean she cannot be raped nor does it mean she consents to sexual acts with everyone. No woman wishes to expose her private life to unnecessary public probing. The state has a legitimate interest in protecting witnesses from harassment and intimidation. Thorough cross-examination is a principal means of ascertaining the truth, but a witness has a "right ... to be examined only as to relevant matter and to be protected from improper questions and from harsh or insulting demeanor." OCGA § 24–9–62. (Georgia's Rape Shield Statute)

* * *

The Occasional Victim Who Recants (Changes His or Her Story)

In 1985, an Illinois rape case received national attention when the victim recanted (withdrew) her accusations that she had been raped by Gary Dotson. At the time, Dotson was serving his sixth year of a twenty-five- to fifty-year sentence for aggravated kidnapping and rape.

The victim appeared in court and testified that she had perjured herself in the rape trial six years earlier. Because of inconsistencies in her story, the trial court refused to vacate Dotson's convictions. These inconsistencies also appeared in the publicly televised hearings conducted by an Illinois board headed by the

Illinois governor. The governor did not pardon Dotson but commuted his sentence to the time he had served. An extensive review of the matter is found in Dotson's appeal from the trial court ruling (*People v. Dotson,* 516 N.E.2d 718). In affirming the trial court's ruling, the court stated the Illinois rule as to recanted testimony as follows:

> Recanting testimony is regarded as very unreliable, and a court will usually deny a new trial based on that ground where it is not satisfied that such testimony is true. Especially is this true where the recantation relied on involves a confession of perjury. The recanting testimony of witnesses will not ordinarily be regarded as sufficient ground for a new trial except in extraordinary and unusual cases. (33 A.L.R. p. 550, note.) The affidavit of a recanting witness is not entitled to so much weight as to justify the conclusion that the evidence given by him was corrupt and willfully false. The conclusion of the jury would rather warrant the presumption that his testimony was truthful and his affidavit false." (344 Ill. 261, 265, 176 N.E. 314, 315.)

C. The Sexual Assault Statutes of the 1970s and 1980s

In the early 1970s, there was much criticism of the traditional rape statutes used by most states. These statutes generally followed the old common law and presented many problems in prosecuting rape offenders. In the mid-1970s, states commenced enacting comprehensive "sexual assault" laws, which brought about some or all of the changes indicated in the chart on page 543.

Danger of HIV Infection (AIDS) to Victims of Sexual Assault

With the spread of HIV infection (AIDS), another very serious risk has been added to other risks faced by victims of sexual assault. A growing number of courts are holding that accused sex offenders be required to submit to HIV tests. In the 1991 case of *Government of Virgin Islands v. Roberts,* 756 F. Supp. 898 (D.V.I.), the federal court held that testing before conviction could be ordered:

- when probable cause existed to believe that a sexual assault had occurred and it was the defendant who had committed the crime, and
- information as to the test results be given only to the defendant, the victim, and the doctors of both parties.

The Court in the *Roberts* case found a "compelling need" to order the test from the point of view of the victim who would have great anxiety and would make medical decisions based upon the outcome of the test. Also, if the victim knew she had been infected, it would affect her decision "to engage in intimate relations" or have children.

D. Homosexual Rape

Males may be raped by forcible anal sodomy and other forms of homosexual rape. Such offenses are not as common as rape of women except, as reports indicate,

Traditional Rape and the New Sexual Assault Laws

Old Common Law Rules Regarding Rape	*Statutory Changes Enacted in Many States*
• Only females can be the victims of rape.	• Any person (male or female) may be a victim.
• Only a male could directly commit the crime.	• Any person (male or female) can directly commit the crime. (See the 1986 case of *State v. Stevens,* 510 A.2d 1070, where it was held an adult woman could be charged with having sexual intercourse with a thirteen-year-old boy.)
• A husband could not rape his wife (under the common law, however, the husband could be charged with assault and battery).	• A husband can be charged with the rape of his wife under the law of states that have made this change from the old common law.
• Rape was defined in one (or at most a few) degree.	• A variety of degrees of criminal conduct are defined in more specific language.
• Rape was defined only as the insertion of the penis into a vagina by force and against the will of the female.	• "Sexual intercourse" is broadly defined not only as vaginal intercourse, but also "cunnilingus, fellatio, anal intercourse, or any other intrusion, however slight, of any part of a person's body or of any object into the genital or anal opening of another, but emission of semen is not required" (Section 940.225[5][c] of the Wisconsin Criminal Code).
• Common law rape did not include the crime of "offensive touching" (however, this could be charged either as disorderly conduct or assault and sometimes battery if there was an injury).	• Many modern sexual assault laws include the offense of "offensive touching" in that they forbid "sexual contact" (intentional touching of an intimate part of another person's body without consent).
• "Utmost resistance" and "resistance" was required under the old common law.	• Resistance is no longer an essential element of the crime of rape. Instead, many states require proof that the sex act was done "without consent" and "against the will" of the victim.
• Rape was classified as a crime against sexual morality.	• Sexual assault is more often classified as a crime against a person.

within prisons. U.S. Supreme Court Justice Harry A. Blackmun wrote in his dissenting opinion in the 1980 case of *United States v. Bailey:*

> A youthful inmate can expect to be subjected to homosexual gang rape his first night in jail, or, it has been said, even in the van on the way to jail. Weaker inmates become the property of stronger prisoners or gangs, who sell the sexual services to the victim. Prison officials either are disinterested in stopping abuse of prisoners by other prisoners or are incapable of doing so, given the limited resources society allocates to the prison system. Prison officials often are merely indifferent to serious health and safety needs of prisoners as well.[19]

The defendant in the 1984 case of *United States v. Boone*[20] testified that he used a razor blade in self-defense because he feared that the complainant was going to forcibly commit anal sodomy on him. As the trial judge did not believe the defendant and concluded that the issue was weak, he did not give a jury instruction on self-defense. The court of appeals reversed, holding that this issue should have gone to the jury. Pointing out that a woman who had alleged such facts after cutting up another person would be entitled to instructions on self-defense, the court held that the results should be the same "unless we are to make sexist differences."

E. "Statutory Rape"

Probably all states have statutes that make sexual intercourse with a female who is not the wife of the perpetrator a criminal offense if the female is under the age stated by the state criminal code. This crime is called "statutory rape." The origin of the American statutes go back to the English statute of 1275, when the age of consent was set at twelve years. In 1576, the age was reduced to ten years. California, for example, enacted its first statute in 1850 making the age ten. In 1913, it was fixed at eighteen, where it remained into the 1980s.

In 1981, the California "statutory rape" statute was challenged before the U.S. Supreme Court, when it was alleged that the statute unlawfully discriminates on the basis of gender, since men alone were criminally liable under the statute. The Court upheld the power of the states to enact such statutes in the case of *Michael M. v. Superior Court of Sonoma County*,[21] holding:

> We are satisfied not only that the prevention of illegitimate pregnancy is at least one of the "purposes" of the statute, but that the State has a strong interest in preventing such pregnancy. At the risk of stating the obvious, teenage pregnancies, which have increased dramatically over the last two decades, have significant social, medical and economic consequences for both the mother and her child, and the State. Of particular concern to the State is that approximately half of all teenage pregnancies end in abortion. And of those children who are born, their illegitimacy makes them likely candidates to become wards of the State.
>
> We need not be medical doctors to discern that young men and young women are not similarly situated with respect to the problems and the risks of sexual intercourse. Only women may become pregnant and they suffer disproportionately the profound physical, emotional, and psychological consequences of sexual activity. The statute at issue here protects women from sexual intercourse at an age when those consequences are particularly severe.
>
> The question thus boils down to whether a State may attack the problem of sexual intercourse and teenage pregnancy directly by prohibiting a male from having sexual intercourse with a minor female. We hold that such a statute is sufficiently related to the State's objectives to pass constitutional muster.
>
> Because virtually all of the significant harmful and inescapably identifiable consequences of teenage pregnancy fall on the young female, a legislature acts well within its authority when it elects to punish only the participant who, by nature, suffers few of the consequences of his conduct. It is hardly unreasonable for a legislature acting to protect minor females to exclude them from punishment. Moreover, the risk of pregnancy itself constitutes a substantial deterrence to young females. No similar

---

Sexual Misbehavior, or a Felony?

An eighteen and a half-year-old high school senior has a fifteen-year-old girlfriend. They have sex together with both parties consenting. Is this a case of "kids will be kids" where both parties are sexually active? Some law enforcement officers, prosecutors, and judges point out that young men have been doing this going back to the horse and buggy days. Are they correct? Do such comments condone and approve of such behavior?

If the girl's parents discover what is going on and very angrily demand prosecution, should a prosecutor charge the young man with a felony? Or if high school officials come upon the couple during a sex act and demand that an example be set, should the young man (an adult) be charged with the felony of having sex with a minor?

If the girl did not consent to the sex, the cases would very uniformly be charged as rape (or forcible sexual assault). However, where the parties are both very young and both consent, very few of the cases are charged criminally.

Should such cases be left to the discretion of parents, law enforcement officers, and prosecutors as they have in past years? Or should state legislative bodies provide additional laws governing such situations? An example of such a proposed enactment provides:

> Criminally charges cannot be issued if the child consents and the offender is no more than four years older than the victim (for example, a nineteen-year-old has sexual relations with a sixteen-year-old).

---

natural sanctions deter males. A criminal sanction imposed solely on males thus serves to roughly "equalize" the deterrents on the sexes.

Many states have statutes that do not permit the defense of mistake as to the age of a minor. In such states, a defendant could not argue before a jury that he honestly made a mistake as to the age of the minor. However, other states do not have such statutes. The 1984 case of *State v. Elton*[22] occurred before the Utah legislature disallowed a mistake of fact as to age of a minor as a defense. In the *Elton* case, the Utah Supreme Court held the defendant could use the defense.

F. Sexual Abuse and Exploitation of Children

In 1982, the U.S. Supreme Court stated in *New York v. Ferber:*[23]

> In recent years, the exploitive use of children in the production of pornography has become a serious national problem. The federal government and forty-seven States have sought to combat the problem with statutes specifically directed at the production of child pornography. At least half of such statutes do not require that the materials produced be legally obscene. Thirty-five States and the United States Congress have also passed legislation prohibiting the distribution of such materials; twenty States prohibit the distribution of material depicting children engaged in sexual conduct without requiring that the material be legally obscene.

The defendant in the case of *New York v. Ferber* challenged the child pornography law of New York. The U.S. Supreme Court stated that:

- nineteen states prohibit the dissemination of material depicting children engaged in sexual conduct, regardless of whether the material is obscene
- fifteen states prohibit the dissemination of such material only if it is obscene
- twelve states prohibit only the use of minors in the production of the material.

The U.S. Supreme Court gave the following reasons for holding that state child pornography statutes do not violate the First Amendment of the U.S. Constitution:

First. It is evident beyond the need for elaboration that a state's interest in "safeguarding the physical and psychological well being of a minor" is "compelling. . . . A democratic society rests, for its continuance, upon the healthy well-rounded growth of young people into full maturity as citizens."

* * *

Second. The distribution of photographs and films depicting sexual activity by juveniles is intrinsically related to the sexual abuse of children in at least two ways. First, the materials produced are a permanent record of the children's participation and the harm to the child is exacerbated by their circulation. Second, the distribution network for child pornography must be closed if the production of material which requires the sexual exploitation of children is to be effectively controlled. Indeed, there is no serious contention that the legislature was unjustified in believing that it is difficult, if not impossible, to halt the exploitation of children by pursuing only those who produce the photographs and movies. While the production of pornographic materials is a low-profile, clandestine industry, the need to market the resulting products requires a visible apparatus of distribution. The most expeditious if not the only practical method of law enforcement may be to dry up the market for this material by imposing severe criminal penalties on persons selling, advertising, or otherwise promoting the product.

* * *

Third. The advertising and selling of child pornography provides an economic motive for and is thus an integral part of the production of such materials, an activity illegal throughout the nation.

* * *

Fourth. The value of permitting live performances and photographic reproductions of children engaged in lewd sexual conduct is exceedingly modest, if not *de minimis.* We consider it unlikely that visual depictions of children performing sexual acts or lewdly exhibiting their genitals would often constitute an important and necessary part of a literary performance or scientific or educational work.

* * *

Fifth. Recognizing and classifying child pornography as a category of material outside the protection of the First Amendment is not incompatible with our earlier decisions.

The McMartin Trial: Longest and Most Expensive Proceeding in the United States

After six years of accusations, the McMartin Preschool child molesting case came to an end in 1990. It had been the longest and most expensive criminal trial in American history. A Los Angeles jury acquitted sixty-two-year-old Peggy Buckey and her thirty-one-year-old son, Raymond Buckey, of fifty-two criminal counts of sodomy, rape, and oral copulation against young children. Several months later, the thirteen counts against Raymond Buckey, on which the jury deadlocked, were dismissed.

The original criminal case involved seven defendants, forty-two alleged victims (all preschool children), and 321 counts of criminal child molestation charges. Charges were dropped against five defendants, which also reduced the number of alleged victims to eleven. The case received national attention over the years it dragged on. The shocking accusations also included satanism, animal mutilations, and conspiracy.

Reputations were ruined and lives were shattered; the school was demolished and the California legal system took a beating. The costs of the criminal proceedings were estimated at $13.5 million. Raymond Buckey was in jail for five years, one of the longest pretrial detentions in U.S. history. His mother, Peggy Buckey, spent almost two years in jail.

The preliminary hearing in the case took eighteen months. At the end of five years of criminal proceedings, the children who were alleged to have been molested when they were four and five years old were nine and ten years old. The former toddlers had grown to adolescence and were testifying on the witness stand about childhood memories that had faded.

Publicity about the McMartin Preschool trial was nationwide. Geraldo Rivera, Oprah Winfrey, and "60 Minutes" were among the many shows that covered the trial. The references to bizarre sex acts and naked children shocked audiences from coast to coast.

The lead article in the December 1989 National District Attorneys *Bulletin* covered the McMartin trial. It stated that "we can all see the mistakes that were made" and asked the question, "Could this happen again?" The McMartin trial will continue to be talked about, written about, and used as an example for years to come.

G. The Crime of Incest

The crime of incest may be committed by adults within a family, but the public concern and prosecution are generally for cases involving children. Like "statutory rape," the crime does not require a showing that force was used (or threatened) or that the victim did not consent. Incest was not a crime at common law, nor was it statutorized in England until 1908. Before that time, the offense was dealt with by the English ecclesiastical (religious) courts. Probably all the states have statutes making the offense a crime.

An article entitled "Incest: The Last Taboo," in the January 1984 *FBI Law Enforcement Bulletin,* states:

> One thing every State has in common is the prohibition of marriage between parents and children, between siblings, between grandparents and grandchildren, uncles and nieces, and aunts and nephews.

Statutes Seeking to Protect Children

All states forbid adults from having sexual intercourse or sexual contact with a child and make such conduct a crime.* Children who have not reached the age of majority are deemed not capable of giving consent to sexual intercourse. The offense of having sexual intercourse with a child is called "statutory rape" or "SIWAC" (sexual intercourse with a child).

Law enforcement officers sometimes come upon persons having consensual sexual relations in cars, parks, and other public places. If the parties are both adults, they often are warned and released. However, charges could be brought against them. If one or both of the parties are minors, most law enforcement officers would bring the parties to the police station or sheriff's office where the parents would be called and asked to come down to the station. After the parents are informed of the facts, the minors are released to the parents who can then determine what further action will be taken, if any.

In Your State: *Statute Number*
Sex with a child under age _____ is _____
Sex with a child under age _____ is _____
Sex with a child under age _____ is _____

How would the following be charged in your state?

	Statute Number
Sexual abuse of a child	_____
Enticing a child for immoral purposes	_____
Sexual exploitation of a child	_____
Incest involving a child	_____
Exposing a minor to harmful material	_____
Other statutes	_____
Does your state have a "sexually dangerous person" statute (or chapter)?	_____
Does your state have a child abuse reporting statute?	_____

*The exception to this is the adult who is legally married to a child as the sexual relations are therefore marital relations

Incest is usually defined as sexual exploitation between persons so closely related that marriage is prohibited by law. While this definition indicates that there is sexual intercourse, it is important to note that not all incestuous relationships involve intercourse. The term "intercourse" refers specifically to sexual activity between two individuals of the opposite sex. Beyond this usual definition are two other types of sexual child molestation that are closely related to incest and share some common features.

The first type, psychological incest, does not require that the individuals be blood relatives. It only requires that the adult assume the role of a parent. This type of incest extends to other nonrelated family members as well, such as step-uncles and aunts and step-siblings. This type of incest often occurs in families that include a step-parent, a foster parent, or a live-in boyfriend of the mother.

The second type of incest involves sexual contact between persons of the same sex, such as father/son, mother/daughter, or siblings of the same sex. Because, father/son and mother/daughter incest are basically unstudied areas, very little can be written about their frequency of occurrence, the dynamics of the situation, the traumatic effects, or mode of treatment. It is known that in these types of incest, the parent is usually either a latent or overt homosexual.

Current Controversy

Should News Organizations Identify Victims of Sexual Attacks by Name?

Some states have laws forbidding the identification of victims of sexual offenses. Florida, for example, punishes the publication by news organizations of the identity of a sex offense victim as a misdemeanor. However, no criminal prosecution has ever been pursued of Florida's eighty-year-old law. Victims have instead chosen to commence civil lawsuits to collect damages for wrongs created by this law. The following two civil cases have come before the U.S. Supreme Court:

Cox Broadcasting Corp. v. Cohn, 420 U.S. 469, 95 S.Ct. 1029 (1975). A Georgia newspaper published the name of a victim of a sexual assault obtained from official court records. The U.S. Supreme Court held that "the protection of the First Amendment" bars (forbade) the civil recovery in this Georgia case.

The Florida Star v. B. J. F., 491 U.S. 524, 109 S.Ct. 2603 (1989). A Florida woman sued the newspaper for publishing her name as a rape victim. The accurate information was obtained from a police report. In reversing her civil recovery, the U.S. Supreme Court held that Florida had to take "more careful and inclusive precautions" in forbidding the names of victims of sexual crimes.

The accusations of rape at the Kennedy Palm Beach Florida estate in 1991 again raised the issue of identifying victims of sex crimes by news organizations. NBC News and the *New York Times* identified the woman in the 1991 Palm Beach case with details so unflattering that a defense lawyer could use such information to discredit the woman (if such evidence could get past the Florida rape shield law).

The Privacy of Victims of Sex Crimes Should Be Respected	*The First Amendment Freedom of the Press Should Prevail*
If names of sex crimes victims are used by news organizations, fewer victims of sex crimes will report offenses. Television and newspaper disclosures embarrass victims and their families. Victims' right to privacy should be respected unless they agree to be publicly identified.	Most news organizations as a matter of policy will not disclose the identity of victims of sex crimes. However, the First Amendment gives news organizations the right to publish this type of information. As the identity of the man accused of rape is published, the identity of the woman accusing him should also be published.

The article also points out that it is estimated that between 60,000 and 100,000 female children are sexually abused annually and that 80 percent of sexual abuse is not reported. It is believed that incest affects more than 10 percent of all American families, with at least 5,000 cases of father/daughter incest.

Penalties for incest, the article reports, range from ninety days to life imprisonment. Enforcement, however, is practically impossible unless a member of the family cooperates. Unfortunately, the credibility of the child victim is often attacked and severely questioned.

In 90 percent of cases, the victim is female and the abuse may commence while the child is too young to realize the significance of the problem. When the child becomes knowledgeable about what has happened, or is happening, the child will probably feel guilt, betrayal, confusion, and fright.

The defendant in the case of *Hamilton v. Commonwealth*[24] was convicted of both rape and incest, resulting from a single act of sexual intercourse with his then ten-year-old daughter. The Supreme Court of Kentucky held that the two convictions for the single act violated double jeopardy and vacated the incest conviction. The conviction for rape was affirmed with the life imprisonment sentence.

H. "Sexually Dangerous Persons" Laws

About half of the states have enacted laws known as "sexually dangerous persons" or "sexual psychopath" laws. These laws permit a prosecutor to seek institutionalization rather than criminal imprisonment of defendants charged with certain sex offenses. In other states, prosecutors can seek treatment in addition to imprisonment.

In 1986, The U.S. Supreme Court heard the case of *Allen v. Illinois*[25] where the defendant was declared to be a sexually dangerous person under the Illinois Sexually Dangerous Person Act. In holding that the Illinois proceedings were essentially civil in nature, the U.S. Supreme Court affirmed the Illinois statute and proceedings holding:

> For the reasons stated, we conclude that the Illinois proceedings here considered were not "criminal" within the meaning of the Fifth Amendment to the United States Constitution, and that due process does not independently require application of the privilege. Here, as in *Addington,* "[t]he essence of federalism is that states must be free to develop a variety of solutions to problems and not be forced into a common, uniform mold" of the sort urged by petitioner. 441 U.S., at 431. The judgment of the Supreme Court of Illinois is therefore *Affirmed.*

Questions and Problems for Chapter 18

1. The defendant lived with his girlfriend for three years during which time they had sexual relations. In the following two years, the defendant did not live with the woman but the two continued to have sexual relations. The defendant was charged with the sexual assault of his former girlfriend a year after the parties ceased to have regular sexual relations. At the defendant's criminal trial, the trial judge would not permit evidence of the past relations of the parties nor would the judge permit the defendant to testify he had sexual relations with the complainant four days before the alleged sexual assault. The woman denied that the parties had sex four days prior to the incident she complained of. Would the rape shield law in your state prevent such evidence from being presented to a jury? *State v. Gonyaw,* 146 Vt. 559, 507 A.2d 944 (1985).

2. The civilian girlfriend of a U.S. Marine private came onto a military base and "partied" with enlisted personnel over a three-day weekend. When the private's sergeant found the woman in the barrack's room, he threatened that he would accuse the private of violation of barrack's regulations unless the girlfriend agreed to have sexual intercourse with the sergeant. Two weeks after having sex with the sergeant, the woman reported him. The sergeant was convicted of rape and extortion and appealed his conviction to the U.S. Supreme Court. Do the circumstances permit inferences that the civilian woman consented to the sex, but later changed her mind? Does the two-week delay in reporting the incident support this conclusion? Should testimony of other female witnesses concerning other similar acts of extortion by the sergeant (defendant) be permitted to overcome the two-week delay in reporting? Should the convictions of both rape and extortion stand? *Hicks v. United States,* 24 M.J. 3, 41 CrL 4097, 484 U.S. 827, 108 S.Ct. 95 (1987).

3. In the late afternoon, a Milwaukee police officer came upon a young man and woman in a parked car engaged in what the officer concluded to be sexual activity. As it was a cold day and the woman was partially undressed, the officer did not have the parties get out of the car, which was

standard and required procedure of the Milwaukee police department.

Instead, the officer cautioned both adults and told them to move on. The young man started the car and drove away with the woman. An hour later, the woman walked into a nearby suburban police department and complained that she had been raped. She stated that the driver of the car had a gun pressed against her when the police officer was talking to the couple. She stated that she did not ask for help because of fear for her life. Should the officer be disciplined for not following departmental procedures in this case?

NOTES

1. Supreme Court of Oregon in *State v. Bashaw,* 296 Or. 50, 672 P.2d 48 (1983).

2. An admitted prostitute may be the victim of a rape. In the case of *People v. Gonzales,* 24 CrL 2194 (N.Y.Crim.Ct. 1978), the defendant did not pay the agreed fee for sexual services but obtained them at the point of a revolver. In affirming the conviction of the defendant, the court held: "It is the conclusion of this court that sexual intercourse with an admitted prostitute accomplished, if proven, by evidence establishing guilt beyond a reasonable doubt, but the coercive force of the weapon described constitutes rape in the third degree."

3. See 131 A.L.R. 1322, 84 A.L.R.2d 1017.

4. 462 S.W.2d 677 (Mo. 1971).

5. 619 S.W.2d 513 (Tenn. 1981).

6. See e.g., *McDonald v. State,* 225 Ark. 38, 279 S.W.2d 44 (1955); *Wilson v. State,* 10 Terry 37, 49 Del. 37, 109 A.2d 381 (1954), *cert. denied,* 348 U.S. 983, 75 S.Ct. 574 (1955); *Commonwealth v. Goldenberg,* 338 Mass. 377, 155 N.E.2d 187 (1959), *cert. denied,* 359 U.S. 1001, 79 S.Ct. 1143 (1959); *State v. Catron,* 317 Mo. 894, 296 S.W. 141 (1927); *State v. Carter,* 265 N.C. 626, 144 S.E.2d 826 (1965); *Commonwealth v. Stephens,* 143 Pa. .Super. 394, 17 A.2d 919 (1941); R. Perkins, *Perkins on Criminal Law,* 160–161 (2d ed. 1969).

7. *People v. Hunt,* 72 Cal.App. 3d at 194, 139 Cal. Rptr. at 676.

8. *State v. Rusk,* 289 Md. 230, 424 A.2d 720 (1981).

9. See *State v. Reinhold,* 123 Ariz. 50, 597 P.2d 532 (1979); *People v. Hunt,* 72 Cal.App. 3d 190, 139 Cal.Rptr. 675 (1977); *State v. Dill,* 3 Terry 533, 42 Del. 533, 40 A.2d 443 (1944); *Arnold v. United States,* 358 A.2d 335 (D.C.App. 1976); *Doyle v. State,* 39 Fla. 155, 22 So. 272 (1897); *Curtis v. State,* 236 Ga. 362, 223 S.E.2d 721 (1976); *People v. Murphy,* 124 Ill.App.2d 71, 260 N.E.2d 386 (1970); *Carroll v. State,* 263 Ind. 86, 324 N.E.2d 809 (1975); *Fields v. State,* 293 So.2d 430 (Miss. 1974); *State v. Beck,* 368 S.W.2d 490 (Mo. 1963); *Cascio v. State,* 147 Neb. 1075, 25 N.W.2d 897 (1947); *State v. Burns,* 287 N.C. 102, 214 S.E.2d 56 (1975), *cert. denied,* 423 U.S. 933, 96 S.Ct. 288 (1975); *State v. Verdone,* 114 R.I. 613, 337 A.2d 804 (1975); *Brown v. State,* 576 S.W.2d 820 (Tex.Cr.App. 1978); *Jones v. Com.,* 219 Va. 983, 252 S.E.2d 370 (1979); *State v. Baker,* 30 Wash.2d 601, 192 P.2d 839 (1948); *Brown v. State,* 581 P.2d 189 (Wyo. 1978). Some jurisdictions do not require that the victim's fear be reasonably grounded. See *Struggs v. State,* 372 So.2d 49 (Ala.Cr.App.), *cert. denied,* 444 U.S. 936, 100 S.Ct. 285, 62 L.Ed.2d 195 (1979); *Kirby v. State,* 5 Ala.App. 128, 59 So. 374 (1912); *Dinkens v. State,* 92 Nev. 74, 546 P.2d 228 (1976); *citing Hazel v. State, supra; State v. Herfel,* 49 Wis.2d 513, 182 N.W.2d 232 (1971). See also *Salsman v. Com.,* 565 S.W.2d 638 (Ky.App. 1978); *State v. Havens,* 264 N.W.2d 918 (S.D. 1978).

10. *People v. Barnes,* 42 Cal.3d 284, 228 Cal.Rptr. 228, 721 P.2d 110 (1986).

11. *People v. McIlvain,* 55 Cal.App.2d 322, 329, 130 P.2d 131 (1942).

12. *People v. Barnes,* 42 Cal.3d 284, 228 Cal.Rptr. 228, 721 P.2d 110, 117 (1986).

13. 42 Cal.3d 284, 228 Cal.Rptr. 228, 721 P.2d 110.

14. However, "if as a result of self-induced intoxication, the defendant believed that the female was consenting, that belief would not thereby become either reasonable or in good faith." (*California Jury Instruction* 4.20).

15. 117 Ill.App.3d 363, 453 N.E.2d 842 (1983). See also the case of *Florida v. Meyers,* 35 CrL 4022 (1984), in which the defendant was convicted of sexual battery. The conviction was affirmed by the U.S. Supreme Court.

16. 450 U.S. 464, 101 S.Ct. 1200.

17. See section E in this chapter on "Statutory Rape" where there is further material on the U.S. Supreme Court, case of *Michael M. v. Superior Court of Sonoma County (California).*

18. 35 CrL 2064. See also *People v. Sandoval,* 135 Ill.2d 159, 142 Ill. Dec. 135, 552 N.E.2d 726 (1990), review denied ___ U.S. ___, 111 S.Ct. 343 (1990) and *State v. Reinart,* 440 N.W.2d 503 (N.D. 1989).

19. 444 U.S. 394, 100 S. Ct. 624 (1980). However, since 1980 prison officials indicate they have better control over prisons. Evidence of conditions that Justice Blackmun refers to today would cause a court order to be issued mandating changes.

20. 483 A.2d 1135, 35 CrL 2070 (D.C.App. 1984).

21. 450 U.S. 464, 101 S.Ct. 1200. Most states probably make their statutory rape statutes applicable to both females and males. There certainly is a justifiable need for states to protect children from adults, whether the child is a girl or a boy.

22. 680 P.2d 727, 35 CrL 2071.

23. 458 U.S. 747, 102 S.Ct. 3348.

24. 659 S.W.2d 201 (Ky. 1983).

25. 478 U.S. 364, 106 S.Ct. 2988 (1986).

Chapter Nineteen

PROSTITUTION, RELATED OFFENSES, AND AIDS

A. Prostitution

The offense of prostitution can be one of at least three nonmarital acts:

1. engaging in sexual relations with another person for a fee or something of value
2. offering (or soliciting) to engage in sexual relations with another person for a fee or something of value
3. requests (or agrees) to pay a fee or something of value to another person for sexual services and acts

The "fee" or "something of value" is most often money. Members of either sex may now be convicted of prostitution as distinguished from the past, when only women could be convicted. Most (if not all) state prostitution statutes forbid prostitution by males selling sexual services to other males. Males who offer to pay a woman to engage in sex acts may also be charged with the crime if the statutes of that jurisdiction apply to both sexes.

Prostitution is often referred to as the world's oldest profession and is described in history's earliest written records. The Bible, for instance, makes many references to whores and whoremongering. Prostitution is an activity that grows and recedes, depending on the changing mores and morals of a particular civilization. Many believe that, like the poor, it will always be with us.

Throughout the world efforts have been made to suppress, control, organize, or discourage prostitution, with varying degrees of success. Prostitutes range from the common streetwalker to the privately kept woman or man. In England and France, prostitution is legal, but publicly soliciting customers is against the law. In some countries, particularly in the Orient, government-inspected houses of prostitution are allowed.

Efforts to decriminalize prostitution in the United States have met with little success. Only one state (Nevada) has legalized prostitution. In Nevada, each county has the option as to whether prostitution will be legalized. Fifteen of Nevada's seventeen counties have decided to remove the legal restraints against prostitution.

Why Do States Make Prostitution a Crime?

Two states (Hawaii and Delaware) give the following reasons in their statutes for making prostitution a crime:[1]

> History has proven that prostitution is not going to be abolished either by penal legislation nor the imposition of criminal sanctions through the vigorous enforcement of such legislation. Yet the trend of modern thought on prostitution in this country is that "public policy" demands that the criminal law go on record against prostitution. Defining this "public policy" is a difficult task. Perhaps it more correctly ought to be considered and termed "public demand"—a widespread community attitude which the penal law must take into account regardless of the questionable rationales upon which it is based.

***

This Los Angeles mounted police officer is part of a special patrol seeking to curb prostitution on Sunset Boulevard near Hollywood. Such law enforcement reflects the "public demand" behind the criminal treatment of prostitution.

Our study of public attitude in this area revealed the widespread belief among those interviewed that prostitution should be suppressed entirely or that it should be so restricted as not to offend those members of society who do not wish to consort with prostitutes or to be affronted by them. Making prostitution a criminal offense is one method of controlling the scope of prostitution and thereby protecting those segments of society which are offended by its open existence. This "abolitionist" approach is not without its vociferous detractors. There are those that contend that the only honest and workable approach to the problem is to legalize prostitution and confine it to certain localities within a given community. While such a proposal may exhibit foresight and practicality, the fact remains that a large segment of society is not presently willing to accept such a liberal approach. Recognizing this fact and the need for public order, the Code makes prostitution and its associate enterprises criminal offenses.[2]

Sexual Conduct that Constitutes Prostitution

Modern prostitution statutes generally forbid not only vaginal intercourse, but also oral sex (cunnilingus and fellatio), anal intercourse, masturbation, and, in many instances, sexual contact.

As most cases that go into a court involve police decoys, solicitation to commit any of these acts are almost always the basis of the criminal charge. Defendants in such cases are women who solicit male undercover officers, men who proposition female officers, and male prostitutes offering sex for a fee.

The very unusual case of *State v. Tarkington*[3] is presented in chapter 7. In that case, a civilian police volunteer went all the way and had sex with women in Honolulu in order to obtain evidence used to convict them of prostitution. The defendants appealed their convictions to the Hawaiian Supreme Court arguing

Old Offenses that are no Longer Crimes or are Seldom Charged

Offense	Definition	History
Bigamy (or polygamy)	Marriage to two or more spouses at the same time	Statutorized in 1604 (prior to that time was an ecclesiastical crime in England).
Adultery	Voluntary sexual intercourse in which one or both parties are married to another person (parties not married to one another)	Goes back in history to old Roman law. It is reported that about half of the states continue to make adultery a crime, but these old laws are rarely enforced. When a woman in northern Wisconsin admitted in a contested divorce hearing in 1990 that she had an "affair," she received national attention when she was charged with the two-year felony. Charges were later dropped.
Fornication	Voluntary sexual intercourse between two unmarried persons	Formerly a crime in all states. Most states have removed this offense and adultery from their criminal codes.
Seduction	Enticement by a male of an unmarried woman of prior chaste character to have sexual intercourse	Was a crime in early English law and in many states.
Miscegenation	Intermarriage (and in some states living together) of persons of different races (generally white and black)	Was a crime in some of the states. Such statutes were declared unconstitutional by the U.S. Supreme Court. See the case of *Loving v. Virginia* in chapter 1.
Buggery (or bestiality)	Any type of sexual intercourse with an animal or, in some states, anal intercourse with a man or woman (now charged under other statutes)	A statutory offense in England until 1967. Some states also used either or both of these terms to forbid this conduct.
Blasphemy, profanity, and indecent language	Cursing or reviling God; unbecoming, not decent, or impious language	Can no longer punish for language violations unless the language falls within one of the crimes listed in chapter 10. England continues to have an early seventeenth-century law that forbids "any contemptuous, reviling, scurrilous or ludicrous matter relating to God, Jesus Christ or the Bible" that is presented in an indecent and intemperate way.
Abortion	Causing the expulsion of a human fetus prematurely	Previously a crime in all states. States may not now make abortion a crime until the third trimester of pregnancy. Some states no longer have a crime of abortion (see chapter 12).

"outrageous government conduct." The court affirmed the convictions but noted that the "police (in this instance) are not to be congratulated." Although this procedure may be legal, most law enforcement agencies and communities probably would not tolerate it in this day of AIDS and other diseases.

Is a Home a Protected Zone of Privacy for Prostitution?

In the 1983 case of *State v. Mueller*,[4] the defendant offered to provide sexual services for hire in the privacy of her apartment. Neither street nor public solicitation was used. The persons involved were consenting adults. There were "no signs of advertising" anywhere in the apartment building.

The Supreme Court of Hawaii affirmed the defendant's conviction, holding that her right of privacy in her home did not give her a right to practice prostitution in her home in violation of the criminal code. The court quoted the U.S. Supreme Court, holding:

> The sum of experience, including that of the past two decades, affords an ample basis for legislatures to conclude that a sensitive, key relationship of human existence, central to family life, community welfare, and the development of human personality, can be debased and distorted by crass commercial exploitation of sex. Nothing in the Constitution prohibits a State from reaching such conclusion and acting on it legislatively simply because there is no conclusive evidence or empirical data.

Organized Crime and Prostitution

The National Advisory Committee on Criminal Justice Standards and Goals makes the following observations in its report on organized crime:

> Prostitution was one of organized crime's early rackets, dating from the turn of the 20th century. Unfortunately, not much has been written about how organized crime got into and ran the operations, or where illegal syndicates were most heavily involved.

* * *

> One form of prostitution—streetwalking—probably became too conspicuous and hard to regulate for organized crime. It is the street prostitute whom the police arrest most frequently, and she may have a bad reputation because of prostitution-related crimes (e.g., robbery of customers, assault, etc.). Also . . . streetwalkers have pimps, who serve the practical functions of providing bail and clients. It has been said that organized crime does not want to be involved with pimps, believing that they are stupid, unreliable, and treacherous. . . . Thus it seems that organized crime, when it is involved in prostitution, has concentrated on call girls and the brothel trade, employing a variety of legal fronts such as massage parlors and "rap" and "encounter" joints.

* * *

> Organized crime has also invented some ingenious gimmicks involving prostitution. For one, prostitutes apply for computer dates, enabling them to obtain economic data on prospective "pigeons" who are then set up to be robbed. Others are placed in public relations companies, which they then represent at business conventions, an ideal situation for blackmailing the men they entice.[5]

Prostitution

Prostitutes may operate (a) independently, (b) under the control of a pimp, (c) as part of an organized syndicate, (d) with persons other than the above.

Type of Operation	Type of Complaint Received by Law Enforcement Agencies
Streetwalkers (and prostitutes who operate out of taverns and bars)	• From business establishments (restaurants, hotels, etc.) when streetwalkers hurt business by driving customers away • From homeowners when streetwalkers are walking in their neighborhood • From women who have been mistaken for prostitutes by cruising men • From men who have been embarrassed or annoyed by prostitutes • From customers complaining of theft, robbery, etc. of their wallets, credit cards, or other personal property *This is the form of prostitution most visible to the public. Streetwalkers are also most susceptible to arrest by law enforcement officers.*
Call girls	• Generally, only customer complaints *Unless call girls have developed their own customers, they must rely on others to pander for them. Pimps, bartenders, cab drivers, etc. could be used to refer customers to call girls.*
Employees of "massage parlors," "artist's studios," "model shops," "escort services," etc.	• Generally only customer complaints. However, legitimate businesses in the neighborhood of "massage parlors," etc. are apt to complain to their local or county government. Persons living in the neighborhood are also likely to complain. See the article "Escort Services—A Front For Prostitution" in the August 1988 issue of the *FBI Law Enforcement Bulletin.* The article points out that crimes "of theft, drug abuse, robbery, and assault and battery are frequently byproducts of an organized prostitution service."
"Sex-for-drugs" prostitution	• Public health officials believe that increases in traditional and rare forms of venereal diseases are linked to an increase in sex-for-drugs prostitution. It is believed that such diseases also make their victims more vulnerable to AIDS.

Procuring, Promoting, and Pimping for the Practice of Prostitution

Many prostitutes operate without pimps or other persons procuring or promoting for them. Some prostitutes, however, have pimps who procure customers and provide protection and bail as needed. In addition to pimps, other persons could obtain money by procuring and promoting prostitution.

Facts and Fictions Regarding Prostitutes

Vice-squad officers and other professions who talk to prostitutes soon become aware of some of the following inconsistencies:

What Prostitutes Say:	*Reality:*
• they make $300 a night	• as they wear the same clothing day after day, it can be assumed that they do not have much of a wardrobe and do not have much money for themselves
• they know all about VD and have tested negative for AIDS	• on questioning, it becomes apparent their knowledge of venereal diseases is not adequate, and in some parts of the United States up to half of the prostitutes have tested positive for AIDS
• they always use condoms for safe sex	• facts show that many prostitutes are not practicing safe sex
• they are working for a goal such as buying a house or getting enough money to go to school	• unfortunately, the goal is seldom obtained

*Cities that Want to Crack Down on Prostitution Are Considering Some or All of the Following:**

- increased fines and jail sentences for prostitutes and johns
- cracking down on male johns to discourage this activity
- compulsory AIDS tests for convicted prostitutes and johns (A California statute mandating the testing of persons convicted of prostitution for AIDS was upheld in the 1990 case of *Love v. Superior Court,* 226 Cal.App.3d 736, 276 Cal.Rptr. 660.)
- confiscation of the johns' cars under forfeiture statutes
- city placing newspaper ads listing names of prostitutes and johns
- consider rewriting statutes or ordinances forbidding "loitering to solicit prostitution" if it is possible to meet constitutional standards. Cases holding that such statutes (or ordinances) were unconstitutional are *Coleman v. City of Richmond,* 5 Va.App. 459, 364 S.E.2d 239 (1988), *Brown v. Municipality of Anchorage,* 584 P.2d 35 (Alaska 1978), *New York v. Uplinger,* appeal dismissed by the U.S. Supreme Court (35 CrL 3101, 1984).

*Private persons who were angry about prostitution in their neighborhood wrote down the license numbers of cruising cars. Police departments in the Milwaukee area cooperated by obtaining the names and telephone numbers of the owners of the vehicles. Police would call the homes to caution the men not to cruise in such neighborhoods. This procedure was used until the police were given inaccurate numbers for a license plate. The angry wife and husband caused the police to discontinue the practice.

Procuring, promoting, and pimping for prostitution are generally forbidden by state criminal codes. Because of financial gains, this group of persons has a motive to encourage and coerce young persons into prostitution. They increase the volume and extent to which prostitution is practiced and often gain a vicious hold over the prostitutes they work with.

The means used to profit and to advance prostitution varies from serious offenses to minor violations. These offenses can be classified generally as follows:

- Criminal coercion by force, drugs, or other means to compel persons to remain in prostitution. This offense is further aggravated when it is used against young persons.
- Advancing or profiting from prostitution by operating or owning a house of prostitution or a business or enterprise involving prostitution. Such a person could be a madam or a person involved in a call girl ring. However, the New Jersey courts held in *State v. Alveario* that the owner of a hotel who rented out rooms knowing that the rooms were being used for prostitution could not be convicted of solicitation.[6]
- Small-scale promoters and procurers, such as taxicab drivers, bartenders, hotel porters, and clerks, who set up customers for prostitutes or provide other services.

B. HOMOSEXUAL SODOMY

Homosexual sodomy has been a crime for centuries. It was an offense punishable by death under Roman law. Chief Justice Burger pointed out that the famous English legal author Blackstone wrote in 1769 that sodomy was a " 'crime against nature' ... of 'deeper malignity than rape,' a heinous act 'the very mention of which is a disgrace to human nature' and 'a crime not fit to be named' " (106 S. Ct. at 2841).

Until 1961, all fifty states outlawed sodomy. During the following years, increased tolerance, greater understanding, and changing moral standards caused many homosexuals to come out in the open. Today, homosexual communities are well organized and very active politically. Gay men and women today may live together in all fifty states, generally without fear of criminal prosecutions.

However, public homosexual acts in parks or other public places are prosecuted as crimes, just as are heterosexual sex acts committed in public. In some urban areas, homosexual "cruisers" are as much or more of a problem to local law enforcement as heterosexual prostitutes. The prostitution statutes in all fifty states apply equally to both heterosexual and homosexual prostitution.

Many states have decriminalized private homosexual acts between consenting adults. Some states, however, continue to include sodomy (homosexual acts) in their criminal codes. Such criminal statutes have been challenged twice before the U.S. Supreme Court. In the 1976 case of *Doe v. Commonwealth*,[7] the U.S. Supreme Court affirmed a State of Virginia statute forbidding homosexual sodomy between consenting adults, holding "that the sodomy statute, so long in force in Virginia, has a rational basis of State interest demonstrably legitimate and mirrored in the cited decisional law of the Supreme Court."

In the 1986 case of *Bowers v. Hardwick*,[8] the U.S. Supreme Court refused to invalidate the homosexual sodomy statute of the State of Georgia, holding:

* * *

Even if the conduct at issue here is not a fundamental right, respondent asserts that there must be a rational basis for the law and that there is none in this case other than the presumed belief of a majority of the electorate in Georgia that homosexual sodomy is immoral and unacceptable. This is said to be an inadequate rationale to support

Crimes Against and by Homosexuals

Murders of homosexuals: Committed by (a) "pickups" or "tricks," (b) persons who hate gays, or (c) lovers or other homosexuals in an angry argument.

"Fag bashing": Persons who hate homosexuals beat them and sometimes rob them (in past years, many of these incidents were not reported to the police). A New York truck driver who said that he sought out gays over the years and beat them "too many times to remember" was found to have AIDS. In the beatings, he often cut his hands.[9]

"Gacy-style" murders: In 1980, John Wayne Gacy slew thirty-three young men and boys in the Chicago area after homosexually assaulting them. In 1991, Gacy and a man named Eyler were awaiting execution in Illinois. Eyler is believed to have killed twenty-three young men in northern Illinois. See 477 N.E.2d 774 (1985).

In 1991, Jeffrey Dahmer confessed to killing seventeen young men in homosexual murders. All of the bodies were then cut up and most disposed of. Dahmer is awaiting trial for sixteen murders in Wisconsin and one in Ohio.

Assaults, batteries, knifings, and disorderly conduct: Result from lovers' quarrels and fights between homosexuals.

---

the law. The law, however, is constantly based on notions of morality, and if all laws representing essentially moral choices are to be invalidated under the Due Process Clause, the courts will be very busy indeed. Even respondent makes no such claim, but insists that majority sentiments about the morality of homosexuality should be declared inadequate. We do not agree, and are unpersuaded that the sodomy laws of some 25 States should be invalidated on this basis.

* * *

Gays in the Military

The policy of the U.S. military forces is set forth in AR 135−178, sec. 10−2:

> Homosexuality is incompatible with military service. The presence in the military environment of persons who engage in homosexual conduct, or who by their statements demonstrate a propensity to engage in homosexual conduct, seriously impair the accomplishment of the military mission. The presence of such members adversely affects the ability of the service to accomplish the enumerated government interests.

This regulation was challenged in a 1990 appeal to the U.S. Supreme Court in the case of *Ben-Shalom v. Marsh,* 881 F.2d 454 (7th Cir.), *review denied,* ___ U.S. ___, 110 S.Ct. 1269 (1990). In refusing to reverse the U.S. Army's decision denying reenlistment to a woman because she was a lesbian, the Federal Court of Appeals held:

* * *

> Homosexuals have suffered a history of discrimination and still do, though possibly now in less degree. We do not see, however, that the new regulation embodies a gross unfairness in the military context so inconsistent with equal protection as to

be termed "invidious." In these times homosexuals are proving that they are not without growing political power. It cannot be said "they have no ability to attract the attention of the lawmakers." *Cleburne,* 473 U.S. at 445, 105 S.Ct. at 3257. A political approach is open to them to seek a congressional determination about the rejection of homosexuals in the Army. We are, however, unwilling to substitute a mere judge-made rule for the Army's regulation or to act in an executive or legislative fashion.

* * *

In 1990, the case of *Watkins v. U.S. Army,* 875 F.2d 699 (9th Cir. 1989), *review denied,* __ U.S. __, 111 S.Ct. 384, was also appealed to the U.S. Supreme Court. Sergeant Watkins had served for fourteen years in the army after disclosing his homosexual tendencies on his army preinduction medical form. His reviews by superior officers were excellent, with one commanding officer writing that Watkins was "one of our most respected and trusted soldiers." The U.S. Supreme Court upheld a lower court ruling that since the army had "affirmatively misrepresented" to Mr. Watkins that his homosexuality would not be a bar to reenlistment, the army had to permit Watkins to reenlist.

Gays in Law Enforcement

Each state may enact legislation as to employment of persons with different sexual preferences (or alternative lifestyles). The 1987 case of *Padula v. Webster,* 822 F.2d 97 (D.C.Cir.) received a great amount of national attention. Margaret Padula applied for a position as a special agent with the FBI and ranked very well on the written examination and oral interview. However, the subsequent background investigation disclosed that Padula was a practicing homosexual. Padula commenced a civil lawsuit after the FBI rejected her application for employment. The Court held that the FBI did not violate equal protection, stating:

* * *

The FBI, as the Bureau points out, is a national law enforcement agency whose agents must be able to work in all the states of the nation. To have agents who engage in conduct criminalized in roughly one-half of the states would undermine the law enforcement credibility of the Bureau. Perhaps more important, FBI agents perform counterintelligence duties that involve highly classified matters relating to national security. It is not irrational for the Bureau to conclude that the criminalization of homosexual conduct coupled with the general public opprobrium toward homosexuality exposes many homosexuals, even "open" homosexuals, to the risk of possible blackmail to protect their partners, if not themselves. We therefore conclude the Bureau's specialized functions, like the Navy's in *Dronenburg,* rationally justify consideration of homosexual conduct that could adversely affect that agency's responsibilities. The judgment of the district court is hereby
    Affirmed.

When Evidence Is Insufficient to Support a Rape Conviction

The criminal charge of sodomy (or deviate sexual intercourse) is generally used only when such acts are committed in public. However, the following cases illustrate the use of such criminal charges for acts done in private:

KELLY v. STATE
Court of Special Appeals of Maryland (1980) 412 A.2d 1274

A woman testified that she was abducted at knifepoint from a shopping mall by the defendant and another man. She was taken to a secluded area, where she was assaulted, raped, and forced to engage in fellatio. She was then released and reported the incident. The defendant and his friend each took the witness stand and testified that the woman voluntarily had sexual relations with each of them and also performed fellatio on each of them several times. The jury found the defendant not guilty on all charges where force or threat of force was an element but found the defendant guilty of count six, "perverted sexual practices." The court affirmed the conviction, holding:

> *Appellant argues that inasmuch as fornication is not prohibited by Maryland law, persons indulging in private, consensual acts of sodomy are denied equal protection of the law. The argument is that there is no essential difference between vaginal intercourse and other sex acts. He also argues that any punishment for sodomy is cruel and unusual. Once again we repeat, we will not invalidate laws of such ancient vintage without clear authority from higher courts.*

STATE v. POE
Court of Appeals of North Carolina (1979) 40 N.C.App. 385, 252 S.E.2d 843, appeal dismissed by 445 U.S. 947, 100 S.Ct. 1593, 27 CrL 4023 (1980)

The defendant was charged with rape and committing a crime against nature with a woman. The Court dismissed the rape charge and the jury found the defendant guilty of sodomy. The defendant appealed, arguing that North Carolina made fellatio a crime between unmarried persons, but it was not a crime if done by married persons in North Carolina. In affirming the conviction, the court held:

> *In this state, fornication and adultery have been proscribed [forbidden] since at least 1805.... We believe the state, consistent with the Fourteenth Amendment, can classify unmarried persons so as to prohibit fellatio between males and females without forbidding the same acts between married couples. We hold that the constitutional right of privacy does not protect in this case.*

C. PUBLIC SEX ACTS

Private sex acts between consenting adults are rarely charged as crimes even if they violate specific sections of criminal codes. Public sex acts, however, are charged as criminal conduct. The following cases illustrate:

UNITED STATES v. LEMONS
United States Court of Appeals, Eighth Circuit (1983) 697 F.2d 832

The defendant and another man were observed in a toilet stall in a Hot Springs National Park men's room engaging in oral sex. Defendant was convicted of violating the Arkansas sodomy statute under the assimilative crimes statutes and appealed. In affirming the conviction, the court held:

> *Lemons contends that public sexuality is not the issue here. To the contrary, we find that Lemons' public sexual conduct is the sole issue here. We remain unconvinced that the constitutional right to privacy extends to Lemons' conduct, much less that the State of Arkansas does not have a compelling interest in limiting sexuality, even*

Regulation of Nudity by States or Municipalities

Place of Nudity	*Manner in Which Nudity May Be Regulated*
Public nudity (public beach or public place, such as street)	May be forbidden or regulated by a specific statute or ordinance.
Nude entertainment or nudity in a place licensed to serve alcoholic beverages	May be forbidden or regulated under the authority given to states by the Twenty-first Amendment of the U.S. Constitution to regulate the sale and use of alcohol. The U.S. Supreme Court stated that "the broad sweep of the 21st Amendment has been recognized as conferring something more than the normal state authority over public health, welfare, and morals." (*California v. LaRue,* 409 U.S. 109, 93 S.Ct. 390 [1972]).
Nudity in a private place (a nudist camp for example) or in a stage play or in a movie (*Hair* and *Oh Calcutta,* for example). Such places do not sell alcoholic beverages nor are they public places in this sense.	May not be regulated unless the conduct or display is obscene. Nudity, by itself, is not obscene, lewd, or indecent. See the case of *People v. Garrison,* 82 Ill.2d 444, 45 Ill.Dec. 132, 412 N.E.2d 483 (1980), where the defendant stood behind a storm door in his home exposing his penis to a woman standing outside. The Supreme Court of Illinois held that this was not private conduct and the defendant had no right of privacy. If a jury found that the defendant exposed his body "with intent to arouse or to satisfy (his) sexual desire," the defendant could be found guilty of the Illinois Public Indecency statute.

if arguably given some constitutional protection, to prohibit oral sex in a public restroom within the confines of a national park.

CAMMACK v. STATE
Texas Court of Appeals (1982) 641 S.W.2d 906, 32 CrL 2137

The defendant was convicted of the Texas public lewdness statute when he followed a police officer into a peep show booth in a porn shop and fondled the genitals of the officer. The court held that the offense occurred in a public place, even though the defendant closed the door to the booth. In affirming the conviction, the court held:

> *The public nature of the booth could not be changed by the appellant, acting alone, closing and locking the door, closeting himself with a stranger. [Note: If the defendant were alone in the booth with the door closed, a right of privacy would exist.]*

STATE v. BLACK
Supreme Court of Arkansas (1977) 260 Ark. 864, 545 S.W.2d 617

The defendant was observed engaging in oral sex while in the "drunk tank" of a jail. Other inmates could observe the two men, and families and visitors coming into the jail had to pass the "drunk tank." In holding that the "drunk tank" was a public place within the meaning of the public sexual indecency statute, the Supreme Court of Arkansas held:

> *Summarizing, what is a public place? Primarily, the circumstances must be considered. While the fact situation was different, the language of the Maryland Court of Appeals in the indecent exposure case of* Messina v. State, *212 Md. 602, 130 A.2d 578, we think, succinctly answers the question asked. There, the court said: "An exposure is 'public,' or in a 'public place,' if it occurs under such circumstances that it could be seen by a number of persons, if they were present and happened to look."*

D. Child Pornography

The U.S. Supreme Court has repeatedly held that states have a compelling interest in "safeguarding the physical and psychological well-being of a minor" and that "the use of children as subjects of pornographic materials is harmful to the physiological, emotional, and mental health of the child" *Osborne v. Ohio, ___ U.S. ___,* 110 S.Ct. 1691 (1990).

Because of these reasons, child pornography is treated differently than adult pornography. Adult pornography is sold openly in many communities throughout the United States. Child pornography is outlawed by the federal government and many of the states.

In the 1982 case of *New York v. Ferber,* 458 U.S. 747, 102 S.Ct. 3348, the U.S. Supreme Court upheld a New York statute outlawing the distribution of child pornography. Enforcement efforts since 1982 against the transportation, sale, and distribution of child pornography have driven the business of child pornography underground. However, there continues to be a market for these illegal products, which continue to be supplied by persons in the United States and foreign countries.

Postal inspectors provided Ohio police with information that a Columbus man, Clyde Osborne, had child pornographic material in his home. The police obtained a search warrant and searched Osborne's home, where they found four sexually explicit photographs of a fourteen-year-old boy. Osborne was convicted under an Ohio law forbidding the possession of child pornography and received a six-month jail sentence. He appealed the conviction and sentence to the U.S. Supreme Court, where the case of *Ohio v. Osborne, ___ U.S. ___,* 110 S.Ct. 1691 was heard in 1990.

Osborne argued that his conviction and sentence should be reversed under the 1969 case of *Stanley v. Georgia,* 394 U.S. 557, 89 S.Ct. 1243, which held that Stanley had the right to possess and look at adult pornography in the privacy of his home. The U.S. Supreme Court refused to expand the *Stanley* case because the "interests underlying child pornography . . . far exceed the interests . . . at issue in *Stanley.*" (109 L.Ed.2d 108) The U.S. Supreme Court upheld the Ohio law forbidding the possession of child pornography, holding:

* * *

> Given the importance of the State's interest in protecting the victims of child pornography, we cannot fault Ohio for attempting to stamp out this vice at all levels in the distribution chain. According to the State, since the time of our decision in

Ferber, much of the child pornography market has been driven underground; as a result, it is now difficult, if not impossible, to solve the child pornography problem by only attacking production and distribution. . . .

. . . the materials produced by child pornographers permanently record the victim's abuse. The pornography's continued existence causes the child victims continuing harm by haunting the children in years to come. . . . The State's ban on possession and viewing encourages the possessors of these materials to destroy them. Second, encouraging the destruction of these materials is also desirable because evidence suggests that pedophiles use child pornography to seduce other children into sexual activity.

Given the gravity of the State's interests in this context, we find that Ohio may constitutionally proscribe the possession and viewing of child pornography.

* * *

The Ohio statute, on its face, purports to prohibit the possession of "nude" photographs of minors. We have stated that depictions of nudity, without more, constitute protected expression. . . . Relying on this observation, Osborne argues that the statute as written is substantially overbroad. We are skeptical of this claim because, in light of the statute's exemptions and "proper purposes" provisions, the statute may not be substantially overbroad under our cases. However that may be, Osborne's overbreadth challenge, in any event, fails because the statute, as construed by the Ohio Supreme Court on Osborne's direct appeal, plainly survives overbreadth scrutiny. Under the Ohio Supreme Court reading, the statute prohibits "the possession or viewing of material or performance of a minor who is in a state of nudity, where such nudity constitutes a lewd exhibition or involves a graphic focus on the genitals, and where the person depicted is neither the child nor the ward of the person charged." 37 Ohio St. 3d, at 252, 525 N.E.2d, at 1368. By limiting the statute's operation in this manner, the Ohio Supreme Court avoided penalizing persons for viewing or possessing innocuous photographs of naked children. . . .

* * *

The case of *United States v. Jacobson,* 916 F.2d 467 (8th Cir. 1990) (review granted by the U.S. Supreme Court, 49 CrL 3021), was in appeal in the federal courts in 1991. Jacobson was convicted of receiving sexually explicit material depicting a minor through the U.S. mail. The Eighth Circuit Court of Appeals summarized the facts in the *Jacobson* case as follows in affirming the conviction:

* * *

We simply cannot characterize the government's conduct in Jacobson's case as outrageous. Having discovered Jacobson's name on a pornographer's mailing list, the government pursued its investigation over a period of twenty-nine months by mailing surveys, letters, and catalogues to Jacobson. Jacobson responded, remitting a membership fee, requesting more information, corresponding with another adult sharing his interest in child erotica, and finally ordering obscene magazines and photographs depicting "young boys in sex action fun." The postal inspectors did not apply extraordinary pressure on Jacobson. The inspectors merely invited Jacobson to purchase pornographic material through the mail. *See Kaminski,* 703 F.2d at 1009 (the offer of reasonable inducements is a proper means of investigation). Unlike face-to-face contacts, Jacobson easily could have ignored the contents of the mailings if he was not interested in them. Similar undercover operations aimed at child pornography collectors "have withstood the constitutional challenge [Jacobson] now raises." *Musslyn,* 865 F.2d at 947 (citations omitted).

Jacobson also contends he was entrapped as a matter of law. We cannot agree. The jury rejected Jacobson's entrapment defense. Jacobson argues, however, the evidence clearly shows entrapment: the postal inspectors originated the criminal plan, implanted the disposition to purchase child pornography into Jacobson's otherwise innocent mind, and Jacobson ordered the illegal magazine at their behest. . . . , we conclude this is not a case in which the government was a manufacturer rather than a detector of crime.

* * *

E. Harassment as an Offense

Cities and states have enacted offenses entitled "harassment," "mashing," "hassling," etc., which prohibit such conduct as improper accosting, ogling, insulting, pursuing, following, molesting, touching a person of the opposite sex. The primary purpose of such statutes and ordinances is to protect women and young persons from behavior that can be menacing and threatening. There are different types of harassment.

Sexual Harassment

Sexual harassment can be a criminal or civil offense. It is defined as unwelcome sexual advances or requests for sexual favors that may be combined with other verbal or physical conduct of a sexual nature. Ordinarily, women and girls are the victims of sexual harassment, but occasional cases concern men who are the victims of unwelcome sexual advances that amount to sexual harassment. Workplace sexual harassment could occur when:

- the boss expects submission by an employee to sexual harassment as an explicit or implicit term or condition of employment
- pay raises, promotions, type of work, etc. is used as a reward for submission to sexual harassment and providing sexual favors
- such conduct interferes with work performance or creates an intimidating, hostile, or offensive working environment.

The U.S. Supreme Court held in 1986 that sexual harassment that caused a hostile or abusive work environment, without showing an economic loss, violated Title VII of the Civil Rights Act of 1964 (42 U.S.C.S. Sec. 2000e-2000e-17). In the case of *Meritor Savings Bank v. Mechelle Vinson,*[10] the female bank employee was subjected to public fondling and sexual demands to which she allegedly submitted out of fear that she would lose her job.

Telephone Harassment

Before 1966, few states had criminal laws dealing with harassing, abusive, or obscene telephone calls. However, because of the increased volume of complaints received during the 1960s, all the states and federal government have now enacted statutes making such telephone calls criminal offenses.[11]

Harassing, abusive, or obscene phone calls include the deliberate obscene call, threats, the cruel hoax, bomb scares and threat of bombs, and the "silent" call, in which the person answering the telephone hears nothing or hears breathing on the other end of the line. Criminal charges may be issued in all of the above cases if it is apparent that the call was deliberate and made with intent to harass, abuse, or threaten another person. However, charges should not be issued if it appears that the person has dialed a wrong number and simply does not explain the error.

The Illinois telephone harassment statute, which outlaws "harassment by telephone," was found to be constitutional by the Illinois Supreme Court in the 1979 case of *Parkins v. Illinois.*[12] The appeal to the U.S. Supreme Court was dismissed for want of a substantial federal question.

Other Types of Harassment

In the 1979 case of *State v. Keller,*[13] the Oregon Court of Appeals held that spitting on another person could be "offensive physical contact" within the meaning of the Oregon statute forbidding harassment. Spitting on another person could also be charged as an "assault" or "disorderly conduct" if such an act violates these statutes.

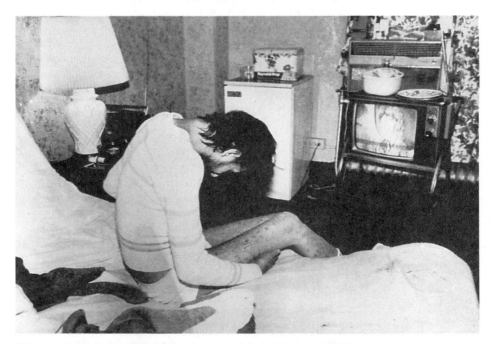

This twenty-four-year-old man shows some of the grim signs of AIDS: sores, lesions, and other infections.

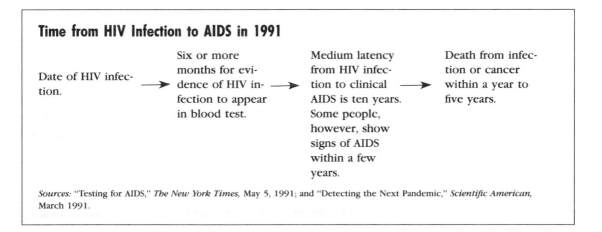

Time from HIV Infection to AIDS in 1991

| Date of HIV infection. | → | Six or more months for evidence of HIV infection to appear in blood test. | → | Medium latency from HIV infection to clinical AIDS is ten years. Some people, however, show signs of AIDS within a few years. | → | Death from infection or cancer within a year to five years. |

Sources: "Testing for AIDS," *The New York Times,* May 5, 1991; and "Detecting the Next Pandemic," *Scientific American,* March 1991.

F. The AIDS Crisis

AIDS became a fast-growing epidemic in the early 1980s.[14] Some experts point out that the rapid increase of the disease occurred at the same time of increased homosexual activity and increased use of dirty needles by drug abusers. It is through these practices that the disease primarily spreads.

At the present time, there is no cure for AIDS. The disease cripples the body's immune system and leaves victims exposed to serious infections and cancers. Half of patients diagnosed as having AIDS die within a year of diagnosis. Fifteen percent have a chance of surviving at least five years. It remains to be seen whether long-term survival is possible for the few persons living beyond five years from diagnosis.

AIDS is not a single disease. There are a variety of reactions to the AIDS virus, and the disease takes different forms. To be diagnosed as having AIDS, the Centers for Disease Control require that a patient must have one or more "opportunistic infections" or cancers in the absence of all other known underlying causes of immune deficiency.[15] Persons having AIDS die from the "opportunistic infections" and cancers, not from AIDS itself.

Doctors estimate that in 1980 approximately 100,000 people worldwide were infected with the AIDS virus. It is estimated that in 1991 8 to 10 million people were infected with the HIV virus worldwide.[16] The medium latency from infection to clinical AIDS is about ten years, although a few persons show clinically recognizable signs of the disease within just a few years after infection.

In 1987, the U.S. Public Health Service estimated that 1 million to 1.5 million Americans carry the AIDS virus. Having the AIDS virus does not necessarily mean that the person will develop the disease. But infection with the virus is a permanent condition the person will have for the rest of his or her life.

Persons who have AIDS and carriers of the AIDS virus can spread the disease to other persons. The infection is spread most often through blood and sperm. Means of transmission of the AIDS virus is presented in the chart on "Possible Transmission of the AIDS Virus." Because of the long time lapse (average of ten years) between the infection of a victim and the appearance of symptoms, an infected person could be unaware that he or she has been exposed to the virus and is spreading AIDS.

"Selling Death": Prostitutes and AIDS

An unknown number of male and female prostitutes are infected with AIDS and could transmit the deadly disease through sexual contact. Those who do are "selling death" in the words of the executive director of the Mississippi Gay Alliance.[17]

The Surgeon General of the United States illustrated the unknown risks involved when he stated that, "We use the numbers of a million or a million and a half. But it could be 400,000, or it could be four million. Those estimates are based on very shaky evidence. We just don't know." The high risk groups are drug users using needles, homosexuals, and persons having sexual contacts with persons in these groups, which includes many prostitutes.

There is a question of what can or should be done when it is determined (or suspected) that a prostitute has been infected with the AIDS virus and is likely to continue having sex with other persons. Public officials have used one or more of the following:

1. Seek the maximum jail sentence for the offense for which the prostitute is being held. However, with a male prostitute, this could mean infecting other male prisoners unless the male prostitute is segregated. After the prison term expires, the person is released.
2. Use of the quarantine laws of the state that were written to protect public health but are not generally intended to regulate sexual activity.
3. Take the person to the local bus station and buy a ticket for the person to a city in another state. This practice has caused officials in other states to ship prostitutes back to the city of origin with loud complaints regarding the practice.
4. Release the person after urging and trying to convince him or her not to have sexual relations with others for fear of infecting them. This practice

A community group billboard in Milwaukee, Wisconsin, raises a newly relevant issue for both potential customers and lawmakers.

is often used when a prostitute permits testing for AIDS in return for a short jail sentence or no jail sentence.

Mandatory Testing for AIDS: California Moving Toward While the State of New York Forbids

The State of California enacted a statute requiring testing for AIDS of persons convicted of prostitution. This statute was upheld against a Fourth Amendment challenge in the case of *Love v. Superior Court,* 226 Cal.App.3d 736, 276 Cal. Rptr. 660 (1990). The usual method in the United States of obtaining consent for AIDS testing is to strike a bargain with the person charged with rape or prostitution (plea bargaining). After the California example, other states may consider legislation mandating AIDS testing.

While California has a law mandating AIDS testing of persons convicted of prostitution, the State of New York has a 1988 law that expressly forbids mandatory testing and contact tracing (the tracing of persons having contact with the infected person).

Medical societies in New York requested the health commissioner to declare AIDS to be a sexually transmissible disease. Once a disease is classified as sexually transmissible, doctors can require a person to be tested if the doctor has reason to believe the person is infected. If the person tests positive, the doctor is then obligated to report the results.

When the New York health commissioner refused to classify AIDS as a sexually transmissible disease, doctors went to court, saying they wanted to slow down the AIDS epidemic. The highest court in New York upheld the health commissioner and his decision not to classify AIDS as a sexually transmissible disease. The 1991 decision went on to point out that New York state law forbids mandatory testing and contact tracing. (See "Citing Privacy Law, High Court Rejects Forced AIDS Tests," *The New York Times,* May 3, 1991.)

As courts in the State of New York cannot order testing in rape or prostitution cases, plea bargaining is the usual way to obtain consent for AIDS testing. This means that prosecutors have to bargain with the accused or convicted person and his or her attorney. In return for concessions from the state, consent for AIDS testing can be obtained in many cases.

The New Crime of Knowingly Transmitting AIDS

Some states have old laws that forbid knowingly transmitting a venereal disease, but many states do not classify AIDS as a venereal disease. Five or more states have created the new crime of knowingly transmitting AIDS. Alabama's statute requires that the offender act "in a manner likely to transmit" a sexually transmitted disease. Nevada's law has provisions for charging attempted murder for prostitutes who continue to sell their sexual services after learning they are infected with the AIDS virus.

Charging Persons Who Endanger Others with AIDS with a Traditional Crime

There are many cases throughout the United States and other countries where a person infected with AIDS has been charged with traditional criminal offenses

Possible Transmission of the AIDS Virus

Issue Concern	*Educational and Action Messages*
Human bites	Person who bites usually receives the victim's blood; viral transmission through saliva is highly unlikely. If bitten by anyone, milk wound to make it bleed, wash the area thoroughly, and seek medical attention.
Spitting	Viral transmission through saliva is highly unlikely.
Urine/feces	Virus isolated in only very low concentrations in urine; not at all in feces; no cases of AIDS or AIDS virus infection associated with either urine or feces.
Cuts/puncture wounds	Use caution in handling sharp objects and searching areas hidden from view; needle stick studies show risk of infection is very low.
CPR/first aid	To eliminate the already minimal risk associated with CPR, use masks/airways; avoid blood-to-blood contact by keeping open wounds covered and wearing gloves when in contact with bleeding wounds.
Body removal	Observe crime scene rule: Do not touch anything. Those who must come into contact with blood or other body fluids should wear gloves.
Casual contact	No cases of AIDS or AIDS virus infection attributed to casual contact.
Any contact with blood or body fluids	Wear gloves if contact with blood or body fluids is considered likely. If contact occurs, wash thoroughly with soap and water, clean up spills with one part water to nine parts household bleach.
Contact with dried blood	No cases of infection have been traced to exposure to dried blood. The drying process itself appears to inactivate the virus. Despite low risk, however, caution dictates wearing gloves, a mask, and protective shoe coverings if exposure to dried blood particles is likely (e.g., crime scene investigation).

Source: U.S. Dept. of Justice. National Institute of Justice Reports (December 1987).

because he or she endangered others with AIDS. Whether the person knew of his or her HIV infection would affect the charge. If the defendant did not know he or she was infected with the AIDS virus, defense attorneys could use this lack of knowledge as a defense to a criminal charge. In the 1989 case of *Brock v. State,* 555 So.2d 285, the Alabama Court of Appeals held the defendant could not be convicted of first-degree assault for biting a correctional officer because he did not know he was infected with the HIV virus and could transmit HIV. The defendant, however, could be convicted of a lesser assault.

The defendant in the case of *Scroggins v. State (Alabama),* 1990 WL 263463, however, knew that he was HIV infected. His conviction for assault with intent to murder was affirmed in 1991. An Indiana defendant was also convicted of attempted murder when he knew he was HIV infected and bit and scratched persons seeking to aid him after a suicide attempt. *State v. Haines,* 545 N.E.2d 834 (Ind.App.1989). In the case of *United States v. Stewart,* 29 M.J. 92 (CMA, 1989), a military court affirmed the conviction for aggravated assault where the defendant knowingly exposed another person to HIV infection.

The following case also illustrates:

Laws Used by States to Obtain Public Order and Protect Public Health

Type of Law   *Examples*

"Sexually danger-   The Illinois sexually dangerous person statute was tested before the U.S.
ous person" laws   Supreme Court in the 1986 case of *Allen v. Illinois,* 478 U.S. 364, 106 S.Ct.
                      2988. In such civil proceedings, the state can order a person who has com-
                      mitted a sex crime to submit to psychiatric examinations and treatment if
                      appropriate (in addition or while serving time for their crime).

                      The Court held: "states must be free to develop a variety of solutions
                      to problems and not be forced into a common, uniform mold."

Quarantine laws   All states have old quarantine laws, which in past years were used to fight
                      contagious diseases such as typhoid, tuberculosis, and occasionally sexually
                      transmitted diseases. Since 1985, nine or more states have amended their
                      old quarantine laws or passed new laws empowering health officials, as a
                      last resort, to quarantine and isolate persons with AIDS who endanger the
                      health of other persons.

                      Female and male prostitutes known to be infected with AIDS have
                      been observed soliciting for prostitution ("selling death"). Warning poten-
                      tial customers, use of criminal statutes, or use of a quarantine law are alter-
                      natives available to public officials.

Licensing escort   The State of Nevada enacted a statute requiring that operators of escort
services   services obtain a license. Failure to not obtain a license is a criminal of-
                      fense. The law forbids escort services from operating in a "sexually ori-
                      ented" manner or advertising in a manner that suggests to a "reasonable,
                      prudent person that sexual stimulation or sexual gratification will be pro-
                      vided." The Federal Court of Appeals for the 9th Circuit held the Nevada
                      law to be constitutional in 1988 case of *IDK, Inc. v. Clark County,* 836 F.2d
                      1185.

Regulations for-   Bars, bathhouses, and theaters have been closed under such regulations by
bidding unsafe   court orders supported with affidavits showing that the business was "an
sexual activities   AIDS breeding ground with profit being the driving force."
and operating   After two months of observations, health inspectors stated in affidavits
AIDS-virus breed-   that they observed 67 incidents of high-risk sexual activities involving 117
ing grounds   individuals in a New York City theater. When the theater owners did not
                      respond to a series of warning letters from the city, a court order was ob-
                      tained to close the theater under a New York statute. See "Gay Movie
                      House is Closed in Raid—Health Officials Call Cinema 'AIDS Breeding
                      Ground,'" *The New York Times,* October 1, 1988.

Zoning ordi-   A Detroit zoning ordinance regulating adult bookstores and theaters was
nances for adult   reviewed by the U.S. Supreme Court in the 1976 case of *Young v. Ameri-*
bookstores featur-   *can Mini Threatres,* 96 S.Ct. 2440, and held valid.
ing sexually ex-   The Court held that interference with First Amendment rights was
plicit materials   "slight" as there were many locations not within 500 feet of a residential
that are not   area and other "regulated uses" as forbidden by the ordinance.
obscene   The Detroit ordinance was shown to have the legitimate purpose of
                      preventing urban blight. Not all ordinances regulating adult bookstores,
                      however, have been held to be constitutional. See also *Renton v. Playtime,*
                      473 U.S. 932, 106 S.Ct. 27 (1985).

continued

Laws Used by State to Obtain Public Order and Protect Public Health (continued)

Type of Law	Examples
Laws permitting buildings to be declared a public nuisance or public health nuisance	The case of *Arcara v. Cloud Books, Inc.,* 478 U.S. 697, 106 S.Ct. 3172 was decided by the U.S. Supreme Court in 1986. Masturbation, fondling, fellatio, and solicitation for prostitution were observed in a New York adult bookstore. Under a court order, the premises were declared a nuisance and closed for one year. In affirming the action, the Court held that the nuisance law "sought to protect the environment of the community by directing the sanction at premises knowingly used for lawless activities." Nuisance statutes have also been used to close crack houses and other drug houses. Such buildings could also be condemned and torn down for building code violations or become the property of the city for nonpayment of property taxes.
Use by a state of their RICO statute to proceed against selling obscenity	In 1989, the case of *Fort Wayne Books, Inc. v. Indiana,* 489 U.S. 46, 109 S. Ct. 916 came before the U.S. Supreme Court. The Supreme Court held that states could use their RICO statutes to proceed against businesses selling obscenity, but that wholesale seizure of the material in question cannot take place until after there has been a full adversary hearing. (See chapter 21 for material on RICO.)

UNITED STATES v. MOORE

U.S. District Court for Minnesota (1987) 669 F.Supp. 289, affirmed on appeal, 846 F.2d 1163 (8th Cir., 1988)

Knowing that he had AIDS and hepatitis, the defendant bit two corrections officers. A jury convicted Moore of assault with a deadly or dangerous weapon after being instructed, "If you're not convinced that AIDS or hepatitis can be transmitted by a bite, you are duty-bound to find James Moore not guilty." The Court of Appeals affirmed, holding:

> *The defendant moves for judgment of acquittal on the ground that the evidence was insufficient to sustain a conviction for assault with a deadly or dangerous weapon. A deadly or dangerous weapon is an object that is used in a manner likely to endanger life or inflict serious bodily harm. The defendant argues that, in order for his mouth and teeth to be a deadly and dangerous weapon, there must be sufficient evidence to show beyond a reasonable doubt that AIDS can be transmitted by a human bite. He believes that the evidence was not sufficient to make that showing or to show that human bites like those here are likely to produce death or great bodily harm. The government responds that the jury was not required to find that AIDS could be transmitted by a human bite in order to convict the defendant of assault with a deadly or dangerous weapon.*
>
> *The evidence showed that AIDS can be transmitted through bodily fluid such as blood and semen. The defendant had been informed both that he had the AIDS virus and the hepatitis antibody and that he could potentially transmit the diseases to others. The defendant bit one officer on the leg twice, leaving a four-inch saliva stain. He bit the other officer on the leg, breaking the skin. After the incident, the defendant stated that he intended to kill the officers. A doctor testified that any human bite can cause a serious infection given the variety of infectious microorganisms present in the human mouth. He also testified that blood is sometimes present in the mouth, particularly if an individual has ill-fitting teeth or gum problems. He testified that the defendant has some false teeth or a bridge. Viewed in the light most favorable to the government, this composite of evidence supports the guilty verdicts. The motion for acquittal is denied.*

Persons infected with the HIV virus have filed civil lawsuits in probably every state where there is a chance of a money recovery from someone who infected them. Not only are there AIDS lawsuits, but there are also civil lawsuits because of infection with herpes, genital warts, gonorrhea, syphilis, and chlamydial infections.

Questions and Problems for Chapter 19

1. The following problem is taken from the 1987 National Institute of Justice publication *Problem-Oriented Policing:*
At 1:32 a.m. a man we will call Fred Snyder dials 911 from a downtown corner phone booth. The dispatcher notes his location and calls the nearest patrol unit. Officer Knox arrives 4 minutes later.
Snyder says he was beaten and robbed 20 minutes before but didn't see the robber. Under persistent questioning Snyder admits he was with a prostitute, picked up in a bar. Later, in a hotel room, he discovered the prostitute was actually a man, who then beat Snyder and took his wallet.
Is it likely that most victims in this type of case will cooperate with the police in attempting to apprehend the robber? Could the police, a prosecutor, or a judge effectively force a victim such as Snyder to cooperate? Explain.

2. Mr. Von Loh was very persuasive in presenting himself as a door-to-door salesman for a well-known local store. Once inside a home he would model men's underwear that exposed his genitals. Women who were alone in the house (or had children with them) became fearful and would have difficulty getting Von Loh to leave. Should this conduct be charged criminally? If so, what would be the possible charges in your state? (*State v. Von Loh,* 157 Wis.2d 91, 458 N.W.2d 556 (App. 1990))

3. Mr. Osborne was a very friendly man. As he greeted a young house guest of his family, he hugged the minor and grabbed her buttocks. If it could be easily inferred that his conduct was done to arouse or gratify sexual desire, could he be charged with a crime under the laws of your state? If your answer is yes, state the offense and elements that would have to be proved to obtain a conviction. (See *State v. Osborne,* 808 P.2d 624, 49 CrL 1063 (N.M. 1991.)

Notes

1. Hawaii Revised Statutes Sec. 721–1200 quoting the Delaware statutes.

2. The National Advisory Committee on Criminal Justice Standards and Goals states, on p. 242 of its report on Organized Crime: "Decriminalization is offered as a serious alternative to prostitution.... Proponents of decriminalizing all aspects of the trade believe that prostitution should be looked on as just another occupation or business, and that any laws or regulations deprive women of their fundamental constitutional rights. Legalization proposals would perpetuate their deprivation, because they generally restrict the women to certain areas and otherwise regulate them. Another argument is that legalization proposals requiring prostitutes to work in licensed brothels simply substitute slavery to a pimp with slavery to the State government, legislators, vice profiteers, and the managers of the house."

3. 67 Hawaii 608, 699 P.2d 983 (1985).

4. 66 Hawaii 616, 671 P.2d 1351.

5. See pp. 225–226.

6. 154 N.J.Super. 135, 381 A.2d 38 (1977). Although the defendant in the *Alveario* case was not convicted of solicitation for prostitution, he could be charged with other offenses for which the likelihood of conviction would be greater. Take, for example, Sec. 712–1204, promoting prostitution in the third degree of the Hawaiian Penal Code. The statute prohibits "knowingly advanc[ing] or profit[ing] from prostitution."

7. 425 U.S. 901, 96 S.Ct. 1489 (1976).

8. 478 U.S. 186, 106 S.Ct. 2841 (1986). In the case of *Bowers v. Hardwick,* the U.S. Supreme Court held that homosexuals do not enjoy a fundamental constitutional right to engage in sodomy and upheld the Georgia statute making sodomy a crime.

Pointing out that sodomy is not "implicit in the concept of ordered liberty" and is not "deeply rooted in this Nation's history and tradition," the U.S. Supreme Court refused to rule that it is protected by a right of privacy. The Court pointed out that a fundamental right of privacy does exist as pointed out in abortion (410 U.S. 113, *Roe v. Wade*), marriage (388 U.S. 1, *Loving v. Virginia*), contraception (381 U.S. 479, *Griswold v. Connecticut*), family relationship (321 U.S. 158, *Prince v. Massachusetts*), and procreation (*Skinner v. Oklahoma,* 316 U.S. 535).

9. See "Man Who Beat Up Homosexuals is Reported to Have AIDS Virus," *The New York Times,* March 22, 1991. The forty-nine-year-old man stated that he did not use drugs or ever contact prostitutes. His wife was not infected and it was concluded by doctors that he became infected with the AIDS virus through cuts on his hands when he beat up gay men.

10. 477 U.S. 57, 106 S.Ct. 2399 (1986).

11. In addition to statutes forbidding abusive, harassing, or obscene telephone calls, federal statutes also forbid other abusive use of the telephone, such as the Consumer Credit Protection Act (Pub. Law. 95–109 Stat. 877), which prohibits debt collectors from "placing telephone calls without meaningful disclosure of the caller's identity"; from "engaging any person in telephone conversation repeatedly or continuously with intent, to annoy, abuse, or harass any person at the called number"; and from "us[ing] obscene or profane language or language the natural consequence of which is to abuse the hearer or reader."

12. 77 Ill.2d 253, 396 N.E.2d 22, 27 CrL 4055.

13. 40 Or.App. 143, 594 P.2d 1250.

14. Evidence is now available showing that the AIDS virus was present in the United States in the 1960s. A fifteen-year-old Missouri boy died in a St. Louis hospital in 1969 of what was probably AIDS. An autopsy found signs of homosexual behavior suggesting that the boy had been subjected to frequent anal intercourse. See "A New Clue in the AIDS Mystery," *Newsweek,* November 9, 1987.

15. The borough president of Manhattan (New York) argued that this definition of AIDS is too narrow and results in undercounting. In his November 23, 1987, article in the *New York Times,* Mr. David Dinkins (now mayor of the City of New York) states that the narrow definition insulates "from the magnitude of the problem and leaves many people whose illness is still deemed unrelated to AIDS ineligible for the benefits that are available only to those who meet the limited definition." (See his article, "For a Broader New York Policy on AIDS".)

16. See the article "Detecting the Next Pandemic" in the March 1991 issue of *Scientific American* and also an advertisement by the same name in the March 8, 1991, *New York Times.* The article was written by Dr. Jonathan Mann, founder of the World Health Organization Global Program on AIDS and professor at the Harvard School of Public Health.

17. See "Dilemma for Southern Prosecutors: Infect Streets or Prisons with AIDS?" *The New York Times,* January 2, 1987.

Part Six

OTHER CRIMINAL CONDUCT

Chapter Twenty

DRUG ABUSE AND ALCOHOL-RELATED CRIMES

A. Drug Abuse

The Frightening Drug Problem

Polls taken in 1988, and since, have identified the drug problem as the principal concern of American voters. The public is aware of the staggering problem of drugs in the United States. Aspects of the problem are presented daily and weekly in newspapers, magazines, and on television.

Illegal drugs cause more violence in the United States than any other single factor. The Attorney General of the United States stated at the 1991 Crime Summit that "drug trafficking and its inevitable handmaiden of violence are the greatest threats to what I have always called the first civil right of every American—the right to be free from fear in our homes, on our streets, and in our communities." The statistics on illegal drugs presented by the Partnership for a Drug-Free America[1] are:

- Americans spend $110 billion annually to purchase illegal drugs.
- Organized crime and terrorism depend on drug money.
- 37 million Americans have tried illegal drugs in the past year.
- 20 million Americans used marijuana in the past month.
- 6 million Americans used cocaine in the past month.
- 6 million Americans use marijuana every day.

Illegal drugs have shattered many lives, caused suicides and murders, and caused serious health problems in many persons. Illegal drugs have disrupted the economies of many countries and many communities in America and elsewhere in the world. Older drug addicts who began using drugs in the 1960s and 1970s are reported to be widely exposed to the AIDS virus.

The combination of drugs and AIDS will continue to drain the resources of all American cities for decades to come. For example, it is estimated that New York City alone has 200,000 cocaine, coke, and heroin addicts and that half are already infected with AIDS.[2] Officials in San Francisco report 4 percent of the city's residents (nearly one person in 20) are infected with AIDS. And federal and state officials are pointing out that this is only the beginning.[3]

Drug lords all over the world have become rich and powerful. They build private armies to protect their illegal operations and to become richer and more powerful. In the Carribean alone, it is estimated that billions of drug dollars are used every year to tempt government leaders who would otherwise be allies of America.[4]

Corruption of American officials has become a very serious problem. On page 1 of the April 11, 1988, issue of the *New York Times,* it was reported that "in some American communities, corruption among law enforcement officials, policemen, sheriffs, jailers, even prosecutors and judges—is out of control."

Drugs have become readily available to anyone seeking them. Not only are drugs easily available, but better quality drugs are sold illegally at prices lower than ever before. The prices and quality make them available to the poor and the very young. Scientists have become very concerned about crack, the smokable concentrated form of cocaine. Studies have shown that persons using crack find it virtually impossible to stop and never go back to it again.[5]

Shooting up: the extreme addiction for drugs
creates a breeding ground for crime.

Recent studies show that a high number of babies are being exposed to cocaine or other illegal drugs in their mothers' wombs.[6] Public service messages on radio and television state, "If you are pregnant and use cocaine just once, you could have a deformed baby." Surveys found that at least 11 percent of women in hospitals studied have used illegal drugs during pregnancy. Experts state that this data suggest that 375,000 newborn babies a year face the possibility of health damages because of their mothers' drug abuse. A doctor commenting on the problem stated, "We are producing a new generation of innocent addicts." Even exposure of unborn babies to marijuana produces a likelihood of the babies being born smaller than normal and having neurological problems.

Some homeless persons are on the streets because of abuse of drugs and/or alcohol. Excessive use of these substances has caused many to lose their jobs. Failure to pay rent or mortgages then brings about loss of homes. Excessive use of drugs or alcohol can debilitate persons to the point where they are unable to work and are very susceptible to diseases.

In 1991, the U.S. Bureau of Justice Statistics showed that total crimes were down but that violence in the United States was up. Minor thefts, such as bicycle thefts, were down 8 percent, but homicides hit a record high of more than 23,000 in 1990. Also rising were violent crimes of assault involving injury, attempted robbery, and larceny involving contact with the victim (purse snatching, etc.).

After a federal drug raid in 1991 of fraternity houses on the University of Virginia campus, the question was asked whether drug use was on the increase at colleges and high schools. Students were concerned about the raid in which twelve students were arrested on charges of selling and distributing marijuana, LSD, and hallucinogenic mushrooms. Surveys of high school and college students have found a "significant downturn" in the use of crack and the use of cocaine.[7]

What Is the Relationship Between Drugs and Violent Crime?

- Researchers have identified three ways in which drugs are related to crime: *psychopharmacological,* in which a drug user commits crime because of drug-induced changes in physiological functions, cognitive ability, and mood
  economic compulsive, in which a drug user commits crime in order to obtain money to buy drugs
  systemic, in which violent crime occurs as a part of the drug business or culture.

- The actual number of drug-related acts of violence is difficult to measure. Three cities, however, have studied the amount of drug-related homicide in their jurisdictions:
  —Of 1,263 homicides reported in New York City in 1984, 24 percent were identified as drug-related.
  —Of 1,850 homicides recorded in Miami from 1978 to 1982, 24 percent were classified as drug-related.
  —In 1985, 21 percent of the homicides reported in the District of Columbia were identified as drug-related, increasing steadily to 34 percent in 1986, 51 percent in 1987, and to as much as 80 percent in 1988.

- Victims across the country reported that they believe their assailants were under the influence of drugs in about 12 percent of violent crime incidents in 1986–87. An additional 2 percent of the victims said their assailants were under the influence of drugs or alcohol, but they were not sure which. In 22 percent of the cases, the victims reported that the offenders were under the influence of alcohol alone.

- Incarcerated adults and youth report high levels of drug use. Among those incarcerated for violent crimes, a third of state prisoners and more than a third of the incarcerated youth said they had been under the influence of an illegal drug at the time of their offense. In the month before the violent offense for which they were incarcerated, 39 percent of state prison inmates reported daily drug use, and 16 percent reported daily use of a major drug (cocaine, heroin, PCP, LSD, and methadone).

  Among the violent offenders in state prison, those incarcerated for robbery were the most likely to have used a major drug daily, (23 percent); those incarcerated for rape and other sexual offenses were the least likely to report such use, 9 percent and 6 percent, respectively.

  Additional data from the surveys shed light on the relationship between drugs and crime, although not available separately for violent offenders.

- Overall, more than half of the state prisoners who had ever used a major drug (cocaine, heroin, PCP, LSD, or methadone) reported that they began their major drug use after their first arrest.

- Major drug use (cocaine, heroin, PCP, LSD, and methadone) is related to the number of prior convictions for state prisoners: the greater the use of major drugs, the more prior convictions the inmate was likely to report.

Source: Violent Crime in the United States, 1991 U.S. Department of Justice
Office of Justice Programs
Bureau of Justice Statistics

While many students and much of middle-class America seem to be turning away from hard drugs, hundreds of thousands of longtime users remain heavily involved with drugs.

Who Uses Illegal Drugs?

The war against illegal drugs is being fought on the "supply side" and on the "demand side." Cocaine, heroin, crack, and marijuana are produced and grown for the most part outside the United States. Great efforts are being made to prevent illegal drugs from entering the United States. However, efforts to win the "supply side" war have been going on since the 1950s with what is estimated as 90 percent of the illegal drugs getting into the United States.[8]

The "demand side" problem is that an estimated 37 million Americans are willing to pay an estimated $110 billion yearly for illegal drugs. It is reported that more money is spent annually in the United States on illegal drugs and legal alcohol than is spent for clothing. As the United States is the biggest market in the world for illegal drugs and the profits are huge, criminals will take great risks to bring the illegal drugs into the United States. The users of illegal drugs can be classified as follows:

- *The "situational" drug abuser* is a person who will use illegal drugs for a specific or "situational" purpose, such as to accomplish some other objective. A person who is under a great deal of stress or tension might use a drug such as marijuana to relax. A performer or a truck driver might use an "upper" for stimulation and to stay awake.
- *The "party" or the "weekend" user* is a drug abuser who might use drugs for "kicks" or just for the "experience." These users and the "casual user" are great sources of profits for drug pushers. U.S. Senator Phil Gramm, in pointing out that interdiction (stopping drugs from coming into the United States) was not working, stated, "The real drug 'kingpin' is the user. It is the casual users who create the profits. But we can't put them all in prison; there isn't room in the jails. We have to use disincentives."[9] Texas Senator Gramm was referring to civil penalties such as increased fines, the possible revoking of eligibility for student loans and grants, etc.
- *The drug addict* is physically and/or psychologically dependent on drugs. He or she cannot perform daily without drug support. The addict has a "monkey on his (or her) back," which could be very expensive to support. To raise the money for the daily supply of drugs ($50, $100, or even $150 per day), the addict will steal, break into cars, commit burglaries, rob, snatch purses, or push drugs. Women or men who trade sex for drugs are the most susceptible to AIDS.

Drug treatment programs are immediately available to persons with medical insurance or money to pay for them. Other persons, however, often have their names placed on waiting lists. In some parts of the United States, the wait can be long.

Observers believe that drug abuse in mainstream America seems to be on a slow decline. Surveys have found a "significant downturn" in the use of crack and cocaine among young persons of high school and college age.[10] Preventive education appears to be getting the message across about the many dangers of drug abuse. There are an unknown number of middle- and upper-class buyers of crack and cocaine, and the damage of the illegal drugs is often not visible among these groups. The most visible damage of illegal drugs can be seen among the poor who, because of drugs, sometimes become homeless or come to the attention of government officials and employees after they abuse their children.

Where Do Illegal Drugs Come From?

Drugs from Naturally Grown Plants.   It is estimated that over $100 billion is spent yearly in the United States for illegal drugs. Foreign suppliers eager to make huge profits provide a large share of naturally grown illegal drugs.

The biggest source of coca is Peru, followed by Bolivia, Ecuador, and Co-lombia. In these countries, coca, "a miracle crop, grows almost anywhere, needs little attention, resists disease and yields 3 or 4 harvests a year."[11] More than eight hundred processing labs have been destroyed by the military in an effort to stop the flow of cocaine and crack from South America. The Drug Enforcement Agency argues that if enough processing labs are destroyed, the price of coca will fall and farmers will switch to a different crop.

Current Controversy
Should Some Drugs Be Legalized?

Problems of Illegal Drug Trafficking:

- Huge profits from selling to the hundreds of thousands of addicts and casual users. The huge profits attract many persons willing to take risks for the money. The profits also fund other criminal ventures and corrupt society.
- Addicts who rob, burglarize, steal, push drugs, and commit other crimes to get money for drugs.
- Drug gangs and organized criminals committing crime and violence.
- Health problems directly and indirectly related to drugs (AIDS, addicted babies, mental and emotional problems, and others).
- Problems such as homelessness, inability to cope with life, suicide, etc.
- Drugs overwhelm the criminal justice system requiring more law enforcement officers, more courts, more prisons, etc.
- The United States now has the highest rate of imprisonment in the world (more than one million persons are in prison serving time or awaiting trial).

Controversial Questions Relating to Legalizing Some Drugs

- Are present efforts to cut off sources of drugs and reduce demand for illegal drugs effective (sources include foreign and domestic; synthetics; and drugs processed from natural products such as the coca leaf)?
- Would making drugs available to addicts cut out huge profits (incentive) and cut down burglaries, thefts, robberies, etc. committed by addicts?
- Which drugs would be made available to addicts? Would addicts have to be certified by doctors to be eligible for drugs?
- If some drugs were legalized:
  —could these drugs be kept out of the hands of minors and others not autho-rized to have them?
  —would government or private companies provide drugs?
  —who would determine the cost of drugs?
  —if addicts didn't have money (and many do not), would drugs be provided free?
  —after drug addiction becomes a health problem instead of a criminal problem, would adequate treatment centers and health care facilities become avail-able?
  —what would happen to the drug gangs and other criminals after some drugs were legalized?
  —would legalizing some drugs work in cutting down crime rates and be a practical solution?

The major opium producing countries are Burma, Laos, and Thailand in southeastern Asia, with Thailand reported to have major refineries and to be the conduit of heroin from that area. In the mideast, the major producers of opium are Afghanistan, Pakistan, and Iran, with Iran reported as the major route for heroin and opium from Pakistan and Afghanistan. Bumper crops of opium poppies, the raw material for heroin, were reported being harvested around the world in the early 1990s. It is estimated that at least 200,000 of the estimated 500,000 heroin addicts in the United States live in New York.[12]

Colombia (South America) is reported to be the largest producer of marijuana, along with Mexico, Jamaica, and Belize. Marijuana is also grown illegally in the United States either in fields or indoors. Magazines giving instructions on how to grow marijuana are available for sale in the United States.

Synthetic Drugs.   Drug experts point out that addicts are often unaware they are buying and using a synthetic. They may conclude they have obtained a finer grade of heroin or cocaine. Illegal laboratories throughout the United States are producing synthetic drugs and selling them in the illegal drug market.

Growing drug-producing plants, refining the natural product, and marketing or smuggling heroin, cocaine, or marijuana is costly and risky. Persons with training or a background in chemistry can instead illegally set up a home laboratory and manufacture a synthetic drug to market.

Synthetic drugs are often produced under few quality controls. Persons producing the drugs may have inadequate knowledge of or experience in what they are doing. They might be negligent or apathetic. Major mistakes have occurred regularly that have resulted in the deaths or serious injury of persons using the illegal drugs. Many addicts and other drug users are aware of these problems. Drug experts believe fear and uncertainty about the quality of synthetic drugs have limited their popularity.

Yet synthetics have a big share of the illegal drug market. For example, it is reported that the State of California produces more methamphetamine illegally than any country in the world.

Another illegal market for synthetics is in counterfeiting legitimate drugs and selling the pirate product for less money. An article in the November 5, 1990, issue of *Newsweek* magazine tells of the worldwide problem of counterfeit drugs, which have killed and crippled many people. The title of the article is "A Really Nasty Business: Fake pharmaceuticals look like the real thing—but they can be lethal." The article points out that drug "piracy has hit the poorest nations [of the world] like a plague," causing many deaths.

B. Drug Laws in the United States

Early Drug Laws

The first drug law enacted in the United States was an anti-opium-smoking ordinance passed in San Francisco in 1875 because of the opium smoking problem there. This was one of the few restrictions in the United States at that time.

In the 1880s and 1890s, persons in the United States could concoct and sell to the American public practically any drug or drug compound they wished.

Drugs were available in stores, through mail-order catalogues, or through traveling vendors and peddlers. Little was known at that time about the effect of drugs on human beings. Drug promoters claimed the drugs cured sickness and other human problems.

A German firm, for example, marketed a newly discovered drug in the 1890s as a cough suppressant. The name the firm gave the drug is well known today—heroin. Heroin did a wonderful job of suppressing coughs, but years passed before people realized the terrible evils and misery of addiction to heroin. Other drugs and compounds were advertised and promoted as cures for everything from ingrown toenails to cancer. Medications were sold that guaranteed sex rejuvenation, the growing of hair on bald persons, the enlargement of women's breasts, a cure for arthritis, etc. Because of these promotions, a drug problem grew in the United States.

In 1910, President William Howard Taft stated that "the misuse of cocaine is undoubtedly an American habit, the most threatening of the drug habits that has ever appeared in this country." In 1906, the Federal Pure Food and Drug Act was enacted because of the concern over heroin addiction. The federal Food and Drug Administration (FDA) requires that a firm or person who wishes to market and sell a drug in the United States must show that:

- the drug or medication is not harmful to humans, and
- the drug or medication will do what it is advertised to do.

Another law enacted at the time was the 1915 Federal Harrison Narcotics Act.

The Uniform Controlled Substances Act

Today, the federal government and all of the states have enacted the Uniform Controlled Substances Act. The Uniform Controlled Substances Act was approved by the National Conference of Commissioners on Uniform State Laws in 1970.[13] The purposes of this act have been stated as follows:

> This Uniform Act was drafted to achieve uniformity between the laws of the several States and those of the Federal government. It has been designed to complement the new Federal narcotic and dangerous drug legislation and provide an interlocking trellis of Federal and State law to enable government at all levels to control more effectively the drug abuse problem.
>
> Uniform Controlled Substances Act, 9 U.L.A., Commissioners' Prefatory Note, p. 188 (1979).

In their Uniform Controlled Substances acts, most states forbid and make it criminal conduct to:

- manufacture or deliver a controlled (forbidden) substance,
- possess with intent to manufacture or deliver a controlled substance,
- create, deliver, or possess with intent to deliver a counterfeit substance,
- offer or agree to deliver a controlled substance and then deliver or dispense a substance that is not a controlled substance,
- possess a controlled substance,
- knowingly keep or maintain a store, dwelling, building, vehicle, boat, or aircraft, etc. resorted to by persons illegally using controlled substances,
- acquire or obtain possession of a controlled substance by misrepresentation, fraud, forgery, deception, or subterfuge.

The Uniform Controlled Substances Act has five schedules of controlled substances according to their potential for abuse, degree of accepted medical use, and relative physical danger to the abuser. These schedules may be summarized as follows:

Schedule I. This schedule contains substances, both narcotics and non-narcotics, which (a) have a high potential for abuse, (b) have no currently accepted medical use, and (c) lack acceptable safety standards for supervised medical use. This schedule includes drugs such as illegal narcotics and hallucinogens such as opiates (heroine and morphine), LSD, marijuana and mescaline. The maximum possible imprisonment for the manufacture or delivery of the narcotic substances is listed in this schedule. Money fines may also be imposed. The penalties for the manufacture or delivery of the non-narcotic substances are also listed in this schedule.

Schedule II. This schedule contains substances, both narcotic and non-narcotic, which (a) have a high potential for abuse, (b) have currently accepted medical uses, even though some uses may have severe restrictions, and (c) may lead to severe psychological or physical dependence. This schedule includes drugs such as opium, coca leaves and their derivatives, opiates (synthetic narcotics such as methadone), amphetamine, methamphetamine, methylphenidate and phenmetrazine. The maximum imprisonment possible for the illegal manufacture or delivery of the substances in this schedule are often identical to Schedule I.

Schedule III. This schedule contains substances which (a) have a potential for abuse less than the substances listed in Schedules I and II, (b) have a currently accepted medical use and (c) may lead to moderate or low physical dependence or high psychological dependence. This schedule includes stimulants such as amphetamines, depressants, such as short acting barbiturates, and certain narcotic combinations such as codeine preparations. Penalties are listed in the schedule.

Schedule IV. This schedule contains substances which (a) have a low potential for abuse relative to the substances in Schedule III, (b) have a currently accepted medical use, and (c) may lead to limited physical or psychological dependence relative to the substances in Schedule III. This schedule includes long-acting barbiturates such as phenobarbital, and "minor tranquilizers" such as meprobamate. The maximum imprisonment possible for the illegal manufacture or delivery of the substances is listed in this schedule.

Schedule V. This schedule contains substances which (a) have a low potential for abuse relative to the substances in Schedule IV, (b) have currently accepted medical use and (c) may lead to limited physical or psychological dependence relative to the substances in Schedule IV. This schedule incudes narcotic drugs containing non-narcotic active medical ingredients, and certain stimulants or depressants containing active medical ingredients. The maximum imprisonment possible for the illegal manufacture or delivery of the substances is listed in this schedule.

Types of Possession of Controlled Substances

The most common criminal (or ordinance) illegal drug charge is that of possession of a controlled substance. Possession must be proved in order to sustain the arrest and conviction. Proof of possession may be either of the following:

- *Actual possession* is possession on the person of the defendant, or within an area of his or her immediate control and reach. Actual possession may be within a container (purse, package, suitcase, etc.) that the defendant

Possession of a Small Amount of Marijuana

The offense of "possession of a small amount of marijuana" is charged in different ways throughout the United States.

Criminal Offense	*Civil Offense*	*Legalizing this Conduct*
If the person is charged and convicted under a statute where the person could receive a jail sentence, the conviction is a criminal conviction and the person has been convicted of a crime.	If the only penalty that can be imposed after conviction is a money fine, the conviction is for a civil offense and is similar to a speeding ticket or a parking ticket. Under these circumstances, the offense of possession of a small amount of marijuana has been "decriminalized" as it is no longer charged as a crime.	If there is neither criminal nor civil punishment of possession of a small amount of marijuana, the conduct has then been legalized as it is no longer a crime or a civil offense. It is reported that Alaska was the only state that had legalized possession of marijuana, and then only for personal use in the home. However in 1991, a new law became effective that makes possession of marijuana a crime in Alaska (any amount and any place).

may be carrying or has within reach. Actual possession may also occur in a vehicle when the controlled substance is under the seat of the person or in the glove compartment of the vehicle owned or driven by the defendant.

- *Constructive possession* of a controlled substance occurs when illegal drugs are in a place immediately accessible to the accused and subject to his or her domination and control. Examples of constructive possession would be drugs found in the trunk of a car where the defendant was the owner or driver of the vehicle, or in a home or business place controlled and dominated by a defendant to such an extent that a strong inference of possession could be drawn by a judge or jury.

(See chapter 3 for additional material on possession.)

First Offense Provision for Simple Possession

Where the criminal charge is simple possession of a controlled substance, the Federal Act, as well as most of the State Acts, provides that in dealing with a person who has not been previously convicted of a controlled substance related offense, the court may accept a plea of guilty, then place the accused on a year or less of probation without entering a judgment of guilty, with the provision that upon satisfaction of the probation terms, the court will dismiss the charge. When this procedure is followed, the accused does not receive a criminal record.

Do Some Drugs Cause an Increase in Violent Behavior?

Marijuana is known as the "entry drug" as it can lead to the use of other drugs. Heroin is reported to maintain users at a consistent level as it ordinarily acts as a tranquilizer.

However, violent behavior has been reported by police and drug treatment experts to be increasing in areas where crack and cocaine are heavily used. Violent, erratic, and paranoid behavior, a condition known as "cocaine psychosis," has been reported to be increasing among cocaine users and crack users.

"Cocaine psychosis" was first described by Sigmund Freud in 1884 after he observed patients who had been given cocaine for periods of time. The world forgot Freud's observations until widespread use of cocaine in the 1970s again produced violence and psychiatric difficulties associated with the use of cocaine.

Experts also associate violence with the use of some of the designer (synthetic) drugs. As crack is a cocaine concentrate, the likelihood of violence is increased.

Delivery of Controlled Substances

Delivery of controlled substances is generally defined as the transfer of a controlled substance from one person to another. "Delivery" statutes are tailored to apply to the "supplier" of drugs. Consequently, most arrests under these statutes involve a supplier either selling a drug to a lower level distributor or selling a drug to the ultimate user. In contrast to crimes of "possession" of controlled substances, which most often are treated as misdemeanors, delivery under both the federal and state statutes is treated as a felony, calling for lengthy terms of incarceration.

Possession of Controlled Substance with Intent to Deliver

The Controlled Substances Act attaches the same felony penalties to "possession with intent to deliver" as it does to actual delivery. A typical case of "possession with intent to deliver" would be the possession by an accused of a kilogram or more of marijuana, scales, numerous small plastic bags, several evenly weighed out one ounce bags of marijuana, a price list, and a customer list. In all cases "intent to deliver" may be shown circumstantially by evidence such as proof of a large monetary value of drugs, a large quantity of drugs, possession of manufacturing or packaging implements, and the activities or statements of the person or persons in possession of the substance.

The "Len Bias" Laws (Drug-Induced Deaths)

Len Bias was a basketball star at the University of Maryland when he died as the result of using cocaine. If the person who supplied the cocaine was committing a felony in supplying the cocaine, the state law would probably justify charging the supplier with felony murder in addition to the illegal drug charge (see chapter 13 for a discussion of "felony murder").

A number of states have enacted what is now called the "Len Bias" law. Such a statute makes a person who illegally manufactures, distributes, or dispenses illegal drugs strictly liable for a death that results from the injection, inhalation, or ingestion of such a drug. The following 1990 case illustrates:

STATE V. ERVIN
Superior Court of New Jersey (1990) 242 N.J.Super. 584, 577 A. 2d 1273

Ervin purchased cocaine, which he and his girlfriend shared. She died as the result of using the cocaine. He was not only charged with possession of cocaine but also possession with intent to deliver and causing a drug-induced death, in violation of the New Jersey "Len Bias" law. In sustaining the conviction for the drug-induced death, the court held:

* * *

The New Jersey Legislature has determined that manufacturing, distributing and dispensing certain illegal drugs, including cocaine which is the substance involved in the present case, are criminal activities which, like the crimes enumerated in the felony murder statute, pose inherent dangers to others including those who use the drugs. Defendant has shown us no basis upon which to conclude that that determination is irrational. N.J.S.A. 2C:35−9b limits criminal liability to cases in which the defendant has illegally manufactured, distributed or dispensed a prohibited substance, death results which would not have occurred but for the injection, inhalation or ingestion of that substance, and "the death was not (a) too remote in its occurrence as to have a just bearing on the defendant's liability; or (b) too dependent upon conduct of another person which was unrelated to the injection, inhalation or ingestion of the substance or its effect as to have a just bearing on the defendant's liability." N.J.S.A. 2C:35−9. These limitations on liability are similar to those imposed on criminal liability for felony murder. . . . By analogy to the felony murder rule, we hold that the absolute or strict liability feature of N.J.S.A. 2C:35−9, limited as it is to deaths which are the proximate consequences of inherently dangerous illegal activities, does not violate due process of law.

* * *

Use of Drugs by a Pregnant Woman: Should She Be Charged with Illegal Delivery of Drugs?

Drugs used by a pregnant woman could have a very serious effect upon the baby. The baby could be born addicted and could have serious physical, neurological, or other problems. The question whether this is criminal delivery of an illegal drug has become a much debated issue in the United States.

Criminal charges are not usually commenced in most situations where a woman has used illegal drugs during her pregnancy. But since 1987, more than sixty criminal cases have been commenced charging women with charges such as criminal child abuse, assault with a deadly weapon, manslaughter, and criminal delivery of drugs.

In 1990, the first woman convicted was Jennifer Johnson of Florida. Her sentence for the drug delivery conviction was one year in a drug treatment program and fourteen years of probation, which included court-supervised prenatal care if she ever becomes pregnant again. Her appeal is expected to receive national attention, partly because her lawyer plans to argue that "we are creating pregnancy police."

Current Controversy

Pregnancy Police? What Efforts Should Be Made to Protect Unborn Babies?

Obstetricians tell pregnant women not to use alcohol and tobacco, as these substances are linked with low birth weight and prematurity. In Seattle in 1991, two young cocktail waiters refused to serve a pregnant woman a strawberry daiquiri. The waiters were fired but became local heroes for showing such concern for the unborn baby. Was this concern none of their business and were they acting as pregnancy police?

Drug use during pregnancy is dangerous to the fetus, particularly in the last trimester. Hard drugs such as crack, cocaine, and heroin have a devastating effect upon unborn babies. The baby can be born addicted and have serious physical, neurological, and emotional problems. Medical bills for the first months of life for such babies often run into hundreds of thousands of dollars.

Women using hard drugs during pregnancy should be charged with illegal delivery of drugs	*Mothers of newly born babies should not be charged criminally*
The public wants such prosecutions. The message is clear what problems the mother is imposing upon the newborn baby. A pregnant woman today knows that drugs will seriously harm her unborn child.	Prosecuting a woman for using drugs during pregnancy is counterproductive. Addicted pregnant women are going to avoid doctors or abort. They are not going to admit using drugs and provide evidence needed to prosecute them. Treatment centers should be made available to such women.

A Michigan Court of Appeals threw out a criminal case against a woman who used crack just hours before her son's birth in 1991. The court in the case of *State v. Hardy* held that the State of Michigan could not proceed with the criminal charge of delivery of drugs.[14] The prosecutor stated that he would appeal the matter to the Supreme Court of Michigan.

C. ALCOHOL-RELATED CRIMES

Alcohol as a Drug

Most persons use some form of drugs every day. Coffee, tea, and cola contain caffeine. Tobacco products contain nicotine. Probably the great majority of medicine cabinets in America contain an assortment of over-the-counter drugs (nonprescription drugs) and also prescription drugs. The nonprescription drugs may include aspirin, digestive medication, and tranquilizers. The prescription drugs might include any of the tremendous variety of modern medication that is available to medical science for the treatment of human diseases and ailments.

Alcohol is a drug used by an estimated 95 million Americans in some form and in varying amounts. It is a mood-altering drug used by many persons as a tranquilizer. It has been observed that, if alcohol were discovered today for the first time, the Federal Food and Drug Administration would be obligated by law to forbid its over-the-counter sale without prescription. This statement is made because alcohol is an addictive drug and because it is toxic, it is a poison. But alcohol has, for a long time, been part of our economic, social, and cultural environment. It is because of the beverage's long history of social acceptance and our society's economic dependence upon it that it continues to be sold openly on the market.

Alcohol is the most widely abused and misused drug in America (and probably in the world). It is related to a substantial number of this country's traffic fatalities, one-half of the homicides, and one-third of the suicides. Alcoholism is one of America's biggest health problems, behind heart disease and cancer.

Arrests for drunkenness are always high on the yearly lists of crimes. Alcohol is also a factor in many disorderly conduct, battery, rape, child abuse, and criminal damage to property offenses committed every year in the United States. The use of alcohol by children and young persons is a problem throughout the country. The movement from other drugs to alcohol is sometimes condoned by parents, who in their relief that their children are not involved in the use of other forms of drugs, do not recognize the dangers inherent in the use of alcohol.

Drunken Driving: The Criminal Homicide Causing the Most Deaths

More than fifty persons a day are killed in the United States because of driving under the influence. In addition, thousands of others are injured every year and billions of dollars of property is damaged or destroyed. Until the early 1980s, more than seventy persons were killed every day in accidents involving drunken drivers. Because of actions taken in every state, the number of persons killed and injured has been lowered.

The National Commission on Drunk Driving reports that in recent years more than 500 laws were passed to discourage driving under the influence. For example, all states have now established twenty-one as the legal drinking age.

More than a dozen states curb (or forbid) "happy hours" where bars have drinks available at bargain prices. Punishment for drunken driving has been increased in all states. Victims of drunken driving can commence civil lawsuits under "dram shop" laws that permit the drunk driver (or his or her estate) as well as the bars (and persons) furnishing or selling the alcoholic drinks to be sued.

Under new laws, driving licenses are suspended and taken away sooner. Insurance companies have always placed persons convicted of drunken driving in high risk categories and slap high surcharges on such auto insurance policies.

The U.S. Congress has amended the federal bankruptcy statutes and classifies driving under the influence as deliberate conduct that prevents offenders from minimizing liabilities by going into bankruptcy.

The general public has become increasingly aware of the problems of drunken driving through newspapers and television. Schools, churches, and other private groups have also drawn public attention to the problem. Organizations such as MADD (Mothers Against Drunken Driving) urge tougher laws and tougher enforcement and advocate "designated drivers" for persons who have been drinking. Business corporations have provided funds or have provided advertising space urging moderation in drinking and the use of "designated drivers" (a nondrinking person who drives for a group).

Fines from drunken driving convictions amount to hundreds of millions of dollars per year. In most states, this money goes into the state's treasury, but by law in some states the money goes back to the local community. New York statutes now provide that drunken driving fines go to the arresting law enforce-

A couple walking their dog were the victims of an alleged drunk driver. The man and the dog were killed and the woman injured when the cab (background) was hit from behind and forced onto the sidewalk.

ment agency, thereby giving the local police department (or sheriff's department) a financial stake in tougher enforcement. The chances of the average drunken driver being apprehended are estimated at only 1 in 2,000, but it is hoped that these odds will be cut.

The Problem Drinker Is the Problem Driver

Many social drinkers have responded to the many messages that driving under the influence is dangerous. Peer pressure from their families and friends have also aided in causing more social drinkers not to drive under the influence.

Experts now point out that it is the driver with a drinking problem who is the problem. Too many persons with severe alcohol and/or drug problems continue to drive while impaired and under the influence.

For a social drinker in good health, there is only a small chance of being arrested if they drive while impaired. The penalties for drunken driving are very steep and no one wants the embarrassment of having his or her name in the newspaper's drunk list. Thus, an increasing number of social drinkers are not driving under the influence. Problem drinkers, however, continue to drink and drive even after their licenses have been revoked. They are generally the danger on the highway. One expert commented on the problem drinker, stating that often, "He doesn't give a damn, especially after drinking."

Detecting Drunk Drivers

Drunk drivers are often detected after they have caused an accident or hit another car or a pedestrian. Drunk drivers are also detected when they commit a moving

Drunk Driving*

- Drunk driving is a serious crime—serious in terms of its prevalence and its consequences. In 1986 there was about one arrest for driving under the influence of an intoxicant for every eighty-eight licensed drivers. The National Highway Traffic Safety Administration estimates that perhaps as many as a quarter of a million persons were killed in alcohol-related motor vehicle crashes over the last ten years. More than 650,000 persons are injured in such crashes every year. The annual cost in property damage, medical costs, and other costs of drunk driving may total more than $24 billion.
- Between 1970 and 1986 arrests for DUI increased nearly 223 percent, while the number of licensed drivers increased by 42 percent.
- Arrest rates for DUI were highest among twenty-one-year-olds and reached their peak in 1983 with a rate of one arrest for every thirty-nine licensed drivers of that age.
- Prior to their arrest for DWI, convicted offenders had consumed a median of 6 ounces of pure alcohol (about equal to the alcoholic content of 12 bottles of beer or 8 mixed drinks) in a median of 4 hours. About 26 percent consumed at least 10 ounces of pure alcohol (equivalent to 20 beers or 13 mixed drinks).

- About 54 percent reported drinking only beer, about 2 percent only wine, 23 percent liquor only, and 21 percent had been drinking two or more different beverages. This last group consumed the most alcohol prior to arrest, about three times more than those who drank only beer.
- For DWI offenders sentenced to jail, the median term imposed was five months; those with prior DWI sentences received sentences that were about twice as long as first-timers.
- About 7 percent of all persons confined in local jails on June 30, 1983, were charged with or convicted of DWI; nearly 13 percent of jail inmates had a current charge or prior conviction for DWI.
- Those in jail for DWI were 95 percent male, had a median age of 32, and reflected a racial distribution similar to the adult general population. Nearly 80 percent were not living with a spouse at the time of arrest, and they were more likely to be unemployed than adults in the civilian labor force.
- Nearly half of those in jail for DWI had previously been sentenced to probation, jail, or prison for DWI, and three-quarters had a prior sentence for any crime (including DWI).

*U.S. Bureau of Justice Statistics released in 1988 on studies of 1986. The Bureau of Justice Statistics define "DUI" and "DWI" as follows: *DUI is the general term for drivers who operate a motor vehicle after having consumed an intoxicant (such as drugs or alcohol); DWI generally refers to inmates in local jails who were charged with driving while intoxicated by alcohol (usually defined by State law as a specific concentration of alcohol in the blood).*

violation such as speeding, weaving or changing traffic lanes without signaling, or running a stop sign or signal light. Efforts used to detect impaired drivers before they have an accident are:

- Roadblocks to check for drunk driver, driver's license, vehicle registration, or equipment.
- One-block detours set up by the police requiring drivers to make a series of turns, or to drive down narrow lanes with plastic traffic cones on each side of the lane. Drivers who do not perform well can be stopped for observation.
- Observing the conduct of persons leaving taverns and night clubs ("watering holes"). Observing the manner in which they handle themselves and their motor vehicles. Ten years ago, newspapers criticized police for this procedure. Today, the same papers encourage and praise police using this tactic.

Laws in Your State

Law   *State Statute #*

Absolute sobriety law (under   _____ years of age
what age drivers may not have
any alcohol in their system)

Blood alcohol content to deter-   _____ %
mine legal intoxication

Aggravated drunken driving   _____ %
(blood alcohol required)

Felony statutes for drunken driving causing:
• death
• aggravated injury
• other injury

Statutes forbidding:
• open alcohol/malt beverage in
  vehicle
• drinking in vehicle (alcohol/
  malt beverage) (Must the vehicle be moving?)

Penalties

| *First* | *Second* | *Aggravated* | *Implied Consent* |
| *Offense DWI* | *Offense DWI* | *Drunk Driving* | *(Refusal to Submit to Test)* |

Questions and Problems for Chapter 20

1. Ripoffs occur regularly in illegal drug transactions. The following situations were not ripoffs, but the defendants sold substances to undercover officers that they presented as and thought were illegal drugs. Oviedo sold what he thought was heroin. Everett sold what he thought to be P-2-P (phenyl-2-propanone). Both sold harmless material to undercover officers. Both were convicted of attempt to sell the drug each thought he was selling. Would the convictions stand in your state? Or would the defense of "legal impossibility" cause a reversal of the convictions? *United States v. Everett,* 700 F.2d 900 (3d Cir. 1983), *United States v. Oviedo,* 525 F.2d 881 (5th Cir. 1976).

2. Based on the information from a reliable informant, Louisville police provided the following in an affidavit in support of a search warrant: "within the past 48 hours he (the informant) was at 4306 South Third Street, the home of Claude Hargrave, and at this time and at this same address he observed a quantity of marijuana." Does this establish probable cause to issue the search warrant? *Hargrave v. Commonwealth,* 724 S.W.2d 202 (Ky. 1986), review denied, 484 U.S. 821, 108 S.Ct. 81, 42 CrL 4005 (1987).

3. A police officer observed the defendant stagger out of a tavern with all the appearances of being very intoxicated. The defendant got into a parked car and inserted a key into the ignition. As there was probable cause to believe that the defendant was legally intoxicated, could he be arrested at this point and required to submit to a breath test under the refusal statute of your state? Or should the officer permit the defendant to drive the vehicle and run the risk of an accident, or the defendant fleeing from the officer at high speeds? Read the statutes of your state before answering. *State v. Mulcahy,* 107 N.J. 467, 527 A.2d 368 (1987).

Notes

1. Partnership for a Drug-Free America is a volunteer, private sector coalition of the communication business presenting a massive media program against drug abuse.

2. See the *New York Times* editorial entitled "The Right Fight Against AIDS: As the Admiral Says, Focus on Addicts," February 28, 1988.

3. See the *Milwaukee Journal* article entitled "AIDS Toll Has Frisco Besieged: About 4% of Residents Have Contracted Disease," August 28, 1988. See the March 1991 issue of *Scientific American* where the founder of the World Health Organization Global Program on AIDS stated that the "pandemic remains . . . dynamic and volatile. We can expect (worldwide) at least six million new cases of clinical AIDS in adults during the 1990s."

4. See the letter to the *New York Times* from the Ambassador to Barbados, July 2, 1988.

5. See the *New York Times* article, "Drug Researchers Try to Treat a Nearly Unbreakable Habit," June 25, 1988.

6. See "Widespread Abuse of Drugs by Pregnant Women is Found" *The New York Times,* August 30, 1988.

7. See "Notwithstanding U. of Virginia Raid, Drug Use on Campuses Seems Less" *The New York Times,* March 26, 1991; "Cocaine on Wane in New York City," *The New York Times,* January 6, 1991; and "Cocaine Use Found on the Way Down Among U.S. Youths," *The New York Times,* January 25, 1991.

8. The problem of drugs in the United States is not a new problem. In 1910, President William Howard Taft said, "The misuse of cocaine is undoubtedly an American habit, the most threatening of the drug habits that has ever appeared in this country." In 1989, New York Governor Mario Cuomo said at a luncheon, "The State of New York has three major problems: drugs first, drugs second, drugs third."

9. See "In the Politicians' War on Drugs, the Rhetorical Guns are Blazing," *The New York Times,* September 11, 1988.

10. See the frontpage article "Cocaine Use Found on the Way Down Among U.S. Youths," *The New York Times,* January 25, 1991.

11. See "Tainted Drug Toll Rises to 10, Officials Say," *The New York Times,* February 4, 1991; and "Cocaine Users Adding Heroin to Their Menu" *The New York Times,* July 21, 1991.

12. See "Search for Better Heroin High Is Fatal Allure of Synthetics" *The New York Times,* February 4, 1991.

13. This act replaced the 1933 Uniform Narcotic Drug Act and the 1966 Model State Drug Abuse Control Act. Uniform Controlled Substances Act, 9 U.L.A. 188 (1979).

14. See "Court Backs Woman in Pregnancy Drug Case," *The New York Times,* April 3, 1991.

Chapter Twenty One

GANGS, ORGANIZED CRIME, AND TERRORISM

A. The Danger of Gangs and Organized Crime

Gangs and organized crime have been a very serious problem in the United States for many years. However, the problems in the late 1980s and 1990s are more dangerous and more serious than ever before. The continuing problems are illustrated by the following quotes from past years:

> **1967** In many ways organized crime is the most sinister form of crime in America. The men who control it have become rich and powerful by encouraging the needy to gamble, by luring the troubled to destroy themselves with drugs, by extorting the profits of honest and hardworking businessmen, by collecting usury from those in financial plight, by maiming or murdering those who oppose them, by bribing those who are sworn to destroy them. Organized crime is not merely a few preying upon a few. In a very real sense it is dedicated to subverting not only American institutions, but the very decency and integrity that are the most cherished attributes of a free society.
>
> *—President's Commission on Law Enforcement*
> *and Administration of Justice in 1967*

> **1970** Organized crime in the United States has three goals: exploitation, corruption and destruction. What it cannot directly exploit, it seeks to corrupt; what it cannot directly corrupt, it seeks to destroy. Its degrading influence can be felt in every level of American society, sometimes in insidious, subtle ways, but more often in direct acts of violence and illegality. It is a malignant growth in the body of American social and economic life that must be eliminated.
>
> *—Former President Richard Nixon*
> *on the establishment of the National Council*
> *on Organized Crime on June 4, 1970*

> **1983** Organized crime today is a more dangerous and pervasive force than ever before. It affects virtually every aspect of our nation and its economy.
>
> *—Federal Appeals Judge Irving Kaufman,*
> *Chairman of the 1983 President's Commission*
> *on Organized Crime*

B. Types of Gangs and Organized Criminal Groups

In outlining the duties and responsibilities of the Pennsylvania Crime Commission, Pennsylvania statutes define "organized crime" as:

> The unlawful activity of an association trafficking in illegal goods or services, including but not limited to gambling, prostitution, loan-sharking, controlled substances, labor racketeering or other unlawful activities or any continuing criminal conspiracy or other unlawful practice which has as its objective large economic gain through fraudulent or coercive practices or improper governmental influence.

Organized Crime Is More than the Mafia

Former FBI Director William Webster stated in testimony before the President's Commission on Organized Crime that organized crime is no longer synonymous

In 1979, four men went into a New York restaurant as Mafia boss Carmine Galente was having lunch. They caught Galente and his companions by surprise, killing them with automatic weapons and shotguns.

with one group—the Mafia or Cosa Nostra—but includes many other groups that present serious growing threats to the nation. The most violent are the drug gangs and street gangs that are waging wars in American cities across the nation.

Webster testified that "although these criminal groups have often been glamorized in books, movies and television, they are associations of career criminals who operate with utter contempt for our laws and the rights of others. In short, they are purveyors of crime, violence, death and human misery."

The Mafia: Are They Losing Their Grip on America?

The legendary Mafia, once prominent in many of America's big cities, is believed by many law enforcement officers to be losing its grip on America. Many former Mafia leaders are serving long prison sentences after convictions under RICO (Racketeer Influenced and Corrupt Organizations Act). Some have been killed, others have died, and some former dons and other Mafia leaders are living in retirement.

The Mafia is known throughout the world. Many law enforcement officers call it *La Cosa Nostra*. It is believed that more than half of the two thousand "made" Mafia members in the United States operate in the New York City area and belong to one of five active New York City families. The Chicago branch is called the "Outfit" by some and is believed to have 100 to 150 members (down from more than 200 in the late 1980s).

Like many other organized groups of mobsters and criminals operating in the United States, the Mafia is primarily an ethnic group. Most members are of Italian ancestry and many have roots in Sicily. The Sicilian Mafia is said to operate independently of the American Mafia.

Law enforcement officers agree that the Mafia has lost much of its former power and remains effective only in New York City and Chicago (and some areas around these cities). But even in Chicago and New York, the Mafia is operating on a smaller scale than in years past. The reasons given for this loss of power are:

1. *Effectiveness of the RICO laws* (a discussion of RICO follows later in this chapter). RICO has proved to be very effective against organized crime. Organized crime task forces have used RICO to obtain convictions against Mafia leaders that resulted in long prison terms.

2. *Loss of efficient leaders.* The Mafia has not been able to recruit effective, competent persons to replace the many leaders lost to them by prison, killings, and death. Mismanagement and inability to cope with many new problems facing the Mafia have also diminished the power of the Mafia.

3. *Changes in large American cities.* At the height of its power, central cities were filled with ethnic groups that tolerated or did business with the Mafia. The Mafia had a political power base and was always strongest in the Italian-American sections of big cities. But the neighborhoods have changed. White populations have moved out of America's big cities and Hispanics and blacks generally will not do business with the Mafia.

4. *Competition.* With the changes in America's large cities, new gangs emerged. Asian, black, Hispanic, and other groups dominated drug trafficking and illegal gambling. Many of the new groups are able to move drugs and money across international borders. It is reported that the American Mafia did not develop adequate drug sources and is not competing successfully with the new drug gangs. Even the Sicilian Mafia, with its European and Mediterranean sources, is competing with the American Mafia.

5. *Legalization of gambling in the United States.* Illegal gambling was once the greatest source of profit for the Mafia. Today, many forms of legal gambling are available in probably every state. With the competition of legal gambling, profits in illegal gambling have gone down. At the same time, risks have gone up with the RICO laws. In addition, blacks and Hispanics in large cities are reluctant to place bets with Mafia bookies.

6. *Breakdown of the code of silence.* For many generations, the Mafia code of silence protected the organization and made it difficult to penetrate the Mafia. Today, the code of silence has been broken so many times that it is no longer unusual to find informants to provide information against the Mafia.

In the 1991 trial of ten defendants charged with bid-rigging in the New York City window-installation business, a former high-ranking Mafia leader, Philip Leonetti, testified for the government against the leader and members of the New York Gambino family. Leonetti testified that he was a member of the Philadelphia La Cosa Nostra family for nine years and that his uncle, Nicodemo Scarfo, was the boss of the Philadelphia family. When asked what crimes he had committed for the Philadelphia family, Mr. Leonetti answered, "Murder, extortion, attempted murder, gambling, loan-sharking, beatings." (See "Ex-Mob Leader Tells Court of Killings," *The New York Times,* April 26, 1991.)

7. *Organized crime as a career choice.* Can the Mafia recruit replacements in the United States or Italy to fill its ranks and return it to the prominence and profits it once enjoyed? This remains to be seen, but the future for the Mafia looks doubtful.

The Problem of Gang Violence in American Cities

In 1987 when gang killings rose to 387, law enforcement agencies in Los Angeles county made more than 12,000 gang-related arrests. In an attempt to keep the estimated 70,000 gang members off balance and on the defensive, it is reported that thousands of "rousts" were made by police in south-central Los Angeles.

Gang violence in the early 1970s in Los Angeles and other American cities was often over neighborhood turf and protecting the gang colors. Gangs would stake out their own turf and fight off intruders. Today, the most powerful and ruthless of the gangs use and sell drugs, and the violence is over selling territory. Rip-offs and drive-by shootings are frequent.

When competition for drug sales caused the price of cocaine, heroin, and crack to drop dramatically, gang members took their trade to other cities. By flying or driving to other areas, they sometimes receive prices four times what they were receiving in their source city.

The August 1988 issue of the *National District Attorneys Bulletin* reported that "to date, 46 cities across the country have reported the presence of Los Angeles gang members, most of them dealing in narcotics." The spread of gangs and the sale of narcotics from source cities to distribution cities has occurred throughout the United States.

Police and other experts report that in many large cities, the police are "outmanned, out gunned and outspent." Weapons such as the UZI and the AK-47 are available in either legal or illegal markets. If such weapons are purchased legally, they can be easily converted to fully automatic by a gunsmith who ignores the law.

Police in large cities are increasingly wearing armored vests. Departments are equipping officers with automatic pistols and rifles to increase fire power. The fight over the legalization of "cop-killer" and "fast" bullets was fought in Congress in 1987. Although now outlawed, such bullets are available on the black market. "Cop-killer" bullets and "fast" bullets can penetrate armored vests and garments.

Many police officers and observers are not optimistic about the outcome of the battles in American cities with drug and street gangs. They point out that the gangs are better armed and more violent than ever before. Like the Mafia, they will learn to become more skillful in evading the law. Huge profits are being made from the sale of drugs. Some of the gangs are reported to have established direct connections with major foreign suppliers and smugglers and are assured of continuous supplies of high quality cocaine and other drugs.

Many of the gangs are made up of national and ethnic groups. The Hispanic, black, and Asian gangs have a continuing source of new recruits from their national and ethnic groups living in American cities. New members can also be recruited from either foreign countries or illegals living in the United States.

The Big Four of Motorcycle Gangs

Of the motorcycle groups thought by law enforcement officers to be dangerous, the following are not only the largest but also the most sophisticated, well-organized groups, with regular organization structures:

Hell's Angels   The oldest and most famous of the gangs, this group concentrates on the West Coast. Its Oakland, California, chapter is considered the most important. Hell's Angels had chapters in Europe, Australia, and New Zealand. The Hamburg, West Germany, chapter was shut down in 1983 with the arrest of 28 members for extortion, white slavery, and other offenses. It is thought that the strong-arm enforcers of the U.S. gang are the "Filthy Few." Motorcycle gangs first received national attention in the United States in 1947. Hundreds of motorcyclists took over the small California town of Holister. They literally tore the small community apart and intimidated everybody with their violence and their numbers. A movie was made of the incident and with their success, membership in the gang grew and they took the new name of "Hell's Angels."

The Pagans   This group is found mostly in the mid-Atlantic states. The Pagans have tangled with the Mafia in Philadelphia and have not backed down from La Cosa Nostra, whom they consider a bunch of old men.

The Bandidos   Found mostly in the Southwest, the strong-arm enforcement group for the Bandidos is thought to be the "Nomads."

The Outlaws   This group is concentrated in the Midwest and on the East Coast. In a clash with the Hell's Angels in Charlotte, North Carolina, members of both groups were seriously injured and killed. T-shirts worn by some members of the group say, "God Forgives, Outlaws Don't."

Other information regarding these gangs thought to be just a step below the Mafia in sophistication:

- The rank-and-file members of the gangs seem to make special efforts to appear menacing and tough. Many never clean their motorcycle vests. Tattoos are common. The tattoo "1%" refers to the statement of the American Motorcycle Association that 99 percent of the nation's motorcyclists are decent, law-abiding citizens.
- It seems that to be a member of one of the "big four" gangs, a person must be white and must operate a U.S.-made Harley-Davidson motorcycle. Imported bikes are commonly referred to as "Jap scrap."
- The gangs are believed to be heavily involved in the illegal drug trade. Fights and disputes between gangs occur apparently over control of illegal rackets.

Jamaican gangs known as "posses" have alarmed law enforcement officials because of both their rapid growth and extreme violence. In 1988, there were estimated to be thirty to forty posses with a total membership of 5,000 or more operating in cities throughout the United States. Many members of the posses are believed to be illegal aliens. Posses are believed to be major distributors of crack in East Coast cities and are believed to be spreading to the Midwest and the Southwest. It is believed that posses work with local groups in opening and supplying crack houses. In many respects, illegal drug distribution systems follow structures used by manufacturers and importers of lawful goods.

In 1989, FBI agents and New York City police officers raided locations of Asian organized criminal groups. They seized heroin with a street value of over $1 billion, found $3 million in cash, and arrested forty-four people in the largest heroin bust to date in the United States. In an article entitled "Asian Organized

"Edges" That Organized Crime Has

In 1983, former FBI Director William Webster testified before the President's Commission on Organized Crime as to the "edges" organized crime has and why organized crime has been successful. He stated:

Such organizations are involved in every conceivable type of crime, including extortion, pornography, labor racketeering, bribery and murder. Their main sources of revenue, however, are narcotics and gambling.

* * *

The activities of organized crime are not limited to open acts of criminality. Today there are few businesses or industries in our communities that are not affected by organized

criminal enterprises. This brand of crime is costing the American people billions of dollars every year. Those engaged in organized crime are "no-holds-barred" competitors who seek an edge. They don't face the problems of legitimate businesses. . . . Instead—and this is their hallmark—they concentrate on intimidation, extortion, fear and the corruption of public officials.

* * *

Still another edge comes from the practice of putting laundered funds from illegal activities into legitimate enterprises. This allows organized crime to undercut competition by reducing the cost of doing business.

Crime" in the October 1989 issue of the *FBI Law Enforcement Bulletin,* an FBI agent commenting on the raid, observed:

> Asian organized crime (AOC) groups are becoming involved at an increasing rate in murder, kidnapping, extortion, gambling, drugs and money laundering. It has been suggested that AOC has the potential to become the future number-one law enforcement problem in the United States.

The *New York Times* gave reasons in 1991 for this prediction. A January 6, 1991, article entitled "New Immigrant Wave from Asia Gives the Underworld New Faces" tells of waves of immigrants from Asia flooding New York City "in search of better lives." Not only are Asian street gangs growing but Hong Kong criminal Triad societies are making efforts to establish a base in New York City and elsewhere. This is being done in anticipation of the 1997 takeover of Hong Kong by Communist China. In 1997, in compliance with a treaty written one hundred years ago, the British will leave Hong Kong and Communist China will take over. Not wanting to live under Communist rule, the criminal Triad societies are seeking bases elsewhere.

The Struggle for Power Among and Within Gangs

Organized criminal groups are not operated on democratic principles. Power in many gangs is obtained by force. When treachery or murder is used to advance, fear and suspicion will almost always continue to exist.

The old saying that there is no honor among thieves is probably true. Terrible violence erupts periodically among criminal groups and criminals. Such murder and violence could be the result of:

A police task force of more than one thousand officers was formed in Los Angeles in 1988 to deal with drugs, street gangs, and street violence. Here, one police officer hands another officer a marble-size piece of rock cocaine found on a teenage member of a Hispanic street gang.

- internal struggles within gangs over money, policy, or power
- warfare between gangs, attempted mob rubouts, family rivalries, or struggle for control of rackets or territories. Continued efforts by Asian organized gangs to expand and grow could trigger violence.
- attempts to retaliate or revenge acts of violence
- belief that an individual has violated the code of silence and has provided information to law enforcement or a rival gang
- an attempt to rob or prevent a robbery of money or drugs (law enforcement officers conducting drug raids have stated that criminals sometimes express relief that it is a police raid and not a raid by a rival, warring gang)

Mafia violence has been portrayed to the public through movies, books, and TV series. Similar wars were fought in the 1980s over the cocaine trade in southern Florida and on the streets of Los Angeles. When cocaine, crack, and heroin reaches the United States, in most instances it is distributed by gangs (Colombians, Cubans, Jamaicans, etc.). Hundreds of murders occur every year in smuggling and protecting the distribution of drugs.

As the profits in the drug trades are gigantic, drug gangs are becoming increasingly well-armed and violent. Elaborate intelligence and counterintelligence systems are used, and suspected squealers may be executed. Drug gangs do not request assistance from law enforcement, nor do they go to the police to report that millions of dollars worth of cocaine or crack have been stolen.

Illegal Gambling in the United States

During prohibition in the United States (1919–33), organized crime made huge profits selling illegal beer and alcohol to the many persons who wanted to drink.

With the legalization of beer and alcoholic drinks, organized crime turned to other illegal activities. It is widely believed that until the 1970s, illegal gambling was the greatest money-maker for organized crime.

With the legalization of many forms of gambling in the United States and with the effective use of RICO, profits from gambling dropped rapidly, while the risks in illegal gambling went up. Illegal gambling is no longer the problem it previously was. Today, many forms of gambling continue to be illegal. The following present information about what is considered illegal gambling:

Distinguishing Illegal Gambling From Friendly Gambling

For a game of chance or lottery to be illegal, it must violate a specific law or ordinance. Illegal gambling is often distinguished from legitimate commercial promotions in that illegal gambling or lotteries have (a) a prize, (b) consideration, and (c) chance elements.

Friendly gambling (office or factory football pool, neighborhood poker game, etc.) can be distinguished from commercial gambling by some or all of the following factors:

- where the game is played and who the players are
- size of the pot
- whether the house takes a percentage of each pot
- whether the players bet against the house, and the house acts as the banker, and whether the house acts as the dealer in such games as blackjack and craps, etc.
- other factors, such as the type of game played

The Federal Crime of Gambling: 18 U.S.C.A Section 1955

"Major gambling activities were a principal focus of congressional concern. Large-scale gambling enterprises were seen to be both a substantial evil and a source of funds for other criminal conduct."

—U.S. Supreme Court, in
Iannelli et al. v. United States
420 U.S. 770, 16 CrL 3127 (1975)

The U.S. Supreme Court pointed out that the federal offense created by the U.S. Congress has the following requirements:

Participation of "five or more persons" as an element of the substantive offense under Sec. 1955 represents a legislative attempt to merge the conspiracy and the substantive offense into a single crime.

* * *

Recognizing that gambling activities normally are matters of state concern, Congress indicated a desire to extend federal criminal jurisdiction to reach only those who are engaged in an illicit gambling business of major proportions. . . . It accordingly conditioned the application of Sec. 1955 on a finding that the gambling activities involve five or more persons and that they remain substantially in operation in excess of 30 days or attain gross revenues of $2,000 in a single day.

* * *

We think it evident that Congress intended to retain each offense as an "independent curb" available for use in the strategy against organized crime.

New terms and phrases are being used reflecting the war for American streets. "Mushrooms" is brutal street gang slang for innocent children or other persons who unexpectedly pop up in the line of fire of a drug gunman. "Street sweeper" is a weapon capable of clearing the streets. If could refer specifically to a double-action shotgun that can fire twelve rounds in less than three seconds. "Rambo weapon" is an automatic weapon or a "street sweeper."

C. CRIMINAL PROFITS: WHERE DO THEY GO?

Who Does the Banking for Criminals?

Most narcotic and other such criminal transactions are cash transactions. The offender often has the problem of determining what is to be done with huge amounts of cash. As $20 bills are commonly used in the purchase of narcotics, cardboard boxes of cash can accumulate quickly.

For example, a suitcase filled with $1 million in $20 bills would weigh just over 100 pounds.[1] The suitcase would be bulky and heavy. Smuggling it out of the United States would not be an easy task.

Taking this money to a U.S. bank or other financial institution would create problems, as large cash transactions are recorded as such and are routinely scrutinized. The Internal Revenue Service would receive such records and this information could be used to build a tax case.

Under federal law, financial institutions (banks, savings and loans, etc.) are required to report currency transactions over $10,000. Currency transaction reports (CTRs) are used by governmental agencies to determine whether tax fraud or criminal activities such as money laundering, illegal drug transactions, racketeering, etc. is occurring. (See *United States v. Anzalone,* 766 F.2d 676 for a discussion of CTRs.)

Criminals do not want their governments to know where they are banking and they want their banking records kept secret. In past years, Switzerland has been a good haven for "flight money." However, under a 1977 treaty between the United States and Switzerland, access to Swiss bank-deposit information is now given to U.S. prosecutors for certain white-collar crimes.

Criminals seek tax havens to deposit "flight capital." Much of the money is used for the purchase of new drug shipments and other expenses. Before the fall of the Noriega government in 1990, Panama was the leading banking system for criminals from all parts of the world.

To ship money out of the United States to a tax haven, the criminal violates a number of laws, including a requirement that a declaration be made when more than $5,000 is taken out of the United States. As illegal drugs are a major source of profits for criminals, law enforcement officers are not only looking for illegal narcotics coming into their country but are also on the alert for large cash shipments going out of the country.

In 1989, federal agents arrested eleven persons in New York City and seized $20 million from Colombian money launderers who were preparing to ship the money to Colombia, South America.[2]

Laundering "Dirty" Cash

Criminals and racketeers do not report to the Internal Revenue Service that they support themselves and their families by committing crimes. They need a source of reportable income for income tax purposes in reporting to federal and state tax departments. The reportable income must be large enough to justify the standard of living of the criminal and his family.

Acquiring a legitimate business is therefore common. Legitimate businesses can be profitable in themselves. "Dirty" money might be held until it can be "laundered" through a legitimate business and returned in a "clean" reportable form to the owner. The owner then reports this amount to federal and state tax departments.

Shipping cash out of the United States is necessary in illegal drug trafficking to pay for further shipments of narcotics in South America and elsewhere in the world. "Laundering" dirty money can also be done outside the United States. This service, when combined with banking criminal dollars, can be profitable.

The article entitled "Laundering Drug Money" in the April 1990 issue of the *FBI Law Enforcement Bulletin* states that illegal drug trafficking revenues are estimated as high as $300 billion annually, with one-third of that collected in the United States. The article describes the three ways that money is moved out of the United States:

- *Smuggling,* which is not a preferred method for large amounts of money because of the possibilities of loss through accident, theft, or seizure by government authorities.
- *Wire transfer,* which requires the cooperation of a financial institution to transfer funds to a bank or other depository in another country. Officials of a Miami bank were bribed and within a thirteen-month period had transferred $94 million before they were apprehended.
- *Conversion* of the money into paper documents such as cashier's checks, letters of credit, etc.

Currency Transaction Reports and "Structured Transactions"

With drug trafficking revenues as high as $300 billion a year, many drug dealers and other criminals reap huge profits. A large amount of such criminal profits are spent purchasing expensive cars, homes, condos, jewelry, furs, clothing, and other luxuries.

Businesses and financial institutions in the United States are required to report cash transactions of $10,000 or more under the Currency Transaction Reporting Act (31 U.S.C. sec. 5311). The currency transaction reports (CTRs) filed by businesses, banks, and other financial institutions are used to determine whether tax frauds or money laundering is occurring. Further investigation could then lead to illegal drug dealings and racketeering.

Unfortunately, business persons who want to make profits will sometimes cooperate with drug dealers and other criminals seeking to hide cash transactions. Car dealers, real estate agents, and jewelers can illegally agree to structure a transaction. In a structured transaction, the buyer makes a series of payments in cash or cashier's checks of under $10,000 over a period of weeks. When the sales price is reached, the dealer or real estate agent turns the car or condo over to the buyer. For a $50,000 Mercedes-Benz or Rolls-Royce, six or seven payments under $10,000 would be the structured transaction.

Another illegal way of avoiding the CTR requirement is to put the title to an expensive car or piece of real estate in the name of a third party. The question is then raised how the third party obtained the $50,000 in cash to purchase a Mercedes-Benz and whether they are driving the vehicle or living in the condo.

In 1990, when analysis showed that Wisconsin was far below the national average in the number of CTRs filed, teams of federal officers were sent to Wisconsin. Undercover agents approached car dealers and other business persons who were suspected of structuring transactions to avoid the CTR requirement. The investigations resulted in a number of criminal indictments. (See the *Milwaukee Sentinel* article "Drug Money Isn't Being Socked Away," September 15, 1990.)

Loan Sharking as a Criminal Investment and as a Criminal Banking Venture

Loan-sharking has always been a profitable source of income for organized crime and racketeers. Not only is it a profitable criminal investment, but the loan shark often acts as a banker for criminals.

The loan shark will finance criminal ventures, such as narcotic purchases. Such loans are made at high rates of interest. Failure to repay a loan could result in brutality or death. Gamblers can borrow money from loan sharks to pay their gambling debts, or they may find if they run up a gambling debt that it has been turned over to a loan shark for collection.

Persons threatened by a loan shark for collection of a large debt will sometimes become police informants or government witnesses as a way out of their dilemma.

D. Organized Crime Investment in Lawful Businesses

An article in the November 1981 *FBI Bulletin,* "How Illicit Funds Are Acquired and Concealed," states:

> Alphonse Capone, the infamous gangster of the 1920's is said to have amassed a fortune of $20 million in a 10-year period through such illegal activities as bootlegging and gambling. Yet, when Capone was sentenced to 11 years in prison in 1931, it was for an income tax evasion conviction, not because he had been charged with any of these illegal activities.
>
> The conviction of Capone taught other organized crime members an important lesson: Money not reported on an income tax return is money that cannot be spent or invested without risk of detection and prosecution.
>
> Since most monies collected by organized crime activities are from illegal sources such as loansharking, prostitution, gambling, or narcotics, the individual racketeer is understandably reluctant to report the income and its source on his tax return. Before spending or otherwise using these funds, it is necessary that these monies be given an image of legality so that they can be reported on a tax return without revealing the true nature of their origins. This process of conversion is known as "laundering."

* * *

While laundering money can be accomplished in a wide variety of legitimate businesses, it should be recognized that certain domestic businesses have characteristics which lend themselves to successful laundering operations. For example, the business selected as a "laundry" must be capable of absorbing a large volume of cash income, since most illicit income is received in the form of cash. The purpose of laundering funds is to commingle licit and illicit monies so that they cannot be separated, while simultaneously preventing the discovery of the introduction of illegal monies into the business. Since almost all checks and credit card receipts are traceable by law enforcement officials, businesses such as restaurants, bars, and massage parlors, which normally take in a high proportion of cash, tend to be more desirable as a potential "laundry" than a business normally receiving most of its income in the form of checks or other traceable financial instruments.

Another favorable characteristic for a "laundry" is relatively fixed expenses which do not vary with sales volume. An example of such a business is a movie theater showing pornographic films. The expenses of such a business (rent, electricity, wages) are almost constant, regardless of whether the theater is full. Illicit income can be introduced and camouflaged in this type of business quite easily, since the additional sales volume does not result in a proportional increase in business expenses. Law enforcement officials who later examine the records of such a movie theater would have a difficult time proving that the actual or "legitimate" income generated by the theater was much less than that recorded on the books and reported to the taxing authorities.

Businesses that normally experience a high rate of spoilage or other loss of goods also have a high potential for being used to launder money. Groceries and restaurants are good examples, since some spoilage of goods is expected during the normal course of business. When such a business is controlled, large blocks of illicit money are introduced into the business and recorded in the general income accounts of the grocery store or restaurant as if this money were received from customers. Fraudulent invoices for produce or other perishable items are then issued to these businesses by other mob-owned or mob-controlled companies acting as suppliers. The grocery store or restaurant either issues checks to these "suppliers" or records the transaction as a cash payment and charges the expenditure to an expense account, such as cost of goods sold. The undelivered produce or perishable items listed as spoiled and discarded are written off the books.

By using this method, the grocery store or restaurant avoids substantial tax liability on large blocks of illicit monies introduced into the business, since this income is offset by corresponding expenses relating to the nondelivered goods. The funds paid to the "supplier" by the grocery or restaurant have taken on an image of legality and may be spent or invested with very little risk of discovery. Within a week of this "transaction," it is almost impossible for law enforcement officials to disprove the story of the grocer or restaurant owner.

E. ILLEGAL PRACTICES AFTER TAKING OVER LEGITIMATE BUSINESSES

When organized criminals take over legitimate businesses, do they run the businesses in a lawful way? The National Advisory Committee answered this question in the Task Force Report on Organized Crime:

In recent years, organized crime has acquired a large number of legitimate businesses—either by direct purchase, using funds accumulated from illegal activities, or by forfeiture because of gambling debts, or through foreclosure on usurious loans. Once acquired, such businesses may be operated legitimately, but, more often than not, illegal practices are used to increase profits. The Task Force Report describes one such practice, involving bankruptcy fraud:

With the original owners remaining in nominal management positions, extensive product orders were placed through established lines of credit, and the goods were immediately sold at low prices before the suppliers were paid. The organized criminal group made a quick profit of three-quarters of a million dollars by pocketing the receipts from sale of the products ordered and placing the firm in bankruptcy without paying the suppliers.

Other types of frauds sometimes perpetrated after an organized crime takeover of a business include fraudulent stock sales and arson of the business property (... to defraud the insurance company).

When organized crime takes over a business or enters the field of labor, it brings with it a variety of criminal techniques that supplement ordinary business activity in a manner designed to extract extra profits. Bribery and illegal kickbacks are used extensively. In addition, the President's task force found that, "Strong-arm tactics are used to enforce unfair business policy and to obtain customers ..." and that "[I]nfiltration of labor unions ... provides opportunities for stealing from union funds and extorting money by threats." ...

The fact that organized crime is heavily involved in commercial vice and illegal activities in connection with otherwise legitimate businesses does not mean that it has abandoned traditional crimes, such as theft and receiving stolen property. Looting and pilferage frequently accompany organized crime's entry into legitimate activities, and receiving stolen property can itself be big business.

F. CORRUPTION OF PUBLIC OFFICIALS

In 1967, the President's Commission on Law Enforcement stated:

> All available data indicate that organized crime flourishes only where it has corrupted officials. As the scope and variety of organized crime's activities have expanded, its need to involve officials at every level of government has grown. And as government regulation expands into more and more areas of private and business activity, the power to corrupt likewise affords the corrupter more control over matters affecting the everyday life of each citizen.[3]

In 1983, the Attorney General of the United States, in testifying before the Senate Judiciary Committee, cited instances of huge payments to law enforcement officials to ignore organized criminal activities. He stated: "The dollar amounts involved are so great that bribery threatens the very foundations of law and law enforcement."

On page 1 of the April 11, 1988, *New York Times,* it was stated that "in some American communities, corruption among law-enforcement officials—policemen, sheriffs, jailers, even prosecutors and judges—is out of control."[4] There is no question that billions of dollars are being used to tempt (or to bribe) American law enforcement officers every year.

The Criminal Justice Standards and Goals Task Force Report on Organized Crime states:

> The primary goals of organized crime, whether through enterprises such as illegal gambling or legitimate businesses such as construction, are the making of money and the maximization of profit. In order to achieve the greatest possible return, organized crime has found it expedient to invest some of its capital in government; that is, to distribute varying sums of money to carefully chosen individuals serving in strategic

government and law enforcement capacities who can provide organized crime with the services it requires. If the individual happens to be a publicly elected official, a bribe may arrive in the form of a cash contribution to the campaign fund or a promise for the delivery of large blocs of votes. Sometimes, though, an individual whom organized crime has designated as desirable to be "in their hip pocket" will refuse to accept a bribe. In such cases, organized crime will seek to corrupt through threats and/or blackmail.

* * *

Failure to arrest and prosecute those whom the officer knows have violated the law is only one form police corruption can take. Herman Goldstein, in his monograph, *Police Corruption,* lists several others:

- Agreeing to drop an investigation prematurely;
- Agreeing not to inspect various locations where a violation may be occurring;
- Reducing the seriousness of a charge against an offender;
- Agreeing to alter testimony at trial;
- Influencing departmental recommendations regarding the granting of licenses, e.g., recommending for or against continuance of a liquor or amusement license by either giving or suppressing derogatory information;
- Agreeing to alter departmental records of arrested persons.

* * *

Of course, not all police corruption is rooted in organized crime. The officer who accepts a bribe from a businessman, even on a continuing basis, not to enforce certain parking regulations is guilty of corruption, but not corruption perpetrated by a syndicate. However, the Knapp Commission testimony revealed alliances between enough police officers and organized crime figures to lend credence to the belief that such relationships exist. And other instances of the phenomenon indicate that such police corruption is not limited to New York City.

Police corruption has other serious implications. In addition to eroding public confidence in the police, both intradepartmental and interdepartmental cooperation is undermined. Officers do not know whom they can trust. Says Cressey, "if a policeman in one city calls the police department of another city to report a piece of valuable information about organized crime activities in either of the two communities, he can never be sure that a corrupt policeman will not answer the telephone."[5]

G. THE INVOLVEMENT OF ORGANIZED CRIME IN VICTIMLESS CRIMES*

Advantages for Organized Crime   The nature of some victimless crimes makes them excellent targets for organized crime. Says one observer: "Organized criminal groups participate in any illegal activity that offers maximum profit at minimum risk of law enforcement interference." Generally, these activities involve something the public wants badly enough to risk criminal sanctions. Providing them requires

---

*This material is from the Criminal Justice Standards and Goals Report on Organized Crime, pp. 218–219.

certain skills and an organization, in return for which there is great potential for profit.

Gambling, drugs, prostitution, and pornography all meet these conditions, and supplying them is relatively free of risk. Because the public tolerates the activity—indeed, a large segment demands it—there rarely is a complainant. Moreover, there is little incentive for strict law enforcement or tough judicial decisions. Even if there were, the laws are extremely difficult to enforce. Evidence is hard to come by, witnesses are scarce, and the organized crime masterminds are insulated from implication in the activities.

Characteristics of Involvement   Organized crime attempts to achieve monopolistic control over specific activities and geographic areas in which it operates. However, there is some dispute over the extent of this control. The Organized Crime Task Force of the President's Commission on Law Enforcement and Administration of Justice (1967) stated that few independent operators exist in cities where organized crime is present. Others agree, saying that where independents exist, they do so at the sufferance of organized crime, and last only as long as they are not a threat or major source of competition to that element. In short, "Until they become a threat to the 'big group' they are permitted to exist and to continue to grow."

It is also probable that organized crime tolerates independents only up to a point, so that "Only when profits are of sufficient consequence do the larger organizations move in to become affiliated with local groups."

* * *

The top echelons of organized crime have established a shield between themselves and the law. Actual street merchandising of illegal goods and services usually is handled by nonmembers of the organization who know little about their suppliers, and thus are unable to inform on them. For those who do know, organized crime figures combine the threat of retribution with a promise to provide a lawyer and court costs in case of arrest, and to care for an individual's family in the case of conviction.

Some observers stress the significance of this buffer, contending that as long as the higher levels of the organization are protected, the supply of goods and services will flow without interruption, because there will never be a shortage of sellers or customers. Others, however, believe this point is exaggerated. They argue that organized crime depends entirely on its market; and if that can be severely disrupted, organized crime will be crippled.

A third point to note is that the survival or organized crime does not depend on a single individual. "Like any large corporation, the organization functions regardless of personnel changes, and no individual—not even the leader—is indispensable."

The next factor to consider is control. Organized crime is able to hold sway over not just its street-level operators but, to some degree, the official forces arrayed against it. There is general agreement that organized crime's illegal activities could not be sustained without the complicity of local law officers, judges, and politicians at all levels. In effect, "The organization . . . provides a systematized method of corrupting the law enforcement process by centralizing procedures for the payment of graft." Corruption has been well documented, perhaps most elaborately by the Knapp Commission in New York City and in a study of Reading, Pennsylvania, by John Gardiner.

The method of corruption varies with the positions of the officials to be corrupted. The higher they are, the more subtle and difficult the corruption will be to trace. Politicians are offered campaign contributions, for example, and there are cases where organized crime has swung an election or affected the course of legislation.

Many authors cite the parallels between organized crime operations and large-scale, legitimate businesses. They may speak, for example, of a "large-scale, organized system, often of national scope, comprising an integration of the stages of production and distribution of the illicit product on a continuous and thoroughly business-like basis."

Thomas Schelling, author of a number of economic analyses of organized crime, adds that because organized crime must use extortion to monopolize its area of activity, the street-level suppliers are vulnerable to this tactic. These suppliers cannot complain to the police, because they are committing crimes. Also, they cannot hide, because they must be accessible to their customers, and they cannot move their businesses out of town.

As with legitimate enterprises, organized crime's "businesses" require certain conditions and characteristics in order to be profitable. Schelling believes that by analyzing the structure and operations of the businesses, a strategy can be devised to affect their profitability, a practice that occurs among competitors in the legal marketplace.

An economic approach might involve "regulation, accommodation or the restructuring of markets and business conditions." If, for example, an illicit operation is profitable because a law "protects" it from legitimate competition, then removal of the law should undercut it. However, if the operation is profitable because it is a monopoly based on extortion, removing the law would have little effect. The end of the Prohibition Period, followed by a free, though regulated, liquor trade, is an example of how competition drove organized crime out of one activity.

H. Should Victimless Crimes in Which Organized Crime is Extensively Involved Be Legalized or Decriminalized?

The National Advisory Committee on Criminal Justice Standards and Goals offered this advice on the above question:

> States and localities should exercise caution in considering the legalization or decriminalization of so-called "victimless crimes," such as gambling, drug use, prostitution, and pornography, which are known to provide income to organized crime because there is insufficient evidence that legalization or decriminalization of such crimes will materially reduce the income of organized crime and on the contrary, evidence does exist that the elimination or reduction of legal restraints can encourage the expansion of organized crime activities.

I. "RICO": Racketeer Influenced and Corrupt Organizations Act

In 1970, Congress enacted a criminal statute with such broad provisions that it has been called the "new darling of the prosecutor's nursery." The Racketeer Influenced and Corrupt Organizations (RICO) Act was enacted as Title IX of the Organized Crime Control Act of 1970.

RICO has proved to be a valuable tool in the fight against organized crime in the United States. Since 1980, senior mob figures from Los Angeles, New Orleans, New York, Cleveland, and Philadelphia have been convicted. A high-ranking FBI agent stated in 1983 that "I think we've proven that the myth of the invincibility of organized crime is total fantasy. You can indict them and you can convict them, but that doesn't mean you can put them out of business."[6]

Gangland executions and mobsters who turn informers also seem to be on the increase.[7] For example, after being criminally convicted and while awaiting

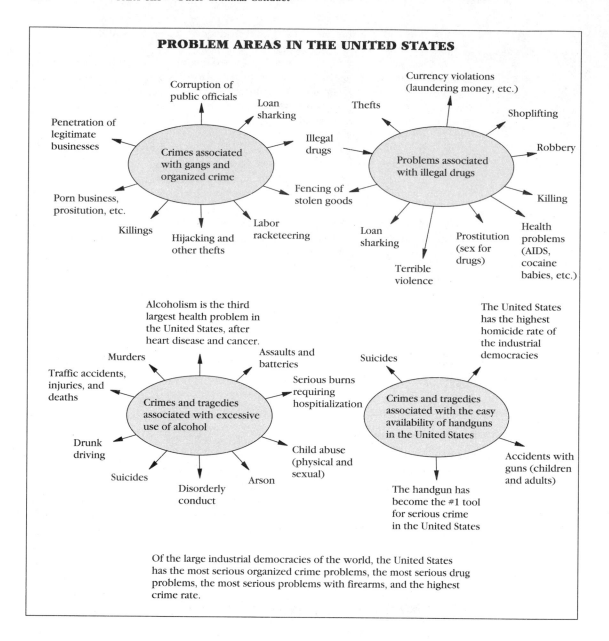

PROBLEM AREAS IN THE UNITED STATES

Crimes associated with gangs and organized crime
- Corruption of public officials
- Loan sharking
- Illegal drugs
- Fencing of stolen goods
- Labor racketeering
- Hijacking and other thefts
- Killings
- Porn business, prositution, etc.
- Penetration of legitimate businesses

Problems associated with illegal drugs
- Thefts
- Currency violations (laundering money, etc.)
- Shoplifting
- Robbery
- Killing
- Health problems (AIDS, cocaine babies, etc.)
- Prostitution (sex for drugs)
- Terrible violence
- Loan sharking

Crimes and tragedies associated with excessive use of alcohol
- Alcoholism is the third largest health problem in the United States, after heart disease and cancer.
- Assaults and batteries
- Serious burns requiring hospitialization
- Child abuse (physical and sexual)
- Arson
- Disorderly conduct
- Suicides
- Drunk driving
- Traffic accidents, injuries, and deaths
- Murders

Crimes and tragedies associated with the easy availability of handguns in the United States
- Suicides
- The United States has the highest homicide rate of the industrial democracies
- Accidents with guns (children and adults)
- The handgun has become the #1 tool for serious crime in the United States

Of the large industrial democracies of the world, the United States has the most serious organized crime problems, the most serious drug problems, the most serious problems with firearms, and the highest crime rate.

sentencing, millionaire Allen Dorfman was gunned down gangland style in a hotel parking lot. It is speculated that Dorfman was killed to prevent him from talking and disclosing information regarding organized crime.

Former FBI Director William Webster pointed out that it was not until the early 1980s that law enforcement officers and prosecutors learned how to use RICO effectively. Many states have enacted similar statutes ("little RICOs"). Webster indicated that new and extensive investigations into such areas as labor racketeering and international drug traffic would be opened up. With RICO, every transaction involving the use of the mail, telephone, or interstate wire facilities creates the potential for criminal prosecution or a civil lawsuit.

RICO (Racketeer Influenced and Corrupt Organizations Act)*

RICO Forbids a Person or Persons From

- using income received from a pattern of "racketeering" activity to acquire an interest in an "enterprise." An "enterprise" is defined as "any individual, partnership, or corporation, association, or other legal entity, and any union or group of individuals associated in fact although not a legal entity" (18 U.S.C. Sec. 1961 [4]). The U.S. Supreme Court held that this included both legitimate and illegitimate "associations in fact" (*United States v. Turkette,* 101 S.Ct. 2524 [1981])
- acquiring or maintaining an interest in an "enterprise" through a pattern of "racketeering" activity
- conducting or participating in the affairs of an "enterprise" through a pattern of "racketeering" activity
- conspiring to commit any of the above offenses.

Criminal Penalties:

fines up to $25,000 and/or imprisonment not longer than twenty years for each offense plus forfeiture of interests acquired in violation of RICO

Civil Penalties:

"any person" may commence a private civil action for treble damages and attorney fees when the forbidden conduct causes injury to "business or property"

The statute numbers of the RICO act in your state are: _____

_____

Designated Potentially Associated Statutes

Mail and Wire Fraud Statutes The two elements for these federal crimes are (a) formation of a "scheme or artifice to defraud" and (b) use of the mails or wires to further the fraudulent scheme.

Travel Act Statute This statute forbids travel in interstate commerce or use of any facility in interstate commerce with intent to (a) distribute the proceeds of unlawful activity; (b) commit any violent crime in furtherance of unlawful activity; or (c) manage, promote, or establish any unlawful activity.

Extortion (Hobbs Act, 18 U.S.C. Sec. 1951) This defines extortion as "the obtaining of property from another, with his consent, induced by wrongful use of actual or threatened force, violence, or fear, or under color of official right."

Obstruction of Justice, Criminal Investigations, and State and Local Governments Unlawful Labor Payments (violation of the Taft-Hartley Act, 29 U.S.C. sec. 186[a][b]) The making of payments by an employer or his representative to a union official, and the receiving of payment by a union official from an employer or their representatives is forbidden. (Specific intent, such as in bribery, need not be proved and only general intent is required.)

*18 U.S.C. Sec. 1961–68 first enacted by Congress in 1970.

J. TERRORISM

Terrorists are persons who operate outside of the law and will use force and violence in efforts to obtain political or racist goals. Terrorists commit crimes because they cannot achieve their political goals through free elections and they cannot convince persons living in democratic countries to adopt their ideas. Former U.S. Supreme Court Justice Douglas stated in the 1951 case of *Dennis v. United States*[8] that:

> [T]he activities of Communists in plotting and scheming against the free world are common knowledge. ... The Communists in America are miserable merchants of unwanted ideas; their wares remain unsold.

The eighteenth-century revolutionary, Sergei Nechayev, wrote, "Whatever promotes the triumph of the revolution is moral, whatever hinders it is immoral. . . . Our business is passionate, complete, ruthless destruction."

Bombings, assassinations, armed robberies, kidnappings, and hijacking are among the many crimes that terrorists have committed in the 1970s and 1980s. The federal criminal code and the criminal laws of each state forbid many of the criminal acts of terrorists. In addition, the following statutes provide additional authority to law enforcement officers:

1. *Chapter XX of the Comprehensive Crime Control Act of 1984* forbids hostage taking and gives federal law enforcement officers jurisdiction outside the United States if: a) the offender or any of the victims are Americans, or b) the offender is later apprehended in the United States, or c) the U.S. government is compelled to take certain actions.

2. *The 1986 Omnibus Diplomatic Security and Antiterrorism Act* gives federal law enforcement agencies jurisdiction when violence or homicide is committed against Americans outside of the United States.

3. *Aircraft Piracy and Related Offenses* (Title 49, U.S.C., App. 1472i-n) wherein pursuant to the Hague Convention, the Federal Aviation Act of 1958 prohibited the seizure, by force or violence, of any aircraft within the special aircraft jurisdiction of the United States, interference with the flight crew while aboard such aircraft, the carrying of concealed weapons or explosives aboard such aircraft and the commission of certain crimes while aboard such aircraft. (Murder— 18 U.S.C. 1111; Manslaughter— 18 U.S.C. 1112; Maiming— 18 U.S.C. 114; Rape— 18 U.S.C. 2031; Assault— 18 U.S.C. 113; and Robbery— 18 U.S.C. 2111)

   This act gave the United States the authority to prosecute aircraft piracy outside the special aircraft jurisdiction of the United States as long as the offender is later found in the United States. The Federal Aviation Act authorized the government to seek the death penalty if the death of another person resulted from aircraft piracy as defined in this statute.

4. *Crimes Committed Within the Special Maritime Jurisdiction of the United States* (18 U.S.C. 7, 113, 114, 1111, 1112, 1201, 2031, 2111) These statutes authorize the United States to prosecute the crimes of murder, manslaughter, maiming, kidnapping, rape, assault, or robbery committed on the high seas or any other waters within the admiralty and maritime jurisdiction of the United States that is outside of the jurisdiction of any particular state. This prosecutive authority exists regardless of the nationality of the persons committing the enumerated crimes if the crimes are committed against United States citizens or are committed on U.S. civil or military vessels.

5. *Piracy* (18 U.S.C. 1651) Since 1819, the United States has had jurisdiction to prosecute anyone who commits the crime of piracy, as defined by the law of nations, on the high seas and is later brought to or found in the United States.

Targets of Political Terrorists

Since World War II insurgencies or wars of national liberation have been conducted steadily throughout the free world. It was not until the late 1960s and 1970s that urban insurgency and terrorism began to appear in the United States.

American law enforcement officers and agencies became the prime targets of these early assaults on public order. The National Bomb Data Center reported that in one four-month period in 1970, 751 assaults were made on law enforcement officers. Thirty-one of the officers were killed as a result of the assaults. There were a total of 509 incidents in which explosives and incendiary devices were used. In commenting on this violence, the executive director of the International Association of Chiefs of Police stated:

> Many of the recent attacks on the police officer have been made not because of who he is, but simply because of what he is. Sniper attacks, ambushing, terrorist bombings, and other assaults on police officers have become a grave threat to the very foundation of our system of government. The officer is now the object of attack, not because of enforcement activity, not because of the necessity of mediating tense situations in our society, but because he stands as the most visible representation of the authority of society.

In recent years the violence directed at law enforcement has diminished to some extent, but terrorism in its many forms continues to be a very serious threat throughout the world.

Is Nuclear Terrorism Possible?

A 1987 report to the U.S. Congress from the Defense Department stated, "Opportunities for terrorist acts, including attempts to steal civil plutonium, will increase substantially as a result of the increased commercial use of plutonium." The theft of any nuclear material by a terrorist group would create an alarming situation. Nuclear blackmail or a tragic incident could result from such a theft.

Other potential for danger exists due to the possibility of a terrorist group making a homemade bomb or a hostile nation supplying material for a bomb. In 1970, officials in Orlando, Florida, received a note stating that unless $1 million was paid, an H-bomb would be set off in the center of the city. A diagram was enclosed showing the thermonuclear weapon to be used. Good police work and a slip-up by the "bomber," however, showed that the whole matter was a hoax by a fourteen-year-old high school honor student who had taken courses in physics. The incident received a great deal of national attention because terrorists or criminal groups could devise such a devastating weapon.

Data for building crude bombs is available in libraries and in government publications. Scientists disagree about the difficulty and degree of danger in creating homemade bombs. Some think that such a bomb could be created in a couple of months with highly trained and skilled engineers, whereas other scientists think that one person might do the job within a couple of weeks. Still, the fact remains that even the most clumsy and crude bomb could be a very frightening weapon in the hands of terrorists or other criminal groups.

K. TERRORIST GROUPS PRESENTING THREATS IN THE UNITED STATES

The entire *FBI Law Enforcement Bulletin* of October 1987 was entitled the "Terrorism Issue." The remaining text material in this chapter (including quotes) is taken from the FBI material identifying the following groups as engaging in terrorist practices:

Domestic Leftist Groups

Members and associates of former groups such as the Weather Underground, the Black Liberation Army, and the Black Panther Party associated in the 1980s with such groups as the May 19th Communist Organization and the Republic of New Afrika to commit armed robberies and other crimes. These leftist organizations were responsible for twenty-one bombings or attempted bombings since 1981 and claimed sixteen of the twenty-six terrorist acts committed during their most active period in 1983 and 1984.[9]

Domestic Right-wing Terrorism

Right-wing terrorism has become an area of focus for law enforcement during the 1980's. Although belief in the white supremacist and antigovernment views of the far right is not illegal, the commission of violent acts to further these views is criminal. These acts have included bombings, armed robberies, assaults, and murder. Much of the rhetoric of the extreme right is particularly volatile and corrosive and is a motivating factor in this violence.

Unlike leftist terrorists, the terrorists of the far right do not leave communiques to claim credit or provide explanations. Therefore, an act that initially appears to be criminal may, in fact, be terrorist related. Although numerous violent acts have been committed by right extremists, the total number of terrorist incidents directly attributed to this faction has been few—two shootings (1981 and 1983) and four bombings and an attempted bombing (1986).

A basic belief of many right-wing extremists is the superiority of the white race. According to this view, blacks, other nonwhites, and Jews are inferior racially, mentally, physically, and spiritually. Much of this is based upon a racist, anti-Semitic religion, the Christian Identity Movement. This religion teaches that the white race is God's chosen race and that whites, not Jews, are the true descendants of Israel. Jews, instead, are of Satan's bloodline. According to Identity doctrine, the Bible is a history and guidebook of the white race that began with Adam. The appearance of the white race on earth (some 7,400 years ago) postdated black, Asiatic, and all other races.

* * *

The most violent far right group active during the 1980's has been the Order, an offshoot of the Aryan Nations. Another name for the group is Bruders Schweigen or Silent Brotherhood. This group was founded by Robert Mathews, who was an Aryan Nations member. Order members were also members of other right-wing organizations and had become disenchanted with their respective groups' lack of action to further the cause. Among the groups represented in the Order were the National Alliance; various chapters of the Ku Klux Klan; and the Covenant, the Sword, the Arm of the Lord (CSA).

* * *

Beginning in 1980, some CSA members were involved in bombings, arsons, robberies, and the murder of a black Arkansas State policeman. During April 1985, the CSA compound was raided by Federal authorities. Military surplus equipment, shoulder weapons, a heavy machine gun, money, handguns, and grenades and other explosives were found in a search of the compound. A total of five persons were arrested, including four Order members, two of whom were fugitives, and CSA leader James Ellison. Other

CSA members were arrested at a later time. Of the CSA and Order members arrested, all either pled guilty to charges or were convicted in Federal or State courts. As a result, the threat posed by these two groups has significantly decreased.

Another far right-wing faction of interest to law enforcement during the 1980's are the tax protest and antigovernment groups. Organizations such as the Sheriff's Posse Comitatus (SPC) and Arizona Patriots view Federal and/or State authority with suspicion. They espouse parochial as opposed to national interests, and they desire that there be as little government involvement as possible in their lives. They advocate nonpayment of taxes and regard Federal and State laws as unconstitutional. The SPC, for example, views the local sheriff as the only legitimate law enforcement authority and the only legal elected authority, and it regards the justice of the peace as the highest court in the country.

Domestic Puerto Rican Leftists

The island of Puerto Rico is a commonwealth of the United States. Puerto Ricans are citizens of the United States. Persons living in Puerto Rico (and corporations) pay no federal income tax. The great majority of Puerto Ricans wish to continue this special relation with the United States, but members of the Puerto Rican radical left seek independence from the United States through violence. When captured, "they consider themselves to be prisoners of war."

The wave of attacks by Puerto Rican groups during the 1970's has carried over into the 1980's. Since 1980, Puerto Rican terrorists in the United States and Puerto Rico have been responsible for more than 70 terrorist incidents. Included in these are bombings, assassinations, armed robberies, and rocket attacks. Targets have been military facilities and personnel (especially in Puerto Rico), U.S. Government facilities, and corporate interests. Seventeen of these attacks occurred in the continental United States.

The Puerto Rican group most active in the continental United States during the 1980's has been the Armed Forces of the National Liberation, or FALN. Since 1974, this group has been responsible for more than 100 terrorist attacks in the United States; however, the group has claimed only 10 bombings since 1980. All of these occurred in 1982.

The FALN was also responsible for takeovers at campaign offices of former President Jimmy Carter and Vice President George Bush during March 1980.

Eleven FALN members were arrested in Evanston, IL, during April 1980, planning an armored truck robbery. An FALN leader, Oscar Lopez, was arrested in Glenview, IL, during May 1981. He was subsequently convicted of seditious conspiracy, armed robbery, and weapons violations. Four other FALN members were arrested during June 1983, in connection with a plan to free Oscar Lopez from jail. Following these arrests, several FALN safehouses were located and searched. Dynamite, weapons, bombing materials, and bulletproof vests were seized. A second plot to free Lopez during 1985 was interdicted and resulted in indictments of several persons, including Donna Jean Willmott and Claude Marks, who are Top Ten fugitives.

Domestic Black Groups

There have been three terrorist incidents attributed to domestic black groups in the United States during the 1980's. All of these 1983 acts were the result of a religious rivalry. In addition, at least one other terrorist incident was prevented by arrests in 1984, and a possible terrorist plot was prevented during August 1986. Some black groups, however, have been involved in criminal activities, such as murder and armed robbery.

The three terrorist incidents were attributed to the group Fuqra, a black Islamic religious sect headquartered in Detroit, MI. In order to further its religious goals, Fuqra seeks to purify Islam by eliminating rival religious sects, such as the Ahmaddiya Movement in Islam (AMI). During August 1983, several terrorist acts occurred against the AMI treasurer but the bombs did not ignite; and an AMI temple was burned. Fuqra was implicated in these attacks because the bodies of the arsonists, Fuqra members, were found at the temple. They had become trapped setting the blaze and died. The gun used to kill the AMI secretary was found on one of the bodies.

Domestic Jewish Extremists

During the 1980's, approximately 20 terrorist incidents and numerous other acts of violence, including extortion and threats, have either been claimed by or attributed to militant Jewish terrorists. Groups claiming credit for these attacks have been the United Jewish Underground, the Jewish Defense League, the Jewish Defenders, and the Jewish Direct Action. Included in these attacks were smoke bombings, fire bombings, and pipe bombings. As a result of these acts, three persons were killed and many more were injured.

Persons, organizations, or other elements deemed anti-Semitic, or overtly supportive of Arab efforts determined not to be in the interests of Israel, are targets of the Jewish terrorists. In the past, Soviet Government interests in the United States have been attacked in protest of the U.S.S.R.'s treatment of Soviet Jews, Arab interests have been attacked because of the anti-Israeli policies of various Arab states, and alleged ex-Nazi's have been attacked because of their reported participation in atrocities against the Jewish people during World War II. The two most recent incidents attributed to Jewish terrorists involved the throwing of a tear gas canister during the performance of a Soviet dance troupe in New York City in September 1986, and an arson at Avery Fisher Hall in New York City prior to a performance by a Soviet symphony orchestra in October 1986. Most of the attacks by the Jewish terrorists have occurred in the New York City metropolitan area; however, attacks have also occurred in California, Washington, DC, and elsewhere.

A major pro-Jewish group in the United States is the Jewish Defense League (JDL). The slogan "Never Again" is the slogan of the JDL. This is a national organization with chapters in numerous American cities. Leaders of the organization have publicly advocated, encouraged, and applauded the use of violence against the enemies of the Jewish people. Although terrorist attacks have been claimed on behalf of the JDL, the violence appears to have been committed by a few of the more militant and hardcore members; the entire JDL organization should not be construed as being involved in these criminal acts.

Illegal Activity in Support of Irish Terrorism

Criminal acts by Irish terrorists occur regularly in Northern Ireland and occasionally in England and in the Republic of Ireland. In recent years violence as a result of the present conflict has not occurred in the United States.

The criminal acts in violation of the laws of the United States include: (1) weapons procurement in the United States and the illegal transport of these weapons to Northern Ireland or the Republic of Ireland, (2) fund-raising in the United States and the illegal transfer of this money to Northern Ireland to support Irish terrorist elements operating there, and (3) Irish terrorists who are in the United States illegally and may be active in the illegal procurement of weapons or funds to support their terrorist activity.

Narcotics and Terrorism

Narco-terrorism, the linking of narcotics traffickers and terrorists, may be a problem in drug-source countries but does not appear to exist in the United States at this time. This may be because in drug-producing countries there is often contact between terrorists and narcotics traffickers in rural areas where narcotics traffickers cultivate their crops. However, in the United States, which is primarily a drug-consuming rather than drug-producing country, such avenues of contact and cooperation are not as likely to exist.

Recent cases in the United States involving contacts between established terrorist groups and narcotics traffickers or individuals involved in a criminal enterprise using narcotics trafficking to finance their criminal activity appear to represent a blending of the criminal activities of the two types of groups. Both narcotics traffickers and terrorist groups, because of their common criminal activity and enterprises, operate in criminal circles. Consequently, it appears that contacts between the terrorist groups and narcotics traffickers are coincidental, resulting primarily from the criminal activity and clandestine nature of the groups.

While there does not currently appear to be linkages between narcotics traffickers and terrorist groups in the United States, such a development is possible. Narcotics trafficking represents a way to raise large amounts of cash in a relatively short time. Consequently, terrorist groups might resort to this type of activity in order to finance their operations. This development, while possible, is considered unlikely. Should it become known that the terrorist group is engaged in narcotics trafficking, financial and moral support by community elements sympathetic to the terrorist groups goals would, in all likelihood, be withdrawn.

International Terrorism

Of the international groups active in the United States, the FBI is most concerned about those associated with Libya and Iran. Both countries have large student populations in the United States which are well organized through societies and clubs and have the potential to serve as an infrastructure to support terrorist activity. The vast majority of these students do not and will not support terrorism; however, a minority within these groups have demonstrated a fanatical dedication to the regimes that control Libya and Iran and these governments have sponsored terrorism. Syria also has been a proponent of state-sponsored terrorism. To date, their activities in the United States have been confined primarily to monitoring and countering dissidents; however, this could well change due to an increasingly vigorous American response to terrorism abroad.

Our Government's military actions against Libya have resulted in threats by Colonel Qadhafi and Palestinian terrorists to export terrorist violence to the United States itself. These threats are taken seriously by the FBI and the U.S. intelligence community. Fortunately, these threats have not developed into terrorist attacks in the United States. Other international groups, such as Sikh and Armenian extremists, continue to pose a serious threat to Indian and Turkish interests in the United States.

The threat to Americans traveling overseas and to American personnel and interests abroad has increased as well. Groups which pose the greatest threat include Palestinian or Arab commando groups, such as Abu Nidal, Hizballah, and the 15 May Organization; shadowy associations, such as Islamic Jihad (Holy War), which is actually a concept or philosophy rather than an organization; and Libyan-sponsored elements. These have been responsible for a cruise ship hijacking (*Le Achille Lauro*) and several airline hijackings (TWA, Pan Am, Egypt Air) during which American citizens, simply because they were Americans, were singled out and murdered. These groups have also been responsible for the bombing of the La Belle Discotheque in West Berlin, West Germany, which was frequented by U.S. Army personnel; for the bombings of the American Embassy and Marine Corps compound and the kidnapping of American citizens in Beirut, Lebanon; and for the assaults at the Rome, Italy, and Vienna, Austria, airports.

In addition, American military personnel and facilities in Europe, especially West Germany and Italy, have been subjected to attacks, mostly by bombing. These have been carried out by domestic groups in those countries, such as the Red Army Faction in West Germany and the Action Direct in France. The threat level to our military and diplomatic personnel in these locations remains high.

Notes

1. See the article "Laundering Drug Money" in the April 1990 issue of the *FBI Law Enforcement Bulletin.*

2. See "$20 Million Seized, 11 Arrested in N.Y.," *Washington Post,* January 6, 1989; and "Laundering Drug Money."

3. p. 6, President's Commission of Law Enforcement.

4. See the article in that paper entitled "Enemy Within: Drug Money is Corrupting the Enforcers."

5. Criminal Justice Standards and Goals Task Force Report, p. 23.

6. "The Mob Taps Out in Vegas," *Newsweek,* October 24, 1983.

7. See the article entitled "Chicago's Mob Figures Run Scared—To Death," *Chicago Tribune,* August 7, 1983.

8. Justice Douglas's statements were in his dissenting opinion, 341 U.S. 494, 71 S.Ct. 857. In the *Dennis* case, the defendant was an officer in the American communist party and was convicted of conspiracy to advocate the violent overthrow of the U.S. government in violation of the Smith Act of 1940 (18 U.S.C.A. Sec. 11). The Smith Act is our basic sedition act in effect today. It forbids the advocation of the forceful overthrow of the U.S. government and forbids the distribution with disloyal intent of matters teaching or advising the overthrow of the government by violence. It also forbids organizing or helping to knowingly organize any group having such purposes.

9. One of the armed robberies committed to raise money for terrorist activities is described as follows in the *FBI Bulletin:*

On October 20, 1981, a Brinks Armored Car Service truck was robbed of more than $1.5 million at a bank in Nanuet, NY. A Brinks guard was killed and another wounded during the robbery. Participants in this crime included black males, who actually committed the robbery, and white males and females, who acted in support roles. The suspects fled the scene in a van but abandoned it nearby for a U-Haul truck. Other suspects accompanied the robbers in a tan Honda automobile.

Police stopped the truck near the entrance to the New York State Thruway in Nyack, NY, to question the driver. Several black males jumped from the back of the truck firing automatic weapons: two police officers were killed and another was wounded. One suspect who had been in the cab of the U-Haul, a white female, was arrested at the scene. Other suspects escaped on foot or in commandeered vehicles.

The Honda and another car sped away from the shooting scene and were pursued by police. During the chase, the Honda crashed and its occupants, a black male, a white male, and a white female, were arrested. The other car was later found abandoned.

The individuals arrested on October 20th were identified as Kathy Boudin (at Nyack), and Judith Clark, David Gilbert, and Samuel Brown (in the Honda). Another suspect, Samuel Smith, was killed in a gun battle with New York City Police Department officers 3 days later, and a second suspect, Nathaniel Burns, was arrested. Several safehouses in the New York City metropolitan area were searched as a result of leads generated by these arrests. Weapons, bombing components, radical literature, and other items were recovered at some of these.

Chapter Twenty Two

THE CRIME OF CONTEMPT AND OTHER CRIMES AGAINST GOVERNMENT

A. CONTEMPT

Contempt is the willful disregard of the authority of a court of law or of a legislative body. Acts that delay, impede, or frustrate the functioning or the dignity of a court or legislative body may be held to be in contempt of that body. The deliberate, willful, and contumacious (obstinate) disobedience of a lawful order is a common reason for finding a person in contempt. The U.S. Supreme Court held in the 1975 case of *Maness v. Meyers:*

> We begin with the basic proposition that all orders and judgements of courts must be complied with promptly. If a person to whom a court directs an order believes that order is incorrect the remedy is to appeal, but, absent a stay, he must comply promptly with the order pending appeal. Persons who make private determinations of the law and refuse to obey an order generally risk criminal contempt even if the order is ultimately ruled incorrect.[1]

Contempt and contempt proceedings originated in early England, when English kings gave their judges the power to punish conduct that interfered with the functioning of the courts. Although many American states have statutes defining contempt, the offense of contempt remains today in England as a common law misdemeanor. The following example of contempt received national attention in November 1983:

EXAMPLE: In a hearing before the U.S. Supreme Court, *Hustler* magazine publisher Larry Flynt became angry and shouted obscenities at the nine justices. The hearing concerned a civil libel suit by a vice-president of *Penthouse* against *Hustler.* Flynt wanted to argue the case himself, but the Court refused and appointed a lawyer to represent him. Flynt (who was in a wheelchair, paralyzed in a 1978 assassination attempt) was taken to a jail and booked on contempt charges. Flynt apologized later and the charges were dropped.

Civil and Criminal Contempt

Contempt is classified as either civil or criminal. *Civil contempt* is used to compel a person to do something they are obligated to do. *Criminal contempt* can be used to punish a person for what they have done. When Larry Flynt shouted obscenities at the nine justices in the courtroom of the U.S. Supreme Court, he was immediately found in criminal contempt and jailed.

Civil or criminal contempt is sometimes used in divorce cases, child custody cases, and other matters to compel persons to comply with court orders. The following examples illustrate:

EXAMPLE: After a divorce, Dr. Elizabeth Morgan (a plastic surgeon) accused the father of her six-year-old daughter of sexually abusing the child. The judge hearing the matter, however, ordered that unsupervised visits with the father, Dr. Eric Foretich (an oral surgeon) continue. Morgan sent the child into hiding with the child's grandparents and would not comply with court orders to produce the child or tell of the whereabouts of the child. Morgan went to jail for twenty-five months for refusing to comply with the orders of the court. The grandparents took the child first to England and then to New Zealand where the whereabouts of the child became publicly known. A New Zealand family court granted custody of the child to her mother while the mother and child remained in New Zealand. The father of the child discontinued legal proceedings. (See *Morgan v. Foretich,* 546 A.2d 407, D.C.App. 1988.)

EXAMPLE: In the 1988 U.S. Supreme Court case of *Hicks v. Feiock,* 485 U.S. 624, 108 S.Ct. 1423, a father who had money refused to make child support payments and went to jail. The question before the Court in this case was whether the contempt proceedings were civil or criminal.

EXAMPLE: When information was received that a mother was abusing her infant son, she was ordered to produce the child as it was found that she could not adequately care for the baby. The mother was jailed by the court until she either produced the baby or disclosed his whereabouts. The U.S. Supreme Court held that the contempt order did not violate the mother's Fifth Amendment privilege against self-incrimination. *City of Baltimore v. Bouknight,* 493 U.S. 549, 110 S.Ct. 900 (1990).

EXAMPLE: Newspaper reporters can be jailed if they refuse to provide information ordered by a court. (Only a few states have enacted a newspaper persons privilege law.) See the December 8, 1990, *New York Times* article, "Texas Reporter Jailed for Contempt of Court," where a defendant in a murder case sought the testimony of a woman newspaper reporter as part of his defense. The reporter went to jail after she refused to answer questions asked by the defense lawyer.

EXAMPLE: Persons who are granted immunity by a court and continue to refuse to answer questions can be jailed for contempt. See the U.S. Supreme Court case of *Shillitani v. United States,* 384 U.S. 364, 86 S.Ct. 1531 (1966), where two men were sentenced to two years imprisonment when they refused to testify after being granted immunity. The sentence was affirmed by the U.S. Supreme Court because either man could be freed anytime he agreed to testify (each man had the key to his own jail cell).

EXAMPLE: Under forfeiture laws, states and the federal government can confiscate profits from criminal activity. Lawyers representing drug dealers and organized-crime figures run the risk that their legal fees will be seized if it is shown that the legal fees were paid out of criminal profits. In 1991, a Manhattan grand jury indicted a defense lawyer for criminal contempt for refusing to disclose the source and amount of legal fees the lawyer received from a drug dealer the lawyer had defended. (See the April 18, 1991, *New York Times* article, "Lawyer Indicted for Refusal to Tell Source of Fees.")

Criminal contempt is designed to protect the public interest by ensuring the effective functioning of the judicial and legislative systems. In 1968, the U.S. Supreme Court stated in *Bloom v. Illinois* that "criminal contempt is a crime in the ordinary sense; it is a violation of the law, a public wrong which is punishable by fine or imprisonment or both."[2] The Court quoted Justice Oliver Wendell Holmes as stating that "these contempts are infractions of the law, visited with punishment as such. If such acts are not criminal, we are in error as to the most fundamental characteristic of crimes as that word has been understood in English speech." The defendant in the *Bloom* case was sentenced to twenty-four months in prison for submitting a falsely prepared will for probate. His demand for a jury trial was denied. In holding that in serious contempt cases the defendant had a right to a jury, the Court stated:

> Prosecution for contempt plays a significant role in the proper functioning of our judicial system; but despite the important values which the contempt power protects, courts and legislatures have gradually eroded the power of judges to try contempts of their own authority. In modern times, procedures in criminal contempt cases have come to mirror those used in ordinary criminal cases. Our experience teaches that convictions for criminal contempt, not infrequently resulting in extremely serious penalties are indistinguishable from those obtained under ordinary criminal laws. If the right to a jury trial is a fundamental matter in other criminal cases, which we think it is, it must also be extended to criminal contempt cases.[3]

Direct and Constructive (or Indirect) Contempt

Contempt is also classified as either direct or indirect (constructive contempt). Direct contempt is committed in the immediate presence and view or hearing of the court or legislative body. Acts of violence, insulting or abusive language, or failure to obey a proper order of the court or the legislative body are examples of conduct that have been held to be in direct contempt. Direct contempt may be punished summarily, since the person is present before the court or the legislative body at the time.

Constructive (or indirect) contempt arises from matters not occurring in or near the presence of the court or the legislative body but that nevertheless tend to obstruct or delay the functioning of the court or legislative body. Failure to appear as ordered or as required would be an example of conduct that could be found to be in constructive contempt. Constructive contempt may not be punished summarily, since the person is entitled to procedural due process. This entitles the person to an opportunity to show cause within a stated time why an order adjudging one in contempt should not be issued; to a hearing after receiving notice of its time and place; to a reasonable time for preparation of one's defense; to a statement of facts constituting the contempt charged; to service on him or her of a copy of any writing or document filed in support of the alleged contempt with such matters set out in an order issued by the court determining to cite the person for contempt.

The Requirement of Intentional Wrongdoing

In the 1976 case of *Commonwealth v. Washington,* the Supreme Court of Pennsylvania quoted other courts, holding:

> There is no contempt unless there is some sort of wrongful intent. *Offutt v. United States,* 98 U.S.App.D.C. 69, 232 F.2d 69, 72 (1956), *cert. den.* 351 U.S. 988, 76 S.Ct. 1049, 100 L.Ed. 1501 (1956). "[A] degree of intentional wrongdoing is an ingredient of the offense of criminal contempt." *In Re Brown,* 147 U.S.App.D.C. 156, 454 F.2d 999, 1006 (1971). "Willfulness is, of course, an element of criminal contempt and must be proved beyond a reasonable doubt." *United States v. Greyhound Corporation,* 508 F.2d 529, 531 (7th Cir. 1974). In *United States v. Seale,* 461 F.2d 345, 368 (7th Cir. 1972), the Court thoroughly discussed the necessity for proof of the element of intent, and concluded that the minimum intent required is a volitional act done by one who knows or should reasonably be aware that his conduct is wrongful.[4]

Contempt

Classification	Type	Procedure Used to Punish
Civil contempt is remedial and is used to force persons to do what they are lawfully required to do (answer questions, identify themselves, pay support money as ordered by a divorce court, etc.)	*Direct contempt* is committed in the immediate presence and view or hearing of the court or legislative body.	*Summary process* Only direct contempt may be punished summarily. If the court or legislative body does not act at the time the contempt is committed, notice and an opportunity for a hearing must be given to the persons.
"Criminal contempt is a crime in the ordinary sense; it is a violation of the law, a public wrong which is punishable by fine or imprisonment or both."* U.S. Supreme Court in *Bloom v. Illinois,* 391 U.S. 194, 88 S.Ct. 1477 (1968).	*Constructive (or indirect) contempt* is committed out of the presence or hearing of the court or legislative body. Although the matter or incident does not occur in or near the presence of a court or legislative body, it must tend to obstruct or delay the functioning of the court or the legislative body.	*Contempt hearings* Notice and an opportunity for a hearing (plus other due process rights) must be given for constructive (indirect contempt) and for direct contempt when the court or legislative body does not act immediately.

In the *Washington* case, the defendant overslept and failed to appear in time at his trial. In reversing his contempt conviction, the Supreme Court of Pennsylvania held:

> Were we to accept the prosecution's argument, any person, judge, attorney, witness, or party, who comes into the courtroom late can be held guilty of contempt of court, regardless of the reason for the lateness. We cannot accept such a conclusion. Unless the evidence establishes an intentional disobedience or an intentional neglect of the lawful process of the court, no contempt has been proven. Such is the case here.
> Judgment of sentence reversed.

In the 1976 case of *People v. Harris,*[5] the defendant failed to pay a fine imposed for a prior criminal conviction. Although the defendant showed that he had no money and was unemployed, he was found in contempt for failure to pay the fine. The Illinois Court of Appeals reversed the contempt finding, holding that there was no showing that the defendant willfully placed himself in a position to be unable to pay the fine.

When the Basis of the Contempt Is a Personal Attack on the Trial Judge

It is a well-settled law that in order to prevent a breakdown of the judicial process, courts have the power to punish persons summarily for contempt of court that consists of personal attacks on the trial judge. In *Mayberry v. Penn-sylvania*,[6] the defendants and two others were tried for holding hostages in a prison break and for escaping from prison. The defendants rejected the court-appointed attorney and represented themselves, using disruptive tactics, which included verbal attacks on the trial judge. Because of Mayberry's disruptions while the judge was attempting to instruct the jury, Mayberry had to be gagged and put in a straitjacket. When this did not work, Mayberry was placed in an adjoining room, where he was able to listen to the conclusion of the trial over a public address system. Before sentencing the defendants on the basis of the jury finding of guilty, the trial judge sentenced Mayberry to not less than eleven or more than twenty-two years in prison on eleven contempt citations.

After the sentence for contempt was affirmed by the Supreme Court of Pennsylvania, the case was appealed to the U.S. Supreme Court in 1971. This Court based its decision to vacate and remand for a new trial on the concept that "justice must satisfy the appearance of justice." The two factors that the Court held did not meet the "appearance of justice" were the length of the sentence and the "appearance" of an angry judge seeking revenge. Justice William O. Douglas wrote:

> A judge, vilified as was this Pennsylvania judge, necessarily becomes embroiled in a running, bitter controversy. No one so cruelly slandered is likely to maintain that calm detachment necessary for fair adjudication.
>
> Justice Harlan wrote in his concurring opinion: "These contempt convictions must be regarded as infected by the fact that the unprecedented long sentence of 22 years which they carried was imposed by a judge who himself had been the victim of petitioner's shocking abusive conduct. That circumstance seems to me to deprive the contempt proceeding of the appearance of even-handed justice which is the core of due process."

The Supreme Court held that "where ... he [the trial judge] does not act the instant the contempt is committed, but waits until the end of the trial, on balance, it is generally wise where the marks of the unseemly conduct have left personal stings to ask a fellow judge to take his place."

But what of the unruly and disruptive defendant who not only attacks and vilifies the trial judge, but also personally insults the second judge who is presiding at the contempt hearing? This question was presented in the 1971 case of *Knox v. Municipal Court of Des Moines.*[7] The defendant was charged with operating a motor vehicle after his driver's license was suspended. He was openly antagonistic to the trial judge and after he was sentenced to five days in jail (maximum sentence was 30 days), he spat at the judge. The trial judge chose to transfer the contempt hearing to another judge. The defendant was so disruptive at the contempt hearing that in addition to sentencing the defendant to six months for the first contempt, the second judge summarily sentenced the defendant to six months for the second contempt. The Iowa Supreme Court affirmed the contempt sentences in a 4−3 decision. The dissenting judge argued that a third judge should have sat on the matter as the second judge himself had been vilified. If the dissenting opinion in *Knox* were followed, the question would then rise as to what course of action should be followed if the determined disruptive defendant vilifies the third and fourth judges hearing the contempt motions.

In *Illinois v. Allen*,[8] the U.S. Supreme Court held that a defendant who continues to engage in disruptive behavior, after being properly warned, can lose his right to remain in the courtroom. Although such defendants have a constitutional right to the confrontation of the witnesses against them, by engaging in disruptive conduct that may affect proceedings to the point where it may be impossible to complete the trial. In addition to summary and delayed contempt against such disruptive defendants, trial judges may have such defendants removed from the courtroom, bound and gagged, or moved to other rooms where they can hear the trial proceedings over a public address system or closed-circuit TV.

Language by a Witness or Attorney that Would Justify a Contempt Finding

While answering a question on cross examination, a witness used the expression "chicken shit." As a result, the witness was found to be in direct contempt for the use of this term in a courtroom. The U.S. Supreme Court reversed the defendant's conviction in the case of *Eaton v. City of Tulsa,*[9] holding:

> This single isolated usage of street vernacular, not directed at the judge or any officer of the court, cannot constitutionally support the conviction of criminal contempt. "The vehemence of language used is not alone the measure of the power to punish for contempt. The fires which it kindles must constitute an imminent, not merely a likely, threat to the administration of justice." *Craig v. Harney,* 331 U.S. 367, 376 (1947). In using the expletive in answering the question on cross-examination "it is not charged that [petitioner] here disobeyed any valid court order, talked loudly, acted boisterously, or attempted to prevent the judge or any other officer of the court from carrying on his court duties." *Holt v. Virginia,* 381 U.S. 131, 136 (1965); see also *In re Little,* 404 U.S. 553 (1972). In the circumstances, the use of the expletive thus cannot be held to "constitute an imminent . . . threat to the administration of justice."

The Power of Legislative Bodies to Punish for Contempt

Constitutions grant legislative bodies the power to legislate. In order to inform themselves as to what laws and measures should be enacted, legislative bodies must gather necessary information on which to base their decisions. They therefore have the power to hold hearings and make investigations into matters relevant to their jurisdiction to legislate. Neither Congress nor the state legislatures possess the general power to make inquiries into the private affairs of citizens that are not relevant to measures they may be considering. Legislatures possess inherent power to protect their existence and their power to proceed in their legislative functions. The following case came before the U.S. Supreme Court in 1972:

GROPPI v. LESLIE
Supreme Court of the United States (1972) 404 U.S. 496, 92 S.Ct. 582

A former Catholic priest, Father Groppi, led a group who seized the Wisconsin Assembly chamber and held it for a short time. Father Groppi was arrested and held in jail. Two days after the incident, the Wisconsin Assembly voted to hold Groppi in contempt and gave him six months in jail as punishment. The U.S. Supreme Court unanimously held that the action violated Groppi's due process rights, as he received a jail sentence without any notice of the hearing and there was no opportunity for him to appear and defend himself.

B. Crimes by Public Officials

If all people were angels and were to live in peace and harmony with one another, then, as James Madison observed in *The Federalist Papers,* there would be no need for governments. But people are not angels, nor are they governed by angels (as Madison also pointed out almost two hundred years ago). The sad fact that in recent years many high public officials have had to resign, or have been convicted of offenses, illustrates this. The Supreme Court of the United States observed that "nothing can destroy a government more quickly than its failure to observe its own laws, or worse, its disregard of the charter of its own existence."[10] In 1928, Justice Louis D. Brandeis stated in his dissenting opinion in *Olmstead v. United States:* "Our Government is the potent, the omnipresent teacher. For good or ill, it teaches the whole people by its example. . . . If the Government becomes a lawbreaker, it breeds contempt for law; it invites every man to become a law unto himself; it invites anarchy."[11]

Cicero wrote long ago in *Pro Cluentio 53* that "we are in bondage to the law in order that we may be free." Calvin Coolidge observed, while president of the United States: "Wherever the law goes, there civilization goes and stays. When the law fails, barbarism flourishes. Whoever scorns the law, whoever brings it into disrespect, whoever connives at its evasion, is an enemy of civilization. Change it if you will . . . but observe it always. That is government."

Categories of Offenses Committed by Public Officials

All public officials, whether they be judges, governors, legislators, or law enforcement officers, are subject to the law and must obey the law of their jurisdictions. Civil and criminal offenses that are applicable to public officials have been categorized as follows:

- *Nonfeasance*—the omission or failure to perform a duty or undertaking that the public official is obligated to perform as part of his or her public office. Failure to execute a writ and failure to obey a court order are examples of nonfeasance.
- *Malfeasance*—the commission of an act that the public official has no right to do and that may be a criminal violation.
- *Misfeasance*—the improper performance of an act that the public official may perform but should not perform in the manner in which he or she acted. Misfeasance is the failure to do a lawful act in a proper manner.

The state of New York has statutorized nonfeasance and misfeasance in Section 195.00 of the New York Criminal Code as follows:

A public servant is guilty of official misconduct when, with intent to obtain a benefit or to injure or deprive another person of a benefit:

1. He commits an act relating to his office but constituting an unauthorized exercise of his official functions, knowing that such act is unauthorized; or
2. He knowingly refrains from performing a duty which is imposed upon him by law or is clearly inherent in the nature of his office.

Official misconduct is a class A misdemeanor.

Malfeasance would include many offenses that are statutorized in every criminal code. The following offenses could be committed not only by public officials, but by ordinary persons:

- Unauthorized (or excessive) use of force (assault and battery)
- False imprisonment
- Extortion or accepting a bribe (accepting unlawful fees)
- Unauthorized wiretapping (federal felony) or bugging (state offense)
- Perjury[12] and subornation of perjury.[13] (The crime of perjury consists of knowingly and materially testifying falsely while under oath; the crime of subornation of perjury is committed when another person is induced or knowingly permitted to testify falsely.)
- Official misconduct and misconduct in public office (using the powers of one's office to obtain a dishonest advantage for oneself or falsifying an entry in a record or report)
- Aiding, assisting, or permitting the escape of a prisoner
- Intimidating witnesses, prisoners, or other persons
- Misprision of felony—"to sustain a conviction . . . for misprision of felony it was incumbent upon the government to prove beyond a reasonable doubt (1) that . . . the principal had committed and completed the felony alleged . . . (2) that the defendant had full knowledge of that fact; (3) that he failed to notify the authorities; and (4) that he took . . . affirmative steps to conceal the crime of the principal."[14]
- Bribery.[15] This offense was described by the Court in the 1976 case of *United States v. Arthur,* as follows:

Not every gift, favor or contribution to a government or political official constitutes bribery. It is universally recognized that bribery occurs only if the gift is coupled with a particular criminal intent. . . . That intent is not supplied merely by the fact that the gift was motivated by some generalized hope or expectation of ultimate benefit on the part of the donor. . . . "Bribery" imports the notion of some more or less specific quid pro quo for which the gift or contribution is offered or accepted. . . .

This requirement of criminal intent would, of course, be satisfied if the jury were to find a "course of conduct of favors and gifts flowing" to a public official in exchange for a pattern of official actions favorable to the donor even though no particular gift or favor is directly connected to any particular official act. *U.S. v. Baggett* (4th Cir. 1973) 481 F.2d 114, cert. denied 414 U.S. 1116 (1973) (Travel Act prosecution involving alleged bribery of Maryland County Commissioner). Moreover, as the Seventh Circuit has held, it is sufficient that the gift is made on the condition "that the offeree act favorably to the offeror when necessary." *U.S. v. Isaacs* (7th Cir. 1974) 493 F.2d 1124, 1145, 15 Cr.L. 2002, cert. denied 417 U.S. 976 (1974) (construing Illinois statute in a Travel Act prosecution). It does not follow, however, that the traditional business practice of promoting a favorable business climate by entertaining and doing favors for potential customers becomes bribery merely because the potential customer is the government. Such expenditures, although inspired by the hope of greater government business, are not intended as a quid pro quo for that business: they are in no way conditioned upon the performance of an official act or pattern of acts or upon the recipient's express or implied agreement to act favorably to the donor when necessary.[16]

- Extortion by a public official or employee in violation of the Hobbs Act, 18 U.S.C.A. Sec. 1951. The public official or employee obtains payment because of his or her office and by use of "force, violence or fear." In *United States v. Swift*[17] the defendant was a city sewer director who received payments from a contractor in return for approval of payments made for work done on sewage pumping stations. In *United States v. Aguon,*[18] a businessman made payments to the defendant government employee so that he would have "no trouble" with a contract he had with government. In *United States v. Holzer*[19] a state judge put pressure on lawyers who had cases in his court to loan the judge money.

C. A FEW OF THE MANY CRIMES AGAINST GOVERNMENT

Sedition Laws

All democratic countries have had to pass laws to protect their governments from overthrow by use of force and violence. The sedition law in effect in the United States is the Smith Act of 1940. It forbids advocating the forceful overthrow of the American government, the distributing with disloyal intent of materials teaching and advising the overthrow of government by violence, and organizing or helping to organize any group having such purpose.

The Supreme Court of the United States affirmed the conviction of an officer in the American Communist party in the 1951 case of *Dennis v. United States.*[20] At that time, Communist literature distributed in the United States urged the violent overthrow of the U.S. government. Following the conviction of Dennis, the American Communist party stopped urging the violent overthrow of our government and now advocates change through peaceful and lawful means.

Sabotage

Sabotage is made a crime by 18 U.S.C.A. Sec. 2155. The offense forbids damaging or injuring national defense material or national defense utilities "with intent to injure, interfere with, or obstruct the national defense." In the 1987 case of *United States v. Johnson,* 41 CrL 2205, the defendant was convicted of sabotage when he put a bolt in an airplane's engine intake because he was "angry," "upset," and "thinking about all of my problems." The defendant was an airman with the U.S. Air Force.

Espionage

Spying or being a party to espionage is forbidden by all democratic countries. Giving or selling national military or defense secrets to a foreign nation is a very serious felony. A shocking number of Americans were charged with or convicted of spying in 1986. Most spies today sell secrets for money (two of the following had different motives):

- *John A. Walker, Jr.* headed a spy ring of family members and friends. Officials called it the most damaging espionage conspiracy in decades. Walker received life imprisonment and said the Soviet Union paid $1 million for his information.

- *Jerry A. Whitworth* was a former Navy radioman and member of the Walker spy ring. Sentenced to 365 years in prison and fined $410,000 for providing details of military communications codes.
- *Ronald W. Pelton* was a $24,500-a-year National Security Agency employee who sold military secrets to the Soviet Union for $13,000. Sentenced to three life terms.
- *Richard W. Miller* was a former FBI agent who became involved with a Soviet woman. As the first FBI employee ever to be charged with spying, he was convicted of espionage after three trials. One conviction was overturned because the trial judge had allowed the results of polygraph tests to be used as evidence.
- *Jonathan Jay Pollard* provided secret information to Israel that was available to him as a U.S. Navy intelligence analyst. He received a long prison sentence.

The Spy Who Got Away[21] is a 1988 book about Edward L. Howard who sold secrets to the Soviet Union as a CIA agent and then in 1985 escaped to Moscow where he is now living.

Obstruction of Justice

The offense of obstruction of justice was a common law misdemeanor that is now part of the criminal code of the federal government and many of the states. The offense seeks to protect the judicial system, both civil and criminal, from intentional acts that would hinder, corrupt, or impede the functioning of the system. Attempting to influence a juror, destruction or suppression of evidence, and seeking to prevent a witness from testifying or attending a trial are some of the acts that have justified charging the offense of obstruction of justice.

In the early days of the law, resisting, hindering, or obstructing a law enforcement officer was a common form of obstruction of justice. Many states, however, have made this offense a separate offense from obstruction of justice. For example, Chapter 843 of the Florida Criminal Code is entitled "Obstructing Justice." Within Florida Chapter 843 are eighteen separate offenses, of which two forbid "resisting an officer." Tampering with evidence (destroying, concealing, altering) is found in Florida Chapter 918.

In 1987, former presidential candidate Lyndon H. LaRouche was indicted and convicted of conspiracy to obstruct justice. It was found that LaRouche had ordered employees to stall a grand jury investigation and had plotted to "fix" and "quash" the grand jury.

A police officer was charged with obstructing justice in 1991 when he pretended to find a bag of cocaine in the vicinity of a person who had just been arrested. An Illinois Court of Appeals held that the officer could be convicted of obstructing justice for attempting to "frame" the arrested person in the case of *People v. Hollingsead,* 210 Ill.App.3d 750, 155 Ill.Dec. 216, 569 N.E.2d 216. The officer's defense was that he was just joking, and then that he was attempting to obtain a confession from the arrested person.

The Crime of Tax Evasion

To operate and provide services, government needs money. Former U.S. Supreme Court Justice Oliver Wendell Holmes pointed out that taxes are the price we pay for civilization.

Much of the money needed to fund government services and activities is obtained through taxes. Deliberate tax evasion and tax fraud are generally punished as crimes. Tax evasion cases that have received national attention are:

- In 1973, the Vice President of the United States, Spiro T. Agnew, resigned after pleading no contest to tax evasion charges. Congressman Gerald R. Ford was Agnew's successor. After the resignation of President Richard Nixon, Ford became the president of the United States.
- Socially prominent hotel owner Leona Helmsley was convicted of failure to report and pay taxes on $1.8 million in 1990. She was sentenced to four years in prison and fined $7.1 million.
- In the 1920s, Gangster Al Capone and his gang had an extraordinary grip on Chicago. Law enforcement officials were unable to convict Capone of any of the many felonies they believed he had committed, but they were able to convict Capone of income tax fraud and send him to prison. Capone was one of the first persons to be convicted by use of the "net worth" method. The U.S. Supreme Court affirmed the use of the "net worth" method (circumstantial evidence) in the 1954 case of *Holland v. United States,* 348 U.S. 121, 75 S.Ct. 127.

Drug dealers and other criminals who live lavishly as a result of their criminal activities must show "legitimate" income to support their high lifestyles. To do this, they must launder dirty money and create sources of "legitimate" income. They then pay taxes to state and federal government on their declared incomes.

In 1985 a prominent Mafia leader was tried. The jury heard a tape recording of the Mafia leader talking to a friend in which the Mafia leader stated, "I surround myself with accountants and lawyers." The Mafia leader had in mind what happened to Al Capone and wanted to avoid being prosecuted in a "net worth" tax case. He was convicted, however, of other criminal violations.

Environmental Crimes

It is reported that today the United States alone produces approximately 125 billion pounds of hazardous waste annually.[23] If not properly handled and disposed of, this waste can foul air, pollute land, poison water, and seriously affect persons, animals, fish, and agriculture.

Until the 1980s, little was done to regulate disposal of hazardous waste. FBI Director William S. Sessions quoted American conservationist Paul Brooks: "In America today [1970s], you can murder land for private profit. You can leave the corpse for all to see, and nobody calls the cops." Sessions pointed out that unfortunately "this was the case 20 years ago. No one could call the police, because no laws had been broken."[24]

In the 1980s and 1990s, laws have been enacted to protect public health and the quality of the environment. The U.S. Congress has added criminal sanctions to a host of environmental laws and in 1990 enacted the Clean Air Act Reauthorization. Vigorous enforcement of these laws has been said to be a top priority. Sessions concluded:

> Environmental crime is a deadly serious subject with devastating consequences. People who endanger the planet for greed and profit must not be allowed to continue to break the law. Our environment is fragile, and it is up to all of us to protect it. Individuals must accept the responsibility for their own communities. Nations must set forth clear policies, laws, and regulations that will protect their environments. And, law enforcement and government agencies must relentlessly enforce these laws and policies.[25]

The Environmental Protection Agency (EPA) and the Department of Justice's Environmental Crimes Section are among the federal agencies combating environmental crimes. All of the states have enacted laws and authorized agencies within the state to enforce these laws. In 1990, the federal government issued 134 indictments against corporations, their top executives, and other persons. Prison terms were imposed in many of the cases where convictions were obtained, and nearly $30 million in fines were imposed.

The worst environmental catastrophe in the United States was the 1989 Exxon Valdez oil spill in Alaska's Prince William Sound. Nearly 11 million gallons of oil spilled when the oil carrier Exxon Valdez ran aground. Twelve hundred miles of Alaska's coastal shores were covered with oil for months. Hundreds of thousands of sea birds were killed along with hundreds of sea otters, harbor seals, bald eagles, murres, sea ducks, clams, and snails. Extensive damage to salmon and other fish was reported.

The Exxon Corporation pleaded guilty to four misdemeanor violations of environmental statutes and agreed to pay a $100 million fine. A settlement of $1.1 billion was agreed upon to settle civil claims from the spill. However, a federal judge would not accept the plea bargain, stating that the fines "do not adequately achieve deterrence." (Exxon's chairman had publicly stated that the fines would "not have a significant effect upon Exxon's earnings.")

Immigration Offenses

Every day, approximately one million persons seek entry into the United States. Some try to sneak in, while others present themselves at one of the hundreds of ports of entry on the Mexican or Canadian border or ports on the Atlantic or Pacific coasts. About 3,000 of these persons are intercepted every day as suspects in illegal entry or other immigration offenses.

Every year, more than one million persons are detained for illegal entry or other offenses and are returned to their native country. Most of the detained persons are not referred for criminal prosecution.

Detained aliens may request a civil (noncriminal) hearing before an immigration officer to determine whether the detained person is legally entitled to remain in the United States. However, only 2 percent of detained aliens request such a hearing, because:

1. the hearing date is usually weeks in the future, which means the person would be held in a detention facility for the waiting time;
2. the formal hearing and the recording of the identity of the person could hurt future chances for a visa and legal immigration into the United States (no record is kept if the alien agrees to deportation without a hearing);

3. at the hearing, the burden is on the detainee to show why he or she should be legally permitted to enter the United States. Without documentation, the detainee will be ordered deported.

For all of the above reasons, most detained aliens do not request a formal hearing and agree to deportation without a hearing. In that case the Immigration and Naturalization Service (INS) does not record the identity of the deported person.

Illegal entry or reentry into the United States accounts for about 46 percent of the suspects investigated. Harboring or bringing in foreign citizens with forged or inadequate documents accounts for about 38 percent of the offenses investigated. Misusing visas or permits accounts for approximately 8 percent of the offenses, and frauds and forgery involving passports and other documents comprise another 8 percent, according to the INS.

Notes

1. 419 U.S. 449, 95 S.Ct. 584 (1975). However, in the *Maness* case, the U.S. Supreme Court held that a lawyer is not subject to the penalty of contempt for advising his client, during a civil trial, to refuse to produce material that would incriminate him. The Court held: "The privilege against compelled self-incrimination would be drained of its meaning if counsel, being lawfully present, as here, could be penalized for advising his client in good faith to assert it."

2. 391 U.S. 194, 88 S.Ct. 1477 (1968).

3. New Jersey courts have held that "before a judge makes a contempt determination the accused should be permitted to speak." 357 A.2d at 276. In the case of *In re Logan Jr.,* 52 N.J. 475, 246 A.2d 441 (1968), the Court held: "The pronouncement of guilt before according that opportunity places the defendant at the disadvantage of trying to persuade a mind apparently already made up, and also puts the judge in the possibly embarrassing position of reversing himself if such persuasion results."

4. 466 Pa. 506, 353 A.2d 806 (1976).

5. 41 Ill.App.3d 690, 354 N.E.2d 648 (1976).

6. 400 U.S. 455, 91 S.Ct. 499 (1971).

7. 185 N.W.2d 705 (Iowa 1971).

8. 397 U.S. 337, 90 S.Ct. 1057 (1970).

9. 415 U.S. 697, 94 S.Ct. 1228 (1974). In a dissenting opinion, Justice William H. Rehnquist suggests "a flat rule, analogous to the hoary doctrine of the law of torts that every dog is entitled to one bite, to the effect that every witness is entitled to one free contumacious or other impermissible remark."

10. *Mapp v. Ohio,* 367 U.S. 643, 81 S.Ct. 1684 (1961).

11. 277 U.S. 438, 48 S.Ct. 564 (1928).

12. In 1968, the President's Commission on Crime noted that perjury has always been widespread and that there must be more effective deterrents against perjury to ensure the integrity of trials. Another writer commented that few crimes "except fornication are more prevalent or carried off with greater impunity." See "Perjury: The Forgotten Offense," *The Journal of Criminal Law & Criminology* 65 (1974).

13. Some of the Watergate defendants were charged with and convicted of subornation of perjury.

14. Court in *United States v. Stuard,* 556 F.2d 1, 22 CrL 2337 (6th Cir. 1977), quoting *Neal v. United States,* 102 F.2d 643 (8th Cir. 1939). See also *Pope v. State,* 284 Md. 309, 396 A.2d 1054 (1979).

15. Operation Greylord of the 1980s is the biggest sting operation conducted by the FBI. As of 1988, more than sixty persons have been indicted for bribery to throw cases in the Chicago court system. Persons convicted include lawyers, bailiffs, judges, and other persons. Charges have been bribery, mail fraud, racketeering, obstruction of justice, etc.

16. 544 F.2d 730 (4th Cir.).

17. 732 F.2d 878 (11th Cir. 1984).

18. 813 F.2d 1413 (9th Cir. 1987).

19. 816 F.2d 304 (7th Cir. 1987).

20. 341 U.S. 494, 71 S.Ct. 857 (1951).

21. Published by Random House, New York.

22. *United States v. Williams,* 649 F.Supp. 1290 (M.D.Fla. 1986).

23. See the article "Environmental Crimes Prosecution" in the April 1990 issue of the *FBI Law Enforcement Bulletin.*

24. See the "Director's Message" in the April 1991 issue of the *FBI Law Enforcement Bulletin.*

25. See the "Director's Message." There are three excellent articles on environmental crimes in this issue.

Appendix A

Applicable Sections of the U.S. Constitution, Ratified in 1788

Preamble

WE THE PEOPLE of the United States, in Order to form a more perfect Union, establish Justice, insure domestic Tranquility, provide for the common defense, promote the general Welfare, and secure the Blessings of Liberty to ourselves and our Posterity, do ordain and establish this CONSTITUTION for the United States of America.

Article I

Section 1   All legislative Powers herein granted shall be vested in a Congress of the United States, which shall consist of a Senate and House of Representatives. . . .

Article II

Section 1   The executive Power shall be vested in a President of the United States of America. . . .

Article III

Section 1   The judicial Power of the United States, shall be vested in one supreme Court, and in such inferior Courts as the Congress may from time to time ordain and establish. . . .

Article IV

Section 4   The United States shall guarantee to every State in this Union a Republican Form of Government, and shall protect each of them against Invasion; and on Application of the Legislature, or of the Executive [when the Legislature cannot be convened] against domestic Violence. . . .

Article VI

This Constitution, and the Laws of the United States which shall be made in Pursuance thereof; and all Treaties made, or which shall be made, under the Authority of the United States, shall be the supreme Law of the Land; and the Judges in every State shall be bound thereby, any Thing in the Constitution or Laws of any State to the Contrary notwithstanding. . . .

American Bill of Rights, Ratified 1791

Amendment I

Congress shall make no law respecting an establishment of religion, or prohibiting the free exercise thereof; or abridging the freedom of speech or of the press; or the right of the people peaceably to assemble and to petition the Government for a redress of grievances.

Amendment II

A well regulated Militia, being necessary to the security of a free State, the right of the people to keep and bear Arms, shall not be infringed.

Amendment III

No Soldier shall, in time of peace be quartered in any house, without the consent of the Owner, nor in time of war, but in a manner to be prescribed by law.

Amendment IV

The right of the people to be secure in their persons, houses, papers, and effects, against unreasonable searches and seizures, shall not be violated, and no Warrants shall issue, but upon probable cause, supported by Oath, or affirmation, and particularly describing the place to be searched and the persons or things to be seized.

Amendment V

No person shall be held to answer for a capital, or otherwise infamous crime, unless on a presentment or indictment of a Grand Jury, except in cases arising in the land or naval forces, or in the Militia, when in actual service in time of War or public danger; nor shall any person be subject for the same offence to be twice put in jeopardy of life or limb; nor shall be compelled in any criminal case to be a witness against himself, nor be deprived of life, liberty, or property, without due process of law; nor shall private property be taken for public use, without just compensation.

Amendment VI

In all criminal prosecutions, the accused shall enjoy the right to a speedy and public trial, by an impartial jury of the State and district wherein the crime shall have been committed, which district shall have been previously ascertained by law, and to be informed of the nature and cause of the accusation; to be confronted with the witnesses against him; to have compulsory process for obtaining witnesses in his favor, and to have the Assistance of Counsel for his defence.

Amendment VII

In suits at common law, where the value in controversy shall exceed twenty dollars, the right of trial by jury shall be preserved and no fact tried by jury, shall be otherwise reexamined in any Court of the United States, than according to the rules of the common law.

Amendment VIII

Excessive bail shall not be required, nor excessive fines imposed, nor cruel and unusual punishments inflicted.

Amendment IX

The enumeration in the Constitution, of certain rights, shall not be construed to deny or disparage others retained by the people.

Amendment X

The powers not delegated to the United States by the Constitution, nor prohibited by it to the States, are reserved to the States respectively, or to the people. . . .

14TH AMENDMENT, RATIFIED 1868

Amendment XIV

Section 1. All persons born or naturalized in the United States, and subject to the jurisdiction thereof, are citizens of the United States and of the State wherein they reside. No State shall make or enforce any law which shall abridge the privileges or immunities of citizens of the United States; nor shall any State deprive any person of life, liberty, or property, without due process of law; nor deny to any person within its jurisdiction the equal protection of the laws. . . .

Appendix B

Glossary of Legal Terms

accomplice   One who aids another in the commission of a crime. An accomplice is generally treated the same as a principle.

actus reus   The criminal act.

affirmative defense   A defense to a criminal charge where the defendant generally admits doing the criminal act but claims an affirmative defense such as duress (he or she were forced) or entrapment (see Chapter 7).

arraignment   Formal assertion of criminal charges against a defendant.

assault   In many instances an assault is an attempt to commit a battery but many states also make other conduct also an assault. Could be combined with a charge of battery to constitute the crimes of "assault and battery" (see Chapter 14).

battery   A successful assault, in which the victim is actually and intentionally (or knowingly) struck by the defendant.

benefit of clergy   A medieval limit on capital punishment. Persons convicted of a capital crime entitled to claim the benefit of clergy (by the 15th century anyone who could read) could not be executed for their offense. By the end of the 18th century the privilege had been eliminated for most crimes.

bill of attainder   Legislative act which inflicts punishment without trial; prohibited by Article I, section 9 and 10 of the Constitution.

burglary   Unlawful entry into the premises of another with intent to steal or commit a felony. Two hundred years ago in England, an illegal entry into the home of another by force and at night was punishable by death if the entry was done to steal or commit a felony (see Chapter 15).

capital punishment   Inflicting deadly injury as punishment for criminal conduct.

certiorari   A form of review of lower court decisions by the Supreme Court. Certiorari is discretionary with the Court, and most petitions requesting it are denied. Traditional legal doctrine is that no conclusion can be drawn from a denial of Certiorari.

clear and present danger   The test used to judge governmental restrictions on speech.

common law   The laws which resulted from opinions of courts and other decision making bodies, as distinguished from laws passed by legislatures.

common law crimes   Crimes created by judges.

condonation   Forgiveness of the criminal act by the victim. Normally not a defense to prosecution.

consecutive sentences   Sentences for conviction of more than one criminal charge which are to be served one after the other, thereby extending the prison time. Concurrent sentences are served at the same time, and thus shorten the prison time for multiple convictions.

contempt   Failure or refusal to obey a court order (civil contempt), or interfering with the functioning of a court or legislative body in a manner which seriously disrupts or insults the court or legislative body (criminal contempt). Criminal contempt which occurs in the presence of the court can be punished summarily: other criminal contempts require the normal prosecution procedures.

corporal punishment   Inflicting nondeadly physical injury as punishment for criminal conduct.

corpus delicti   In all criminal cases, the government must prove that the crime charged was committed (corpus delicti) and that the defendant was party to the crime (committed the crime or was an accomplice). (see chapters 3 and 13).

criminology   The sociological study of the causes, development, and control of crime.

de novo   A hearing or review in which the reviewing authority may decide the question presented as though it were the initial decision maker, and without being bound by the decision or findings of any previous body deciding the question. Contrasts with normal appellate review, where the appellate court is bound by many findings made by the court being reviewed.

depraved-mind   The rule that one who knowingly acts with reckless disregard for the lives of others possesses the requisite malice for conviction of murder, should another be killed by such acts.

double jeopardy   A defense, stated in the Fifth Amendment, to prosecution on the grounds that the defendant has been tried before on the same charge, and acquitted.

due process   The Constitutional guarantee that criminal arrests and trials must meet certain minimum standards of fairness (procedural due process), and that laws not violate constitutional rights (substantive due process).

duress   A defense to criminal prosecution on the grounds that the defendant was forced to commit the criminal act to avoid death or serious injury to himself or others.

electronic handcuff   Electronic sending device attached to person of defendant for purpose of monitoring movement. Used as an alternative to imprisonment.

entrapment   The defense that a law enforcement officer used excessive temptation or urging to wrongfully induce the defendant to commit a crime he or she would not have ordinarily committed.

ex post facto   Criminal law made retroactive to punish prior conduct not criminal when done. Prohibited by Article I. section 9 and 10 of the Constitution.

exclusionary rule   Rule that prohibits a federal or state prosecutor from using evidence that was obtained by improper or illegal means by a law enforcement officer. In may instances, a constitutional right of a defendant has been violated.

extortion   Obtaining property by threats of future harm. Differs from robbery in that robbery requires threat of immediate harm.

federalism   The principle defining the division of power between the states and the federal government, in which the federal government has only those powers specifically delegated in the Constitution.

felony murder   All states and the federal government have felony murder statutes which punish as murder the causing of death of another while the defendant is committing a felony of violence. A felony murder conviction does not require a showing of malice or deliberate intent to kill (see Chapter 13).

felony   The most serious grade of crime; usually includes possibility of prison sentence.

fighting words   Speech which, because it will likely incite immediate violence, is not protected by the First Amendment.

forensic   Pertaining to Courts of law.

grand jury   The group of persons charged with determining whether a crime may have occurred, and who should be indicted to stand trial for that crime.

hearsay   Second hand evidence. Hearsay testimony results when one person, the witness, testifies that she heard another person, the third person, say something. Such testimony is generally not admissible in trials if it is offered to prove the truth of what the third person said.

habeas corpus   A writ which compels the authority holding a person in confinement to explain the basis for that confinement. Used frequently as a method for state and federal prisoners to attack the constitutionality of their imprisonment. Both the federal government and states have some form of a Habeas corpus law, often called "post-conviction relief" laws.

immunity   An exemption from criminal prosecution, which can be limited to prosecution for a specific crime (transactional immunity) or for any crime related to the testimony or conduct for which immunity is granted (use immunity). Diplomats and legislators also enjoy immunity from prosecution in many circumstances.

imperfect self-defense   The rule that excessive force used in self-defense which results in death subjects the actor to liability for a lesser crime than murder, even though the actor intended to cause death.

impossibility   A defense to guilt based on some fact's presence or absence which makes the commission of the crime impossible. Most states reject the defense, saying a defendant can be convicted of the attempt to commit a crime which could not actually be committed.

inchoate crimes   Criminal acts which lead to or are attempts to commit other crimes.

indeterminate sentence   A sentence for a criminal conviction which provides for a broad range of prison time, based on factors such as the good behavior of the prisoner. The recent Federal Sentencing Guidelines have moved away from this approach in favor of well defined, often mandatory sentences.

indictment   A formal criminal charge brought by a grand jury against a defendant.

injunction   A court order prohibiting a person from engaging in defined conduct. A violation of an injunction can be criminal.

interdiction   The name given the government's attempts to stop the import of illegal drugs into this country.

jury nullification   The name given the result when a jury acquits a defendant who has committed the crime because the jury rejects either the crime or the punishment given for the crime.

justification   The general doctrine of non-liability for actions otherwise criminal based on recognized categories of excuse. Self-defense, necessity and duress are examples of justification categories.

larceny   The general category of theft offenses, which includes robbery, embezzlement, shoplifting, and other forms of unlawful taking.

lesser included offense   A criminal offense which is necessarily included in commission of some other offense. The crime of unlawful entry (or breaking and entering) is included in the crime of burglary. Normally one can not be convicted of both offenses for the same acts.

M'Naghten rule   The insanity defense rule requiring proof that the defendant did not know the scope or character of his actions.

Magna Carta   The document signed by King John in 1215 giving certain rights to his nobles. Successive kings affirmed this charter before Parliament.

malum in se   Evil or wrong in itself. Murder is wrong with or without a law prohibiting it.

malum prohibitum   Conduct made wrong by law, but which is not criminal by itself. Failure to file an income tax, if made criminal, would be malum prohibitum.

manslaughter   Criminal homicides other than murder. Most states provide for two degrees of manslaughter, voluntary and involuntary.

menacing   Intentionally placing or attempting to place another in fear of immediate serious physical injury.

mens rea   The criminal intent or state of mind.

misdemeanor   Offenses which carry punishment of a degree less than felonies. Usually misdemeanor crimes do not involve prison sentences.

misprision of a felony   Failing to report or concealing a known criminal.

model penal code   Proposed criminal law developed by the American Law Institute, a group of lawyers, judges, and teachers. Many states have modeled their criminal codes on the MPC.

necessity   A defense to criminal prosecution on the grounds that the harm to be avoided outweighed the harm caused by the crime committed. Necessity will not justify taking another persons life.

no contest plea   A plea to a criminal charge which does not admit guilt, but does not contest the charges filed. In most instances this plea will be treated as a guilty plea for sentencing and other purposes. (Sometimes called "nolo contendre")

nuisance speech   Speech which, because of its intrusive quality, may be regulated in time and place of its exercise.

nulla poena (CRIMIN) sine lege   The principle of legality; no act should be made criminal or punished without advance warning in the form of legislative act.

obscenity   Communication which the average person, using contemporary community standards, would find appeals to the prurient interests, or depicts sexual conduct in a patently offensive manner, and which, taken as a whole, lacks serious artistic, literary, political or scientific value.

overbreadth   The Constitutional law doctrine which invalidates laws which regulate conduct so broadly as to interfere with individual freedoms.

Penumbra Doctrine   The doctrine used by the Supreme Court to find rights in the Constitution which have no direct textual location. The existence of certain rights, under this doctrine, implies the existence of others.

police power   The inherent power of every state and local government, subject to Constitutional limits, to enact criminal laws.

presumption   A rule of law that the trier of fact shall assume the existence of a state of facts without evidence being produced. Presumptions are rebuttable or irrebuttable.

privilege   A defense to criminal prosecution on the grounds that the person was in good faith discharging some duty of her public office when the criminal act occurred.

proximate cause   The ordinary and probable cause of a result.

prurient   A prurient interest is an excessive, shameful or morbid interest in sex.

rape shield laws   Laws passed by many states to limit the extent to which defense attorneys in a rape case can inquire into the victim's past sexual life.

recidivist   One who is a habitual criminal.

regulatory offenses   Crimes relating to conduct effecting the health and welfare of the general public in areas where federal or state governments may lawfully regulate the conduct. Manufacture and sale of drugs and storing and selling food for human consumption are examples of areas where the government can regulate, and can thus create regulatory crimes. Many regulatory crimes are "strict liability", and require no guilty intent.

rehabilitative ideal   The theory of punishment with reform of the criminal as its justification.

retribution   The theory of punishment with payment in the form of criminal punishment as its justification.

RICO   The Racketeer Influenced and Corrupt Organizations Act. Passed by Congress to enable prosecutors to charge all persons engaged in unlawful activity who own or invest in an enterprise which effects interstate commerce.

scienter   A form of specific intent requiring a showing that the actor knew of the existence of certain facts. For example, one cannot be guilty of possession of stolen property if one does not know property is stolen.

sedition   The crime of advocating the forceful overthrow of the established Government. In this country, the Smith Act makes such advocacy a crime.

sequester   To isolate. A jury may be sequested when the court believes the publicity surrounding the case is such that the jury may be unlawfully swayed by the publicity.

sexual assault   The crime in most states which includes the crime of rape, as well as other lesser degrees of assault.

sexual harassment   Unwelcome sexual advances, with or without physical contact; in the workplace, creation of a "hostile environment", such as belittling or embarrassing an employee or co-worker who has refused sexual advances, can be sexual harassment.

shoplifting   Stealing goods from retail stores by concealment, generally on the person of the defendant. Commission does not require removal of the goods from the store.

solicitation   Attempting to get another to commit a crime.

specific intent   The intent necessary for one or more elements of an offense. Murder, for example, requires the specific intent that the act be done intentionally or purposely.

status crimes   Criminal laws which punish a status, such as drug addiction, with no act requirement.

statutory rape   Sexual intercourse with a minor female under a certain age, usually 18. Consent, and generally mistake as to age, are not defenses to this crime.

stop and frisk   A form of lawful search which is generally less intrusive than a search based on a search warrant.

strict scrutiny   The balancing test used by the Supreme Court to test the validity of state or federal laws that interfere with certain individual rights.

tort   A noncontractual civil wrong.

transferred intent   The doctrine that one who intends to inflict harm on one person but injures another instead is presumed, for purpose of criminal prosecution, to intend the actual result.

uttering   Putting into circulation a check known to be worthless.

venue   In criminal prosecutions, the proper location for the criminal trial. Venue is usually in the county in which the crime is alleged to have occurred.

vicarious liability   Criminal liability of one person, with or without culpability, for the criminal acts of another. Usually imposed where the defendant occupies some relationship to the person committing the crime, such as employer-employee, which charges the defendant with the duty to control the other person.

void for vagueness   The constitutional law doctrine which invalidates criminal laws which are written in such a manner as to make it unreasonably difficult for a defendant to know whether or not conduct is prohibited by the law.

Wharton Rule   The requirement that crimes needing more than one person for commission, such as bigamy, require three or more persons for a conspiracy conviction.

| Table of Cases

The principal cases are in bold type. Cases cited or discussed in the text are roman type. References are to pages.

INDEX